PENGUIN BOOKS

AT HOME WITH THE MARQUIS DE SADE

Francine du Plessix Gray is the author of *Rage and Fire,
Lovers and Tyrants*, and *Soviet Women*, among other
books, and contributes regularly to *The New Yorker* and
many other publications. She lives in Connecticut with
her husband, the painter Cleve Gray.

At Home with

with

PENGUIN BOOKS

the

Marquis de Sade

A LIFE

Francine du Plessix Gray

PENGUIN BOOKS
Published by the Penguin Group
Penguin Putnam Inc., 375 Hudson Street,
New York, New York 10014, U.S.A.
Penguin Books Ltd, 27 Wrights Lane,
London W8 5TZ, England
Penguin Books Australia Ltd, Ringwood,
Victoria, Australia
Penguin Books Canada Ltd, 10 Alcorn Avenue,
Toronto, Ontario, Canada M4V 3B2
Penguin Books (N.Z.) Ltd, 182–190 Wairau Road,
Auckland 10, New Zealand

Penguin Books Ltd, Registered Offices:
Harmondsworth, Middlesex, England

First published in the United States of America by Simon & Schuster, 1999
Published in Penguin Books 1999

10 9 8 7 6 5 4 3 2 1

Picture research by Natalie Goldstein, New York, and Kate Lewin, Paris

THE LIBRARY OF CONGRESS HAS CATALOGED
THE HARDCOVER EDITION AS FOLLOWS:
Gray, Francine du Plessix.
At home with the Marquis de Sade: a life/Francine du Plessix Gray.
p.   cm.
Includes bibliographical references and index.
1. Sade, marquis de, 1740–1814.   2. Authors, French—18th Century—Biography.
I. Title.
PQ2063.S3G73   1998
843'.6—dc21   98-34224
CIP [b]
ISBN 0-684-80007-1 (hc.)
ISBN 0 14 02.8677 2 (pbk.)

Printed in the United States of America
Set in Galliard

To Alex and Melinda
with gratitude and love always

Contents

Foreword

Since therefore the knowledge and survey of vice is in this world so necessary to the constituting of human virtue, and the scanning of error to the confirmation of truth, how can we more safely, and with less danger, scout into the regions of sin and falsity than by reading all manner of tractates and hearing all manner of reason? And this is the benefit which may be had of books promiscuously read.

—Milton, *Areopagitica*

☐

DONATIEN ALPHONSE FRANÇOIS, Marquis de Sade (1740–1814), is one of the few men in history whose names have spawned adjectives (others who come readily to mind are Plato, Machiavelli, and Masoch). He may well be the only writer who will never lose his capacity to shock us. And over the past century, he has evoked more mixed epithets than any other writer in memory: "the freest spirit who ever lived,"[1] "a Professor Emeritus of Crime,"[2] "the most lucid hero of Western thought,"[3] "a frenetic and abominable assemblage of all crimes and obscenities,"[4] "the one completely consistent and thorough-going revolutionary of history."[5]

Yet when I steeped myself in the scandalous marquis's correspondence, I became entranced by the more modest, familial motifs of his saga. I soon realized that few writers' destinies have been so powerfully shaped by women, that few lives provide a more eloquent allegory on women's ability to tame men's nomadic sexual energies, to enforce civilization and its attendant discontents.

This millennial conflict is exemplified by the complex triadic relationship Sade evolved with the two central female figures in his life: with his devoted wife, Renée-Pélagie de Sade, and with his vindictive, brilliant mother-in-law, Mme de Montreuil, each of whom, in her own way, dealt with the taboos that imprisoned Sade the man and liberated Sade the writer.

For it is Sade's consummately proper mother-in-law who was responsible for his decades of imprisonment and was thus a muse (if she'd only known!) of his feral texts. It is Sade's prudish wife who fostered his talent during his years of detainment and preserved his scabrous correspondence, perhaps the most remarkable part of his oeuvre. What was it like, I began to wonder as I read on, to be at home with the Marquis de Sade? What was it like to be the Marquise de Sade, a pious, very decorous woman married, throughout the decades that preceded the French Revolution, to one of the most depraved mavericks of recent times? What was it like to be Sade's mother-in-law, a highly ambitious bourgeoise struggling to protect the fabric of a family that her renegade son-in-law constantly threatened to destroy? And beyond his real-life orgies and delirious fictional debauches, what kind of husband was Sade to write the following letter, from his jail cell at Vincennes, to his prim and pining wife?

> Rest assured, soul of my soul, that the first little errand I will make upon being sprung, my very first action as a free man, after kissing your eyes, your nipples, and your buttocks, will be to purchase . . . the totality of the works of Montaigne, Voltaire, J.-J. Rousseau. . . . [And] why the refusal of the peach wine? . . . Could one or two bottles of peach wine, my Poopsie, subvert the Salic Law, or threaten the Justinian Code? Hark ye, Minerva's favorite, only a drunkard should suffer such a refusal: but I who am solely inebriated by your charms and am never sated by them, O you Olympian ambrosia, shouldn't be denied a little peach wine! Charm of my eyes, I thank you for the fine Rousseau print you sent me. Flame of my life, when will your alabaster fingers come to exchange the irons of [my jailer] for the roses of your breast? Adieu, I kiss it and go to sleep. This 24th [of November 1783] at one A.M.[6]

It is, in part, the irony and rage and tenderness of the Marquis and Marquise de Sade's correspondence that incited me to write this book. The writer's task is to probe the mystery of personality, the mystery of human incompleteness, particularly the mystery of love and of evil. And one cannot hope to explore the most hidden recesses of the mortal cave without giving equal time to yogis and to commissars, to heroes and to cowards, to kings and to knaves, to demons and to saints. In this family portrait, I have tried to shed light on the enigmas of guilt and grace evoked by Sade's fate and bring to life the extraordinary women who shaped it.

Part One

I

Youth

*I assumed that everything must yield to me, that the
entire universe had to flatter my whims, and that I
had the right to satisfy them at will.*

—*Aline et Valcour*[1]

□

THE CHILD STOOD in the palace courtyard, shouting. Donatien Alphonse François, Marquis de Sade, a ravishing blond four-year-old, was giving the first public display of his dreadful temper.

"That is mine!" he yelled at his playmate, eight-year-old Prince de Condé, a prince of the royal blood. Donatien may have been clamoring for his toy horse, his miniature sword, his skip rope. It could have been one of many objects, but it was the one currently in his friend's hand, and Donatien, fearing that the little prince would choose to keep it, demanded that it be returned to him that very instant.

Upon being denied his toy, the four-year-old threw himself fiercely upon his dearest playmate, the beloved companion in whose home he had been brought up since birth, and started pummeling the young Prince de Condé's chest with his tiny fists, smacking the face ten inches above his own, continuing to bellow out his rage, howling urgently for his possession. Young Condé, who as head of the junior branch of the Bourbon family was a prince of the royal blood and already aware of his exalted station, cried out for his friend to stop. Soon the warring pair was surrounded by dozens of palace personnel—gentlemen of the bedchamber and tutors and governesses, equerries, grooms, and valets, all shouting for the little marquis to desist. It took the strength of several adults to separate the battling children. Young Sade's voracity, his need to have every appetite instantly indulged—which most humans begin to curb at the age of seven or eight—was a trait this particular boy would seldom in his lifetime be willing to control.

The struggle took place in 1744 at the Condés' palace, Paris's largest private residence, whose hundreds of acres of park and scores of superbly furnished rooms overlooked the entire expanse of what is now the Luxembourg Gardens. Born in 1740, the little Marquis de Sade had been brought up in this palace alongside young Prince de Condé, his mother being a relative of the prince's father and a governess and lady-in-waiting to the prince.

Whether the young noble was bruised or bloodied by Donatien's blows, or whether just his feelings were hurt, is not known. There is only one fact we are sure of: shortly after this confrontation, the four-year-old Marquis de Sade suffered the first of his many banishments. In the following weeks, he was shunted out of Paris to his paternal grandmother's home in Avignon, the region of Provence where his ancestors had exercised their feudal rights with legendary arrogance.

The young marquis's nascent hubris cannot have been diminished by the greeting he received upon his arrival in Avignon. He was met by a delegation of the most distinguished citizens of Saumane, one of the several neighboring villages owned by his father. They came, in the delegation's own words, "to compliment M. Marquis de Sade, son of M. le Comte, lord of this place, on his happy arrival in Avignon, and to wish him long and happy years as his presumptive heir."[2] A score of adults bowing, scraping their hats upon the floor, to pay homage to the three-foot-high Donatien: he must have relished it.

In his first and most autobiographical novel, *Aline et Valcour*, written decades later at the Bastille, Sade would describe this childhood quarrel, which he viewed as his first dishonor, and his subsequent dismissal from the Condés' court:

> Connected, through my mother, to all the greatest powers in the kingdom and, through my father, to the most distinguished families of the province of Languedoc; born in Paris in the bosom of luxury and plenty, I believed, from the very first moment I could reason, that nature and fortune had collaborated to lavish me with their gifts; I believed it because people were foolish enough to tell me so, and this ridiculous prejudice made me haughty, despotic, and choleric. . . . I shall relate just one feature of my childhood to convince you of the dangerous principles that were so ineptly allowed to flourish in me.
>
> Since I was born and raised in the palace of the illustrious prince to whom my mother was honored to be connected, and

who was my contemporary, I was encouraged to be constantly in his company . . . but during one of our youthful games, my vanity . . . was ruffled during a quarrel over an object; and since [the prince] seemed to think he was entitled to it through sheer rank, I avenged myself for his resistance with repeated blows which were beyond my control, with the result that only violent force could separate me from my adversary.[3]

There is hubris in this passage, and much preening about origins. Young Donatien came from the kind of Provençal nobility that bristles with self-serving legends. The names Gaspar and Balthasar having recurred frequently in the family—they were widespread throughout the region—the Sades even promoted the myth that they were directly descended from one of the three Magi. What is far more certain than that zany delusion is that the family had been rooted in the Avignon region since at least the tenth century and bought a title of nobility after growing rich in the textile trade, having specialized in the processing of hemp. From then on, their progeny abounded with high-ranking civil servants and clerics—many bishops, eight Knights of Malta, scores of magistrates and high dignitaries of Avignon's papal court, and also numerous priests and nuns, who would later fuel Donatien de Sade's erotic imagination.

The marquis's ancestry begins to be precisely chronicled with one Louis de Sade, a textile magnate who in 1177 helped to finance the building of the Pont Bénézet, Avignon's oldest bridge and the subject of that popular French children's ditty "Sur le Pont d'Avignon."[4] It was Louis's great-great-grandson Hughes who initiated the most romantic legend attached to the Sade clan: he married a woman called Laure de Noves, who became fabled throughout history as Petrarch's muse. The poet began his lifelong obsession for Laure de Sade upon glimpsing her at Sunday mass in Avignon when she was a young married woman of twenty-three. She remained the dark lady of his sonnets until she died of the plague, twenty years to the day after their meeting. Opinions have varied on whether Laure ever returned Petrarch's love. Arguments for her chastity emphasize the several children she had already borne her husband, the bard's many complaints concerning his muse's coolness, his repeated praise for her moral virtue, and the theme of "unattainability" and "distance" central to Petrarch's oeuvre and to the general traditions of fourteenth-century courtly love. The case for her surrender stresses that it would have been difficult for any woman to resist, for twenty years, the love of Christendom's most famous poet, especially in a society of such notoriously loose mores: medieval Avignon was a city of easy virtue, in whose convents some of the region's lewdest orgies were held.

Whether or not Laure gave in to the poet—contemporary scholars tend to deny that she ever did[5]—she wove a phenomenal spell on the Sade family's imagination. For many centuries, nearly every generation of Sades has included her in their daughters' baptismal names. Her most illustrious descendant, the marquis, her great-grandson twelve generations removed, was haunted by her legend throughout his life. And her fascination continues undiminished to this day—a noted twentieth-century offspring is Philippe de Montebello, director of New York's Metropolitan Museum and a direct descendant of the marquis, who like every member of his generation of Sades has called his own daughter Laure.

The family entered the late seventeenth century through Gaspard-François de Sade, Donatien's paternal grandfather. He was the first in his family to urge his offspring to set their ambitions on Paris. This was a significant step, for until then the Sades, like the great majority of Provençal nobles, had looked on the capital with a mixture of envy and mistrust, and had never attempted their fortunes outside the confines of their province. Gaspard-François was also the first Sade to call himself Marquis. The title had recently come into wide usage, and Provençal nobles tended to enjoy its flamboyance. (The alternation of titles in the Sade family has caused great confusion. The first marquis's oldest son, Jean-Baptiste de Sade, Donatien's father, reverted to the less flashy status of count. Upon Donatien's birth, shortly after the first marquis died, his parents decided he should bear his grandfather's title—French government authorities, however, would frequently use "Count" as a designation for young Sade.)

Comte de Sade, Donatien's diplomat father, was one of the more illustrious rakes of Louis XV's reign. He had an unusually complex and close relationship with his only child, but he saw little of Donatien during the boy's first ten years, being constantly engaged in diplomatic missions in foreign lands. Donatien's indolent mother, who spent much of her life sponging off relatives and religious orders, was equally absent from Donatien's orbit. She accompanied her husband on his foreign assignments, not out of a marital devotion—the Comte and Comtesse de Sade were notoriously inimical to each other—but in order to get him out of his many scrapes. So when four-year-old Donatien was exiled to Provence after his struggle with Prince de Condé, it was his paternal grandmother he first lived with. This convivial matriarch, who doted on her only grandson, lived in the palatial Hôtel de Sade, which still stands in the center of Avignon and now serves as its prefecture.

Grand-mère de Sade was visited often by her five daughters. Her youngest child, Donatien's aunt Henriette-Victoire, a notoriously promiscuous beauty, was particularly fond of her turbulent little nephew and loved to indulge him. She had married a great lord of Provence, the Marquis de Villeneuve-Martignan, who built her a splendid palace, a few blocks from her mother's house, which now houses the Musée Calvet. The dowager marquise's other four daughters were nuns. Convents being relatively worldly in prerevolutionary days, these ladies, during their frequent forays into the secular world, doted on Donatien as lavishly as the rest of his female kin. Aunt Gabrielle Laure, his father's eldest sister, a forceful personality with a taste for wild game and truffles, was abbess of the convent of Saint-Laurent in Avignon. Aunt Gabrielle Éléonore was abbess of a nunnery in nearby Cavaillon, a town renowned for its succulent melons. Aunts Anne-Marie Lucrèce and Marguerite-Félicité also belonged to monastic communities in the Avignon region. In addition, one of Donatien's paternal uncles, Richard-Jean-Louis de Sade, was a knight of the Order of Malta and served as grand prior of the city of Toulouse; the boy's other uncle, Jacques-François-Paul-Aldonse de Sade, was a worldly cleric whose influence on Donatien would be fully as great as the child's father's.

The religious vocations that prevailed in that generation of Sades had a crucial impact on young Donatien's character. With the exception of the Marquise de Villeneuve, who had several daughters, none of his aunts or uncles had children. Thus the hot-tempered boy was the only male descendant of a family that took its distinguished lineage all too seriously. His status was further enhanced by his connections to Paris society. His father was the first Sade to take part in the court life of Versailles; his mother, being related to the great Condés, could claim descent from the most hallowed monarch in the nation's history, thirteenth-century king Saint Louis. Moreover, Donatien, a round-faced, blue-eyed boy with curly blond hair and a memorably sweet voice, was said to be so handsome that women stopped in the streets to stare at him. The doting grandmother and the coddling aunts lavished all manner of affection on the child. Plying him with toys, candy, and caresses, they indulged his most capricious whims, with the result that the apprentice tyrant, as he was the first to admit, became more unruly than ever. "My father being busy with diplomatic negotiations, my mother having followed him," he later wrote, "I was sent to the home of a grandmother . . . whose overly blind tenderness fostered all the faults I have acknowledged."[6]

Comte de Sade must have learned that his son was being spoiled rotten by his female relatives and decided that Donatien's character needed to be honed by male authority. So the little marquis went into his second exile, this time with his paternal uncle Abbé Jacques-François de Sade, a cleric and scholar. The abbé's official functions, at his tiny abbey in the Auvergne, took up only a few months of the year. He spent the rest of his time at the family castle of Saumane, some thirty-five kilometers from Avignon and equidistant, by some six kilometers, from the towns of Fontaine-de-Vaucluse and L'Isle-sur-la-Sorgue. Saumane, which one of the Avignon popes had offered the Sades centuries back as a reward for their services, belonged officially to Donatien's father, who had given his younger brother a lifelong lease on it. The little marquis, now six or so,[7] was in for a grim surprise.

One can still see the château of Saumane as it was when Donatien first entered it. A sinister former fortress whose foundations date back to the twelfth century, it retains the ominous air of a military stronghold. It is built upon the steep rocky crag that overlooks its tiny village, and is perpetually shrouded by dense groves of evergreens and oaks. Its high crenellated ramparts of dark-gray stone, the gray of an unkempt tomb, are still dotted with openings for artillery pieces and Judas windows, and they overlook a foreboding twenty-foot-deep moat hollowed out of the rock. And one cannot look at this oppressive residence without recalling the fortress of Silling, the forbidding fictional citadel in which the morbid orgies of Sade's *The 120 Days of Sodom* are held: "A very narrow, very steep spiral staircase with three hundred steps . . . descended through the entrails of the earth toward a kind of vaulted dungeon sealed by three iron gates and containing all that the cruelest art and most refined barbarism could invent in the way of atrocity."[8]

Luckily for Donatien, the master of this somber estate had a temperament and manner radically at odds with his surroundings. Jacques-François de Sade was an amiable forty-year-old priest and scholar with an ardent love life, who was much admired for his gallantry and literary skills. Like his brother Comte de Sade, he was well known in Parisian society and was a friend of Voltaire's and of the philosopher's companion, the eminent Mme du Châtelet. "I love you with all my heart," Voltaire had written the abbé a few years before Donatien arrived in Saumane. "I shall be devoted to you throughout my brief life."[9] Voltaire and Châtelet often worried that the abbé's Enlightenment ideals would eventually be dimmed by his clerical vocation: "[Abbé de Sade] is one of the men I like best," Châtelet wrote to a friend she shared with Donatien's uncle. "Unless four or five years of priestifying have terribly spoiled him, I'm sure that his wit and character have pleased you."[10]

Voltaire, also hoping that the abbé would retain his hedonistic bent, dedicated the following verses to him: "However much of a priest you are, / O Sir, you'll continue to love; /that is your true ministry, / Be you a bishop or the Holy Father. / You will love, you will seduce / and you'll equally succeed / in the Church and in Cythera."[11]

Voltaire's predictions were on the mark. Part of the abbé's charm, to his generation of libertines, was that he remained an active debauchee while acquiring considerable standing as a linguist and scholar. He held true to the Sades' fascination with their ancestor Laure de Sade by writing a three-volume biography of Petrarch. The work would take him twenty years—it was published in 1763, the year of Donatien's marriage —and came to be looked on as an unexcelled cultural chronicle of fourteenth-century Italy. He also authored a book on the French poets and troubadours of the Middle Ages and translated numerous Latin texts.

For relaxation, "the priest of Epicurus," as the abbé was often referred to, enjoyed liaisons with women of very diverse social milieus (he was also known as "the sybarite of Saumane"). His greatest love was Mme de La Popelinière, a noblewoman who was the official mistress of the powerful Maréchal de Richelieu. But the abbé also frequented Paris's most ribald bordellos, an inclination that led to at least one arrest. In fear that his police record be reopened, he tended to keep away from the capital and confine his lust to Provence. During the years he welcomed the young Marquis de Sade to Saumane, the abbé was keeping simultaneous company with two women, a mother and her daughter, who resided in his house; with a maid called Marie, for whom he had arranged a marriage with a local youth; and with a notorious prostitute in the nearby town of Bonnieux, whom he rewarded handsomely.

But such seemingly lurid details are mitigated if set into the context of the abbé's milieu. The ethics of Provence's clergy, and of its nobility, were even looser than in the rest of France. The French Crown had granted the papacy a vast tract of land in the Avignon area in the thirteenth century, when the Pope sought refuge from the political turmoil of Rome; and until the Revolution, Avignon would remain under the notoriously lax jurisdiction of the papal police. The region had long been renowned for the debauchery of its brothels and taverns. It was also an asylum for countless criminals ("a sewer where all the muck of the universe collects,"[12] Petrarch called Avignon in the thirteenth century). Moreover, during the popes' seventy years in Provence, their penury had incited them to evolve a uniquely corrupt system of indulgences. Here, for instance, are some legal stipulations issued by the Avignon papacy, which intended to raise cash by absolving sinners of some of the worst crimes in Christendom:

A nun who has given herself to several men, simultaneously or successively, within or outside her monastery, and
wishes to achieve the rank of abbess, will pay 131 livres, 15 sous.

For all sins of fornication committed by a layman, absolution will be given for 27 livres. Add an extra 4 livres for incest.

Adulterous women can receive absolution, be shielded
from any pursuit, and receive dispensation to continue illicit
relations, for 87 livres, 5 sous.[13]

The aura of dissipation that permeated the Marquis de Sade's childhood later supplied him with his favorite moral fodder: he would frequently excuse his own depravity by flaunting the profligacy of various
kin and male surrogates. "Priest though he is, he still keeps a pair of
trollops in his house," Donatien wrote his aunt Gabrielle Éléonore of
Cavaillon at the age of twenty-five, as he described her brother's household. "Is his château a seraglio? No, better, it's a bordello," he added in
response to one of her scoldings. "Forgive my mischief . . . I'm taking
up the family spirit, and if I have anything to reproach myself for, it's to
have the misfortune of being born into it. God keep me from all the
foolishness and vice with which it is rife."[14]

SETTLED WITH this curious surrogate family, a "bordello" whose members seem to have shown Donatien great kindness, the child grew very
fond of his uncle. Abbé de Sade was clearly intrigued by this choleric,
imperious but emotionally fragile boy who was also capable of great
gentleness, and he took his ward along on most of his excursions. They
often visited a Sade estate, La Coste, which the marquis's later antics
would make notorious. They shared many excursions to the village of
Fontaine-de-Vaucluse, a bare six kilometers' distance from Saumane,
where the Sorgue River begins its tumultuous course. It was in Fontaine-
de-Vaucluse, on the banks of the Sorgue, that Petrarch lived for seventeen years while nursing his hopeless passion for the beautiful Laure de
Sade. The site of the little riverside house he lived in, and in which he
composed scores of sonnets to his muse, remains little changed to this
day. As Petrarch's biographer, Abbé de Sade often entranced his nephew
with accounts of the poet's love for their ancestor. Through such excursions to places that had been linked to his family for centuries, Donatien
learned to love this region of Provence—the verdant rolling hills that
stretch between the peaks of the Lubéron and Ventoux mountain chains,
the groves of olive, fig, cherry, pear, and quince trees that thrive in their
valleys, the steep hilltop villages clinging to their slopes.

Every few months, the abbé's household took off a day to travel, by coach, the twenty miles to Avignon, referred to as "the city." Mail from "the city" reached Saumane only once a week; news of Paris was far less frequent and seemed to come from another planet.

Like most youngsters his age, Donatien enjoyed helping with simple rural tasks: milking the cows and goats, collecting eggs, helping to herd sheep, learning to fish for the fine trout—a favorite fare of his uncle— found in the waters of the speeding Sorgue. It was also at the abbé's estate that Donatien acquired his attachment to dogs; he would continue to love them as an adult, often asking permission, decades later, to keep dogs in his jail cells to allay his solitude. He frequently socialized with local children, sons of peasants or of the few bourgeois—doctors, lawyers—who lived in nearby villages and from whom he acquired his fluent knowledge of the Provençal dialect.

The days, the years, passed uneventfully. The abbé occasionally left his seraglio at Saumane to oversee a dilapidated Cistercian abbey in the Auvergne, whose administration was his principal source of income. Its community consisted of four monks in various phases of senility. Donatien, who accompanied his uncle on most such journeys, may later have transmuted this particular memory of ramshackle priories and sinister friars into his fiction. Back at Saumane, the abbé's concubines—the mother-and-daughter pair, the maid Marie—caressed Donatien like a pet and exclaimed, as all women did, on his beauty. When his uncle was home, there were occasions when Donatien might have heard sounds of much heaving and laughter emerging from the "seraglio" in which Uncle Jacques-François cavorted with his paramours. And yet Abbé de Sade retained a rigorous sense of protocol: on the occasions when a bishop or fellow cleric came for lunch—Monseigneur l'Évêque de Mon-télimar, Monsieur le Curé from the nearby town of Apt or Mazan—back to their rooms the ladies retreated, back went the white clerical collar on Abbé de Sade's black garb.

Beyond his lofty social status, there was a particular way in which the young Marquis de Sade must have felt his difference from the children he played with. It can be safely assumed that most of his peers in the tranquil village of Saumane had a mother. And it may have been harder for Donatien than for many other young aristocrats to explain why he seldom saw his own *maman*—why, indeed, he had seen her so seldom that he could barely describe her. He could not have known much about Comtesse de Sade beyond the fact that she spent a lot of time dressing up to look well at the court of the great Condé family, and accompanied his father on his important diplomatic trips. Questions about his father were far easier to answer, for though Papa was a very busy diplomat, he sometimes found the time in between his official trips to come to Provence to see the boy, and teach him swordsmanship, and tell him about his trips to Germany and Russia.

Donatien's inner thoughts about his female parent, however, were possibly more bitter than any he communicated to his playmates. A hatred of motherhood as virulent as that which prevails throughout Sade's writing—a loathing of procreation, of all manifestations of the maternal principle—is not likely to arise full-blown in adulthood. He may have already felt resentment, by the age of ten, toward the glacial, self-absorbed mother who seemed too lazy to come see him in Provence, too lazy, perhaps, to even love anyone. Upon seeing the children of Saumane being hugged by their mothers, he may well have felt a wave of anxiety at the possibility that he would never be tousled, cuddled, caressed, with the kind of passion that only a mother can bestow.

Fortunately, beyond his uncle's attachment to him, young Donatien was solaced by yet another source of affection, even of purity. Understandably concerned by the limited education his only son was getting in the barnyards and boudoirs of Provence, Comte de Sade had asked his brother to find a preceptor for his child. Sometime between Donatien's ninth and tenth years, the abbé hired a gentle twenty-six-year-old bachelor who was also called "Abbé," because he was studying for the priesthood and, though he had not yet been ordained, wore his hair tonsured like a cleric's. It was "Abbé" Amblet, a native of Annecy, who with great patience taught Donatien the fundamentals of reading and arithmetic, of geography and French history. This "steadfast and highly intelligent man, a most fitting overseer of my education," [15] as Sade later described him, was the only member of the child's male entourage who was not the least bit interested in keeping company with women. And Sade would remain deeply devoted to this mentor for the rest of his life, taking great pains, even in his own moments of greatest penury, to provide him with financial support.

ONCE HE HAD learned to read, Donatien had plenty of free time, during Abbé Amblet's periods of personal study, to browse through his uncle's library, as extensive and progressive as that of any liberal nobleman in France. Along with the classics of previous centuries—Cervantes, Boileau, Racine, Molière—every major text of Enlightenment thought was included in the abbé's collection: Locke's *Essay Concerning Human Understanding;* Thomas Hobbes's and Montesquieu's works; all of Rousseau, Voltaire, and Diderot; and the many contemporary works of anthropology and comparative religion that had been banned by the

Church and were the *dernier cri* of the French intelligentsia. The abbé's library, like any accomplished eighteenth-century gentleman's, was also rich in erotic literature. It included Aretino's famous *Book of Postures* and scores of salacious contemporary volumes such as *Venus in the Cloister, or the Nun in Her Nightdress* and *The Bordello, or John the Fucker Debauched*. Such books sometimes bore equally lewd publishers' addresses: "At Incunt, c/o Widow Big Mound's" (*"À Anconne, chez la veuve Grosse-Motte"*).[16]

Even as a child, Sade was a voracious reader, and he tells us that by the age of ten he knew the holdings of Saumane's library so intimately that he could locate almost any volume with his eyes closed. The abbé would have been the last man to put areas of his collection off limits to his nephew. There is no way Donatien could have missed the kinds of books intended, as the French euphemism went, "to be read with one hand." I doubt if he could have overlooked their illustrations, many of which displayed persons in religious garb performing curious acts upon each other—monks mightily whipping bare-bottomed nuns who kneel at their prayer stools, wearing the same kind of religious attire and floating white headgear as Aunt Gabrielle Laure of Avignon, Aunt Gabrielle Éléonore of Cavaillon. Such books, such images, were an important part of the education Donatien received during the last years he spent with his uncle "the sybarite of Saumane."

II

The Father

"How many crimes are incited by my prick," Noirceuil *cried out. "What atrocities I commit in order
to make it lose its sperm with a little passion! There's
no object on earth which I'm not ready to sacrifice to
it! It's a god for me, Juliette, let it also be yours:
Adore this despotic phallus, offer incense to this superb
deity. I would like it to receive homages from the
entire planet. . . ."*

—*Juliette*

□

IT WAS A FAMILY rife with licentious behavior.

On a fine autumn evening in the 1730s, a few years before his son, Donatien, was born, Comte Jean-Baptiste de Sade was strolling in the Tuileries Gardens, looking for a good time. Having spotted a young man whose charms he admired, he struck up a conversation and then invited the fellow to join him behind a clump of bushes. Unfortunately for the count, his prey turned out to be a *mouche*, or "fly," one of the thousands of undercover agents employed by Louis XV's police to monitor the mores of his subjects. Within a few minutes, Comte de Sade was surrounded by a police squad and put under arrest. The police report reads as follows:

> When the young man passed him by, he [Comte de Sade] . . . made various lewd propositions. . . . He would invite him to dine and go to bed with him. . . . And he would have taken him immediately behind the trees, but the young man was unwilling to go along and proposed instead that they go to his room, which was not far away. . . . Sieur de Sade agreed to this. As the two got up and started on their way . . . the officer of

the watch, who had observed them and who learned from the young man's signal that a reprobate was actively soliciting him, attempted to arrest the man but in view of his quality did not, and instead released him after taking his name and address.[1]

LIKE MANY of his playboy peers, Comte de Sade was bisexual, and needed street boys to fully satisfy his impulses. His erotic exploits with men, a fairly minor part of his sexual proclivities, were the only ones that were caste-blind. For most of his pleasure was sought with women of quality—women, in fact, with the most distinguished titles and the most powerful connections in the kingdom.

Upon arriving in Paris from Provence in 1721, Comte de Sade made friends, through family acquaintances, with the very unpopular but powerful Prince de Condé, father of the young noble who would be roughed up by little Donatien. He obtained a captaincy in Condé's regiment. And he soon began a liaison with the prince's sister, Mlle de Charolais, the most beautiful of the Bourbon princesses and one of the more dissolute women of the French court. She ordered her portraitists to depict her in the garb of a Franciscan nun, not out of any religious devotion but as a way of sexually arousing the lovers to whom she offered these images. "The singularity of the adventure entices me as much as it does you," Mlle de Charolais once wrote Donatien's father when he suggested some particularly exotic orgy, "and the curiosity of knowing if this debauch will suit me leads me to accept your proposition."[2]

Comte de Sade's erotic activities, like his brother's in Provence, should be seen in the context of a particularly libertine phase of French culture. Donatien's father arrived in Paris in the last years of the Regency, the eight-year interlude that began in 1715 with the death of Louis XIV and ended when his only legitimate offspring, his thirteen-year-old great-grandson Louis, was crowned King Louis XV. The Regency was the most dissolute period in French history and might well vie with the late Roman Empire as the most debauched era of Western civilization. Indeed, Mlle de Charolais's capers seem fairly innocuous compared with the excesses of her peers.

The permissiveness of Regency society was in part a rebellion against the rigid etiquette of Louis XIV's court and the austere protocol imposed by his last consort, or morganatic wife, Mme de Maintenon. But it also took its moral tone from the proclivities of the regent himself, the Duc d'Orléans, Louis XIV's nephew, who ruled France between Louis XV's fifth and thirteenth years. A brilliant, industrious statesman, the regent was also an indefatigable playboy and voyeur, who took up with a new batch of paramours at least every fortnight and enjoyed witnessing, if not participating in, some of the most outlandish bacchanals of the time.

In a frenzy of pleasure-seeking, members of the regent's circle held nightly "suppers" at which, after hours of serious drinking, the highest nobility in the land reenacted the illustrations of various classics of erotic literature. Or else they watched as Prince de Soubise got his lover, Mme de Gacé, thoroughly inebriated and ordered a group of valets to take their pleasure with her. "Our state of general debauch is dreadful," the regent's mother commented about the morals of her son's entourage. "Youths of both sexes . . . have the conduct of pigs and sows. . . . Women . . . particularly those of our highest families . . . are worse than those in houses of ill repute. . . . I'm amazed that France is not totally drowned, like Sodom and Gomorrah."[3] The prudish Mme de Maintenon readily concurred. "I prefer not to paint you a picture of our current mores; I would sin against the love one should have for one's country,"[4] she wrote about the era that followed her consort's reign.

The period of French history into which Comte de Sade was born has been eloquently represented by the refined hedonism of Watteau's and Boucher's paintings and has primarily been known as the Age of Pleasure-Seeking. But one could also look on it as the Age of Cruelty. A perfect example of the vicious eighteenth-century French aristocrat was Comte de Charolais, the brother of Prince de Condé and of Comte de Sade's mistress. Charolais was particularly detested for the ferocity of his pleasures. "His heart was cruel and his actions were bloody. . . . Orgies of all kinds were to his taste," a contemporary described him.[5] Drunk more often than not, Charolais killed peasants for sheer sport the way other men went hunting, and fired at workmen repairing roofs in the village adjoining his castle. Attempting to avoid prosecution, he once begged Louis XV's forgiveness for such murders. The monarch replied: "The pardon you seek is granted . . . but I shall be even more pleased to pardon the man who kills you."

"Sublime reply!"[6] the Marquis de Sade later commented on this royal mercy. During his childhood, Donatien had been closely acquainted with Charolais, who was the legal guardian of his childhood playmate Prince de Condé, and he would later draw heavily on him to portray the depraved protagonists of his novels.

In one brutal prank, Charolais got the Marquise de Saint-Sulpice drunk, then placed two ropes of explosives under her skirt and ignited them. His victim was taken home wrapped in a tablecloth, with dreadful burns on her stomach and thighs. This caper was celebrated with a ditty that swiftly made the rounds of Paris: *"Le grand portail de Saint-*

Sulpice / Où l'on a tant fait le service / est brulé jusqu'aux fondements."
("The great portal of Saint-Sulpice [one of Paris's most celebrated churches], / Which was the site of so many services, / Has been burned down to its foundations.")[7]

Such was the milieu that young Comte de Sade chose as the power base for his attempted rise in Paris society. Such were the examples set for his son.

LIKE HIS BROTHER the abbé, Comte de Sade had literary aspirations, which he expressed in heroic verses, novellas, comedies, and tragedies. But unlike his brother, who left a lasting work of scholarship in his biography of Petrarch, the count never published his writings. Donatien's father exemplified the type of man described by the French phrase *petit maître*—the gay blade endowed with a superficial scribbler's talent who gets ahead in the world through his abundance of facile charm. Of his large literary output, only the count's letters, filled with racy documentations of mid-eighteenth-century Parisian mores, remain of interest to posterity.

Observing society from the homes of the capital's most exalted aristocrats—the Condés, the Rochefoucaulds, his distant cousin the Duchesse de La Roche-Guyon—the count served as confidant to the city's liveliest dowagers: "She tells me that her love is so violent that it is her very first passion,"[8] he commented about a sixty-year-old duchess who had taken a twenty-two-year-old lover. "Mme de Clermont could not resist the pleasure of simultaneously cuckolding two men,"[9] he wrote about another Parisian grande dame. His correspondence with his own paramours is filled with ironic reversals of accepted pieties. "How can one not be unfaithful, my queen?" he wrote to one of his most beloved mistresses, Mme de Raimond, whom young Donatien would eventually look upon as an adopted mother. "Only idiots are constant. . . . One must submit to whatever temptation presents itself. . . . I've sometimes known faithful lovers. . . . Their sadness, moroseness, would make you tremble. If my son were to be faithful, I would be outraged."[10]

Comte de Sade's eventual social decline was based not only on his lack of scruples but on an astonishing lack of judgment. He seems to have made a grave miscalculation, for instance, by choosing the Condé-Charolais family as his central power base, for they were as despised by their fellow nobles, and by the general public, as any aristocrats in France. The count's fall from grace would also be caused by the fact that his sensual impulses all too often got in the way of his good sense.

Having received all the favors he needed from Mlle de Charolais,

he moved on to affairs with dozens of other highborn mistresses, including the second wife of his principal protector, Prince de Condé. She was
a beautiful fifteen-year-old German princess, twenty-five years Condé's
junior, and she was harder to seduce than most other Parisian women
because her husband guarded her with particularly fierce jealousy. But
no moral scruples ever stood in the way of Comte de Sade's appetites,
no means were too crude in achieving his end. In order to "be closer to
her and obtain permission to see her at all hours,"[11] as he wrote in a
memoir, he decided to court and marry one of Princesse de Condé's
ladies-in-waiting, Mlle Maillé de Carman. Aristocratic but penniless, she
was a distant cousin of the Condés. She would eventually become the
Marquis de Sade's mother.

Comte de Sade readily admitted to the cynical manner in which he
contrived his marriage. As the first phase of his strategy, he secured
Prince de Condé's agreement to the union by claiming that he was
marrying her solely to remain close to his protector. Touched by his
courtier's devotion, the prince paid for the couple's bridal clothes and
all other details of their nuptials, which took place in 1734. As the timid
young Comtesse de Sade prepared for her wedding night, she begged
her own protector, Princesse de Condé, to remain by her bedside. A
piquant vision: the princess observed her lady-in-waiting being deflowered by a man who was in fact lusting for her, the witness. Here is how
Comte de Sade describes the scene in a memoir written some years later:

> The presence of the princess heightened my rapture and
> made me keener and more eager than ever to remain in her
> company. . . . Everyone seemed pleased. . . . Notwithstanding
> her dearth of assets, my wife had found a husband . . . [the
> princess] had a lady-in-waiting on whom she could rely . . .
> and I—I had an engaging wife, the prospect of a regiment that
> [Prince de Condé] had promised me, and the hope of being
> loved by a charming young princess. I pointed out to her that
> I had sacrificed my material security by marrying a girl without
> dowry . . . for the sole purpose of being closer to her and ob-
> taining permission to see her at all hours. My marriage afforded
> me considerable familiarity [with the Princess]. I could enter
> her quarters anytime.[12]

These Casanova-like tactics eventually backfired. Comte de Sade
was soon confronted by his mistress's jealousy of his wife and had to
promise Princesse de Condé that he would sleep in a separate bed. Com-

tesse de Sade learned about the lovers' trysts and threatened to tell all to the powerful prince. The call of military duty saved Comte de Sade from the wrath of his protector; he was ordered to join his regiment three months after his marriage. The ensuing events read like a Marivaux comedy: Shortly after Sade's departure for the army, Princesse de Condé took another lover. Upon returning from his military tour, Comte de Sade, with characteristic lack of scruples, sought revenge for her infidelity by telling the prince about his wife's new paramour. The infuriated prince consequently increased the surveillance of his spouse and dismissed all her ladies-in-waiting with the exception of Comtesse de Sade —the only one of the lot, he thought, who would remain beyond reproach.

Both couples then settled down to the task of begetting children. In 1736, the Condés had a son, Louis-Joseph, the playmate who would be so roughly treated by the little Marquis de Sade. In 1740, a year after her first child, Caroline-Laure, had died at the age of two (one could surmise that her grief over this loss led her to withdraw emotionally from her next child), Comtesse de Sade gave birth to the future marquis. A curious incident occurred when the infant was baptized: unattended by his parents or any other relatives, he was carried to the church by two absentminded servants, who forgot the precise names his parents intended to give him, Donatien Aldonse Louis, and instead had him baptized Donatien Alphonse François. Throughout his life, the marquis would resent not having the privilege of being called Louis, the baptismal name of all the Bourbon kings. When he reached adulthood, he would recover the sign of distinction by signing most official documents "Louis Aldonse Donatien de Sade." This habit would have serious repercussions for him during the 1789 Revolution, when he was forced to shed his title of nobility, yet continued to intimate his kinship with royalty by calling himself Louis Sade.

What did the marquis's father gain from all his scheming? The young woman Comte de Sade married because of his lust for another was not only dowerless but indolent and self-absorbed, yet her pedigree was as lofty as any rake could have hoped for. As a distant cousin of Prince de Condé, she offered Sade a connection to the junior branch of France's royal family. In 1741, a year after Donatien's birth, Sade's enhanced social status enabled him to obtain a diplomatic post to the court of the Elector of Bavaria. He lived in high style, incurring large debts as he maintained the most sumptuous household of Bavaria's diplomatic corps.

The next stages of his career were far less successful. He soon managed to argue with the elector, and in 1745, during one of the frequent border skirmishes between Bavaria and Austria that occurred in the wake of the War of Austrian Succession, he was jailed by troops loyal to Empress Maria Theresa of Austria, France's enemy in that particular conflict. Neither of the clashing factions seemed eager to liberate him. He lingered in prison for seven months, writing poetry and prose fiction, cheered solely by correspondence from Paris friends, including Voltaire, who sent him his newest plays.

In the middle of his jail term, Comte de Sade had yet one more picaresque adventure, which attests to his occasional sense of honor: An Austrian citizen, the Countess of Metternich, who seems to have been yet another of his conquests, decided to engineer his escape by dressing him up in women's clothes. At the last minute the count demurred, fearing that he might compromise her. ("I felt ashamed of the dangers she was risking for my sake," he recounted in a memoir. "I got out of the woman's vestments and returned them to her."[13]) Only the efforts of Comtesse de Sade, who in one of her rare moments of energy pleaded with the highest powers in Europe for the release of her husband, returned him to freedom.

Shortly after he came back to Paris, Comte de Sade was accused of having committed several irregularities during his ambassadorial term, such as collecting excessive stipends. This marked the beginning of his social decline. Louis XV's minister of foreign affairs, the powerful Marquis d'Argenson, had long looked on the comte as a mere minion and puppet of the Condé family, "a fop of some intelligence but no substance."[14] This was the view held by numerous French grandees, who hated the arrogant Condés but did not dare attack them head-on. After Prince de Condé's death, in 1740, when the reputation of his minion, Comte de Sade, became officially blemished, Donatien's father was relentlessly persecuted.

The count's fortunes plummeted even further when he incurred the disfavor of King Louis XV by criticizing one of his mistresses, Mme de Châteauroux. For this imprudence he would suffer the rest of his life. He was thereafter assigned only the most trivial diplomatic missions and was ostracized from all positions of power. Forced to live very modestly, he was largely supported by the revenue from his lands in Provence and by the stipends he received from the honorary governorship of four small provinces in the Savoy region. (It usually took a few generations for the offspring of noble families to go bankrupt, but Comte de Sade had managed it in one.) By the time the young Marquis de Sade came of age, his own social status would be compromised by his father's bad reputation, and his own social demise can in part be traced to his parent's disgrace.

In the eyes of his peers, there was not much that Comte de Sade had done right. Involved as he was in the calculating life of the courtier —choosing his mistresses out of a blend of snobbism and lust, marrying a woman because of his passion for another—he found release for his innate recklessness in wilder, more impulsive experiences. In 1726, when the count was twenty-four years old, there was published in Paris a collection of doggerel verses that narrated the antics of various Paris homosexuals. They were to be sung to the tune of a familiar ditty called "J'ai du Mirliton," roughly translatable as "I Have a Reed Pipe." ("You rejects of Sodom . . . ," one couplet goes, "I summon you to bring / Your cute bums to the rendezvous.") The ballad singled out various Parisian nobles, such as the Duc de La Vrillière, a member of the regent's circle, as notorious sodomites. ("Does one withdraw, at your age, / From the handsome La Vrillière? / Up with your ass!") Another of the song's couplets, all of which ended with the refrain "I have a reed pipe," went on to specify Comte de Sade:

"You seem pretty wan / With your seigneurial air, / Yet, Comte de Sade, / Just to prove my vigor / I have a reed pipe. . . ."[15]

Some of the count's own writings have a bisexual tone. Here are two poems in which he expressed the complexities of his erotic tastes:

"When I pay you my respects I fulfill many appetites, / In your company I frolic with both woman and boy. / I adore the fickle female in you, / The wise companion, the delightful catamite."

Also from the count's pen: "Like a citizen of Sodom / I play the woman's role with a man— / That's what puts you in a rage. / But why get angry, ladies? / You alone make me happy: / With women I am all man."[16]

Might one say that Comte de Sade's picaresque androgyny is one of the traits that kept him from becoming another preening courtier? That he was too imprudent, too foolhardy, to be a mere fop? That is the impression he wished to give when, toward the end of his life, he wrote a memoir much colored by the reawakened religiousness of his old age. Here is how he explained his botched career: "What stood in the way of my success was that I was always too much the libertine to bide my time in an antechamber, too poor to bribe my servants to serve my interests, and too proud to flatter the favorites, the ministers, and the mistresses. I've said it a hundred times: I am a free man."[17]

The self-portrait is somewhat disingenuous. Sade *père* fawned all too ardently on the favorites, ministers, and mistresses. And he was not nearly as free a man as he thought, for the simple reason that he lied too frequently to others and to himself.

This is the enigmatic father with whom Donatien began to make friends at the age of ten, when the count called him back to Paris. Extremely ambitious for his only child, Comte de Sade had decided, with good reason, that his son needed a more solid education than he was getting at the abbé's seraglio in sunny Provence.

III

Wild Oats

More than three hundred persons were already assembled, all of them naked. They were busy sodomizing, whacking each other off, whipping each other, engaging in fellatio, coming to orgasm—all of this in the greatest calm; one could only hear whatever noise was necessitated by the circumstances.

—*Juliette*

□

WHEN THE TEN-YEAR-OLD Marquis de Sade arrived in Paris, his speech was still colored by the Provençal accent he had acquired during his years in Avignon and Saumane. It seems that this rustic youngster did not take easily to formal studies. His name is not found in the lists of prize-winners published yearly by the school his father had chosen for him, the Jesuits' College Louis-le-Grand. But then the challenge had been formidable: it was the most prestigious and rigorous educational institution of its time, and its three thousand students included the offspring of France's most powerful families.

Young Donatien did not have to confront Paris by himself. His tutor, Abbé Amblet, retained to oversee his schoolwork, accompanied him to the capital. A private tutor was a prerequisite of all noble families, even in a household as impoverished as Comte de Sade's. Louis-le-Grand's wealthier student boarders lived in fancy private suites at school with their mentors and private valets. Due to his father's straitened circumstances, Donatien had to be a day student; he probably lodged nearby in Abbé Amblet's modest flat on Rue des Fossés-Monsieur-le-Prince.

Despite Donatien's lack of academic distinction, his three and a half years of Jesuit education profoundly marked his character, the nature of his sexuality, and the erotic fantasies he would express in his works. For among the most distinctive traits of Jesuit schools in eighteenth-century France were their emphasis on corporal punishment, their reputation for sodomy, and their tradition of staging lavish theatrical productions.

The practice of whipping students was hardly exclusive to Jesuits in Sade's time. The most important pedagogical textbook of the century, the *Instruction Manual for Christian Schoolmasters,* specified that although blows to the head and stomach should be avoided, "the rod [on the buttocks] is necessary. . . . It produces good behavior, and it must be used."[1] As practiced by Jesuits, who held their whippings in front of the assembled student body and had a notoriously heavy hand, the experience was particularly humiliating. Moreover, floggings can be sexually arousing and often generate what came to be called sadomasochistic behavior. As an adult, Sade would seldom be satisfied by "normal" sex, and in many ways his carnal preferences seemed arrested at an infantile anal level.

The Jesuits' bent for severe floggings was made all the more onerous by the sodomistic inclinations alleged to prevail in the order. A popular French euphemism for pederasty was *molinisme,* after the eminent sixteenth-century Jesuit theologian Luis de Molina. The ditty that cites Comte de Sade's sexual proclivities includes an explicit couplet concerning Jesuits: "And you, Messieurs Jesuits, / Come one and all, come swiftly— / Do not delay in sampling my reed pipe."[2]

The goal of young Sade's sophisticated teachers, who were the finest educators of their time and imposed a far less pious routine than other religious schools—only three brief prayer sessions a day—was to turn out worldly leaders with a wide range of culture. The dramas, operas, and oratorios performed five times a year at the Jesuits' Paris lycée were intended to encourage "the boldness and discernment necessary to public speaking" and "train them for [vocations] in the Church and the Law."[3] The Jesuits' stagings, in the eighteenth century, tended to a physical splendor and scale seldom achieved before in France: some stages were over five hundred feet deep; performances lasted for as long as eight hours and could have up to twenty-five set changes. Lycée Louis-le-Grand's theatrical storerooms were vaster than those of the prestigious Comédie Française;[4] and the general grandeur of its productions—replete with gold and marble trappings, majestic mansions and landscapes—was not surpassed by any thespian group in Paris. Professional dancers and singers from the Paris Opéra often performed alongside the students. The plays drew large audiences from outside the school, attracting court nobles and Paris bourgeois as well as students' families.

Only the highest-ranking pupils were allowed to participate in these productions. Donatien did not receive good grades, so it is probable he never had a chance to take part in them. His lifelong infatuation with the stage may have been all the more passionate because it was frustrated in his youth. All of Sade's biographers have emphasized that the theatricality of Sade's fictions—with their tableaux vivants, complex sexual choreographies, and balletic poses—was influenced by the flamboyant performances he attended during his student days.

The Jesuits' attitude toward the sacrament of confession also affected him deeply. The importance of diagnosing the roots of our sinfulness is emphasized more by Jesuits than by any other Catholic order. In their view, the diligent dissection of trespasses is at the core of the spiritual life. It could even be said that Jesuit-style confession tends to be lenient toward sin by valorizing the process of analyzing it. Throughout his life, Sade would resort to a typically Jesuitic form of casuistry to justify the abundance of crimes and debauches limned in his fictions: he defended them as indispensable to our deeper knowledge of the human heart. As he wrote in an essay on the novelistic process: "The profound study of man's heart—nature's labyrinth—alone can inspire the novelist, whose work must make us see man not only as he is, or as he purports to be—which is the duty of the historian—but as he is capable of being when subjected to the modifying influences of vice and the full impact of passion. Therefore . . . we must know them all, we must employ every passion and vice, if we labor in this field."[5]

DONATIEN'S ROUTINE during school months was worse than spartan. According to survivors of the Jesuit regimen, the food offered to the young nobles at Lycée Louis-le-Grand was nauseating and the bedding often ridden with vermin. Nor were Donatien's lycée years softened by any maternal solicitude; Comtesse de Sade remained as glacially aloof as ever. Within a few years of his return to Paris, she moved into a Carmelite convent on Paris's Rue d'Enfer, convents offering housing that was extremely popular among the indigent nobility. However, Donatien's solitude was again allayed, as it had been during his stay in Avignon, by the presence of adoring women.

The youth's first summer vacation from the lycée was spent at the Château de Longeville, some eighty kilometers east of Paris, with his father's former paramour Mme de Raimond. She had only a daughter, and she quickly grew so fond of Donatien that in her letters to Comte de Sade she always referred to him as "our son" or "our child," while Donatien addressed her as "Maman." Mme de Raimond had an entourage of equally doting ladies, two of whom—Mme de Saint-Germain and Mme de Vernouillet—played central roles in Donatien's emotional life between his tenth and fourteenth years. The beautiful Mme de Vernouillet (yet another former paramour of Donatien's father) delighted in turning the child's head, and at the age of thirteen he fell hopelessly in love with her, to the amusement of his hostess.

"He is truly in love with her," Mme de Raimond wrote the Comte de Sade. "It made me laugh so hard I cried. . . . He evidently experienced sensations which he could not express, which astonished him and drove him wild. His confusion was charming. He was angry, then he stood still, and later he gave way to fits of jealousy and other signs of the most tender, the warmest love. And his 'mistress' was indeed touched and moved. She said, 'This is a most unusual child.' " [6]

So DURING THE VACATIONS of his early adolescence, Donatien was once more surrounded by flirtatious, caressing women who spoiled him rotten and incited his first sensual impulses. At the end of one school furlough he burst into sobs when the time came to say good-bye to his "maman," Mme de Raimond. "Alas, our child has departed and left us in sadness," she wrote his father. "He has a heart, this charming boy. . . . Tell him how much I love him and am touched by his thoughtfulness. . . . I love him too as if he were my child. I hope he loves me as a mother." [7]

Young Donatien seemed to be as irresistible to women as his father had been. During his school years he was also invited to spend time at the country home of Mme de Saint-Germain, whose maternal sentiments were as deep as Mme de Raimond's. She became so attached to him that she often refused to send the boy back to his uncle or his father, begging them to let her keep him a while longer.

"Yes, I take pleasure in loving your child," she wrote the Comte de Sade, who seemed very pleased by his son's first social successes. "Time, which consumes all things, only increases my passion for him. . . . Your brother [Abbé de Sade] has been trying to take him from me for the past two weeks. I am pained to the point of distraction. . . . Can you be so cruel as to deprive me of my child, to deny me the only pleasure I ask of you on bended knee?" [8]

The relationships Donatien forged in his youth with these women remained deep and doggedly loyal. He would idolize Mme de Saint-Germain for the rest of his life. Writing to his wife from jail decades later, he described Mme de Saint-Germain as "the one woman in the world I love most after you, to whom I surely owe as much as a son can owe his mother." [9] "If she has died," he wrote another time, "do not tell me, because I love her, I have always prodigiously loved her, and I would never get over it." [10]

THROUGHOUT DONATIEN'S last year with the Jesuits, Comte de Sade was pulling all the strings he could to prepare his son for an army career. Toward the end of 1754, when Donatien had just turned fourteen, the count took him out of the lycée and placed him in a prestigious military academy. There he would be trained to serve in the light cavalry regiment of the king's guard, one of the most elite units in the country. Somewhat similar in prestige to the "Musketeers" of Dumas fame, it comprised only two hundred guardsmen and nineteen officers, drawn from the highest nobility in the land. Such an abrupt change of schooling was frequent among Louis-le-Grand students, the great majority of whom were destined for military careers. (It was not unusual for boys to join regiments at the age of twelve and to be accompanied to the battlefield by their tutors. Some honorary officers were so young that they had to be carried on their mentors' shoulders.)

Young Sade entered the king's light cavalry regiment in the last weeks of 1755, after twenty months of training, with the grade of sublieutenant. Soon thereafter he went into battle. The Seven Years' War, in which, through a radical reshuffling of political alignments, France, Russia, and Austria joined in a coalition against Prussia and England, had just begun. Donatien had his baptism by fire at the age of fifteen, when the French seized the British site of Port Mahon, the most impregnable fortress in Europe after Gibraltar. Leading four companies of grenadiers, Lieutenant de Sade distinguished himself in a particularly dangerous assault, during which the French troops lost over four hundred officers. "At ten o'clock at night, all batteries having ceased their fire," the *Gazette de Paris* reported, ". . . the Marquis de Briqueville and Sieur de Sade energetically assaulted the queen's redoubt, and after a heated and rather deadly exchange of fire, managed, by frontal assaults . . . to grasp hold of the objective and establish a position there." [11]

By the time Donatien began military service, his father seemed to have but one goal left in life: having ruined his own career and squandered most of his inheritance, he longed to see his child obtain all the glory and stability he himself had never been able to achieve. Comte de Sade began to wield whatever influence he still had at court to get his son into a unit even more prestigious than the king's light cavalry. The Carabiniers de Monsieur were commanded by a member of the royal family, usually by the king's brother, who was known as "Monsieur."

Only men the French then considered very tall, at least five feet four inches, were allowed into the Carabiniers, and Donatien was only five feet two, but his father prevailed upon a friend of Mme de Pompadour, then Louis XV's "official" mistress, to get him in. So at the age of sixteen, Donatien became the standard-bearer of an entire cavalry company.

Alarmed by reports that the Carabiniers' mores were notoriously loose, Comte de Sade followed his son from garrison to garrison like a duenna, visiting Donatien's superiors and begging them to observe closely the morals of their troops. He expressed his concerns to Mme de Raimond. "My polite entreaties are meant to say: 'Gentlemen, do not seduce this child! What good would it do you to turn him into a libertine? Aren't there enough of you already? Respect his naïveté.' "[12] So the rakish Comte de Sade, attempting to restore the family reputation his own haplessness had tarnished, became very puritan about the behavior of his precious son. Mme de Raimond complimented her friend on his paternal devotion.

> . . . in reading your letters I feel that no father is more affectionate or more concerned with making his son virtuous. A libertine would not take such care. Where can one find a father who follows his son to his regiment, who subjects himself to the boredom of courting all the officers, old and young, who finds associates for him, who is sensitive enough to fear that the passions may speak more loudly than reason, and who sets such an example?[13]

In 1758, as Donatien turned eighteen, his military superiors' satisfaction with him enabled Comte de Sade to relax his surveillance. Beyond his courage, the character trait most often stressed in army reports on the young Sade was "his extreme gentleness." The count was consoled by this praise. His finances had been further reduced since his dismissal from the diplomatic corps. And that year he was left particularly destitute by the death of Mlle de Charolais, with whom he had retained a warm platonic friendship and whose home, for reasons of economy, he had shared for over a decade. In order to pay the debts incurred by his son's education, he had even thought of cutting his expenses by retiring to a monastery.

Instead Comte de Sade, upon being comforted by good reports on his son, went to live for a while in Avignon, with his eighty-three-year-old mother. Mme de Raimond warned the count that he might be jeopardizing Donatien's future by leaving Paris, but she could not dis-

suade him. He wrote her a letter in which he expressed his bitter disillusionment with the city he once considered a gateway to all kinds of
glory.

"I went to see the queen," he wrote, describing his last visit to
Queen Marie Leszczynska, wife of Louis XV. "She said, 'M. de Sade, it
has been a long time since I last saw you.' I thought of telling her, 'Alas,
you will see me no more. . . .' What a difference, my dear countess, to
see the court as one who is leaving rather than as one who clings to it!
What madness to have gone there in search of happiness! Slavery is all
that is to be found."[14]

Meanwhile Donatien was promoted to the rank of captain. More
winsome than ever, he now strutted about in a gleaming blue cavalry
uniform with crimson lining, cuffs, and collar. While stationed in Germany, he decided to learn the local language.

> I was told that to learn a language well it was necessary to
> sleep regularly . . . with a woman of the country. Convinced of
> the truth of this maxim, I equipped myself, in my winter quar-
> ters in Cleves, with a nice fat baroness three or four times my
> age, who educated me very nicely. After six months I spoke
> German like Cicero.[15]

But Donatien's liaison with a "nice fat baroness" was the least
of his father's concerns. As Mme de Raimond had feared, the count's
retirement to Provence, and the cessation of his constant scrutiny, provoked Donatien to far more serious dissipation. The first report of trouble came in Donatien's nineteenth year, from a fellow officer who had
befriended him: "Your dear son is doing marvelously," the young man
wrote the Comte de Sade. "He is friendly, easygoing, and amusing. . . .
We're taking care of him. . . . His little heart, or, rather, *body* is furiously
combustible. German girls, look out!! I will do my utmost to keep him
from doing anything stupid. He's given me his word not to gamble
more than a louis a day."[16]

The count sent a copy of the letter to his brother the abbé, with the
following annotation: "As if that scoundrel had a louis a day to lose! He
promised me not to risk a cent. But you can't ever trust him to keep his
word." In the same mailing, the count included a "confessional letter"
that Donatien had sent to Abbé Amblet, asking his former tutor to pass it
on to his father. This missive, which responds to harsh paternal criticism
concerning Donatien's increasingly promiscuous conduct, is the budding libertine's first surviving letter and his first self-portrait.

The number of mistakes I made during my stay in Paris, my dear Abbé, and the manner in which I behaved to the world's most affectionate father, make him regret that he ever brought me there. But I am amply punished by the remorse I feel at having displeased him, and by my fear of losing his friendship forever. Of those pleasures which I believed to be so real, nothing remains but the pain at having irritated the most affectionate of fathers and the best of friends.

I woke up every morning looking for pleasure. This sole idea made me forget everything else, [and] I was happy the minute I found what I was looking for. But this supposed happiness vanished as quickly as my desires turned to regrets. At night I turned desperate. I acknowledged my misdeeds, but only at night, and the very next day my desires returned and sent me out again in pursuit of pleasure. . . .

Note the recurrence of the key word of that century, "pleasure." One is also struck by the reiterated expressions of tenderness for the increasingly judgmental, critical father and by young Sade's desire to make a Jesuit-style "general confession" to pacify his parent.

A moment ago, I received a letter from my father in which he asks me to make a *general confession*. I shall make it, and I assure you that it will be sincere. I cannot equivocate anymore with a father who is so tender and who is still willing to forgive me if I admit my faults.[17]

The following year, aged twenty and apparently indulging in increasingly dissipated behavior, Donatien again sought to recapture his parent's affection through a Jesuit-style "confession." This time it was written directly to Comte de Sade.

You ask me for a report on my life and occupations. I'll give you a detailed report in all sincerity. People reproach my fondness for sleep. It's true that I suffer somewhat from this fault, I go to bed early and get up very late. . . . I act in accordance with my thoughts, good or bad. I speak my mind to people and am praised or blamed in proportion to whatever common sense there is in my ideas. Sometimes I pay visits, but only to M. de Pouyanne [Sade's regimental general] or to my former comrades in the Carabiniers or the king's regiment. . . . I know I'm not doing myself any good. One has to pay court to succeed, but I don't like doing it. . . .

"To be courteous, honest, dignified but not proud, obliging but not tepid," so the young man's credo continues, "to do quite often the little things we enjoy when they do no damage to ourselves or to others. To live well and have a good time without harming ourselves or losing our wits. . . ."

The following lines are crucial to our understanding of young Sade's disaffection from his peers, his growing distrust of humanity in general, and his greatest terror—losing the love of the only parent he knows:

> [I have] few friends, perhaps none, because I know no one who is truly sincere and who would not sacrifice you twenty times if he found the slightest advantage in it. . . . Whom can we trust, anyhow? Friends are like women: when put to the test, the goods often prove defective. That is my full confession. I open my heart to you, not as to a father whom one often fears and does not love, but to the most honest of friends, the most tender friend I deem to have in the world. Give up your reasons for pretending to hate me, give me back your love and never deprive me of it again, and believe that I will do everything in my power to try to preserve it.[18]

Yet another desperate appeal for love from the parent who may have been all the more embittered by his son's flaws because they mirrored his own. Throughout Sade's youth he constantly tried, and failed, to regain his father's affection. At the same time, he remained totally alienated from a mother who was alive and well in Paris. As his surrogate mothers—Mme de Saint-Germain, Mme de Raimond—understood so well, Donatien's flippancy and dissipation concealed a hypersensitive character starved for tenderness. In 1762, his grandmother, the dowager Marquise de Sade, died at her home in Avignon. The loss seems to have created yet another void in the young man's life. "I adored her and she brought me up," Sade would write later.[19]

IN FEBRUARY 1763, when Donatien was twenty-two years old, the Seven Years' War came to an end. France, resoundingly defeated, emerged from the conflict weakened and humiliated, stripped of its most lucrative colonies, including Canada, and most of its West Indian holdings. Great Britain now ruled the seas. Frederick II of Prussia was the true victor of the war and was remodeling his nation on efficient, rational principles derived from the philosophers of the French Enlightenment, thinkers who were having little impact on their own rulers.

Aristocratic mores may have become a trifle more decorous under Louis XV's reign than they were under the Regency, but excesses were still rampant. The monarch, upon being denied the sexual favors of Mme de Pompadour, a brilliant woman who had never had much fondness for sex, created the legendary private brothel called Parc aux Cerfs, a mansion near Versailles where a select group of adolescent beauties destined for the king alone were lodged. By 1763, French citizens had begun to display a measure of the discontent that would eventually be unleashed in the fury of the French Revolution. Louis XV, the "dearly beloved" monarch of earlier decades, was being referred to in the increasingly powerful satirical underground press as the "vile, imbecilic automaton," "the father of thieves and of harlots." [20] Tensions between the Crown and the increasingly powerful merchant and magistrate classes grew apace. It was seen as a bad omen that a mentally unbalanced man who served as a domestic in a family of magistrates, a valet called Damiens, had scratched the king lightly with a knife and suffered a sensational public execution.

But Donatien, who was demobilized toward the end of the war, still thought of little beyond his "pleasures." Having been in army service since the age of fourteen, throughout the entire duration of the Seven Years' War, he now launched into Paris social life without a care in the world. The document testifying to his honorable army discharge offers a laconic appraisal of his character: "Deranged, but extremely courageous." [21] And the activities he engaged in after his stint in the army make it clear that the term "deranged" referred to his dissipations. He frequented houses of prostitution, ran up large gambling debts, and was particularly noticed for his failure to pay court to the king. Comte de Sade, endeavoring to curb his son's excesses, returned to Paris from Provence in the winter of 1762—he lived in modest lodgings at the foreign ministry headquarters on Rue du Bac. The count was increasingly infuriated by his only child and complained in a letter, "My son never misses a ball or a spectacle; everyone is indignant." [22] He described Donatien as "riffraff . . . devoid of one good quality," [23] his head "filled with wind" and an insatiable appetite for pleasure. "I have never known one like him," the count concluded. "He will force me to leave Paris in order that I may never hear about him again." [24]

In short, Comte de Sade was mortified to see that his once beloved offspring had not only followed his dissolute example but was threatening to better him. There was only one way out for the now ailing, increasingly destitute count, who still hoped that his son might eventually redeem his own disgraces: he must marry Donatien off as soon as possible, and for a handsome sum of money.

IV

Settling Down

It is so delicious when the movements of one's heart
are in accord with the laws of society and with its
sacred pledges. . . . Our wife is simultaneously our
mistress, our sister, our God.

—*Aline et Valcour*

□

"I'VE ALWAYS FELT I should marry him off early," Comte de Sade wrote
one of his sisters about Donatien in 1762. "No one believed me, I was
told it wasn't urgent, but now I know it's time."[1] The count had been
negotiating with various families for two years. His first bridal prospect,
a noblewoman in northern France, had been flawed by her ripe age—
thirty years—and her modest dowry. A damsel from Avignon of equally
distinguished pedigree did not offer the fortune the count hoped for. In
the last months of 1762, he finally struck gold: a friend of his—the
director of the Invalides—talked to him about his niece Renée-Pélagie
de Montreuil, approximately Donatien's age, who was the oldest of six
children of a high-ranking Paris judge. Unlike the earlier candidates, the
Montreuils belonged to the recently ennobled bourgeoisie rather than
the "true" aristocracy, but they offered a very promising income and
unusually powerful connections at court. The count began his siege, and
within a few weeks he managed to have a marriage contract drawn up.

A family of bourgeois origins may seem like a singular choice for
arrogant patricians such as the Sades, who prided themselves on their
kinship with the French royal family. But marriages between the ancient
noblesse d'épée and the rawer *noblesse de robe,* who were descended from
middle-class magistrates and merchants, were increasingly frequent in
the eighteenth century. Such alliances were based on the growing penury
of the more ancient nobility, of which Comte de Sade was a perfect

example. It had been Louis XIV's strategy to weaken the power of the aristocracy by drawing them to Versailles and creating a court society in which prestige depended on flamboyant display. Since his reign, many aristocrats had lost their wealth by living far beyond their means.

How desirable a groom was the young Marquis de Sade? He was not altogether without assets. Beyond his lofty name, he was known for his attractive bearing, lively wit, and sprightly conversation; for his already exceptional literary culture; and for his charming singing voice. His income was modest but not totally negligible. He received some ten thousand livres a year from his honorary governorship[2] of four provinces in Savoy, posts that Comte de Sade had recently transferred to his son with a view toward making him a more attractive marital prospect. He was also the sole heir to the Sades' estates in the Provençal towns of La Coste, Saumane, and Mazan, and to a large, prosperous farm near Arles called Mas de Cabannes. These passable resources, however, were handicapped by the twenty-two-year-old marquis's reputation for licentiousness. "All earlier marriage prospects have foundered on his bad reputation,"[3] the count himself admitted.

The Montreuils, on the other hand, were a family of perfect stability and uprightness, qualities found more readily in the bourgeoisie than in the relatively dissolute aristocracy. Much of their wealth had been only recently acquired by M. de Montreuil's father, Jacques-René Cordier de Launay, who served as treasurer for a few prosperous northern towns. The year of his son's marriage to Marie-Madeleine du Plissay, daughter of a secretary in the king's household, M. Cordier acquired a baronial land in Normandy called Montreuil-Largillé. It was then that the family name was changed to "de Montreuil." Donatien's future in-laws exemplified the growing power and prestige of the French middle class: most of their own siblings had also married "up." Mme de Montreuil's sisters were wed to a baron and a marquis, and M. de Montreuil's sisters had done as well with a count and two marquis.

But the family's handsome means was far more important to Comte de Sade than their social standing. Whereas his financial situation now restricted him to cheap furnished rooms and public transportation ("We should have a carriage to look decent compared to them,"[4] he complained to his brother), the Montreuils' fortune allowed them to live in a large house staffed with scores of domestics in one of Paris's most fashionable areas, Rue Neuve-du-Luxembourg, near the Madeleine. And they had been able to acquire for their youngest daughter, Anne-Prospère, who would play a crucial role in Sade's later life, the rank of canoness in the Society of the Ladies of Malta, a religious order reserved for members of the nobility.

Soon after the family name was changed, M. de Montreuil had been appointed chief judge of one of Paris's most important courts of law, the Cours des Aides, which oversaw the functioning of government finances. After an early retirement, he remained its honorary president for the rest of his life. Hence the designation given his wife, who was known in Paris society as "la Présidente de Montreuil," a title ideally suited to her dynamic and uniquely commanding character. Her husband, as self-effacing a Milquetoast as could be found in his generation, was usually referred to as "M. de Montreuil."

Comte de Sade at once saw the advantages of this match for his black-sheep son: "The more I think about this marriage, the more I like it," he wrote in April 1763 to his brother the abbé, who retained a keen interest in Donatien. "M. de Montreuil will have at least eighty thousand [extra] livres upon [his mother's] death. . . . M. de Montreuil's offspring might each have incomes of twenty-five thousand livres [a year]. . . . This is not an ephemeral property subject to ups and downs like a businessman's. . . . The mother [is] a gay, devout woman, a worthy woman of great intelligence. . . . In all respects . . . excellent people with whom my son would be quite happy."

He ends this accounting with a comment about his twenty-two-year-old son: "As far as I'm concerned, the best thing about [the marriage] is that I'll be rid of that boy, who has not one good quality and all the bad ones."[5] "To get rid of him I did things I'd never have done if I'd loved him tenderly," he added a few weeks later. "I couldn't have paid too high for the pleasure of not hearing about him anymore."[6]

Writing to his sister Gabrielle Laure, the abbess of Cavaillon, the count pretended to feel guilty at the prospect of deceiving fine folk such as the Montreuils with a rotten bill of goods. "They're the best and the most honest people in the world. . . . I pity them for making such a bad purchase, capable of making all kinds of trouble."[7]

THROUGHOUT THE SPRING of 1763, the count kept panicking at the prospect that his son might jinx this carefully planned alliance. His misgivings were prescient. In the first months of that year, until a few days before the scheduled wedding, Donatien, who had not even met Mlle de Montreuil, was doing his best to get out of the marriage. He was desperately in love with a young woman who belonged to one of the most illustrious families of Provence. Her father was the Marquis de Lauris, sovereign lord of Vacqueyras, a town still known for producing one of the finest wines of the Rhône region, and like the Sades, he could trace his lineage back to early medieval times.[8] The damsel's name was

Laure-Victoire de Lauris, and one cannot help but wonder whether this double measure of the sound "Laure," with its recall of the Sade family's most beloved forebear, cast an additional spell on Donatien.

Laure-Victoire seems to have begun her relationship with Donatien in the last months of 1762, during one of her stays in Paris. A letter written by Donatien to his father during the final weeks of that year states that he has no intention of marrying anyone other than Mlle de Lauris. "As for getting married, I'm still very determined to not marry anyone except the [person] whom I've had the honor of mentioning to you. . . . I beg your pardon if I've resolved never to be counseled by anything else than my heart. . . . You have been kind enough to assure me that you would never trespass against my sentiments."[9]

In March 1763, while his father was putting the finishing touches on the marriage contract with the Montreuils, Donatien went off to Provence, having apparently received Laure's promise that she would join him there. But she reneged on her vow and remained in the capital. Deciding that she was betraying him with another suitor, the young marquis grew belligerent. Laure's alleged perfidy incited Donatien to write her an eight-page letter, which is precursory, in the rage of its invective and its torrent of conflicting emotions, of the frenzied missives he would later pen from his various jails.

> Liar! Ungrateful wretch! What became of your promise to love me as long as you lived?? Who is forcing you to infidelity? Who is persuading you to break the bonds that were to unite us forever? . . . Your family no doubt influenced your decision. . . . You're afraid of being reunited with the one who worships you. The links of an eternal bond were weighing on you, and your heart, exclusively captivated by falseness and frivolity, was not subtle enough to appreciate all its charms. . . . My love was not enough for you. . . . Monster, born to make me miserable, go ahead, never leave the city!! May the betrayals of the rascal who will replace me in your heart make Paris as odious to you as your deceptions have made it to me!!

In characteristically romantic fashion, the lover then recants his fury and tries persuasion.

> . . . But what am I saying? Oh, my dear beloved! My divine friend! Heart's sustenance, sole delight of my life, my dear love, where is my despair taking me? Forgive the outbursts of a miserable man who no longer knows himself, who, after losing

his loved one, can only hope for death. . . . Who could possibly
reattach me to a life of which you were the only delight? I lose
you, I lose my existence, my life, I die the most cruel death.

And then a less romantic issue is introduced: Donatien, who has
just learned that he suffers from the century's most dreaded disease,
accuses his mistress of having infected him, and alternates threats with
additional declarations of love:

> The story of the [clap] should convince you to deal gently
> with me. I admit that I shall not hide it from my rival and that
> it won't be the only confidence I'll share with him. I swear, I'd
> be capable of every possible horror. . . . But I blush to think
> that I'd have to resort to such means to hold on to you. I will,
> I must, speak to you only of your love. . . .
>   Love me always. Be faithful to me lest I die of sorrow.
> Farewell, my beautiful, I adore and love you a thousand times
> more than my own life. Though you tell me to leave you, I
> swear that we'll always remain together.[10]

It is improbable that such threats of blackmail could have won over
any mistress; and it is possible that it was Donatien who infected the
lady. By this time, his father had found out about the illness and was
demanding that the young man return to Paris to appear at the festivities
attendant on his marriage to Mlle de Montreuil. But Donatien stayed on
in Provence, despondently taking the mercury cure, which was then the
most popular remedy for his ailment, while making a last-ditch attempt
to recapture Mlle de Lauris's love.

"Please, just talk about his bouts of fever; that's what I'm saying up
here," the desperate Comte de Sade wrote his sister the abbess in early
May, a fortnight before the scheduled wedding. "Nothing is more important, and easier, than to hide the nature of his illness. . . . If the issue
comes up, one could say that it's nothing but malevolent provincial
gossip."[11]

Time was running out. In mid-May, four days before the wedding,
Donatien still had not returned to Paris. Terrified that news of his son's
Provençal romance threatened the security he'd worked so hard to attain, the count started paying even more feverish court to the Montreuils. "I help things along a little with my concern, courtesy, and
attention," he wrote his sister. "The family seems very pleased with me;
I dine with them and visit them every day. I don't see anyone else,
and their thoughtfulness toward me is beyond imagining."[12] "He's still

capable of messing up the deal," he also ruminated. "I won't be sure until I see them at the altar. . . . [The Montreuils] would call off the marriage if they dared. . . . I'm not strong enough to sustain all these setbacks."[13] "Don't trust my son with any dishes," he had instructed his brother the abbé about Donatien's impending return to Paris. "He'd sell them on the way. Nothing is sacred to him."[14] It was clear that Donatien had "no sentiment or sense of honor," he wrote his sister the abbess about his enfant terrible.

Meanwhile, as the last details of the wedding arrangements were being made, Comtesse de Sade made one of her rare appearances, creating countless complications for her family. As stingy and distrustful as she was self-absorbed, and well forewarned of her son's prodigality, she refused to have Donatien stay with her when he came to Paris for the prenuptial festivities. ("My son will have to stay with me," the count complained. "His mother no longer wants him."[15]) What was far more serious was the countess's adamant refusal to contribute a cent to her son's marital assets and her particular unwillingness to offer him as much as one of her diamonds, a traditional parental wedding gift. "Mme de Sade held us up for three days, making new difficulties every day," the count complained to his brother in May. "She's a terrible woman. Her son will take after her."[16]

According to Comte de Sade, the countess talked so disparagingly about their son that Donatien's prospective in-laws came to his defense. "Ah, madame, what a terrible impression you're giving me of your son!!" the Présidente de Montreuil is said to have exclaimed to Donatien's mother. "If you think him capable of such things, I'm very unhappy to give him my daughter. But I have a higher opinion of him than you do."[17] In fact, it is interesting to note the vehemence with which the Présidente defended Donatien to both his parents throughout the young couple's engagement and in the early stages of their marriage. Her support was duly noted by Comte de Sade. "I've never known one like him!" he griped again to his brother. "[But when I complained about him] the young woman's mother [rallied to his side]: 'Has there ever been a young man incapable of foolishness?' she said. 'Let's always surge ahead to the future.' "[18]

The count's last instructions to his son, when Donatien finally agreed to travel back to Paris, concerned an ancient Provençal custom: the groom must bring a pâté of thyme from Avignon, and also a few dozen artichokes, traditional wedding fare not always available in the capital. On this point Donatien obliged: he arrived in Paris a mere twenty-four hours before his appointed wedding day, bearing the specified delicacies. The count's strategy was finally secure. And the Montreuils were fulfilling their own most fervent hope—to marry their daughter into the highest aristocracy. The wedding contract, which had been signed in Versailles two weeks before the church ceremony, in the absence of the groom, had been witnessed by His Majesty King Louis XV, an honor conferred upon only a handful of families in France. Other witnesses included the most distinguished members of the royal family: the dauphin and dauphine; Comte de Provence (the future Louis XVIII) and his sisters, Mesdames de France; and His Most Serene Highness the Prince de Condé, playmate of Donatien's youth. The religious ceremony was at last held on May 17, in the church of Saint-Roch.

WHAT OF DONATIEN'S new bride? Renée-Pélagie de Sade, whom he did not meet until the eve of their wedding, was not endowed with those attributes then called "physical graces." Only one portrait of her survives, an ineptly drawn profile of very doubtful origin. Official papers issued to Renée-Pélagie during the Revolution tell us that she was four feet ten, four inches shorter than her husband, and had a round, full face, gray eyes, brown hair. Her plainness, though never directly stated, was several times intimated by relatives. "I didn't find the young woman ugly," Comte de Sade wrote his sister earlier that spring. "She is very nicely built, with a pretty bosom and very white arms and hands. Nothing offensive, a charming character."[19] This judgment on the part of a jaded libertine was more enthusiastic than that offered on several occasions by the bride's own mother. "The gentleness of her character," she wrote to Abbé de Sade the week following the marriage, "her attachment to her husband . . . and to the entire house to which she now has the honor of belonging, will make up for her lack of natural graces."[20] She also wrote to the abbé: "When she will have the honor of meeting you, I hope that she will incite your genuine interest, at least if only for her reasonability and gentleness; good looks and graces are gifts of nature over which we have no control."[21]

Renée-Pélagie's plainness was not redeemed by her intellectual qualities. Her parents seemed to have neglected her education; the Présidente's own literary style—the syntax, spelling, and general eloquence of her letters—was strikingly more developed than her daughter's. Yet what Renée-Pélagie lacked in beauty and polish she redeemed by strength of character and sterling independence. She was a resolute, homespun young woman, totally uninterested in the machinations of social life. In a letter to her husband, she once described French high society as "a bunch of riffraff, the most successful of whom are the most fraudulent."[22] Notwithstanding the exuberant coquetry of her time, an

era when the cult of feminine "charm and graces" reached unprecedented heights, she seemed devoid of regrets concerning her looks and
utterly lacked any affectations or vanity. In fact, Renée-Pélagie (whom I
shall henceforth refer to as Pélagie) had singularly frugal tastes, preferring old clothes and resoled shoes. She was a tomboy of sorts, and when
staying at her husband's family estate at La Coste in later years, she
would display a lusty appetite for rustic outdoor work such as pruning
fruit trees and splitting wood. The most striking aspect of Pélagie's
character was her capacity to withstand the force of her mother's personality. In a culture of brilliant and powerful women, the Présidente de
Montreuil had a personality as commanding and seductive as that of any
female citizen in the kingdom.

While the sedate, self-effacing Marquise de Sade steps out from a
Millet painting, robed in sober hues of dun and earth, her mother
waltzes out of a Greuze portrait, a flirtatious virago adorned in rose and
pale violet, as sprightly of wit and polished in her conversation as she was
cunning in her social tactics. Forty years old at the time of her daughter's
marriage, the Présidente looked far younger and remained playfully coquettish. A description of her by a close family friend, written some
fifteen years later, depicts her as "a charming woman, a good storyteller,
with a very fresh complexion, short rather than tall, with a pleasant
figure, a seductive laugh and eye, a mischievous wit . . . shrewd as a fox,
yet eminently likable and attractive."[23] And an early chronicler of the
Sade family, writing in the 1920s, elaborates thus on the Présidente's
character:

> She is a creature of force and action well suited to her
> milieu and her generation. She is determined, utterly self-
> controlled, prudent to the last, and yet endowed with more
> heart and audaciousness than most of her peers. Her patterns
> of thought are prompt, exact, and orderly. It is she who leads
> everything, and it's to her that everyone, including the
> marquis, appeals.[24]

The Présidente de Montreuil exemplified that eighteenth-century
French phenomenon, the formidable authority of women; M. de Montreuil's meek, submissive persona was all the more pronounced. Good-
natured but colorless, utterly dominated by his wife, he seemed to have
long ago given up the prospect of making any decisions, or even making
himself heard, in his own home. Whether through her husband's willing
capitulation or through the sheer power of her own personality, the

entirety of the Montreuil family's business dealings—the most minute details of its income, house mortgages, loans, marriage contracts, and wills—was exclusively in the Présidente's hands. It is she who dictated the terms of such transactions, drew up and signed the papers that pertained to them, and generally ruled over her family as if it were the world's most orderly and important little kingdom.

The Présidente had been exhilarated at the prospect of marrying her plain daughter into one of France's most distinguished families. "I could not be more touched by all the reassurances you're good enough to offer me concerning the alliance we have the honor of contracting with you," she wrote Abbé de Sade upon meeting Donatien the night before his marriage. "The reasonableness, gentleness, and fine education which you seem to have fostered in your nephew make him as lovable and desirable a son-in-law as one could find. My daughter is as grateful as she could be for all the kindness that you've shown her; she sends you her respects and urges you to be persuaded of the great desire she has to please you and to win your friendship and that of the entire family that she has the honor of entering."[25] "I have unreserved gratitude to you for having sent me a son-in-law so worthy of his lineage and his education," she wrote the abbé a few days after the wedding.[26]

Despite her enthusiasm for the match, the marriage contract drawn up by this iron lady was shrewdly calculated. She was well advised of the Sades' profligacy. So in order to make the deal irresistible to Comte de Sade, she promised the bride and groom a handsome sum in the somewhat distant future—a sparkling three hundred thousand livres[27]—while confining them to a very modest income in their first decades. Under the terms of the agreement, the Montreuils pledged to provide the young Sades with room and board for the first five years of their marriage and with the services of a chambermaid and valet, either in the Montreuils' *hôtel particulier* in Paris or at their château at Echauffour, Normandy, where they often made extensive stays. After five years, the marquis and marquise would receive ten thousand livres with which to furnish a home of their own.

This arrangement ensured Mme de Montreuil tight surveillance of Donatien. Yet however he might have chafed at it, for the first months he behaved like an exemplary husband and son-in-law. He was attentive to the Présidente, wielding his great talent for sweet talk, witty repartee, and the art of flattery. In part because of his disdain for the court and his sense of superiority to most of his aristocratic peers, Sade was in his own way very much a family man and felt far more at ease with his wife and an assorted group of relatives than with any member of Parisian "society." He loved the familial games and rituals—charades, cards, chess and checkers, blindman's buff, hide-and-seek—and excelled at all of them, remaining at center stage.

So despite reports of his previously debauched conduct, Mme de Montreuil fell quickly under the spell of her high-spirited son-in-law. She clearly had not had a hilarious time, over the two decades past, with her prosaic husband, and the beguiling young man was injecting unprecedented fun and excitement into her rigorously duty-bound life. "Ah, the funny kid! That's what I call my little son-in-law," she wrote to her faithful correspondent the abbé a few months after the wedding. "I sometimes take the liberty of scolding him. We have a falling-out, we make up immediately; it's never very serious. . . . Unless I misread him, he has already improved." [28]

Throughout that first summer she accompanied the newly-marrieds many times a month to the theater, to concerts, to balls, to that northeastern periphery of Paris then called the Remparts or the Boulevard. Graced by grand trees and wide alleys, flanked with chic stores, cafés, small theaters offering the more offbeat theatrical productions, this lively thoroughfare also presented a variety of street spectacles—Spanish dancers, mimes, acrobats, jugglers, circus artists, handlers of exotic animals. It was a favorite site for promenades and general recreation.

"They spend at least a louis a day for spectacles, they go to the boulevards day and night," Comte de Sade, both impressed and disgruntled by this high living, wrote in midsummer about the cheerful, inseparable triad. "Mme de Montreuil bends to all of my son's fantasies," he added. "She's crazy about him; her family doesn't recognize her." [29]

Donatien got along quite as well with his meek father-in-law. In August, when the entire family retired to their country estate, Donatien and M. de Montreuil seemed to enjoy a joint overnight visit to the nearby abbey of La Trappe, founding home of the Trappist order. ("I hope he [Donatien] finds the visit edifying," the Présidente remarked pointedly in a letter to the abbé.) There were also deer hunts in the forest, horseback rides, long walks. Most important to Donatien, there was the theater. At last able to satisfy that passion for drama inspired by his years at the Jesuit lycée, he began that year to stage amateur theatricals at his in-laws' château. Most every member of the Montreuils' extended family and assembled guests participated in his productions, and Donatien shrewdly offered the Présidente all the leading female roles.

All the while, the cunning Présidente continued to observe her son-in-law closely. "The tranquillity of the countryside is good for his health; he's plumping out," she wrote Abbé de Sade, "but I don't know if it satisfies him. His spirit and his tastes are lively, they need fodder.

Fortunately there are always two remedies, sleep and reading. You surely know the taste he has for both." [30] (It is interesting to note that because of his careful avoidance of Paris, the abbé and the Présidente would write each other loyally for some fifteen years without ever having the pleasure of meeting.)

During these first months, the Présidente displayed her attachment to Donatien by supporting him in the most bitter dispute he had yet had with his father. It was caused by the fact that the count had done away with some twenty thousand livres—income from the four southeastern provinces whose governorship he had reassigned to Donatien. What no one knew until the marquis's marriage is that the count had failed to transfer the attendant revenues to his son and continued to collect them himself. In the heated correspondence that followed this disclosure, the count tried to justify himself by asserting that he had used the funds to pay for Donatien's upkeep; but that argument only made him seem more hypocritical in the Montreuils' eyes, not to speak of his son's.

"I can find no wrongdoing on the part of my son-in-law, in either substance or form," the Présidente wrote the abbé. She went on to insinuate that Donatien was being unjustly maligned by his own father. "A certain person is complaining about him to the family to which he has just been joined by marriage . . . and perhaps even [complaining] to the public, as though he were an ungrateful and unnatural son." [31]

Infuriated by the duplicity, Mme de Montreuil tried to persuade the count that his son was of far finer mettle than he realized. "I'm perhaps speaking to you too frankly, monsieur," she wrote Comte de Sade after having stated Donatien's right to the disputed revenues. "But if I ever have the honor of getting to know you well, you will understand my feelings: [your son's] heart is fundamentally better than . . . you can even imagine. Only his excess of vivacity could possibly flaw his character. . . . I vouch for his heart. I would be so happy to see you reunited in trust and confidence." [32]

The count was not moved. "He's so turned Mme de Montreuil's head that she's sure he's right," he griped to his brother the abbé. "That's how I'm rewarded for all I've done for him. . . . He hasn't given me an hour of contentment. . . . Please write her so she might hear the voice of reason." [33] The count's ire was further fanned by his son's stubborn negligence of court life. "Alas! I came here [the court at Fontainebleau] and arranged for him to be a member of the king's hunting party," he wrote to Provence the summer after his son's marriage. "He said he'd go, but after all the trouble I took, he never did." [34] ("It's beyond me to play the role of a fop," Donatien had already warned his father the previous year.)

Relations between the two men grew so strained that Donatien refused to visit his father, who was living that season in modest lodgings right around the corner from the Montreuils. "For a week I've been at his very door, and he hasn't deigned to see me even once," the count wrote to one of his siblings. Come autumn, the two men's relations so deteriorated that the count, upon returning from a trip to Provence, accused his son of turning him out of his in-laws' house. "Arriving in Paris," he wrote his sister, "I wanted to sleep . . . at the Montreuils'. My valet went ahead of me to make up my bed. The porter told him that there was a standing order forbidding me to sleep there. I subsequently learned that M. le Marquis was [responsible]; for such an order, alas, could not have come from the masters of the house."[35]

Shortly thereafter the Montreuils, with great apprehension, arranged for the two men to meet at their country house in Normandy. The reunion was as violent as they had feared it would be. According to Mme de Montreuil, the count treated his son "horribly," disparaging him in front of his in-laws as "a bad sort." In a letter to the abbé, after once more outlining all the reasons why her son-in-law was in the right and his father in the wrong, she reported that even her own mother had entered the fray to defend Donatien. "[The scene] led my mother to say, 'I think, sir, that an excess of temper leads you to say all that. If he were all that you accuse him of being, it would be up to us to complain; *you* gave him to us, and we accepted him with the reputation of his goodness.' "[36]

In the same letter, the Présidente chides the abbé for not stating his support of Donatien strongly enough. "Your nephew . . . loves and respects you, and what he fears most is to displease you. You hold the number-two spot in his heart, and I am not jealous; I shall be content to hold the third."

The abbé's second-place ranking in Donatien's heart suggests that the young marquis had formed affectionate bonds with his wife.

DESPITE THE LAXITY of sexual mores in eighteenth-century France, the freedoms offered the female gender were reserved to married women of the high aristocracy. A rigid double standard obtained between women of recently ennobled bourgeois background, such as the young Marquise de Sade, and noblewomen of court circles. As the mother of France's regent once pointed out, to love one's wife was considered downright uncouth in the higher ranks of the French nobility. "One can still find faithful couples among the inferior classes, but among persons of quality I don't know a single example of reciprocal affection, or of fidelity."[37]

Young women of the bourgeoisie and the high nobility shared one common fate, however: thrust into the marriage bed with total strangers —often not acquainted with them, as in Pélagie's case, until the night before the wedding—they were mere passports for their parents' social advancement and financial ambitions. After the bearing of a few children to ensure the survival of the family name, most marriages ended in some kind of tenuous peace. At that point another class difference arose: whereas in the older aristocracy, particularly in court circles, both spouses were free to enjoy adulterous liaisons, most women of bourgeois origins had to resign themselves to suffering at home. The less fortunate of such wives, particularly those devoid of "natural graces," often sank into depression or sought refuge in their religious faith. But Pélagie de Sade, although she was plain and came from the puritanical bourgeoisie, was of a totally different mettle.

There are some women who turn to self-sacrifice with the same wholehearted grace that the most inspired priests or nuns commit to their vocations, and Pélagie was one of them. Throughout her husband's scandals she would retain her faith in him without sinking into the moroseness or cynicism of other deceived wives, and accept his transgressions with wondrous stoicism and calm. Indeed, the great mystery of the Sades' marriage is that this puritanical young woman so worshiped her husband that she was able to suspend all moral judgment of him: the moral scruples that would have alienated a woman of her ilk from a debauchee such as Sade seemed to bind these spouses all the more.

Yet Pélagie's acquiescence was not caused by weakness of character. It was solely traceable to her loyalty, and to the depth of her passion for a man whose seemingly supernatural magnetism was not diminished by the bizarreness of his sexual practices. The young marquise did not necessarily enjoy her early experiences of sodomy, which would prove to be her husband's favorite sexual workout. But she clearly underwent some gradual process of eroticization, for the kind of marital fervor she displayed is inconceivable without an involvement of the flesh. Her devotion to her husband, indeed, had a kind of mystic force: "I still adore you with the same violence,"[38] she would write the marquis in one of the many periods of dejection he suffered during his jail terms. "I've made no other oath but to adore you";[39] "I have only one happiness in life, to be reunited with you and to see you happy and content. . . . We shall live and die together."[40]

In part because of the byzantine complexity of his character, in part because none of the couple's early correspondence survives, young Sade's emotions toward his wife are far more difficult to decode. Upon reading his later letters, one is constantly struck by his rage at the manner

in which he had been "sold" to a family of such undistinguished pedigree as the Montreuils; ceaselessly deriding his in-laws' mercantile background, he often sneered that "Cordier," the original name of M. de
Montreuil's father, revealed the family's past in the rope trade. His elitist
disdain for these homespun origins may have further incited him to drag
their honor in the mud.

On the other hand, the remarkable mettle of the women with whom
Sade enjoyed loyal platonic friendships—Mme de Saint-Germain and,
later, Mlle de Rousset—shows him to have been a very discriminating
judge of character. He was astute and decent enough, in his own way, to
appreciate Pélagie's mettle and intelligence, and was perpetually terrified
of losing her esteem: his first plea, upon falling into any scrape, was
"Don't let my wife know." If one cannot describe his complex emotions
for her as passion, his letters often express feelings of admiration, gratitude, and devotion. A decade and a half into his marriage, in his correspondence from jail, Donatien would refer to Pélagie as "beloved soul,"
as his "dear and divine friend," as "you whom I shall love throughout
all as the best and the dearest friend who could ever have existed for me
in the world." And perhaps because of his high regard for his wife, Sade
developed a notably idealistic view of marriage. With one exception, all
of his liaisons were held with courtesans, whores, and young domestic
helpers, and he prided himself immensely on never affronting "the sanc-
tity of wedlock" by committing adultery with a married woman.

There was yet another interesting aspect to the young Sades' marital
concord: both of them had been lonely, affection-starved children. Pélagie had suffered throughout her youth from her father's aloofness ("You
know well that my father is not a loving man," she would write her
husband[41]). Mme de Montreuil's flaunted preference for her younger
daughter, the ravishing Anne-Prospère, whom Pélagie referred to as "my
mother's beautiful Dulcinea,"[42] was even more painful to her. She seems
to have realized that in Donatien there lurked a hypersensitive child who
had suffered, as she did, from a dearth of parental love. So for much of
their married life these spouses would cling to each other like two neglected orphans contesting together, in an often lawless manner, the
detestable adult world of sycophancy, social clambering, and material
gain. Indeed, a token of the intimate bond formed by them is their
forthright use of the familiar *tu* form of address: it was a custom of the
peasant and working class, very rare among spouses of their aristocratic
milieu.

"Their tender friendship seems very reciprocal," the Présidente reported to the abbé about the young Marquis and Marquise de Sade's
relationship four months after the wedding ceremonies. "So far there is

only one affliction in their union; it's of not being able to assure us —you and me—of the attribute of 'grand' [she means grandmother, granduncle] . . . but I wait without impatience, for neither of them is of sterile lineage."[43] The following month, after mentioning Donatien's "vivacity" of character, she shrewdly sized up the power of Pélagie's passion for her husband: "[Your niece] . . . will never scold him. She will love him beyond one's wildest expectations. That is fairly simple; he is lovable. Thus far he loves her mightily, and no one could treat her better."[44] Even Donatien's contentious father had to agree that the marriage seemed to be going splendidly: "He's getting along very well with his wife. As long as that lasts I'll forgive him the rest."[45]

And yet five months into this serene new family life, as the newly-weds continued to display an unusual degree of mutual affection, the Marquis de Sade plunged into his first scandal.

V

The First Outrage

*What are religions but the restraints which keep the
strong from overwhelming the weak? . . . Is there one
not marked by imposture and stupidity? What do I
see in all of them? Mysteries that insult reason, dog-
mas that go against the laws of nature, grotesque
ceremonies which only inspire derision and disgust.
But if one of them particularly merits our scorn and
our hatred . . . isn't it the barbaric Christendom into
which we were both born? Is there a more odious one?
Is there one which more offends the heart and the
spirit?*

—Justine

□

IN MID-OCTOBER 1763, after a peaceful few months in Normandy, Sade
left his in-laws' estate for the Paris region, ostensibly on a business trip.
As a token of a partial reconciliation with his father, he intended, or so
he told his new family, to travel to Louis XV's court at Fontainebleau
and call on the Duc de Choiseul, France's all-powerful foreign minister,
to solicit a position from him. He would next go on to Dijon in order
to be officially acknowledged lieutenant governor of the four provinces
—Bresse, Bugey, Valromey, and Gex—he had inherited from his father.
His wife and in-laws saw him off, with all possible displays of affection.

But once in the capital, Donatien did not proceed to the king's
court at Fontainebleau. Instead he headed for one of several *petites
maisons*, "little houses"—the phrase then denoted trysting places for
members of the aristocracy—he had secretly rented in the Paris area a
few weeks after his marriage. He had acquired one in the city, near Place
Saint-Marceau, another in Versailles, yet another in the suburban village
of Arcueil. It was a tradition among libertines to hold their trysts in a

variety of rented sites. This allowed them to cover their tracks and avoid the recriminations of the women they enlisted; and if very kinky sex acts were involved, it protected them from the wrath of procuresses.

First notice of the scandal: two weeks after Donatien's departure from the Montreuils' family nest in Normandy, Comte de Sade wrote his brother the following letter concerning his son's true activities on that alleged business trip:

> A little rented house, its furniture bought on credit, an outrageous debauch which he went about *coolly, all alone.* Dreadful impieties, whose details the girl thought obliged to testify about. The culprit was arrested, taken to M. de Saint-Florentin [Louis XV's minister of the royal household, somewhat akin to minister of the interior], who upon the grounds of the girl's deposition, which he showed the king, recommended that the king punish [the culprit] with the greatest rigor. . . .

> Every three months I seem destined to have some terrible blow. I kept to my bed Thursday and Friday, with fever. Alas, why did I survive my last illness??

The count now displays a newly fervent religiosity:

> My mishaps are a punishment for my crimes. I kiss the hand that strikes me and submit to it. . . . This all happened two weeks ago. . . . I much feared telling you about it. . . . Don't talk about it to our sisters. I'm most unhappy.[1]

Until a few decades ago, no one knew the precise nature of Sade's misdeeds on that October day of 1763. But in the 1960s, a French bibliophile discovered the pivotal document relating to this episode, a deposition made by a prostitute to a high-ranking commissioner of Paris's police force. The testimony accuses Sade of the following transgressions: On October 18, Sade offered a twenty-year-old unemployed fanmaker and sometime whore called Jeanne Testard the sum of forty-eight livres—an enormous sum to give a harlot in those days—to accompany him to one of his rented lodgings in Paris. The marquis, prettily dressed in a bright-blue cloth jacket, red cuffs and collars trimmed with silver buttons, had driven Mlle Testard by coach to a little house with a bright-yellow carriage gate on Rue Mouffetard, near Place Saint-Marceau. Sade led the girl to a second-floor room, locked and bolted the door. He asked her if she had religion; she answered that she believed in God, Jesus, and the Virgin Mary and abided by all practices of the Christian religion. The marquis then blurted out a stream of atrocious insults and profanities. After telling her that he had proved that God did not exist, he masturbated into a chalice, referred to the Lord as "motherfucker" and to the Holy Virgin as "bugger," and asserted that he had recently taken two Communion hosts, placed them in a woman's vagina, and entered her, shouting, "If thou art God, avenge thyself!"[2]

Sade next pushed Testard, who protested that she was pregnant and did not wish to see anything that might frighten her, into another room. As she entered, the young woman saw a curious collection of objects hanging from the wall: four cane whips and five sets of cat-o'-nine-tails —three of hemp, two of iron and brass. Alongside them hung several religious articles—ivory crucifixes, engravings of Christ and the Virgin —which in turn were intermingled with several prints and drawings that Mlle Testard testified were "of the greatest obscenity."[3]

"Having made her examine these different items," so went the young woman's deposition, which was recorded in the third person by a police official, "[M. de Sade] told her that she must whip him with the cat-o'-nine-tails after heating it in the fire until it glowed red, and he then would beat her with whatever other whip she wished; although he pressed her hard, she did not agree to being whipped herself. . . . After that he took two of the crucifixes off the wall, one of which he trampled on while masturbating with the other, after which he ordered her to do the same. . . . While showing her two pistols that lay on the table and holding his hand on his sword, menacing to pierce her with it, he asked her simultaneously to blaspheme the deity by speaking the following impieties: "B[ugger], I don't give a f[uck] about you."[4]

After having refused the marquis's orders to commit a few more such sacrilegious acts, Mlle Testard, who like many prostitutes appeared to be very devout, spent the night with her tormentor, during which he read her poetry "filled with impieties and totally contrary to religion."[5] In the dawn hours the marquis announced that he intended to sodomize Mlle Testard, a mode of congress she adamantly refused. He then made her promise that she would return the following Sunday morning, when they would go to a nearby church, steal two Communion hosts, burn one, and use the other as an instrument of sexual pleasure. He also made her pledge that she would never reveal to anyone the events of their first encounter.

At the end of this hectic night, at nine A.M., the procuress who had introduced Sade to Mlle Testard came to fetch her. The two women went directly to a high-ranking police commissioner, to whom the prostitute gave her deposition. As a result of this swift action, the Marquis de Sade was arrested ten days later on the king's orders by Inspector Louis Marais, a prominent official of Paris's police corps, and taken to the dungeon of Vincennes. This historic fortress in the eastern suburbs of Paris, built in the fourteenth century as a royal residence, two centuries later had been transformed into a royal prison.

FOR THE NEXT DECADE AND A HALF, Marais, the French police's leading authority on libertinage, would be charged with the constant surveillance of the Marquis de Sade, leaving posterity a highly detailed chronicle of the marquis's romps for most of his years as a free man. Marais's official title was Commissioner of the Palais-Royal (a notorious site for prostitutes since the beginning of the century); but he was also known in French society as "the monitor of Cythera."[6] He had acceded to his post in 1757. A few years earlier, the Duc de Gesvres, First Gentleman of the King's Bedchamber, whose sense of Louis XV's tastes was very keen, had ordained that the sexual excesses of Paris citizens should be recorded more thoroughly than ever and their chronicles passed directly to the aging monarch.

Such reports had a definite purpose. The king and his official mistress, Mme de Pompadour, had ceased a decade back to have carnal relations—as she reached her middle years, Pompadour finally told her monarch that she had never had much of a taste for sex. So the couple went on to find much delight in perusing reports of their citizens' sexual prowess, which Marais documented by following debauched priests, visiting houses of prostitution, persuading pimps and procuresses to reveal the secrets of Paris's bordello networks. Whores and courtesans also confided in Marais and were probably rewarded handsomely for their information. Through their accounts he drew up detailed summaries of their clients' most bizarre requests and depravities.

Marais then forwarded these bulletins to his superior, one of the country's most powerful men—Antoine de Sartine, lieutenant general of the entire Paris police corps. Sartine's superefficient methods of surveillance were so highly esteemed that monarchs from all over Europe —Maria Theresa of Austria and Catherine II of Russia among them— asked for copies of his documents. After editing Marais's reports, Sartine passed them on directly to Louis XV. "Such tattles," Sartine's biographer reports, "were the highest source of delectation for the king and Mme de Pompadour."[7]

□   □

As FOR the psychological motivations that prompted Sade to commit the bizarre transgressions that led to his first confrontation with the law, three aspects of the incident are particularly striking:

First, masochistic sexual practices such as Sade's demanding to be whipped—he commanded the girl to whip *him* with a "red-hot" iron instrument but did not insist on whipping *her*—were banal in the eighteenth century. Perhaps incited by the frequent floggings young men endured, as Sade did, in school, flagellation of male clients was a more than common bordello practice. Inspector Marais offers the following comment on this activity: "There is no public house today in which one does not find cane whips in large numbers. . . . Moreover, this passion is strangely prevalent among clergymen. . . . In these sorts of establishments I have found many men who came looking for a good thrashing . . . including [a] librarian . . . on whose body two women used up two entire brooms, after which, having run out of cane, they were forced to take straw from a doormat. When I came in, his entire body was dripping blood."[8]

Second, although Sade terrorized the young woman and seems to have caused her considerable psychic pain, he did her no physical harm. The only *official* allegations against Sade, in fact, were those of "blasphemy and incitement to sacrilege," crimes for which, notwithstanding the considerable secularization of Enlightenment society, persons not protected by high social rank were routinely put to death. (A few years before Sade's scandal with Mlle Testard, a nineteen-year-old scion of the minor nobility named Jean-François de La Barre was decapitated and burned at the stake for the sole charges of "impieties and blasphemies.") In fact, the outward trappings of Catholic piety had remained so de rigueur that even the least devout members of the French aristocracy took pains to observe the major Church rituals and sacraments, as a means of self-protection. Sade, clearly, was constitutionally incapable of such cautionary, and often hypocritical, behavior.

Third, even though, as his writings would later show, the marquis had a virtually paranoid loathing for institutional religion, one marvels at the naïveté of the blasphemies he was alleged to have committed with Mlle Testard. Why should a man who so adamantly denied the existence of God be driven to such juvenile ranting against Him? The answer lies not so much in the nature of Sade's atheism as in the workings of his peculiar sexuality. In a book written three decades following the Testard incident, *Philosophy in the Boudoir,* Sade reveals some of the motives that repeatedly incited him to apostasy. Having noted that the desecration of Christian symbols is no worse than "the degradation of a pagan statue," he states that blasphemy is amply justified whenever it is a stimulus to erotic pleasure. He goes on to emphasize the sexual importance of what we might today call "sheer shock value."

"In the inebriation of pleasure, it is essential to utter powerful or dirty words, and blasphemous ones are particularly serviceable. . . . One must spare nothing; one must adorn these words with the greatest possible luxury of expression; they must scandalize as forcefully as possible; for it is so sweet to scandalize. . . . It is one of my secret delectations: few moral pleasures better ignite my imagination."[9] That candid admission offers an important key to Sade's psyche: an innate exhibitionism, coupled with a subconscious need to seek punishment, incited many of his actions. Donatien's tantrums against the Deity were not so much fueled by his desire to deny God's existence as by his wish to heighten his sexual pleasure through the uttering of profanities; on the more subliminal level, it might also have been incited by an impulse to provoke attention by insulting the sensibility of his peers.

As for Comte de Sade's reaction to his son's first official disgrace: "An outrageous debauch which he went about *coolly,* all *alone.*" The emphasis is the count's. The most appalling aspects of the Testard episode, in the count's eyes, were its glacial, meticulous programming, and its *solitude.* "All alone"—in the old roué's eyes, that may have been the scandal's most inexplicable feature, the one most contrary to his own generation's mores. In the count's own heyday, Prince de Soubise had a score of chums at hand when he offered the inebriated Mme de Gacé to gang rape; Comte de Charolais was attended by numerous comrades when he ignited the pubic (and public) area of Mme de Saint-Sulpice. How bizarre to hold a *solitary* orgy! Beyond his very occasional encounters with male prostitutes, Comte de Sade's own sexual activity had mostly been confined to women of quality; and most of the aberrant saturnalias he had engaged in had probably been shared with a few peers. His son, on the other hand, would remain singularly alone throughout most of his debauches, seeking only the occasional company of a social inferior, his valet.

And there is that other shocking attribute of the marquis's conduct, equally underlined by the count's anguished letter: its *coolness.* Until the religious awakening that attended his last decade, Comte de Sade's life had been motivated solely by ambition, lust, and sheer frivolity. It had exemplified that Dionysian quest for pleasure which reached its acme in eighteenth-century France. But the Testard episode was the opposite of frivolous. It was, to the contrary, clinically methodical. How could the count comprehend his son's carefully programmed assault on the national sensibility? Like his future fictional protagonists, young Sade seldom gave himself to pleasure nonchalantly; rather, he coolly studied the most efficacious methods of achieving it. The father's sexual style is as starkly different from his son's as is the voluptuous abandon of Watteau's *Embarcation for Cythera* from the icy debauches of *The 120 Days of Sodom*.

UPON BEGINNING his first jail term at Vincennes, Sade, surprised and confused by the uproar he had caused, immediately started writing letters to get out of his predicament. The first of them, to the celebrated Lieutenant General de Sartine, humbly asks the police official's pardon for his "errors" and begs him above all to allow his wife to visit him in jail.

"This is a favor I dare to ask you on my knees, with tears in my eyes. Be kind enough to reconcile me with a beloved person whom I was weak enough to offend so grievously. . . . I beg you, monsieur, do not refuse me the privilege of seeing the dearest person I have in the world. If she had the honor of being acquainted with you, you would realize that her conversation . . . is capable of restoring to the straight and narrow path a wretch who feels unsurpassable despair at ever having left it." [10]

Shortly thereafter, Sade again petitioned M. de Sartine for a visit with Pélagie. (Though informed that her husband was in prison for some form of misconduct, she knew nothing of the nature of his misdeeds, for her mother shielded her carefully from all such information.) In this second missive, the marquis adds a surprising request: he wants to see a priest!

"Unhappy as I am, sir, I do not deplore my fate; I deserved God's vengeance, and I'm experiencing it. Crying for my sins, loathing my errors—those are my only occupations. Alas! God could well destroy me without giving me time to acknowledge my misdeeds and repent for them."

Young Sade goes on to simulate, most cunningly, a very Jesuitic form of "examination of conscience."

"How many redemptive actions must I engage in to be allowed to see into myself! Give me the means to do so, I beg you, monsieur, by permitting me to visit with a priest. Through his good guidance and my sincere repentance, I hope to soon be allowed to share in the sacred emotions whose very neglect was the principal cause of my ruin."

The letter ends on this plaintive, juvenile note: "Don't let anyone tell my relatives of the details of my conduct, as it might make them miserable." [11]

Thanks to his family's diligent pleading with the highest powers in the land, Sade's first incarceration lasted only three weeks. On November

13, the governor of Vincennes received orders from the summit to set the marquis free:

"I am writing this letter to tell you to [release] the Lord Comte [*sic*] de Sade, whom you are holding at my castle of Vincennes." The missive was signed "Louis." The king's decision was immediately conveyed to the Présidente de Montreuil, who for the next few years received—and single-handedly masterminded—all legal communications concerning her son-in-law's misdoings.

An interesting confluence of pressure had liberated Sade: on one front, Comte de Sade had traveled to the court at Fontainebleau to beg for Louis XV's mercy, and the monarch had been moved by the pleas of his former ambassador. On the other front, Donatien's in-laws put pressure on M. de Sartine and on various magistrates with whom they had a warm acquaintanceship because of M. de Montreuil's distinguished career in the law.

For the next months—no specific interval was defined—the marquis was under royal order to live exclusively at his in-laws' country house at Echauffour, where he would remain under the surveillance of the wily Inspector Marais.

"It will behoove your nephew to replace his past behavior with an irreproachable future conduct," Mme de Montreuil wrote to the abbé in mid-January of 1764, two months after Donatien's release. "Since he has been restored to us, we are content. M. de Montreuil and I did what we would have done for our own son . . . believing that such procedure will have a good effect on a soul that well born. As for my daughter— you can imagine how sorrowful she has been. She has chosen to play the role of a virtuous woman. It's not up to me to praise her for it; I will allow her to be judged by the family to which she has the honor to belong. . . ."[12]

Notwithstanding the scabrous details of the Testard episode, the Présidente felt as proud as ever of the distinguished family into which she had married her daughter. She continued to act on the certainty that marriage would "put lead" into her son-in-law's head and that he would benefit from her counsel and surveillance; and she continued to intimate, to Pélagie, that his jail term had been incurred by debts. She informed the abbé of another reason for her current satisfaction: Pélagie was three months pregnant.

VI

A Peaceful Interlude

*Never, I repeat, never shall I portray crime other
than clothed in the colors of hell. I wish people to see
crime laid bare, I want them to fear and detest it,
and I know no other way to achieve this end than to
paint it in all its horrors. Woe to those who surround
it with roses! Their views are far less pure, and I shall
never emulate them.*

—Reflections on the Novel

□

THE MARQUISE DE SADE's pregnancy was ideally timed, coinciding as it did with the legal confinement imposed on her husband in Normandy. If anyone asked the Présidente why her family was breaking precedent by staying in Normandy throughout the winter, she had no need to mention her son-in-law; she could simply answer that country air was the best thing for an expectant mother. Meanwhile Donatien consoled himself in his temporary exile by devoting himself to his first love, the theater.

Amateur theatricals had been the rage since the late seventeenth century, and most every gentleman of substance in France had a theater on his estate. The young marquis took over the theater appendant to the château of M. de Montreuil's sister Marquise d'Évry, close to his in-laws' country house. There he produced and acted in a number of popular works that had been first staged at the prestigious Théâtre Français, such as Voltaire's *Nanine*. In addition to the marquis, the cast of actors included his wife; Mme de Montreuil, to whom Donatien assigned the leading role; their hostess, Mme d'Évry; Mme de Plissay, mother of the Présidente; and an assortment of other relatives and houseguests.

Unlike seventeenth-century theater, which was dominated by the art of tragedy, the French eighteenth century witnessed the triumph of comedy and of lighthearted, gossamer plays best exemplified by Marivaux. They were filled with complex interlacings of marital and extramarital intrigues, erotic innuendos and swift-witted repartee, and the deft wordplay that came to be known as *marivaudage.* In home performances, verses were traditionally improvised as the finale of each play. For the comedy *L'Avocat Patelin,* staged in May 1764, six months after his incarceration at Vincennes, Sade composed lyrics that expressed his promised reform.

"Happiness was far from us; / Now it rules my heart," the hero of the play, Valère, played by Sade, sings to the ingenue, Henriette. "Rest assured of my fidelity. . . . / There is only one step from wickedness to virtue. . . ."

"Dear Valère, there is danger / When one feels the power of love," Henriette, played by Pélagie, replies to her husband. "But I have no more fears: / We'll soon pass from wickedness to virtue."

Three couplets later—Donatien had written eight of them, assigning the Présidente to sing the last one—came the following verses, meant to depict the bliss of a united family:

"This site is the picture of delight; / The master of the house makes it so. / All that surrounds him is happy / And is the model of virtue. Ah! How sweetly one tastes with him / The sweet bonds of friendship."[1]

Indeed, serenity and order seemed restored to the Sade-Montreuil clan. In April 1764, Donatien received Louis XV's permission to visit Paris and its immediate environs: this, again, was perfectly timed to Pélagie's condition, for she had to return to the capital toward the end of her pregnancy for medical reasons. The following month, His Majesty reluctantly authorized young Sade to travel to Dijon in order to attend the parliament of Burgundy and officially receive the post of "lieutenant governor," passed on to him by his father. The speech the marquis delivered on this occasion is notably obsequious:

> To speak in praise of each of you, messieurs, is beyond my capacity and my age. But to find myself in your midst, messieurs, transports me to the acme of happiness. . . . Your approval, your esteem, your kindness, are more essential to me than all else. . . . To be worthy of you, that is my ambition; to have you, one day, judge me worthy of you—that is my dearest wish.[2]

Notwithstanding these honorable declarations, Sade, upon returning to Paris, launched into a new phase of sexual activity, one safely confined to liaisons with prominent actresses and dancers. By the summer of 1764, he was head over heels in love with one of the most sought-after performers in Paris, the tall, shapely Mlle Colet.[3] Her erotic skills were so notorious that a prominent member of the British aristocracy, Lord Elgin, who was living in Paris at that moment of his youth, paid her a whopping 720 livres—the approximate equivalent of 2,800 contemporary dollars—for a single night.

Sade met the eighteen-year-old Mlle Colet after seeing her perform at the Théâtre des Italiens. She allowed him to accompany her home. A few hours after he had left her bed, he dispatched to her a message, which included the following endearments:

> It is difficult to see you without loving you, and even more difficult to love you without saying so. I have remained silent for a long time, but can no longer keep my peace. . . . Please send me a word in answer, I beg you. If I, the most sincere of men, am fortunate enough not to be rejected by you, grant me a rendezvous at which we might make some arrangements; but I warn you that I wish to make them for life. . . . My happiness is in your hands, I cannot live without you anymore.[4]

But Mlle Colet, who had started plying her trade in her midteens and who currently was financed by at least two prodigally generous men, would not dispense her favors to any newcomer until she had upped his bidding to the highest possible price. She used a tactic favored by the most seasoned women of pleasure: upon perusing the marquis's letter, she sent his valet back with a barbed reply that feigned a tantrum of anger and outraged virtue. A few hours later, Sade was begging for her forgiveness.

> Oh, dear God! I am at your feet, mademoiselle, attempting to repair the outrage you accuse me of! I, capable of offending you! I would rather die a thousand deaths! . . . Did you think that I was offering you my fortune to buy your favors? Delicate and sensitive as you are, you were certainly right to hate me, had I tried to obtain them in that manner! My tears, my sighs, my fidelity, my obedience, my remorse, and my respect: those are the only wages of a heart such as yours, of the only heart that can make my life a happy one.[5]

Nevertheless, Mlle Colet kept Sade waiting several months before granting him another appointment. Meanwhile Pélagie's pregnancy came to term, but her baby girl lived for only two days. Donatien seemed sincerely to mourn the death ("I was not destined to be a father for long," he wrote his uncle in Provence). But his pursuit of Mlle Colet, and of other Parisian pleasures, was not in the least affected. By the early winter, Inspector Marais reported that Donatien was paying Mlle Colet some six hundred livres a month,[6] although she was simultaneously dallying with a young Marquis de Lignerac. Sade was also seeing many lowly whores, since he could not ask a prominent courtesan such as Mlle Colet to satisfy his more kinky impulses—she would have sent him packing. Moreover, Marais had warned every substantial madam in Paris to refuse Sade's patronage if he "exercised his temperament"[7] in an indecent way. As a result, he could only turn to the most wretched, least protected girls for his more bizarre demands. By this time Sade was well aware of the police surveillance, and one can imagine the extent of the loathing he felt for his constant nemesis, Marais, and for Marais's superior, Lieutenant General Sartine, whom he would later describe as being "descended from the left side of Torquemada . . . sacrific[ing] men like cannibals . . . the most politically corrupt and consummately depraved wretch ever to light up the sky."[8]

As the winter wore on, Sade found himself in a difficult position with the gifted Mlle Colet. The precision of Marais's report on this issue displays the particular solicitude with which he trailed the marquis, who seemed to be his favorite prey. "M. le Marquis de Lignerac, upon the orders of his family, has been forced to abandon Mlle Colet," he wrote, ". . . and to abandon her totally to M. le Comte [*sic*] de Sade, who is very embarrassed by this development, for he is not wealthy enough to sustain by himself the burden of a lady of the theater."[9]

Marais's assiduous surveillance continued throughout the Christmas holidays. He noted that Sade "slept with [Mlle Colet] again three times" between December 21 and 28. He also reported that Mlle Colet had recently seduced one of the wealthiest men in the kingdom—the Duc de Fronsac, son of the famous military hero Maréchal de Richelieu —and that he had offered her a pair of earrings, costing three thousand livres[10] for Christmas. Young Lignerac, meanwhile, was not totally out of the picture: although relegated to the modest role of *greluchon*—an earlier French word for "gigolo"—he was still visiting her backstage, "hiding under her dressing table," as the inspector reports, each time anyone knocked at her door.

Enter the Présidente. Marais seems to have kept her informed of every stage in her son-in-law's liaison with Mlle Colet. Always brilliant in her timing, she chose just the right moment to intervene. She ambushed Donatien in that very span of days when, furious at the ascendance of

Mlle Colet's affluent new devotee, yet ambivalent about having to bear the brunt of Colet's expenses by himself, he was, for once, confused. "By convincing him of her infidelities . . . I succeeded . . . in separating him from Colet and leading him back to reason," she would write the abbé a few months later. "I successfully . . . wrested him from that girl's door,"[11] she added, intimating that she had marched into the young woman's lodgings, unannounced, and proved to Sade the extent of Mlle Colet's philanderings.

The affair ended, as most affairs did in those years, with the betrayed lover demanding to have his letters returned. Exhilarated to have one of the most illustrious nobles in France, the great Richelieu's offspring, tucked into her bed, Colet seems to have answered Sade's missives in a very insolent manner, for his last letter to her runs thus: "What have I done to deserve such treatment? And why are you vicious enough to humiliate a man whose only fault was to have loved you too much? . . . Who are you? You're making it only too clear. Who am I? Your buffoon. Which of us plays the more humiliating role? . . . May this incident forever spare me from such a lethal passion!"[12]

According to Marais's reports, Mlle Colet was abandoned a few months thereafter by the affluent Fronsac. And while continuing to allow young Lignerac, "her only true love," to linger under her dressing table, she again accepted Lord Elgin's favors in order to pay off her large debts. She died a year later, at the age of twenty, of causes unknown.

So GREAT was Donatien's spell over his mother-in-law that the Colet escapade failed to diminish her affection for him. Sophisticated enough to recognize the disparity between aristocratic mores and those of her own bourgeois background, she may have looked on such frolics as the price she had to pay for having married her daughter to a high-ranking nobleman. The Présidente de Montreuil knew only too well how downright ordinary such comportment was for a patrician of her time—liaisons with actresses, opera girls, dancers, were the conventional fodder of any proper aristocrat's life. Moreover, considering the drabness of her own love life, might Inspector Marais's detailed accounts of Donatien's capers have aroused her dormant sexuality and offered her the same voyeuristic thrill they provided France's monarch?

As for Donatien, he seems to have made a coolheaded decision to play his mother-in-law's game, at least temporarily. For the next several years, the complicity that bonded Donatien and the Présidente remained the dynamic center of the Sade-Montreuil clan.

The central goal of their alliance was to keep pure, innocent Pélagie sheltered from the cruel realities of the outside world. Sade had developed very warm bonds with his wife, created an intimate domain that he could leave and reenter at will but wished to keep untainted by any harsh truths. Upon the disclosure of each of his misdemeanors, Donatien's first step was always to inquire how much his wife knew about his conduct and to beg all those informed to keep her in total ignorance. The gambit succeeded. Thanks to her husband's and mother's joint efforts, for the next few years Pélagie would continue to believe that Sade was imprisoned for financial reasons.

So the Présidente's relationship with Donatien remained strong. She turned to her husband at those critical moments when she needed him to pressure high circles of power into settling some family crisis, but she appeared to confide far more in Donatien than in her spouse. It is her son-in-law rather than her husband who seemed to console her in her deepest sorrows, such as the occasion of her father's death, in the mid-1760s. "Didn't I wipe your tears when you lost your beloved father," Donatien would write her a decade later, "and didn't you find my heart as sensitive to your griefs as to my own?"[13] However he may have resented the restraints she imposed on him, Donatien seemed to take the Présidente into his confidence whenever he needed her. She may have been the only person in the world, in those first years of his marriage, to whom he truly opened himself; in fact, she was the most steadfast source of motherly affection he had ever known. ("O you whom I used to call mother," he would write her, "you whom I came to claim as such . . ."[14]) So a modus vivendi had been worked out. The Présidente was content to minimize the damages caused by Donatien's adventures; she would wait for his youthful turbulence to pass, still believing that the institution of marriage "put lead" into men's heads. And she remained very proud—this is the irony—that the young Marquis and Marquise de Sade offered a far more intimate, more harmonious public image of married life than most aristocrats of their time.

Donatien's next scandal would erupt in Provence, outside the Présidente's vigilance, at his ancestral family home of La Coste, which would become more closely linked to his name than any other site in France.

VII

La Coste

O tender creatures, divine works created for men's
pleasures! Stop believing that you were made for the
delight of only one man; trample fearlessly on those
absurd bonds which chain you to the arms of a single
spouse and forbid the bliss awaiting you with a precious lover! . . . Did nature dictate that you should
be the captive of a single man, when it gave you the
strength to exhaust four or five of them in a row?

—*Juliette*

□

LA COSTE, a hilltop settlement that in Sade's time counted a few hundred inhabitants, is situated in the sloping hills of the Lubéron, a forty-
minute drive east of Avignon and twenty minutes from Cavaillon. It is
one of the most romantic sites in France, a steep-pathed pinnacle of
pale-gray fieldstone dominated by the Sades' ancestral castle, commanding breathtaking three-hundred-sixty-degree views over the verdant valleys of the Vaucluse. Like many similar structures in that area of
Provence, the château of the Sades dates back to before the tenth century, when it served as a refuge and stronghold against Saracen invaders.
Around the year A.D. 1000, shortly after the Saracens had been driven
out of southern France, the citadel of La Coste became the property of
powerful Provençal nobles, the Simianes, who owned scores of other
fortresses in the area. In the seventeenth century, when the family's only
male descendant died without progeny, the castle was inherited by one
of his nephews, Marquis Gaspard-François de Sade, Donatien's grandfather.

Two features distinguished La Coste from its adjacent communities.
Unlike its nearest neighbors, Ménerbes and Bonnieux, it lay within the
borders of the French part of Provence, just outside the frontiers of the

Comtat Venaissain, the vast terrain that from the thirteenth century until
the time of the Revolution was held by the papacy. Thus La Coste was
directly responsible to the King of France, not, like nearby settlements,
to the Pope. This detail would affect Donatien de Sade's frequent clashes
with the law. And unlike most Provençal villages, La Coste's population
had been predominantly Protestant[1] since the sixteenth-century wars of
religion. Throughout the following century, this persuasion incited the
French Crown to impose severe economic sanctions against the Costains, as the village's inhabitants call themselves, and to carry out several
brutal campaigns in which as many as three-quarters of the residents
were killed. La Coste's Protestant affiliation may also have affected the
marquis's convictions. It could be ventured that his loathing for the
Church of Rome was exacerbated by the vehement antipapism that prevailed in France's Protestant settlements. In several passages of his writings, he virulently censures those church and state authorities that
collaborated in the persecution, and occasionally the massacre, of
Provence's Protestant communities.

The castle of La Coste became dilapidated from the mid-
seventeenth to the mid-eighteenth century, because Donatien's grandfather chose to make his home at Mazan, some forty kilometers away.
Donatien's father began to renovate La Coste when he inherited the
settlement in 1740, upon his own father's death. The count made minimal improvements—enlarging the castle's narrow medieval windows,
rebuilding the inner courtyard, installing a kitchen—but within a few
years, ruined by his improvidence, he was too broke to maintain, or live
on, any of his Provençal estates. So for the first decades of Donatien's
life, La Coste was largely uninhabited, used only for a few weeks of the
summer by his grandmother, the dowager Marquise de Sade, or his aunt
the Marquise de Villeneuve, as a cool summer retreat from their native
Avignon.

Sade had visited La Coste as a boy, during his prolonged stay with
his uncle the abbé, but he does not seem to have gone there again until
the spring of 1763. During the months preceding his marriage, while he
pined in Avignon for Mlle de Lauris's return, he made a brief trip to La
Coste and fell deeply in love with the property and the terrain that
surrounded it. He remained enamored of it for much of his life. The
romantic, feudal character of the site—the conical hill surmounted by its
phantasmagoric castle, like some vision in a Hieronymus Bosch painting
—struck some central chord of Sade's imagination. In the next years he
came to think of La Coste as his only roots, the only true home he had
ever had.

Shortly after his marriage to Pélagie, Donatien asked his father's permission to take care of the domain and live in it at his will. The count readily agreed. "My son has just asked me to allow him to live in La Coste with the furniture that's there, while he pays the upkeep," he wrote one of his sisters in the sullen tone that marked most of his dealings with his offspring. "And I gave it to him. . . . He can let it go if he wants, sell the furniture if he wants. . . . Let him abuse it sooner or later; it's his business." And he added: "We'll see him soon living at La Coste. There's no great harm there."[2] By which the count meant let the rogue stay there out of sight, with fewer temptations than in the capital. But at the beginning of his marriage, Donatien was either too absorbed by his Paris bacchanals, or too confined by royal punishment, to visit Provence. He did not return to La Coste until the spring of 1765.

ON A BRILLIANT May day in 1765, a cavalcade of villagers congregated at the gate of the Château de La Coste to greet their lord—"Moussu lou Marquis de Sade," he was called in Provençal dialect—as he arrived for his first official stay at his estate. A group of young people dressed as shepherds and shepherdesses—the girls in brilliant-hued, beribonned headdresses, the boys holding bright-colored banners—had assembled, on muleback or on foot, behind the mayor of the town, who carried a lamb festooned with ribbons and flowers. As the villagers sang a ditty composed especially for this feudal ritual of greeting, their lord, the young marquis, stood at the gate of his castle, on his arm a prettily dressed lady who was assumed to be his wife. The song specifically celebrated the marquis's marriage, on which the Costains had not yet had a chance to congratulate him because of his years of absence. Based on the traditional *pastorale* form and sung to the tune of an ancient Provençal folk melody, "Couci-Couca," the musical greeting went this way:

"O la nouvelo huruouso / que venoun d'announssa—/ derida! / Nouoste marquis espouso / uno jouino beouto. / Couci-couca! / Veleissa veleissa!"[3] ("Oh, the happy news / that's just been announced — / all cheer! / Our marquis has married / a young beauty. / There she is! There she is!")

As the marquis greeted his vassals in the bright Provençal sunshine, there was no way for them to know that the young beauty on his arm was not his wife but an eminent Parisian demimondaine with whom he'd been dallying for some months. Did Sade introduce his paramour outright as his spouse, as the more malevolent local gossip would have it? Or, with typical Sadeian nonchalance, did he simply forget to warn the villagers that he was coming to La Coste with "a friend"? Or else, as yet other observers claimed, did he introduce Mlle Beauvoisin as a "relative" of the marquise, who could not travel to La Coste that summer because she still suffered from her sorrowful confinement of the previous year?

However Donatien identified his companion, he acted as if it were the most normal relationship in the world. And for the next month he proceeded to offer fête after fête at his domain, staging theatricals in the north wing of the castle, inviting scores of nobles from neighboring communities to these revels. One of his more enthusiastic visitors was Abbé de Sade, who tarried at La Coste for an entire week and seemed never to have raised his voice about the pretty guest with whom his nephew was sharing his first summer at his estate.

As for Mlle Beauvoisin, there is as usual no better authority on her provenance than Inspector Marais's reports. This "very amiable young person," the inspector tells us, was originally the housemaid of a Paris surgeon. She was launched into prostitution by the most famous pimp in Paris, "Comte" du Barry, brother-in-law and initiator of the former whore who three years thence would become Louis XV's official mistress. "She is handsomely furnished, few women have as fine a wardrobe as [Mlle Beauvoisin] or a larger collection of lace," writes Marais. "One finds her at home . . . in the most seductive dishabilles, and no one knows how to better enhance her figure. She is considered to be one of our prettiest women."[4]

Like most women of her profession, Mlle Beauvoisin did not limit herself to one lover at a time. Marais's first account of Sade's involvement with her reported that she was being kept in part by a M. de la Boulay, "who lavished her with favors," and in part by M. de Sade, who paid out some five hundred livres a month to cover the costs of her "wardrobe and theatrical expenses." All the while she was also enjoying a younger gentleman as her *guerluchon*. At the time of her arrival at La Coste she was three or four months pregnant, most probably not by Sade. This condition did not seem to diminish the marquis's lust. Indeed, throughout his life he would be drawn to pregnant women.

Mlle Beauvoisin's presence at the festivities she cohosted with the marquis soon put the abbé in an embarrassing position. He had seldom been able to pass up a good time, and he missed no parties held at La Coste during his week-long stay there. Upon returning to Saumane, he heard the outraged gossip concerning Mlle de Beauvoisin's alleged imposture as the marquise. Only then did he realize that his presence at his nephew's revels indicated that he condoned them. He first pretended that he had not attended any of Donatien's parties and was not even on speaking terms with him. "I never see my nephew," he told his Provençal friends. "I'd be ashamed to see anyone who behaves so badly."[5] When eyewitnesses began to report that they had indeed seen him at La Coste, the abbé shifted strategies and dashed off a letter to the person whose criticism he most feared—his eldest sister, the abbess of Cavaillon— severely denouncing Donatien's behavior. The abbess, suffused with traditional monastic piety, then sent Donatien a stinging letter accusing him of passing off "a trollop" as his wife.

The missive did not elicit the contrition she had hoped for. Replying to his aunt, the marquis denied that he had passed any woman off as his wife and, with studied insolence, called into question the behavior of several other members of the Sade family, focusing his sarcasm on the abbé and his aunt the Marquise de Villeneuve.

> Your reproaches are out of control, my dear aunt. To tell you the truth, I didn't expect to hear such strong words from the mouth of a saint. I do not allow, do not suffer, do not authorize anyone to identify the person living in my house as my wife; I have told everyone the contrary. . . . "Let people say what they want, even though you're telling them the exact opposite," the abbé told me. . . . I'm just following his advice. When one of your married sisters [Mme de Villeneuve] lived here publicly with her lover, did you look on La Coste as an accursed site? My behavior is no worse than hers, and neither of us deserves much blame. As to the one who provided you with all this information [Abbé de Sade], he may be a priest, but he always has a couple of trollops living with him—excuse me for using your very language. Is his château a seraglio? No, better, it's a bordello.

The letter concluded: "I'm taking up the family spirit, and if I have anything to reproach myself for, it's to have had the misfortune of being born into it. . . . God spare me the follies and vices with which it is rife. . . . Do accept, dear aunt, all assurances of my respect."[6]

The abbess passed this communication on to the abbé, and as a result Donatien was estranged from his once cherished mentor for several months.

MEANWHILE, BACK IN NORMANDY, the Présidente de Montreuil was feeling growing anxiety. She had initially been delighted by Donatien's plan to travel to Provence, thinking that he would benefit from the advice of the abbé, whom she revered. But within a fortnight of his departure, she began to fuss about the lack of news from her son-in-law. Her worries may have been fanned by Comte de Sade, who greatly disapproved of his son's trip to La Coste, probably fearing that his off-spring would cheat him out of property he still owned. She began to suspect that something was wrong, and in late May she expressed her fears to the abbé.

> Your nephew left on the 9th of this month; neither my daughter nor I have had news since. I believe he went to Avignon. . . . I do not cease to sorrow about our dearth of news, so I'd be infinitely obliged to you, sir, if you could let me know as soon as he's arrived. He's in great need of counsel from you to reform his frivolous ways. . . . You have to go easy with a spirit like his, for his initial impulses are violent, and hence fearsome. But he can be reasoned with. . . . I'm a fine one to be telling you what your nephew's like . . . you surely know him better than I do, and need no advice. . . . It was up to him to let me continue my praise of his character, but he didn't hold to his promise. I know that one must be lenient toward persons of his age, but one must also require decency of conduct.[7]

Angered by the disparaging comments his nephew had made about him to the abbess, the abbé retaliated by informing the Présidente of the true situation at La Coste. She responded the following month with a ten-page letter, which reveals how betrayed she suddenly felt by her son-in-law. She was only too aware of the considerable spell he'd wrought on her, and her rage suggests that of a deceived lover.

> I'm fascinated, monsieur, by what I learn from you. Prepared as I was to accept absolutely everything from M. de S., I didn't think that his demented passions could lead to such excessive indecency. . . . His covert infidelities are an affront to his wife and to me, but this public offense that confronts his entire province is an insult to his neighbors and will be of irreparable harm to him if it becomes known up here—how could it fail to be? Even though I've slaved to advance his career and his fortune, even though he's indebted to his wife and to us for hushing up wrongdoing that could ruin him forever and earn him years of imprisonment, here are his tokens of gratitude!!

How well the Présidente sizes up the actor always lurking in Sade:

> Later, in earnest tones, he'll complain about his destiny,
> about the violence and wildness of his passions, about his re-
> grets concerning the unhappiness he causes to those who love
> him. We aren't perpetually masters of our hearts, but we can
> certainly control our behavior, and it's on the basis of our
> conduct that we're judged.

The Présidente then reprimands the abbé, as she will several times
in the course of that summer, for having dishonored her family by taking
part in, and thus tacitly approving, the revels at La Coste.

> I'm startled, sir, that you had the patience to witness such
> an extravagant scene and never even denied the mistaken im-
> pression, doubtless blindly propagated by servants, that [Mlle
> Beauvoisin] was Mme de Sade. This delusion is simply too
> humiliating to her. . . . I can only lament, and hope that you
> still care enough for him to help him curb his passions. . . . He
> was never as extravagant in his conduct and expenditures dur-
> ing the six years he was in the charge of the army and of his
> father. So severity served him better than our kindness.

She now threatens Donatien with what he most dreads—the possibility of Pélagie's learning the truth about her husband's frolics at La
Coste.

> He can rest assured that even though I've hidden his fol-
> lies from his wife . . . in order to spare them from lifetime es-
> trangement . . . when he'll be in danger of even worse errors
> and misfortunes I shall firmly inform her, and convince her of
> her unhappy fate.[8]

Pélagie indeed knew next to nothing about the situation in
Provence. Summering with her parents in Normandy, she remained as
sheltered as ever by her mother's and her husband's complicity. The
Présidente had told her that Donatien was too absorbed with directing
and acting in plays staged for local gentry to write her from La Coste,
and she had believed it.

As for Abbé de Sade, he apparently made a brief second stay at La
Coste and gave Mme de Montreuil even more scabrous details about

the situation there. The Présidente's wrath grew as she wrote him her longest missive to date—twenty-five pages of reproaches.

> A marvel, sir! I'm only sorry that being in such good form, you left the party so fast. In your absence that girl will have restored her ascendance over him. . . . He'll doubtless return here to see me, sooner or later; he'll make handsome promises of good conduct and moderation . . . he'll flatter himself for having persuaded me, it'll limp along that way for two or three months, he'll go back to Paris and start everything over again, and all will go from worse to worse.

And then the recurrent maternal concern, to keep her daughter totally ignorant of the truth.

> For the time being [Mme de Sade] is convinced that he's on his way. . . . I didn't tell her I'd had news of you. . . . That's why I always have your letters forwarded from Paris in double envelopes, so that no one can detect their provenance. . . . My daughter's fate depends solely on you.

One can imagine the Présidente's pen flying over the pages as she sits at her writing desk, planning, scheming all the subtle traps whereby her wayward son-in-law might be snared back into the marital nest.
"Should one force them [Donatien and his Beauvoisin] to separate?" the Présidente muses in a postscript.

> I could arrange that with no difficulty by going through the proper ministry, but it would cause an uproar and be dangerous for him. . . . The only way to deal with him is to never let him out of your sight, never leave him alone for a moment. That's how I succeeded last year in separating him from Colette [*sic*] and in forcing him to be reasonable, after convincing him that she had been unfaithful to him. . . . Under the pretext of business—something about real estate—please return to La Coste to see what's happening there, whether he's still as smitten as ever. Shout at him, speak firmly, and you will at least convince him . . . to behave more decently, to spend less, to lead a quieter life. . . .
> Moreover, his presence here would worry me. . . . If he lost interest in this mistress, he would take another. I prefer that he find one in Provence. He might be fortunate enough

to attach himself to a married woman. They're always less dangerous than courtesans. [9]

But the abbé did not go to La Coste again as urged; he did not scold his nephew; he now seemed largely indifferent to the young man's fate. The abbé was at heart a courtier and loathed confrontations. And like most of Donatien's relatives—his slothful, frigid mother, his aloof uncle the Knight of Malta, his pious, scandalized aunts—the abbé was a consummate egoist who would not lift a finger for his family's only male heir. At the end of summer, as the abbé still refused to act, the Présidente took him to task:

> Your letter . . . distresses me more than I can say. I'd counted on your support. . . . Seeing that he's decided not to seek you out—he's probably held back by that girl, who fears your influence on him—in your place I would have found the courage to go to La Coste to confront him . . . to speak to him with reason and firmness. . . . Instead you honored him by continuing to attend his revels, which gives the appearance of approving them.[10]

By September, the Présidente seemed to have been informed—by Marais, of course—that Donatien was back in Paris. "I know that his valet has arrived with his luggage," she wrote the abbé. "He says that his master has sent him ahead, that he'd arrive in a few days. I'm absolutely persuaded that he's already here and that he's lodging with his damsel. . . . If I were in Paris I'd go myself to wrest him from that girl's door, as I successfully wrested him from the other one."[11]

Finally, in mid-September, Donatien's coach drove through the gates of the château of Echauffour. He appeared cheerful, relaxed, loving, as if he'd been away on a respectable business trip. In a conversation with Pélagie's paternal grandmother, he vowed that he wished to "let the past be forgotten by his attentive and correct behavior." And he expressed the hope that his wife would never learn of his capers and would "maintain a high opinion of him." ("Amen!" the Présidente commented to the abbé upon communicating these intentions.)[12] As for Pélagie, still quite ignorant of her husband's infidelities, she welcomed him with joy, and in the following weeks they conceived another child.

A modicum of order was restored to the Montreuil-Sade clan. Clearly, the Présidente had little to do but play a firm, prudent waiting game with her fractious son-in-law. "He answers my admittedly tough letters with much honesty, with gentleness even, with a trust that can only be guided by friendship," she reported to the abbé soon after Donatien came back from La Coste. "But is he sincere, or faking it?"[13]

Two months after his return from Provence, Donatien left hurriedly for Paris to tend to Mlle Beauvoisin, who was suffering a malaise related to her impending confinement, but the Présidente did not seem much concerned. "In her current state, I can't imagine that she offers him many sources of pleasure,"[14] she commented wryly to the abbé.

A month after Donatien had rejoined her in Paris, Beauvoisin, her pregnancy having come to term, started appearing again at the Théâtre des Italiens and, according to Inspector Marais, was more beautiful and admired than ever. "Her maternity has much embellished her," Marais reported, naming five different noblemen who were jostling for her favors. In this contest against the scions of illustrious families, Donatien ultimately lost out. Cursing his paramour of the last six months, he sought pleasures with a "tall, most amiable girl,"[15] whom he shared once more with Lord Elgin; and also with a Mlle Le Clair, an Opéra dancer with the distinctive reputation of being the official whipper of the Count of Bintheim, who was notorious for demanding to be flogged into a bloody mess. Mlle Le Clair carried out the command "with such grace, and such theatrical gift,"[16] according to Marais, that this customer satisfied every one of her most outlandish whims.

Whatever shreds of a relationship Donatien retained with Beauvoisin, it was very stormy, for in mid-January of 1766, he wrote her a furious letter:

> There you are unmasked, you monster!! Your villainy is without equal. . . . I shall loathe you all my life, you and your kind. I'll take no vengeance, you're not worth it. Don't worry, a sovereign disdain is the only sentiment I can have for you. Adieu, grab your latest conquest, and get rid of him by the same vile tricks you used with me . . . you monster of ungratefulness and falseness. . . . With what delight I think that at this time tomorrow I'll be fifty leagues from you![17]

Although he would see Beauvoisin briefly two years later and did not cease to sport with dozens of other actresses, singers, dancers, and common prostitutes, for the next few years the Marquis de Sade did not form any other binding relationships. He spent the summer of 1766 at La Coste quite alone, in apparent chastity. His wife had been hoping to join him there for her first visit to Provence, but she was grieving over a second unsuccessful pregnancy—the child, this time, had been stillborn.

Donatien gave himself fully that summer to his infatuation with his family estate at La Coste.

THE CASTLE AT LA COSTE is set on a flat, rocky two-acre plateau that surmounts its cliffside village like some hovering eagle. Sacked by insurgent peasants during the Revolution and plundered repeatedly into this century, the castle retains only its moat, sections of its walls and ramparts, and a few half-demolished rooms. From the distance, the structure now evokes the toothless face of a ravaged colossus. Yet this arid, treeless site, scorched by sun in summer, ravaged in winter by icy winds, in every way extreme, is as evocative a ruin as one can see in Europe. Along with Saumane, it was a muse for the awesome fortresses, bloodthirsty monks, villainous noblemen, deflowered and persecuted virgins, that saturate Sade's novels more flamboyantly than any other French fiction of his century. Like the dominant patterns of Sade's destiny, La Coste is an archetypal outlaw's landscape, communicating defiance and disdain for the conventions of the world below, rebellion against most laws of moral gravity.

The village of La Coste was similar to many settlements of its size in that rocky, arid region of the Vaucluse; it was already very poor in Sade's time, having been made all the more destitute by the persecutions effected against Protestants by the French Crown. The key to its backwardness was its archetypally feudal character. For many centuries it had been owned by two families of absentee landlords, the Simianes and the Sades, so its citizenry paid rigorous dues to rulers who may not have visited more than a few times in a decade. The lord of La Coste was the sole possessor of the key to the village jail, which for over seven centuries had been situated inside the bowels of his castle.

These aspects of the village also appealed to Sade. Unlike other patricians of his time, who tended to look on their domains as mere sources of revenue, Sade had a very romantic attachment to La Coste, which was connected to both his neuroses and his archaic political ideals. That ideology—a very bizarre blend of robber-baron elitism and radical libertarianism—infused him with a nostalgia for those anarchic eras of the early Middle Ages, before the rise of nation-states, when every warrior lord had total control over his vassals and was not constrained by the edicts of any other ruler. At La Coste, Sade could retain precisely that illusion of archaic autonomy, could feel like the feudal suzerain whose most deviant whims could remain unchallenged. As his transgressions multiplied, Sade's Provençal retreat would grow increasingly talismanic to him. It became the only dwelling where he felt totally safe, a utopian refuge from family reprimands, social rebukes, and the meddle-some interventions of the Crown.

In the summer of 1766, Sade, during his first solitary stay at La Coste, began the extensive, meticulously programmed remodeling he had planned for the estate. At the northern end of the plateau, which overlooks the arid expanse of the Ventoux mountain chain, he fashioned a labyrinth of evergreens copied from the black-and-white motif of the floor in the cathedral of Chartres. Upon the western end of the ridge he planted groves of fruit trees—quince, cherry, almond, pear. His land-scape-design specifications were fussy and precise. He stipulated that his orchard be planted in the medieval quincuncial pattern, in groups of five trees—four at the points of a square, one in the middle. He particularly cherished his fruit trees and, years later, would continually worry about them in the letters he wrote his wife from prison. ("How is my poor cherry orchard?" such a query would go. "See to it that the park be well tended . . . tell them to replace that little hedge of hazelnut trees." [18])

Sade also lavished great expense on redecorating the castle's forty-two-room interior. One of his first projects, when summering there the previous year with Beauvoisin, had been to install a private theater. Dur-ing the chaste ensuing summer, he enlarged it into a stage space of some three hundred square feet and a hall that could seat an audience of sixty. He also continued working on his private apartment, which, situated in the southernmost and warmest wing of the château, overlooked an ex-panse of rolling hills and the beautiful village of Bonnieux. He spent particular care on building and furnishing a new apartment for his wife, which comprised a winter bedroom, a summer bedroom, a boudoir, and a study.

The marquis, who was very particular about matters of personal hygiene, did not stint on any luxuries his era offered and was especially attentive to Pélagie's needs. By the mid-1770s, when the first inventory of La Coste was made, her bathroom, whose walls were of flowered Indian cotton, was equipped with a bathtub and a copper water heater, and the château commanded fifteen portable toilets, or *chaises percées,* and six bidets. The marquise's boudoir was hung with a gray-and-green *toile de Jouy* design representing Normandy landscapes; her bedroom walls were of gold-trimmed blue moiré, with matching bedspreads and baldachins. Tapestries covered the walls of the main salon, which was furnished with numerous sofas, bergères, and card tables. Paintings in the castle's other public rooms centered on popular eighteenth-century themes—the school of Athens, the death of Alexander, Joshua stopping the sun in its course, Mary Magdalene—and included a portrait, inherited from Comte de Sade, of the lascivious Mlle de Charolais attired as a Franciscan nun. In the summer of 1767, Sade began to install a "secret apartment" at La Coste, which contained vaguely pornographic curiosities; the only item of this kind precisely described in the inventory is a large collection of enema syringes, which were decorated with drawings of persons kneeling before naked behinds and saluting them.

Of course, like any proper gentleman of the Enlightenment era, Sade began to assemble a library of erotic and anticlerical books. They included pornographic classics of the midcentury that he might have perused in his uncle's collection when a child, such as *The Voluptuous Life of Capuchins, Tales of Priests and Monks' Fornications,* and *Thérèse the Philosopher.*[19] The author of that last volume was said to be a Provençal noble, the Marquis d'Argens. In the next two decades, yet another nobleman of that region, the future revolutionary leader Comte de Mirabeau, who was a distant cousin of the Sades, would write some of the finest erotica of the century. Sade's later proclivity for writing pornography was not an isolated phenomenon; the practice seemed to be particularly common among the Provençal aristocracy.

During this quiet, monastic stay at La Coste, Donatien visited often with his uncle, with whom he'd become reconciled. Writing to the Présidente, Abbé de Sade expanded on his nephew's unusually docile summer and went on to muse about the tumults that Donatien might still incite in the future:

> Only you and I, madame, are capable of having some influence on him. But what can we do? Not very much for the time being. He must sow his wild oats. You're right to say that he must be dealt with in a measured manner. It would be dangerous to confront him against the grain, as his father tends to do. It's only through gentleness and persuasion that one might hope to lead him back to us. You couldn't have gone about it better, madame.

The next paragraph of the abbé's letter, in which he hints at a central flaw in Donatien's and Pélagie's marriage, must have been somewhat painful for the Présidente.

> As you can imagine, I talked to him at great length about his wife. He recognizes her great qualities; he has praised her lavishly to me; he has friendship for her, and much respect; he would despair to ever displease her, but he finds her too cold

and too devout to his taste, hence his impulse to look for amusement elsewhere.[20]

The following winter, a few months after he had returned to Paris, Donatien suffered his first painful loss. In January 1767, his father died, at the age of sixty-five. Like many libertines of his generation, Comte de Sade had in his final years been finding his principal consolation in religion. His last will and testament was filled with the traditional pieties of the Roman Catholic Church: "By the intercession of our Lord J.-C. and of the glorious Virgin Mary and of all the saints, into whose communion I had the grace to be received by Holy Baptism, I very humbly beseech divine Mercy to pardon my sins, and also hope it will accord me the grace of remaining until my death a true child of the Apostolic Roman Catholic Church. I give my soul to God my creator, and my body to the earth from which it was formed. . . ."[21]

Most of Comte de Sade's former mistresses had died, and he had been living in recent years on the Montreuils' charity, in a property they owned in Versailles. He had spent his last decade attempting to pay off some of his debts and engaging in his favorite avocation, literature. He edited the writings of his youth, composed memoirs on the court of the "much beloved" Louis XV, compiled an anthology of "English anecdotes," and wrote essays on history, morality, and philosophy. However strained his relations with Donatien had been, nearly all his writings were dedicated to his son.

The count had suffered for some time from a disease that kept him in bed for weeks at a time, probably some form of dropsy. In his final weeks, his condition improved; Donatien went to see him shortly before his death and found him in stable condition, rising every day and moving about his flat. But four days after his son's visit he collapsed and within a few hours died.

In a journal entry, M. de Montreuil, in his prosaic style, describes the burial of one of the most illustrious rakes of Louis XV's reign:

My son-in-law and I had his body watched for twice twenty-four hours. We followed the procession to the church of Le Grand-Montreuil, in which he was buried at ten-thirty in the morning. The procession and burial were most dignified. The church had been draped in black. Twelve paupers bearing torches attended the burial. In his home we found twenty-four or twenty-five pages written in [the count's] hand that were full of anecdotes about the court and reflections on morality;

they deserve to be printed. He was buried in the church of Le Grand-Montreuil opposite the left pulpit.[22]

The major part of Comte de Sade's correspondence and literary efforts were discovered only a few decades ago, in the attic of one of his descendants, their margins carefully annotated with comments by his son. Notwithstanding their many disputes and estrangements, the two men had had very deep bonds, intensified by the aloofness of Donatien's mother. Years later, in one of his missives from jail, Donatien would refer to his father as "the only trace of family" he ever had. Upon the count's passing, he seems to have felt genuine sorrow. Whatever animosity Mme de Montreuil had harbored toward Donatien since the Beauvoisin episode, she was much moved by his expressions of grief. "The way in which his son was affected by his loss has quite reconciled me to him," she wrote the abbé. "Be a father to him, sir, he could not find one finer than you."[23]

Comte de Sade's death revealed yet another curious behavior pattern in his son's life. Since the seventeenth century, Sade family tradition had dictated that the titles Comte and Marquis would so alternate from father to son that during his father's lifetime, Donatien was to be referred to as Marquis de Sade, but he should assume the title of Comte upon his sire's death. However, for reasons unknown—his behavior is all the more mysterious in the light of his strong sense of feudal protocol—Donatien defied this convention and until the Revolution continued to refer to himself as Marquis. This is in contrast to the title of Comte used by government authorities in their all too frequent official dealings with him—in police reports, in arrest warrants. Donatien's unorthodox use of the title Marquis after his father's death, and his reference to his wife as Marquise, has never been explained. One might speculate that his tormented love for his father incited him to retain the Marquis title to maintain the illusion that his father was still alive. One could just as readily conjecture that his affection for his rigid, authoritarian parent was tinged with resentment, that his refusal to assume his father's title was another way of distancing himself from him. One could also link this idiosyncrasy to the capricious manner in which he would alter his various first names—Aldonse (or its Provençal form, Aldonze); Alphonse; François; Donatien; and the invented royal Louis—at whim, often as a way of eluding the police.

One should also note that owing to the dreadful reputation gleaned by *the* Marquis de Sade in his lifetime, all family protocol of alternating titles ceased immediately after Donatien's death. To lessen the stigma Sade-the-writer had cast on the family name, all his progeny, well into the twentieth century, would be known as "Comte." The tradition of integrating both titles has been reconsidered only in the past few decades, by Donatien's great-great-grandson Xavier de Sade.

NOT FOR LONG did Donatien's bereavement restrain that all-consuming search for pleasure which had obsessed him since his early youth. After a month of official mourning, he threw himself into yet another round of bacchanals, continuing to rent little apartments and houses in different parts of Paris for his recreations. None of his partners for the rest of the winter are identified. He seems to have looked for sexual experiments as unsavory as those he'd imposed on Mlle Testard—carousals for which he had to go to the lowliest, least protected whores, those not available to Inspector Marais's surveillance. The upper crust of purchasable ladies —women such as Colet and Beauvoisin, or even the harlots of prosperous bordellos—were usually protected from whipping, blasphemy, and the harsher forms of physical and mental abuse. Upon mere mention of such mistreatment, such women would have reported the marquis to their madams and to Marais's network.

In late April of 1767, Donatien very briefly resumed his relations with Beauvoisin and took off with her for a fortnight in Lyons. This strained Mme de Montreuil's patience again, for Pélagie was five months into her third pregnancy and her family did not think her husband was being attentive enough. "The father does not seem that eager, he is occupied with matters far more interesting to his taste," she wrote to the abbé. "I fear that the mother's suffering will overwhelm her." [24]

The denouement of Donatien's Lyons journey, however, eventually led the Présidente to rejoice: it marked the definitive end of the marquis's involvement with Beauvoisin. Although she would not die until 1784, leaving a considerable fortune, Donatien, as far as we know, never saw her again. After his last showdown with the lady, he went straight to La Coste. He spent another chaste summer there, greatly enjoying his domain and the feudal rights he had over its villagers, whom he looked upon, quite literally, as his serfs.

During his summer stay in 1767, Sade imposed an archaic exercise on the Costains. He ordered his business manager, M. Fage, a notary from the nearby town of Apt, to arrange an official ritual of "homage" from the La Coste community. Within a few weeks of Sade's arrival, La Coste's mayors and "consuls," [25] assisted by four specially selected deputies, executed the following folderol, following a custom that dated back to the twelfth century:

[They] did homage to the high and mighty lord Louis
Aldonse Donatien, Marquis de Sade, seated in an armchair,
[the consuls] kneeling before him, heads bared, without sashes
or arms, their hands clasped inside those of the lord marquis,
who, as a sign of the received homage, released the hands of
said mayors and consuls and received from each of them and
from each of the deputies the traditional kiss. . . . Said mayors
and consuls and deputies . . . further promised and swore to
be, in the future as in the past, good, loyal, and faithful vassals
of their lord marquis and his heirs, to keep his secrets, to refrain
from doing him harm . . . and not to repudiate or evade his
jurisdiction.[26]

During this ceremony, reference was made to similar homages received in 1551 by the marquis's great-great-granduncle Balthasar de Simiane, in 1668 by his great-uncle Octavien de Simiane, and in 1732 by his
father. Apart from this particular festivity, the marquis seems to have
spent a quiet summer at the Provençal home he increasingly loved,
overseeing the progress of all the works he had started the previous
summer and visiting frequently with the abbé. Even Mme de Montreuil
reported that he was writing his wife faithfully.

By midsummer, Pélagie's pregnancy was coming to term. Donatien
returned to Paris in time to attend the birth, on August 27, 1767, of his
son Louis-Marie, the first of his children who would survive into adulthood. Soon afterward baptism ceremonies were held at the chapel of the
Hôtel de Condé. The baby was held over the church font by several
members of that illustrious family, among them Louis-Joseph de Condé,
the comrade whom Donatien had assaulted so fiercely as a small child.

The Présidente had hoped that fatherhood would help the marquis
to settle down, but no such blessing occurred. By mid-October, Inspector Marais was on his trail again, reporting that Sade was "pulling out
all the stops" to persuade a Mlle Rivière, of the Paris Opéra, to live with
him, offering her several hundred livres a month to stay at his "little
house" in Arcueil on the days when she was not scheduled to perform.
The actress was reluctant to commit herself, having a large circle of
devotees to choose from, but the marquis's efforts to persuade her lasted
several months. Meanwhile Donatien was also trying to convince Mme
Brissault, one of the capital's most notorious madams, to supply him
with some of her own girls. "We'll soon be hearing about M. de Sade's
horrors again," Inspector Marais's report ended. "Very soon, certainly,
we'll hear about him again."[27] The inspector's predictions were realized
six months later.

VIII

Easter Sunday

"Are you a whipper, my dear?" "Ah, until blood shows, darling girl ... and I also delight in being whipped. I've never found a more delicious passion; flagellation is doubtless the best remedy to restore the vigor depleted by excessive orgasms ... it is the sovereign remedy for exhaustion."

—*Juliette*

□

NINE A.M., EASTER SUNDAY, April 3, 1768, at Paris's Place des Victoires, by the entrance to the church of the Petits-Pères, or "Little Fathers." The Marquis de Sade, attired in a gray frock coat, holding a muff of white lynx fur in one hand and a cane in the other, leans against the grillwork that surrounds the equestrian statue of Louis XIV. As bells ring to indicate the end of mass, a woman exits the church and stops a few yards away from the marquis, thrusting her hand toward passersby to ask for alms. Her name is Rose Keller. She is a native of Strasbourg and speaks French with a heavy German accent. The thirty-six-year-old widow of a pastry cook, she is a cotton spinner, currently unemployed. A man walks by her, offers her a coin.

The marquis, standing by the statue, beckons the beggar and promises her two livres if she agrees to follow him. "But I'm not that kind of woman!" she protests. The marquis reassures her: she misunderstood him; all he needs her for is housework. On that condition, Rose agrees to follow him. Shortly thereafter, the marquis and Rose Keller are riding in a coach toward his country cottage at Arcueil, an hour out of Paris, one of the "little houses" he has been renting for his secret trysts. Don't worry, the marquis tells the woman as they start their journey, you'll be well fed in your new job, well taken care of. Then he shuts the wooden windows of the coach, closes his eyes, and sleeps, or pretends to sleep.[1]

A little after noon, the coach stops on the fringes of Arcueil and the marquis opens the door. He ushers Rose Keller through a little green gate and, crossing a small courtyard, into his cottage. Taking his visitor to a dark second-floor bedroom, furnished with two baldachin beds, he tells her, Make yourself at home; I'll get you some food and drink. He leaves the room, locking the door behind him, and does not reappear for an hour. (Earlier that day, two prostitutes were brought to the house by Sade's valet; they have been waiting for their customer on the ground floor.)

When the marquis returns to fetch Rose Keller, he is holding a lighted candle. "Come with me, my dear," he says. He leads her down the stairs, into another small, dark room. As soon as they've entered it, he orders the woman to take off her clothes. "What for?" she asks. "For fun," he answers. She protests again that she did not come with any such intent. The marquis warns her that if she refuses his orders he will murder her and bury her in the garden. He leaves the room for a moment. Keller, terrified, starts to get undressed but keeps her chemise on. The marquis soon returns, a white kerchief wrapped around his head, his torso bare under a sleeveless vest. He rages that he wants Keller to be totally naked; she protests that she would rather die than follow his orders. He strips off her chemise himself, pushes her face down into a bed upholstered in red-and-white chintz. Then he covers her head with a bolster and his fur muff to stifle her cries, and still holding a candle in his left hand, he starts to whip her, flaying her alternately with a bundle of cane and a cat-o'-nine-tails.

Two or three times during the course of this scourging the marquis stops to rub the victim's wounds with what feels to Keller like molten wax—lying on her stomach, she cannot see his implements. Keller implores him to stop because she is terrified of dying without having done her Easter duties. He replies that he doesn't give a damn, that he can confess her himself. As Keller screams louder, his strokes become more rapid, and suddenly the flagellator himself, in the victim's words, gives out "very loud and very terrifying shrieks." The Marquis de Sade has come to orgasm, and Keller's ordeal reaches its end.

Sade releases his victim, goes to fetch her a pitcher of water and a bowl, and tells her to get washed and dressed. He leaves briefly and returns with her dinner—bread, boiled beef, a carafe of wine—and leads her back to the upstairs room. Again he locks Keller in, asking her to keep quiet and not go near the window. He tells her that she'll be free to return to Paris that very evening.

Left alone, the prisoner tears the sheets off the two beds and knots them together. Then, having attached them to the window casing and torn through the wooden shutters with a knife she has found in the room (the marquis nonchalantly forgot it there), she drops the bedclothes into the garden below and slides down them into the garden. She swiftly climbs a little stone wall and jumps into the yard beyond it, lacerating her arm and hand. As Rose Keller runs down the village street, the marquis's valet, Langlois, chases after her, waving a purse full of money. He catches up, tells her that she will be handsomely paid if she returns to the marquis's house. But Keller shoves him aside and keeps running.

Three local women stop her, noting her disheveled, bloodied state. Sade's victim breaks into sobs as she tells them her misfortunes. "But that man must be a demon!" the women cry out. They take her into a courtyard, examine her wounds, then accompany her to the home of a local lawyer, who in turn sends her to the château of the chief bailiff of Arcueil, a M. Lambert. The bailiff being momentarily absent, Rose Keller repeats her woeful tale to Mme Lambert, who is so stricken by the account that she is forced to retire to her room. Within the next few hours, Keller's story is heard again by a local police officer, who takes her deposition and has her examined by a surgeon. That night, she is sheltered by another friendly villager. The following day, Mme Lambert having recovered from the emotional upheaval wrought by Keller's tale, the victim is offered a room at the Lamberts' château.

A few hours after his last glimpse of Rose Keller, at around six P.M. on that Easter Sunday, Donatien de Sade returns to Paris, to his wife and in-laws.

ON EASTER MONDAY, April 4, the chief judge of Arcueil hears Rose Keller's deposition. On Wednesday, April 6, the judge receives testimony on the Keller episode from four witnesses. The same day, some member of the Montreuils' household is warned that legal proceedings are being brought against Sade. The marquis, breaking with his previous custom of sheltering his wife from all details of his escapades, informs her fully of Sunday's events. On the following day, the young Marquise de Sade suddenly emerges from the shadows and begins to play a prominent part in her husband's defense, taking on the role of protector previously assumed by her mother.

At dawn on the seventh, the marquise summons Abbé Amblet, Donatien's friend and former tutor, and another family acquaintance, a lawyer. She calls for her mother, and the women inform their friends of the accusations made against Donatien by a prostitute. They ask the two

men to proceed immediately to Arcueil and persuade Rose Keller to
drop her charges.

Abbé Amblet and the barrister visit Keller at the château of the
town bailiff, M. Lambert. They find her in bed, declaring that she does
not feel well enough to sit up yet and that she will be "unfit for service"
for a long time. When the visitors ask whether she might be persuaded
to drop her charges, she replies that she will do so in exchange for 3,000
livres (the equivalent of about 12,000 contemporary dollars). The sum,
the Sade-Montreuil delegation answers, is too high. Keller seems all too
aware of the benefits she can gain from her situation, and the two sides
negotiate strenuously. The abbé and the lawyer hold out for 1,500 livres.
Keller insists that she will not accept a penny less than 2,400. The sum
still sounds very steep to the negotiators, and they return to Paris to
check out the deal with the Marquise de Sade and her mother. They are
ordered to settle immediately for the amount being demanded.

Returning to Arcueil, the two men find the victim sitting up in bed,
chatting excitedly with several women. "You're not as sick as you claimed
to be," the lawyer comments. He hands her a legal document. Rose
Keller signs it. She is handed the 2,400 livres she insisted on, plus some
200 livres "for her bandages and medications." Armed with that sum,
Rose Keller would soon marry an agreeable new husband.

THE SADE-KELLER CASE tells us much about the eighteenth-century
French legal system, which operated on two judicial structures that were
independent of each other and often at odds. There was "royal" justice,
which was decreed at the whim of the king and his ministers. The second
system, which had become increasingly powerful during the reign of
Louis XV, was governed by the nation's thirteen Parlements, each of
which controlled a specific region of the nation. The nature of France's
Parlements had nothing to do with the familiar British-style Parliament,
on which the American political system is in part based. They were,
rather, assemblies of jurists that served as the last court of appeals for
civil lawsuits and for the more prominent criminal cases. Their consent
was also required for any legal or financial innovations the king might
want to effect. As the Parlements grew in power and prestige throughout
the eighteenth century, the Crown was more and more reluctant to
exercise its prerogative of vetoing any of their rulings, particularly the
judgments handed down by the most powerful assembly of all, the
Parlement of Paris. Neither elected nor appointed by the king, members
of the French Parlements purchased their offices from the government.
These magistrates were automatically ennobled after twenty years of

service (hence their designation *noblesse de robe*). They thus constituted a powerful network of vested interests, and often were at odds with the Crown and with the older *noblesse d'épée*—nobility of the sword—to which Sade belonged.

King Louis XV was notoriously more lenient on the issue of noblemen's sexual misconduct than were the predominantly bourgeois Parlements. So the proper strategy for any well-connected family dealing with a scandal such as Sade's Arcueil episode was to persuade the king and his ministers to keep the case within their own network of jurisdiction and not allow it to be tried in a Parlement. The most efficient tactic, for a family so afflicted, was to obtain a *lettre de cachet*, or "sealed letter," an arbitrary order of arrest and detention, used since the Middle Ages, which could be issued and signed only by the king and was looked on as an ultimate symbol of the monarch's divine right. One of the most arbitrary and detested features of the ancien régime, it could imprison any citizen for life without his ever being granted any kind of legal hearing, the length of the prison term depending solely on the king's pleasure and will.

Beyond serving as weapons for the king's personal vendettas, *lettres de cachet*, which would play a central role in Sade's life, were regularly employed against political dissidents or authors deemed seditious or indecent by the Crown—Louis XVI would issue one against Beaumarchais in an attempt to stop the production of his bold play *The Marriage of Figaro*.

The *lettre de cachet* was also commonly used by powerful families, which petitioned the king for the sealed warrant to get a fractious relative out of the way. Such a victim was the future revolutionary leader Mirabeau, a distant cousin of Sade's, who was immured for some years through a *lettre de cachet* obtained by his father on grounds of filial insubordination. Yet ironically, in certain instances *lettres de cachet* could also serve as a protective measure for the highborn. In the reign of the relatively permissive Louis XV, *lettres de cachet* issued for sexual scandals committed by an aristocrat such as Sade might ensure a far briefer and more comfortable prison term than arrest warrants issued by Parlement. And by preventing any kind of court trial, such arbitrary warrants could hush up most scandals and keep the culprit's reputation intact.

THE LEGALLY ASTUTE Présidente de Montreuil acted instantly to retain Donatien in the king's system of justice. Shaking her husband out of his habitual lethargy, she ordered him to pressure his most high-ranking friends in government into obtaining a *lettre de cachet*. The speed with which the petition was granted says something about Mme de Montreuil's power as a lobbyist: the warrant was issued within twenty-four hours. By Sunday, April 10, a week after the Keller episode, M. de Sartine, head of the French police, had received the king's orders to seize the Marquis de Sade and take him to the royal prison in Saumur. That very evening, the marquis was again riding toward a jail, one far more distant than Vincennes—Saumur lies some two hundred miles southwest of Paris, halfway between Tours and Nantes. He was in the company of Abbé Amblet. This was yet another royal favor obtained by the Montreuils to safeguard the family honor: traveling to a penal institution in the company of a friend promised a far greater measure of secrecy than being escorted by police guards.

THE MOST STRIKING aspects of Sade's conduct throughout this episode are his recklessness and his total inability to foresee the legal consequences of his offenses. In Arcueil, he left his victim in an unguarded room, not even bothering to check the windows. Moreover, Sade was astonished each time by the ruckus he created. One can explain his lack of contact with reality only through his grandiose self-image and his ridiculously inflated sense of caste. Since childhood, he had believed himself to be as exalted a seigneur as any in France, superseded in rank only by the princes of the blood, and thus he had considered himself above the law. Unleashed licentiousness was a traditional privilege of the high aristocracy, so what was all this fuss about whipping a whore?

And then would come the inevitable jolt into reality—the arrest. Whenever confronted with a jail term, Sade would first react by safeguarding himself from his family's censure. Upon arriving in Saumur, Donatien immediately wrote his uncle to apprise him of his misfortune. Well aware of the surface decorum demanded by his fellow roué, he offered, with dubious candor, the following act of contrition:

> Throughout the calamity that afflicts and pursues me, I hope that you deign to forgive me all the wrongs I have done you and to bear this adversity, my dear uncle, in a spirit of peace rather than of the vengeance which I well deserve. If the episode is talked about in your part of the country, you can deny it all and say that I have joined my regiment."[2]

Their prodigy locked up in His Majesty's jail, the Marquise de Sade and her family were content for a few days, assured that Donatien's incarceration—the length of the prison term was never specified ahead of time—spared him from the malice of gossipmongers. But their peace of mind was brief: the marquise and her mother were sadly out of touch with the power of public opinion, which was increasingly receptive to the new mass media and to a vast samizdat of antiroyalist and antiaristocratic literature. Since midcentury, the French middle class, its interests represented by the Parlements, had become increasingly outraged by the lenient punishments meted out to debauched bluebloods. This was one of several reasons why the Parlement of Paris seized on Sade's case within a week of his incarceration at Saumur. On April 15, a member of the Parlement's criminal chamber took the floor to denounce "a horrible crime that took place in Arcueil" and offered his colleagues a few choice details. In the days that followed, the chamber launched a thorough investigation into the Sade-Keller affair and, even though the culprit was already held in a royal jail, issued its own warrant for Sade's arrest. Within a few days, news of the Arcueil scandal had spread throughout the nation.

There were several reasons why the Parlement singled out Donatien for punishment, rather than the scores of other patrician rakes who engaged in the popular aberration of whipping their sexual partners. The most immediate reason was the influence wrought by the president of the Parlement of Paris, the notorious jurist Charles-Augustin de Maupeou. A bitter adversary of the Montreuils, Maupeou was one of the two or three most influential figures of Louis XV's reign; later that year, he would become France's Chancellor. Even as bland a man as the Président de Montreuil was bound to have made a few enemies during his decades as a high-ranking judge, and Maupeou found an ideal opportunity for revenge by attempting to prosecute his adversary's dissolute son-in-law.

Donatien's vulnerability was in part grounded in his own family history. He still suffered from the dishonor incurred by his father's unfortunate career. Comte de Sade's disrepute as a diplomat, his indiscretions and financial fiascos, all were recent enough to tarnish his son's reputation. Equally at cause was Donatien's social isolation. At a time when good connections and proper patronage were the principal roads to success, he had neglected to protect himself. Not only did he take pride in his refusal to visit the king's court, a serious enough social failing; he had not made even one friend among his peers since adolescence. As a result, he had become, like his father before him, a marginal and powerless member of the nobility. The Arcueil affair revealed Sade's dangerous solitude: he had no social moorings beyond his feudal roots in Provence, no allies beyond in-laws whom he would soon grow to resent greatly.

In the larger political context, Donatien was also the victim of a power struggle between Louis XV and the French Parlement system. These assemblies, frustrated by their failure to make a dent in the power of the Crown, had been all too happy to lash out against vulnerable members of the more ancient, far less puritanical aristocracy. Sade as convenient scapegoat, Sade as whipping boy for bourgeois jurists trying to create exemplary legal cases against patrician debauchery: this is precisely the issue that most upset Donatien's devoted friend Mme de Saint-Germain, who wrote to Abbé de Sade a few days after his nephew had been jailed:

> Public hatred is aroused against him to inconceivable heights. People are even saying that he committed this flagellation—can you imagine!—in derision of [Christ's] Passion.[3] . . . For the past fifteen days no one has talked about anything but this ridiculous incident, embroidering one imagined detail after another. What with the civil courts being kept at bay, I thought the issue was closed, and then a treacherous counselor began to denounce him, forcing the chief prosecutor to take action. . . . The marquis is a victim of public ferocity.

Mme de Saint-Germain went on to mention three notorious libertines of Donatien's generation whose escapades, considerably more violent and heinous than his, had gone unpunished and unpublicized because these nobles had remained solely in the king's jurisdiction. It is also possible that their revels seemed more tolerable because they had been engaged in with peers, a more "acceptable" style of depravity than Sade's lonely debauches. "M. de Fronsac's misdeeds, and those of so many others, are equal to [your nephew's] actions," Mme de Saint-Germain lamented. "D'Olonne and Montbossier find far greater grace in the public eye than your little libertine. . . . In the past ten years, the horrors committed in court circles are absolutely beyond belief."[4]

TEN DAYS AFTER the Marquis de Sade was incarcerated at Saumur, the Parlement heard dozens of depositions concerning the Keller episode. Witnesses included the gardener of Sade's little house at Arcueil, the village women who first encountered Rose Keller when she escaped, the notary M. Lambert, who had sheltered her in his château, and Abbé Amblet. The latter was not a wholly credible witness, since he continued to receive a modest annual pension from the marquis. Amblet testified that he had "known M. de Sade since his childhood . . . and had always recognized in him an ardent temperament which induced him to seek pleasure, but that he had always known him to have a good heart, one incapable of the horrors being alleged against him; that at school he was beloved by his comrades, as he was in the military regiments in which he had served; that he had seen him commit many kind and humane actions."[5]

Donatien remained at Saumur for barely a fortnight. In an attempt to protect him from the furor of the public courts, his family had pleaded that he be taken into tighter security. So upon the king's orders, he was moved on to the royal prison of Pierre-Encize, near Lyons, where he was to remain in his room and have no communication with any other prisoner. This time the marquis was allowed to be accompanied by his valet—a special favor granted because he suffered from a severe case of hemorrhoids (the disease would plague him much of his life) and his manservant was "accustomed to change his dressings twice a day."[6]

The official assigned to oversee Donatien's transfer to the Lyons area was none other than Inspector Marais, the eloquent chronicler of the marquis's past debauches. Visiting Sade in Saumur toward the end of April, Marais had been perplexed to see that the prisoner was in a state of virtual liberty inside the fortress. He found him dining at the table of the warden, who had apparently been quickly charmed by his guest. According to Marais's reports, Donatien, once assured that he would be treated quite as well in his new prison, was most accommodating during the long eastward journey across France, some four hundred kilometers, from Saumur to the Lyons region. Chatting amiably throughout the trip, Sade assured Marais that he had done nothing to Mme Keller beyond whipping her and that if Parlement ordered an investigation by expert surgeons, they would find "no trace of scars."

"Everyone in the provinces knows his story, in Saumur, Lyons, Moulins, Dijon," Marais added, commenting on how celebrated the Arcueil episode had become since Parlement pounced on it. "It's the hottest news of the day [*l'histoire du jour*] . . . but at heart [the prisoner] is still the same."[7]

Within a few days of Donatien's arrival at Pierre-Encize, the Marquise de Sade was writing to the king's highest ministers, pleading that her husband be offered more freedom of movement within the grounds of his new jail. Mme de Montreuil, meanwhile, was trying to redeem Donatien's image in the eyes of his own family. "Your nephew's adventure is an inexcusable act of folly or libertinage, but it is devoid of all the horrors alleged to have accompanied it," she wrote to the abbé, who notwithstanding the entire family's pleading had not bothered to come to Paris to help with Donatien's defense. "Much prudence and careful planning are needed in this matter. . . . Let's not even speak of Mme de Sade. It's easy to understand her afflicted state. Her son is well. He's about to cut his first teeth."[8]

In early June, Sade was taken to the prison of the Conciergerie in Paris, again in the company of Inspector Marais, to testify in front of the parliamentary body investigating his alleged crimes. The humiliating procedure demanded that he appear at court "on his knees, his head bared," to answer the prosecutor's questions. It is in this servile stance that he delivered his testimony, which differed from that of his victim on the following points: (1) He categorically denied the victim's accusations that he lacerated her with "a small knife or blade" (the surgeon's deposition corroborated Sade's). (2) He denied that he applied ointment with the purpose of heightening Keller's pain and insisted that, quite the contrary, he applied "a salve consisting of white wax . . . for the purpose of healing her wounds."[9] (3) He maintained that Rose Keller was a whore and insisted that she had agreed to be engaged for sexual purposes (one should note that Place des Victoires and its parish church, the Petits-Pères, were notorious places to meet prostitutes on Sundays).

After his appearance, the prisoner was taken back to Pierre-Encize by Inspector Marais. Within a few weeks of Sade's deposition, Parlement approved a royal "letter of annulment," which greatly lightened his sentence. Beyond serving a few more months in jail at the king's discretion, the only punishment meted out was that Sade contribute one hundred livres in alms "to purchase bread for the prisoners of the Conciergerie." Mme de Montreuil expressed her delight to her faithful correspondent in Provence. "A disreputable and unforgivable action could not have had more reputable consequences."[10]

UNTIL DONATIEN'S RELEASE from Pierre-Encize in the fall of 1768, Pélagie would remain the dominant protagonist in his struggle for freedom and for increased comfort in jail. This period of her life remains undocumented by her own letters, but surviving missives from government officials to the marquise attest to the numerous entreaties she made in those months: that her husband be allowed more fresh air, more walks, better medical services, and, above all, more frequent and longer visits with her. In late July, she arrived in Lyons, having acceded to Donatien's plea that she remain there for the duration of his captivity. She sold her diamonds to pay for her trip and her lodgings, a detail she judiciously hid from her mother.

In principle, Pélagie was allowed only two or three visits with her husband during his entire incarceration, but the young couple managed to charm the commander of the Pierre-Encize fortress into granting the prisoner many unauthorized diversions. Sade was permitted to take supervised walks, and he was allowed to see his wife far more frequently, and in considerably more intimate circumstances, than the king's decrees had specified. In the last months of Donatien's imprisonment, the Sades conceived another child.

THE IMPACT of the Arcueil episode on Sade's life went far beyond a temporary loss of freedom. It turned him overnight into a media celebrity. Up to then he had been just another patrician playboy. The Arcueil case endowed him with a legendary new persona—as the epitome of the debauched aristocrat, a reincarnation of the murderer Gilles de Rais, the fifteenth-century nobleman who was put to death for slaughtering scores of children and originated the Bluebeard legend throughout the West. Since the French press under Louis XV was forbidden to mention any crime committed by a member of the aristocracy, particularly if he was an officer in the king's army, accurate reports of Sade's case were omitted in the official French press. The information vacuum was filled by French-language periodicals published in foreign countries and by the clandestine, often sensationalistic broadsheets beginning to proliferate in France. This erratic coverage emphasized two interesting themes: experimental drugs and Sade's alleged "insanity."

Both motifs were elaborated by the foreign French-language press, which mostly catered to the nobility and tried to be lenient toward its miscreant members. The most popular of these publications, *Gazette d'Utrecht*, alleged that Sade's mind was known to be "unhinged" and took pains to emphasize that his victim had dropped her charges. It indulged in the current vogue for the natural sciences by tracing Sade's misdeeds to his interest in scientific experiment, and reported that after his balm had been applied, the victim "was so perfectly healed . . . that there were no traces of wounds."[11] This medicinal interpretation seems to have been particularly popular in French aristocratic circles. It was the one seized on by the hostess of Paris's most prominent salon, the Marquise du Deffand, nine days after the Arcueil episode. Writing to her close friend Horace Walpole, Deffand admits that Sade committed "an execrable deed." But she goes on to say that he "claimed to have done a useful thing and to have rendered a great service to the public by discovering a balm capable of healing wounds on the spot. . . . It had that effect on this woman."[12]

These amicable reactions were chiefly expressed by patricians. How did Sade's gambol play with the increasingly powerful French middle class? Far less well. After describing the Arcueil affair in his journal, a Paris bookseller—this vocation was becoming more powerful than any other in shaping public opinion—made the following comments: "If the courts do not deal with [Sade's] behavior, which is so peculiar as to be vile and disgusting, by imposing exemplary punishment, the case will offer posterity one more example that in our century even the most abominable crimes meet with impunity so long as those who commit them are fortunate enough to be noble, wealthy, or well connected." [13] It is precisely this kind of prerevolutionary rage toward the impunity of the old "nobility of the sword" that had motivated the Parlement's swift vengeance.

As SADE'S SUCCÈS DE SCANDALE was being played out, the struggle for his freedom and his good name was joined by a very unusual protagonist —his own mother. In May, Comtesse de Sade had emerged from her habitual torpor and dashed off an angry letter to Interior Minister de Saint-Florentin, complaining that her son was not being well enough treated in prison. Two weeks later, the countess turned her guns onto Lieutenant General Sartine, this time to protest a less than favorable article in a popular foreign periodical.

It isn't possible for me to ignore the most ignoble calum-nies that have been uttered against my son. . . . I have learned that the whole unfortunate matter has just been recounted in the *Gazette de Hollande* in the grimmest possible terms. A scurrilous attack of this kind is enough to dishonor a person throughout the world. The scoundrels responsible for this vile offense should be locked up for the rest of their lives.

"No one who has dishonored a person so closely related to me will escape punishment," [14] the letter concluded. Comtesse de Sade's intercessions in behalf of her son must have been as persistent as they were ferocious. It was her mediation, for once, that seems to have set him free. The first official document to mention his release, after seven months of captivity, was a letter to the countess from Minister de Saint-Florentin, announcing that Donatien was being granted a qualified lib-erty. Upon an order of Louis XV, which was to be considered "as binding as the one that had detained him at Pierre Encize," [15] Donatien was released on the condition that he retire to his estates in Provence and not move from them until further notice.

As the marquis and marquise enjoyed a few peaceful days together in Lyons, Donatien prepared to return to his cherished La Coste. Pélagie, who had never visited the estate, intended to spend the winter there with her husband. But several factors persuaded her to return to Paris and let him go on to Provence alone. Given her medical history, she had to sustain her fourth pregnancy in conditions that were as safe as possible. It had been five months since she had seen her son, Louis-Marie, whose upbringing had been relegated to Mme de Montreuil as Pélagie became increasingly involved in the formidable enterprise of rescuing her husband. "I would hope that your nephew has reflected enough on his fate not to give his wife or his family any more grief or anxiety," Mme de Montreuil wrote the abbé upon Donatien's release from jail. "Your grandnephew is very well and is walking on his own. . . . The care I give him is inspired by my affection for his parents." [16]

But there was yet another reason for Pélagie's reluctant separation from her husband: she had to attend to his severe debts. Until now he had been able to hide them from his wife and in-laws, pretending that he had paid cash for all his extravagances, but his recent detention allowed the Montreuils to scrutinize his finances closely. They discovered that most of his properties had already been mortgaged to pay off his father's large debts and that he owed 7,400 additional livres to his regiment. In addition to squandering his own modest funds, Donatien had also consumed most of his wife's dowry—66,000 livres—to pay for his "little houses," his procuresses, his opera girls and actresses. Moreover, he was heavily in debt to his mother; the diamonds whose sale Pélagie had so carefully hidden from Mme de Montreuil not only paid for her stay in Lyons but served to reimburse the large sum Sade owed the countess on her pension. The exhaustive letter Mme de Montreuil wrote to the abbé in early 1769—a document of some five thousand words—outlines the debits noted above, as well as other material griefs. Her criticism of Sade's continuing prodigality is colored, this time, with more than bitter disillusionment.

> A little nothing could totally finish him off. . . . At the very time that his gratitude should have attached him ever more to his wife and to me, your nephew's innumerable misdeeds oblige me to terminate all correspondence with him and kills all sentiments I had for him, all my hope for his return to the straight path, which alone had guided me in all that I've done to repair his misfortunes. . . . Your behavior toward your nephew will be guided by your own feelings. For my part, I wash my hands of him. I shall concern myself solely with my daughter and her unfortunate children. . . .

I'll allow the torrent to flow. I want the second [child] to arrive safely despite the many sorrows inflicted on its mother, not to speak of the ones her husband still has in store. Our little one is in excellent health and—grandmother's partiality aside—is very handsome. He frequently kisses the portrait of his father that hangs in his mother's bedroom. This sight, I admit, breaks my heart.[17]

AWARE THAT HE HAD HAD a very close call, Donatien led a sedate life at La Coste that winter. But as spring approached, after months of languishing quietly in his castle, he held a series of parties and theatricals, to which he once more invited the local nobility. Many of them stayed away, the Arcueil affair having been the leading media event of the year. Snubbed by his peers, Donatien swallowed his pride and invited the local bourgeoisie, the kind of villagers who wore their Sunday best when they went to visit *Moussu lou Marquis* in his castle. And of course he had as constant guest his uncle Abbé de Sade, who seldom turned down a good time.

Mme de Montreuil thought it outrageous that a man so ridden with debts should be throwing a series of theatrical soirees, and the abbé's participation in Donatien's social gatherings once more incited her wrath. The sixty-four-year-old roué, restricted to a tediously tranquil rural life by his abiding dread of the Paris police, was far more interested in sharing Donatien's fun than in offering him moral counsel. The Présidente obviously had not yet gauged the abbé's true proclivities. A particularly fierce letter she wrote him at the end of the winter sums up the contrast between the Montreuils' ethos and the Sades', between the bourgeoisie's frugal, puritanical attitude to pleasure and the insouciant hedonism of the nobility into which her daughter had married.

I can't help but express my surprise, sir. . . . Instead of occupations suitable to [his] situation . . . I learn through hearsay that he gave a gala, a ball, a comedy, and all the accompanying frills, and with what actresses! . . . I've been told that you honored these social occasions with your presence. . . . Is it fitting that instead of striving to restore his reputation, a man who has only been free for a short time, whose pardon is not complete, whose misfortunes are so recent, amuses himself by throwing parties. . . . Such expenses, when they not only disable us from acquitting ourselves of debts but further increase them, are odious.

The Présidente twists the knife. "I wouldn't have been as indulgent as you were. I would have set fire to the room in order to stop such proceedings."[18] "Is it true," she asks in a postscript, "that his health is not well, that he's still so impaired by his hemorrhoids that he can't ride horseback?"

Thanks to the joint lobbying of the marquis's mother and his wife, in the late spring the king allowed Donatien to return to his in-laws' country house. It was still a limited liberty: Sade had to stay out of Paris, see very few people, and attend to healing his hemorrhoids. Donatien's family, in fact, had greatly exaggerated the urgency of expert medical treatment for this ailment, which could have been equally well dealt with in the medical facilities of Montpellier, a few hours' ride from La Coste. But in those days hemorrhoids were an excellent alibi: a very common and openly discussed ailment, it particularly affected "career officers" such as Sade, because it prevented them from riding horseback. Writing to the abbé, the Présidente praised the efficacy of this excuse: "He's coming back to see his wife and family and to be treated for a dangerous infirmity which has taken a critical turn and requires skilled surgeons and prompt therapy. That's all one needs to say in Provence, as well as here, when word of his return gets out."[19]

Once more, Mme de Montreuil's mounting ire toward Donatien was temporarily suspended. She was too enthused by the fact that he could attend the birth of his next child, due in June. And in the following months, by the time her son-in-law settled back into his family routine, Pélagie's impending confinement seemed to have greatly increased Donatien's solicitude. "Since his return," the Présidente reported to the abbé, "his assiduity to Mme de Sade is exemplary of a good husband. . . . Only time will tell whether his attitude is based on politics, friendship, or gratitude."[20]

The Marquis de Sade's second son, Donatien-Claude-Armand, was born on June 27, 1769. The spartan family intimacy in which the baby was baptized reflected the social stigmas now affecting his father. Instead of the hoopla that had attended his brother's baptism, held at the Hôtel de Condé and witnessed by the highest princes of the blood, the infant was held over the font of a country church near the Montreuils' Normandy estate. His godparents were his maternal grandfather, M. de Montreuil, and his paternal grandmother, Comtesse de Sade. "Please receive the mother's homages," the Présidente wrote the abbé as she ended her description of the ceremony. "The older brother assisted at his sibling's baptism. He is in fine health and simply beautiful. His father seems to take care of him with great pleasure."[21]

❑   ❑

A FEW MONTHS after his return, Sade enjoyed his freedom by making a month's trip to Holland, which he documented in his letters home. "In general they seem to be good people, keen about business, totally absorbed by the ideas of always acquiring new wealth. . . . The women . . . are not particularly likable . . . one sees few slender waists. . . . Immoderate use of very hot tea and coffee completely ruins their teeth, to the point where it is all but impossible to find four women in Holland with a good set." [22]

Upon the marquis's return to the capital, the young Sades spent a good part of the winter of 1769–70 trying to salvage whatever standing was left to them in Paris society. They attended receptions almost daily. Some visits were to old friends like Mme de Saint-Germain and the Prince de Condé. Others were more challenging, such as a courtesy call upon Interior Minister de Saint-Florentin, the official who had signed the warrants for Donatien's arrest. The visit seemed to go so well that a few weeks later, Mme de Montreuil wrote to Saint-Florentin asking him if her son-in-law would be received at Versailles—after his close call, Donatien even felt ready to "pay court" to his monarch. But the minister decided that such an ambition was still premature.

"The adverse impressions that [M. de Sade] might have made upon His Majesty are still too fresh to be forgotten. . . . Thus I felt it best not to pursue the issue, for . . . if he was refused, as there is every reason to believe he would be, it would do him a great deal of harm." [23]

In August 1770, after a season dedicated to clearing his name, Sade concentrated on reviving his military career and left for the Poitou to rejoin his regiment. The experience was not pleasant. Prejudiced by Sade's dreadful reputation, his regiment commander refused to allow Captain de Sade to carry out his duties and forbade junior officers to follow his orders. The marquis, piqued, left his unit. We know next to nothing about his activities in the following months beyond the fact that he and the marquise conceived yet another child. In the spring of 1771, with the support of his childhood friend Prince de Condé, Donatien applied to the minister of war for a commission as cavalrymaster. His request was granted, a consent prompted, in the minister's words, by "favorable testimony" concerning his past military service. The King of France personally had to approve all such commissions. This had been the acid test, and Donatien had passed: Louis XV had symbolically cleansed him of his past errors.

The Sades' third child and first daughter, Madeleine-Laure, was born in April. "Confer on her your wit, sir," her maternal grandmother wrote to Abbé de Sade, "and I shall offer her my patience, the virtue most essential to women." Mme de Montreuil went on to say that the

Sades' oldest child, Louis-Marie, was growing into "the most beautiful possible creature." "The younger one interests me less," she admitted. "He's handsome, but there's no way of judging his intelligence or character—he's barely begun to speak. And then the oldest one was in my arms, in my safekeeping, during our most unhappy times. . . . He has inspired a more affectionate concern." [24]

However serene the appearance of his family life, the marquis was still facing arduous financial problems. The letters he wrote later that spring to his business agent in Provence, Maître Fage, were desperate. He needed sixty thousand livres, the equivalent of some two hundred and forty thousand present-day dollars, to get out of debt. His letters indicate the marquis's abiding fear of his wife's disapproval. "All [these loans] must be found instantly, otherwise I shall be lost in my wife's eyes." [25]

But credit was not readily available, and that summer Sade had to sell the cavalry commission he had so proudly acquired earlier that year, thus putting a definitive end to the often distinguished military career he had begun at the age of fourteen. Because of his debts, he spent several weeks in jail at Fort l'Évêque, near Paris—not that disgraceful a way to pass the summer, for that is where France's bluebloods often bided their time when they were hard-pressed for cash. After Sade regained his liberty, his thoughts centered on one goal: to establish himself for as long as possible at La Coste.

"I wish to enjoy the fruits of the garden next summer, and this will not happen if you neglected to follow my directions concerning the plantings," he scolded his estate manager, M. Fage. "So I urge you to remedy your negligence forthwith."

He intimated that he was about to make his first extensive stay at the estate. "Please don't overlook any detail of all that I had asked you for my stay at La Coste, which promises to be more imminent and longer than you may imagine: garden, farmyard, cheeses, firewood, etc.—get all that moving, so that upon arriving in the fall I'll find everything on which to live economically. I approve the landscaping plans for the garden, etc." [26]

And so in September 1771, the marquis set off for his cherished Provençal retreat, accompanied for the first time by his wife, and also by his sons, Louis-Marie and Claude-Armand, his five-month-old daughter, Madeleine-Laure, and the children's governess, Mlle Langevin.

IX

A Winter in Provence

*I'm alone here, I'm at the end of the world, protected
from the gaze of all others, no other creature is able
to reach me; no more barriers, no more restraints.*

— *The 120 Days of Sodom*

□

DURING THE 1760s, Louis XV had endured his greatest sorrows and
increasingly lost the affection of his people. In 1764, he had mourned
the love of his life, Mme de Pompadour, who died of cardiac complications
after a twenty-year reign over the court of Versailles. In the next
four years, the king would grieve over the deaths of his oldest son and
daughter-in-law, the dauphin and dauphine, who left in his care their
five children, one of whom was to become Louis XVI. During that span
of time Louis would also lose his wife of four decades, Marie Leszczynska
for whom he felt the same fondness he might have had for a dull,
cherished aunt, but who was one of the only links left to his youth.

However, the nation remained at peace. The king was managing to
keep the fractious Parlements under control. He had chosen as his chief
adviser Charles-Augustin de Maupeou, the jurist who was instrumental
in publicizing the Marquis de Sade's depravity. In 1770, Louis enjoyed a
very brief renewal of popularity when his oldest grandson, the seventeen-
year-old dauphin, married the ravishing fourteen-year-old Marie-
Antoinette, archduchess of France's most treasured ally, Austria. That
spring, several hundred thousand cheering citizens gathered on Place
Louis XV, now Place de la Concorde, to watch fireworks honoring the
marriage. But the festivities were flawed by a bad omen: the devices
caught fire and whizzed toward the tightly packed crowd, panic erupted,
and one hundred thirty-two persons were crushed or trampled to death.

Louis XV's popularity would once more be frayed by the ascendance

of his new official mistress, Mme du Barry, born Jeanne Bécu, illegitimate daughter of a seamstress and a monk. By the early 1770s, innumerable popular ditties were portraying the king as an impotent debauchee
ensnared by a harlot. The talk of the court in 1771 concerned du Barry's
annual pension, the equivalent of six million contemporary dollars, and
the disdainful conduct of Dauphine Marie-Antoinette toward the
profligate royal mistress, whom she had never once addressed. It took
scores of scolding letters from Empress Maria Theresa to persuade her
daughter that the core of Europe's balance of power—the Franco-
Austrian alliance—was of greater importance than her pride. The peace
of the royal family, and perhaps of Europe, was restored on New Year's
Day of 1772, when Mme du Barry, filing past the dauphine with the rest
of the court, heard Marie-Antoinette murmur to her, with visible effort,
"There are many people at Versailles today, madame." [1]

BUT THROUGHOUT THAT WINTER, the Marquis de Sade, snugly sheltered at La Coste with his family, remained indifferent to all that lay
outside his ancestral Eden. It was his very first family stay there, and a
new cast of characters was now entering the Sadean stage. It included
the marquis's favorite valets—a picturesque buffoon called Carteron,
and another called d'Anglade, known as "Latour," a strapping fellow
said to be of noble descent, perhaps an illegitimate son of the Duke of
Bavaria. Equally important to the household was the housekeeper, Gothon, a comely native of Geneva, endowed, in the marquis's own words,
with "the sweetest ass ever to leave Switzerland," who engaged in
steamy trysts with Carteron. Three other residents of Provence would
from now on be constantly drawn into Sade's catastrophic predicaments:
his estate and business manager, M. Fage; Ripert, the overseer of the
castle of Mazan, another ancestral domain of the Sade family, which the
marquis was about to visit for the first time; and the jurist Gaufridy—
Donatien's favorite playmate during the childhood years he spent with
his uncle in Saumane—who would later serve as Sade's legal counselor
and general gadfly.

Another new character, more fateful than any other, made a debut
this season at La Coste: the marquis's sister-in-law, Pélagie's youngest
sister, Anne-Prospère de Launay. She glided into view that autumn like
some angel in a Botticelli Annunciation—blithe, ethereally beautiful,
and unpredictable. She would have considerable impact on Sade's fate,
for it was in part due to Anne-Prospère's romance with her brother-in-
law that the Présidente would eventually deprive the marquis of freedom
for thirteen years of his life.

Anne-Prospère, nine years younger than her sister, was born in 1751. Her parents had given her one of the family names of M. de Montreuil's father, Jacques-René Cordier de Launay, a frequent custom among the eighteenth century's "new" nobility. The Montreuils' most winsome and most cherished child, she was twenty years old the autumn she arrived at La Coste. She had come straight from the convent in which she had been living for some years, a Benedictine priory in the Beaujolais area, east of the Auvergne. This was a semimonastic community reserved for daughters of the aristocracy. Its acolytes took no vows, remaining free to marry and return to the world. Applicants had to prove at least three-quarters noble blood to be admitted. Since Anne-Prospère displayed no leanings toward the monastic life, the Montreuils seem to have cloistered her in this particular abbey for the exclusive purpose of augmenting their standing in society and enhancing her marital prospects. As for the young woman's sudden appearance in Provence in October 1771, a few weeks after the Sades' arrival there, it was probably motivated by a recent bout of poor health and her need for curative country air. "Please remember about the bathtub, I've been ordered to take baths for my health. . . . I badly need my baths to restore [it],"[2] she would write to Fage a few weeks after settling at La Coste.

Because of the long gaps of years left undocumented in the Sade family's correspondence, Sade scholars have traditionally inferred many biographical details from the marquis's writings. No portraits of Anne-Prospère have survived, and the following passage found in the marquis's papers after his death—he described it as a portrait of "Mlle Delaunay, aunt of the younger Comte de Sade"—has often been resorted to for descriptions of his alluring sister-in-law:

> Julie is at that happy age when the heart is becoming ripe for the sentiment of love. Her charming eyes announce this by their most tender expression of sensuality; her interesting pallor provokes desire . . . the zephyr's tender whiff is less pure than her breath; her smile is like the rose blossoming out from the sun's rays. Julie is tall. Her waist is slender and elegant, her demeanor noble, her walk easy and graceful, as is everything she does. What grace! And how rare it is!

This enamored portrait goes on to praise Julie's character and focuses particularly on her gift for "philosophy," a euphemism, in eighteenth-century France, for "free thinking" liberated from the restraints of religious bigotry.

Julie combines the delightfully natural spirit of her age with the gentleness and worldliness of the most amiable and sophisticated woman. . . . From very early on she learned to let her reason speak, and using philosophy to shake off the shackles of [her] upbringing, she learned to understand and to judge at an age when her peers scarcely know how to think.[3]

We are treading here on the very heart of Sade's emotional life. Did the marquis and the fetching quasi-nun fall in love that autumn at La Coste? Or had Sade and Anne-Prospère begun their liaison in previous years, during the young woman's visits home from the convent? If, as some biographers have speculated, the latter scenario is accurate, her mother and sister may have encouraged the reunion in Provence as a means of preserving familial honor by "keeping the scandal in the family." All we know is that the marquise would soon be aware of the liaison. Some months later, in one of the many petitions she drafted in her attempts to preserve her husband's freedom, she dictated these impressions to her lawyer (the third person was always used in legal documents):

> She [Madame de Sade] was with the Marquis de Sade, her husband, at the estate of La Coste in Provence. . . . She was joined there by Mlle de Launay, her sister, who came on the pretext of keeping her company and enjoying a calmer atmosphere. . . . The attentiveness of her husband prevented her from suspecting that a fatal passion was soon to cause a series of sorrows and calamities.[4]

Since no correspondence between Sade and his sister-in-law now exists—their letters were probably among the first documents Mme de Montreuil destroyed—the chronology of this particular affair of Sade's may never be established. But enough of Anne-Prospère's missives to other family members, a few of which one can see at the Bibliothèque Nationale, have survived to shed light on her education and character. They display a strikingly orderly hand, an elegant turn of phrase, and fine spelling; these talents, a rarity among women of her day, show that the Montreuils had lavished far more attention on their younger daughter's education than on that of Pélagie, whose vivid but appallingly misspelled letters could have been written by a literate peasant. The letters that offer the clearest insight into Anne-Prospère's temperament are those she wrote to Abbé de Sade. At the age of sixty-six, this seasoned roué was clearly infatuated with his delectable relative. Within two weeks

of her arrival at La Coste, he sent Anne-Prospère a little Corsican horse
as a present; like the rest of her surviving correspondence, her thank-you
note to him reveals a playful and undeniably flirtatious character.

> I beg you to believe that my sentiments for you far tran-
> scend my desire for the little Corsican horse. . . . Only the dic-
> tates of my heart lead me to reassure my uncle of my
> attachment to him. . . . Your little niece is very sad not to be
> able to tease you in person; she was so looking forward to
> teasing you that she is very pained.[5]

These two charmers, the abbé and Anne-Prospère, visited with each
other extensively. She frequently played the lute for him. And at some
point in their relationship the old rake, undaunted by the forty-six years
that separated them, must have declared his love for the young woman,
for she scolded him for jeopardizing her "honor, reputation, and perhaps
[her] very life."[6] Here are excerpts from the chastened abbé's long reply,
in which he attempts to restore her esteem for him:

"Nothing is dearer to me on earth than *your honor* and *your life*. . . .
Let's reach an understanding and once and for all impose some boundaries
between us. . . ." Elaborating on the impact of environment on human
emotions—a reductionist argument endemic to eighteenth-century
thought—the abbé refers to the harsh climate of the Auvergne, an
area not far from the convent where Anne-Prospère had been immured.

> I know no one as charming as you and I was born in a hot
> climate; these two factors can only give rise to a very vivacious
> friendship, which is the kind I have for you. You wish me to
> suppress that sentiment and substitute for it a more tranquil
> emotion. . . . You wish a Provençal to love in an Auvergnat
> manner, and that is impossible. . . . The sun lashes at the face
> of a Provençal, while snows cool the emotions of an Auvergnat.
> Whence the difference between various ways of loving; it is not
> surprising that a Provençal's friendship might be taken for love
> by a woman who has spent her life in the Auvergne. . . .
> I would like to spend my life with you; I shall not be able
> to. . . . I shall not go. If I followed my heart's desires, I'd write
> you every day, my letters would be filled with tenderness and
> fire; but to please you I'll write you from time to time glacial
> missives in which I'll try to emulate the style of the Auvergne.

Citing a phrase that the teasing schoolgirl wrote him in one of her
earlier letters ("Ah, my dear uncle, since I've met you you've been

constantly on my mind"), the abbé then berates her for having led him on.

> My niece, is that phrase in the style of friendship or of love? . . . If you continue to write me such things I'll lose all self-control; I'll call forth all my fires, I'll go on to melt all your glaciers, and I'll turn them into a torrent that will drown you. Don't you find it amusing, dear niece, that I'm the one who finds your expressions too powerful and complains of your excessive tenderness? [7]

So much for the abbé's dalliance with Anne-Prospère. How could such a frolicsome beauty not have ignited equal lust in the marquis? We know that Donatien and the playful twenty-year-old belle engaged in affectionate bantering. Anne-Prospère often acted as Donatien's secretary. At the end of a letter the marquis dictated to her, she wrote the following postscript to its addressee, M. Fage: "Having just served as the M. de Sade's scribe—I've just sent him packing because I'm tired of writing—I'll now speak for myself and beg our dear attorney not to forget, as he has done thus far, the four pads of paper I've asked him to send me. . . . My brother-in-law has told me about your concern for my health, and I thank you for it." [8]

Intimate attachments could readily have prospered in the confined spaces of La Coste, and there were many other aspects of Mlle de Launay that may have aroused the marquis's quirky lust. A virgin imbued with religious principles and still dressed in a nun's garb, made all the more forbidden by being his wife's sister, she characterized certain themes and taboos that Sade would later glorify in his fictions: defloration, apostasy, incest. Whether his passion for her was nascent or well developed at the time of her arrival at La Coste, there is further proof of the marquis's fascination with his sister-in-law: he gave her the leading roles in every play he staged that season at La Coste. For in the winter of 1771–72, now that he was settled in his favorite domain, Sade could at last fully indulge his passion for the theater.

THE THEATER at La Coste, which the marquis had built a few summers back, could now seat an audience of sixty persons, with standing room for an equal number. Its blue stage curtain was fitted with an intricate mechanism that allowed it to be operated from the lobby; the theater was lit by sixty-five metal candleholders and twenty-four fairy lights. The permanent scenery represented a salon, as was customary in the eighteenth century, but this setting could be altered by adding back-drops of painted canvas (the other two panoramas used at La Coste depicted a town square and, ominously, a prison).

There were clearly delusions of grandeur about the theatrical season Sade planned in Provence that winter. Not content to hold it exclusively at La Coste, he extended it to another ancient family domain of the Sades, the Château de Mazan, an estate to which he turned his attention for the first time that winter.

Mazan, some thirty-five miles to the north of La Coste, had been acquired by the Sades in the fifteenth century through a great-granddaughter of Hughes de Sade, widower of the marquis's legendary ancestor, Laure. A spacious dwelling in the center of a town significantly larger and wealthier than La Coste, Mazan was far more of a cradle of Donatien's forefathers than either of the marquis's other major proper-ties, Saumane or La Coste. It was the birthplace of Donatien's paternal grandfather, Gaspard-François, who called himself Marquis de Mazan; of his father; and of all his uncles and aunts, including Abbé de Sade.

If Donatien had acted solely upon his strong emotions for family lineage, he might well have been more drawn to Mazan than to La Coste. But the Château de Mazan is a conventional urban manor in the middle of a prosperous market town that is set in a quiet valley, and it was ingrained in Sade's character to prefer the rugged, phantasmagoric setting of La Coste. In the winter of 1771–72, however, as he began to plan for a touring company that could alternate between two separate Provençal communities, he started to see Mazan as a fitting place in which to establish his reputation as a theatrical impresario. (To this day the mayor of Mazan claims that thanks to the Marquis de Sade, La Coste and Mazan hosted "one of the world's first theater festivals.")

Due to the improvidence of Comte de Sade, the Mazan estate had been badly neglected for several decades. Donatien corralled a large segment of Mazan's working population—the town's most able contrac-tors, carpenters, and engineers—into restoring it and building its the-ater. He was fortunate to have a very capable employee, M. Ripert, an obliging man whose own father had been the manager of Mazan, to oversee the remodeling. For a man constantly bordering on bankruptcy, Sade's theatrical ambitions were outlandish. Beyond the expensive stage props, one single theatrical production necessitated wigmakers for the actors, extra men to change decors and snuff candles between the acts, several horsemen to provide police protection to the audience, enough candles, tables, hot-water dispensers, carafes, and glasses for dozens of guests. The festival, intended to run from March to November of 1772, was to include a cycle of twenty-four plays.

In the 1770s, the "theatromania" that had pervaded Europe throughout that century was at its height. Sade's ultimate ambition was to create a dramatic troupe that would move beyond "society theater" and become thoroughly professional. In yet another grand, delusionary scheme, he invited eight of the Comédie Française's leading actors to join his Provençal troupe[9] and act alongside a group of amateurs that would include himself, his wife, and his sister-in-law. This request having been turned down, in February 1772 Sade hired twelve actors and actresses—second-rate but seasoned professionals—who agreed to perform in exchange for room, board, and a salary of eight hundred livres. (The Sades' finances were so sloppily run that back pay was still owed to two of the performers, a couple by the name of Bourdais, after the 1789 revolution!)

Sade fulfilled his grandiose impulses through the programming of his plays: literally every one of the nineteen productions he scheduled for 1772—Diderot and Voltaire are the only authors on the list who made a mark on posterity—were being played that same season at the Comédie Française. The only exception to his roster of Parisian box office hits was one of his own dramas, a melodrama "in the English taste" called *The Marriage of the Century,* in which Mlle de Launay starred as the heroine, the marquis played her husband, Mme de Sade played her confidante, and various domestics were put onstage as soubrettes and valets.

During the months of May and June, the repertory schedule ran as follows:

May 3, La Coste: *Le Glorieux* by Destouches and *Les Moeurs du Temps* by Saurin.

May 10, Mazan: Same program.

May 17, La Coste: *Beverly* by Saurin and *Le Retour Imprévu* by Regnand.

May 24 to June 7: Spring recess.

June 12, La Coste: *Le Déserteur* by Mercier and *Le Somnambule* by Pont de Veyle.

June 15, Mazan: Same program.

June 22, La Coste: *Le Philosophe Marié* by Destouches and *Heureusement* by Rochon de Chabannes. (The latter play had been staged successfully eight years earlier at Sade's in-laws' château in Normandy.)

What an itinerary! Few aspects of Sade's life are more bizarre, more manic, than the travel schedule he imposed on his family and retinue in the first half of 1772 to fulfill his thespian ambitions. The communities of La Coste and Mazan are thirty-five miles distant and separated by some of the most arduous terrain in Provence. Today it is a fifty-minute drive

from La Coste to Mazan on winding, often hilly roads, so the trip must
have taken the Sade entourage at least twelve hours by muleback or
horse-drawn coach. Imagine the baroque cortege: the marquis in his
double role of feudal seigneur and ambulant theater director, shuttling
every few days between the two towns at the head of a procession
that comprised his wife and children, his sister-in-law, his housekeeper,
Gothon, his valets, maître d'hôtel, cooks, and the score of technicians
and actors hired for his repertory.

The procession's path can be more or less retraced because it would
have tried to follow the few stretches of flat valleys between La Coste
and Mazan. It would have headed toward the little river—the Calavon
—that flows between La Coste and the villages of Goult and Gordes and
now runs parallel to Route 100, and crossed the stream either at Pont
Julien, a third-century Roman bridge that is still used today, or at a
bridge at the nearby settlement of Les Beaumettes. The cortege would
then have headed north-northwest toward L'Isle-sur-la-Sorgue, following, for a few miles, the turbulent green waters of that river. It might
occasionally make a small detour to stop at Saumane, where members of
the cavalcade could count on rest and refreshments with Abbé de Sade,
and then it would have headed due north to Mazan via the great medieval town of Carpentras, past the vineyards and fruit groves of a fertile
plain where, in springtime, groves of cherry and apple trees blaze against
the snow-capped peaks of the Ventoux Mountains.

These expeditions did not become more comfortable when Sade's
party reached Mazan. However well equipped its new *salle de spectacles*,
the château's living quarters remained primitive; the Sade family and a
few of their retainers stayed in the town house of the overseer Ripert,
while less ranking members of the entourage slept in dozens of beds that
had been set up in the château's living room. Once arrived from the
arduous journey, Sade had barely two or three days to mount a brand-
new production; he had to rehearse his actors, attend to decors, direct
technicians concerning the raising of curtains and the lighting of candles,
approach notaries and creditors to find additional funds, all the while
taking a leading role in each play. The energy involved in these multiple
functions is mind-boggling, as is Sade's apparent delight in fusing fact
and fantasy, in assigning semifictional roles to his sister-in-law (heroine),
to his wife (heroine's confidante), to his authentic servants (dramatic
soubrettes and valets). But if the marquis's exertions seem extraordinary,
one must remember that the art of theater was the central paradigm of
his life. Sade had chosen all his paramours from the ranks of actresses,
dancers, singers, as was a convention for most noblemen. What is more
relevant is that the mise-en-scène of his sexual exploits—the meticulous

choreography of the apostasy scenes programmed for Mlle Testard, the careful premeditation of the Arcueil whippings, even the choice of costume planned for the event (naked to the waist, a white kerchief about his head)—suggest that Sade was continually *onstage,* if only for his own voyeuristic delight.

The marquis had to hustle hard, however, to get a proper audience to his chaster spectacles. Provençal society was well used to Abbé de Sade's classic brand of libertinage, but Donatien's reported antics seem to have struck them as beyond the pale. The obsequious missives the proud seigneur sent to one of his neighbors, a M. Girard of the nearby village of Lourmarin, intimate that the local gentry was not that eager to associate with the rogue whose fame had spread through France in the wake of the Arcueil episode.

> I have not yet had the happy privilege of your visit, so I desire it ardently; could I hope that the occasion of a comedy I have staged, which will play on the 20th of the month and which I would be most grateful to have your opinion on, might finally satisfy the long-awaited pleasure of meeting you? Spectators and critics as enlightened as you are, sir, are precious, and I do not hide the fact that you will cause me much sorrow if you do not accept the urgent invitation I extend to you for that day. If the weather were not so bad, I would have gone to your house to beseech you in person, etc. [10]

Ultimately, so few "enlightened" guests appeared at his performances that Sade allowed access to any villager who wished to attend, hiring several additional constables to make sure that no "tumult" would be occasioned by the rabble.

And there was always the issue, both on and off the stage, of what would become another Sadeian obsession—money, money, money. The *train de vie* at La Coste was extravagant enough without his theatrical spectaculars. With the marquis's family, his children's governess, the personal maids attending Pélagie and her sister, his secretary, personal valets, and resident actors, his maître d' and the diverse other domestics, cooks, and gardeners tending to daily life at La Coste, Sade's retinue constituted at least thirty persons. This entire crowd had to be fed, clothed, shod. Archives reveal that in the winter of 1771–72, a M. Silvestre, cobbler of Ménerbes, designed scores of shoes commissioned by the marquis for himself, his secretary, his valets, his maître d' (who alone received two pairs of day shoes and a pair of evening slippers), and Pélagie and her sister, who each ordered pink silk mules for their stage performances. In addition, both the marquis and the marquise were great gourmets, if not gluttons. Early in 1772, a M. Légier, confectioner, delivered to La Coste "almonds and marzipan, refined and brown sugar, pralines, quince preserves, jellies and marmalades, Portuguese oranges, orange blossoms, mustard and white pepper, lavender water and soaps. . . ."[11] Sade's entourage, probably too voracious for its own good, also needed medical services. This was provided by Dr. Terris of the nearby village of Bonnieux, who came to La Coste sixty-three times in the first two months of 1772 to attend to a variety of the castle's inhabitants—the marquise and her sister, their maids, the maître d', the governess, the scullery boy, and the hired actors.

DURING THE PAST MONTHS, Pélagie has come to love La Coste quite as ardently as her spouse, but her dedication to it is markedly more altruistic than his. She is sensitive to the well-being of the villagers and of anyone in her direct employ, undertaking the task, for instance, of teaching some local children to read and write. Her frenzied approach to everyday life is well expressed in her sprawling handwriting, replete with deletions, chaotic attempts at rephrasings, and stupendous grammatical mistakes. Like many women who take on more duties than they can handle, she is an absentminded and rather helter-skelter housekeeper and is also prodigally charitable toward her domestic help, so much so that they take advantage of her, stealing and cheating on their accounts, provoking mild fits of indignation on her part that never quite assure her authority over them. But then, disdaining high society as much as she does, Pélagie has lived most of her life in the company of domestics. Somewhat like her husband, who would shock his peers by sharing sexual exploits with his valets, she feels more at ease with her servants than with any other social group. One of the keys to the Sades' amazing marital harmony, in fact, may be their shared sense of marginality toward their aristocratic milieu, which would readily lead them to become outcasts. However tinged with seigneurial disdain their intimacy with "the people" might be, even their habit of addressing each other with the informal *tu*—a usage then largely confined, among spouses, to peasants and humble artisans—displays their earthiness, their familiarity with the customs of the more modest classes.

Occasionally, discreet archival details such as medical visits and laundry lists, yield glimpses into the Sades' emotional life. Witness a notation in the diary of their attending physician, Dr. Terris, in May 1772, shortly after he has recorded two calls paid in one day to the marquise's sister: "In riding to the castle to see [Mlle de Launay], as I'd promised her

I'd do . . . I met her riding horseback . . . in good health, coming to Bonnieux with M. le Marquis."[12]

Witness, too, a curious notation the marquise made the same month on the margin of an inventory of family linen compiled by the Sade children's governess, Mlle Langevin, and Mlle de Launay upon arriving at La Coste: Pélagie's scribbling consists of words so disconnected that they seem to have been jotted down in the process of trying out a new pen; their content is somber: "I we / killed / bad project / horrible / horrible . . ."[13]

Juxtapose the doctor's glimpse of Anne-Prospère on that May day and the marquise's daily reality: the flirtatious canoness, dressed in her nun's habit, is frisking on her little Corsican horse alongside the marquis through the two miles of gently rolling fields that separate La Coste from Bonnieux. She wears around her neck the octagonal gilded cross (an exact replica, by coincidence, of the design in the Sades' coat of arms) that Louis XV bestowed upon the members of her convent. They ride through fields ablaze with the violet of Judas trees, sparkling with crimson poppies, redolent with the scent of thyme, lavender, and rosemary.

Back at the craggy, sun-drenched mountaintop castle, calm, sturdy Mme de Sade, dressed in her sensible shoes and her dun-hued mended clothes, ambles briskly from kitchen to laundry to vegetable garden to larder, a bunch of keys always dangling from her waist as she attends to her children's and guests' needs, managing details of the domestic schedule with obsessive dutifulness.

She is indefatigable, filled with an energy that's almost as manic as her husband's. At La Coste, the marquise enjoys the most menial country tasks, and even though scores of villagers could be hired for such chores, she puts on thick, mannish leather gloves to chop the firewood, prune the fruit trees, lend a hand in the vegetable garden. Her friend Milli de Rousset, who later will play a major role in the Sades' lives, describes her as constantly pacing through the property at terrific speed, "with giant's footsteps."[14] And indeed there is a virile streak to this brawny, willful creature who seldom reveals her innermost feelings, who throughout her husband's most bizarre erotic intrigues will never admit that she holds anything but first place in his affections, however many sun-drenched promenades he enjoys with her beautiful sister.

EVEN AT A TIME of cheap labor, it was an expensive venture to mount a theatrical company in two separate communities, and by the spring of 1772, older members of Sade's family were again commenting on the extravagance of his enterprise. "My nephew's passion for comedy . . . is carried to the extreme," Abbé de Sade wrote to his nephew's business agent, Maître Fage, in those months, "and could well lead to his ruin if it lasts. . . . I'm observing with pleasure that the complications he faces in reconciling the actors to each other and handling their perpetual fraudulence, his difficulty in finding money to finance all [these specta- cles], the obstacles that constantly arise . . . are beginning to discourage him; he might have already dropped it all if his wife agreed to cooperate with me, and if she were less accommodating to every one of his whims." [15]

And what about Mme de Montreuil's state of mind throughout these long months when both her daughters were immured with the marquis? Her correspondence this season reveals her to be anxious, per- plexed, not quite knowing which leg to stand on, what tack to take. Her daughters had barely communicated with her since their arrival at La Coste, and in the spring of 1772 her letters to Provence did not have their habitual driving clarity. They were elusive, rambling, and for once rather confused, as if she was having trouble choosing the right strategy with which to defy the Sades' alarmingly volatile life.

"Not having received news of my children for a long time, I'm anxious about their health," she wrote to the abbé in May. "I hear that all their theatricals keep them constantly on the move, so I don't even know which town they're living in at this moment. . . . Such spectacles are reasonable enough when engaged in with one's social equals but tend to become very ridiculous . . . when they're indulged in without restraint. . . . The entire province . . . is very shocked by them."

She then turns her attention to the impact Sade's way of life was having on her daughters and, of course, on family finances.

"[Theater] has always been his dominant passion—if not his folly —but it would be sad if [this obsession] would further compromise his wife and his sister-in-law. . . . That would be an indignity that I would immediately rectify, if he doesn't upstage me by becoming reasonable of his own will. What is the purpose of all these spectacles and festivities? Totally to decimate his fortune, which he's considerably diminished al- ready through every possible extravagance? . . . I'm weary of being a dupe; I'm ready to sacrifice myself for honest, reasonable ends, but [I refuse] to encourage excesses."

The Présidente's next thought reveals the depth of her disillusion- ment with Donatien.

"When he will have dissipated all he has, he will send me back his wife and children, for whom he has little concern, and whom I'll surely take in. . . . And he will face an unfortunate, miserable fate." [16]

Donatien himself was very aware of the financial strains caused by his thespian spectaculars. Right in the middle of his theater festival, on June 22, 1772, he left La Coste with his valet Latour to obtain cash in the prosperous metropolis of Marseilles. However, in his century as in our own, Marseilles was a city renowned for its easy mores, and the two men were readily distracted from their business dealings.

X

The Orgy

Soft and voluptuous creatures who are led by libertin-
age, sloth, or adversity to the delectable and lucrative
vocation of whoring, follow the following advice, the
fruits of wisdom and experience: practice sodomy, my
friends, it's the only way to earn money and amuse
yourselves. . . . Prudish and delicate wives, take the
same course; become Protean with your husbands in
order to attach them to you. . . . You will run infi-
nitely fewer risks, both for your happiness and for
your health: no children, seldom any illnesses, and a
thousand times greater pleasure.

—*Juliette*

☐

MARSEILLES, TWELVE NOON of Saturday, July 27, 1772: a little third-floor flat of 15 *bis* Rue d'Aubagne, at the corner of Rue des Capucins. Enter a gentleman—"average size," "blond hair," "handsome face," "full features"[1]—wearing a gray coat with blue lining and a vest of marigold-yellow silk with matching breeches; there is a dapper plume in his hat, a sword at his side; he carries a gold-knobbed cane. The visitor is in the company of his valet, who is slightly taller than his master and has long hair and a face pitted by smallpox; he wears a blue-and-yellow-striped sailor's costume. When addressing each other, the two men swap social roles: Sade calls his domestic Monsieur le Marquis and Latour addresses his employer as Lafleur, the plebeian name Sade will later bestow on a fictional valet in his novel *Philosophy in the Boudoir*.

The flat the two men are visiting belongs to the prostitute Mariette Borelly, one of four girls hired by the marquis for this particular party. Sade's hunt for big-city pleasure began four days earlier, upon his arrival in Marseilles. After dropping off his bags at his hotel, he went several times to a brothel on Rue Saint-Ferréol-le-Vieux to visit a nineteen-year-old prostitute called Jeanne Nicou. Meanwhile Latour was scouring the back alleys of the port district, assigned by his master to recruit some "extremely young girls" for a special debauch.

The company has finally assembled, and besides the hostess of the party, twenty-three-year-old Mariette, it consists of eighteen-year-old Marianne Laverne and two other professionals, both twenty years old, Mariannette Laugier and Rosette Coste.

The four young women are gathered in the room, waiting for the marquis. Immediately upon arriving, he seizes a handful of large coins from his pocket, holds out his clenched palm. "There'll be enough money for everyone!" he announces. Whoever comes closest to guessing the number of coins in his hand, he adds, will have the honor of being first. Each girl guesses a number, and Marianne Laverne "wins" by coming closest.

In the first scene, the Marquis de Sade locks the door and orders Latour and Marianne to lie down on the bed. He whips the prostitute with one hand while masturbating his servant with the other, calling him "Monsieur le Marquis." Then Latour is asked to leave, and exits rather dejectedly. Left alone with Marianne, the marquis offers her a gold-rimmed crystal candy box containing pastilles of Spanish fly—cantharides is the chemical name of the substance—coated with anise-flavored sugar. He tells her to eat plenty of them in order to bring about the desired flatulence: he has specified that he wishes her to fart and let him "take the wind in his mouth," but she refuses to consume more than seven or eight. The marquis then says that for an extra coin she can be sodomized by him or by his valet—take your choice, he offers. When Marianne turns down both options (or so she will claim in her deposition to the police, sodomy being a crime for men and women), Sade hands her a scroll of parchment bristling with misshapen nails and asks her to whip him with it. She cannot manage to give him more than three blows. He orders her to continue, but she pleads that she feels faint. He then asks her to find a heather broom, which she goes to fetch in the nearby kitchen. Less fearful of this household implement than of the metal scourge, Marianne strikes the marquis with it several times, as he cries out that she must strike him harder. Suddenly Marianne moans that she feels sick to her stomach. She rushes to the kitchen to get a glass of water from the maid. Feeling even sicker, she asks for a cup of coffee. Another set of performers gathers to play out the marquis's fantasies.

In the second scene, while Marianne is recovering in the kitchen, Sade invites Latour to return, in the company of Mariette. Sade tells her to undress and to crouch at the foot of the bed. He gives her a few strokes with the broom and asks her to do the same to him. While Mariette repeatedly whips him, the marquis, using his penknife, records on the wooden mantelpiece the number of blows that he receives: . . . 179 . . . 215 . . . 225 . . . 240 . . . After a total of 758 blows, he throws the girl down on the bed, face up. He takes his pleasure with her in the conventional manner, while masturbating his valet and then being sodomized by him. Then exit Mariette, enter Rosette.

The antics of the triad in the third scene duplicate those of the previous one, with a few minor variations: the marquis orders Rosette to undress and watches his valet take her in the missionary position. Latour and Sade next take turns masturbating each other, while Rosette thrashes the marquis with the broom. Sade then offers the girl extra cash to be sodomized by his valet. She refuses (or so she will testify) and leaves the room, making way for Mariannette.

In the next scene, Sade first caresses the prostitute and then tells her he will whip her because "he still has twenty-five blows to administer." Seeing the blood on the scourge of nails he is holding (it is his own blood), she takes fright and tries to leave. Sade forcibly prevents her and calls for the first whore, Marianne, to rejoin them. He offers candies to both girls. Mariannette tries a few and spits them out. Marianne refuses the sweets, saying she has already eaten too many. After giving a few blows of the whip to both girls, one of the girls' police testimony went, "the man . . . whipped both of us with the broom whisk he had asked for, then threw the witness on the bed face down . . . stuck his nose between the cheeks of her buttocks so as to inhale her wind, and asked the victim to masturbate his domestic again. This she refused to do."

Then, having ordered Mariannette to watch the proceedings, Sade sodomizes Marianne while being sodomized by his valet. Mariannette turns away and weeps by the window (or so she will testify), saying she does not wish to watch such spectacles. The marquis again orders her to masturbate Latour, but she refuses and tries to leave. Marianne, still lying face down on the bed, also weeps. Now both girls beg to leave. At first Sade threatens them, then he dismisses them, giving each six livres and promising ten more if they will accompany him that evening on a moonlight sail in Marseilles harbor.

Thus ended an interlude that the marquis's enthusiastic pioneer biographer, Gilbert Lely, called "Cytherean." Sade went back to his hotel room for his afternoon siesta, enjoying, as usual, a sleep as deep and untroubled as a child's. But the prior events had been merely an hors d'oeuvre. He planned to leave for La Coste the next day and could not face an evening devoid of novelties. After his siesta, he sent his lackey to Marianne and Mariannette's bordello to pick them up for his projected sailing party, but they refused to go. Latour then scoured the streets of Marseilles for fresh meat (one is constantly reminded, throughout this picaresque episode, of Don Giovanni and his manservant, Leporello). He found a whore standing before her door, twenty-five-year-old Marguerite Coste, native of Montpellier, who was willing to receive the marquis in her room. Leaving her a small advance, Latour rushed back to find Sade, who was dining at his inn with an actor, and whispered news of his great find. Dinner and guest were quickly dispatched, and the two men set out for the fifth prostitute's room.

In the final scene, Sade and his valet climb the two flights of stairs to Marguerite Coste's room. Upon arriving, the marquis dismisses Latour, who again leaves with a look of frustration. Sade puts down his cane and sword and offers the girl his crystal candy box, from which she eats several pieces of sugar-coated Spanish fly. He tries to persuade her to take more, but she declines. He insists, telling her that all the girls he consorts with eat a great deal of these bonbons, and she finishes the contents of the box. He then proposes to "enjoy her from behind and in other yet more horrible manner," but she refuses, asking him to take her only "in the way God wills it." [2] Sade leaves the lady, paying her six francs.

At dawn the next morning, the marquis and his valet set off in a three-horse coach for Aix-en-Provence, first relay stop on their way home. Little did they know that their last prey, Marguerite Coste, made very ill by an overdose of Sade's candies, was setting in motion the judicial system of the entire Marseilles region, which was under the jurisdiction of the Parlement of Aix-en-Provence. After Sade left her room, she had vomited "black fetid matter" and suffered from fever and severe intestinal pains. Compassionate neighbors called the police, and Mlle Coste was diagnosed by surgeons and pharmacists. Along with the four prostitutes who took part in the marquis's earlier revel, one of whom had a milder form of the symptoms plaguing Mlle Coste, she would be thoroughly cross-examined by policemen and prosecutors later in the week. On Saturday, July 4, one week after the marquis's "Cytherean" frolic, the king's prosecutor would issue a warrant of arrest for the Marquis de Sade and his valet, M. Latour.

SPANISH FLY, a substance extracted from the body of a green-hued Mediterranean insect, has been renowned for its aphrodisiac properties since antiquity. It enjoyed a renewed vogue in Europe during the Renaissance and became particularly popular in mid-eighteenth-century France, where it was used extensively—and notoriously—by one of the most popular military heroes of those decades, Maréchal de Richelieu (candies made with this ingredient soon became known as "pastilles à la Richelieu").

It is very doubtful that Sade employed this venerable substance with the intention of harming his sexual partners. Even Mme de Montreuil, who by now had become her son-in-law's bitterest enemy, vigorously denied any possibility of malicious intent on his part. "Why on earth," she commented, "would a man give poison to girls he had never seen or heard of and whose profession offers no occasion for love, jealousy, or benefit of any kind?"[3] But it was in Sade's nature to be sloppy about preparing such potions, and the doses he forced upon the girls were irresponsibly large, the traditional dosage being two pastilles in twenty-four hours. Sade made excessive use of the drug because his intent went beyond mere sexual arousal. Incited by what psychiatrists call "coprophilic perversion"—a neurotic pleasure derived from the smell of feces —he wished, above all, to stimulate the prostitutes' intestinal functions and have them produce a maximum of gases. So he covered large doses of Spanish fly with a coating of anise, equally known for its capacity to increase flatulence.

Sade's disregard for the potentially fatal effect of this pharmaceutical experiment inevitably brings up the issue of his brutal elitism and that of his entire caste: most every member of Sade's society was indifferent to the fate of whores. The fact that a man of his rank could be condemned because of a whore's illness—he considered all such women to be "vile creatures"—was an indignity Sade would never be able to fathom. As an affront to the judicial system that condemned him (he later described the members of the Aix Parlement as "a bunch of tuna merchants and petty seamen, a crowd of riffraff with whom the nobility should have nothing to do"), he even refused to admit that he had offered the prostitutes any sweets. He insisted that the women had simply been made ill by their overindulgence at the dinner table. His disdain for the legal proceedings set against him is displayed in a letter he wrote some five years later. Continuing to assert that gluttony had been the sole cause of the girls' illnesses, he claimed that "a mild disturbance of the entrails is a very prevalent illness in Provence" and derided the prosecutors of his case in his novella *Le Président mystifié* as "a pack of scoundrels . . . return[ing] a verdict of 'poison' in a case involving a few strumpets with colic."[4]

But the nature of Sade's intent was never examined by the French judicial system. Once again Sade was not only victimized by his own psychopathic follies and his dreadful reputation; he was also a casualty of the social conflicts that continued to be played out in France. In 1772, the French political system was more dominated than ever by the Montreuils' bitter enemy M. de Maupeou. Louis XV would die in 1774, and in the last two years of his reign, Maupeou, his chancellor, wielded greater influence than ever. Although he had risen to power on the basis of his popularity as a leading member of the French Parlements, by 1772 the mercurial chancellor was locked into a fierce struggle with these increasingly fractious institutions. He had exiled thousands of magistrates throughout the country and replaced them with men loyal to him. So the indictment on charges of poisoning and sodomy brought against Sade and Latour by the Marseilles court was maneuvered by jurists appointed by Maupeou, who did his bidding. Moreover, the lawsuit incited by the Marseilles incident was the most serious one yet brought against the marquis; sodomy, theoretically, carried the death penalty. So the police detail that arrived at La Coste on July 9 to arrest Sade was out for blood. Much chagrined were they to be met at the gate of the château by M. Fage, Sade's notary, and to hear that the marquis and his valet had been gone for a week and had not been heard from since their departure. After a careful search of the castle, the police went on to question servants and villagers, who also claimed, most loyally, that no one had seen the men for many days.

Sade had escaped just in time. Two days earlier, during rehearsals of two plays scheduled to be performed at La Coste on July 9, one of which was Voltaire's comedy *Adélaide du Guesclin,* an actor in Sade's troupe had come to warn him that he was accused of having poisoned several prostitutes and that an arrest warrant was imminent. Because of its exposed topography, the village of La Coste is perilous for anyone seeking cover; every slope of its barren peak is clearly visible from the plain that surrounds it. But most of its adjoining terrain, the area now called the Vaucluse, is perfect for escapees. (The word *maquis,* a term for the underground fighters of World War II France, is derived from the thick, low shrubbery that covers much of that region and makes it ideal for outlaws.) So the marquis and his valet had fled La Coste for safer hiding places in their own province. But they had not escaped alone. They were in the company of Sade's sister-in-law the canoness, Anne-Prospère de Launay.

The fugitives probably found refuge not far from home: at Saumane, with Abbé de Sade, who would have been delighted to feast his eyes on the ravishing Anne-Prospère, or in Mazan, with the devoted overseer of Sade's estate, M. Ripert. Whatever site of Provence the marquis and his companions hid out in, soon after their attempted arrest the Marseilles court returned a verdict of guilty against them. Police officers came back many times to La Coste, seizing and marking, as specified by law, all of the marquis's property and sources of revenue—his château, his farms and estates in the region, and any rents and revenues deriving from them.

And then three weeks later, as mysteriously as she had left, Anne-Prospère returned alone to La Coste, to be with her sister. Did the marquise *ask* Anne-Prospère to escort the marquis in order to increase his safety, by making his wanderings seem like a peaceful family trip? Or did this impulsive, confused schoolgirl decide on her own to accompany him? Did she return out of religious scruple, or out of ambivalence toward the marquis's sexual requests, or out of loyalty to her sibling? Whatever her intentions were, by the time the enigmatic Anne-Prospère reappeared at La Coste she was not in great shape. Her state of emotional turmoil is portrayed in a petition to legal authorities, drawn up by the Marquise de Sade some time later, which describes the events of the summer of 1772. (It is the same chronicle in which the marquise intimates that her husband had conceived a "fatal passion" for his sister-in-law.) After describing the state of shock she herself suffered in the weeks after her husband's indictment, Pélagie states the following:

> She [Mme de Sade] strives to quiet her anguish, to soothe her state of alarm; she addresses herself to her sister, but the disarray she witnesses in [her sister]'s soul, the hesitation and wavering of her answers, only heighten her own state of agitation. . . . Her sister's very dejection diminishes her own strength.[5]

Notwithstanding their shared anguish, soon after Anne-Prospère's return to Provence the sisters went off together to Marseilles, determined to bribe the prostitutes into withdrawing their accusations before Sade's case went on to the court of Aix-en-Provence for appeals. They were armed with four thousand livres, which Pélagie—in direr financial straits than ever, since the police had seized all her husband's properties —managed to raise with the help of M. Ripert, Abbé de Sade, and even the impoverished Abbé Amblet, who contributed a thousand livres. Her search for cash had been frantic. She had first turned to her mother, who by this time was fully apprised of her younger daughter's liaison with Donatien, and this time the Présidente refused her. No letters of Mme de Montreuil's have survived from that summer, but her state of mind is made clear in Pélagie's aforementioned petition:

> The petitioner . . . imagined that she would find comfort in the tenderness of her parents. She addressed herself to Mme

de Montreuil, her mother; she made every possible effort to move her but did not find any of the kindness she had counted on; [her mother informed her that] to solicit for her husband would be tantamount to being the accomplice of his transgressions.[6]

So in the summer of 1772—her husband in hiding, her mother estranged—Pélagie was left with no support whatever. The Présidente's state of mind can be readily inferred: How could she continue to assist the rake who had deflowered her most treasured child, the dazzling beauty whom she had groomed to further enhance the Montreuils' social standing by a brilliant marriage? Obviously, Mme de Montreuil had sent her oldest daughter packing. And from now on the enmity between the two women would grow apace.

Their estrangement was not without benefit to Pélagie. Once she realized that she was on her own, she acted with quite as much imagination and dynamism as her parent; her mission in Marseilles was highly successful. In exchange for handsome payment (they probably received over a thousand livres apiece), the two prostitutes responsible for Sade's indictment, Marguerite Coste and Marianne Laverne, signed documents withdrawing their charges.

But this was a small victory in light of the new crop of legends and outlandish gossip that flared up against the marquis a mere six weeks after his Marseilles caper. The writers of the "Bachaumont" newsletter, one of France's most popular social gazettes, published the following fable:

> Friends write from Marseilles that M. Le Comte de Sade, who caused such an uproar in 1768 . . . gave a ball. . . . Into the dessert he slipped chocolate pastilles so good that a number of people devoured them. . . . He had mixed in some Spanish fly. The effect of this preparation is well known. It proved so potent that those who ate the pastilles began to burn with an unchaste ardor and to carry on as if in the grip of the most amorous frenzy. The ball degenerated into one of those licentious orgies for which the Romans were renowned. Even the most respectable women could not resist the uterine rage that swept through them. And so it was that M. de Sade enjoyed the favors of his sister-in-law, with whom he had fled to avoid the punishment he deserves. Several persons died of their frightful priapic excesses, and others are still quite sick.[7]

News of Sade's latest fling quickly spread to the highest Parisian circles. Three weeks after the Marseilles episode, M. de Saint-Florentin, the minister of the interior, wrote to the governor of Provence: "One hears a great deal, sir, of a very serious incident in Marseilles that involved M. de Sade and of which the Parlement has been apprised. I can't help but express my surprise at the fact that you have not yet informed me of it directly. It is my duty to keep the king informed of all the important happenings that occur in the provinces."[8]

A renowned bookseller who also published a popular newsletter, M. Hardy, made far graver accusations. Sade, he alleged, had been found guilty of "having conspired with his servants to poison his wife, incited by the violent passion he had conceived for his sister-in-law."[9]

Such reports were all too frequently brought to Pélagie's attention. One can imagine her state of anguish as she sat out the summer at La Coste. How could she make the public understand that her husband's latest fling was just another case of licentious excess, so many thousands of which had gone unpunished? How could she make this truth be heard by a sensation-starved public? Above all, how could she surmount this grimmest crisis to date without her mother's help? Somehow her pessimism never daunted her spirits.

THE MOST UNEXPECTED EVENT yet to occur in this agitated summer was the arrival of M. de Montreuil at La Coste. It was his first visit there. Despite his advancing years and his passive inclinations, he had traveled four hundred thirty miles, braving the summer heat of Provence, to do what he could to safeguard his family's reputation and perhaps bring solace to his eldest daughter. "La Coste is not a very extensive estate, but it is most seigneurial,"[10] he recorded in his diary.

Did the lethargic jurist come to Provence to offer Pélagie the help his wife refused to give, or was he merely carrying out the Présidente's commands? Whatever his intent, after ten days at La Coste, M. de Montreuil visited all possible relatives and acquaintances who might aid the family. He went to Saumane to commiserate with the abbé and to Mazan to dine with the resourceful M. Ripert. He met with the oldest of the marquis's uncles, Richard-Jean-Louis de Sade, commander of the Order of Malta, who had recently returned to Provence after a stay of many years abroad. The commander was the family's most respected and powerful member, and it is in his company that M. de Montreuil called on several influential jurists of Aix-en-Provence, whose Parlement was about to review the verdict handed down by the court of Marseilles. Even though he never intended to publish his diary, the cautious M. de Montreuil was so secretive about his mission that his journal entries do not mention his two daughters; they only once refer to his son-in-law, alluding to him in the context of M. de Montreuil's visit to Ripert's home at Mazan (it is probable that he secretly met there with Donatien).

Meanwhile the judicial system was proceeding, as it always did in Donatien's cases, with uncanny speed. In the first days of September, the Parlement of Aix upheld the verdict of the Marseilles court, finding Sade and Latour guilty as accused, "M. de Sade of the crime of poisoning and M. de Sade as well as Latour of the crime of sodomy." And a harsh sentence was imposed: The two men were condemned

> to make a public confession in the courtyard of the cathedral of [Aix], and there, kneeling, hatless and in bare feet, rope about their necks . . . ask forgiveness from God, from the king, and from Justice, and this done, to be led to a scaffold erected on Place des Prêcheurs, where Sieur de Sade will be beheaded and Latour will be hanged or strangled on a gibbet until found dead; then the bodies of Sieur de Sade and Latour will be burned and their ashes thrown to the winds.[11]

Thus Sade was sentenced to a double execution—he was to be beheaded for the crime of poisoning, burned for the crime of sodomy. The day after the court delivered its judgment, one of the eighteenth century's most picturesque scenarios of public disgrace was acted out on Aix's Place des Prêcheurs: the two culprits were executed in effigy— rustic mannequin likenesses of the men were burned after a beheading and a hanging, in the manner spelled out in the sentence. Such allegorical death sentences, not unusual in the eighteenth century, were primarily designed to have an edifying effect on the public. A bonfire was built well ahead of time, and the large crowds in attendance, misled by the thick clouds of smoke shrouding the mannequins, often believed they were witnessing the real thing. As imposed on Sade, such an illusory execution was strictly symbolic; with the possible exception of political treason, under the ancien régime no physical torture or death sentence was likely to have been imposed upon such a high-ranking lord. Yet the chastisement signified another kind of decease, Sade's civil death. Precisely because he did not appear at his own trial and was condemned in absentia, under France's statutes of limitations the marquis was stripped for thirty years of all possible citizen's rights; his wife inherited all his property, and his increasingly detested in-laws, the Montreuils, now became his children's legal guardians.

The injustices of Sade's trials have been commented on extensively, even by his most bitter and prudish enemies. Documents concerning Sade's indictment and sentence drawn up four years later by Louis XVI's advisers would note "a number of absolute and even radical irregularities." The eminent young jurist Joseph Siméon, who four decades later would serve as minister of the interior in the cabinet of the ultraconservative monarch Charles X, was particularly incensed by the high-handed inequity of Sade's trial. Asked to write a report on the legal consequences of the Marseilles episode, Siméon harshly criticized the initial indictment for being "devoid of any factual foundations" and noted that the entire procedure was characterized by "such precipitous haste that one can only conclude that it was provoked." All critics of Sade's trial agreed that the charge of poisoning was particularly outrageous. The Aix courts never even took note of the fact that the two prostitutes, both of whom had fully recovered from their candy binge within a fortnight, had withdrawn their accusations on that count. Nor did the courts take note of the apothecaries' report, which, however archaic its methodology, exonerated the marquis of attempted poisoning.

The charge of sodomy was more complex, for it was shrouded in countless layers of judicial and social hypocrisy. Eighteenth-century French law specified that both males *and* females indulging in that practice were to be burned at the stake. Yet every citizen in his right mind knew that the custom had been widespread in bordellos for centuries and that no prostitutes or other women had ever been punished for it in any way. Moreover, only seven of the tens of thousands of men registered by the police as homosexuals throughout the eighteenth century were put to death, all of them defenseless members of the lower middle class. A few years after the civil death meted out to Sade for the Marseilles episode, a French police official commented on the blatant hypocrisy of his contemporaries' attitudes toward homosexuality: "Punishment . . . falls . . . not on the most criminal but on the least protected of the guilty. . . . Pederasty, in the long run, is only allowed to be the vice of great lords." [12]

The key phrase here is "least protected of the guilty." Due to the ascendance of Chancellor de Maupeou, by 1772 this was clearly the category Sade had once more fallen into. For this time, Maupeou, being in total control of the judiciary branch of government, was out for Sade's head; the marquis's fugitive status, which sabotaged any possible defense strategy, was a trump card in the hands of the chancellor's minions.

How did the marquis react to his symbolic execution? Many Sade scholars have drawn on a passage from *The 120 Days of Sodom* in which a debauched aristocrat learns that he has been sentenced to be burned at the stake in effigy: "When informed of the news that he was to be burned in effigy, the Marquis de ··· pulled his cock out of his trousers and yelled, 'Fuckgod! Now I'm where I always wanted to be, heaped with scandal and infamy! Wait a minute, I must jerk off!' And so he did, at that very moment." [13] Reading flesh-and-blood facts into Sade's fictions, biographers intimate that upon hearing of his public burning, the marquis acted just like his fictive libertine and cheerfully masturbated. Many Sade studies have been tainted by equally questionable tactics.

Whatever his reaction to the news, by the time he had heard of his death sentence Sade had fled to Italy. His wife having arranged every step of his triumphant evasion of the police, he was traveling in the company, again, of his valet and his sister-in-law. This time he had concocted yet another pseudonym from his repertory of names—Comte de Mazan.

WHAT ABOUT PÉLAGIE, who once more remained at La Coste alone to engineer mercy for her husband? How might she have felt about his choice of traveling companions? Such speculations must take into account the extraordinary attitude Mme de Sade had toward her marriage. One cannot decode her through traditional concepts of wifely love, for her fixation on Sade far transcended most such attachments. Her obsession for her husband was analogous to the most perfect monastic dedication, to that total surrender of self achieved only by the most perfect nuns. Like an exemplary Christian whose love for a sinner must match the enormity of the sinner's transgressions, she seems to have felt that if Sade became a monster of immorality, she must all the more become a paragon of devotion. Most persons who knew Donatien well—Mme de Saint-Germain, his military superiors, even, initially, his mother-in-law —detected a secret gentleness in him, which may well have been at the heart of his terrible charm. Pélagie seems to have been acutely conscious of this trait, for she would continue to act throughout their years together as if his excesses were motivated by a totally innocent impulse for experiment, by the same ingenious curiosity that incites a child to pull a butterfly's wings apart.

We've never had access to the Sades' bedroom. Perhaps, when he returned to his wife after his revels, filled with the contentment he achieved through orgy, Donatien expressed his love for her more ardently than ever. Perhaps, when he took her in his arms, she felt their bond was strong enough to withstand any and all transgressions. Whatever inner rhetoric Pélagie took solace in, her spouse was her mission on earth, and she had so totally subjugated herself that she was incapable of judging him. Her marital ardor, in fact, may have been unique in her generation of women. It has a legendary, mythical streak. It is akin to the devotion displayed by wives of ogres in European fairy tales—peerlessly domestic women who, constantly stirring delectable stews, keeping immaculate households and perfectly made beds, shut their eyes to their spouses' most gruesome murders. However the world would pity her—for being deserted again and again for sluts, for having a husband more vilified than any other nobleman in the realm—Pélagie appears to have found such felicity in serving Donatien de Sade that she never considered herself an unhappy woman.

So Pélagie's love was a kind of sublime folly and had most of the lineaments of the loftiest romances: a serene capacity for self-sacrifice; ardent admiration for the cherished one; a voluntary servitude to him, coupled with great disdain for those who had not grasped her beloved's splendor of soul. There was only one essential lineament of "love" as most of us know it that did not infuse Pélagie's obsession with her husband: the desire to possess the being by whom we are possessed. Her love seems to have been too exalted, too selfless, for such a commonplace aspiration. And that may be why she was able to remain at La Coste alone, doggedly struggling for the marquis's freedom, while he lived an incestuous idyll with her little sister in Italy.

XI

The Prisoner

Should we allow anyone to punish our thoughts? Only God has the right to do so, for only he truly knows them.

—Letter to Gaufridy, 1774

□

THWARTING THE PROGRESS of many a biographer, there occasionally appear persons so mercurial that our quest for their identity resembles the search for a rare butterfly. The elusive Anne-Prospère de Launay is precisely that kind of creature. Her mother, in her perpetual crusade to safeguard her family's standing, seems to have efficiently destroyed all of Anne-Prospère's correspondence with her brother-in-law and most other evidence of this illicit liaison. So all chroniclers can do is report on the path of their own footsteps as they lurch and grasp, net in hand, for every vestige of this baffling maiden's presence in Provence, Paris, or Italy.

It is quite certain that Anne-Prospère's second rendezvous with her brother-in-law did not last much longer than the first. Having accompanied the marquis to Venice in early September, Mlle de Launay sampled its beauties for only a few weeks. By October 2, she was back at La Coste with her sister, again in a state of great pique at the marquis, having fled him in such haste that she left all her luggage behind with him.

We are once more driven to conjecture: even though she was not a model of primness, did the fleet-footed beauty rebel against the nature of her brother-in-law's sexual demands? Or did she quickly weary Sade and fall out with him over a revel he enjoyed with another woman? The second alternative is likely. In a document drawn up by Pélagie that relates the events of that year, she describes her younger sister's state of mind when she returned from Italy: "Even Mlle de Launay joins [the accusers], expresses her resentment, and paints the Marquis de Sade in the darkest colors."[1]

In any case, there the two sisters are, biding their time in the glorious autumn of La Coste, with little besides Pélagie's obstinate fortitude to sustain their morale. As for the marquis, shortly after Anne-Prospère left him, he returned from Italy by ship via Nice. He stayed on French territory only long enough to drop off his sister-in-law's baggage and to obtain some badly needed cash from his business agent in Marseilles. Then he headed for safety on foreign soil. Chambéry, now part of France, belonged then to the duchy of Savoy, which in turn was under the jurisdiction of the kingdom of Sardinia-Piedmont. Traveling incognito, as he had since the Marseilles episode, Sade arrived in Chambéry in the company of three persons: his faithful first valet, Latour; the roguish new second valet, Carteron, also called La Jeunesse ("Youth") and Martin Quiros; and a woman, who had accompanied the three men from Italy and whose identity remains unclear: we know that she was not Mlle de Launay, for by the end of October Anne-Prospère was on her way to Paris with her sister.

In Chambéry, the marquis stayed for a few weeks at an inn called Auberge de la Pomme d'Or; early in November, his female companion returned to Italy, escorted by Latour. A few days after her departure, Sade moved into an isolated country house near Chambéry, which he had rented from a local nobleman. Still under the nom de guerre of Comte de Mazan, he lived there reclusively in the company of Carteron, ordering all his meals from a local tavern. Toward the end of November, Latour returned from his mission of accompanying the mysterious lady to Italy. The valets then switched assignments. Latour took charge of Donatien's modest household, while Carteron was sent to Paris to deliver an important letter to Mme de Montreuil. The sending of that missive was yet another extravagantly reckless act.

Donatien's letter to his mother-in-law rashly announced where he was living. The iron lady must have gasped with joy: the rascal had given away his whereabouts! Her prey was a few easy paces away. She instantly contacted France's minister of foreign affairs, the Duc d'Aiguillon. Within a few days, Aiguillon had petitioned the Sardinian government for Sade's arrest. The King of Sardinia-Piedmont, Charles-Emmanuel III, replied that he was "most pleased" to render this service to the French crown, and on December 8, at nine P.M., the royal orders were enacted. As a squadron of police silently surrounded Sade's villa, a Sardinian officer appeared at his door and informed him that he had a warrant from the king for his arrest. Donatien, who was as usual spending the evening at home alone with Latour, was asked to surrender his arms, and he handed over a pair of pistols and a Damascene sword. "As surprised as he was upset,"[2] he was left for the night under two adjutants' surveillance. At dawn the next morning, he was put into a coach and accompanied by mounted escorts to his new jail, the fortress of Miolans, some twenty-five miles from Chambéry. Latour followed his master on horseback.

A few hours later, Donatien de Sade had his first glimpse of Miolans, known throughout Europe as the "Bastille of the Dukes of Savoy." A majestic sixteenth-century citadel perched on a seven-hundred-eighty-foot-high promontory overlooking the valley of the Isère, it was encircled by three thick walls and a double moat. Underneath the drawbridge, at the base of a crenellated tower that loomed two hundred fifty feet over the citadel's ramparts, was a network of dark, perpetually frigid cells that were known as "Hell." Above this were "Purgatory" and "The Treasury," cozier chambers allotted to less dangerous prisoners. The uppermost floor, destined for the *crème de la crème* of inmates, held two suites, "Petite Espérance" to the north and, to the south, "Grande Espérance," whose heavily barred windows offered a magnificent view of the Alps. This was the apartment assigned to the Marquis de Sade, who always seemed to be given lodgings with ironic designations (ten years later, his apartment at the Bastille would be in an area of the prison called "La Liberté").

The commander of the fortress of Miolans, M. de Launay (no relation to Anne-Prospère's paternal grandfather), was a Savoyard army officer who had been in charge of Miolans for over fifteen years. He was under orders to treat his new guest with all the respect due his station, while taking every precaution against the possibility of his escape. Like most captive noblemen of the time, Sade was allowed to outfit his rooms with his own hangings and furniture and to have his first valet live in his suite. He could take daytime walks within the dungeon's inner walls, under the surveillance of guards. He was also permitted to keep two dogs for company (this had been one of Sade's first requests). But visits from anyone but his second valet, Carteron, were strictly prohibited, and his correspondence was heavily censored. This proscription was the hardest for Donatien to bear: M. de Launay was to screen all letters addressed to the marquis, pass on to him only those he approved, and hold on to the others until the captive was freed.

Some highlights from the next few months of Sade's incarceration at Chambéry:

December 16: Sade receives a visit from his second valet, who brings him news of his family in Paris. The marquis orders Carteron to go to Nice to fetch his sister-in-law's suitcases, which he left there upon returning from Italy. (Throughout the next months, an incessant tug-of-war would be played out between Mme de Montreuil and Donatien over this luggage, the Présidente struggling to retrieve it to destroy any incriminating correspondence concerning her daughter, Donatien attempting to keep it from her sight.)

December 27: Chafing against the round-the-clock surveillance—it is constantly being tightened, at the command of his mother-in-law, who is obsessed by the possibility of his escape—Sade sends one of his numerous letters of protest to the governor of the duchy of Savoy, M. De la Tour. He complains that the prison commander, M. de Launay, has been addressing him "in a tone, and with manners, which my birth and military rank clearly do not permit me to tolerate." [3]

December 31: Having learned that Sade has tried to bribe some of his officers with gifts of wine, coffee, and chocolate, Commander de Launay beseeches the governor of Savoy to relieve him of any responsibility for this "dangerous" prisoner: "This lord . . . is as capricious as he is hot-tempered and unreliable, and he could harm me terribly by bribing someone into helping him to escape, having even made frivolous propositions of that kind to me. Therefore it would be wise for his relatives to have him transferred to a fortress in France. One cannot be sure of anyone with so volatile a mind." [4]

January 15: Mme de Montreuil sends the Sardinian ambassador a memo concerning the luggage being sent to the prisoner from Nice and asks that the following items be immediately seized and forwarded to her in Paris: all manuscripts and correspondence, along with any "books harmful to mores"; and also all china of good quality, of which the prisoner is "well capable of making dangerous use." [5]

January 17: The captive, who detests eating meals alone without civil conversation, has taken to dining with a fellow prisoner and gourmet, Baron Songy de L'Allée, who is described in police reports as "a man who becomes very dangerous through drink, is a threat to public peace, and readily threatens to kill others." Relations between Sade and de L'Allée soon become strained as the two men quarrel violently over their card games, which the baron wins too often for Sade's pleasure. For several weeks the two men do not speak.

February 5: Commander de Launay again petitions the governor to relieve him of the dreadful duty of being Sade's custodian. If only Sade were transferred to a French jail, de Launay adds, he would owe the governor "a lifetime of gratitude. . . . It is always dangerous to be in custody of an eccentric like M. de Sade, who in no way acts like a man of his high birth," de Launay notes. [6]

February 14: Sade asks the governor to transmit to the King of

Sardinia a document he has just drafted for the monarch concerning Mme de Montreuil: "A mother-in-law guided by the most detestable self-interest, and who aspires to nothing short of my total ruin, profits from my woes by imposing the most rigorous restrictions upon me . . . and obliging me to be exiled forever." Sade expresses his hope that "the fairest, most sensible of monarchs" will cease to collaborate "with this persecution and injustice," which only aims "to protect avarice and self-interest." If His Majesty ever knew of the lies through which he has been duped, Sade adds, he would not hesitate to liberate him and to expose "the horrors which [Mme de Montreuil] has heaped on me, and renews daily, with the purpose of forever entombing me."[7]

FOR SEVERAL DECADES, the more conservative foreign observers had identified French women as Europe's most dangerous species, deploring their astounding social and political influence. According to David Hume, the French nation "gravely exalts those whom nature has subjected to them and whose inferiority and infirmities are absolutely incurable."[8] Joseph Addison noted that the French tend "to make the [female] sex . . . more *awaken'd* than is consistent either with virtue or discretion."[9] And Mme de Montreuil was as "awaken'd" and commanding a woman as could be found in the kingdom. One is astounded by the efficacy of her three-hundred-mile-distant surveillance of Donatien throughout his imprisonment and by the extraordinary authority she wielded with his captors. Apprised of Sade's every move and conversation, tolerating certain freedoms offered him and prohibiting others, constantly scolding, threatening, and bullying prison authorities and far more lofty government officials of several realms, the iron lady managed to have every one of her orders followed to the last detail. From the jail wardens of Miolans to the governor of Savoy to the ministers of the king of Sicily's cabinet—none of these excellencies could move fast enough to satisfy Mme de Montreuil's wishes.

This authority over others was made all the more striking by the fact that the Présidente, though fairly wealthy, was of undistinguished birth. If she so readily bent the law to her will, it was in part because she had the luck to live in a society that rewarded women of outstanding intelligence with a considerable degree of social mobility; in part because she had, as her son-in-law was the first to emphasize, "the charm of the devil"; and in even greater part because her brilliance shone forth so radiantly from her letters.

For the spell Mme de Montreuil wove over men of high station went beyond the particulars of her own society. It also illustrates the seductive force of rhetoric at any time of history, a skill she displayed in her letters as well as most any woman of her time. Beyond their energy and clarity, her missives blended stylistic elements highly prized in the eighteenth century: shrewdly simulated forthrightness, an unfailing sense of the *mot juste,* fetching female strategies of sentiment and flattery. Here's a brief sample of her authoritative voice as she specifies the degree of freedom Donatien might be permitted during his stay in Miolans:

> He must be treated with all the respect and comfort due his high station and permitted whatever pleasures might soothe the distress of his situation. . . . If [his missives] only beg for goodness and understanding . . . and attempt to justify his most recent misdeed, there should be no obstacle to their passage. But if they contain false and injurious statements concerning his wife's family . . . it would be cruel to allow these imprudent texts to impose yet more lies on the public and the court.[10]

In 1774, Mme de Montreuil's obsession concerning Sade's contacts with the outside world was motivated by an increasingly urgent priority: Anne-Prospère, now going on twenty-three, needed to be married off as soon as possible. In the course of that season, a superb match, Vicomte de Beaumont, came the Montreuils' way. He belonged to a grand and ultraconservative family—the young man's uncle was the archbishop of Paris, Christophe de Beaumont, one of the most powerful French prelates of the century. A man as rigidly entrenched against Enlightenment ideas as anyone in Europe, the archbishop was engaged in a constant crusade against *philosophes* and freethinkers, and had condemned Rousseau's novel *Émile* as the most dangerous book of its time. What a scandal would erupt if the venerable cleric's own nephew were to marry the mistress of a debauchee who had been sentenced to death for sodomy!

So it's understandable that the Beaumonts would consent to the marriage only on condition that Sade remain imprisoned for life. The Présidente, worried by the threat that Donatien might ruin the match by breaking out of jail or by publishing some scabrous text, marshaled all her energies to prevent such a disaster. For some years, she had allowed "the torrent to flow," as she put it. She had now reached the stage where she had to start building her dam.

□   □

WE RETURN to the chronicle of the Marquis de Sade's incarceration at the "Bastille of the Dukes of Savoy."

February 26: The Sardinian ambassador to France informs M. de Launay that the Marquise de Sade has just left Paris. She claims to be headed for Provence, he reports, but there is every reason to believe that she is headed for Savoy in order to attempt a visit to her husband. M. de Launay is cautioned about the dreadful risks of such a meeting—such warnings all originate from Mme de Montreuil—and is instructed to take all precautions against the marquise's visit.

March 5: Staying at a tiny inn some twelve miles from her husband's prison, Pélagie writes another letter to the governor of Savoy, one of the first precisely dated letters of Pélagie's that have survived, begging him to allow her to visit her husband. "I took the road to Grenoble with the intention of visiting my husband," she pleads. "Duty decreed this step, and the dictates of my heart made it a necessity. Your Excellency surely could not disapprove such motives." [11]

Moving from village to village, shifting locations like a convict on the lam, Pélagie fires off an emotional letter to the King of Sardinia himself.

> No, Sire, my husband must not be confused with the numerous scoundrels who should be purged from this planet. An overly vivid imagination motivated him, Sire, to commit a misdemeanor; our judicial system, displaying its full thunder, made a crime of it. And for what kind of a misdeed? For a youthful misadventure which neither harmed anyone's health, or honor, or reputation. He has been locked up at Miolans to calm the fires of an overly tempestuous imagination—this measure only aggravates the harmful proclivity which is in need of being cured. It's for all these reasons, Sire, that I beg Your Majesty to restore my husband to liberty and to permit him to remain in your country. [12]

March 10–17: Having been repeatedly denied the right to visit her husband, Pélagie now turns to cloak-and-dagger tactics. On March 10, the Savoy authorities are apprised that two French citizens, traveling under the pseudonym "frères Dumont," have registered at an inn some six miles from the fortress and that one of these travelers is the Marquise de Sade, disguised as a man. The genuine male of the pair, a M. Albaret, whom the marquise has hired as her private secretary and messenger, has been dispatched by Pélagie to Miolans to deliver a letter to the prisoner.

March 17–24: Pélagie's mission proves futile. Albaret/Dumont is finally allowed to see M. de Launay and asks permission to see the marquis for fifteen minutes in order to give his wife a firsthand report on his condition. But because of Mme de Montreuil's repeated warnings that any communication between Pélagie and her husband would have "fatal consequences," the prison commander turns down even that modest request.

Pélagie does not yet lose heart. She moves on to Chambéry and sends her traveling companion directly to M. de La Tour, the governor of Savoy, with the same request. Citing direct orders from the King of Sardinia, the governor also refuses her a visit with the marquis. But he warmly assures the marquise that her husband is in marvelous shape, agrees to pass on her letter to him, and advises her to spare her own health by leaving the "foul inn" where she is staying. Pélagie next toys with the notion of calling upon the King of Sardinia himself, in Turin, to ask permission to see her husband; but she finally loses heart and, turning back toward Lyons, makes her way to La Coste.

The same week, the Sardinian ambassador to the French court, Count Ferrero de La Marmora, expresses what may well be the first recognition of Sade's literary gifts. He writes a memo to the governor of Savoy, reminding him that no text written by the Marquis de Sade must ever be allowed to circulate outside the fortress, for the prisoner "inundates us with rhapsodies and memoirs in which facts are as false as they are artistically presented." [13]

March 26: Count Ferrero de La Marmora transmits to the governor of Savoy Mme de Montreuil's very deep gratitude for the "firm and courteous manner" in which he thwarted all of the Marquise de Sade's attempts to see her husband. The ambassador urges the governor to prevent Sade from "inundat[ing] the public with his dreadful writings and with his memoirs, which only aggravate his guilt in the eyes of reasonable people." [14]

But then, that very week, M. de Launay informs the governor that "M. de Sade is beginning to become more reasonable" and that "only his tendency to write too much, and to not submit himself to his parents' will, has delayed his process of maturation." [15]

April 15: The Marquis de Sade sends a message to the commander of Miolans, announcing that he has made up with his former companion the Baron de L'Allée and asking permission to share his meals with the baron, "wanting with all his heart to reassure him of the sincerity of his reconciliation." [16]

□   □

IT IS EVIDENT that toward the middle of March Sade had chosen to switch strategies toward his jailers and feign a more compliant attitude. As Easter Week approached, the consummate actor in Sade decided to make the most of it. Midway through Lent, he sent a letter to the governor of Savoy, in which he stated his wish to take the path of "submission" recommended by his jail commander. Expounding on his in-laws' decision to confine him, he says it was solely to assure the end of his liaison with his wife's sister, which he described as "a misplaced and unfortunate intrigue."

> They carry their rancor too far, for I have with the greatest sincerity declared that I renounced [this affair]. . . . I break off all communication, I offer to return all letters, I swear never to go within a hundred leagues of Paris for as long as they wish, and I promise to suppress any memorandum, petition, or injurious statement that might undermine or interfere with a venture . . . that I desire perhaps more than they.[17]

That first phase of Sade's new strategy worked wonders. The prison commander soon began to boast to all his peers about his captive's metamorphosis. What thrilled M. de Launay most of all about Donatien's reform was that he "discharged his Easter duties as a good Christian," an allusion to Sade's request to take confession and communion at that most sacred time of year. A few days later, the governor of Savoy himself took pains to report that after doing his "Easter duties," Sade was "suddenly quite changed in disposition and behavior." This happy improvement, the governor concluded, "clearly seems to have been effected by the grace of the sacrament."[18]

By the middle of April, the prison commander was reporting that both Sade and the tempestuous Baron de L'Allée had been "much edified" by fulfilling their religious duties and equally soothed by their determination to drink only water. The two captives were now allowed to resume dining together, and to walk together a few hours a day within the fortress walls.

It is this renewed solidarity with a skilled fellow convict that enabled Sade to make his sensational escape from the "Bastille of the Dukes of Savoy."

XII

On the Lam

He was at home . . . in a safe country, in the depths
of an inhabitable forest, at that heart of the forest
which only birds could reach, he was there as in the
very entrails of the earth.

— *The 120 Days of Sodom*

☐

THE MARQUIS DE SADE'S quarters at Miolans were at the opposite end
of the fortress from the prison kitchen. In the last week of April 1773, he
complained that the meals served to him and his dinner companion,
Baron de L'Allée, were arriving to their table cold. He asked the jail
commander if they might dine as close as possible to the canteen, on the
ground floor. M. de Launay, now filled with much goodwill toward both
men, was happy to allot them a room adjoining the kitchen in which to
take their meals. That particular area of the prison comprised a storage
room, whose window, the only one in the entire fortress to be devoid of
bars, was only some thirteen feet up from the ground.

On the evening of April 30, at seven P.M., the marquis and the
baron arrive at the kitchen quarters for their supper and are served by
the marquis's valet. Latour waits for the moment when the cook and her
staff begin their own dinner, then he proceeds to the storeroom, having
seized the keys to it sometime earlier. Within a few minutes, the three
men easily crawl through the unbarred window of the storeroom. Below
them waits an accomplice, an eighteen-year-old Savoyard mountain
guide with whom the marquis has been having clandestine communications. A few steps down, and they're free. Under the young man's guidance, the three fugitives proceed swiftly toward the French border, only
ten miles away.

At about nine P.M., the night watchman assigned to guard the marquis takes up his post by the captive's door. Looking through the keyhole, he sees a light burning and concludes that the marquis is playing his habitual game of checkers with Baron de L'Allée. He does not dare disturb the noblemen, whose violent tempers incited them to raise a great fuss the last time he came into their lodgings at night. So the watchman lies down and falls asleep, waiting until the baron is ready to be accompanied to his cell. He wakes up at three A.M., sees that the marquis's light is still on, suspects trouble, and rushes to the jail commander's quarters to warn him. M. de Launay, accompanied by guards, opens the door of Sade's cell. It is empty. Candles, nearly spent, are burning on the table. Alongside are two letters, one from each of the deserters. The Marquis de Sade's missive displays his habitual braggadocio.

"Sir," it begins, "if anything can spoil the joy I feel in freeing myself from my shackles, it is the dread that you may be held responsible for my escape. After all your decency and kindness toward me, I cannot conceal from you that this thought much troubles me."

Sade reassures the prison commander that he is innocent of having abetted his escape. "Your vigilance delayed me by several days. . . . I owe . . . [my success] solely to my own stratagems." After a few more such gallant consolations, Sade, pretending that he is supported by a network of redoubtable mercenaries, warns the commander that he must not attempt to pursue him. "Fifteen well-mounted, well-armed men await me at the base of the castle. . . . They are all sworn to risk death rather than see me captured again." If the commander were to send the garrison after him, Sade warns, there would be a danger of "many people being massacred," and in any case, the marquis would not be taken alive, for "I shall defend my freedom if it costs me my life." After a few more such intimidating cautions, Sade threatens the revenge of his entire family: "I have a wife, and children, who would pursue you unto death if you harmed me." (The eldest of his children, all of whom have been living in Paris with their grandmother for the past year, is not yet six years old!)

"I solely desire my freedom and only wish to be liberated from the intolerable bondage effected by the whims of my mother-in-law," Sade concludes. "A day will come, I hope, when I shall be allowed to fully express the sentiments of deep appreciation . . . with which, my dear commandant, I am honored to be your most humble and obedient servant."

The marquis had taken pains to draft a meticulous inventory of all the personal effects left behind in his cell. In addition to Sade's bed, mattress, linens, silver-plated coats of arms, and the six ancient maps that had decorated the walls of his cell, the list, drafted with obvious sarcasm, included his bidet, his chamber pot, and its accompanying pierced chair. He also mentioned some dear companions he was forced to leave behind —"two sleeping dogs, one all black, the other black and white, to which [I am] extremely attached."[1]

THE DETAIL OF TROOPS sent by Commander de Launay arrived at the French border a few hours too late. By that time, the three truants were well on the road to Grenoble. And for several months through the spring and summer of 1773, Sade's trail goes totally cold. We know only that he was in Bordeaux in late July, whence he wrote his mother-in-law to send him the funds he needed to flee to Spain. In view of her present obsessive enmity toward him—she had received the news of his escape "with the most extreme sorrow and chagrin"[2]—this unrealistic demand was most probably a false lead, intended to cover up his tracks. We do not reencounter Sade until that autumn, when, back in Provence, he lived once more like a member of the *maquis,* never staying in one place more than two or three days. At first he shuttled between several locations in Mazan, which had the advantage of being in papal territory and thus less accessible to French police. Later that fall, he settled very cautiously at La Coste, the most hazardous of his sites, seldom venturing outside his estate. He spent long hours walking in its park with his cherished dogs, Dragon, Thisbée, and Gros-Dodu. He hobnobbed with a few trusted workmen employed at the castle. And he often retreated to his study to read. Throughout this time, he got along better than ever with his wife, with whom, according to friends' reports, he had never been on more harmonious, loving terms.

NOTWITHSTANDING their vast differences in sexual temperament, the Sades shared many traits of character, most prominently that of prodigality. From his late teens on, Sade had indulged himself in services and material possessions chimerically unsuited to his modest finances. His frantic impulse to "spend" too much seems to have been as compulsive as his need for taboo sex. Pélagie was equally extravagant and, moreover, was always ready to fulfill every one of her husband's imprudent whims. In the following few years, the Sades would search for loans and promissory notes in a totally heedless manner. That winter at La Coste, they pawned all their family silver and indebted themselves so heavily to one of the many Jewish financiers settled in the Carpentras and Mazan region of Provence, a M. Beaucaire, that he was driven to barge into La Coste and "make a great din." During the months following Donatien's escape from Miolans, Pélagie even borrowed money from the priest of La Coste. Having no response to the notes he had written to the marquise, after some months the poor man complained to Mme de Montreuil about the unrequited loan.

"Madame," Father Testanière wrote, "the interest you have in the affairs of M. and Mme de Sade allow me to presume that you would not find it ill-advised of me to address myself to your charity in order to be reimbursed for the eight gold louis [one hundred sixty gold francs, the equivalent of some six hundred contemporary dollars] I had the honor of lending them last year. . . . This little sum [is] totally necessary to my survival: a village priest on a modest pension needs every cent he earns to survive." [3]

Seeing that the Sades were destitute and that the marquis's fugitive status should have incited them to live in frugal secrecy, the extravagance of the food and furnishings supplied to La Coste in the fall and winter of 1773–74 is stupefying. A crew of upholsterers and carpenters was called in to redecorate the castle. The marquise's orders of meat, vegetables, fruit, lard, and "those particularly delicious sausages" could have fed a garrison. An additional chambermaid was engaged by the marquise, along with a game warden, a guard, and an additional gardener (it is possible that she was replacing some of her staff with domestics who had never heard of the Marseilles scandal).

Such was the sumptuous life being led at La Coste until the night of January 6, 1774, when a villager loyal to the marquis ran up to the castle to warn his suzerain that a large detachment of troops was on the way to arrest him and would reach the castle in half an hour. The marquis immediately fled.

THE COMMANDO RAID staged at La Coste that night, for which Mme de Montreuil was responsible, was most fully described by Pélagie. Again written, for judicial purposes, in the third person, it begins with an invocation against her mother's treachery and goes on to describe the events of that evening.

A squadron of Parisian police approaches La Coste, in the depths of Provence, escorted by four archers and an additional detail of local marshals. . . . This troop arrives in the night of January 6, 1774. Their ladders are set up, the walls of the castle ascended; they break in, a pistol in one hand, a sword in the other. This is the manner in which the leader of the detail presents himself to the petitioner: the full ferocity of the event expressed on his face, uttering the most appalling profanities and obscenities, he asks her where he can find M. de Sade, tells her that he must have him, dead or alive.

THE PRÉSIDENTE had in fact met ten separate times with Lieutenant Goupil of the Paris police, whom she commissioned to lead the raid on La Coste. Together they had planned every detail of the foray, down to two sets of peasants' clothing—Mme de Montreuil's ingenious idea—which officers wore on scouting expeditions prior to the attack.

> She [Pélagie] answers that her husband is absent [the marquise's report continues]. This word triggers the most appalling outbursts. The group branches out into the property. One detail of men guards the approaches to the castle, the others, weapons in hand, spread through the house to search its every corner. . . . The futility of their quest increases the men's furor; in the Marquis de Sade's private study, family portraits are torn apart and slashed by the captain of the squad; he breaks into all desks and cupboards, seizes all documents and letters; some of them he burns, he sorts out others, which he keeps, without giving the petitioner any notion of their content. . . .
> This particular man has the insolence forcibly to tear out of the petitioner's hand . . . a tobacco box of gold-rimmed tortoiseshell embellished with a miniature [probably of the marquis]. . . . No manner of insults, no manner of infamous invective against the marquis, are omitted.

Pélagie once more singles out her mother's responsibility for the attack (the marquis may well have dictated part of the letter):

> If any remorse for this event had risen to the police captain's conscience, it would have been instantly dissipated, like a brief spark, by the force of Mme de Montreuil's orders; he admitted that he was merely executing them. What is truly inconceivable is that some of the men were barbaric enough to announce that they were under orders to shoot the marquis and bring his cadaver to Mme de Montreuil.[4]

"She does all that is necessary to achieve her goal," one of the Sade family's earliest biographers commented about the Présidente. "The means she employs to reach her ends are as supple and varied as her goal is clearly defined. . . . She knows at once to seduce, intimidate, and corrupt. . . . She is skilled at the most cunning, treacherous procedures and always uses the best means to overcome an obstacle. . . . All is revealed to her at the hour it needs to be, and she never has to regret a failure. . . . She is as devoid of regrets as she is of remorse. . . . All capitulates to her willpower or to her mere influence."[5]

The marquise's instincts concerning her mother's responsibility for the police raid concur perfectly with this description. One cannot underestimate the frenzy of the Présidente's wrath against her son-in-law. It had become a loathing as fanatical in its force as Pélagie's devotion to her husband.

In every woman there is a potential for destruction and revenge that is part of a far greater communal female energy. It erupts whenever men threaten the structure of the hearths women have patiently built over the millennia and menace the calm, conservative harmony of family life. Few are summoned to unleash this force. But when they do, women's tumult of rage, their "blood-dimmed tide," as Aeschylus called it, is terrifying in its power, because it is deeply encrusted in the bed of childbirth, in the archaic impulse to protect the future of their young. And that is why it is so often successful.

Ever since Donatien de Sade seduced her favorite daughter, the vendetta Mme de Montreuil waged against him exemplifies this primitive female fury, a rage that is unquestioning in its self-righteousness. Like the Eumenides shouting for revenge against Orestes' murder of his mother, like Demeter in her battle to liberate her daughter from the primal rapist of the Underworld, the Présidente had now unleashed her wrath against Donatien de Sade, and woe to anyone who thwarted her intent to destroy him. Observing the savage ire with which she was weaving her net about him, with tactics all the more ruthless because her preceding ploy to confine him had failed, one can only think of the last lines of Aeschylus' *Libation Bearers:* "Where will it sink to sleep and rest, / this murderous hate, this Fury?"[6]

There had also been a pragmatic maternal intent to the commando raid the Présidente staged at La Coste: she was making one last desperate attempt to marry off her younger daughter. In 1774, Anne-Prospère's prospective in-laws, the Beaumonts, were setting increasingly rigorous conditions for the alliance. Besides demanding that the marquis be incarcerated for life, they were requesting that all incriminating letters relating to the young woman's liaison with her infamous brother-in-law be destroyed. The Présidente had tried to fulfill both of these requirements by commissioning the attack on La Coste. Admittedly, she did not necessarily instruct the squad leader to proceed in a violent manner, as her daughter alleged; the police detail had simply run amok, as police have since time immemorial.

This botched assault cost Mme de Montreuil a huge sum. It had taken months to plan. The policemen's round trip—Paris to La Coste to Paris—took twenty additional days. Lieutenant Goupil alone received over eight thousand livres, the equivalent of thirty-two thousand present-day dollars, for his services. Stressing the fact that she was subsidizing the upkeep of her grandchildren, the Présidente claimed that this fee put a terrible strain on her finances. "I find myself . . . in the most urgent distress," she wrote to her friend Mme Necker, wife of the future minister of finance and mother of the writer Germaine de Staël. "The entire family . . . has to be supported. I have done all I could, but I am drained." [7]

Several key persons in Provence had tried to help Mme de Montreuil and Lieutenant Goupil in their aborted mission. Among them was the cynical Abbé de Sade, who was fed up with the insurmountable task of taming his nephew. Another was the marquis's heretofore trusted notary, Maître Fage, who was bullied by the Présidente into giving the commandos a few tips as they assembled for their raid in the nearby village of Bonnieux.

It had not been easy for Mme de Montreuil to win Fage to her cause. The notary was too well acquainted with his local terrain and the shrewdness of the Présidente's prey. "I very much doubt that you'll ever be able to capture him," he wrote her a few days before the attack. "For the time being he is as if in the center of the earth—short of blasting the castle down to its very foundations and burying him in its remains, it will be very difficult to execute such a mission." The Présidente persisted in requesting his aid, and Fage tried to dissuade her again by pleading that such a mission would have disastrous effects on her family. "Ah, the cruel assignment you impose upon me! . . . What will happen to the respectable [Mme de Sade]? What dreadful mayhem I foresee! . . . I repeat, what a sad chore for me! It makes me suddenly wish I had never even known this family! . . . Again, what a blow to that fine lady, what a scandal for the entire province!" [8]

However adamant Fage's disapproval of the enterprise, the Présidente ultimately convinced him to confer with the Parisian police. The day after the failed attempt, Fage, furious that he'd been coerced to participate in a fiasco, accused Mme de Montreuil in a stern letter of having "deeply compromised me in associating me with [an] operation . . . which was repugnant to me." [9] The Présidente angrily replied that her only option was to have Sade imprisoned and, displaying the depth of her estrangement from Pélagie, made markedly disparaging statements about her daughter. "The style in which Mme de S[ade] was exploiting others . . . embittered many people and proved that there had been no change in her way of thinking and acting."[10]

Fage, so the marquis and marquise discovered soon after the raid, had been treacherous in more ways than one. They realized that he had misappropriated the marquis's funds for the past year—an easy task, since Pélagie, now exclusively in control of the family finances, was totally chaotic about business matters. So the police foray did bring one benefit to the Sades: they fired Fage and replaced him with Gaspard Gaufridy, "attorney at the bar and royal notary of the city of Apt."[11] Gaufridy's father had administered Comte de Sade's property, and young Gaufridy had been a favorite companion during the childhood years Donatien spent in Provence. Gaufridy would remain in charge of the marquis's estates and funds for the next quarter of a century. And notwithstanding his excessive indolence, he would be fairly loyal to Sade, and to the marquise, throughout those decades.

From the night of the police raid, Sade became a truly hunted man. Realizing that his mother-in-law would pursue him to the bitter end, he was now forced to find a new refuge every night. Within a few weeks, Pélagie and he decided that his only chance to remain free was to leave French soil and return to Italy.

On March 11, after raising money from yet more loans, the marquis boarded a boat down the Rhône, headed for Marseilles. He was dressed as a priest, having borrowed a cassock from the brother of M. Ripert, his agent in Mazan. One incident on this journey particularly delighted Donatien: while the ferry was crossing the Durance River, which was made turbulent by the recently melted Alpine snows, its rope broke and the vessel went adrift for a few hours. Convinced that they were facing disaster, the passengers, noticing Donatien's clerical garb, gathered about him and begged him to hear their final confessions.

ON MAY 10, 1774, at three-fifteen in the afternoon, King Louis XV died of smallpox. He had enjoyed the second-longest reign—fifty-nine years —of any monarch in the history of France. Hundreds of courtiers were assembled around him in Versailles as he drew his last breath. His grandson the dauphin, with his wife, Marie-Antoinette, waited alone in their quarters, across the courtyard from the royal apartment. They watched a candle set in the king's window, which, as tradition dictated, was to be snuffed out at the moment of his passing. A few seconds after the flame was extinguished, the dauphin and dauphine heard "a terrible noise absolutely resembling that of thunder." It was the entire court, racing down the corridors of Versailles to pay them homage. The panting mob stopped, astonished, at the threshold of the youngsters' room. The new king, Louis XVI, and his queen were kneeling on the floor, tears running down their cheeks, crying out, "Protect us, O Lord. We are too young to reign!"[12]

At first the Marquise de Sade was jubilant about the potential benefits the new regime might bring to her husband's legal status. Any *lettre de cachet* issued by Louis XV for Sade's arrest would not be valid under his successor. Moreover, Louis XVI soon dismissed from his government the marquis's most assiduous persecutor, Maupeou, and reinstated the very members of France's regional Parlements whom Maupeou had fired two years back. There was now a fair chance, or at least a better chance, that the court judgment made against Sade by Maupeou's minions at the Marseilles trial could eventually be appealed and overturned.

But the marquise was not taking into account her mother's swift diligence. Mme de Montreuil instantly began petitioning Louis XVI for a new arrest warrant. She went about it through her friend the Duc d'Aiguillon, the foreign affairs minister, who was the only high-ranking official the young king had retained from his grandfather's government. The Présidente's new trump card was that Louis XVI was considerably more devout and priggish than his grandfather and would be delighted to send libertines of Sade's ilk to jail.

During the months it took for this order to be processed, and as Donatien began his second Italian journey, Pélagie acted boldly on her own to set her husband free. Eager to take advantage of any changes wrought by the new regime, she left La Coste for Paris on July 14 to carry out two distinct legal moves. She wanted to prepare the ground for Donatien's appeal on the Marseilles ruling (this judicial issue was referred to in the Sade-Montreuil clan as "the big deal," *la grande affaire*, to distinguish it from the marquis's numerous other problems). Pélagie also wished to subpoena her mother to one of the nation's highest courts of law, Paris's Châtelet, and bring a civil suit against her for masterminding the assault on La Coste. Pélagie was again attended, on this chimerical mission to Paris, by Anne-Prospère, whose inclination to remain in her sister's company is as mysterious as all other aspects of the women's relations. The marquise clearly relished the cloak-and-dagger tactics her husband's outcast state imposed on her. She traveled incognito, unbeknownst to her mother, and though she put up at a small hotel near Saint-Germain-des-Prés, she asked her new business manager, Gaufridy, to forward her correspondence through a tailor at the other end of Paris, because she considered all hotels to be unreliable, "accomplices of the police."[13]

Pélagie's stay in Paris was longer than she had intended it to be, a tedious two months, for her legal dealings dragged on interminably. The royal prosecutor, unused to seeing young women attempting to subpoena their own mothers, dismissed Pélagie as demented. "He's taking pains to announce to everyone that I'm a madwoman. I've already been saluted with that compliment, and I'm sure I shall be again." [14] Toward the end of her stay in Paris, Pélagie heard some totally unexpected gossip: it was being reported in the capital that the Présidente was madly in love with the marquis and felt far more hostile toward her daughter than toward her son-in-law. "That's all I need," [15] Pélagie quipped when she heard the rumor.

Meanwhile the marquis, lingering in Italy, was apprised of his wife's every move by the loyal Gaufridy. "For heaven's sake," he wrote his agent, "give madame courage, advise her well, and urge her to do all in her power to complete this business within the next four months. . . . In God's name, may she manage to put an end to the nomadic vagabond's life I'm leading! I've come to realize that I'm not made to be an adventurer, and my need to play that role is one of the greatest torments of my present state." [16] Sade also continued his incessant polemic against his mother-in-law (it would gush from his pen with increasing rage for the following two decades). "Don't you agree that Mme de Montreuil's mania for refusing any accommodations is most extraordinary?" he wrote Gaufridy. "What does she gain in her persistent enmity? She perpetuates the dishonor . . . of her daughter and grandchildren, imposes frightful disorder upon our finances, and forces me to lead the saddest and most miserable of lives." [17]

Pélagie returned to Provence in late summer, when she realized that her case against her mother was hopeless. For the Châtelet court, where M. de Montreuil still had numerous acquaintances, was the Présidente's most familiar corridor of power. Not only had she been able to block her daughter's every legal move; she also received detailed reports on Pélagie's activities in Paris. Rather than disdain them, she was more likely left puzzled by this plucky creature whose iron will matched her own but who was so radically unlike her in her capacity for love. She may even have experienced a fleeting sense of admiration for this plainspoken woman who went out to battle alone, as if with a toy sword, against the whole of society, for the love of a man whose spell over her seemed unshakable.

As autumn approached, Pélagie began to pressure her husband to return to Provence. "Everyone is convinced that he is still here [at La Coste], I constantly hear that speculation, so it's equally safe for him to *really* be here," she argued in a letter to Gaufridy. "His return would save us a lot of money and will make it easier for me to transmit any news that I can glean." [18] The marquis, acceding to his wife's wishes, returned to France in the fall. The spouses had an affectionate reunion in the city of Lyons and again proceeded to throw all caution to the wind.

THIS IS THE POINT at which Donatien de Sade's quest for pleasure crosses the line between obsession and some kind of dementia. More broke than ever, more hunted than ever by the police, an outlaw who had recently suffered his longest, toughest incarceration, he now chooses to hold his most extravagant, outrageous bacchanal to date. Upon meeting in Lyons, the Marquis and Marquise de Sade spent some weeks engaging a large roster of additional servants to bring back to La Coste —all very young and nubile, all obviously chosen for purposes of sexual exploitation. In the face of the increasingly severe punishments being imposed upon them, the Sades' foolhardiness and delusions test the limits of one's comprehension. It is abundantly clear that the marquis had discarded, to a greater degree than most of his peers, all traces of those Christian teachings that instill us with guilt or remorse. But given Sade's formidable intellectual gifts, what kind of character flaws deprive a man of all sense of cause and effect? Faced with the growing enigma of Sade's behavior, the biographer, this once, is impelled to glean some insights offered by the psychoanalytic profession. [19]

The marquis's most famous neurotic symptom, "sadism," a term first coined by the pioneer psychiatrist Krafft-Ebing in 1888, has been much discussed. But "sadism" is only one small feature of Sade's deviances. And the full pathology of the marquis's personality has been plumbed by surprisingly few psychoanalysts—so few, in fact, that one can easily draw up a résumé of their findings. [20] Such studies single out a half-dozen biographical details that shaped the patterns of Sade's neuroses.

—Sade's earliest years were spent in the shadow of the young Prince de Condé, whom little Donatien seems to have looked upon as both an "idealized self" and a rival—a rival because Donatien's mother, Comtesse de Sade, had served as a lady-in-waiting and governess to the prince.

—Four-year-old Donatien's fit of murderous rage against young Condé caused his traumatic subsequent banishment from court life and from the presence of his mother, who would seldom reenter his orbit.

—The child was exiled for a few years, beginning at the crucial age of four, with his doting grandmother. The overindulgent matriarch encouraged Donatien to retain the "grandiose, archaic self" of his early childhood—a necessary stage in human development, which turns to megalomania if retained into adulthood, and which the little marquis had evolved with particular loftiness to compensate for his early traumas.

—During the long absence abroad of both his parents, Donatien spent several years with affectionate abbés—his uncle and his tutor—who failed to deflate the overblown ego the child had evolved as a defense mechanism.

—The young marquis suffered the continued absence of maternal affection during his school years in Paris, which were also marked by the often erotic masochistic experiences of being flogged by his preceptors.

—In Donatien's adolescence, there emerged what some of Sade's biographers have called "a negative oedipal complex"—a savage resentment toward the cold, neglectful mother and an equally fierce but frustrated love for his father. There was the subsequent sorrow, as he grew into adulthood, of experiencing his father's rejection.

As psychiatrists see it, the consequence of these aberrant developmental stages was a personality that refused to endure the renunciations essential to the Reality Principle: an individual who, in order not to lapse into total psychosis, needed to retain the grandiose delusions of the very young child into adulthood. Throughout his life as a free man, Sade's extravagant behavior was characteristic of individuals struggling against the threat of psychic disintegration through the mechanism of regressive neurosis. The regressive states singled out by psychoanalysts (this list is hardly inclusive) also comprise the following symptoms:

Narcissism: Sade had an early sense, candidly admitted to in his writings, that "the entire universe had to flatter [his] whims, and that [he] had the right to satisfy them at will." Be it his yearning to whip women with cat-o'nine-tails, or his urge to create a sodomitic daisy chain with several prostitutes and his valet, or his craving to stage orgies at his castle with a company of nubile youngsters, no threats or public censures could persuade him to curb his most offensive demands. Each of Sade's sexual infractions also reinforced what some psychiatrists call "narcissistic cement," offering him an illusory but exhilarating sense of control over others.

Delusional identities: Sade's illusory immunity to the law—the very fantasy that blinded him to the inevitable causality of crime and punishment—buttressed his narcissistic chimeras. Retaining an "idealized self" based on the exalted status of his young playmate Condé, he saw himself as a kinsman of the French Crown, permitted, like royalty, to indulge his most outrageous whims with impunity. "I know no master other than the king," he would write a few years later to his wife. ". . . I am not subservient to anyone below him, for between him and the princes of his royal blood, and myself, I see only inferiors." [21] (If the transgressions incited by Sade's delusions of grandeur seem improbably repetitive, one must keep in mind that any delusionary self is perpetually threatened and must be continually reaffirmed.)

Infantile anality: The whipping of buttocks and the demand to be beaten himself; the bisexual sodomitic exploits of the Marseilles orgy; his pleasure in inhaling prostitutes' farts—throughout these exploits, the marquis's sexuality centers about the anal area, the principal site of a small child's pleasures, and retains the pregenital character of the true pervert. In Sade's writings, the female genitals, referred to as "this unworthy part" or "this accursed slit," are always found inferior to "the other temple." And that "other temple" is even worthier if it is a male's. An example from *The 120 Days of Sodom:* "The President penetrated indiscriminately all holes, though that of a young boy's bottom was infinitely more precious to him." [22]

Exhibitionism: Throughout his years as a free man, Sade's sadomasochistic perversions were always performed with enough indiscretion to evoke punishment. For the individual whose self-identity is threatened, shocking the community, forcing attention through sadistic acts, is yet another means of attaining a sense of heightened power and control. The only constant in the marquis's offenses is that they served to reassure him that *he was not being ignored,* that he was having an impact on his audience, which quite soon became the entire French nation.

This brief psychoanalytic résumé may help to explain the following sequence of events.

THE HIRING for Sade's newest extravaganza was done one hundred fifty miles from La Coste, in Lyons and in the adjoining city of Vienne, where news of the marquis's Marseilles caper might have been less familiar than in Provence. Among the new staff was a fifteen-year-old secretary, André, and five girls of approximately the same age. The makeup of the entourage has led biographers to label this particular escapade of Sade's the "Little Girls Episode." Also engaged that season was a twenty-four-year-old chambermaid known as Nanon, who, the marquis later alleged, was "an official madam" and had procured the youngsters for him. Two somewhat older girls—a dancer from Marseilles, Mlle du Plan, "of age and condition not to be recalled by her parents," and a damsel called

Rosette, officially engaged as "governess" for the Sade children—joined the group a few weeks later. All of these newcomers were put under the charge of the "sweet-assed" housekeeper, Gothon, who was still trysting with Sade's first valet, Carteron/La Jeunesse.

It is abundantly clear that Madame de Sade knew the purpose of hiring the Ganymede "secretary" and the accompanying nymphets, and that she played a central role in choosing them. During the preceding weeks, she had even prepared the ground by a shrewd bit of duplicity. If the parents of the children asked him which branch of the Sade family was employing their offspring, she instructed her lawyer, Gaufridy, under no circumstances should he reveal that they were "the Sades of La Coste." There were several other branches in Provence he could mention—the Sades of Eyguières, of Tarascon, etc., all of them distant cousins of the marquis. Further, Pélagie deceived Gaufridy by telling him that for reasons of "order and economy" she had fired all but one of her former servants, thus making the hiring of new personnel seem perfectly reasonable. These tactics were most deliberate and clearly not coerced. Pélagie had inherited her mother's realistic outlook. Beyond her husband's unearthly spell on her, there was a pragmatic reason for her readiness to collaborate with the marquis: she wished to confine the scandal within the walls of her home rather than let it erupt outside.

So it is that in December, when the spouses returned to La Coste with their freshly gleaned young retinue, Pélagie began to conspire with her husband—amiably, efficiently—in his most scandalous antics to date. In Sade's subsequent letters to his wife, it is clear that she either participated in, or amply witnessed, the debauches that occurred that winter within the secrecy of their household. Some years later, discussing, as he often did in his letters to her, the quasi-epileptic nature of his orgasms, Sade wrote Pélagie: "You saw samples of them at La Coste. . . . You saw it all happen."[23] (Some of Sade's commentators, among them Simone de Beauvoir, have traced his outlandish sexual appetite to the uniquely turbulent nature of his climaxes, and to the fact that he often had great trouble achieving them.)

Many of us would have a lot of tough questions to ask Pélagie: How did she manage to suspend her moral judgment, her ethical scruples, the entirety of her conscience? Did she miss the sacrament of confession and the solace it has often brought to downtrodden women? (even in an era of often licentious clergy, one doubts if any priest could have listened calmly to her accounts of Sade's misdeeds.) Was she ever able to transcend her individual plight and marvel at the atrocities women can commit, or allow themselves to suffer, in order to retain their men's love?

The answer lies, I think, in the fact that the initially timid, sheltered Pélagie had been sexually aroused by her husband, intensely so, and may have been further stimulated by witnessing his carousings. Throughout his few long-term relationships, the marquis had a way of casting a magnetic spell over his women through a blend of eroticism, tenderness, and despotism, which galvanized them into limitless devotion. Even that season's adventures did not seem to affect the Sades' conjugal sex; and the following spring Pélagie may have been briefly pregnant. But the blind folly of her marital ardor brings up yet more questions: What about her deep devotion to her children, two sons and a daughter, now aged seven, five, and three? There they were in Paris, being brought up by her most implacable enemy, her own mother, with whom she had ceased to communicate. How did she deal with that anguish? Many women, in different phases of their lives, must make the bitter choice between wifehood and motherhood and spend some years sacrificing their off-spring to their men. The renunciation of motherhood Pélagie endured throughout the 1770s helps to explain the outburst of maternal guilt and commitment that would consume her a decade later.

As the Sades settled down at La Coste with their new staff, they did not seem to take any extensive safeguards to avoid the outbreak of a new scandal. There are only two intimations of caution in the marquis's dealings that winter: he commissioned the enlargement and strengthening of the castle's redoubts, specifying that the fortifications achieve a thickness of two feet. And a letter he sent to Gaufridy shortly after he had come home with his nubile domestics expressed a heightened wariness.

So we're expecting you on Tuesday, dear attorney. . . . I beseech you to come early, or in any case for dinner, which is at three o'clock. You'll accommodate me by observing the same schedule each time you visit us this winter. . . . We've decided, for many reasons, to see very few people this season. . . . I take to my study in the evenings, while madame keeps company with her ladies. . . . Consequently, the château is locked up tight after dusk, the lights are extinguished, the kitchen is closed.[24]

*Laure de Noves, the Sades'
beloved thirteenth-century ancestor, said to be the "Laura" of
Petrarch's sonnets. Anonymous.*

Below: *Marie-Éléonore de
Maillé de Carman, the
marquis's mother. Anonymous,
eighteenth century.*

Below right: *Jean Baptiste
François Joseph de Sade, the
marquis's father. Painting by
Jean-Marc Nattier.*

1

2

3

Pencil drawing of Sade in his early twenties, by Van Loo.

The Marquise de Sade, engraving. Posthumous imaginary portrait. Anonymous, nineteenth century.

Louis-Marie de Sade, the marquis's oldest and most beloved child. Anonymous, early nineteenth century.

Louis-Henri, Duc de Bourbon, Prince de Condé, the Marquis de Sade's distant cousin and his closest friend in early childhood. Attributed to Jean-Honoré Fragonard.

Ruins of the château of La Coste, in the Vaucluse region of Provence, for many years Sade's favorite residence.

8

9

Saumane, another Sade family estate, some twenty kilometers from La Coste.

Facade of the Palais de Condé in Paris, where the Marquis de Sade was born.

10

Illustration for a nineteenth-century edition of Sade's works showing several fortresses in which he was detained. Clockwise from the top: Miolans, in the Savoie; the Bastille; Pierre-Encize, near Lyons; and Vincennes, in the Paris region, where he was incarcerated from 1777 to 1784.

Closeup of the fortress of Miolans, from which Sade escaped in 1773.

11

12

The Bastille, where Sade was imprisoned from 1784 to 1789, and its surrounding area, the Porte Saint-Antoine, a traditional site of political agitation.

13

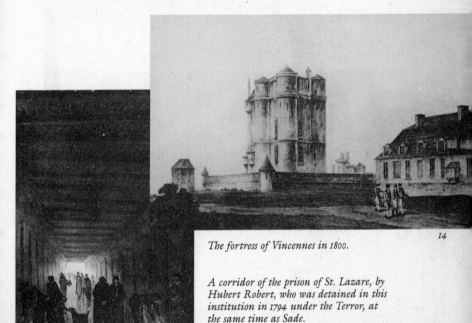

The fortress of Vincennes in 1800.

14

A corridor of the prison of St. Lazare, by Hubert Robert, who was detained in this institution in 1794 under the Terror, at the same time as Sade.

15

16

Paris citizens and Revolutionary troops arresting M. de Launay, commander of the Bastille, on July 14, 1789. De Launay is in center foreground, disarmed.

Another of the Sades' family homes in Provence: château de Mazan, in the town of the same name, some forty kilometers northwest of La Coste.

17

afin que... les traces de ma tombe disparaissent de dessus de la surface de la terre,
comme je me flatte que ma mémoire s'effacera de l'esprit des hommes... D.A.F. SADE.

*Imaginary portrait of the Marquis de Sade, painted by Man Ray in 1938, a decade
after Sade had become a revered hero of the surrealist movement.*

Imaginary portrait of Sade,
circa 1791.

20

19

21

Allegorical portrait of Sade by
H. Biberstein, circa 1839.

Imaginary portrait of Sade,
circa 1840.

Sade in his jail cell in the company of three fictional characters. Imaginary drawing by the philosopher Pierre Klossowski, brother of the painter Balthus and a prominent figure in Sade studies.

Imaginary drawing of Sade by the twentieth-century French artist Gévaudon.

Imaginary drawing of Sade by the surrealist artist Hans Bellmer.

23

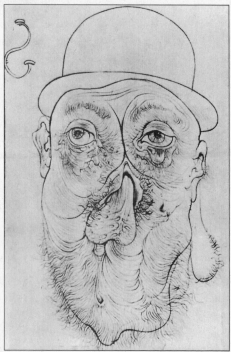

24

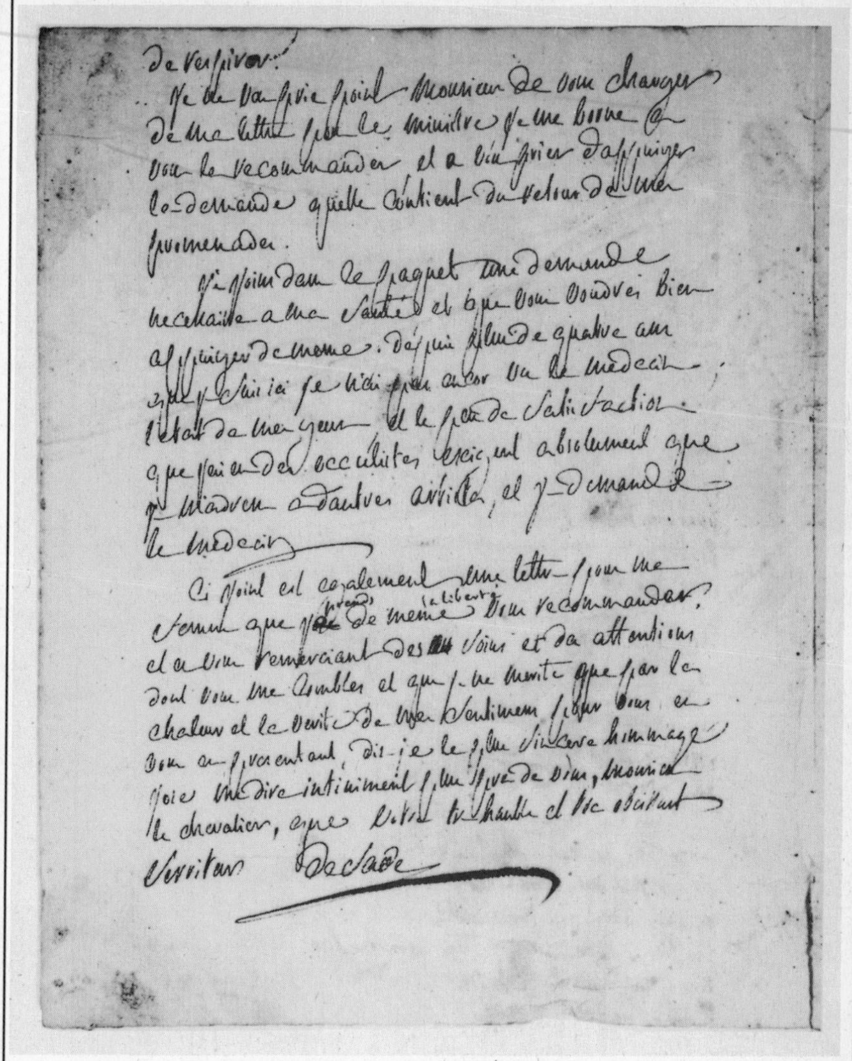

A sample of Sade's handwriting.

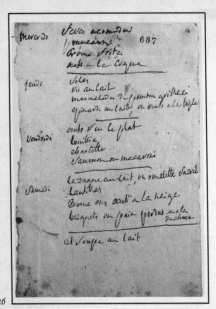

25

26

Ideal menus drawn up by Sade during his incarceration at the Bastille, 1784–89.

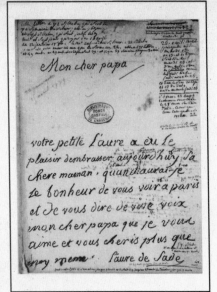

27

Letter from Madeleine-Laure de Sade, the marquis's seven-year-old daughter, written to her father in 1779, the third year of his incarceration at Vincennes.

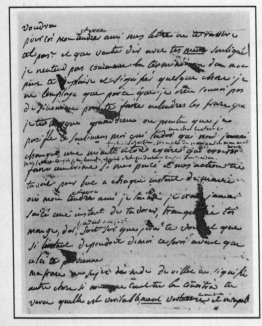

Letter from Mme de Sade to her husband (1781) which the marquis, in a fit of jealous rage about an affair he alleged she was having, stained with his own blood and annotated with obscene comments. Below line seven, to the right, "Lefèvre," the name of his suspected rival.

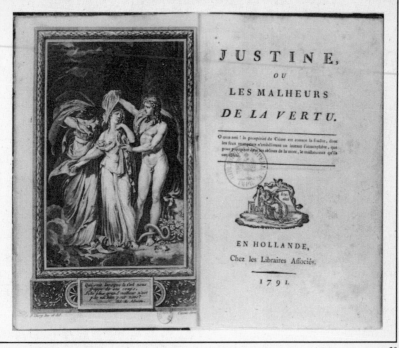

Frontispiece of the original edition of Justine, 1791.

Example of anti-aristocratic pornography in the same years. The caption reads, "Oh, oh! There's my portrait!" The engraving singles out a member of the distinguished Polignac family.

Example of anti-clerical pornography published in France in the first years of the Revolution, probably 1791. The caption is a pun on vivant (alive) and vit (a slang word for penis).

32

Illustration from an eighteenth-century edition of Justine.

Illustration by the engraver Bornet for a late-eighteenth-century edition of Juliette.

33

34

Drawing by André Masson
for a twentieth-century
edition of Justine.

Painting by Félix Labisse, La
Matinée Poétique, *1944, that
features persons whom the
artist considers prominent
members of the surrealist
movement. From left to right:
Jean-Louis Barrault, Alfred
Jarry, William Blake,
Guillaume Apollinaire,
Félix Labisse, Pablo Picasso,
and Robert Desnos. At the
extreme left, from the back
and barely seen, the Marquis
de Sade.*

35

René Magritte: La Philosophie dans le Boudoir, *1948, gouache.*

XIII

The Last Fling of Liberty

> *Pleasure is nothing more than the shock of voluptuous*
> *atoms, or the emanation of voluptuous objects, firing*
> *the electrical particles that circulate in the hollows of*
> *our veins. Therefore the optimum pleasure is attained*
> *by the most violent possible shock.*
>
> *—Juliette*

☐

DECEMBER 1774. Newly reinforced fortress walls, the bliss of increased isolation. Sade's bedroom, with its gorgeous view of the hill town of Bonnieux, adjoined that of the housekeeper, Gothon, and was situated right below the rooms in which the five young servant girls were lodged. Some biographers, speculating on the events of the six winter weeks that would seal Sade's fate, have exploited these domestic details and referred to that wing of the castle as the "laboratory of sadism." One "Sadologue" describes the marquis's erotic stagings in the following manner:

> It is an unleashed witches' sabbath participated in by the domestics. . . . Gothon probably rode astride her broom without participating in the dance, but Nanon took a part in it that would lead her waist to swell; the marquise's young seamstresses offered their flanks to some gashing, and the young secretary had to play the role of flutist.[1]

Most of us would be loath to engage in such detailed conjectures. Speculating on the bacchanals held at La Coste during those winter weeks, one can do no more than recall a few choreographies central to Sade's earlier revels, as well as the bordello exploits favored by many noblemen of his time: yet more whips and cat-o'-nine-tails; a great deal of sodomy, both homo and hetero; plenty of daisy chains—for once, there was an abundance of participants young enough to be easily sub-dued. And one should add another staple of erotica that had not yet been recorded in Sade's sexual repertory: the deflowering of five virgins. One can surmise that this particular enticement was central to the mise-en-scène of that winter season.

But the general style of Sade's new debauches can also be deduced from the fastidious *theatricality* of his previous revels. Fantasies of total control would always remain at the heart of his real life and his fictional orgies. The stage directions he had given to his partners in Marseilles—the meticulous regulation of every protagonist's postures and gestures, the "now you do this with him/her" instructions—are mirrored on a grandiose scale in all his novels, with an often hilarious sense of parody: "Two or three extra cocks might be needed." "Let's please put some order into these orgies." So given the relative helplessness of his young partners, it is likely that the same fantasies of absolute power were now enacted at La Coste. He prescribed partnerships, assigned the distribu-tion of pleasure over various parts of participants' bodies, controlled their emissions—dictated, in sum, the protocol of every sexual ritual. "Order," wrote one of Sade's most gifted commentators, Roland Barthes, "is essential to transgression."

There is another feature of Sade's revels that may strike the contem-porary reader as arcane: the use of literature to debauch the young. Particularly when dealing with adolescents, it was common practice in the eighteenth century to bring out luridly illustrated volumes—the very kind little Donatien had perused as a child in his uncle's library, *Venus in the Cloister* or *John the Fucker*—and tell the kids to do the same things. For libertines of Sade's generation, the thrill of deflowering pu-bescent girls or boys was far more than physical. The general process of corrupting minors, and instructing them in the art of dissipation, had been a popular form of debauchery since the Renaissance. *The 120 Days of Sodom* is subtitled "The School for Libertinage." "The Libertine Instructors" is the subtitle of *Philosophy in the Boudoir*. "How delicious to corrupt, to stifle all semblances of virtue and religion in that young heart!"[2] exclaims the chevalier, one of *Boudoir*'s depraved protagonists, about his chaste fifteen-year-old acolyte.

And there was also the thrill of psychic terrorism: Sade's brand of sadism was often more mental than corporeal. Throughout his previous saturnalia, he had clearly relished frightening his partners as much as he enjoyed any physical act of control (one recalls his threats to kill Mlle Testard and Mme Coste). This winter in Provence, there he was with his new cast, six minors and a few resolute adults such as Gothon, La Jeunesse, and perhaps his own wife, to help him discipline his young prey. Since the village jail, for many centuries, had been situated in the cellars of La Coste, and only Sade had the key to it, it is probable that one of his tactics was to menace the youngsters with confinement if they did not comply with his demands.

How did Pélagie relate to these ignoble doings? She is reported to have remained gentle—indeed, comforting—to the hired youngsters. They unanimously praised her.

WHAT CALM, what debonair serenity, the marquis displayed during those hectic weeks! As the captive youngsters wept and his wife sublimated, or hid, or repressed, her distress, Sade spent his days in occupations archetypal of the rural Enlightenment gentleman. He corresponded about the possibility of obtaining a harpsichord for La Coste; read and studied extensively; fussed about which bilingual editions of Virgil he could order; and generally tended to his growing library, which, alongside the usual erotica, contained plenty of serious volumes: Pascal's *Pensées,* Montesquieu's *Persian Letters,* and many works of other Enlightenment *philosophes.* He was particularly devoted to La Mettrie and Baron d'Holbach, proponents of the most radical materialism professed by any eighteenth-century thinker. He was equally fond of religious works, and his collection included *A Treatise Concerning the Existence of God* and *The Life and Mystery of the Most Holy Virgin.*

Sade also busied himself that season with the care of his estate and lavished special attention on the planning of the gluttonous meals served at La Coste. One order of food sent on to Gaufridy specified the marquis's desire for the following produce, to be sent immediately: "chard, cauliflower, asparagus, navy beans, green peas, carrots, parsnips, artichokes, truffles, potatoes, spinach, radishes, turnips, chicory, lettuce, celery, chervil, watercress, beets, and other vegetables." [3] As for company, Sade continued to avoid members of his own class. He preferred to hobnob with workmen on his estate and the local bourgeoisie—the mayor of La Coste, "friend Paulet," and the faithful Ripert and Gaufridy, both of whom enjoyed discussing religion. That winter, the marquis even pretended to worry about his villagers' morals. When a group of traveling actors arrived at La Coste, presenting a double bill of plays— with the titles of *The Cuckolded Husband, Battered and Content,* and *The Chastised Cad*—Sade ordered that their posters be taken off the walls of the village, because they were "scandalous, and harmful to the autonomy of the Church." [4] Was he performing the role of the virtuous ruler tongue-in-cheek? Not entirely. In those years, aristocratic protocol dictated that erotica should be severely restricted to the educated upper classes, since it could pose dangers to the psyche of the hoi polloi and incite them to misconduct.

THE "LITTLE GIRLS EPISODE" lasted only six weeks. One wonders how long the bacchanal would have continued, how long it would have taken for Sade to grow sated and bored, if the news had not leaked out. For of course people in the village, in the surrounding hill towns, began to talk. The first inkling of trouble came when the parents of four of the young girls filed charges in Lyons, complaining that their offspring had been "abducted against their will and through a process of seduction."

With the help of her housekeeper, Gothon, Pélagie immediately mapped out the principal lines of strategy needed to rebut these accusations: First, whatever the extent of their hostility, Abbé de Sade and Mme de Montreuil must immediately be mobilized into a communal effort to silence the charges, if only for the sake of "family honor." Second, negotiations with the youngsters' parents must begin instantly, in hope of cajoling them, with proper sums, into dropping their complaints. Third and most important, since the "little chicks," as Mme de Sade called the young domestics, could not be returned to their parents as long as their bodies still bore marks of the marquis's abuse, they must be shipped out to various sites where their prattle could be silenced.

One girl chose to remain with the marquise as scullery maid; convents were the safest choice for the four others. Three of the nymphets were sent to nunneries in the Provençal towns of Caderousse and Jumiège, where the nuns were instructed to pay no attention to their ravings. The most "damaged" youngster caused the greatest difficulties. In great secrecy, she was taken to Abbé de Sade in Saumane, to whom she immediately related the miseries the marquis had inflicted on her. The abbé wrote the Sades that he could no longer keep her and would ship her back to her home town of Vienne. The marquise's savage rebuttal, with its look-who's-calling-the-kettle-black tone, suggests that the abbé's morals had not improved with his advancing years.

When, this past season, rumors spread throughout Provence that you were hiding in your château a girl whom you were said to have snatched from her parents and that your secretary, upon your orders and pistol in hand, opposed their attempts to retrieve her; when two women from Lyons recently came to me to complain of some very harsh treatment they claimed to have received at Saumane, I quieted things down, kept everything under wraps, and did all I could to deny such dreadful defamations. I hope that you will be kind enough to do the same in my case—disprove this girl's statements and above all see to it that she does not return to Vienne . . . which is dangerous, because she is spreading any amount of appalling tales.[5]

PÉLAGIE WENT ON to tell some outrageous lies, such as that "her husband had not set foot in La Coste in over a year."[6] But her criticism of the abbé seems to have been based on fact, for he was briefly silenced into submission and agreed to keep the abused teenager for a while. Some weeks later, he started fussing again and this time begged Gaufridy to take her off his hands. He had kept her at Saumane, he said, "for the sake of persons who deserve nothing from me and with whom I do not wish to have any further communications."[7]

In a maelstrom of greedy parents, rebellious captives, mutinous servants, accusations false and true, and threats of blackmail on all sides, total chaos reigned in the Sades' lives for the next few months. The three girls sent to convents managed to escape, were abducted by older members of the Sades' staff, and were sent to yet other religious institutions. The mother of the youngster who had chosen to remain in the marquise's service arrived at La Coste to demand her daughter, but through "cajoling and a few trinkets"[8] was readily swayed by Gaufridy into leaving her there.

Yet another problem arose in March 1775. Nanon, the voluptuous twenty-four-year-old head maid hired the preceding fall, gave birth to a child and alleged that Sade was the father. (The accusation is not necessarily true, since to the best of our knowledge she had entered the Sades' service in October.) When the Sades threatened to have Nanon arrested, she left La Coste, shouting "a million impertinences," and took refuge in a neighboring hamlet. The marquise worried that Nanon, joining the group of parents who had brought charges against the Sades, might spread nasty new rumors throughout the province.

To silence Nanon, Pélagie had to seek help, for the first time in some years, from her mother. Incited by her need to retain a decorous image, the Présidente responded efficiently and went about getting an official government warrant for Nanon's arrest, but the girl was capable of doing a great deal of harm during the weeks the warrant was processed. Panicking, and willing to commit any crassness for the sake of her husband, Pélagie accused Nanon of having stolen three silver plates. Nanon, sensing the danger, sought refuge with the prior of the convent of Jumiège. When the Sades sent three servants to the abbey to seize her, the prior not only protected her but angrily complained to Abbé de Sade, advising him to have his nephew incarcerated for the rest of his life. It was clear, the prior added, that the Marquise de Sade was no worthier than her husband, since "no one from their house made Easter [Communion], and because she allows her young male servants to have affairs with a married Lutheran woman"[9] (the absurd reference is to the Protestant housekeeper, Gothon, and her paramour, La Jeunesse).

The situation was further confused when the mother of young André also arrived at La Coste to reclaim her offspring, even though she had heretofore advised her son to devote himself to his employers. For the rest of the year, the "Little Girls Episode"—the dark pith of Sade's life—continued to be swathed in layers of lies, cowardly silences, deceitful silences, betrayals, threats. The events of those months can principally be decoded through a few legal documents and through the majestic reentry of Mme de Montreuil into her children's desolate affairs.

THE PRÉSIDENTE DE MONTREUIL has been much maligned by Sade's biographers. The reader is urged to consider the very narrow spectrum of her options: What, indeed, were her alternatives? Her patience was deservedly worn out. For the first decade or so of the young Sades' marriage, her forbearance and devotion exceeded the call of duty. Not only did she rescue Donatien from each of his scrapes, restore him to freedom, and save him from bankruptcy and other forms of dishonor, she was also the only human being, outside of his wife, to display genuine affection for him, and she had offered him the most constant maternal love he had ever known. She was tough on him, but she was passionately tough, which is more than one could say about Donatien's selfish, indifferent relatives.

Yet her letters reveal that however furiously she might have been pursuing Donatien for the past few years, when she was informed of the Little Girls Episode, her loathing for him became even more intense. She had discovered in her son-in-law a dimension of corruption that even she had not suspected—beyond the bitterness of betrayal, she may have experienced the chagrin of being deluded.

The Présidente reentered the Sades' orbit in early 1775, a few weeks after the parents of the abused children had filed charges against the marquis. Writing to notary Gaufridy, with whom she had recently started a correspondence, she discussed such issues as the proper handling of the "damaged" girls—how to quicken their process of healing and the timing of their return to their parents. But her most pervasive anxiety concerned the marquis's disastrous influence on his wife. "Can a mother be calm when she knows that her daughter is locked up under the roof with such a man and is not even certain whether reports of her child's fate are true or altered?" she wrote Gaufridy. "If at least they were not together, I would be calmer. But the way it stands, each letter I open makes me shiver." The Présidente fretted particularly about Pélagie's total subservience to her husband: "Never expect to hear a complaint from her. She would allow herself to be chopped to pieces rather than admit that he could ever do her harm." Mme de Montreuil even intimated that Pélagie, through her constant acquiescence to her husband, might be a bad influence on *him*. "When he's in his castle with her, he thinks of himself as too powerful, too secure, and he permits himself all kinds of excesses. Elsewhere, he controls himself better."

In this long, distressed letter, the Présidente alleges that her daughter is literally imprisoned by the marquis. "Could you not confer with Saumane [Abbé de Sade] on how we could assure some safety, some solace, to this poor prisoner, for it is said that all is locked up [at the castle] and that she is not allowed to leave. Everyone dreads him too much, and this capacity for evoking fear, which he has cultivated, is part of his power and his wretchedness."[10]

No wonder Mme de Montreuil had started writing to Gaufridy. For the past months, infuriated by Abbé de Sade's sloth and cynicism, she had suspended her decade-long habit of consciousness-raising with him. One of her last letters to him reads thus:

> The philosophical indolence which you and M. le Commandeur [Donatien's oldest uncle] displayed in those critical moments which demanded the most energetic action have made me incapable of ever hoping for any help on your part. . . . Is it possible that in a numerous family of so distinguished a *name* . . . no one had the resolve to reason forcefully with him and make him take a suitable course? . . . His family . . . stepped totally aside, and his accusations and furor fell exclusively upon me: calumnies, libels, nothing was spared me. . . . He holds his unfortunate wife captive, forces her to be the agent of his infamous maneuvers. . . . You're just twelve miles away! And you're not able to make the trip in the company of a reliable person and impose some order! And speak firmly![11]

A few months later, Mme de Montreuil resumed her efforts to settle "the big deal"—the reversal of the Marseilles verdict against the marquis. Her attempt to persuade the abbé to travel to Aix and speak to the prosecutor incited him to rebel against her. "No, I shall not go to Aix to make an absurd request from the prosecutor," he wrote Gaufridy. "I shall not make this trip until a decree has been obtained reassigning jurisdiction in this case. . . . That is my family's view, and I shall abide by it, sorry as I am that it does not coincide with the ideas of that woman [Mme de Montreuil], who looks on us as automatons designed to carry out her will and perpetually rants against me and what she alleges to be my iniquities."[12]

Mme de Montreuil's principal motive was always to secure her grandchildren's future by rescuing her family's reputation. As long as Donatien was no longer talked about, she would have been satisfied to see him exiled to some foreign country. Abbé de Sade, having no off-spring to protect, had far more ruthless views. By the spring of 1775, he simply wished to get his nephew jailed for life and out of the way. He suggested that the only way out of the quandary was to have the marquis put "in the king's custody," seeing that his actions had "blemished his entire family."[13]

In the midst of the brouhaha at La Coste, Mme de Montreuil was distressed to hear from acquaintances in Provence that her daughter was pregnant, a possibility that "would be a great misfortune for her and a considerable source of worry for me." Pélagie may or may not have had an early miscarriage. In either case, her mother's fears soon proved unfounded.

As for the other pregnancy that concerned the Sade-Montreuil clan that season, Nanon's, it had been resolved in a manner that shows both families in their ugliest light. Thanks to the Présidente's diligent lob-bying in the Paris courts, a warrant for Nanon's arrest was finally issued. She may well have been the procuress who furnished the marquis with that winter's nubile prey, and like other participants in the winter revels at La Coste, she indulged in crass blackmail tactics, offering to drop her accusation against the Sades if she was paid a certain sum. But one can only deplore the fate imposed on her by the Sades and Montreuils. By midsummer, she was locked up in a house of detention at Arles person-ally chosen by the Présidente, and she was not informed for months after the fact that her baby had died in wet nurse. Mme de Montreuil consid-ered the Arles institution to be just right for the young woman, provid-ing as it did "everything necessary: humanity but also secrecy and security." Nanon would not leave that prison for three years.

□   □

FOR THE FIRST MONTHS of this uproar, the marquis remained unruffled. With bemused satisfaction, he wrote to Gaufridy about his growing reputation as the Gilles de Rais, the Bluebeard, of Provence. "I'm being taken for the *werewolf* in these parts. Those poor little chicks with their *terrified* comments." [14] But by midsummer he began to feel threatened. The young secretary's mother was still hounding the family, and the marquise had to take the boy to Aix and pay his mother off.

At the end of July, another abortive police raid was staged at La Coste. The marquis, hiding for hours under the eaves of the roof, barely avoided arrest. For this incursion he again accused his mother-in-law, who replied that she had had nothing to do with it and once more lamented the Sades' disastrous influence on each other. "If they stay together . . . he will drag her into the abyss with him," she wrote Gaufridy. "One would have to turn the world upside down to protect her from her own weakness. . . . Her unhappy children, who're right here under my very eyes, break my heart, but I can't accomplish miracles, since both their parents keep ruining my work each time it's nearly finished." [15]

The latest police raid seemed to have shaken Sade. The sense of security he had always enjoyed at La Coste suddenly waned. Perhaps Gaufridy persuaded him that he should leave the country for a while. In late July, he once more fled for Italy, in the company of La Jeunesse and another traveling companion, the postmaster of the nearby town of Courthézon. He traveled again as "Comte de Mazan, colonel in the French army."

THE MARQUIS'S first two journeys to Italy are barely documented. Beyond the fact that at least ten days were spent in Venice, we have no notion, for instance, of which cities he visited in 1772, during the short, stormy trip he shared with his sister-in-law, or during his brief getaway two years later. But the 1775 excursion is amply chronicled in a journal, which was published only in 1995, under the grand name the marquis himself gave it—*Voyage d'Italie, ou Dissertations critiques, historiques et philosophiques sur les villes de Florence, Rome et Naples, 1775–1776*.[16] The writer's calling seemed to have been edging up on Sade, as this is the first of his literary efforts that he seems to have intended for eventual publication. He was so serious about this work that toward the end of his trip he even hired an artist of some repute, Jean-Baptiste Tierce, to illustrate it.

Numerous European aristocrats were publishing travel memoirs in the eighteenth century. Most of them spent a great deal of space com-

menting on that most fashionable tenet of the Enlightenment, the relativity of human mores. It is the principal trait they shared with Sade's
Voyage d'Italie, which stands out among others through its author's
unusually wide range of interests, his insatiable need to judge, admire,
and criticize an immense variety of social and aesthetic issues. Veronese
and Titian were the marquis's favorite painters, and his most admired
artworks were Raphael's *Transfiguration* and, in the way of antiquities,
the Uffizi's Hermaphrodite and its Medici Venus. "One is filled with a
gentle and holy emotion when admiring it," he writes about the latter.
"The proportions of that sublime statue, the grace of its face, the divine
contours of each limb, the harmonious modeling of the throat and the
buttocks, are masterly and could rival nature." [17]

Elaborating on the mores of the Florentines, the marquis displays a
surprisingly sacramental and egalitarian view of marriage and of women.
He observes a "horrendous coolness in the marital bond," which alien-
ates women "from the spirit of that institution, a sacred spirit that increases the delicacy of every sensitive soul." The marital mores of
Florence, indeed, remind him of "those ancient Roman marriages in
which, as soon as a woman had borne her husband a few children, she
was incarcerated in her apartment and judged useless to society." [18] And
while in Florence, where he witnessed a public execution, Sade also
elaborated on his ardent opposition to the death penalty, a belief unusual in the eighteenth century, even among progressive Enlightenment
thinkers.

Sade remained in Florence from early August until late October,
and then he headed for Rome, whence he immediately wrote his wife to
send him a new "trousseau" of ten suits and twenty-four shirts. In the
Holy City, Sade looked up a notoriously debauched churchman,
Cardinal de Bernis. Bernis, the French ambassador to Rome, had trysted
in the cellars of the Vatican with numerous society women and was a
good friend of Casanova, with whom he had shared the favors of two
Venetian nuns. He provided Sade with a living first draft for an important
character in his novel *Juliette,* in which he appears under his own name.
Though our traveler did not succeed in securing it, he seems to have
asked the cardinal to obtain for him a private audience with the Pope,
Pius VI, whom he would also portray in that novel, in a totally fictional,
scabrous way. Sade's attendance at the Holy Father's coronation was
instantly trumpeted throughout Provence by the marquise, who tried to
turn it to her husband's advantage. Having seen the Holy Father in the
flesh, Pélagie announced, the marquis was close to being reconverted to
the Church! "News is being broadcast in the province concerning M. de
Sade's devoutness," she wrote Gaufridy. "In order that you not register

surprise, I'm advising you that I'm telling everyone he has seen the Pope."

Despite his keen interest in the Holy See and his frequent censures of Italians' depravity, Sade continued throughout his journey to pursue his own amorous interests. One of several conquests was a beautiful young Florentine matron, Chiara Moldetti, wife of a customs official. The mother of five children and again pregnant, she was seized by a violent passion for the marquis. He responded in kind, but after some weeks he tired of her, and the power of his spell over women was once more made evident by the dozens of desolate letters the abandoned lady wrote him at the end of their affair. "Forgive one who loves you with the most ardent sentiments of a sincere heart," she laments in one of her missives. "How you make me quake with rage and pain at receiving so cold and undeserved a letter when I was expecting just the opposite. . . . Ah, my treasure, if you abandon me . . . I will know that your heart is one of the most barbarous and insincere that ever was. . . ."[19] Notwithstanding her initial bitterness, Sade stood as godfather of Chiara's child, born a few weeks after their last tryst.

From Rome Sade went on to Naples, whose inhabitants he held in even lower esteem than those of Rome or Florence. They led him to yet more moralizing: "It is painful . . . to see the world's most beautiful country inhabited by its most brutish species."[20] "Those delicious emotions, . . . which alone can polish and civilize moral conduct, are totally unknown in Naples and will probably long foster that indecent and rude conduct which scandalizes us in the more distinguished societies."[21] "What have virtue and health become in a population whose morals are so degraded, where the smallest temptation of financial profit is enough to lead to crime and overthrow all notions of probity, honor and virtue!"[22] But the marquis's loathing of Naples was well founded. It is there that "Comte de Mazan, colonel in the French army," had his most unpleasant adventure. Through a case of mistaken identity caused by his pseudonym—his *noms de guerre* would always get him in serious trouble —he was confused with another Frenchman currently traveling through Italy, a salt-tax collector who had embezzled the equivalent of several hundred thousand dollars from his government and was hiding in Naples under an assumed name. The French chargé d'affaires in that city investigated and was told by French army officials that there was no officer in their ranks by the name of Mazan. Thus to avoid arrest Donatien revealed his true name. The authorities did not trust his documents, so he was placed under surveillance by the Neapolitan police and his correspondence was censored. Having failed to present himself to the King of Naples, as was the custom, because of his habitual disdain for court life, he could not seek recourse in royal circles. His quandary was so serious that Pélagie considered traveling to Naples to come to her husband's rescue; she was held back only by lack of funds.

The imbroglio was finally resolved when a high official at the court of Ferdinand IV who had befriended Donatien assured French authorities that the marquis had nothing to do with the embezzler being sought for arrest. Sade was eventually introduced to the king and so charmed him that he was offered a position at court. But the incident had alarmed Sade; and he missed his wife. Realizing that he ran a greater risk than ever of being unmasked, he left Naples in May of 1776 and headed back to France by way of Bologna and Milan.

Throughout those months, Sade's correspondence continued to be filled with invectives against his mother-in-law. "Put yourself in my place and sense the full horror of my situation," he pleaded with Gaufridy.

> . . . In truth, Mme de Montreuil wishes my ruin and that of my children. . . . That dreadful creature, through a charm (which she received from the devil, to whom she doubtless leagued her soul) that casts an inconceivably powerful spell on others, overpowers all that she touches. . . . As soon as her magical attributes have blinded someone's eyes, I am abandoned and am not worthy of anything but being thrown to the dogs. All concerned . . . complain of everything she does to me . . . yet no one dares to take the side of the oppressed, powerless one. . . . As long as I am not rehabilitated, not a cat in the province will be whipped without everyone saying, "It's the Marquis de Sade's doing."[23]

Little did Sade know that he had experienced only an illusion of safety and freedom during his year in Italy. Thanks to his mother-in-law's perpetual vigilance, Inspector Marais, his nemesis of the past decade, had tracked every step of his journey through the peninsula.

XIV

The Trap

Circular steps, four rows of them, surrounded the dinner table. There, fifty of Rome's most beautiful courtesans, hidden under banks of flowers, let only their behinds peek through, in such a way that their asses, grouped among lilacs, carnations, and roses, presented all the most delicious aspects of nature and sensuality.

—*Juliette*

□

DURING HER HUSBAND'S ABSENCE, the Marquise de Sade had lived through the most difficult winter of her life. Despite her mother's useful interventions concerning the "little girls," she continued to suffer from her hostility. Three of the teenagers, having escaped their convents, were still at large in different corners of Provence, threatening trouble if they talked to the authorities. The youngster who had been lodged with Abbé de Sade was shunted to the hospital of L'Isle-sur-la-Sorgue, then on to Ripert's house in Mazan, whence she fled to return to her parents in Vienne. She began to "yap," as Pélagie put it, to a local judge. The teenager who had remained in the marquise's service came down with measles. Notwithstanding daily visits from the Sades' physician, Dr. Terris, she died, which could hardly benefit the legends that increasingly tainted the Sades' household.

Pélagie also faced penury. In the fall, she reported to her mother that she did not even have the funds to repair La Coste's broken windowpanes before the winter set in. Beyond the domestic problems surrounding her, Mme de Sade was at odds with the village pastor, "that dog of a priest,"[1] as she called him, who constantly usurped her administrative rights as chatelaine of the village. Moreover, the judicial "big deal," the appeal on the Marseilles ruling, dragged on interminably. Only a royal decree would assure that it would be brought to court. And no one was willing to speak to Louis XVI directly about the Sade issue, for fear of shocking the puritanical young monarch ("It is not fitting to sully a young king's imagination with the scabrous details of such episodes,"[2] declared Mme de Montreuil, who herself was working hard for a reversal of the Aix verdict, if only for her grandchildren's sake). Furthermore, Abbé de Sade continued to agitate for Donatien's internment, and Pélagie's efforts in Aix only incited his derision. "That lady will make a very poor impression in that city, where everyone knows she is the accomplice of her husband's last debauches. I know that those events at La Coste much cooled the goodwill of the counselors and prosecutors."[3] Apprised of events at home through his correspondents, the marquis was angered by the hostility shown his wife. "Is it fated that I can't turn around without the world seizing upon my poor little wife and advising her to commit all kinds of follies?"[4] he wrote Gaufridy from Italy.

Sade returned to Provence in the summer of 1776 after a few weeks in Grenoble, where he hired a young male "secretary" to replace the one who had left after last winter's scandal (he would dismiss him in a few weeks for yet another, even younger). Back at La Coste, Sade resumed his favorite schedule—tending his property, reading, studying, and fretting about the various books he needed to order, such as additional histories of the church. He took great pleasure in an occupation favored by innumerable eighteenth-century noblemen, organizing the collection of "antiquities and curiosities" that he had purchased on his Italian journey. Although his lawyer in Aix, M. Reinaud, an old acquaintance, judged that it was "the worst kind of folly" for a man with Sade's legal problems to send himself such extravagances by the public mails, Sade doted on the six hundred pounds of objects he had sent back to La Coste: Greek amphora, antique lamps and marbles, funerary urns, hunks of Vesuvian lava, Etruscan vases, marine sponges, hundreds of seashells, two chests of drawers made of Vesuvian marble, and quantities of books, among them treatises on the existence of God, rhyming dictionaries, and original manuscripts of Mme de Pompadour's letters.

Sade spent the afternoon hours in his study, writing his *Voyage d'Italie* in the expectation that literature might open a new career to him, a new source of funds. His wife referred to him proudly as "the author." He corresponded with a few friends in Italy whom he'd engaged as research assistants for his literary project and who sent him reams of material from archives and libraries. For a few months he seemed to experience the bliss offered him only at La Coste, the primeval sense that as long as he remained within the walls of his own domain he was safe. It was that very delusion of impregnability which always led to his downfall. Once more impelled by a megalomania that by now reached mythic proportions, Sade, after two months of rural seclusion, had his horses saddled and headed for the town of Montpellier, with no purpose in mind other than to hire more young domestics.

Now the marquis's behavior grows even more incomprehensible. Were his delusions so measureless, the desires incited by his "archaic, grandiose self" so frenzied, that he was incapable of controlling them even when they clearly jeopardized his last chance of freedom? Was he one of those gamblers whose pleasure is heightened by the most reckless risk-taking? He chose this most vulnerable moment in his life—a time of respite from the increasingly violent storms gathering about him—to get into yet another scrape.

Upon arriving in Montpellier, he persuaded a young woman named Adelaide to accompany him to La Coste, with the assurance that she would have nothing to complain about at his castle beyond "solitude." He then enlisted the help of a Montpellier friar to recruit another girl. Having assured the young woman's father that the Sades' household was "quite like a convent" in its moral rigor, Father Durand set up Sade with one Catherine Trillet, the pretty twenty-two-year-old daughter of a local weaver. A few days later, the priest accompanied Mlle Trillet to La Coste, where the marquis gave her a new name: Justine.

But a mere two new recruits in his harem did not satisfy Sade, who wished to re-create the kind of group revel he had enjoyed at La Coste the previous year. A few weeks after coming home from his hiring trip in Montpellier, he asked Father Durand to provide him with four more young domestics: a chambermaid, a scullery maid, a wigmaker, and another secretary. Apart from her worries concerning the expenses he was incurring through hiring additional "household staff," the marquise did not seem fazed by her husband's whims. Was she growing jaded by his excesses? Was she more determined than ever to collaborate in his bacchanals in order to retain his love? All we learn from Pélagie's letters in those months is that food was getting short at La Coste, as were firewood and clothing. And what with the many broken windowpanes, on those days when Provence's brutal winter wind, the mistral, howled through La Coste, Pélagie often had to take to her bed to stay warm.

In the winter of 1776, Mme de Montreuil finally sent her daughter some money, via Gaufridy, with severe restrictions upon the way it could be spent. It was to be used only for food and essential repairs on the château, and the notary had to give the Présidente an accounting of how every cent was disbursed. The marquise was distressed by what she took to be another example of Mme de Montreuil's despotism. If her mother wanted to help her out, why couldn't she send her the money directly? "These convoluted arrangements of hers make no sense and will cause a lot of trouble for you," she wrote Gaufridy. "I haven't a cent. . . . I'm short a thousand ecus [three thousand livres] of what I need to make it through the winter."[5]

In late December, the additional set of youngsters hired by the marquis appeared at La Coste in the company of Father Durand. They did not remain long. The night of their arrival, after they had gone to bed in the servants' quarters on the château's uppermost floor, each of the teenagers, in turn, heard a knock at the door. It was the marquis, holding out a purse of money, offering them rewards if they acceded to his wishes. All of them refused (or so they later claimed), and they began to confer with one another as soon as the marquis had left their floor. With the exception of Catherine/Justine—the first girl to have been hired for this new cycle of revels, who chose to stay behind—by dawn the youths had fled the castle and were on the road back to Montpellier.

For a while the drama being played out at La Coste degenerated into farce. The young fugitives went straight to Catherine's father. Outraged, M. Trillet ran to the abbey and informed Father Durand's superior of the events at La Coste. Father Durand, chastised, pleaded that he had indeed heard talk of the Marquis de Sade's lurid character but had been told that he had repented and even been reconverted to the Holy Roman Church. Nevertheless, Father Durand was banished from the monastery, and the angry father of Catherine/Justine went to La Coste to demand justice. He burst into the castle on a Friday evening, demanding to see the marquis. A violent confrontation ensued, and the two men came to blows. As Sade struggled to evict Trillet from the castle, the intruder shot his pistol—it turned out to contain a blank cartridge—two inches from the marquis's chest. Trillet then fled down to the village, spreading rumors about the Sades. His daughter, who throughout this fracas remained well disposed toward her master and refused to go home, attempted to "settle [her father's] raving mind."

Sade's assailant does not seem to have been the most stable of fellows. In the next two days, Trillet was said to consume a great deal of wine as he wandered throughout La Coste,[6] negotiating with various representatives of the marquis, such as the mayor, in hope of a bribe. Having been offered a gold louis for his traveling expenses, he went home the following Monday, announcing that he was about to file charges against the marquis. That same week, the marquis went to see his notary with the intention of preparing a suit of his own against his aggressor.

□   □

FOR THE FIRST TIME in his life, Sade had survived an episode that induced a painful bit of soul-searching. His dearest and oldest friend, Gaufridy, was categorical about the dangers of Sade's going to trial against Trillet. Sade had become too visible, the lawyer argued, and another bout of publicity might undo him totally. Better lie low and do nothing. As Sade continued to argue in favor of a suit, Gaufridy consulted the prominent Aix lawyer M. Reinaud. Reinaud agreed with Gaufridy. The king's prosecutor in Aix took a very dim view of Sade, he asserted, and such a case had a good chance of going against him. In his view, the entire episode, which the Sades had hoped to keep quiet, had already attracted a great deal of notoriety and could have very serious consequences, Reinaud told the marquis.

Sade began to realize the precariousness of his position. Even though he had not received due legal process, French society at large had judged him to be guilty. Now even his own attorneys were not sufficiently convinced of his innocence to defend him publicly. Was he, Donatien Alphonse François de Sade, a relative of the reigning Bourbon family, a descendant of King Saint Louis, so far gone that he could be shot in his own home and see his assailant go scot-free? Not only his personal safety but his entire sense of caste, his general view of a hierarchical society, were threatened. "I could hardly bow down before a man who insulted me," he wrote to Gaufridy in his most lordly tone, "for this might have set a very bad example, particularly within my own domain—a domain . . . where it is so essential that vassals be obliged to show me respect." The next sentences display the disdain with which the future revolutionary held most people of La Coste, a disdain that ran counter to the deep love he had for his property and its surrounding terrain. "I've come to the conclusion that all Costains are beggars fit for the wheel, and one day I'll surely prove my contempt for them. . . . I assure you that if they were to be roasted one after another, I'd furnish the kindling without batting an eyelash."[7] There follows a pitiful *cri de coeur*, which reveals Sade's growing sense that the entire world was turning against him: "I'm persuaded that if this man had *killed* me, it would have been said that *I was in the wrong.*"[8]

In addition to his heightened sense of legal vulnerability, Sade had also been terrified by that gunshot two inches from his heart. There are plenty of nonviolent sadists, and the marquis was one of them. Throughout his life, he would detest bloodshed. Although he was said to have been as brave a soldier as any, unlike many members of the aristocracy he had never been involved in a duel, and he probably had never even

hunted down an animal. Moreover, his chimeras of seigneurial invincibil-
ity had evaporated. Now it seemed that any man could kill him *in his
own house, within his own feudal terrain,* and be acquitted, both legally
and by public opinion. Sade had to face the painful fact that in the
minds of others, he had degenerated to the status of a total outlaw. The
delusions of grandeur he had evolved since childhood suddenly collapsed
like a house of cards. Only this deep sense of crisis, of an abruptly
dissolved self-identity, explains the fact that Sade suddenly turned to
Mme de Montreuil for help, even though he had recently written her a
ten-page letter that led her to renounce forever any dealings with him or
her daughter. A series of "menaces . . . invectives . . . and infamies"—so
she had described his missive. Since then Mme de Montreuil's own
communications had been filled with veiled threats against both Sades.
"If they attack me as they threaten to," she announced ominously in a
note to Gaufridy, "I have the means to respond, and I have no fear of
anything in the world." [9]

Deaf to the Présidente's threats, Donatien was so desperate, his
contact with reality so minimal, that he began to look on her again as his
court of last resort. If he could not be given justice in Provence, he'd go
get it in Paris, he wrote Gaufridy concerning the Trillet affair, which he
was still determined to bring to court. Surely, he added, Mme de Montreuil would be able to get "that man" arrested. Attempting to prove
that he still had some base of support in society, he prepared to leave for
Paris in February 1777, with the notion of seeking a reconciliation with
his mother-in-law. Sade had also learned in mid-January that his mother,
Comtesse de Sade, had fallen very ill and might be in her last days.

And so the Sades left for Paris, even though most members of their
entourage warned them against it. "The marquis is foolishly sticking his
head into the lion's den," attorney Reinaud predicted in a letter to
Gaufridy shortly after the Sades' departure. "His mother-in-law . . . is
planning a subtle maneuver to seize by cunning what she could not seize
by force. Upon my word, he'll be behind bars before the month is
out." [10]

The couple traveled in separate coaches. Donatien rode with La
Jeunesse, Pélagie with an unexpected companion, young Catherine/
Justine Trillet, who had begged the Sades to take her to Paris with them.

The trip was exhausting, the roads were wretched; the coaches kept
breaking down. Upon reaching Paris, Donatien learned of his mother's
death, three weeks earlier. "The impact of [the news] on him was all the
more powerful because he had been hopeful about her condition," [11]
Pélagie reported in a letter to Gaufridy. The night of their arrival, the
marquis went to stay with his former preceptor, Abbé Amblet. The

marquise slept in her late mother-in-law's flat at the Carmelite convent on Rue d'Enfer and the following day moved into the Hôtel de Danemark on Rue Jacob.

Whatever feelings he had at the passing of his enigmatic mother, the Marquis de Sade did not hesitate to seek "pleasure" in the capital. A few days after arriving in Paris, he wrote a letter to an old acquaintance, yet another abbé; he intimated that he had come to Paris in hopes of placating his in-laws, with whom he "was not yet perfectly reconciled," and asked him to arrange a good party. Having entreated his boon companion to inform no one of his return to the capital, he wrote: "I have a burning desire to see you, to tell you of my exploits, to hear about yours, and to share some together. . . . Do specify a rendezvous in some site that is not too public, or at your home, and whatever time of night it might be, I will be there punctually, and we'll do a bit of hunting." [12]

But the marquis most probably did not have time to enjoy another Paris bacchanal. At nine P.M. on February 13, 1777, as he was visiting his wife in her bedroom at the Hôtel de Danemark, there was a knock on the door. It was Sade's enemy Inspector Marais, whom he had not seen for six and a half years. Marais was holding an arrest warrant—a *lettre de cachet*—signed by King Louis XVI.

That night, the Marquis de Sade was taken to the royal fortress of Vincennes to begin a jail term that would be ended only in the course of the French Revolution, thirteen years later.

He was placed in cell number 11, which was called "a room with a view" because its windows were a trifle higher than the walls of the ancient fortress.

Two reflections, written within a week of his incarceration:

Mme de Montreuil: "Things could not be better or more secure; it was about time! . . . All is now in order." [13]

Abbé de Sade: "The man has been arrested and locked up in a fortress near Paris. So now I am at peace, and I believe everyone will be content." [14]

Part Two

XV

The Child of the Government

"I'm forty-five years old," Minsky said. "My erotic capacities are such that I never go to bed without having come to orgasm ten times. . . . Since I hope that we come to orgasm together, it is essential that I warn you of the terrifying symptoms this climax provokes in me. Horrendous screams precede it and accompany it, and the sprays of sperm then emitted spring to the ceiling, often in fifteen or twenty spurts. No multiplicity of pleasures can exhaust me: my ejaculations are as tumultuous, as abundant, the tenth time round as they were the first time, and I've never woken up fatigued by the former night's excesses.

"Concerning the member that causes all this, here it is," Minsky said, unveiling an organ eighteen inches long by sixteen in circumference, surmounted by a crimson mushroom as large as the crown of a hat. "Yes, here he is, always in the same condition as you see it now, even while sleeping, even while walking. . . ."

—*Juliette*

☐

DONATIEN AND PÉLAGIE would not see each other again for four and a half years.

Sade's antagonists—Mme de Montreuil, the authorities bullied into arresting him, his own relatives—seemed united by a central obsession: to keep him incommunicado from his wife. The spouses' brazenness, when mutually reinforced, was apparently viewed as a threat to the social order. So Pélagie was kept ignorant of her husband's whereabouts for the first four months of his imprisonment. From his late mother-in-law's secluded flat at the Carmelite convent, Pélagie wrote to Donatien at the Bastille, convinced that this was where he was being held, and the police amiably forwarded her letters to Vincennes.

"How did you spend the night, my tender husband?" Pélagie began her first letter to Donatien, some forty-eight hours after his arrest. "Even though I'm told you're well, I'm plunged in terrible sorrow. I'll only be content when I've seen you. Keep calm, I beg you. . . . Calm down, don't start thinking that there's an effort to separate us," she lied, knowing all too well that such a conspiracy existed but determined to appease her spouse. "Everyone knows that this would be impossible." [1]

Pélagie started making visits to various government ministers, begging for visiting privileges with her husband. She walked for days on end around the walls of the Bastille, reporting her anxiety to her only confidant, the Sades' Provençal lawyer, Gaufridy. "The bridges are always raised and the guards keep anyone from even looking at the site," [2] she wrote. "Even though it's in the center of Paris, [the Bastille] is the most secret site in the universe . . . but . . . I'm solely motivated by my husband's well-being. He's my only raison d'être; the world is nothing to me without him." [3]

"My good friend, I beg you most ardently to . . . not give in to your depressions," she urged Sade a few weeks into his jail term. "Adieu, my good little boy. I kiss you." [4]

Referring to a popular Paris tailor from whom Sade had immediately ordered many elegant outfits to wear in jail: "Carlier has promised to hurry in the making of your little summer redingote. You'll simultaneously receive your four linen bonnets and four pairs of cotton stockings." [5] (His coquettishness would remain unallayed throughout his jail term. "Send me a little prune-colored redingote, with suede vest and trousers, something fresh and light but most specifically not made out of linen; as for the other costume, make it Paris Mud in hue—a fashionable color this year—with a few silver trimmings, but definitely not silver braid." [6])

During those stretches of weeks when her loved one's correspondence was scant, Pélagie suffered. Had she said something to offend him, or were prison authorities intercepting his missives?

"When I don't receive news of you I invent a thousand fantasies that drive me to despair," she wrote him a few months into his term. ". . . Yet God keep me from ever reproaching you. I'd feel like the guilty one if I ever caused you, even unwittingly, the slightest grief." [7]

In June, Pélagie finally learned that her husband was not at the Bastille but at Vincennes. And with typical brashness, she started to make plans for his escape. The perfect time, she decided, would come during the trip he must eventually make to Aix to stand retrial.

"This will be an occasion upon which no money should be spared," she wrote Gaufridy. "You should hold him in a very secure site. . . . You could simply signal to me that [the marquis] is returning to Paris with his guards."[8]

A few weeks later, she wrote to her husband: "I love you and will never cease loving you. . . . I kiss you with all my soul."[9]

COMPOUNDING PÉLAGIE'S general distress was the anxiety with which she tried to fulfill the marquis's extravagant orders of clothes, gourmet foods, medications, and cosmetics (prison authorities allowed him two such packages every fortnight). Has the ointment she sent him helped his hemorrhoids? she asks. Enclosed in her last packet, she reassures him, were two pounds of face powder, a puff of swansdown, two packs of toothpicks, several hair ribbons, new gloves, and six pairs of cotton stockings. Carlier is making him a pair of summer trousers "in the narrow style,"[10] as the prisoner has requested.

And yet Sade constantly griped about her failure to fulfill his sartorial and culinary orders, drawing profuse apologies from Pélagie. "I didn't lose a minute amending for my previous mistake. I've just made you a pot of beef marrow with hazelnut oil. . . . I'd been assured that the eau de cologne I sent you was better than the last one. . . . As for your mirror, it was the best I could do."[11] In a characteristic letter, the marquise enclosed a list of staples she had just sent her husband; in addition to numerous gourmet items, the packet includes face pomade, bedroom slippers, eight pounds of candles, more cologne, six additional pairs of cotton stockings, six waistcoats, a variety of hair ribbons, bonnets, and gloves. (One marvels at the narcissism that motivates a man allowed out of his cell only a few hours a month to order such an extensive wardrobe.) Pélagie always placed reassurances of her passion in her care packages. "Love me well, say it to me often. . . . My consolation is to repeat a thousand and a thousand times that I love you and adore you as violently as it is possible to love, and well beyond all that can be expressed in words. When shall I be allowed to kiss you again? I think I shall die of joy."[12]

As Christmas approached, the marquis must have asked Pélagie again for news of their children, who remained in the care of their maternal grandparents and were being schooled in a village some two hours south of Paris. Pélagie wrote him the following report:

I'm so exclusively preoccupied by taking care of you that I rarely see them. I leave them exclusively in the care of their grandmother. . . . One can't yet know much about your daughter's looks or character [Madeleine-Laure, now six years old, is in convent school]. . . . She's still too young. She states her desires very violently.

As for your son [Louis-Marie, the eldest, now ten], he's gentle as a lamb yet of a singular vivacity that can be curbed only by keeping him very busy, which is easy to do because he wishes to know everything and could well spend his entire day buried in books. He will make a very fine citizen.

The chevalier [the Sades' younger son, Donatien-Claude-Armand, eight years old] continues to be good-looking and gentle but has less aptitude for learning. . . . He's more readily affectionate and will be more gregarious. I always kiss him twice because of his resemblance to you . . . whom I love with all my soul." [13]

"What you write me about our children gives me great pleasure," the marquis had written Pélagie a few months after beginning his jail term. "You doubtless know the delight with which I shall embrace them, even though . . . I'm aware that it's for their sake that I'm presently suffering." [14]

Sade's paternal feelings, like all of his emotions, were highly volatile. And they were made all the more ambivalent because he knew that his imprisonment had much to do with his in-laws' desire to salvage his children's reputation.

FIVE MONTHS after Sade's arrest, his distant cousin Comte de Mirabeau —one of the numerous Provençal nobles who, like Sade, would join the revolutionaries' side in the upheavals of 1789—was incarcerated at Vincennes upon a *lettre de cachet* obtained by his own father on grounds of filial insubordination. Here is how the most fiery orator of the future revolution described the jail where Sade began his thirteen years of prison correspondence with his wife:

"The dungeon of Vincennes, begun by Charles de Valois and finished by Charles V [1338–80], is so solidly built that it still shows no signs of age. One would need cannons of the heaviest caliber to make a dent in it. Three moats forty feet deep and twenty yards wide surround it. . . . They are so secure that without outside help, a man stranded in one of them would be as safely imprisoned as in a high tower."

As for the prisoners' cells, Mirabeau continues, "those somber lodgings would be steeped in perpetual night if chips of opaque glass did not occasionally let through a few feeble rays of light."[15]

In the first weeks of his detention in the grim fortress, Donatien's lengthy missives to Pélagie expressed the same emotions of sorrow and tenderness as hers.

"Oh, my dear friend, when will my dreadful plight come to an end?" he wrote her as soon as his letters were allowed out of Vincennes. "When will I be released from the tomb where I've been buried alive? . . . All I have here are my tears and my moans; when will my dear friend finally be able to share them? . . . Adieu, my dearest friend; all I ask you is to love me as deeply as I suffer."[16]

"Dear one, you're all that I have left in the world. Father, mother, sister, friend—you're everything to me," he also wrote. "I beg you not to abandon me."[17]

The spouses' communication was made all the more difficult by the fact that their letters were opened by prison authorities and heavily censored. And however cheered she was by finally knowing where her love was being held, Pélagie's morale was shaken by the marquis's frequent threats of suicide: "If I'm not out in four days' time I'm sure to smash my head against the walls," he wrote her a few weeks into his jail term. "This should satisfy your mother, who told Amblet that my death would be the best means to end this entire affair. . . . If my life is still dear to you, go and throw yourself at the feet of the minister, of the king if need be, and ask them to have your husband returned to you. Could they refuse you? If they do, they'll simply be capitulating to your mother's cruelty."[18]

"In the sixty-five days I've been here," he wrote another time, "I've breathed only five hours of fresh air, on five separate occasions, in a sort of cemetery some forty feet square, surmounted with walls over fifty feet high. . . . Ten or twelve minutes a day, I'm in the company of the man who brings me my food. I spend the rest of the time in solitude, weeping. . . . Such is my life."[19]

WHENEVER HE PETITIONED authorities, Sade's first request was that his wife be allowed to visit him. "I love this comrade in suffering with all my heart," he wrote to M. Le Noir, Sartine's successor as lieutenant general of the French police. "It would be infamous to profit by my situation through separating me from the only friend I have left in the world. . . . I have children, sir, who will thank you one day for having kept their father alive!"[20]

But after the first plaintive weeks, the tone of the marquis's correspondence became manic, alternating between despondency and rage,
tender supplications and savage accusations, terms of endearment and
bitter insults. In his many moments of glacial insolence, he addresses his
wife as "madame," and whenever he can, he turns his guns against Mme
de Montreuil. In his letters to Pélagie, she is denoted as "your fucking
bitch of a mother," "your whore of a mother,"[21] "a brothelkeeper,"[22]
"a venomous beast," "an infernal monster."[23] Equally aggressive are the
passages that concern the date of his release from jail: throughout his
imprisonment he would remain obsessed with the notion that Pélagie
knew the length of his prison term and refused to communicate it
to him.

"As long as you insist on denying me the only thing I demand—*to
know the length of my prison term*—you will allow me, dear friend, to
look on your fine expressions of tenderness as mere poppycock."[24]

Sade even accuses his wife of collaborating with her mother, of
being no more than a "marionette" in her shrewish hands. "Go on,
good luck with your pretty words, they're divine, as well as the delicate
role you're being forced to play. . . . You're offering me . . . as my main
course . . . the black and bitter bile distilled by the odious fury who
guides you."[25]

Sade may have reviled his mother-in-law all the more because she
refused to offer him the reconciliation he had sought with her just before
his arrest. Having previously looked on her as his principal protector and
problem-solver, he now saw her as a personification of society's censure
and the detestable Law.

"Adieu, and if, as I suspect, your whore of a mother reads this letter,
let her know the maledictions I'll curse her with upon my death. . . .
Adieu forever to you."[26]

After Pélagie had again tried to pacify the marquis by intimating
that her mother was trying to improve his legal status:

"You can tell . . . your fucking tramp of a mother . . . that I increasingly wish to see her perish, and what's more, I'd like it to happen in
harrowing suffering."[27]

In his more deranged moments, Sade didn't even spare his children,
as he demanded, for the umpteenth time, to know the date of his release.

"You . . . will repent for all the sufferings you've imposed on me for
the sake of those wretched brats, whom I abhor as much as I abhor you
and all that has to do with you."[28]

"Bedded on the floor like a dog, treated like a savage beast, perennially alone and locked up . . . my health is all but gone and your infamous

conduct is finishing me off. . . . Yet once more, the date of my release!
. . . If you refuse to [tell it to me], I'll never see you again, either you or
your children."[29]

"Your threat of abandoning me and the children and moving
abroad is quite the most terrible blow you've given me,"[30] was Pélagie's
response.

It is clear that this orgy of invectives, some twenty pages a day, was
Sade's only means of maintaining some measure of sanity. Particularly
when writing to his wife, the prisoner displayed an obsession with numbers. Attempting to determine the duration of his jail term, he imagined
that his correspondents were communicating it to him in some cryptic
numerical code. In June 1777, for instance, he noted on the margin of a
letter from Pélagie: "Received on the 29th, plus 9 equals 38, which leads
to August 1780."[31]

Or else: "I'm constantly finding marks on every 36 lines. I was
hopeful that it meant '36 weeks.' But . . . what do they mean? Do they
refer to months?"[32] Some of the marquis's biographers have ventured
that these bizarre numerological speculations, which he referred to as
"signals," were inspired by his reading of the Cabbala, a very fashionable
subject among the intelligentsia of his day. Sade not only tried to decode
the date of his release through the numbers cited in his correspondence
but, somewhat like the cabbalists, invented a bizarre alphabet wherein
each number "signaled" certain human emotions—hope, aggressive-
ness, deceit, etc.

Notwithstanding his rage against Mme de Montreuil, a few weeks
after his arrest Sade began writing her directly, practicing, as usual, outlandish emotional blackmail. His mournful discourses concerning his
late mother, for instance, were of dubious sincerity.

Of all the possible means that could be incited by vengeance and cruelty, madame, you chose the most horrible.
Having traveled to Paris to hear my mother's last sighs, I had
no other aim but to see her and embrace her one more time
. . . and that's the moment you chose to victimize me again! I
recently asked you whether I would find a mother or a tyrant
in you; you didn't leave me in the dark for long. . . .

My unfortunate mother beckons to me from her tomb.
She seems to open her breast and call me to it, as if it were the
only asylum left me. I would be happy to follow her closely,
and I ask you as a last favor, madame, to have me buried next
to her.[33]

A few weeks later, he wrote:

> If a soul capable of violating the most sacred principles—
> those of humanity by having a son arrested at his mother's
> coffin, those of hospitality by betraying one who was about to
> throw himself in your arms . . . if in such a soul some traces of
> pity survived, perhaps I could try to awaken them. . . . I have
> been your victim for a long time, madame; don't attempt to
> make me your dupe. The former condition is occasionally in-
> teresting, the latter one is inevitably humiliating.[34]

On the third day of 1778, Sade resorted to an even more histrionic
tactic, sending his mother-in-law a New Year's letter scripted entirely in
his own blood.

> Oh! You whom I once addressed with such pleasure as
> "mother," you . . . who have offered me only shackles instead
> of the consolations I expected, allow yourself to be moved by
> the tears and blood-drenched letters with which I have com-
> posed this missive. Do realize that this blood is also yours, since
> it runs in the veins of beings whom you cherish [the Sade
> children] and in whose name I implore you. . . . Alas! Dear
> God, see me at your knees, bursting into tears, begging you
> again to offer me your kindness and your commiseration. For-
> get all, forget all, forgive me, deliver me.[35]

Was Sade still able to talk himself into the possibility of a reconciliation with the Présidente? If so, were his powers of self-delusion so great
that he could summon renewed tenderness? Or was this consummate
actor merely assuming false emotions? All these questions are raised
again in a letter Sade wrote Mme de Montreuil in late May of 1778, in
which he expressed, more candidly than usual, his abiding desire for
parental tenderness, his need, above all, *to be mothered*.

> The pain of having lost my father and mother—a frightful
> sorrow—still afflicts me much, and these days I can't even hope
> to address you and M. de Montreuil with those consoling
> terms of endearment which were once allowed me. They are
> revoked, madame, and *here I am the child of the government,
> when I would only like to be yours!* Ah! . . . If the past could be
> brought back to us! Your hatred might well be softened, and
> you might then cease to bring sorrow . . . to one who has never
> ceased to love you and who sincerely renounces all the actions

that could have alienated him from your esteem and *all the tribulations* they caused, which were incited *only by his despair.*[36]

The marquise was battered from both sides, for although she tried to avoid head-on confrontations with her mother, she continued to be at odds with her. In her letters to Gaufridy—who notwithstanding his devotion to the Sades reported a great deal to Mme de Montreuil— Pélagie fumed about her mother's apathy toward Donatien's plight. Mme de Montreuil was indifferent to her son-in-law's suffering, she complained, and remained satisfied on all counts as long as she could gaze on "her Dulcinea" (Pélagie's sister, Mlle de Launay). "Once I get out of these particular quandaries," Pélagie quipped, "I'd rather become a farm laborer than fall back into [my mother's] claws."[37]

In fact, the Présidente, out of her perpetual concern for her grand-children's future, was trying tirelessly to improve Donatien's legal status. Petitioning various officials through visits and countless missives, she was working fiercely, on "the big deal"—obtaining an appeals trial for the marquis's conviction in Marseilles. She had learned from Gaufridy, for instance, that certain "compromising" objects had been left by the Sades at La Coste (the marquis himself had written Gaufridy that he had abandoned some "troubling" papers there). And although the Présidente did not know in which way these objects were "compromising," she was obsessed by the need to destroy all traces of them. "Are they writings?" she queried Gaufridy. "Or are they mechanical gadgets alleg-edly used there?" (By "mechanical gadgets," she meant seating contrap-tions that when tipped back forced their occupants' legs wide open— very popular among eighteenth-century libertines as instruments of rape.) "One must abolish and bury one hundred feet underground all traces of articles that can lead to hearsay and rumors."[38]

THE PASSION EXPRESSED in Pélagie's letters to her husband, to her "good little boy,"[39] would endure throughout the first decade of his imprisonment. "I still adore you with the same violence,"[40] she wrote him in February 1778. "I shall love you and adore you always with the same violence, until there's a breath left in me,"[41] she repeated two months later. That same spring: "this 17th of May, a day particularly consecrated to loving you."[42]

And then, in mid-June, the Sades' correspondence is cut off for the entire summer. Unbeknownst to Pélagie, Sade's enemy of the past fifteen years, Inspector Marais, had fetched him from his jail cell and accompanied him to his appeals trial in Aix-en-Provence. Once more, her mother made sure that Pélagie be kept in strict ignorance of her husband's whereabouts.

Upon learning of his impending trip, Sade made several interesting requests of the authorities. He wished to be allowed to kiss his children good-bye and to be accompanied to Provence by his wife. (However nasty his diatribes against Pélagie, she was growing increasingly talismanic to him. As Mme de Montreuil had remarked shortly before his arrest, "he feels safe only with her.") In case he could not be accompanied by his wife, he wished to be taken to Provence by no one else than Inspector Marais. This particular request was granted, and it raises interesting questions about the complex bonds that can develop between prisoner and jailer. Had Sade formed some kind of masochistic attachment to the person who, along with his mother-in-law, had become his most frequent oppressor? Or did he simply derive comfort from the prospect of a very familiar routine?

DONATIEN'S TRIP to Aix might well be seen as a posthumous triumph for his uncle Abbé de Sade, who had died on December 31 of the previous year, at the age of seventy-seven. For years the abbé had been arguing that Donatien would never regain liberty if he remained a fugitive from the law, that his first step toward freedom was to present himself in Aix for a retrial. This was quite different from the strategy initially championed by the Présidente, who had always feared the disgrace of such a public appearance. The two had argued bitterly over the issue.

"The sybarite of Saumane," who at the time of his death was writing a history of the troubadours, had retained his libertine ways to his last day. He cohabited in his fortress with a Spanish lady and her daughter, expiating his lust by saying mass in the chapel that adjoined his sumptuous bedroom. The handling of his inheritance revealed the Sade family's most venal traits. In his last will and testament, Abbé de Sade had left all his worldly goods to his brother Richard-Jean-Louis, commander of the Order of Malta. But this bequest consisted mostly of his library and his collections of botanical curiosities. The abbé had only a life lease on Saumane, and the property now reverted in its entirety to Donatien and his wife. Yet the commander, taking advantage of the mayhem prevailing in his nephew's affairs, acted as if Saumane and all its trappings were suddenly his. He not only transported the domain's furnishings, silver, horses, and vehicles to his own manor house in Mazan; he even had Saumane's trees pulled out and replanted in his property. Furthermore, he refused to pay for his brother's burial. Since the Marseilles edict had given her control of all her husband's worldly goods, the Marquise de Sade made some erratic attempts to recoup some of Saumane's belongings for the sake of her sons, but she was either too inept in financial matters, or too busy tending to her captive husband, to accomplish her goal.

We do not know of Donatien's reaction to his uncle's death. He may not even have been apprised of it until six months after the fact, in June 1778, when he traveled to Aix-en-Provence with Inspector Marais, hoping to be cleared of the charges of poisoning and sodomy he had been convicted of seven years earlier in Marseilles.

XVI

Freedom, Almost

Saint-Fond's discharge was brilliant, audacious, un-restrained; he pronounced the most energetic and im-petuous blasphemies with a very loud voice; his emissions were considerable, his sperm was boiling, thick and savory, his ecstasy strenuous, his convulsions violent, his delirium extreme. . . . He asked me, when he was finished, if his sperm was indeed excellent. . . .

"Pure cream, My Lord," I answered. "Impossi-ble to find better."

—Juliette

□

UPON ARRIVING at the royal prison at Aix, the prisoner immediately started "proving his kind heart,"[1] as Inspector Marais put it in his journal, by ordering extravagant gifts of food for his fellow prisoners. In the three weeks he spent in that jail, he even managed a flirtation, almost surely platonic, with another detainee, a woman he referred to as "the Dulcinea with mirror,"[2] with whom he would exchange billets-doux for a few years.

The first half of the legal proceedings were held without Sade and progressed with extraordinary speed. The Marseilles women had long ago dropped their accusations of poisoning, and however outrageous Sade's trespasses, the haste and sloppiness with which the court had come to a guilty verdict had been widely criticized, particularly in Provence. Moreover, the judges of the current Aix Parlement, those enemies of Maupeou's who had been reinstated by Louis XVI, tended to reverse any court decisions masterminded by the hated former minister. Even the glacial Commandeur de Sade testified on his nephew's behalf, asserting that "Libertinage deserves punishment but hardly warrants the same penalties as crime."[3]

The atmosphere outside the Parlement chambers was festive. Hundreds of citizens had gathered, hoping to hear a verdict of not guilty for their local boy. The housekeeper of La Coste, Gothon, sent the marquis an enormous bouquet of flowers and a loving letter stating her delight at Sade's return to his province: "As soon as I heard of your return . . . I was filled with immeasurable joy. . . . God will it that you might be freed from all your worries and live at peace for the rest of your days. . . . I've been most dejected by your absence and the uncertainty of your condition."[4]

SIX DAYS AFTER Sade's arrival in Provence in late June, Inspector Marais came to fetch him at his temporary prison and accompanied him, in a chaise, to the chambers of the Aix Parlement. Upon entering the courtroom, the captive, ever prone to theatrics, fell upon his knees. The president of the court immediately bade him stand up. After a few hours of testimony from Sade's young defense lawyer, M. Siméon (who a half century later would serve as King Charles X's minister of the interior), the judges annulled the Marseilles verdict. They dismissed all charges of poisoning and ordered more testimony on the counts of debauchery and sodomy. As the marquis left the courthouse to return to his prison cell, his supporters crowded at the door, but Marais had taken the precaution of shutting the curtains of his chaise.

In the next days, when testimony on the remaining counts was heard, Mme de Montreuil's efforts concerning "the big deal" finally bore fruit. She had given Gaufridy large sums with which to wine and dine the prostitutes who had shared in Sade's Marseilles fling, and the ladies amiably agreed to testify that they had never seen the marquis commit sodomy. On July 14, the Aix Parlement found Sade innocent of all original counts beyond those of "debauch and outrageous libertinage." Besides a modest fine of fifty livres, his penalties were nil; he was officially admonished to "show more decent conduct in the future" and was forbidden to visit or live in Marseilles for three years. Once the fine was paid, so the verdict read, "the prison's doors would be opened for him, and his jail term would be annulled."[5] Equally important, his citizen's rights were now fully returned to him. He regained legal charge of his children and the control of all his worldly possessions.

At last, Sade may well have thought as he rode back to the Aix jail to attend to the last formalities, at last he was free! Free to live out his days at his cherished La Coste! He was taken back to his cell, looking forward to the rest of his life. Thus one can imagine his astonishment and rage when he was wrenched out of his bed at three A.M. the following day and informed by Marais that he was being returned to Vin-cennes. What kind of nonsense is this? the marquis might well have exclaimed. I've just been found innocent! But that is only one system of justice, Marais may have reminded him. There is also the royal justice. We do not know at what point Marais showed Sade the new *lettre de cachet*, signed just nine days earlier by Louis XVI, which reactivated the arrest warrant issued the previous year. Mme de Montreuil's diligence remained unsurpassed.

So Donatien dejectedly set out again toward Vincennes, this time in the company of Marais, Marais's brother, and two other policemen. Marais, whose diary entries were usually ample, did not record the pris-oner's mood or conversation during the first two days of the journey, which took the group through the suburbs of Avignon (the city itself was avoided, because Sade was too well known there) and up the banks of the Rhône, through Tarascon and Montélimar. Marais began chroni-cling the journey at the town of Valence, where Sade made another of his sensational escapes.[6]

AT NINE P.M. on July 16, the coach arrives at Valence's most popular inn, Le Logis du Louvre. Having been led to his room, Sade remains at the window, looking out onto the main road below, until the moment he is called to dinner by his traveling companions. The men are served in the prisoner's quarters. But Sade insists that he is not hungry and wants to skip dinner. He paces up and down the room as his four companions start eating, and then he asks permission to go out for "a pressing need." Marais's brother accompanies him to the facilities, which are right outside Sade's room, and waits for him in front of the door. After a few minutes, Sade manages to leave the nook and head toward the stairs. As he approaches the first step, his guard notices the subter-fuge and reaches for him. Sade pretends to stumble, causing the police-man to fall. The cop, caught off balance, is not able to control his prisoner, who rises to his feet very swiftly and bounds down the stairs, into the inn's courtyard, onto the open road, and out of sight. Mean-while the Marais brothers and their helpers, certain that Sade is hiding inside the inn, rush through every wing of the building, searching its cellars, attics, and stables. Marais sends out a member of his squad onto the road south to Montélimar, another onto the road north to Tain, but they return empty-handed.

First thing the following morning, Marais appears before the local constabulary and gives details concerning the fugitive. A dozen men immediately start searching the surrounding countryside, while another group police all the roads leading to the banks of the Rhône. The search lasts until dusk and yields no trace of the fugitive. That evening, doing his best to save face, Marais draws up an official police report, which is attested to by various local officials.

So far we have followed Marais's account of Sade's escape. There is a wholly other account—Sade's own chronicle of his evasion, which asserts that Marais's men assisted in his flight. Composed a few days after the fact in the guise of a letter to Gaufridy and widely distributed to all his Provençal relatives, it is filled with the self-serving flourishes all too frequent in Sade's correspondence and autobiographical texts. His purpose is transparent: the police officers' cooperation would have nullified any charge that he was once again "escaping from the law."

> I noticed that [my guards'] watchful diligence decreased
> as our journey advanced. Hardly had we arrived [in Valence]
> than the inspector in charge of me led me to understand, in
> very clear terms, that my return to Vincennes was a mere for-
> mality and that if I wanted to avoid it by escaping I was free to
> do so; that they, on their part, would pretend to be in rigorous
> pursuit. . . . These two conditions fulfilled, if I [henceforth]
> behaved in [an honorable] manner . . . I would have nothing
> to fear anymore.[7]

Those tempted to accept Sade's version must ask what might have motivated Marais to collaborate with the captive's flight. Could Marais have been paid off by the ingenious Pélagie? One wonders how she would ever have raised the funds. On the other hand, how could a man deprived of exercise for sixteen months so easily evade four skilled members of Europe's most redoubtable police force?

It seems that Sade spent the night in the outskirts of Valence, in a grange in the middle of wheat fields. At dawn the following morning, two peasants took him to the banks of the Rhône and helped him find a dinghy, in which he paddled downriver to Avignon. After disembarking at six P.M. in the city of his forefathers and dining at the home of friends, he hired a coach and set out for La Coste.

HE ARRIVED HOME at eight A.M. the next morning, exhausted but delirious with joy. He was back in his heart's home, in his eagle's nest, in the talismanic fortress that always gave him a sacred sense of security and wholeness. He walked through the apartments filled with cherry-wood gaming tables and chairs upholstered in *toile de Jouy*, gazed at family portraits of his father and wife and children, of Mlle de Charolais dressed as a Franciscan nun. He could sit in his library, able to peruse volumes of Lucretius or Montesquieu or the Church Fathers—or outrageous pornography. He could admire the groves of quince, cherry, and apricot trees Gothon had cared for during his absence, enjoy the hot dusty smell of the boxwood labyrinth he had designed ten years back for his park. He strolled through the cobblestone streets of his village, bantering with the artisans, tradesmen, and farmers whose company he far preferred to that of his own caste.

> I arrived worn out, dying of exhaustion and hunger [he wrote Gaufridy the morning of his arrival]. I caused Gothon a terrible fright; I'll tell you everything; it's like pure fiction. Please come to see me as soon as possible.
>
> Please send me, by return post, some lemons and all the keys. . . . I'm going to eat and sleep, and I kiss you with all my heart.
>
> I think you were right when you told me that I would not be *pursued*.
>
> I ardently hope to dine with you tomorrow night. Lemons and all the keys, I pray you.[8]

Some days later, another note to Gaufridy, still brimming with the bliss of his restored freedom: "When are you coming? I've seen everyone. The priest and I are lavishing affection on each other. I think he's in love with me."[9]

The marquis began to receive numerous letters of congratulations on his evasion. "With what pleasure I congratulate you!" wrote his admirer Reinaud, the Aix lawyer who had warned him against traveling to Paris the previous year. "Nothing surprises me more than the way in which you managed to humanize those Cerberuses. Oh, what a delicious figure the chief [Marais] must have cut! I can just visualize his lowered head! . . . His little group will make a triumphant return to Paris. Mme de Sade will laugh her head off and will soon be on your traces."[10]

News of Sade's flight had spread throughout Provence. Although their congratulations were admixed with pleas for more decorous conduct, the marquis's four aunts also celebrated his escape.

"Have no doubt of the part I took in the happy conclusion of an episode which so involved the honor of our family," wrote his glamorous Avignon aunt, Mme de Villeneuve-Martignan, who had always had a particular fondness for Donatien and admired him as the only "true Sade" of his generation. "I hope that you will not put us under such stress again. . . . Return to your family, if you can, the luster it has lost." [11]

Donatien's three other aunts, all nuns, also exulted.

"Your letter, dear nephew . . . filled me with intense joy," wrote Sister Gabrielle Éléonore de Sade, abbess of the Convent of Saint-Benoît in Cavaillon. "Be circumspect, careful and wise: that is the advice of an aunt who loves you and only wishes for your well-being, your repose, and your tranquillity." [12]

"I want you to know of the great satisfaction with which I learned the happy end of the most unfortunate episode an honest man could suffer," wrote Sister Marguerite-Félicité, the most modest of Donatien's religious aunts, who was a simple nun at another convent in Cavaillon. "I wept too hard over your death not to rejoice in your resurrection. . . . May you give your family as much consolation in the future as you have given it sorrow in the past." [13]

And finally there was the oldest of the aunts, seventy-eight-year-old Gabrielle Laure, abbess of a convent in Avignon. Traumatized by the passing of her brother Abbé de Sade, she wrote in a shaky, barely legible hand:

"Exhausted by a very advanced age, deep sorrows, perpetual and distressing anxieties, the death of a brother whose tender and recipro-cated affection allowed me to savor the miserable remains of a life I had devoted to him . . . nevertheless, I relish the happy outcome of your misfortunes." [14]

THE AUNTS' JUBILATION was hardly echoed in Paris. In a letter to Gau-fridy written a few weeks after her son-in-law's escape, Mme de Mon-treuil expressed her rage and stated that she wished to keep her daughter ignorant of the facts as long as possible, intimating that she would have Pélagie locked up in a convent by force if she thwarted her mother's will. Not until the end of July did the Présidente inform Pélagie that the marquis had left for Provence the previous month and had been exoner-ated at his retrial. With equal caution, she avoided telling Pélagie of his flight to La Coste, simply stating that he was due to be returned to Vincennes. According to Pélagie, the encounter at which this informa-tion was exchanged (and withheld) was explosive.

"I had a terrible row with my mother the day she told me of the outcome of the trial," Pélagie wrote Gaufridy when she learned that her husband was being returned to jail even though proved innocent. "She announced her intention to have him detained again with a revolting haughtiness and despotism. So much so that I was as miserable as I would have been if the outcome of the trial was unfavorable. . . . She told me that the families (she's awfully strong with that word) would not suffer to see him free. What plagues her most is to realize that my ideas and observations come directly from me and not from M. de S., who she thought influenced my every word, as if I were a parrot." [15]

A few days later, Pélagie finally learned about her husband's escape, and she wrote him at La Coste: "Now do you believe I love you, little friend whom I adore a thousand times? Take care of your health, don't let yourself be in dearth of anything. . . . Gaufridy will give you money; all you want." [16]

News that Pélagie was determined to join her husband in Provence exacerbated the Présidente's wrath. She threatened to have Pélagie arrested if she tried to leave Paris. "She's like a lioness on that issue," [17] Mme de Sade described her mother. The Présidente's own correspondence with Gaufridy shows that Pélagie was not exaggerating.

"Regarding Mme de Sade, I'll tell you in all honesty that her family —to whom her honor belongs, above all that of her mother and father —would never permit her to let herself be further disgraced and compromised by rejoining her husband, unless a long experience of *good conduct* reassured us. . . . Let her help her husband. But let her stay in Paris." [18]

Knowing that her mother was perfectly capable of using armed force to keep her from joining the marquis, Pélagie decided to remain in the capital. From her monastic little flat at the Carmelite convent, she continued to lobby incessantly for an annulment of Sade's *lettre de cachet*. Tensions between mother and daughter escalated. In mid-August, a month into Donatien's freedom, Mme de Montreuil wrote Pélagie that she had received a letter from the marquis and was determined never again to open any of his missives. "They'll be sent back without being opened. . . . When M. de Sade defies the king's own law, how proper is it for me to correspond with him and to be suspected of being his supporter? . . . I refuse to be his dupe or his confidante. . . ."

She continues, threatening: "As your mother, I must prevent you from lapsing back into the dangers we've already suffered from. . . . You must listen to me and realize that the ease with which I could act on this issue is as great as the danger it would pose to M. de Sade." [19]

The marquis did not seem to notice his mother-in-law's growing fury. During his last brief happiness at La Coste, the pendulum of his fondness and hate toward the Présidente swung back to the side of filial affection. In the same delusional manner in which he had sought a reconciliation with her the previous year, he once more convinced himself of her warm feelings toward him.

Here is how he phrased these chimeras in a letter to Gaufridy:

Everywhere throughout these subterfuges I shall never cease seeing . . . the hand of my mother-in-law; do be sure . . . of what I've always maintained: Mme de Montreuil has never hated me, she wished to work to my advantage . . . and in order to succeed she had to wrap herself in the trappings of hatred and vengeance. Rest assured . . . I'm not deluded. I've known her longer than you have. . . .

For personal reasons, Mme de Montreuil must pretend that she is avenging herself, that she hates me, and under that veil, she will weed out my friends from my enemies and some-day will warn me properly. . . . She is a shrewd and deceitful woman, and I don't think you've figured her out properly. To soothe the Parlement's feelings, Mme de Montreuil has had to make believe that she wishes to imprison me for life, and she intends to soften her approach as soon as she obtains the desired results.[20]

These rationales are as illusory as any we've yet heard from Sade. It does not even dawn on him that forces far more powerful than his mother-in-law—those of a government outraged by the humiliation of its top police officers—are now after his head. Sade's delusions are not only induced by his extravagant need for parental love (as he had written the iron lady the previous winter, he does not wish to be "the government's child"; he wishes to be her child). They also originate in his paranoid sense of Mme de Montreuil's omnipotence: earlier that year, he had written his wife that all the king's men were mere "lilliputians" compared to the omniscient, all-powerful mother figure who governed every aspect of his fate.

XVII

An Utterly Chaste Romance

> *Miserable creatures thrown for a moment onto the surface of this little heap of mud—it seems predestined that one half of the flock should persecute the other half. O mankind, is it up to you to pronounce what is good—or what is evil; is it up to a puny individual of your species to assign limits to nature, to decide what she tolerates, to declare what she forbids—you, to whom the most ephemeral operations of nature are still a riddle . . . ? Just explain to me why a stone falls when it is flung from a height—yes, make this consequence palpable, and I shall forgive you for being a moralist when you'll have become a better physicist.*

> —"Étrennes Philosophiques"
> (Letter to Mlle de Rousset,
> January 20, 1782)

□

ONE CANNOT END this chronicle of Sade's last stay at La Coste without a portrait of the woman who stands at the heart of it: a childhood acquaintance who was to be the great platonic love of his life, Mlle Marie-Dorothée de Rousset. Milli de Rousset, as the marquis called her, was the daughter of a local Provençal notary, but far more cosmopolitan than the average woman of the provincial bourgeoisie. This very plain, highly educated spinster, four years Sade's junior, had lived for some years in Paris. She was widely read, had equally superb Provençal and Latin (an unusual accomplishment for a woman of her time) and a biting wit. Mlle de Rousset was also a skilled painter and bookbinder and a fine belletrist. The verve and eloquence of her letters give her a high rank amid the mighty *épistolières* of the century, a talent not lost on Sade.

"Like a new Don Quixote," he would write her, "I'd break my lances to proclaim to the rest of the universe that of all the little female beasts breathing between the earth's two poles, you are the one who writes the finest prose. . . . Yes, my dear saint, you fill your pages gallantly and *voluptuously*." [1]

Having been brought up in Saint-Saturnin-d'Apt, a village some fifteen kilometers equidistant from Saumane and La Coste, Milli de Rousset had been acquainted with the marquis since his childhood years with Abbé de Sade. They met again during Sade's stay in Provence in 1763, just before his marriage. Her friendship with both Sades was cemented in 1771, when the couple settled for good at La Coste. One might well compare Milli de Rousset to those serviceable old maids and poor relatives long described in countless family plays and novels (Chekhov and Austen come particularly to mind): adroit, zealous, occasionally meddlesome, they earn their bed and board by their loyalty, resourcefulness, and skill for conversation. Milli de Rousset, who was amply endowed with all these gifts, was as cherished and trusted by the Marquise de Sade as by the marquis and remained devoted to both of them until the end of her days.

In February 1777, when her husband had just been interned at Vincennes, Pélagie had asked Milli de Rousset to take over as *gouvernante* of La Coste (the word literally means "governess" but can denote the role of glorified housekeeper assumed by many genteel spinsters). She was thus engaged when Sade deepened his friendship with her in July 1778; he found her at his estate after fleeing once more from the clutches of the law.

Milli de Rousset was one of those smart women who take lightly to their plainness and whose very lack of "natural graces" fuels a wry, self-deprecating humor. Here is how she explained her disadvantages to Sade: "My temperament would be as unleashed as yours if I didn't contain it, but since I convinced myself long ago that reason should rule over all, I've had little concerns about being pretty or plain. . . . You, who're a handsome lad, propel your full fire toward the world. From time to time we all get singed by it. I, who contain it, often fear that it might stifle me." [2]

Milli had turned her celibacy into a conviction. Her conversations with Sade—a blend of learned banter and semiamorous persiflage— must have resembled encounters between two equally agile duelers. Instead of allowing his lust to be fired, as a few other chaste women had done, Milli persuaded Sade to accept a mildly flirtatious but strictly platonic friendship. He called his friend "Saint Rousset"; she called him "Mr. Thorny" [3] and signed her letters with endearments such as "I love

you and kiss your little finger." [4] In those precious five summer weeks at
La Coste during which she served the marquis as confidante, secretary,
and general troubleshooter, Milli de Rousset gained a very special place
in Sade's heart. He would later describe her as "a very rare and precious
spirit," [5] as "the second-closest and -dearest friend" [6] he'd ever had, after
his wife. The most singular aspect of Mlle de Rousset, in fact, was that
she may have been the only woman in Sade's adult life to whom he
could truly talk. And so she became the recipient of some of his most
remarkable letters.

"O man, how vain and insignificant you are!" he would write her
the following year concerning the injustices of prison life.

> Hardly have you had a chance to see the sunlight, hardly
> have you brushed with the universe, and you already focus on
> the cruel task of oppressing your fellow creature! What grants
> you that right? Your pride? . . . Have you more eyes, more
> hands, more organs, than I do? Unfortunate worm who has
> only a few hours to crawl about, enjoy life and do not trouble
> me. Curb that pride which is founded only in folly, and if
> you've accidentally been placed higher than I—if you graze on
> grass in a better site than I—benefit from it in such a way that
> you will make me happier. [7]

We know from their correspondence that the two friends held most
of their conversations on a stone bench in the park of La Coste; and that
Milli tried to talk Donatien into improving his future conduct, injunc-
tions he seemed to accept only from her. They also shared solid intellectual conversations, which Sade could have had with very few women of
his time—about philosophy, the nature of just government, literature
ancient and contemporary. And if, early on, Sade ever made any erotic
advances toward Milli, she certainly censured him with some piquant
rebuttal, which he took in good spirit. "She does everything she wants
with her five fingers," he wrote his wife in the following months concerning Milli's dexterity at many artisanal skills. "At La Coste, there's
only one thing I wanted her to do with her five fingers, but she always
refused." [8] And thanks to the stylish tact of Milli's rebukes, he would
come to think of her as "a very dear and respected friend . . . whose
honest and sensitive soul is admirably fashioned to enjoy all the charms
of the purest friendship." [9]

□   □

AND SO SADE formed a new circle of devotees at La Coste that summer. Beyond Milli de Rousset, he kept company with Sambuc, brother of the mayor of La Coste, who served as guardian of Sade's estate; with Father Testanière, the village priest, who seemed to have forgotten about the debts the Sades had owed him in past years and showered the marquis with affection; and with the curate of the neighboring hamlet of Oppède, Chanoine Vidal, a learned man who ran a small tutoring school in his parish. This little clique had its dining rituals, its small talk, its intrigues.

At some point Mlle de Rousset and Sade's other acolytes decided that Gaufridy should be dismissed as Sade's confidence man—it is probable that Vidal wanted the job for himself—and tried to convince Sade of Gaufridy's treacheries. Sade, already apprised that his lawyer reported faithfully to Mme de Montreuil, wisely decided not to alienate a childhood friend who could still be very useful to him. Instead he amused himself by teasing Gaufridy about his role as double agent and taunted him into increased fidelity. "I've always been aware of the great delicacy with which you've informed me of your correspondence with Mme de Montreuil," he wrote him. "Mme de Montreuil finds it very useful and advantageous that I go to jail. I look on the opposite state of affairs as very useful and advantageous. Which opinion do you hold to, hers or mine?" [10]

This tactic was effective. Sade was able to confide in Gaufridy when the first warnings of trouble came three weeks after Sade's return, in the form of an anonymous letter warning the marquis to remain on guard. The fugitive, living comfortably in the eye of a cyclone, brushed off the warning with disdain. "Well! More stupidities, as usual, more platitudes!" he wrote Gaufridy. "I suspected they would come. All those alleged plots are merely farcical, and [the police] have no more desire to recapture me than I have to drown myself." [11]

Far greater threats of danger surfaced some ten days later. Sade described them in a letter to his wife a few weeks after the fact.

> On the evening of August 19, I was calmly strolling in the park with the priest and Milli Rousset, when we heard someone walking in the copse of woods with an agitation that caused me great alarm. I called out several times to ask who was there; no one answered me. I went ahead and saw the elder Sambuc, his head somewhat clouded with wine, who told me, with an air of great anxiety and fright, to flee at once because the village tavern was filled with persons who looked very suspect. Milli Rousset went down to the village to look around and returned

an hour later, totally misled by the banter of two spies assigned to reconnoiter the place, assuring me . . . that they were just who they said they were—silk merchants—and that there was absolutely nothing to fear.

The following passage illustrates the marquis's continuing dependence on his wife: "You wouldn't have been misled that way, for one of the men belonged to the group that arrested me at your place in Paris. So I wasn't that wrong to want you near me. Nothing ever happened to me at La Coste when you were there with me." [12]

But Pélagie, his protector, was absent. Upon hearing of the strangers stalking his village, Sade, for the first time, grew scared. In fact, he was panicked enough to leave town that night and seek shelter in Oppède with Chanoine Vidal. Milli de Rousset was to stay at La Coste, sending him messages twice a day to keep him abreast of the situation. In the next twenty-four hours, as reports became more ominous, Sade sought refuge in an abandoned grange just outside Oppède. (His anxiety did not deter him from trysting there with Vidal's housekeeper, obligingly sent him by the curate, who would later father a child with the same lady.) While in his lair, the marquis beckoned yet another old friend to his side: Dr. Terris of Bonnieux, who had so faithfully attended the Sades some years earlier when they were living at La Coste with Mlle de Launay. Complaining, according to the doctor's notes, of "a simulated ailment," [13] the marquis asked him to prescribe a medication. Were his nerves so unsteady that he feared for his health? Or was he preparing to plead a severe illness that would incapacitate him from traveling to jail in case he was arrested? When Vidal came to visit him in his hideout on August 23, he found him in a state of extreme agitation. (The following account comes from a letter Sade wrote later that year to his wife.)

"What's wrong?" Vidal exclaimed.

"I've got to get out of here . . . ," Sade answered.

"And where do you want to go?"

"Back home."

"You're mad!"

"I'll go on alone."

"I beg you, give it further thought."

"I have thought it all out. I'm going home."

"You're being blind to the danger of it. . . ."

"Okay, okay! It's all a bunch of fables; there's no danger. Let's go!"

"Let's wait at least four days!"

"I've told you, I can't; I want to go home!" [14]

Realizing that he couldn't hold Sade back, Vidal accompanied him to La Coste, where the outlaw arrived in a state of exhaustion. His nerves seemed so frayed that in order to assure him a night of rest, his friends decided not to warn him again of the dangers threatening him. A day later, on August 25, he received a comforting note from Pélagie, which made him feel safer. But his sense of security was short-lived. The following night was his Waterloo.

The most vivid account of the events was rendered in the following months in a letter Sade wrote his wife, and this time it can be trusted as accurate, for its details were corroborated by several observers. (In translating this text, I've retained Sade's brusque alternations of the present and past tense.)

> On the night of the 26th, at 4 A.M. Gothon, naked and in a state of terror, runs into my room . . . shouting, "Run away!" What an awakening! Still in my nightclothes, I flee . . . and impulsively climb toward an upstairs room. . . . I lock the door; a minute later, I heard noises so frightful in the stairwell that I thought for a moment thieves had come to strangle me. They shouted, "Murder! Fire! Thief!" and a moment later the door is broken open and I'm simultaneously seized by ten men, some of whom shove the tip of their swords against my body; others thrust the edge of their pistols against my face. Then a deluge of insults spouts from Marais's mouth; my hands are tied; and from that moment until I reach Valence, I didn't cease to suffer from this man's invectives and vileness, details of which I shall not repeat. They too deeply humiliated a man you love, and I prefer to silence them than to repeat them to you.[15]

Sade goes on to describe the chagrin he suffered as he passed through communities so familiar to his childhood, where dozens of his relatives still lived. As his chaise crossed Cavaillon, the entire town turned out to stare at the nobleman surrounded by guards. In Avignon, several hundred persons assembled to see him, a detail particularly poignant to Sade because he feared that his oldest aunt, the abbess, would hear of his public disgrace.

Marais's brutal treatment of Sade had several witnesses: Mlle de Rousset, Chanoine Vidal, the village priest, and the mayor of La Coste, Sambuc, all of whom had been alerted by Gothon when the posse arrived. Mlle de Rousset's description of the arrest, which she addressed two days later to Mme de Montreuil, corroborated Sade's account. The Présidente would soon quote from it in her correspondence, focusing on Marais's invectives against her son-in-law. Even the Présidente finds the policeman's conduct and language inexcusable and prudishly uses ellipses rather than quote Marais's precise words:

> Mlle de Rousset wrote me, on August 28, that M. [Marais] told him, in arresting him [Sade]: "Speak, speak, little man, you who're going to be locked up for the rest of your days for having done . . . this . . . and this . . . thing in a dark room which contains corpses."

Mme de Montreuil was aghast that Marais had addressed a high-ranking nobleman as *tu*.

> If he said such things, which is probable since they're being repeated, having Chanoine Vidal, the priest, the mayor, and the policemen as witnesses, he must have been drunk; . . . it is not pardonable to hold forth in such a manner under those circumstances. I lodged a formal complaint; [Marais's] conduct is being verified, and if it was such as was described, he will certainly be punished for having violated his duties and disregarded the moderation prescribed . . . [to anyone] executing the king's orders.[16]

There was another damning detail: the patrolman heading Marais's troops, a M. Simiot, was so outraged by his superior's conduct that he threatened to withdraw with all his men. Soon thereafter Marais would indeed be issued a severe admonishment—Louis XVI's government was loath to see any nobleman, however delinquent, so roughly treated. Marais's wages were cut, and he was fined the entire cost of his expedition against Sade, a considerable humiliation for any police officer. Yet . . . is it not understandable that Marais lost control? One can readily imagine the magnitude of the loathing Louis Marais had for Sade—the most intractable, explosive, imaginative prisoner he ever had to handle. Well might he have said, in unison with Donatien's own father, "I've never known one like him." Police officer Marais died two years after his disgrace.

But on August 26, 1778, it was Marais who led the procession triumphantly returning the Marquis de Sade to Vincennes.

"What a sight, dear God, what a sight!" Sade mourned to his wife in the long letter in which he would describe his arrest.

After having been congratulated by my entire family . . .
after having spread the news that my tribulations were over,
that the trial had canceled all punishment . . . after all that, to
be arrested with a rage, a zeal, a brutality, an insolence that
would not be used toward the worst rascals of society's scum,
to be hauled—tied and muffled—throughout one's own province and through the same sites in which one had just publi-
cized one's innocence . . .[17]

The prisoner and his jailers reached Vincennes at eight-thirty at
night, after a thirteen-day journey. Marais himself accompanied Sade to
cell number 6.

The Marquise de Sade learned of her husband's arrest a few days
before he reached jail, in early September. She wrote a mournful letter
to Mlle de Rousset, imploring her to join her in Paris as soon as possible.

Dear God, what a blow! What an abyss of sorrow am I
plunged in again! Whom to believe, whom to trust? . . . If
you've written the details to my mother, you've done well by
me, but if you're already on the road to Paris you've done even
better. Since the events [Sade's arrest], I don't see her anymore, and I've vowed eternal hatred and vengeance against her
if within three days she doesn't arrange for me to join my
husband, wherever she has him transferred to. . . . I'm sick and
tired of being duped by everyone in the past year and a half.
. . . I don't want to return to the tribulations I've endured in
the past; I've suffered too much.[18]

XVIII

"Monsieur le 6," 1778–84

> *I would authorize all libertine or immoral books. I*
> *believe them very essential to the happiness of man,*
> *useful to the progress of philosophy, indispensable to*
> *the extinction of prejudices, and in every way useful*
> *to increase the sum of human learning.*
>
> —*Juliette*

□

MANY OF THE CHARACTER TRAITS that flawed the pathologically shy Louis XVI's rule—indecisiveness, fear of wielding power—were traceable to the humiliations he'd suffered in his youth at the court of his overbearing grandfather, Louis XV. Four years into his reign, this solitary, puritanical monarch remained "so savage and rustic he might have been brought up in a forest."[1]

The king's inferiority complex could only have been aggravated by his inability to consummate his marriage for seven years. The problem was caused by an ailment called phymosis, a condition of the foreskin that makes intercourse very painful. During a visit to Paris, Emperor Joseph II of Austria, after a heart-to-heart talk with his sister Marie-Antoinette, drew up the following report on her husband's impairment: "Louis has strong, well-conditioned erections, introduces the member, stays there without moving for perhaps two minutes, and withdraws without ejaculating but still erect and says good night."[2]

At the discreet suggestion of the Austrian emperor, French court doctors are said to have performed light surgery on the royal member. This procedure inspired the following ditty to be sung throughout Paris: "A filament has been cut / From an ineffective prick—/ Take your cap off, chief of France, / But please get your hard-on quick." (*"D'un Pri-*

ape sans conséquence / On vient de couper le filet— / Décalottez, chef de la France—/ Mais bandez avant, s'il vous plaît.") [3]

The intervention was apparently successful. On August 18, 1777, the news spread through the court, and the rest of Europe, that the Queen of France had finally been deflowered by her king.

In part because of his ungainly demeanor, Louis XVI's finer character traits have been often overlooked. "Simple and natural in his conversation, he saw through fibs and flatteries and was free of all vanity, ostentation, arrogance": so one contemporary saw him. "[He was] as harsh on himself as he was on others—beneath the aloof, prickly deportment was an excellent heart and a sense of justice." [4] Until his last day, this churlish, well-meaning ruler, who had far more social conscience than his predecessors, remained maladapted to the hypocrisies of court life. Beyond his dedication to hunting, his favorite relaxation was locksmithing, particularly the fabrication of keys. This avocation led Marie-Antoinette to compare her marriage to that of Vulcan and Venus, a simile she qualified in the following manner: "My taking on the role of Venus would displease him even more than other tastes of mine of which he disapproves." [5]

Louis XVI's eventual success in the marital bed was bound to increase the Austrian beauty's magnetic sway on him, and the political consequences were disastrous. ("The king has only one man—his wife," [6] the future revolutionary Comte de Mirabeau would comment.) Although Louis had been immensely popular in his first years, his reputation was soon tainted by the levity of his foreign queen and her courtiers. Paying for the frivolity of his own grandfather, under whom the ancien régime had been fatally weakened by losing the people's trust, Louis XVI was too chaste, too serious, and too indecisive to resuscitate the monarchy's authority. And this simple, honorable man, ill-suited to statesmanship, walked as if backward throughout his reign, moving directly against the general tide of public opinion and against the numerous reformist ideologies that would culminate in the uprising of 1789.

By 1770, the number of French periodicals and officially published books was double what it had been at midcentury, and the printing of clandestine antimonarchist works had just about tripled. From 1776 on, the American War of Independence much fired the French nation's zeal for political renewal. (France's support of the American cause, initially incited by its traditional enmity with England, would also deal a catastrophic blow to the country's shaky finances.) By the end of the decade, the progressive ideas of two writers Sade read diligently, Rousseau and Voltaire—both of whom died in 1778, the year Sade was returned to jail

—had been absorbed by the majority of literate French citizens. During the following decade, a significant part of the aristocracy would itself become committed to reform, lobbying for a repeal of *lettres de cachet,* expressing outrage about jail conditions, and demanding curbs on their own outlandish privileges.

Louis XVI—isolated, wary of the people's will, the queen's palace intrigues, and the machinations of his treacherous brothers—continued to flounder on his often incoherent course. He would alienate conservatives by attempting to initiate reforms, then lose liberal support by his failure to put them through. He would never give enough backing to the efforts of revisionist ministers such as Turgot or Necker to stabilize the kingdom's tottering finances. Attempting to curb the French intelligentsia, he would further estrange public opinion by banning the books of Voltaire and prohibiting the performance of the decade's most popular play, Beaumarchais's *The Marriage of Figaro,* in each case suffering the humiliation of having to rescind his orders.

These are just a few of the problems confronting the ancien régime as it lurched through its last twelve years. But the Marquis de Sade, immured in cell number 6 of the royal dungeon of Vincennes, had once more lost touch with most of the reality of his time. If the texts and letters he composed during his next years of detention seem outlandishly savage, perhaps his writings have not been enough analyzed in the context of prison literature. As Albert Camus would write about Sade, "Long or unjust jail terms do not inspire conciliatory attitudes. Intelligence in chains loses in lucidity what it gains in intensity. In prison, dreams have no limits and reality is no curb."[7]

For the first few years of Sade's longest captivity, the fluctuation of his moods and the many events of his daily life were best recorded in the letters he exchanged with his favorite confidante, Mlle de Rousset.

MILLI DE ROUSSET left Provence for Paris as soon as she was beckoned there by the marquise. Once reunited, the two women began sharing a life of "angelic monotony." "We sew and mend our clothes," Milli would report, "we eat and sleep. . . . Those are our days."[8] Mlle de Rousset became indispensable to her hostess, offering the kind of loving solicitude Pélagie had never received from her own family, worrying about all the weight she had lost since her husband was in prison—habitually sturdy, the marquise had grown very thin in the past year. Milli often criticized her friend for overindulging her intolerably demanding husband. No wonder Sade committed so many outrages, she once quipped; he needed a partner with "nerve," whereas Pélagie's gentle character seemed to have been "woven by spiders."⁹ But she remained doggedly loyal to her friend, helping her to lobby ministers and assemble the prisoner's fortnightly care packages.

The women's lives were to grow increasingly drab and reclusive. There were many days when Pélagie barely had the equivalent of twenty dollars in the house. In order to economize, she soon moved, Rousset and La Jeunesse in tow, into a smaller apartment at the Carmelite convent, and later into an even tinier and cheaper flat in the Marais.

Milli diligently pursued her correspondence with Sade. She tried to uphold his morale and chided him for the ill humor with which he criticized the packages she and Pélagie sent him in jail. "You would drive a wooden capuchin to despair with your outbursts and your ill humor!" she wrote him at Christmastime in 1778, a few months after he'd been returned to Vincennes. "How crazy women are to attach themselves to a boor like you! We fly to action to do everything that could possibly please you. We do everything as well as we can. Monsieur is never satisfied."¹⁰

Sade and Rousset were both great teasers, and as a New Year's present the marquis sent his friend some toothpicks from his precious collection of beauty aids. Telling him that this offering pleased her more than "a fifty-louis gift" and "shook up [her] soul in a most singular manner," she responded with her special brand of semiamorous banter: "Please heaven that you never have the least little infatuation for me! I'll give you a devil of a time. . . . Ugly girls are more agile than pretty ones. You've always seen me scolding, moralizing. . . . If you turn the portrait around, you'll see a more velvety side of me, which is not deprived of appeal and of a certain roguishness. . . . You'll fall into my net yet!"¹¹

Sade sent his friend another New Year's gift, a pious poem concerning the joys of friendship. Its sentiments are radically different from the writings he later became famous for, and he himself referred to it as "two-penny verse."

> *You will still bring me joy*
> *Through the cares you employ,*
> *And your pure and true friendship*
> *Is nature's path to redemption,*
> *Soothing the sorrow*
> *That may come tomorrow.*
> *Dear one, it's in you that God built*
> *A sacred shrine to a cult,*
> *So that one can render homage*
> *And enjoy as image*

> *Not the laurels of love's pleasures,*
> *Which soon wither through time's measure,*
> *But the crown which it fashions*
> *To pure and chaste passions.*[12]

Much of their correspondence, however, was more coquettish than platonic:

"Which of us will be the most adroit in subjugating the other?" Milli wrote. "Don't be so sure that you could win that struggle. The women in your life have cherished your passions and your money. But that's not any kind of bait for Sainte Rousset!"[13] The friends often exchanged missives in Provençal dialect, and they could be particularly tender: "My dear Sade, soul's delectation, it kills me not to be with you. When will I be able to sit on your lap, put my arm around your neck, kiss you at will, whisper pretty things in your ear."[14]

Sade was strikingly forthright with the spinster about his practice of masturbation, a regular feature of his jail life. "I've found in what you call *the Holy Father's Ass*[15] all the graces—efficient, victorious, sufficient, preemptive, habitual, congruous, persevering, subsequent, actual, virtual, gratuitous, sanctifying, increasable, natural, interior, exterior, expiring, inspiring, operative, and cooperative—that I might hope for!"[16]

In one of his chaster letters, the marquis wrote Milli about the joy with which he had prepared for an imaginary meeting with her in jail.

> Well, dear saint, New Year's Day has passed by, and you didn't come to see me. I waited for you the entire day; I'd made myself into a handsome lad, I'd put on powder and pomade and was freshly shaven, I wore . . . a beautiful pair of green silk stockings, red pants, a yellow vest, and a black jacket, all with a handsome silver-trimmed hat. In sum, I was a very elegant lord. My pots of jam were ready to do battle. I had also arranged a modest concert: three drums, four timbals, eighteen trumpets, and forty-two hunting horns; all of them were prepared to play a pretty little romance I'd written for you. Your eyes, your ears, and your heart would have been truly delighted by the little party I'd prepared in your honor. But to no avail: I stayed alone with all my spread! It will be for another year.[17]

Sade also turned to Milli in his moments of greatest dejection.

> You who've been able to read the most private, secret dictates of my heart, what do you think of the state of my soul?

Should I still hope, or should I totally abandon myself to my sorrow? . . . How is my wife faring? Don't lie to me. Surely you've found her changed. It's painful to face the fact that they wish us both to die. . . . Help put an end to my exile, and we'll start again on new grounds. You'll help me.[18]

At times Mme de Sade teasingly intruded on the friends' correspondence, feigning to be jealous about their intimacy. "What do you think of her sainthood?" she wrote her husband in a postscript to one of Rousset's letters. "She's losing her virtue and saying pretty things to you. Might she want to undercut me? Gently, kids. I'm adamantly opposed to it. I forbid you to go any further than I wish you to. . . . Have fun, you two, as long as you never get closer."

Milli added a post-postscript: "She's indeed displaying jealousy. Would you still be my lover? If your tender and loyal half won't give us permission, there's no way to proceed. Shall we deceive her? We're both too fastidious."[19]

AT SOME POINT in 1778, Mlle de Rousset started talking about eventually going to La Coste to look after the marquis's affairs. He tried to make her promise that she would not leave for Provence before his release, and recalled the good times they had shared there the previous summer:

> Go to La Coste in August, I condemn you to, you'll sit down on that bench. . . . You know it well, that bench? . . . And when you'll be settled there you'll say . . . "He was there just a year ago, at my side . . . he opened his heart to me with that naive candor which proved how well he thought of me" . . . and then you'll go into the little green salon and you'll say, "There was my table, where I wrote all his letters. . . . He used to sit in this armchair . . . and from there used to say: 'Please write. . . .' " You'll think you see me, and it will only be your shadow; you'll think you hear me, but it will only be the voice of your heart.[20]

Rousset described Sade's infrequent good moods as "rare clearings" between long storms "whose downpours of hail stab at our hearts."[21] Some months later, the marquis, following his bent for ruining his few close friendships, wrote a scathing letter to Milli about the possibility that she might return to Provence without him, threatening that he would never see her again if she did so. She tried to reassure him, with no success, that she had no imminent plans to go anywhere; but as a matter of principle she balked at his insistence that she wait for the end of his jail term to leave Paris. The rift in Rousset's friendship with Sade begins with the following letter:

> Monsieur, May the good Lord bless you with His grace . . . and may He offer me the patience to keep myself from telling you to go fuck yourself a thousand times! One couldn't be more unfair than you are. If I didn't remain deaf to your nonsense you'd drive me to insanity. . . . It must be a pleasure for you to mortify people. . . . What have I done to make you hate me so? You make it seem as if I'm constantly at your heels, playing the role of traitor. . . . Calumniator! . . . Yesterday you sent me two thousand kisses, the next day two thousand insults. Such conduct so disgusts me that my pen is about to jump out of my hand and never answer you again. If my communications displease you, I'll stop them this very moment. . . . Let's cease writing each other—okay, monsieur? [22]

Apart from one more cool note Milli wrote Sade a few weeks later, concerning some domestic details at La Coste, the friends' correspondence stops for about two years. "For six months he has not inquired whether I'm alive or dead," [23] Milli commented to attorney Gaufridy in the autumn of 1779.

THERE WERE good reasons for Sade to grow even more thorny during the second leg of his stay at Vincennes. Beyond the fact that he had been proved innocent under the national system of justice, his new prison cell, number 6, was even less comfortable than his former lodgings and had no fireplace to keep him warm in winter. Three months passed before the prisoner was allowed paper and pens. It would take him a year to be permitted a few short walks a week. His most distinguished jailmate, his distant cousin Comte de Mirabeau, attested to the fact that Vincennes prisoners often found "horrible filth" [24] in their food and that the scheduling of their meals—they received no nourishment between five P.M. and 11 A.M.—was direly unhealthy.

So Sade may not have exaggerated much when he complained that he now lived "up to the neck in garbage and filth, devoured by lice, fleas, mice, and spiders, fed like a pig." [25] "Rats and mice keep me up all night," he complained to his wife. "When I beg them to put a cat in my room . . . to kill them, they answer that animals are forbidden. To which

I answer, 'You idiots, if animals are forbidden, rats and mice should be also!' "[26]

An even greater target of the marquis's wrath was the warden himself, M. de Rougemont. The illegitimate son of a high-ranking nobleman, Rougemont was often petty with his prisoners. When Sade asked the warden, in 1781, the baptismal name of the dauphin (Louis XVI's first son, whose birth led to one of the last great celebrations of the decade), Rougemont reprimanded the captive, forbidding him ever again to ask questions about events outside the prison. Mirabeau lambasted Rougemont as a man with "all the swagger of the most prideful ignorance . . . a wind-filled balloon . . . inflated by the sense of his own importance."[27]

A far more diplomatic jailbird than Sade, Mirabeau, whose transgressions included incestuous relations with his sister and who wrote a spate of pornographic novels while at Vincennes, made that assessment only after his release. The marquis went much further while still in the warden's power.

Sade thrashed Rougemont as "an idiotic automaton,"[28] as "a personification of execrable vice, a lowly scoundrel in stockings and waistcoat who . . . starves his detainees to death to accumulate the lucre that will finance his infamous debauches . . . a buffoon, in sum, who . . . without the caprices of fate . . . should have been only too happy to be my scullery boy if we had both remained in the station into which fate thrust us."[29] Within a few months of his second imprisonment, Sade had scribbled on a wall of his cell the following verses about his oppressor:

> Here lies the warden of Vincennes—
> Vile, cuckolded, ugly he's been,
> In men's tears he delighted
> And in the sorrow of the benighted.
>
> The world well knows his reputation.
> Passerby, here's the situation:
> No use asking if his soul persisted—
> In this motherfucker no soul existed.[30]

Sade's relationship with jail authorities would come to a head a year and a half after his return to Vincennes. His obsession with "signals"— the illusory numerical codes he deciphered in his correspondents' letters —had totally disappeared during his weeks of freedom in Provence, but it reappeared in full force as soon as he returned to jail. In an episode that shows him in his most psychotic state, he raged because the "signals" he was receiving from the outside world informed him that he was about to be shipped off to one of France's island colonies in the Caribbean. Sade feared and detested sea trips ("I'd rather be chopped to pieces on some shore than set foot in a ship," [31] he wrote his wife) and spent an agitated night. The following day, after an altercation with his guard, he fainted, spit up blood, and remained unconscious for several hours.

Two days later, Sade learned that his treasured walks had been rescinded on grounds of his insubordination. In yet another brawl with his guard, Sade called the man "John the Fucker" and threatened to kill him. He then went to his window and, identifying himself in ringing tones as "the Marquis de Sade, cavalry officer," shouted invectives against his mother-in-law and the king's ministers. As he called out to his fellow prisoners for support, he heard a noise across the courtyard: it was Mirabeau, knocking at his door to call for fresh water. Sade yelled out that Mirabeau was responsible for the loss of his walks, insulted him as "the commandant's catamite," and told him to "go kiss the ass" of his protector. "Answer me if you dare, fucking bugger," he bellowed across the yard, "so I can cut off your ears as soon as I'm released!"

"I'm an honorable man who never carved up or poisoned women," Mirabeau shouted back, "and who will write that gladly on [Sade's] shoulders with his razor, if Sade doesn't go to the wheel first." [32]

When the ruckus was over, the vengeful Mirabeau would sign a report, addressed to M. Le Noir, lieutenant general of the French police, alleging that it was customary for Sade to incite the Vincennes prisoners to revolt. Sade would take his revenge, years later, by defaming his cousin in his novel *Juliette* as a man who "wished to be a libertine to be someone and who never in his life will amount to anything." "One of the best proofs of the delirium and irrationality that characterized France in 1789," so Sade continued his diatribe against his cousin, "was the ridiculous enthusiasm inspired by this vile spy for the monarchy . . . an immoral and turgid man . . . a knave, a traitor and an ignoramus." [33]

SADE OFTEN MENTIONED his children in his correspondence from jail, but what kind of father was he? Since the notion of the nuclear family was barely nascent in his time, the answers are complex.

Although his paternal emotions were clouded by the sense that he was serving time for the sake of his children's reputation, Sade was anything but an indifferent father. His strong elitist streak led him to honor dynastic ties. He took great interest in his children's social status, health, and education, and also in their looks; he often asked for miniature portraits, and samples of their handwriting, as keepsakes for his jail cell.

"You did well to shave off your son's hair. . . . I owe my head of hair to the fact that this precaution was taken as soon as I caught small-pox," he wrote Pélagie concerning their eldest child's bout with the same disease. "Don't be alarmed by the way he looks today; it'll all straighten out. I can just see him—he'll be slender, graceful, with a fine figure and a devilish wit. With such attributes a man always finds more women than he needs to make him unhappy."[34]

"I'm crazy about them," he wrote her another time about their children. "If you could hear me speak aloud to them [in my cell] . . . you'd think I'd gone off my rocker. Not one night passes without my dreaming about them."[35]

"Here's a letter for those poor little darlings whom I love more than you can imagine," he also wrote Pélagie. "I was right last winter when I constantly dreamed that they would be fully grown when I saw them again. Oh, dear God, they won't even recognize me. Is it worth having children if you can't enjoy them; for this is the moment when they're so pleasurable; later on they only make trouble."[36]

By 1778, when Sade began his second term in Vincennes, his son Louis-Marie de Sade was eleven. Donatien-Claude-Armand, nine, was already referred to as the chevalier, because like many second sons he was destined for a religious vocation and aspired to enter the religious and military Order of Malta. Both boys had been sent that year to Valéry, near Sens, two hours southeast of Paris, where the Montreuils had property. They started their formal schooling there under their grandmother's surveillance, studying with the village priest. They were also accompanied by their governess, Mlle Langevin, who had been with them for nearly a decade. This was one of the only decisions Pélagie had made concerning his offspring that Sade approved of. Far too egotistical to realize that the extravagant demands he imposed on his wife left her no time whatever to bring up their children, he often berated her for allowing them to remain in the Montreuils' care and for abandoning them to a mediocre provincial education.

"Your children's writing is beautiful, to be sure, and the style . . . tell me what lackey wrote all that!" he inveighed a few months after being returned to Vincennes. "Oh, it's surely the secretary of the Valéry parish!! Both handwritings, especially the chevalier's, have regressed to half of what they were the previous year. By Jove! Bravo for progress and village schooling! How appalling, however, to have even sacrificed your children's education to enjoy the delicious pleasure of thrusting your vengeance upon their father."[37]

A short while later, the volatile Sade veered around and hailed his offspring's achievements and charms.

"I was enormously gratified by your news of my son's progress," he wrote Pélagie two months later concerning the academic prowess of Louis-Marie. ". . . His translation [from the Latin] seems to be extremely advanced for his age. This doesn't diminish my affection for the chevalier. You know I've always loved him best. But all the good news I receive about our eldest makes him amazingly dear to me. I'll write the chevalier, as you suggest, to encourage him to study better." [38]

As for the Sades' daughter, Madeleine-Laure, her father barely knew her. She had lived in the country with a nurse until the age of seven,[39] when she was sent to board in a convent. "I don't know if I'll love her, that one; she doesn't move me as much as the two others," he wrote Pélagie." [40] But he often inquired about precise details of her life, such as the kind of attire she wore at school. Little Laure, in fact, was the child who most worried her family, because her plainness, the most worrisome flaw a girl of her time could display, could pose grave threats to a "solid" marriage. Numerous comments by her parents pointed to that concern:

"Yes, your daughter is called Laure but does not sustain that name through any beauty," Pélagie wrote her husband, referring to the legendary beauty of the ancestor after whom his daughter was named. "I imagine that as she gets older she will be less ugly, and her name will not look like a joke." [41] Another time: "Concerning your daughter: in effect, as you guessed it, she is cross-eyed. . . . Since she has no dowry, one should not try to marry her off but rather make her a canoness." [42] In a letter to Milli de Rousset, the marquis also commented, more optimistically than his wife, on his daughter's lack of "natural graces": "In sum, my daughter is ugly. You tell it to me most honestly, I see that she's ugly. Well, too bad for her! Let her have wit and virtue, that'll serve her better than a pretty face." [43]

Alas, Madeleine-Laure's character and aptitudes did not seem any more commendable than her looks. At the age of eight, the girl still needed to have her hand held when she tried to write her father a few lines of greetings. "After two years of schooling," her mother commented, "she doesn't know how to write a word!" [44] A few months later: "Her flaws of character are her stubbornness and her total lack of amiability." [45]

As late as 1780, Sade's children did not know that their father was in prison. Their mother had told them that he was "traveling in Spain," and in order not to raise their suspicions, she did not immediately pass his letters on to them. ("Your son said to me: 'How I would like to be traveling with Papa Sade!' " Pélagie wrote her husband. "And I tell him to work hard in order to be able to travel with him." [46])

The Sade children's letters to their father are written in a tone of
filial submission required by the protocol of their time, but they also
reflect genuine affection. They make it clear that the letters they received
from their absent parent were filled with exhortations to good conduct
and better study habits.

Louis-Marie de Sade, December 29, 1778

We cherish the instructions of a tender father. . . . We burn
with desire to throw ourselves around your neck and prove that
we cherish you with all our hearts. . . . I thank our Lord for the
joyful guidance you have kindly given us, in the spirit of a
father who loves his children and wants to make them happy.
Thus incited by the example of such a good father, I shall work
very hard at school. . . . Your letter is engraved in my heart,
and I've already begun to translate it into Latin.[47]

Donatien-Claude-Armand de Sade, December 29, 1778

This New Year's Day is an occasion for me to ask you a
little place in your heart and to merit the honor of your friendship. . . . I will do all I can to work hard and enjoy your kindness, my dear Papa. I hope, my dear Papa, that you will be
happy with my handwriting.

Madeleine-Laure de Sade, April 13, 1779

Your little Laure had the pleasure today of being able to
kiss her dear mama. When will I have the happiness of seeing
you in Paris and of telling you that I love and cherish you more
than myself?

Louis-Marie, December 26, 1779

I'm doing all that's possible, my dear Papa, to be worthy
of your tenderness and goodwill. . . . I'm writing commentar-
ies on Justinian, Cicero . . . and Virgil. I'm learning the rules
of versification; I hope to start writing some verses next month.
I'm also memorizing the Fables of La Fontaine.

Donatien-Claude-Armand, December 29, 1779

Since I had the honor of last writing you, I've applied
myself hard to my writing in order to please you with my
progress. . . . I've almost finished the history of Louis XIV. . . .
I pray to God every day for you, dear Papa, and beg him to
make me worthy of your tenderness. If you would be kind

enough to assign me the theme for a little essay, I would do all that is possible to please you.

Donatien-Claude-Armand, December 30, 1780

May the renewal of the year reanimate the prayers I sent to the Lord for your good health. When shall we have the happiness of seeing you? We wait for this moment with great impatience. How happy it makes me to remind you of my tenderness, however distantly.

In 1781, the boys would leave the Montreuils' village to board at a small tutoring school in Sèvres, in the Paris area. Abbé Amblet, Sade's former tutor, would be in charge of taking them out on their days off. Their father seemed to have been pleased by this change of schooling.

Louis-Marie, December 31, 1781

Deign to receive the good wishes of one who desires above all to merit the tenderness of a father whose son I'm so happy to be. When will I have the happiness of seeing you, dear Papa? With what impatience I long for that moment! When shall I be able to manifest, at your feet, the profound respect with which I remain, my dear Papa, your very humble and obedient servant and son.

Donatien-Claude-Armand, December 31, 1781

Your little chevalier is racking his brain trying to make you a compliment, though he does not need it to tell you that he loves you. That's the extent of my eloquence, dear Papa. I hope you will not disdain my wishes, since they're informed by heartfelt sentiments.

CARTERON, OR LA JEUNESSE, a tall, sturdy man with a heavily pock-marked face, whom the marquis often addressed by the picaresque nick-name "Martin Quiros," had been in Sade's service since the early 1770s. He had often played Sancho Panza in Sade's searches for kinky sex, and his libido seems to have been as unfettered as his master's. But unlike the relatively abstemious Sade, Carteron indulged heavily in alcohol, spending entire days away on binges. Literate enough to have exception-ally clear handwriting—valets of high-ranking nobles were often well educated—Carteron had been Sade's ideal attendant, able to copy his texts as efficiently as he masterminded his trysts. As they had traipsed about in search of mischief, the dapper marquis and his lumbering valet recalled the colorful servant-master relationships in Molière's *Don Juan* or Beaumarchais's *The Marriage of Figaro*.

Carteron's loyalty to both Sades was total. When the marquis was first imprisoned, his valet continued to work for the marquise for a pittance, attending to her every household need, and he even made herbal potions for Mlle de Rousset's frequent chest ailments. Soon after being returned to Vincennes, Sade began to write a series of plays; Carteron enjoyed transcribing the dramas and copying Sade's abundant notes on Petrarch. He complained, in fact, that his master did not give him enough to do: "I beg you send me some work, for I'm becoming besotted in my idleness. Stupid you left me, stupid I'll be restored to you." [48]

Carteron's most precious contribution to his master during the Vincennes years was the comic relief he offered in his letters. These affectionate, unwittingly hilarious missives were filled with garbled allusions to classical antiquity that made Sade laugh for days on end. "Only Pluto, smeared with excessive debauch, could have vomited such a conflagration," [49] Carteron wrote about a recent eruption of Vesuvius. "Martin Quiros" often described himself as an army general battling various animals and depicted himself in one letter as being mounted on "an old hornless goat who wrought greater ravages on enemy troops than Darius' elephants on Alexander's army." [50] In one of Sade's favorite notes from Carteron, the valet berated his master for his rushed, garbled handwriting, which he was having trouble deciphering: "I hear that you've applied yourself to the art of literature, but I see that your handwriting's the same, as if a swarm of bees had pastured on it." [51]

In turn, Carteron's buffoonish style inspired some of Sade's most picaresque prose. Such is the following missive, jestingly written to rebuke Carteron for criticizing his master's handwriting.

> Martin Quiros . . . you're getting insolent my boy if I were there I'd give you a thorough thrashing. . . . I'd tear out your f*** toupee, which you patch each year with pubic hair left in the bidets of Paris bordellos how else would you repair it you old mongrel yeah how would you?
> . . . You motherfucking ape, you crabgrass face smeared with blackberry juice, you prop of Noah's vine, you rib of Jonah's whale, you discarded match from a bordello's tinderbox, you rancid twopenny candle, you rotten thong of my wife's donkey . . . you old pumpkin stewed in cockroach juice, you third horn of the devil's head, you with a cod face, with

oysters for ears, you old pimp's shoe . . . if you were at hand, how I'd smear your dirty potato face in it, your mug that looks like burning chestnuts, to teach you not to lie to me that way.[52]

A few months later, Sade, addressing Carteron in mock-elegant style, once more inveighs against the jail term imposed for his transgressions.

My sorrows are finally drawing to an end, M. Quiros, and thanks to the kindness and the protection of Mme la Présidente de Montreuil, I hope, M. Quiros, to be able to give you [my New Year's wishes] in situ five years from tomorrow. Cheers to authority, Mr. Quiros! . . . For you know, Monsieur Quiros, that in France one is punished for any lack of respect for whores. One can malign the government, the king, religion— sheer trifles. But a whore, Monsieur Quiros, zounds! one must never insult a whore, for the Sartines, the Maupeous, the Montreuils, and other frequenters of bordellos will instantly come in a soldierly fashion to support the whore and incarcerate intrepidly a gentlemen for 12 or 15 years. . . . So there's nothing more beautiful than the French police. If you have a sister, a niece, a daughter, Monsieur Quiros, advise her to be a whore; I defy her to find a more handsome vocation. Beyond luxury, indolence, the continual inebriation of debauch, in what situation could a girl enjoy as much support, honor, protection as the most honest bourgeoise! . . . I give you my word, Monsieur Quiros, if fate had not given me enough sustenance to support my daughter, I'd instantly turn her into a whore. . . .
Speaking of which, Monsieur Quiros, be kind enough to tell me whether you're staying in fashion, whether you have gay blade shoes, full armor, and a windmill on your head. I have a particular desire to see you adorned in this style. . . . And your fleshly pleasures, how are they, Monsieur Quiros?[53]

Carteron's loyalty to the Sades was more than reciprocated. In 1785, when he came down with a fatal illness, the marquise nursed him with unfailing devotion, seldom leaving his bedside; and notwithstanding her penury, she offered him the most expensive medical care. Carteron would die "with all his wits and in a state of good religious emotions,"[54] Pélagie wrote Gaufridy, adding, a few days later, "I'm heartsick. I don't have poor La Jeunesse to write for me anymore."[55]

□   □

ON FEBRUARY 16, 1779, Sade fell asleep in his cell while rereading his uncle's book on Petrarch. The next morning, he opened his heart to his wife. In one of his most renowned missives, he wrote of his veneration for his thirteenth-century ancestor Laure de Sade and revealed yet once more his acute need for maternal love:

> . . . My only comfort here is Petrarch. I read him with delight, with a passion like none other. . . . How beautifully written the book is! . . . Laura turns my head. I am like a child. I read about her all day and dream about her all night. Listen to a dream I had of her yesterday, while all the world was taking its pleasure.
>
> It was about midnight. I had just fallen asleep with the life of Petrarch in my hand. Suddenly she appeared to me. . . . I saw her! The horror of the tomb had not impaired the splendor of her beauty, and her eyes had the same fire as when Petrarch sang of them. She was draped in black crepe, with her lovely blond hair flowing carelessly above it. . . . "Why do you groan on earth?" she said to me. "Come and join me. No more ills, no more sorrows, no more troubles in the vast expanse that I inhabit. Have the courage to follow me there." At these words, I flung myself at her feet, calling, "Oh, my mother!" And my voice was choked with sobbing. She held out her hand, and I covered it with my tears; she, too, shed tears. "When I dwelt in the world that you loathe," she said, "I used to enjoy beholding the future; I counted my descendants until I reached you, *and none did I see as unhappy as you.*"
>
> Then, engulfed in tenderness and despair, I threw my arms about her neck to hold her back or to follow her . . . but the ghost had disappeared. All that remained was my grief.

> *O voi che travagliate, ecco il cammino,*
> *Venite a me se'l passo altri no serra.*
>
> *[Oh, you who're suffering, come to me,*
> *Here's the way, if no one stands between us.]*
>
> —Petrarch, Sonnet 59 [56]

Several aspects of this letter deserve close scrutiny:

—The lines of Petrarch cited at the letter's end are in fact from Sonnet 81 of the poet's *Canzoniere*.

—The consummate blasphemer Sade might not have caught the

following irony: the Petrarch text he quotes from was inspired by the New Testament, Matthew 11: 28: "Come to me, all who labor and are heavy laden, and I will give you rest." In a trope central to the traditions of courtly love, Petrarch was expressing a need to purge himself of his physical love for Laura.[57]

—The name Laura might have had several phonetic associations for Sade, who read Italian and Latin well: *l'aura,* meaning breeze, wind, sometimes used metaphorically as "the breath" of creative genius; *l'aureo,* meaning halo, golden immanence, and, by extension, lucrative gain; and *laureo,* meaning laurel, the emblem of the poet's gift (Sade was keenly aware that he was just beginning his literary vocation). Petrarch made puns on all these highly charged words in the following quatrain from poem 246 of his *Canzoniere:*

> *L'aura, che 'l verde laureo e l'aureo crine*
> *soavemente sospirando move,*
> *fa con sue viste leggiadre e nove*
> *l'anime da' lor corpi pellegrine.*

> *("The breeze that, when gently sigh-*
> *ing, moves the green laurel tree and the*
> *golden mane of hair, through its gracious*
> *and novel movements also leads souls to*
> *escape from their bodies.")*

—Sade makes some especially revealing comments in his letter: "I am like a child." "I flung myself at her feet, calling, 'Oh, my mother!' " His dream came a few weeks after the second anniversary of his mother's death. He is dreaming of the ideal woman most every man longs for and whom Sade, son of a glacially aloof woman, has particularly good reason to desire—the idealized mother who will never leave him.

"The horror of the tomb had not impaired the splendor of her beauty, and her eyes had the same fire as when Petrarch sang of them." Even in death, Laura's beauty and seduction remain unmarred, thus protecting Sade himself from the threats of physical disintegration that are at the core of the psychotic or merely narcissistic personality.

Finally, was Sade's description of "joining" his ancestral "mother" yet another blackmail tactic toward his wife? Could he have been warning Pélagie that if not released very soon from the tortures of jail, he would join his idol, Laura, in her "vast expanse" of death?

◻   ◻

SADE'S REFERENCES to Mme de Montreuil, sprinkled throughout the letters he wrote his wife during his second jail term at Vincennes, speak for themselves:

July 3, 1780
No, I don't think it would be possible to find, in the entire world, a creature more loathsome than your infamous mother: Hell does not vomit equally abominable women.[58]

September 1780
Ah, the execrable creature! How I abhor her! May she be aware of the full extent of my hatred! And why is there no language strong enough to express the extent of my loathing for her? . . . Truly, do the heavenly powers not tire of leaving such a Fury on earth that long?[59]

April 1781
The devil take me if I find other desires in my heart beyond the one of putting to the wheel the slut who, after nine years of sucking my blood and dishonoring my children, is not yet sated with the horrors she has committed![60]

Sade frequently invented dreadful tortures for his archenemy.

February 1783
This morning, in the midst of my own suffering, I saw her, the bitch, being flayed alive, dragged upon a heap of burning coals and then thrown into a vat of vinegar. And I addressed her thus:
Execrable creature, here's for having sold your son-in-law to executioners!
Here's for having pimped out your two daughters!
Here's for having ruined and dishonored your son-in-law!
Here's for having led him to loathe the children to whom you sacrifice him!
Here's for having made him lose the finest years of his life, when it was up to you to save him. . . .
And I augmented my torments, and insulted her in her pain, and forgot my own.[61]

By the time Sade was returned to Vincennes, the on-and-off honeymoon he'd been having for many years with Mme de Montreuil was over. He had finally reached a plateau of unadulterated loathing. And his conviction that she alone was responsible for every one of his misfortunes grew all the more paranoid. The Présidente seemed to circumscribe his universe, governing the entire system of imaginary "signals" that dictated his fate. Convinced that she programmed every aspect of his destiny, he dismissed the notion that any other person or faction, such as the most puritanical French king in centuries, the humiliated and enraged French police, or public opinion at large, wanted him locked up. He looked on such forces as mere "lilliputians" compared with the all-powerful mother whom he accused of single-handedly masterminding his downfall. Convinced that each jailer and official he came in contact with was Mme de Montreuil's agent, he held her responsible for every misfortune that befell him in jail: taboos on walks, authorities' refusal to inform him of the length of his prison term, the barber's failure to attend to him, the guards' delay in sweeping his cell or hanging curtains on his windows—"such is the amusement sought by Mme de Montreuil."[62]

He even held her responsible for his eye ailments, which plagued him increasingly from the 1780s on and for which he was treated by King Louis XVI's own oculists, the brothers Grandjean. (The diagnosis was keratitis, a chronic pneumococcus infection that affects the cornea. He was advised to take up knitting to strengthen his eye muscles and was also urged to write rather than read at night, which may have helped to incite the amazing pace of literary activity he began at Vincennes.)

Describing, in his letters, his mother-in-law's malfeasances, Sade often resorts to metaphors of cosmic forces: if anyone were to thwart her will by informing him of the date of his release, "The elements [earth, fire, water] would be merged, lightning would burst out, the Présidente would stop shitting."[63] Such metaphors of excretion abound in his references to Mme de Montreuil: "What did she eat throughout Lent, to have such overflowing between Easter and Pentecost!"[64] he exclaims when he senses an overload of "signals" in his correspondence from the outside world. Sade also has many repellent fantasies about his mother-in-law's excess of "bile," a bodily compound that in the eighteenth century symbolized the venom of rage. He describes one such grotesque vision in a letter to his wife:

I sometimes imagine your infamous mother before the abscess of her stinking bile started overflowing on me drop by drop. I've made a little drawing of the scene. . . . She's lying naked, like one of those monsters the sea washes up on the shore. . . . M. Le Noir [the chief of police], who holds her pulse, says, "Madame, your bile must be punctured or else it will stifle you." . . . Marais . . . holds the candle and occasionally takes a taste of the substance to check on its quality. . . . R[ougemont] . . . holds up the plate and says, "Courage, courage, that's not enough to pay for three months' rent on my little trysting place."[65]

Such acute persecution manias are common among those incarcerated for criminal acts. Psychoanalysts suggest that since the human psyche is better organized to struggle against the hostility of the exterior world than against aggressions that arise in the inner self, the illusion of being an innocent victim can allay a prisoner's sense of guilt or responsibility. And so Sade's polemics against the Présidente continued unabated throughout his stay at Vincennes.

And this woman is devout, and this woman takes communion. . . . One would need only one example of this kind to turn the world's most pious man into an atheist. . . . Dear God, how I hate her! And what a moment it will be for me when I'll learn of the end of her abominable life! I most earnestly pledge to donate two hundred louis to the poor upon that day, and fifty to the domestic who will announce it to me or to the postal worker who will hand me the letter.[66]

The marquis was not alone in his condemnation of the Présidente. There is no keener reporter of the iron lady's connivance, and of her harsh treatment of her daughter, than Milli de Rousset. Some four months after the marquis was returned to jail, Milli described to Gaufridy the brusque manner in which "the heroine of treachery" visited her and Pélagie in their little convent flat during one of the marquise's illnesses.

Her hatred [for her daughter] is hidden with great art. Her daughter being ill, but gravely ill . . . she comes to visit her, stays at her bedside for a brief while . . . then goes to see the chambermaid . . . and says to her with her elevated little air: "It's unfortunate that my daughter is so in love with her husband!" "It's natural that she love a husband who's always treated her so well," the woman answers. This response seemed to have incurred the dowager's indignation; she took to criticizing everything: "This is not swept; this is not tidied; this casserole is not clean; adieu, take care of my daughter."[67]

Rousset then expounds on the Montreuil family's heartlessness: "I suspect . . . that this woman's plan is to leave M. de Sade in jail for a long time. . . . One of the marquise's maternal uncles wrote her at New Year's: 'You're wrong to fight so hard for your husband. . . . You should remember that you still have brothers and sisters to marry off.' "[68]

PÉLAGIE'S CONTINUAL PLEA that her mother lobby for Sade's release, and the Presidente's unrelenting hostility, were amply reflected in their correspondence. A few months after the marquis's return to jail, Mme de Montreuil wrote Mme de Sade:

> M. de Sade . . . is contrite, you tell me, and has resolved to behave properly. I want to believe it, and I hope it's true. But will anyone believe us? . . . No. One predicts the future through the example of the past, and therefore we cannot mention freedom now. . . . For finally, madame, let's speak plainly. You who know a great deal (though perhaps not all) are aware that he certainly did what he did. If he acted in full possession of his senses and with a cool head, he certainly deserves at the very least to be prevented from doing it again.[69]

Mme de Sade answered her mother several days later:

> The more time goes by, the more I worry about M. de Sade and the more clearly I see that people wish him to die. . . . Having been arrested despite his good conduct in the most ignominious possible manner, and having been told publicly that he'll remain incarcerated for the rest of his life, has he not every reason to think that his family desires his death? . . . And when my children are of age to understand such things, they will have much to reproach those who will have caused their father to lose his life or his sanity in jail.
> Ponder these truths well, my dear Mama, I beg you. . . . How sweet it would be for me to owe you gratitude for my life's solace! The bitterness that fills my days makes me long for death. See to it that my husband is returned to me, dear Mama. I would then owe you my life twice over, and I remain, with the utmost respect, your most humble and obedient servant.

Within the fortnight, Mme de Montreuil answered her daughter:

> You may assure M. de Sade, madame . . . that I forgive
> him from the bottom of my heart for all the wrongs I might
> reproach him for. . . . I pity his situation and would help him if
> I were able to, as I always did at the times when he slandered
> me to his heart's content; however, the indelible memory of
> the past . . . forbids me to have any direct contact with him.

But Pélagie fought on, desperately trying to convince her mother
and the world that the marquis was on the path of reform. "My good
friend," "My tender friend," "My good little boy," "My good and
tender little boy," "My good little fellow," the marquise continued to
address her husband, her love for him defying her parents' opprobrium,
public opinion, the king's law.

DURING HER HUSBAND'S years in jail, food served as a central staple of
the Sades' folie à deux. Some of the marquis's most vicious rages were
incited by his wife's failure to fulfill his culinary orders properly. ("The
Savoy biscuit isn't at all what I'd asked for: I wished it to be iced all
the way around its surface, on top and underneath."[70]) Conversely,
his sporadic bouts of tenderness were often prompted by a particularly
successful care package: "I've received all of your mailings. This time
they're charming, dear heart, and I thank you with all my soul. . . .
Pheasant worthy of appearing at the table of a prison commandant,
exquisite orange flower liqueur . . . all is very beautiful and delicious. . . .
I assure you that my only cheerful moments are those in which I look
forward to our reunion. . . . Oh, it's been too long, in truth too long!"[71]
    During his years of confinement, fantasies of exquisite mealtimes
often replaced sex as the marquis's main obsession. Along with a phenomenal amount of sweets, he craved such traditional rural delicacies as
quail en brochette wrapped in vine leaves, pots of beef marrow, pâtés of
fresh salmon, little grilled cabbages, madeleines. His food orders were
made with finicky exactness, and like many aspects of his jail life, they
displayed an obsession with numbers: "I wish it to be a chocolate cake,
and of chocolate so dense that it is black, like the devil's ass is blackened
by smoke."[72] "Please send me: fifteen biscuits made at the Palais-Royal,
the finest possible, six inches long by four inches wide and two inches
high, very light and delicate."[73] (The specificity of Sade's requests was
not limited to foods. Within the very same letter to Pélagie, he requested: "the architectural plan for the new Théâtre des Italiens and

the announcement for their opening play . . . an embroidered silk vest, patterned on a green background, without any silver trimming . . . and a very young puppy dog, very young so that I may have the pleasure of training it, either a water spaniel or a setter; I only want one of those two breeds."[74])

A menu that Sade would order, a few years thence, from the chef of his next jail, the Bastille, displays the same precision.

MONDAY

DINNER
—An excellent soup (I will not repeat this adjective: soups must always be excellent, morning and night)
—Two succulent and luscious breaded veal cutlets
—Porridge
—Two cooked apples

SUPPER
—Soup
—Four fresh eggs

TUESDAY

DINNER
—Soup
—A mouthwatering half chicken
—Two little vanilla custards
—Two cooked apples

SUPPER
—Soup
—A small hash of the morning's leftover chicken . . .

SATURDAY

DINNER
—Soup
—Two delectable mutton cutlets
—A coffee custard
—Two cooked pears

SUPPER
—Soup
—A little sweetened omelette made of just two eggs and extremely fresh butter

SUNDAY

DINNER
—Soup
—Sausages
—Two very tender leaves of chard in gravy
—Two cooked pears

SUPPER
—Soup
—Apple fritters[75]

This surprisingly moderate fare would get good ratings from contemporary dieticians. Sade's utopian menus are notable for their lack of
sauces or spices, which he abhorred, and draw nicely from the "major
food groups." Cooked fruit was consumed every day, easing a digestion
upset by lack of exercise and thus allaying hemorrhoidal pain, a chronic
ailment for both Sades. And the marquis was fairly abstemious in his use
of alcohol, preferring very good aged Burgundies or small quantities of
fruit liqueurs to hard spirits.

The one aspect of Sade's regimen that would be censured in our
time is his mania for sweets. Along with two boxes of face powder, twelve
pairs of socks, six ties, and other folderol that suited his vanity, an average
fortnightly package sent Sade by his wife might comprise the following
items: thirty large macaroons, twelve iced cakes, a large box of marshmallows, several pots of greengage, purple plum, and raspberry jams, a box
of candied fruit, jars of canned peaches, an almond cake, and chocolate,
always more chocolate. "[I want] a thick chocolate cake; and the vanilla
cream inside very unctuous; if it's not good, I'll send it back. It must be
iced on top. And [also] some chocolate pastilles."[76] One is struck by
the infantile regression embodied in these treats: marshmallows, sweet
fillings, cake frostings—bland, creamy nursery foods, the fare dreamed
of by children recovering from surgery or direly needing maternal affection. No wonder the marquis grew excessively fat during his sedentary
years in jail.

The menus Sade would devise for his fictions were as exacting as his
real-life diet and far more lavish. A systematic alternation of bed and
table is an intrinsic part of the Sadean orgy, for only delectable repasts
can restore his heroes' psychic and physical energies. "Our cocks are
never as stiff as when we've just completed a sumptuous feast,"[77] Noirceuil explains to Juliette. "Nothing more titillates my imagination than
the fumes of these delectable meals, which caress my thoughts and pre-

pare them for the delights of vice," Gernande exclaims in the middle of a bacchanal.[78] Unlike the gorgings devised by Rabelais, who seems to have had a prodigious influence on Sade but whose excesses always remain plausible, Sade's fictional feasts are as improbable as his protagonists' orgasms (Noirceuil criticizes Juliette's frugality when she plans a menu of a mere fifty courses). In Sade's more murderous tales, such as *The 120 Days of Sodom,* providers of food—cooks and their aides—are the only individuals immune to persecution. Like a caste of high priests, they also tend to remain chaste. Hands off my kitchen personnel! Sade is saying about those fictional chefs whose delicacies he craved in the isolation of his jail cell.

IF ONE WERE to single out the most pivotal impulse that dominated Sade's actions and fantasies, it would be his constant attempt to achieve the illusion of power. The penniless scion of a moribund caste, held at the king's whim in France's most impregnable fortress, he was understandably impelled to seek dominance over the only realm available to him—his wife's emotions. His need to exert maximum control over Pélagie, coupled with his paranoid imagination, his wildly fluctuating moods, and her innate submissiveness, are the essential components of what one might call, these days, the Sades' "classic sadomasochistic relationship" (it was a quirk of fate that such ideally matched personalities had found each other through the random process of a prearranged marriage). And throughout the 1780s, the most painful aspect of her husband's conduct, to Pélagie, was the alternation of intense tenderness and violent loathing that he poured into his letters from jail.

A few examples of the loving husband's voice:

"Here I am returning to you, dear companion, to you whom I'll always cherish as the best and most beloved friend I've ever had in the world."[79]

"Cherished friend, I assure you that . . . my only cheerful moments are occasioned by thoughts of our reunion. But they're making me wait too long for it!! Oh, it's been too long, in truth, too long!"[80]

He seemed to miss her increasingly every year: "Beg the minister to offer me [the favor of your visit] in exchange for two additional years of prison. . . . I would give them [half my worldly goods] to see you one hour alone. . . . In God's name, come to see me for an hour, or I'm not responsible for my life anymore."[81]

And there was the most famous of Sade's letters to his wife, in which he thanked her for her diligence in fulfilling one of his more quixotic requests—the portrait of "a beautiful young man." "You sent me the beautiful boy, my darling turtledove. The beautiful boy! How sweet that word is to my rather Italianate ear! *Un bel' giovanetto, signor,* they would say to me if I were in Naples, and I'd answer, *Sì, sì, signor, mandatelo, lo voglio bene.* You've regaled me as you would a cardinal . . . but unfortunately it's only a drawing."

It is symptomatic of the marquis's weird sexuality that he showered his wife, in the very same letter, with an unprecedented number of endearments. "My little darling," "my puppy dog," "Mahomet's delight," "celestial kitten," "fresh pork of my thoughts," "star of Venus," "soft enamel of my eyes," "image of divinity," "violet of the Garden of Eden," "effusion of the angelic spirits," "miracle of nature," are only a few such appellations, more of which occur in the playful passage that ends the missive:

> Rest assured, soul of my soul, that the first little errand I will make upon being sprung, my very first action as a free man, after kissing your eyes, your nipples, and your buttocks, will be to purchase . . . the totality of the works of Montaigne . . . Voltaire, J.-J. Rousseau. . . . [And] why the refusal of the peach wine? . . . Could one or two bottles of peach wine, my Poopsie, subvert the Salic Law, or threaten the Justinian Code? Hark ye, Minerva's favorite, only a drunkard should suffer such a refusal: but I, who am solely inebriated by your charms and am never sated by them, O you Olympian ambrosia, shouldn't be denied a little peach wine! Flame of my life, when will your alabaster fingers come to exchange the irons of [my jailer] for the roses of your breast? Adieu, I kiss it and go to sleep.[82]

But to Pélagie's anguish, the anger and vile derision could flare up at any time: "the only cause [for your tormenting me] is your horrendous, somber cruelty, or rather your weakness and humility toward those scoundrels who lead you by the nose. . . . Can't you see that you're only trying to torture me through your execrable letters, instead of bringing me consolation?"[83]

In the face of such accusations, Pélagie would defend herself as best she could:

"Your mind is so bizarre when you misinterpret what I write. . . . When you return to me I'll lock you in my room and you won't leave it until you've read, confronted everything you said in your letters and admitted to me, 'My little wife, I must do justice to you.' "[84]

□   □

NOTWITHSTANDING his frequent affronts to her, throughout his years at Vincennes Sade's physical longing for Pélagie's presence seemed to grow deeper. Much of what she touched acquired a talismanic importance for him. He insisted that only she embroider his vests for him. He reiterated his pleasure at having her copy and annotate his writings: "How I'd love to see one of my works totally copied out in your handwriting, with little notes on the margin that would praise or criticize certain passages." [85] And it is clear that the plain, prosaic marquise was central to her husband's sexual fantasies. Her erotic spell over him is chronicled in a diary he started keeping when he began his jail term, the "Almanach Illusoire," in which he faithfully recorded his masturbations. Many if not most of these episodes were incited by fond memories of his wife,[86] for whom he devised the erotic code name "Hélène" (for such entries he dubbed himself "Moise").

In the third year of his prison term at Vincennes, the marquis's letters expressed his longing for his wife with increasing urgency. Oh, when would she come to visit him? he wrote her. Did she realize that it made him "horny as hell" [87] to remain so long without "measuring" her (presumably one of the spouses' euphemisms for making love)? He asked her to send him the sleeve of one of her dresses. The once prim Pélagie forwarded parts of a taffeta gown; she had grown sophisticated enough to realize that her husband's request had to do with his autoerotic practices. This was hardly the only instance of the striking sexual explicitness that prevails in the Sades' correspondence; it displays a marital candor uncommon for any time of history and any class of society. In a letter of 1784, for example, which prison censors may have kept her from seeing, the marquis gave his wife an astonishingly candid description of his solitary orgasms. This curious document is known as the "Vanilla and Manilla" letter. In his erotic fantasies, *vanille* denotes aphrodisiacs; *manille* designates the very specific kind of masturbation he engages in. Another key word is *prestiges,* his very personal euphemism for a dildo.

> I know well that *vanille* is stimulating and that one must use *manille* with moderation. But there it is! When it's the only thing you've got . . . One good hour in the morning dedicated to five *manilles* . . . three more for at least a half hour of the evening, artistically graduated . . .

Elaborating on what seemed to be a critical feature of his sexuality—his great difficulty in reaching orgasm—Sade uses two other key words, "bow" and "arrow," to designate genitals and semen.

It's not that the bow is insufficiently rigid—oh, don't worry, there's all you might want there—but the arrow doesn't want to leave, and that's a killer, because one so wants it to leave. In dearth of a [sexual] object, the imagination leads the way, and that doesn't arrange things. And that's why I'm telling you prison life is so bad—since solitude gives greater force to one's ideas, the disturbances that ensue are stronger.

The prisoner expounds further on the pain he suffers on those occasions when he is able to ejaculate (his allusion makes it clear that his wife witnessed, if not participated in, his sexual adventures at La Coste).

When [the arrow] has as much as pierced the air, it's truly like an epileptic attack. . . . And convulsions, and spasms, and aches—you saw samples of it at La Coste. It has doubled in strength, so you can imagine.

He resorts to a strikingly primitive diagnosis of the pain he suffers during ejaculation.

I've tried to analyze the cause of this syndrome, and I think it is incited by the extreme thickness. —It is as if one tried to squeeze cream through an overly narrow flask. This thickness swells the vessels and tears them. To this one might reply: the arrow must leave more often. —I know that it should.— But it doesn't want to. . . . If I only had those other means I have when I'm free [i.e., sexual partners], the arrow being less reluctant and leaving sooner, the crisis of its departure would not be as violent, or as dangerous. . . . The less often [the arrow] leaves, the more the imagination heats up. . . . If the arrow does not leave and is constrained: horrible swooning; if it succeeds: dreadful crisis. And if one does not succeed: the mind goes to the devil.

The marquis states his intention to seek medical advice as soon as he's liberated, for he is sure that he suffers from "a rare structural flaw." "Answer me if you have any insights into this matter, and remain certain of all my affection," [88] he signs off this letter to his wife. Sade does not seem to have imposed any perversions on his wife more exotic than sodomy, and the notion that she might have any medical insights into his very complex sexual problems is comical. A close reading of this letter intimates that like many of his fictional protagonists, he frequently had trouble coming to orgasm, and that without a partner, he could achieve ejaculation only by an immense effort of the imagination. (Simone de Beauvoir referred to Sade as "semi-impotent."[89]) Furthermore, the nature of his orgasms—one recalls the "loud and terrifying" screams he emitted during his whipping of Rose Keller—makes it clear that the very pain he claims to have suffered upon reaching climax satisfied his masochistic impulses. As for a diagnosis of his painful orgasms: it is probable that the marquis suffered from a benign, undiagnosed case of venereal disease rather than from some "structural flaw."

OTHER SEXUALLY EXPLICIT letters to his wife make it clear that the kind of *manille* Sade preferred was not any garden-variety manual masturbation but an autosodomization achieved with certain objects. A few years into his jail term, Sade began to plague his wife with bizarre requests for such appliances. He asked her to supervise the manufacture of "pocket flasks" or "cases" that could hold "maps, engravings, and several little landscapes I have executed in red ink"[90] (or so he put it for the sake of prison authorities). He was particularly finicky about the measurement of these *prestiges,* as he called them. They had to be twenty centimeters long by sixteen centimeters in circumference, the size of "Moïse's actual *prestige*"[91]—i.e., the alleged size of his own sexual organ when erect. In short, these objects were dildos, camouflaged as "flasks" or "cases" for the eyes of prison censors, with which Sade intended to heighten the kind of painful pleasures he had described in his *vanille* and *manille* letter. The *prestiges* were to be carved of only the smoothest wood, rosewood or ebony, and they must be custom made by a noted Paris cabinetmaker, Abraham, who, Sade assured his wife, had provided objects "of the same measurements for His Eminence the archbishop of Lyons."[92]

The marquise, for once, was rebellious about fulfilling her husband's fantasies. Craftsmen "laughed in [her] face"[93] because of these objects' specified dimensions. They refused to fill her orders, she complained, and treated her "like a madwoman or an imbecile."[94] Some demanded money up front, fearing that these outlandish articles would never be claimed. "I beg you to release me from this errand—you'd bring me much pleasure,"[95] she finally pleaded with the marquis.

But the prisoner was as stubborn and exacting about this request as he was about his gastronomic fancies and his coquettish attire. "You know perfectly well that this flacon is worthless as a pocket flask," he complained about one model he returned to her. ". . . It's far too small."

Pélagie's continual complaints about this assignment led her husband to scribble ribald comments on the margins of her missives to him. On the edge of a letter in which she remarked that a particular flask was too long to fit into his pocket, the marquis scrawled: "I don't put it into my pocket. I put it elsewhere, where it still turns out to be too small."[96] He would make an equally scabrous comment when, their correspondence having lagged, she complained that her imagination was "filling with all kinds of things." "So's my ass,"[97] the marquis noted on the edge of her notepaper.

Incited by his usual mania for numbers, Sade obsessively recorded the number of "introductions" (by which he seems to mean sodomitic masturbations, with or without orgasms) he enjoyed with the help of his devices. It is hard to know how seriously this mathematical exercise should be taken. By December 1, 1780, only two and a half years after his return to Vincennes, he had recorded 6,536.

XIX

The Jealous Husband

*The police tolerate everything; the only thing they
don't tolerate is insults to whores. One can be capable
of all possible injuries and infamies, as long as one
respects whores' asses: . . . that's what I must try myself
when I get out of here, put myself under police protection: I have an ass like a whore's, and I'd be grateful
if it could be respected.*

—Letter to Mme de Sade, 1783

□

FINALLY, prison authorities relented; the day came when Donatien and
Pélagie were allowed to see each other. The conditions of the visit, on
that long-awaited hour of July 21, 1781, were not ideal. The spouses were
not allowed to meet alone in the marquis's cell, as they had asked, but
were consigned to a downstairs parlor, with a prison official present.

But still, after four and a half years, consider the elation they would
feel on such an occasion. Consider the careful cosmetic preparations any
wife would make for such a reunion, planning the costume, the coiffure,
especially if she was the Marquise de Sade, especially if she was as insecure
as Pélagie and as filled with passion for her husband.

Think, too, of the prisoner's thoughts when he sees his wife for the
first time in four and a half years, dressed to kill in a décolleté white
dress, her hair curled in the latest style. While I'm here, as good as dead,
he might well think, she's out there enjoying the world, a world filled
with potential rivals. I find her desirable, thus they find her desirable,
thus she is / is about to be / already has been unfaithful to me.

So although we have no account of the meeting, we know that it
could not have been as calm or joyful as Pélagie had imagined it might
be. A week later, she received a letter from her husband—the angriest

he'd ever written her—expressing his wrath at the coquetry of her attire. After complaining that she was "dressed like a whore," he informed her that he would refuse to see her if she ever arrayed herself again in that manner.

> Tell me, would you go do your Lenten duties in that mountebank's or quack doctor's garment? You wouldn't, would you? Well, the same sense of reverence that informs your Lenten duties should inspire your visits here; grief and sorrow should produce, in your case, what piety and divine respect produce in other souls. . . . If you're a decent woman, you must solely please me, and the only way you'll please me is through the greatest decorum and most perfect modesty. . . . In sum, I demand that you come . . . coiffed with a very large bonnet . . . without the smallest hint of curl in your hair, a chignon and no braids; your throat must be extraordinarily concealed, not indecently uncovered as it was the other day, and the color of your vestment must be as somber as possible.[1]

Pélagie's seductive getup led to one of the more impassioned polemics the marquis had yet delivered on the issue of women's adultery and even elicited one of his rare mea culpas. "Conserve your virtue!" he inveighed like some fanatic preacher. "Virtue is the only thing that makes me ashamed of my digressions, only virtue can make me hate them. . . . All my own misfortunes are traceable to the examples of vice set before me."

He lamented how comforting it had been, after all his tribulations, to look forward to a happy old age in the arms of a faithful friend. And how despicable she was to deprive him of even that gentle hope! He'd never be able to respect her again! And of course it was all the fault of "the monsters" who counseled her. . . . Dear God, let him never leave jail! He'd rather die there than witness the effects of his disgrace! For she had become the instrument of his torture. . . . Yes, her monstrous mother has taken everything away from him, even his wife's devotion! "Oh, my dear and divine friend, oh! ancient soul-friend, no, I won't survive it!"

Reading this letter, one wonders whether the actor in Sade wasn't merely enjoying a brand-new role—that of the passionate, jealous husband. His missive ended on an equally melodramatic tone of abjectness: "I'm left with only one claim upon you, which the entire universe could not deprive me of—I'm the father of your children. Well, perhaps you'll relent, if only for their sake! If you're dissatisfied with me, I agree to die in order to liberate you from me! But first let me weep at your feet, let me kiss your knees once more and hear your verdict from your own voice, and I'll die happy."

In the following weeks and months, the marquis would inveigh repeatedly against his wife's treachery, modulate his sorrow in various keys of rage and betrayed tenderness, even identify certain individuals whom he suspected of being her lovers. One butt of his wrath was Pélagie's relative the Marquise de Villette, a kind and learned woman who was a close friend of Voltaire's (he died in her house) and was known in Paris by the philosopher's epithet for her, "Belle et Bonne." Thirteen years younger than Pélagie, Mme de Villette had married an uncle of Pélagie's who was famed for his homosexuality and his progressive ideas. They had recently befriended the penniless Pélagie and with characteristic hospitality had invited her to live with them. This move the marquis had forbidden Pélagie to make, on the grounds that Mme de Villette was "a big fucker" and "a bit of a Sappho."[2] He didn't even want his wife to attend the marquise's lively, freethinking salon.

Pélagie's reactions were as docile as ever: "I who only live . . . for you, here I am, suspected and insulted. . . . No, it's not possible for you to believe what you're writing."[3] "I renew my oath not to go to Mme de Villette's," she wrote him a few days after their reunion. "In order to keep you from tormenting yourself in this manner, I'll seek out a convent."[4]

The marquis must have continued to vent his jealous anger, for she had to repledge her oath many times. "I promise you that I never have and will never lodge at Villette's," she repeated a few weeks later, "and that I'll instantly leave my flat . . . to live in a convent, and see only persons useful to you, and will continue to do so until the time of your release, when I shall be reunited with you forever."[5] ("You were right, mademoiselle, my visit did more harm than good,"[6] Pélagie wrote Milli de Rousset shortly after her first reunion with her husband, adding that he had also accused her of being pregnant from an illicit liaison.)

An equally absurd object of the marquis's jealousy was a Provençal youth of modest origins named Lefèvre. This native of Mazan had been taught to read and write by Abbé de Sade while serving him as valet and later had briefly worked as the marquis's secretary. The only mention of him Pélagie ever made in her correspondence was that Lefèvre had once bought some books for her husband. At the artist's request, she subsequently sent the inmate a little drawing Mlle de Rousset had made of Lefèvre. That was enough to set Sade's imagination on fire. Describing his suspected rival as "a peasant of the vilest species to whose father I gave alms," he lacerated the portrait and attached it to a letter that he spotted with his own blood and annotated with obscenities, such as the size of his alleged rival's penis. "Here's how . . . a riffraff of this species," he ranted in that note to his wife, "merits to be treated when he forgets the respect he owes his master, and here's how I hope to treat him."[7] (Some decades later, Lefèvre became a subprefect of the city of Verdun and published a study on eloquence.)

OVER THE ENSUING WINTER, the marquis gradually got over his jealousy. "Six visits have sufficed to bring me back from my illusions," he wrote Pélagie the following year. "They outraged you; that's enough for me to never have any more such fantasies. I know enough to esteem those I love."[8] So Pélagie had the satisfaction of having her husband apologize for his folly. "The only vengeance I reserve myself is to pull your ears upon your release," she wrote him gleefully, "and force you to agree, before a witness . . . that all the illusions that filled your head were outlandish."[9]

The marquis's jealous rages were clearly incited by his paranoia concerning his mother-in-law, whom he always suspected (with good reason) of scheming to estrange him from his wife. "A month doesn't go by when I don't dream . . . the same thing," he had written Pélagie shortly before their reunion. "I see you far older than the age at which I left you, always keeping a secret from me which you don't want to share, and always unfaithful to me, *to the full extent of that word,* at your mother's instigation. I must have dreamed this five hundred times."[10]

Sade's jealousy was exacerbated by his surprisingly traditional view of family life. His views of marital bonds were diametrically opposed to the savage sexual anarchy he hailed in his writings and pursued in life. In letters to his wife and Mlle de Rousset, he preached that men should hide their peccadilloes "from the public, and particularly from your children . . . and your wife, [who should] never doubt a thing. Fulfill your duties toward her *in every possible way.*"[11] (Sade obviously wishes to emphasize the duty of conjugal sex, which he seemed to enjoy as much as his kinky capers.) He took great pride in never having committed adultery with a married woman. "For a dozen girls . . . I've tried to seduce," he wrote Rousset, "you won't find three married women."[12] As steeped in rigid double standards of sexual behavior as any of his peers, he grew apoplectic at the notion of female adultery. "Women's infidelity . . . has such fatal and dark consequences that I've never been able to tolerate it."[13]

The marquis's possessiveness created a radical change in his wife's life, one that would deeply affect their marriage. In order to keep her husband from "tormenting" himself, Pélagie decided to leave the little apartment in the Marais she had occupied for the past year and again enter a monastic community. "I'm going to put an end to it all by going to live in a convent," she explained to Mlle de Rousset.[14]

Since the early Middle Ages, many thousands of wellborn women who were forced to live alone—spinsters and widows, abandoned wives, women who like the marquis's own mother disliked family life or who like Pélagie were just poor—had chosen to rent lodgings in Parisian convents. Since the Church owned some twenty percent of the real estate in Paris, such establishments were numerous and offered a wide variety of living quarters, which ranged from the menial to the opulent. (The custom of renting lodgings in nunneries would last well into the nineteenth century; George Sand's mother resided in a convent, and Mme Récamier, the greatest fashion icon of the postrevolutionary years, held her last salon in a convent flat.)

In the 1780s, Paris boasted about two hundred religious communities, which occupied some three thousand buildings. Pélagie's letters indicate that she had first tried to join a society of Carmelite nuns referred to as *Anglaises* because they were dedicated to praying for the conversion of the British nation, but they were very popular and she could find no room with them. So she settled for the convent of Sainte-Aure, on what is now Rue Tournefort in the fifth arrondissement. Like most establishments of its kind, it doubled as a school for young women. Sainte-Aure, which was run by Augustinian nuns, seems to have been a particularly devout community. Beyond their function as educators, the nuns—officially known as Perpetual Worshipers of the Sacred Heart of Jesus—were pledged to the daily worship of the Blessed Sacrament.

At Sainte-Aure, Pélagie first occupied two small rooms on the convent's second floor, next to the bakery. Her closest neighbor was a merchant's widow, "talkative, amiable, and well mannered." "Boarders" such as Pélagie and her neighbors were not asked to take any vows, but they were expected to participate in the nuns' religious services, and Pélagie reported that Sainte-Aure required "great assiduity in the choir." Creature comforts at this nunnery were extremely modest, the fare being "barely sufficient to not die of hunger." For food and board, which included hovel-like quarters for La Jeunesse and her maid, Pélagie paid five hundred livres a year, approximately half of what she had to pay for Sade's food and board at Vincennes, not counting all the delicacies and toiletries she sent him. Pélagie remained so perennially short of cash that she even had to sell her silver shoe buckles, a prized possession at the time, for which she received a thousand livres.

The marquis evidently had no sense of his wife's sacrifices, her struggle to make ends meet. He threw tantrums, in fact, when she mentioned any of the numerous fiscal disasters confronting them at La Coste and elsewhere. In response to one of her SOS's, he reassured her in a tone of merry insouciance that his family could survive perfectly well in the event that his castles were "burned to the ground and all his worldly goods pilfered." His solution was a career in the theater. "One less thing to worry about . . . I'll go write comedies in Prussia," he quipped, "and you'll play the guitar. We'll earn our living, the five of us."[15]

Although Pélagie seemed initially to deride Sainte-Aure's fervent piety, in time this devoutness pleased her, and she began to take a religious attitude toward her suffering: it would improve her soul. "With a little devotion, I would be a perfect creature," she had written Milli de Rousset in 1781, shortly after her friend returned to Provence.

Stoicism was of the essence, for Pélagie's new surroundings did not bring her luck. In their first year there, both she and La Jeunesse were repeatedly ill. Moreover, soon after she moved to Sainte-Aure, her tiny flat there was torn down to make place for additional nuns' cells. She was moved to "a hole in the attic wall" and now had to receive guests in the common parlor, a situation she found ironic, since she owned "three castles, which are deteriorating through lack of occupants."[16] But she loved the convent. Its seclusion suited her reclusive streak, which was now vigorously encouraged by her husband. "I'd accept ten thousand such discomforts if my husband were granted justice,"[17] she commented about her abject quarters.

One can become pious through hypocrisy, or through conviction, or through osmosis. Pélagie's renewed faith was of the latter kind: she assimilated the aura of the nuns amid whom she lived. Paradoxically, the ultimate apostate Sade contributed to her growing devoutness by demanding that she cloister herself increasingly from the world. "Above all, love God and flee men!"[18] he thundered. "I consign you to your room," he commanded her, "and, through all the authority that a husband has over his wife, forbid you to leave it, for whatever pretext."[19] That comment is simply another instance of Sade's rhetorical delirium. In reality he expected his wife to leave her convent as often as possible to visit him, trot all over Paris assembling his treats, and generally attend to his needs.

The irony is that the marquis greatly undermined his own struggle for liberation by isolating Pélagie, since he deprived her of any access she'd ever had to Paris's power structure. His taboo on the Marquis and Marquise de Villette, for instance, cut her off from progressive, influential people who, as their friendship with the often embattled Voltaire attests, were constantly campaigning for "good causes." Progressive ideas were ultrachic in the 1780s, and Villette was a man who would gladly have signed ten petitions a week for some jailbird's release. Such peers would have been highly beneficial to the Sades if the marquis had been less intractable. But he was not that kind of citizen. "Kill me or take me as I am"—this might well have been his epitaph—"for I shall never change." [20]

As SADE RAGED about his wife's alleged infidelities, the only person who could have brought some conciliation between the spouses—Milli de Rousset—was nearing her end.

Mlle de Rousset had returned to Provence in the spring of 1781, shortly after she resumed, after a two-year silence, her correspondence with Sade. She spent some months in Avignon, trying to mend her health, which was beginning to be ravaged by tuberculosis. Proceeding to La Coste, where she first stayed with the village curate, Father Testanière, she immediately visited the marquis's château. And she found there a condition of anarchy that was characteristic of many French grandees' estates in the decade preceding the Revolution: an increasing segment of the population were defying seigneurial privileges—hunting on aristocrats' land, plundering their forests, pillaging their homes. At La Coste, a remote and often persecuted community whose Protestant roots tended to make its citizens all the more rebellious, the situation seemed to be even worse than it was in northern France.

"Any madman could come to murder me in my bed," [21] Mlle de Rousset wrote Gaufridy in 1782 when she moved into the château itself, at the Sades' request, to protect it from further destruction. All of the marquis's former vassals and domestics, such as Sambuc, the guardian of the estate, had become very "impertinent," she complained. Gothon, who for the past years had been much in love with a local carpenter, had neglected most of her housekeeping duties. ("Love makes us so foolish," Milli commented on Gothon's passion. "I'm so happy to be exempt from it.") The filth of the Sades' kitchen, Milli griped, "would make thirty-six cats vomit." Hunters from Ménerbes and Bonnieux were breaking into La Coste, one of the marquis's farms was set on fire, his grapes had been pilfered, and scores of his beloved fruit trees were cut down. She felt "as if all the devils were unleashed in this infernal house," as if she were living "amid enraged wolves."

La Coste's dilapidated state made the winter months barely tolerable. In the abandoned château, walls were crumbling, roof tiles and great hunks of plaster ceilings were crashing down "with the regularity of church bells."[22] A stone weighing more than thirty pounds fell down and nearly crushed Milli's legs. The fireplace in her room collapsed from the huge winds. Her tuberculosis grew worse, causing her to spit up blood more frequently than ever.

Having resumed his correspondence with her, in January 1782 Sade sent Mlle de Rousset a long, reflective New Year's letter, which he called "Étrennes Philosophiques" ("A Philosophical New Year's Gift"). Intended to win back her friendship, it elaborated more lyrically than usual on the injustice of his plight and on the anarchic-pacifist philosophy he was evolving in prison.

> Wheresoever you may be, mademoiselle—near or far, among Turks or Galileans, with monks or comedians, jailers or honest folk, reckoners or philosophers—I am not allowed a dispensation from the yearly renewal of the sacred duties imposed by the bonds of friendship—upon which, according to ancient custom and with your kind accord, I shall give myself to some philosophical reflections generated from innermost experience.
>
> . . . You who send human beings to the gallows for actions that in the Congo are rewarded with crowns . . . abandon your false cunning . . . delight yourself, my friend, delight and do not judge . . . remain aware that it is in order to make your fellow creatures happy, to tend them, to help them, to love them, that nature sets you among them, not to judge them and punish them and above all not to lock them up.
>
> If this little bit of philosophizing pleases you, mademoiselle, I shall have the satisfaction to send you more, with my next new year's wishes. . . .
>
> From the hen coop of Vincennes this January 26 after 59 months and a half of extortion and truly without success . . .[23]

However dashing the marquis's prose, Mlle de Rousset was not that easily reconquered. Her response was downright acerbic. "We are neither Democritus, nor Heraclitus, nor Seneca," she wrote her erstwhile friend, inveighing with particular severity against his moral relativism. "We are born French. . . . Our laws, customs, usages, are structured the way we know them, and not as we desire them. Crowns in the Congo are bestowed on the basis of [that people's] notion of the beautiful, the glorious, the just. Death by hanging, in Paris, is the reward of any transgressor of our laws who is mad enough to think that he lives in the Congo."[24]

The cooling of Rousset's feelings for Sade were in part caused by her discovering the darker aspects of her friend's past. Before leaving Paris, she had read part of a police dossier on Sade and learned more about the nature of his misdeeds—the apostasy committed with the prostitute sixteen years earlier, the details of the "Little Girls Episode" at La Coste; and she had begun to see sense to his imprisonment. "Mme de Montreuil is not as guilty as one might think,"[25] she wrote Gaufridy. "There are grave, very grave offenses, which lead me to fear a very long captivity."[26]

Mlle de Rousset also criticized the marquis for depleting his wife's puny funds through his extravagant orders of victuals, books, and cosmetics. The cost of his fortnightly orders, she estimated, amounted to some two thousand livres a year. And she had grown equally critical of Pélagie for being so compliant to her spouse. "She might have spared me thousands and millions of annoyances if she'd had more education, more greatness of soul, or that delicacy of sentiments given by birthright. . . . There are individuals so baroquely organized that they inspire more pity than anger."[27] So the Sades' spell on Milli de Rousset had weakened. It was a test of the "saint" 's compassion that she maintained some sympathy for their dilemmas and continued to do all she could to make life easier for them.

Rousset showed great loyalty to Gothon, for instance, in her last illness. Gothon had contracted puerperal fever after delivering the child she had conceived with her lover (they had married a few months before their baby boy was born). She died in October 1781, six days after giving birth. Milli had remained at Gothon's bedside throughout her illness. Sade was extremely affected by Gothon's death. He paid for any debts she had incurred and underwrote her child's baptism and a funeral mass in her memory. In a letter to Rousset, Sade wrote a homage to Gothon in which he praised the young woman's devotion and stated that the moment in which "we learn of the death of our faithful vassals" offered a poignant reminder of our own mortality.

Notwithstanding her friend's continued eloquence, Milli de Rousset once more refused to rekindle her platonic passion for Sade. This valiant spinster who had been so obsessed by the oppression of women and the mystery of love may simply have been too tired, too ill. In a businesslike tone, she merely responded that she had "a great desire to see . . . and to kiss"[28] the marquis. The following year, Sade again attempted to resurrect Milli's friendship with a lyrical missive. This particular letter, which was written partly in verse, began with the description of a church bell near the Vincennes prison, which made "a hellish sabbath of a sound." It went on to delineate, in plaintively melodic prose and verse, the delusions and temptations suffered by prisoners:

A prisoner always takes everything personally and always imagines that everything that is done has to do with him, that all that is said is said on purpose—I was obsessed with the notion that the damned bell talked to me and told me, very distinctly:

I pity you, pity you,
the only end for you must
be in dust, in dust.

I rose out of my chair in a state of inexpressible wrath, wishing to slaughter the bell ringer, then realized that *the way of vengeance* was still closed. Then I sat down again—took up my pen again—I thought I must respond to that riffraff in his own tone . . . and I said:

From pleasure and joy
You'll have to part,
My heart, my heart

Friars, monks,
Allay the heart's ache
With hands that shake, that shake

But here—what troubles!
The only hand divine
Is mine, is mine

So come, pray come
And with your cunt
My need confront, confront

Half of me, half of me
Turns, so piteous,
Into Tantalus, Tantalus

Ah, what a fate, what a fate!
It's all too trying—
I'm dying, dying

Wheat dies when not tended
At least come and feed
The seed, the seed

> *What martyrdom—what martyrdom*
> *One must suffer and bend*
> *Without end, without end*

The final phrases of the letter recaptured the erotic tone of Sade's and Rousset's earliest correspondence:

> Adieu, beautiful angel, think of me occasionally when you're between two sheets, your thighs open, and your right hand busy . . . looking for fleas. Remember that . . . the other hand must also be active, otherwise there is only half the pleasure.[29]

The marquis's poem is strikingly experimental for its time, precursive of Verlaine in its languid rhythms and its odd blend of sentimentality and libertine audacity. The French reads, in part:

> *Je te plains—je te plains*
> *il n'est plus pour toi de fins*
> *qu'en poudre, qu'en poudre*
>
> *De plaisir, de jouir*
> *il faut donc vous désaisir*
> *mon âme, mon âme*
>
> *Capucin, capucin*
> *rencontre au moins, une main*
> *qui b . . . —qui b . . .*[30]
>
> *Mais ici—quel souci*
> *pour tout bien j'ai dieu merci*
> *la mienne, la mienne*

There is no indication that Rousset ever responded to this renewed expression of Sade's affection. By this time she was far too sick. The following autumn, the bitter north wind of Provence, the mistral, further aggravated her chest pains. Alone in the freezing, dilapidated house she had persisted in tending, she wandered from room to room, pitifully thin, blown about "like a feather" by the brutal wind, sleeping on the kitchen floor to avoid the bitter cold.

The Marquise de Sade's attitude toward this brilliant, learned woman must have been complex. She once described herself to Milli as "a pathetic creature, writing humbly and thinking prosaically,"[31] implying that her feelings toward her friend were tinged by a strong inferiority complex. Yet the two had been united by their mutual devotion to the marquis, and as Milli's health declined, Pélagie worried more than ever about her, begging her to hire a domestic to help her at La Coste, reassuring her of "all the gratitude and appreciation"[32] she and her husband owed her.

As for Rousset's own attitude to her fatal disease, it was very detached and, as ever, wryly stated. "If I were British, I'd shoot myself in the head. Being French . . . I fear death,"[33] she wrote Gaufridy. One wonders what incited her to stay on in the gloom of that decaying house. Her poverty? The depth of her not uncritical devotion? Or might she have been motivated by the most striking trait of her character, her devouring curiosity concerning the nature of love? One can imagine her, candle in hand, searching through all the secret drawers and trunks that Sade had permitted only her to open, bending over some papers that Inspector Marais had searched for but never found. Perhaps she was seeking the secret of that baffling human force which she had never experienced, sexual passion.

Milli de Rousset died in early 1784, alone, the way she had always lived. It was the day after her fortieth birthday. "Few people knew the beauty of her soul,"[34] Pélagie would write upon her death.

Sade's wife protected him so carefully from all perturbing news that he may not have learned about Milli's death until he walked out of prison eight years later. After a year of not hearing from her—he had occasionally sent her greetings through his wife—he seems to have grown resigned to her silence.

For the next several years, Sade would also remain ignorant of the death of another woman he had much loved—his sister-in-law Mlle de Launay. Still unmarried, she had succumbed on May 13, 1781, to smallpox complicated by an abdominal infection, probably peritonitis. For a long while, Mme de Montreuil was inconsolable.

Mlle de Rousset's death occurred just before a momentous new development in Sade's life. On February 29, 1784, at nine P.M., Sade was dragged out of his cell at Vincennes, "as naked as when I left my mother's belly,"[35] or so he claimed, and taken across Paris to an equally notorious royal jail, the Bastille. There was an uncanny coincidence about the date of his transfer: three years earlier, in the spring of 1781, he had calculated that according to his "signals," he would remain in Vincennes until February 29, 1784.

Sade's transfer was not politically motivated. The fortress of Vincennes had been singled out for destruction, and by 1784 only two prisoners were left there besides Sade—a Comte de Solages, also interned by his family on a *lettre de cachet,* and a Comte de Whyte de

Malleville, certified insane. Yet however bitterly the marquis had complained about Vincennes, he vociferously protested his relocation, pleading that he'd gotten quite used to his former dwelling. He raged to Pélagie in his first letter from the Bastille:

> Thirty-four months after . . . having asked for the favor of being left in peace where I was, however dreadfully I was treated there . . . thirty-four months later . . . to have me forcibly carried out, with no forewarning, with all that secretiveness, all that burlesque clandestinity . . . and to take me where? To a jail where I'm a thousand times worse off and a thousand times more oppressed than the miserable place I was in before. Whatever odious lies cloak these somber doings, you'll admit, madame, that such procedures lead me to the peak of my hatred for your infamous family.
>
> I'm in a room half the size of the one I had before. . . . I'm held at bayonet point, as if I'd tried to overthrow Louis XVI! . . .
>
> Well! My very dear and above all very forthright wife, how prettily you deceived me when you promised . . . that it is you who would fetch me [from Vincennes], that I would come out of it a free man and see my children! Is it possible to be a more revolting, outrageous cheat and liar? [36]

XX

The Tower of Liberty:
1784–89

*What right does this crowd of leeches who feed on the
misfortune of the people and . . . cause that pitiable
class—whose only wrong is to be weak and poor—to
lose either honor or life . . . what right, I ask, do such
monsters have to demand virtue? . . . I see them sacrificing millions of the king's subjects to satisfy their
avarice, their ambition, their pride, their greed, their
lust. . . . Whence their immunity? How will they ab-
solve their infamies?*

—Letter to Milli de Rousset, 1783

□

IT IS AN IRONY of French history that the 1780s were the most reform-
minded years of the century. Liberalism had become very fashionable, in
part because the anglomania that began under Louis XV's reign entailed
admiration for a constitutional monarchy. Taking part in what some
historians have called "the collective masochism of the French aristocracy,"[1] many influential members of the nobility devoted themselves to
progressive causes. They included the Marquis de Lafayette, Vicomte
de Beauharnais, Vicomte de Noailles, the Duc de Broglie, Donatien's
kinsmen Comte de Mirabeau and Comte de Clermont-Tonnerre, Mme
de Sade's kinsman the Marquis de Villette, and Louis XVI's first cousin
Philippe, Duc d'Orléans.

Among such reformers, changes in prison legislation were an urgent
priority. There had been particular agitation since the 1770s against the
institution of *lettres de cachet,* which were seldom used after 1780 and
would be declared illegal by the Parlement of Paris in 1788 (Sade had

missed out by just a few years). It was clearly under the pressure of his aristocratic peers that Baron de Breteuil, minister of the King's House (a post that made him responsible for the functioning of royal jails), undertook a case-by-case review, in the last months of 1783, of all prisoners who were being detained on the basis of *lettres de cachet*.

A devious, pragmatic man, Louis-Auguste Le Tonnelier de Breteuil, who had worked hard to become one of Marie-Antoinette's most trusted advisers, was a reactionary at heart; but he occasionally backed progressive measures to remain popular with his peers. He would be praised, for instance, for releasing the adventurer and memoirist Latude, who had been incarcerated for writing threatening letters to Mme de Pompadour. The movement for prison reform had grown so powerful that even though Latude had made a series of sensational escapes during his twenty-eight-year jail term, upon regaining his freedom he became a national hero and was the beneficiary of a public fund.

Breteuil's guidelines for releasing *lettre de cachet* prisoners were roughly the following: The only persons who should receive unconditional life sentences were the certifiably insane. Those jailed for "excessive libertinage"—transgressions a few notches less serious than Sade's—should be treated with indulgence and freed after a term of two or three years. The liberation of those who had committed depravities equal to Sade's, or any other crimes that threatened "public safety," depended above all on "their state of repentance," to use Breteuil's words, "and their explicit resolve . . . concerning the use they would make of their liberty, if it were returned to them."[2]

It is with these conditions in mind that Breteuil had appeared in Sade's jail cell in Vincennes on December 7, 1783, to decide whether this notorious rogue was worthy of release. He was in the company of Sade's old acquaintance M. Le Noir (referred to in the marquis's letters as "a fucking blockhead" and "an archprotector of Parisian bordellos"), who was serving one of his last years as lieutenant general of the French police. There is no eyewitness account of this meeting, but it would not have been in Sade's style to be gracious or accommodating. And one must step into the shoes of the cautious Breteuil, who, having read through reams of Sade's correspondence intercepted by prison censors, had to decide whether this inmate showed the "repentance," and the "resolve" for improvement, that would merit a release.

How would the following passages concerning the futility of the prisoner's punishments, for instance, have fared with Breteuil?

> If my freedom depended on my principles or my inclinations . . . I would sacrifice a thousand lives and a thousand free-

doms. . . . I hold on to those inclinations and principles to the point of fanaticism. . . . The gallows would be there, and I wouldn't change my mind.[3]

All you do is sour my blood, heat my imagination, incite me to curse my family and wish for their death. . . . This rigor is useless, since in the midst of its worst anguish I protest that nothing in the world would be capable of changing *my habits or my way of thinking.*[4]

By constraining me to be atrociously abstinent in sins of the flesh . . . you've led me to create fantasies that I'll need to fulfill. . . . When a horse is too tempestuous, one lets him gallop at will, one does not lock him up in a stable.[5]

Or, even more provocatively:

Well, here's a letter that will doubtless prolong my detention, right? You might well tell those prolongers that their prolongation is a sheer waste of time, for even if they left me here ten years they wouldn't see any improvement, believe me.[6]

Other aspects of Sade's correspondence that were bound to offend the minister were its sexual explicitness and its militant atheism. Breteuil, after all, had to heed the moral tone of his immediate colleagues and superiors. His companion on the Sade visit, Le Noir, was a bourgeois who tended to be far more puritanical than his aristocratic peers. His monarch, Louis XVI, was the most pious and prudish ruler in several centuries of French history. In view of their zeitgeist, how would the following passage have fared?

"I kiss your buttocks and am about to put my wrist to work in their honor!!" Donatien had written Pélagie in 1783, in one of his more affectionate moments. "Don't go telling the Présidente, for she's a good Jansenist who doesn't like the notion of women being *molinized* [French euphemism for sodomized]. She asserts that M. Cordier solely *buggered* her in the *vase of propagation,* and that whoever strays from *the vase* must go boil in hell. And I who was raised by Jesuits . . . cannot agree with *Maman Cordier.*"

Now comes a crucial passage, which sheds much light upon the Sades' own marital practices and which couldn't have escaped Breteuil's attention. (The word "philosophical" must be read in its eighteenth-century meaning: "convinced of Enlightenment principles," "enlightened," "progressive," or even "libertine.") "But you're philosophical, you have a very beautiful alternate side, movement and narrowness in the alternate side and heat in the rectum, which leads me to get along excellently well with you."[7]

And how would the following salvo have fared with God-fearing Catholic gentlemen monitoring prisoners' mores? "Good night. Go and chew on your little God and assassinate your parents," Sade had recently signed off a note to his wife. "I'm going to jerk off, and I believe that I'll have done far less evil than you."[8]

Salaciousness was hardly the only issue. Not an ounce of the "repentance" demanded by Breteuil was found in Sade's frequent polemics concerning the disproportion between his crime and his punishment. He had been deprived of his freedom and his manhood, he alleged, for his offenses against a species of humanity he disdained above all others —prostitutes; he'd been put in jail for "not respecting a whore's ass."[9] "Here's French justice for you!" he stormed. "A gentleman who has served his kingdom well and, if I may say so, has a few qualities is sacrificed—to whom? to whores! One's blood boils, the pen falls out of one's hand, when one reflects on such infamies."[10]

Finally, Sade had impugned the morals of his jailers, repeating ad nauseam the infantile rationale that "I merely did what everyone else in power does." "It is not up to bandy-legged folk to mock cripples," he had written, "not to the blind to govern the one-eyed."[11] Also, "Let those whom destiny raises to the highest tasks have an irreproachable conduct, and they'll gain the right to demand it of us."[12]

And so instead of being liberated at Breteuil's orders, as many hundreds of his compatriots would be that year, the marquis was transferred to the Bastille on a February night in 1784, to continue a jail term that, if history had not intervened, might well have lasted his entire life. For the rest of his days, Sade's written words would seal his fate.

HOWEVER POTENT A SYMBOL it was of royal despotism, the Bastille, which was built in medieval times as a defense against the English, was a relatively small jail. Eighteenth-century iconography greatly exaggerated its size for propaganda reasons, but in fact it had room for only three dozen inmates, and at the time Sade arrived it held only thirteen. Of the eight round towers that punctuated the fortress's outermost wall, the one Sade was assigned to was named "La Liberté."

Like most of the other towers, "Liberté" comprised six floors, each containing one whitewashed, high-ceilinged, octagonal room, some sixteen feet in diameter and twenty feet high. Sade soon brightened his bleak quarters with tapestries and family portraits and with the large bouquets of flowers he requested from Pélagie. Although he would have been the last to admit it, the relative humaneness of the Bastille regimen was attested to by several of his contemporaries. The meals, served at seven A.M., eleven A.M., and six P.M., were said to be far superior to the diet at other prisons. Walks were permitted in the several interior courtyards of the fortress and, with special permission, on top of the towers; eventually Sade was allowed a daily promenade in both these areas.

The trial of Sade's stay at the Bastille would once more be the jail commander. Bernard-René de Launay (no relation to the commander of the Miolans prison) was a dour, efficient fifty-four-year-old career officer who had been born in the Bastille, his father having governed it for many years. Sade lost no time in deriding de Launay as "a so-called marquis . . . whose great-uncle was a stable groom and who thinks he can control his prisoners with a horsewhip, the way his family's stable was ruled."[13] De Launay, in turn, would soon report to police Lieutenant General Le Noir that Sade was of "extremely difficult and violent" character, that he constantly insulted the sentinels, that his letters were filled with "horrors regarding his wife, his family, and us."

Notwithstanding these tensions, Sade would be far happier at the Bastille than he had been at Vincennes, being allowed many more visits from his wife. The spouses would see each other for a few hours every fortnight or so and as often as once a week in the year before the Revolution. And at the Bastille Sade finally found a peer with whom he could talk. The engaging assistant warden, Pierre François du Rivière du Puget, a cultivated, highly progressive scion of the Provençal gentry, offered the marquis the only true companionship he would enjoy during his prison years. Sade and Puget, who had both served in the Seven Years' War, discussed politics, literature, and philosophy, and Sade enjoyed Puget's careful critiques of his writings. Puget seemed to have a soothing influence on his friend. Perhaps because he could rant to his fellow Provençal about most every injustice, real and imaginary, that plagued him, Sade's violent fits of temper decreased at the Bastille. Two years into his stay, he would compose the following quatrain for his comrade:

> *You who like the sun we adore*
> *Spread your beneficent rays*
> *And change what were sorrows before*
> *Into warm-hearted grace.*[14]

The good company of M. du Puget, and Mme de Sade's frequent visits to the Bastille, produced a radical change in Sade's letters to his wife.

Having ceased to serve as his principal emotional outlets, his written communications became far less frequent. They lost the playfulness of his Vincennes letters and turned considerably more morose, consisting chiefly of requests for creature comforts, derisive comments about Pélagie's increasing devoutness, and continued insults to his mother-in-law. In this new phase of the spouses' correspondence, the marquis most often referred to himself in the third person—"he," "one"—and to Pélagie as "madame": "One beseeches you to only buy comedies published this year"; "Mme de Sade is beseeched to instantly send the prisoner . . ." He now addressed his wife as *vous,* employing the familiar *tu* only once in the five remaining years of his jail term.

Seemingly undeterred by this coolness, Pélagie devoted herself as ever to fulfilling her husband's exorbitant requests—chimerical flasks, nonexistent books, rare delicacies, pens of unusual shape ("very spread out at the top, with fine and hard tips"), clothes that he often sent back to her with sarcastic complaints: "I received yesterday an old pair of boots lined with dirty, stitched-up yellow stuff that might have belonged to the first cousin of the distant ancestor of the grandfather of the registrar of Vincennes."[15] Or: "We're sending back to Mme de Sade the useless bonnet; we doubt it would even fit a five-year-old child."[16] Or: "I . . . praise the agility with which you find excuses to have fun in the country while I'm in need of everything."[17]

And the marquis continued to pester his wife with yet more finicky requests: "A vest and matching pants of alpaca cloth, cut in the same style as the cotton pants and vests you sent me in previous winters. . . . A pint each of eau-de-vie, rose water, orange water, and eau de cologne. Six pairs of long cotton stockings, made in Paris and not in Troyes." Pélagie persevered; in June 1784 alone, Bastille archives reveal, she brought her husband twelve packages of strawberries.

But there were new sources of friction between the spouses. Pélagie had been fairly negligent, much of her life, about church rituals. And having been forced by her husband's jealousy into a devout convent life, she now saw herself derided for her growing piety.

> You haven't chosen a date for your visit. Be kind enough to inform us of the one on which you'll grace this site with your presence. The Feast of the Annunciation is in a fortnight. Would that be suitable to your sexts, matins, and nones? But then you can't come on the Annunciation, I don't believe you can, without announcing news at least equal to those which Gabriel whispered to Mary.[18]

Sade must have stepped up his criticism of Pélagie's devoutness, for a few weeks later she protested—ever so delicately—with the following words:

> Fasting at Lent, far from harming my health, is a healthy regimen, and I'm never ill during that period. . . . You fall into another error if you believe that religiousness is melancholy. True piety, you'll see, is not at all alienating or somber. For I shall not abandon my religious commitment when you're liberated. . . . One of its essential duties is to help make happy all those who surround us.[19]

Another letter expresses Pélagie's grief concerning her husband's paranoid accusations.

> How to answer your long letter, dear friend? The more deeply I love you, the more impossible it becomes; my poor heart is too hurt to see you entertain such thoughts. . . . If I thought [your letter] could be seen by anyone, I'd burn it in a minute. Don't fear that it might alter my feelings for you, for those feelings are beyond anything that you could say or do, and the deeper, the more inalterable they are, the sadder I feel to see you give in to such aberrations. . . .

The delicacy of the next sentence is heartbreaking:

> The satisfaction felt upon insulting a person is at least a proof of our existence.[20]

The Sades' marriage was also being strained by the marquis's preoccupation with literary style. He was becoming a prolific man of letters, consuming several dozen notebooks every fortnight. With callous injustice, he often criticized the prosaic phrasings of Pélagie's missives and their emphasis on domestic issues, which, he complained, bored and depressed him.

> You don't seem to have bathed today, for it is impossible to read anything drier than your letter. Lighten up your style, one begs you. One is in jail and one needs to be diverted. The most monotonous things can be written about with gaiety.[21]

You've sent me three pages of idiotic ramblings which the devil would not understand a word of, a thousand times more unintelligible to me than Hebrew or Chinese. But it's in your manner to say stupidities, to have your reason go off track.[22]

The marquise would counter, quite rightly, that his writing style was the source of all their problems—they angered government authorities and impeded his release. "What you write is doing you dreadful harm. . . ."[23] "Curb your writings, I pray you. . . . Above all, don't write or speak out the aberrations . . . through which the world might choose to judge you."[24]

In Sade's eyes, the most insulting words his wife ever wrote him were the following: "What is the use of your futile writings?"[25] ("I'll remember that phrase," Sade wrote angrily in the margin of her letter.)

And yet very occasionally—this may have been a secret of Pélagie's ethereal devotion to him—the marquis continued to reward his wife with sentiments of great delicacy, gratitude, and concern. He wrote her that upon being liberated, one of his greatest consolations would be "the very soothing satisfaction of having you all to myself . . . and dedicating the little I have left to your needs, to your desires, to the unique charm of knowing you are all mine."[26] Similar emotions are expressed in the following note, which thanks Pélagie for a portrait of herself she sent him.

Certain things offer one such pleasure that words fail to be adequate to our emotions. The soul is too moved; it needs to fold back upon itself awhile to enjoy all that it's feeling. . . . Such are the sentiments of one who thanks you for the delicious present you've just offered him . . . cherished and divine gift, which will offer constantly increased emotions and, in spite of evildoers, will sow thousands of ever renewed flowers upon his life's thorns.

He kisses you and will thank you even more fully when he will be able to hug you in his arms.[27]

During his term at the Bastille, Sade still wrote letters in which he took on the role of the Infinitely Concerned Husband. One such missive is worth quoting at length because it exposes the rage and perhaps the guilt Sade felt whenever he realized that his destitute family was being denied the privileges suiting their noble rank.

So now I've learned the reason for that excessive heat you suffer from, that horrible state you're in, each time you come to see me: it's because you come on foot, like a street vendor, like a street whore. . . . And your parents suffer this, and your sluttish servants don't restrain you! What vileness! What infamy! . . . I have only one thing to say: if you happen to arrive once more in that state, I swear on all that is most sacred . . . that I'll go back up immediately to my cell and never in my life come down to see you again. What is the motive that incites you to such disgrace? If you truly felt friendship for me, wouldn't you safeguard yourself, wouldn't you realize that my only happiness, my only hope, is to find you again in good health someday? Why do you want to mock this dear and sole hope of my life by risking to kill yourself as you're doing? A woman alone, on foot, out in the streets?? There might be a drunk . . . a stone could be hurled at you by some riffraff . . . a roof tile might fall on your head. . . . In truth you must be mad, but mad, undescribably mad, to take such chances. . . . And have you thought of the worry they cause me? Isn't my situation piteous enough without you aggravating it yet further by the worries that such imprudences cause me? . . . Don't protest that it's all for the sake of exercise. When a woman of your station needs to exercise, she goes for walks in gardens; many in Paris have been created for that purpose; and she does not pay her visits on foot. . . . It is proved that a day does not go by that someone doesn't perish from having an accident in the streets of Paris.

The next and last lines display a selflessness extremely unusual to the author.

Is it my expenses that constrain you, and must we both refuse ourselves everything? . . . Well, count on me; I'll suffer from them all alone, these privations, I'll go without everything, I'll eat only bread and sleep on the floor, in order to be sure that you lack nothing. . . . Allow me some peace, I beg you; let me know that you swear that you'll never come again on foot.[28]

How long could Pélagie continue to tolerate such brusque alternations of derision, deep affection, and violent rage?

XXI

Reading and Writing: The Budding Novelist

French citizens, strike the first blows. . . . Replace the religious inanities which you're imposing on the minds of your children with excellent social principles. . . . Instead of futile prayers . . . let them learn their responsibilities to society . . . let them know that happiness consists in making others as fortunate as we would wish to be ourselves.

—*Philosophy in the Boudoir*

☐

THE LIBRARY Sade assembled at Vincennes and the Bastille would eventually number some six hundred books and was of striking variety. It included the classics that had surrounded him since his childhood at Abbé de Sade's—Homer, Virgil, Lucretius, Montaigne, Tasso, Ariosto, the *Contes* of La Fontaine, Boccaccio's *Decameron*. There were the science titles essential to any Enlightenment gentleman: an "Essay on Fluids," "The Elements of Physics," Buffon's *Natural History*. Books of fiction and drama abounded: the collected works of Beaumarchais, Marivaux, and Voltaire, translations of Defoe's *Robinson Crusoe* and Fielding's and Smollett's novels, and some twenty other fictions published between 1777 and 1783. Of that period he particularly favored *Manon Lescaut* by Abbé Prévost, whom he referred to as "the French Richardson" and considered to be the greatest novelist of his time. We know from Sade's journals that Choderlos de Laclos's immensely popular *Les Liaisons Dangereuses* also had a considerable impact on him, but he never expressed an opinion on it in his correspondence, and it is possible that he was very jealous of this colleague's considerable fame. Travel chronicles, such as Captain Cook's and Bougainville's, were numerous in Sade's library, as were historical works: a history of Malta, of the Wars of Hanover, of the thirteenth-century War of Beauvais; an "Account of Modern History from the Fall of the Western Empire Until the Peace of Westphalia" and a twenty-eight-volume set of the history of France. Sade's library also included curiosities such as a history of vampires and a translation of Shakespeare's *King Lear*—somewhat unusual among readers of the marquis's generation, since Shakespeare would not be staged in France for another four decades.

Over the years, Pélagie had also sent her husband the erotica he'd requested ("a few novels that are rather free and . . . you understand me well . . . bring me pretty thoughts in my solitude"[1]). Yet another favorite —Sade had always been fascinated by religious thought—were the sermons of Father Massillon, a popular devotional author, which elicited the following comment from Sade: "How I love Massillon's Sermons! They elevate me, they enchant me, they delight me. . . . What purity! What morality! What a felicitous mixture of simplicity and force!"[2]

However, to the great displeasure of this voracious reader, one of the two contemporary works he most desired—Jean-Jacques Rousseau's *Confessions,* which was published posthumously, and to some scandal, in 1782—was denied him by prison authorities. This incited many a sardonic comment from the prisoner, who had long been a devotee of Rousseau's fiction, even though he loathed his Deism. "Alas! They do me a great honor to think that a Deist author can have a bad influence on me. . . . I much wish I were still at that stage!" he wrote to Pélagie. "Rousseau can be a dangerous author for heavy bigots of your kind and becomes an excellent book for me. Jean-Jacques is to me what *The Imitation of Christ* is to you."[3]

Another much desired work Sade had trouble getting in jail was Baron d'Holbach's *Système de la Nature,* an extremist summation of Enlightenment materialism (he would plagiarize from it extensively, inserting large hunks of Holbach's text into his fictional protagonists' polemics against the notions of Soul or Deity). Referring to this work as "truly and incontestably the basis of my philosophy," a book he would "defend unto martyrdom,"[4] Sade even begged Pélagie to borrow a copy of it from the freethinking Marquis de Villette, even though he'd earlier ordered her to shun his company.

During his first two years at Vincennes, Sade's literary efforts had focused on revising his Italian travel notes. But he then began to write a series of verse plays, the genre he had felt most drawn to since his youth. He thought so highly of his dramas that he even considered sending them to the Comédie Française, where they could be staged professionally. One must emphasize that Sade's fondest aspiration, throughout his life, was to enjoy a widespread and *respectable* success as a dramatist. He looked on such an achievement as a means of social redemption. "It would doubtless be a great pleasure for me to see my works played in Paris," he wrote his former tutor Abbé Amblet shortly after his transfer to the Bastille, "and if they were successful, a reputation for being a man of intellect might perhaps lead people to forget my youthful trespasses and would in some way rehabilitate me."[5]

He sent all his plays to his wife and Amblet, whom he looked on as his most astute literary critics. "Your drama is excellent," Pélagie wrote him about the first of these works, *Le Capricieux*, "the characters are well drawn. . . . This work is sure to be applauded."[6] Of the four plays he would write in 1782, she preferred one called *Deux Jumelles*, which she judged to be "very honest and quite fitting to a convent."[7] The next few plays—he would write some twenty plays in jail, all of them as decorous as Pélagie implied—were received with less enthusiasm.

Some weeks later, Amblet made a specific assessment, most of it negative, of some other plays. The marquis did not take well to criticism, and the abbé's "venomous" comments led him to sulk for a while. Ironically, it is this setback in his self-esteem as a "respectable" dramatist that led Sade to try his hand at prose fiction and, ultimately, pornography. He announced to Amblet that he had qualms about his gift for drama and planned to "abandon Molière's brush for that of Aretino,"[8] by which he meant that he would turn from the dramatic genre to erotica.

The very first of these efforts was the monumental catalogue of sexual perversions known as *Les 120 journées de Sodome (The 120 Days of Sodom)*, written at the Bastille in 1785. Its composition was as bizarre as the book itself. In order to ensure its safety, Sade transcribed it, in nearly microscopic handwriting, onto a series of five-inch-wide sheets of paper, which he glued together into a roll forty-nine feet long. Such a minuscule folio, tightly wound, could be easily hidden in the crevices of a prison cell's wall. Working on it from seven to ten each evening, he finished transcribing his last draft in thirty-seven days, an amazing speed for a manuscript of some 250,000 words.

The virulent atheism and systematic pessimism that had character-ized Sade's thinking since his youth are displayed in *120 Days* on a titanic scale, magnified by the writer's gruesome sexual imagination. His four central characters are powerful and depraved men, grown rich during Louis XIV's military campaigns, who hold a months-long orgy in a remote medieval fortress in the Black Forest. A duke, a bishop, a magis-trate, and a financier, they represent the four social groups responsible for maintaining law and order in France and, at least symbolically, for keeping Sade in jail. These thoroughly bisexual villains; who like many of Sade's fictional personages take women "from both sides" but prefer boys, rant on a great deal about the inferiority of female sexual organs and all aspects of the procreative, maternal impulse (reflecting on Sade's writings, the philosopher Gilles Deleuze sees sadism as "an active negation of the mother and an exaltation of the father who is beyond all laws").[9] They are accompanied by their four wives and a harem of twenty-eight young victims of both genders: although in the totality of Sade's oeuvre the majority of victims tend to be female, a pattern of persecution that makes his books intolerable to most women, in *120 Days* the violence is gender neutral. Also attending the house party are four aging female storytellers whose debauched lives offer a narrative frame —along the line of *The Thousand and One Nights* or Boccaccio's *Decameron,* two favorite texts of Sade's—for the hundreds of sexual deviations and perversions described in the novel.

As we suffer through the book's icy, monstrous orgies, whose diversions range from bestiality to coprophilia and the most repellent forms of torture, we often hear the author's voice striving to clarify his intent. He claims to have an edifying purpose: he wishes to instruct his readers, and lead them to hate vice all the more, by revealing all the "secret horrors" that men experience "when their fantasies take fire." He asserts that the writer who could "delineate and categorize these perversions would provide as fine a work on morals as one could wish for, and perhaps the most interesting."[10] He wants to describe "in the greatest detail and in due order every one of debauchery's extravagances, all its divagations, all its ramifications."[11] Such encyclopedic aspirations—the claim that *all* branches of knowledge, down to sexual perversions, can be exhaustively categorized, that he can compose a definitive Dictionary of Perversions—reveal Sade as a true child of the Enlightenment.

But no writer in history has depicted more nauseating vices. And in reaching toward the furthest frontiers of the moral imagination—toward what Sainte-Beuve would later call the "literary Kamchatka"—Sade reveals an impulse far less typical of his time: his manic need for extreme sensations. Through these libertines who reappropriate, behind the walls of their sumptuous enclave, the unlimited power once conferred on them by the feudal system, he wishes to jolt the world by presenting "the most impure tale that has ever been written since the world exists."[12] In this stated aim, if in no other, Sade succeeds. However prophetic it is of Krafft-Ebing and Freud, *120 Days* is the crudest, most repellent fictional dystopia ever limned, the creation of a borderline psychotic whose scatological fantasies have grown all the more deranged in the solitude and rage of his jail cell. Written in a glacially terse, bureaucratic style and totally devoid of any cosmeticization of the sex act, it is certainly not the kind of "erotica" that intends to arouse the reader sexually, for its repugnance makes it far more conducive to chastity (as Simone de Beauvoir puts it, Sade's "perverse bucolics have the grim austerity of a nudist colony"). *120 Days* is, rather, the brutally dehumanizing kind of pornography that annihilates the human person, reducing it to a disposable pleasure machine. Lacking the vengefulness that is the wellspring of Sade's writings, the eighteenth century's truly erotic works, like those of Sade's kinsman Mirabeau, who wrote several scabrous novels while jailed at Vincennes, seem like valentines in comparison with *120 Days*. And even the most brazen scenes of contemporary pornography seem dainty after a reading of Sade's first major text.

Yet there are passages of *120 Days* that can fascinate us through their monumental recklessness and daring; their awesome ritualism, which recalls the Aztecs' human sacrifices; their regression to a primeval, cannibalistic stage not yet curbed by the most fundamental taboos; their modernist transgression of all the norms of what we still call "art" and "literature."

As a historical curiosity, *120 Days* is also notable for the revolutionary and indeed sadistic relationship it creates between the reader and the author, who bullies his audience as ruthlessly as his protagonists victimize their captives. For those who take to Sade's work, his fascination comes from the dual movement of attraction and revulsion he exerts on us, a relationship that forgoes all traditional narrative "pleasure" and deals instead with insult, alienation, and boredom. The critic Georges Bataille suggests that this very boredom of Sade's texts, which are "more like prayer books than books of entertainment," gives them their significance.[13] It is all these aspects of *120 Days* that have exerted a morbid influence on Flaubert, Swinburne, Baudelaire, Apollinaire, Octavio Paz, Luis Buñuel, Pier Paolo Pasolini, and numerous other artists of the past century, not to speak of the entire surrealist movement and some of the most macabre cultural productions of our own time.

Sade looked on his 1785 version of *120 Days* as no more than a working draft. Its intended length (one trembles at the thought) was double or triple the existing work. Although one might venture the guess that it repelled even *him* too much (Sade as masochist was constantly trying to terrify himself, and in *120 Days* the pain principle might have exceeded his pleasure in it), we may never learn why he did not try to finish it in jail. Neither can we guess whether he would have dared to publish this gruesome text if it had remained in his possession throughout his lifetime. To his chagrin, the manuscript would disappear after the seizure of the Bastille; it was not officially published for almost a century and a half, until the 1930s.

The Bastille, curiously, seems to have acted as Sade's muse. His prolificity during his last years at the fortress is attested to by the astonishing number of writing implements he requested from Pélagie. On one particular visit she brought him nineteen notebooks; two weeks later, she brought him twenty more, and twelve pens. He wrote several other major works while at the Bastille: the final draft of the polemical essay *Dialogue Between a Priest and a Dying Man;* the novella *Eugénie de Franval;* an early draft (written in a fortnight in 1787) of his famous *Justine,* initially entitled *The Adversities of Virtue,* and the relatively chaste novel *Aline et Valcour,* which demands our attention because of the extensive commentary it elicited from the Marquise de Sade.

Aline et Valcour is a sprawling novel with three distinct story lines. The central narrative, that of Aline and Valcour proper, is a tragic family saga recounted in the epistolary style popularized by Richardson's *Clarissa.* The secondary narrative is an account of voyages to exotic lands— in the general style of Swift's *Gulliver's Travels* or Montesquieu's *Persian Letters*—undertaken by an enlightened traveler called Sainville. The third subplot, and the weakest, concerns the adventures of a persecuted young woman, Léonore, sister of Aline and wife of Sainville, who manages to preserve her virtue by cheating and lying.

In the primary narrative, the mutual love of Aline and the penniless aristocrat Valcour is abetted by Aline's virtuous and devout mother but thwarted by the heroine's debauched magistrate father, the Président de Blamont. A cynical materialist motivated solely by his quest for perverted pleasures, Blamont wants to marry his daughter to a wealthy, equally corrupt lecher, Dolbourg, in order to commit incest with her at his whim. After all attempts to kidnap Aline or assassinate Valcour fail, Blamont poisons his wife in order to deprive his daughter of her only remaining ally, leading the ever righteous heroine, Aline, to commit suicide. Sade, who relished creating extreme contrasts as much as he enjoyed eliciting extreme sensations, seemed particularly proud of the vast spectrum of good and evil limned in this work and boasted that "such singularly contrasting [characters] had never before been drawn by the same pen." [14]

It is through *Aline et Valcour*'s second subplot, the traveler Sainville's visit to the mythical kingdom of Tamoé, that Sade first elaborates on the anarchic sociopolitical beliefs that color his entire oeuvre. Tamoé is a socialist utopia, ruled by a benevolent vegetarian king called Zamé, which "should serve as model to all of Europe." In describing his utopia, Sade emphasizes that the duty of the good king is to advise his people rather than rule them. Since such institutions as jails and the death penalty run counter to the spirit of a happy society, they should be immediately abolished. The overthrow of any ruler is justified if his reign limits his subjects' freedom.

This overlong, occasionally interesting novel, which Sade worked on between 1785 and 1788, would be well suited to the ideals of the French Revolution. And just before publishing it, in 1795, Sade was able to radicalize it further with many patriotic grace notes. "The atrocities committed by France's monarchs," the sage King Zamé tells Sainville, "will compel its citizens to throw off the yoke of despotism and enjoy a free and republican government." [15] "A great revolution is brewing in your country," the sage speculates. "France is sated with your sovereigns' crimes . . . their debauches and their ineptitude; it is sated with despotism, about to break its chains." [16]

Some twenty pages of Mme de Sade's observations on *Aline et Valcour,* which she sent her husband in June 1789, on the eve of the Revolution, have survived. They offer some perspicacious literary insights. The marquise begins her critique by highlighting those aspects of her husband's book that impress her the most, such as his gift for dialogue and characterization, but she soon quibbles with his need to expose the fundamental evil of mankind through the baseness of his villains:

> One must expose [such persons], so your argument goes, in order to hate them and defend oneself from them. There's truth in that, but when this becomes the only goal of the work, there's a point at which the process [of depicting evil] must stop. . . . Such details make [the book] unreadable to honest people, and that's a pity. . . . You have charming and virtuous characters, superb maxims and reflections, accurate and just. It's too bad that you let them shine by powerful effects that only desolate and revolt [the reader]. . . .

The marquise elaborates on that point, criticizing the grossly melodramatic effects achieved by the contrast between Aline's vile father, Blamont, and the rectitude of his wife and daughter.

> Madame de Blamont, drowning in her sorrow, is too credulous, and I already foresee that her heart, her desire to reconcile everyone, will lead her to stupid actions. . . . It is improbable that [M. de Blamont] does not perceive his wife's and daughter's virtue, and he should sense that his odious

behavior will be an obstacle to his goals. . . . Being of too extreme a character, he unfortunately loses originality.

Pélagie has praise for her husband's depictions of the utopian state visited by Sainville and of its benevolent ruler, Zamé.

> The benevolence, the kindness, and the fine manners of the island's inhabitants inject balm and peace into the reader's temper and ideas. One hopes to be finally rid of the horrors glimpsed earlier [in the book]. . . . The details of [Sainville]'s arrival . . . , however simple, incite enthusiasm and admiration. . . . One devours [the book] as if starving; that's the effect it had on me. . . . The description of this island is charming; the ruler so affable, in every way so guileless. . . . I'd be loath to find a fault with Zamé. A prince as perfect as he will never have any defect.

The marquise goes on to state her strong reservations about the extreme ethical relativism that prevails in Sade's anarchist utopia, and uses *Aline et Valcour* as a springboard to expose the vast differences of opinion concerning morality and religion that are increasingly heightening the tensions in their marriage. "Truth," she reminds him, is that which contributes to "the maximum happiness of the people." Society direly needs laws, because crimes are a reality of life and run counter to the public good.

> When you arrest an assassin, a madman, what would you do with him? . . . It's not to buy back the life of a dead man that one punishes an assassin with the death penalty; it's to protect society from someone who is destroying it, since he might kill yet another man. It's true that the evil is doubled, but in allowing [the assassin] to live, one could multiply evil to infinity.

Pélagie also detests Sade's cult of ruthlessness, his ethic of survival of the fittest, tenets strikingly precursory, to the contemporary reader, of Nietzsche's. She states that she does not want to confront him on the issue of religion ("Since we do not agree on that issue, it would lead to discussions that you don't like"). She reminds him that "only savages equate ferocity with courage" and delicately compares his egotism to Christian altruism, to "that greatness of soul which leads some to risk their lives . . . to bring aid to the helpless." The marquise also counters

the crude Sadeian materialism (derived from two of his favorite Enlightenment *philosophes,* La Mettrie and Holbach) that denies the existence of
soul and reduces all universal happenings to the organization of matter.
"How could the amalgamation of matter produce a soul, which thinks,
reasons, and deducts such contrary ideas? Nature cannot produce spirit:
what is created is always inferior to its creator." And she offers a color-
fully pious argument for the existence of the human soul.

> The soul is immaterial and does not die when it separates
> itself from the body. . . . The soul does not grow like the body,
> but, enclosed in that little body, it develops as it grows larger,
> for he who shaped the soul allows it to evolve only at the rate
> and in the manner he has prescribed: be [the soul] that of a
> madman, an imbecile, a relatively enlightened being, its prog-
> ress is governed by laws that we cannot understand any more
> than an earthenware pot can understand its maker, who must
> exist because the pot has been made.

Finally, with great common sense, Pélagie takes her husband to task
for throwing out the baby with the bathwater when he denies the validity
of all laws. Religious as well as secular governments have indeed had
their evil excesses, led as they are by individuals who, like all human
beings, can be carried away by their passions. But "the abuse of an
institution," she reminds him, "does not make that institution immoral
per se." "King Zamé should be led by the following maxim," she suggests to the author. " 'I would like to have my hands tied for the committing of evil and free to do good.' "[17]
One marvels at the way Sade, in his consecutive writing of *120 Days,*
Aline et Valcour, and *Justine,* alternated pornographic and chaste fiction.
This oscillation may well correspond to two contradictory and equally
powerful impulses in his character—the need to shock and the need to
gain social approval. It is also possible that the frustrated society dramatist resorted to smut, a highly remunerative industry in his time, with a
view to making money when he got out of jail. Whatever his incentives,
to the end of his days he would vaunt *Aline et Valcour* and his virtuous
dramas as the best of his works and deny that he ever authored pornographic novels or any works even vaguely off color.

IN PART BECAUSE of Pélagie's careful critiques and constant encouragement, by 1788 Sade took himself seriously enough as a writer to draw up
a catalogue raisonné of the works he had written during his jail term (less

than half of them would survive the coming revolution). The catalogue comprised eight novels and volumes of short stories, sixteen historical novellas, two volumes of prose essays, an edition of his diary notes, and some twenty plays, with enticing titles such as *The Ruse of Love, The Siege of Algiers, Azelis, or the Punished Coquette, The Enchanted Tower, The Unsuspecting Husband*. He was now thinking of himself as a full-time writer. When his oculist had decreed that he should reduce eye strain by taking up knitting, his reply was that he wished the doctor to prescribe "some occupation worthier of a man of letters." [18]

Throughout these years of literary creativity, Pélagie served as not only her husband's principal literary adviser but also his researcher. (Amblet disappeared from the marquis's correspondence in 1784, and it is possible that he died that year.) Sade's complex requests for information are displayed in the following note, which demands that his wife provide him with details on several towns in Spain and Portugal where he was setting parts of *Aline et Valcour*.

> In what language must I tell you that I only need, for Lisbon, the name of a hotel, the name of its manager, the name of the street where it is situated and of the buildings that surround it; same details for Toledo and Madrid, and more-over, for Toledo, the names of two or three elegant streets in the courtesans' part of town and the names of the principal promenades of those three towns. And also some details on the forms of Spanish currency, and information on whether the ways of torturing nobles is the same in Spain as it is here; and how it differs from ours." [19]

One is at a loss to know how or where Pélagie could have gleaned such information. Perhaps because of her limited capacity for research, Sade's narratives of foreign lands are extremely haphazard in their details. The rivers of his African landscapes, for instance, are edged with lilies, jonquils, and tulips.

XXII

The Children, the Future

*Perfidious abuse of tyranny! . . . O Frenchmen, when
will you rebel against these horrors? When, weary of
slavery . . . will you lift your head above the chains
with which these crowned scoundrels bind you, and
reclaim the freedom for which nature destined you?*

—*Juliette*

□

BY 1784, SADE'S CHILDREN, whom he had not seen for seven years, had
become adolescents. By the time the marquis was transferred to the
Bastille, his eldest son, Louis-Marie, had grown tall and slender, just as
his father had predicted. A star student, he was reading Boileau and
Pliny's *The Ruses of War,* memorizing passages of Horace every morning, and studying fencing, dance, music, and drawing. As for his brother,
Donatien-Claude-Armand, his schoolwork seemed to have improved
and he showed enthusiasm for literature, mathematics, and dance. Their
mother was extremely proud of them but continued to worry about her
very plain daughter. She described Madeleine-Laure as being "choleric
as a turkey," "absolutely . . . her father's character,"[1] and, even more
harshly, "backward in every way," "a big lazy lout" devoid of any "natural gifts."[2]

In early 1784, just as he was being transferred to the Bastille, the
marquis confronted his first major crisis with his children. Louis-Marie,
having turned seventeen, was expected to join the army. Admission into
a prestigious regiment was a far more potent token of social status in the
eighteenth century than admission into an Ivy League college has ever
been on these shores; since the time of his older son's birth, Sade had
taken it for granted that he would serve in the same elite regiment Sade
had belonged to in his youth—the Carabiniers de Monsieur, which had

traditionally been headed by the king's brother, Comte de Provence. And so he flew into a rage when he heard that the Montreuils had arranged a lieutenancy for his son in only the second-most-prestigious military unit in France, the Régiment de Soubise. The first letter Sade wrote to his wife on this issue was filled with somber warnings.

> If you allow him to enter [that regiment] against my will, I give you my word of honor that I will force him to leave it. . . . Consider the chain of misfortunes that would result from your mother's stubbornness. . . . I absolutely refuse to see him serve anywhere but in the Carabiniers. I've had that planned for him ever since his eyes were opened. . . . I beg you to forbid him to write me until he swears that he'll obey me. [3]

Dismissing the fact that he was one of the most discredited noblemen in France and that only families of impeccable social standing could hope to enlist their sons in the Carabiniers, Sade confronted his son directly.

> I've just learned, sir, that your mother's relatives are planning a sublieutenancy for you in one of the lowest-ranking infantry regiments in France. I forbid you, sir, to accept this commission. . . . If notwithstanding my explicit refusal you still accept it and I learn that you're weak-willed enough to obey relatives to whom you owe no allegiance while your father is still alive, you can wish me adieu forever, for I shall never see you again. . . . I curse you with my malediction if within two months you do not reassure me, in writing, that you will carry out my orders.
>
> The Comte de Sade, your father [4]

It is significant that the prisoner reverts to his official title of "Count," which he has avoided for the past decades, at the very moment when he most needs to stress his legal authority over his children. To further emphasize his status as head of his family, for the first time in his life he addresses his wife as "Madame la Comtesse." [5]

For Sade's rage concerning the issue of his son's army service went far beyond his loathing of the Montreuil clan, who in his view had assumed undue influence over his offspring. His loss of paternal prerogative was the most potent reminder of his powerlessness. This was a time of history, after all, when children could be disowned, or jailed under *lettres de cachet*, as Mirabeau had been at the age of twenty-seven, if they failed to follow their father's orders. For a man as controlling as Sade, losing jurisdiction over a seventeen-year-old son must have been the most bitter of blows. This crisis led him to make explicit, in a letter to Pélagie, all the ways in which he planned to assert authority over his children in the future.

> I hope, madame, that you will have communicated to your parents the substance of our recent conversation concerning the ridiculous employment to which they've engaged your son. I urgently beg your mother not to meddle with my children. I have no need whatsoever of her little airs. . . . To place my son into military service, I only need my liberty. . . . I've written and told you a thousand times that neither of my children will leave either their school, or their home, without my spending a good year with him. . . . Neither one nor the other will join any regiment without having learned to ride a horse properly and without being assigned a valet of my own choice.[6]

Sade went on to set more conditions concerning his sons' future. Although Mme de Montreuil had probably been planning a "beautiful marriage" for them a few years thence, he reminded Pélagie that he would never consent to any wedding plans until they were twenty-six (the age at which young men legally became "adults"). He also asserted that it had always been his intention to live in Provence after his release from jail and he fully expected his children to "follow" him there. Indeed, he specified that neither of his sons could marry "elsewhere than in *Lyons* or *Avignon*," and in no case could they ever settle in Paris, a dictate that reflected his abiding love for southern France and his dislike for the Parisian region, which in his eyes incarnated the despotism of the court. "A *père de famille* is the master of his children," he sternly reminded Pélagie, "and it is impossible to strip him of that authority."[7]

Throughout the rest of his jail term, the marquis would elaborate on the issue of his older son's marital prospects. He would express rage, and a childlike jealousy, at the notion that his offspring might rehabilitate their social standing through fine alliances, while their father would be left to languish and die in jail. This confronts us with a complex nuance of Sade's emotions toward his sons: he was serving time for the principal purpose of rescuing their standing in society! He who had once been the Présidente's and the Marquise de Sade's most beloved "child," whose liberation and happiness had been a central goal of those two women's lives, had been totally displaced in their affections by his "brats." The narcissistic infant lurking at the core of Sade's personality often shouted out its jealous rage, as it did in the following letter to Pélagie, with its melodramatic projection of his impending death:

> Here you are, enjoying the sweetness of widowhood, here's your son, M. le Comte, about to inherit. Young, handsome, wealthy, no more father who would cause him to blush. . . . What a marriage, what a settlement! . . . At least a princess . . . [and] that poor little chevalier, who might weep a bit because he gains nothing by my death and he's such a gentle child. . . . But he doesn't know me. How old was he? Four years old at the most when I left him. . . . If such major issues leave you a second, Mme la Marquise, to think of the one to whom you owe those very offspring for whose sake you're sacrificing your husband, you'll recall that it's been a year since I haven't been allowed to take air.[8]

Sade's attempt to control his sons did not succeed. Louis-Marie ignored his father's wishes and joined the Soubise regiment. This defiance was all the more insulting to the marquis because it had been masterminded by Pélagie's brother-in-law, a veteran of that corps. Sade held firm to his threat of stopping all correspondence with his offspring, for there seems to have been no more communication between them until after the Revolution. And his letters to Pélagie would continue to be tinged with resentment and jealousy concerning their children. "The needs of your son . . . come at a very bad moment, since it's the time when because of the change of season I need [money] even more than he does," he wrote Pélagie when she mentioned the debts Louis-Marie, following in his father's footsteps, was running up during his army leaves. "He needs to be told that . . . as long as his father is at the Bastille, the pleasures of Paris are not suitable for him."[9]

In 1787, on the tenth anniversary of his incarceration at Vincennes, Sade was once more legally stripped of all authority over his children and over his funds—standard procedure after ten years of a prisoner's "absence" from society. The lieutenant governorship of four provinces that he'd inherited from his father, which provided a trickle of revenue, had been sold a decade earlier to a distant Provençal cousin, Comte de Sade d'Eyguières, into whose family his younger son would eventually marry. As for control of the marquis's estates and the guardianship of his children, those prerogatives were handed over to Pélagie and to his one surviving uncle, the indolent eighty-three-year-old Richard-Jean-Louis de Sade, commander of the Order of Malta, the pompous windbag who had plundered the Saumane estate two decades earlier.

□   □

WHERE HAS the Présidente de Montreuil, who betrayed the prisoner by "sacrificing" him to his own children, been all this time? Confident that his jail term would last his lifetime, she had ceased all interference in his affairs. Having long mourned her favorite child, Mlle de Launay, she had spent the last few years trying to restore the social status of her grandsons, Louis-Marie and Donatien-Claude-Armand, and settle them into their vocations, and in this she succeeded well.

It was a centuries-old tradition in France for the older son to enroll in the army and younger sons to enter religious orders (the very protocol followed by Comte de Sade and his two younger brothers). Now that Louis-Marie had been placed in a fine regiment, the major portion of Mme de Montreuil's correspondence, from 1785 on, focused on her desire to settle Donatien-Claude-Armand in the military and religious order of the Knights of Malta, of which his great-uncle was a high-ranking member.

The Knights of Malta, also known as the Knights Templar or the Order of Saint John of Jerusalem, was founded in the eleventh century, at the beginning of the Crusades, with a dual purpose: to wage war on the Muslims and to establish a network of hostels for pilgrims who fell ill on the way to the Holy Land. Grateful gentlemen healed in these refuges bestowed part of their funds and their estates on the order, which in a few centuries became immensely wealthy and eventually acquired the island of Malta, which they ruled as an independent state. After the Muslim threat receded, the knights continued to dabble in charitable works and to nurture their large domains throughout Europe.

It was these landholdings that were at the heart of Mme de Montreuil's strategy: they provided a very lucrative means of livelihood for those privileged members of the order who could attain to the rank of commander and, even higher, grand prior, the status achieved by Richard-Jean-Louis de Sade in the last year of his life. There were six hundred seventy-one commanderies and twenty-two grand priories in Europe on the eve of the Revolution, and the Présidente's obsessive goal was to have her grandson rise in the ranks and achieve the management of some sumptuous estate, whose revenues he would share with the order. As Grand Prior de Sade's indulgent life had proved, this was as comfortable a livelihood as a European gentleman could enjoy.

But the ascent to those ranks was demanding. As with all privileged clerical and military posts (since the mid-eighteenth century, every bishop and army officer in France was a member of the aristocracy), even the lower ranks of the Knights of Malta were reserved to those with impeccable credentials of nobility. So throughout the 1780s Mme de

Montreuil devoted herself to assembling the records needed to validate four generations of her grandson's patrician lineage—marriage contracts, certificates of baptism and of baronial ownerships. Great-uncle Richard-Jean-Louis, who took years to answer any letter, constantly had to be begged to lobby the Order of Malta for his nephew's son. Attestations of Donatien-Claude-Armand's splendid character and Christian resolve had to be documented and formalized. The young man was finally certified as Chevalier of Malta in 1785.

In order to remain in the order, however, a knight had to take a vow of chastity at the age of twenty-five. On this issue young Sade, who had been happily deflowered in his midteens by a Provençal cousin, seemed to be extremely undecided. "Is it wise to make such vows," the youth wrote his mother, to whom he was deeply devoted, ". . . when I could get along with a less substantial career that would still be adequate? . . . I'm permitting myself to state my reasons," he continued obediently, "and henceforth I'll do whatever you wish." [10]

In 1788, within three years of Donatien-Claude-Armand's entering the Knights of Malta, his great-uncle the grand prior would suffer a severe stroke. And the Sade-Montreuil clan would be discomfited to learn that he had never lifted a finger to arrange a commandership for his nephew, nor had he fulfilled his promise to provide for him in his will. Great-uncle's only stipulated legacy to Donatien-Claude-Armand, in fact, was his dog.

Yet amid these busy family dealings, the Présidente's life, from the mid-1780s on, was graced with a new kind of peace: her increasingly cordial relations with her daughter Pélagie. The women's correspondence, in these years, shows no remains of tension. In a letter to her mother in September 1786, for instance, Pélagie chats at length about the slender revenue due from her husband's lands in Provence and about a woman guest she had met at the grand prior's who seemed to wield considerable power over the host and drank "at least half a bottle of champagne more than the rest [of the guests]" [11] over dinner. "Do accept, my dear Mama, my most tender and respectful homage," she ended her missive.

In the decades-long rivalry between the Présidente and the Marquis de Sade over Pélagie's affections, the iron lady seemed finally to be getting the upper hand.

XXIII

A Royal Scandal and
Its Aftermaths

*O my God, I have only one favor to ask of you, and
notwithstanding my prayers, you're not according it
to me: This grace, this insignificant favor, would be,
O my God, not to choose my wardens among men
even more vicious than I, not to deliver a man capable only of very trifling and slight trespasses to hardened riffraff who, mocking your laws, enjoy
transgressing them at all moments of the day. Place
my destiny, O my God, in the hands of the virtuous;
they are your image on earth, and only those who
respect it should be allowed to reform vice.*

—"Evening Prayer to God," Vincennes, 1782

REVOLUTIONS ARE BRED not only by economic crises—the last years of
the French monarchy were acutely plagued by those—but also by gossip
and calumny. In 1785, the greatest royal scandal of the century, one that
would have a direct impact on Sade's prison routine, further undermined
the ancien régime. Known as the Diamond Necklace Affair, it starred
the luxury-loving Marie-Antoinette and featured a supporting cast of
swindlers and charlatans of legendary proportions.

At the center of the imbroglio were the country's highest prelate,
the notoriously vain, frivolous, and popular Cardinal de Rohan, grand
almoner of France, the scion of one of its wealthiest and most venerable
families; a deeply indebted Paris jeweler, M. Böhmer, who was desperately trying to sell the world's most expensive diamond necklace to
Marie-Antoinette; and a gang of thieves led by a rapacious adventuress

named Jeanne de La Motte, the illegitimate daughter of a member of the ancient Valois family, who was determined to gain fame and fortune at the court of Versailles. La Motte planned to capitalize on Cardinal de Rohan's desire to gain the queen's favor—the flamboyant prelate had been detested by Marie-Antoinette's family during his tenure as ambassador to Vienna, and the queen shared her relatives' distaste for him.

To this end La Motte persuaded Rohan that she was a close friend of Marie-Antoinette, upon whom she had never even laid eyes, and that she could help him enter into the queen's favor. Forging documents from the queen that promised the prelate an eventual audience, pretending to hand his own letters to her "dear friend" the queen, and emptying his pocket at every turn, La Motte finally arranged a trumped-up encounter between Rohan and Marie-Antoinette. A cocotte was hired to impersonate the queen and, shrouded with thick veils, granted the deliriously happy cardinal a very brief evening meeting in the gardens of Versailles.

Enter Böhmer the jeweler, more desperate than ever to unload his necklace in a time of deepening national crisis. A rivière of 579 diamonds —2,800 carats' worth of them—he had designed it for Mme du Barry, who never bought it because of Louis XV's sudden death. Böhmer had turned to La Motte for help. Couldn't she persuade her "dear friend" the queen to buy the trifle? La Motte was savvy enough to know that the public's plummeting confidence in Louis XVI's leadership, and a national debt of unprecedented proportions, would deter the king from lavishing 1.6 million livres on yet another trinket for his extravagant wife. But La Motte had a brainstorm: Why not persuade Rohan to cement his new friendship with the queen by offering it to her? The cardinal once more fell prey to La Motte's ruse. Another forgery of Marie-Antoinette's handwriting authorized him to make the purchase. The gleaming trinket was then brought to the cardinal, who, besotted with the prospect of being in the queen's good graces, handed it to a minion of La Motte's posing as the queen's messenger; whence it passed, of course, into the adventuress's own hands. She sold the necklace's component stones in London and for a few months lived like a potentate from *The Thousand and One Nights,* acquiring a grand château and so many luxurious furnishings that it took forty-two coaches to carry them.[1]

But from then on La Motte's ploys faltered. She had not counted on the jeweler's diligence. Within weeks, M. Böhmer visited Marie-Antoinette to deliver some far more modest adornments she *had* ordered (only too aware of the public opinion mounting against her, the queen had recently tried hard to be less ostentatious). At their meeting, the jeweler asked her about the diamond necklace she was purchasing with

Rohan's help. "What necklace?" asked Marie-Antoinette. Within a few minutes, the jeweler and the Queen of France learned that they had been the victims of a spectacularly audacious swindle.

The denouement, which occurred a few days later, was as theatrical as any event in that most theatrical of centuries. The queen, not knowing enough about the plot to realize that Rohan had been as victimized by La Motte as she, begged her husband to arrest the cardinal. Without even examining the details of the charges or asking for documents, the king, being utterly subservient to his wife, agreed.

On August 15, 1785, which was the Feast of the Assumption as well as the queen's name day—Rohan was about to celebrate both occasions by saying high mass in front of the assembled court—the royal couple received the cardinal in their private apartments. They were in the company of the queen's most trusted adviser, Minister de Breteuil, the grandee responsible for Sade's continued incarceration, who was one of Rohan's greatest enemies. The cardinal acknowledged that he had been a pathetic dupe. The king replied that since Rohan had defamed the queen's name, there was no choice but to arrest him. Upon which the four eminences walked together into the Hall of Mirrors, where thousands of courtiers were waiting for mass to begin. The cardinal, in scarlet cassock and full clerical regalia, looked pale and frazzled. Behind him stood Breteuil. "Arrest the cardinal!" he barked out to the captain of the guards, his eyes sparkling with pleasure. The crowd was stupefied. No mass was said at Versailles that day. The cardinal, who enjoyed vast popular support, was hauled off to the Bastille like a common pickpocket. Once there, he received such an unending stream of friends and luxuries—a vast retinue of servants lived with him, daily collations of oysters and champagne were brought to his cell—that for reasons of security the Marquis de Sade's walks, and his visits with his wife, were suspended for ten months, the duration of the cardinal's stay. As Pélagie wrote to a Gaufridy that winter, "The uproar concerning the cardinal prevents me from going to the Bastille. It is very disagreeable to spend one's life being the victim of others' fantasies."[2]

ON MAY 31, 1786, the Rohan case was brought to court before the Parlement of Paris. Tens of thousands of Parisians spent the night in front of the Palais de Justice to hear the verdict. The judges deliberated for sixteen hours, then acquitted the cardinal by twenty-six votes to twenty-two, "without a stain on his character." La Motte and her accomplices were found guilty. The scoundrel was sentenced to be flogged publicly and imprisoned for life in the Salpetrière.

The most visible person in the scandal, the Queen of France, also received a life sentence of sorts. As the cardinal emerged from the Parlement building, greeted by huge crowds voicing their support— "Long live the cardinal," they shouted, instead of the customary "Long live the king!"—the queen wept bitterly in her apartments. She was clever enough to know that a blow had been dealt to the monarchy from which it might never recover. To many enlightened citizens, the scandal had exposed, more nakedly than ever, the debility of Louis XVI's rule, his wife's frivolity and cupidity, and the corruption of the entire ancien régime. All ranks of society, including much of the nobility, were incensed by the royal pair's behavior. Philanthropy and prison reform being the fashion, even some of the queen's most intimate friends, such as Princesse de Polignac, manifested compassion for the poor "victim" La Motte. They collected money in her behalf, sent her gifts. It became the latest thing to visit her in her jail cell. When, within two years of being convicted, La Motte mysteriously escaped from prison and fled to England, many believed that the escape had been engineered in exchange for her promise to keep quiet about the queen's role in the necklace affair. In fact, she used her exile to launch a vituperative propaganda campaign against Marie-Antoinette, which found a ready-made audience in France.

When a building is rotten enough, the withdrawal of one nail can bring the entire structure to the ground. From the summer of 1786 on, the criticism that focused on the queen grew uncontrollable. She became the scapegoat for every problem plaguing France, including the aristocracy's corrupt conduct and the country's increasingly shaky finances. Shortly after Rohan's victorious trial, it was revealed that during the past decade, Louis XVI's government had been forced to borrow the sum of 1,250 million livres. Throughout the kingdom, "l'Autrichienne," Marie-Antoinette, began to be referred to as "Mme Deficit." The slander was laced with sexual innuendos. Hundreds of lampoons published in the next years accused the queen of having slept with dozens of persons of both sexes, including Cardinal de Rohan, the king's brother, and Jeanne de La Motte herself.

The first time the queen appeared at the theater after Rohan's exoneration, she was greeted with such loud hisses that from then on she stayed out of public view. Atoning, too late, for past excesses, she made considerable reductions in her expenditures. She stopped buying diamonds, cuts amounting to more than a million livres were made in Versailles's housekeeping and stables. The most potent single symbol of royal frivolity, gambling—the queen's brother, Joseph II of Austria, had accused her of turning Versailles into a gambling den—was banned in the palace. And Marie-Antoinette, a chaste, innately melancholic woman whose search for constant diversions had allayed her frequent depressions, found her principal solace in the company of the royal children, to whom she was an exceptionally devoted mother.

A LETTER SADE WROTE to the lieutenant general of police shortly after Rohan landed at the Bastille reflects the impact of increased security measures on Sade's prison schedule. It was the first letter he had ever written directly to the official.

> To the Lieutenant General of Police:
>   Show me the legal code which dictates that fantasies executed with whores earn a gentleman tortures as long and arduous as mine! . . . There is no statute against what I have done . . . which condemns a man . . . to . . . be treated with such inhumanity.
>   Pray, sir, tell me if the Messalinas, the Sapphos, the incestuous, the sodomites, the public and private thieves . . . who constitute that respectable Montreuil family of which you are the slave—all knaves, whom I'll introduce you to whenever you wish—tell me, pray you, if any of them have suffered the tortures I've been victimized with for thirteen years. . . . Isn't it because they had money and whores to offer the judges? . . . Cease, sir, cease the consummate injustice you have singled me out for. . . .
>   May the Eternal One someday reject you with the brutality with which you have rejected me.[3]

Sade's moroseness and impatience, demands and grievances, grew apace during the year of Rohan's stay at the Bastille. He harassed his jailers with complaints about prisoners who disturbed his nocturnal writing schedule by singing too loudly or caused his eyes to smart by making fires in their rooms. His requests from Pélagie—particularly for the best wines, and for such Provençal delicacies as nougat, truffles packed in oil, candied fruits and delicate jams (his favorite was chinois, a preserve of tiny green oranges)—were as finicky as ever and continued to be haughtily phrased in the third person:

"Some Vin de la Veuve as soon as possible. One so trusts it that one is persuaded that if one drinks seven or eight hundred bottles of it at the Bastille, all of one's ailments will be healed."[4] ("Widow's wine" refers to one of the many vintages produced by the widows of provincial wine growers.)

In the second half of the 1780s, letters between the spouses often focused on a new issue, the marquis's unmanageable girth. He had put on so much weight during his decade in jail that he could not dress himself anymore. So for an extra three hundred livres a year he was permitted to hire a retired soldier to serve him as orderly and valet. "He's so fat that he can't change his shirt alone. He risks getting pneumonia when he becomes too hot,"[5] Pélagie wrote prison authorities to persuade them that her husband needed a full-time helper. And yet Sade did not seem at all embarrassed by this infirmity; he even referred to his obesity with a kind of archaic pride. He wrote Pélagie in 1787:

> As soon as you've received this note, find out from a good tailor how many yards of very thick alpaca wool are needed to make—for a man whom you'll describe as even fatter than I am—a redingote that said man will put on top of a thick jacket and a thick vest. The information received, . . . you'll choose the thickest, the warmest, and the most long-haired [fabric]. You'll send it immediately with a note that will contain the following phrases: *Mr. So-and-so, tailor, of Rue* _____, *has certified that this length of cloth will suffice to make a very ample redingote for the fattest man in Paris.* . . .
>
> You will bring without fault, I pray you, upon your next visit, a pair of very warm and very large lined boots: the fattest leg in Paris must be able to enter a soft boot.[6]

Ironically, Sade's last year at the Bastille was by far the most comfortable of his term. In the fall of 1788, he was finally transferred to a quieter and more airy cell, on the sixth floor of the "Liberté" tower, which he had long asked to move into. He was now allowed to keep abreast of current events by receiving some newspapers and periodicals. And in addition to his usual promenade in the interior courtyard, he was allowed an hour's walk daily on the ramparts. These improvements were doubtless due to Sade's friendship with the assistant warden, Puget, who had risen in the ranks and continued to lobby for prison reforms. In fact, Puget had joined a widespread national movement that was lobbying to have the Bastille torn down.

Sade treated himself to another luxury in his last year at the Bastille: he asked Pélagie to have a bookcase installed in his cell, equipped with lockable doors, and to hire a professional librarian to help him catalogue his book collection. These additional expenses were hard on Pélagie. Not daring to ask her parents for such funds, yet feeling that "it would be cruel"[7] to refuse her husband these comforts, she had to borrow money from friends. And for once the marquis expressed deep gratitude for her sacrifices. For the first time since he had been at the Bastille, he addressed his wife with the affectionate *tu*.

> You can't imagine how your condition worries me [*Tu ne saurais croire combien ton état m'inquiète*] and how desolate I am to cause you financial worries at this time . . . but when I started engaging in these expenses I didn't know your troubles. . . . If you wish me to remain well in this pathetic situation, don't worry, for I'll be as comfortable as one can be in jail. . . . I kiss you and beg you to take care of yourself.[8]

The marquis had good reason to be worried about his wife. She had begun to suffer from weakness and poor digestion, and she was walking with increasing difficulty. For the first time in her stalwart life, she was complaining about her own ailments. "I've totally lost the use of my legs, perhaps because of having been forced to walk too much," she wrote Gaufridy. "I'm told they'll get better; I don't believe a word of it."[9] "I'm getting old and infirm," she repeated to her friend in Provence a few months later. "I can't go out alone; it would be too risky," she wrote. "I'm growing fat from lack of exercise."[10] She was forty-eight years old.

Donatien had other kinds of worries about Pélagie. Might her devotion to him have begun to waver? These apprehensions surface in a letter of December 1787, in which threats again mingle with endearments and expressions of sexual desire.

> I have a powerful need to scold you. The manner in which you waste time with your silences is horrible, truly unimaginable. One never knows whether to trust you, and that is horrible. . . . You have changed, my dear, in the time we've been separated. . . . You can imagine that I'm very angered by your conduct. Good night. This evening, as of this writing, I'm in need as if I were a beast, a donkey, a Spanish stud; so I salute you. Come to visit me, I beg you, come when you wish; your visit will always be a pleasure and an honor, and you can be sure that notwithstanding all the sorrows you've brought me, you'll be embraced, yes, embraced with all my soul.[11]

But despite such occasional outbursts of lust, during his wife's visits the marquis must have continued to criticize her relentlessly and given vent to his dreadful temper. In a letter of December 1788—she was replying to a note he had placed furtively in her muff during a recent meeting—she addressed him, for the first time in their decades of correspondence, in the formal *vous*. The marquis had apparently accused her of not paying enough attention to him or to his requests.

> In reply to your secret letter handed me during my recent visit.
> It shook my heart with the keenest sorrow. I was so unspeakably upset by it. . . . Your letter cannot be shown to anyone. I feel the full pain of your injustice toward me. I, refusing to see you and to hear you!! [12]

Other instances of Sade's angry behavior toward his wife were chronicled by prison commander de Launay, who in the summer of 1788 wrote the Ministry of Police that the inmate continued to be "extremely difficult and violent" and that he showered his wife "with torrents of injuries and abuse." "The truth is that if someday he were to be set free, she would fear for her life," [13] de Launay added.

The commander may have exaggerated the captive's violence as a ploy in his perpetual campaign to be relieved of Sade, but the marquis could indeed have accused his spouse of dealing improperly with his manuscripts. The country's growing political unrest had evidently led him to worry about the safety of his writings. In her last letters to her husband, Pélagie often discusses the manner in which she was secreting his manuscripts out of the Bastille.

> I took the papers and the confidential packages with me; I opened those which you told me to open; those you wished sealed remained sealed, ready for you when you get out. At that time you'll be fairer toward me, I'm sure. . . . When you are free, you'll very much regret that you suspected me of being one of your enemies. [14]

The phrase "you'll very much regret" would turn out to be prophetic, yet for the time being, the marquise did not cease to lobby for her husband's creature comforts. "The excessive cold must be even worse in his cell," she wrote Commander de Launay on New Year's Eve, 1788, during a bout of particularly bitter weather. "I hope you see to it that he doesn't suffer from it, and even change his room, if there's a warmer one. I find him sad, melancholic. I fear that the length of his term is carrying him to despair and that some disaster might occur in that lonely tower. It would offer me great peace of mind if someone could watch him throughout the night."[15]

Six months later, in June 1789, the marquise would write her husband two of the very last letters he is known to have received from her at the Bastille. One of them, displaying Pélagie's ever growing piety, begged him to rectify his own relationship with God. "My tender friend, if you were of good faith, God would not refuse you grace. . . . He is a good God. . . . He asks nothing better than to forgive, but He knows the recesses of human hearts. . . . My happiness consists of seeing you happy in this world and of hoping for your happiness in the next."[16]

The second letter was dated June 21, 1789, a week after she had brought him her critique of his novel *Aline et Valcour*. She apologized for not being able to see him the following Monday because her "habitual affliction"—hemorrhoids—caused such pain that she was unable to ride in a coach. At letter's end, she kissed him and promised to send him some shirts a few days thence. The following week, the same ailment caused her to cancel their meeting once more.

That had been her last chance to see her husband at the Bastille.

XXIV

The Revolution
According to Madame de Sade

> *O centuries of barbarism, ferocious centuries in
> which the vanquished enemy served as fodder for its
> conqueror and as ornament to its triumph, you do
> not approach the atrocity of our own times!!*

> —Letter to Mlle de Rousset, 1783

☐

EVEN THE WEATHER in the year 1788 was a disaster. In July, a hailstorm
flailed through much of western France, ravaging wheat crops and causing the price of bread to rise meteorically. The summer's political events
were equally turbulent. Attempting to resolve the nation's severe financial crisis, Louis XVI had tried unsuccessfully to force the Paris Parlement
to levy a new stamp tax. Conflicts between parliamentarians and the
Crown had come to a head in the early months of 1788. The magistrates
then declared that only the Estates General—a representative assembly
founded in the fourteenth century, which represented the three societal
orders of clergy, nobility, and commoners, and had not met since 1614—
had the right to levy new taxes. More desperate than ever—he was
reported to have gone to the queen's apartment every day to weep
"at the critical state of the kingdom"[1]—Louis once more recessed the
Parlement and arrested two of its dissenting leaders. All of the nation's
regional Parlements declared solidarity with the Parisian assembly, and
the fate of the ancien régime was sealed.

In the following months, antiroyalist demonstrations spread
throughout the kingdom's major cities, drawing on all classes of society,
from peasantry to nobility. In July 1788, it grew particularly violent in
Grenoble, whose royal governor resigned after his men were assaulted

by rioting mobs and whose regional Parlement's call for the Estates General was echoed by every Parlement in the nation. Brittany's uprisings were equally fierce: when a delegation of Breton gentry came to Versailles to present their grievances, Louis XVI could think of nothing better than to jail them in the Bastille. The fortress's schedule was disrupted for the duration of the Bretons' stay, once more causing all prisoners' visiting schedules, including Sade's, to be canceled for the rest of the summer. The country's morale did not improve that August, when the government announced that France was officially bankrupt and that all its payments would be temporarily suspended.

That summer, the Marquise de Sade's letters to attorney Gaufridy, who had loyally supervised the Sades' Provençal estates for fifteen years, began to reflect on the nation's disorder. "It's [politically agitated] here the same as with you and throughout the kingdom," she wrote him in June, "except that here people are not charitable, so that the humble people die of hunger. It fills you with pity."[2]

"We've been in an uproar of scandals, fear, promissory notes, bankruptcy, joy, rebellion. . . . Necker is chief of finances; he's lending eight million to the king," she wrote a while later about the Swiss financial wizard, a national hero whom Louis had fired seven years back but was now forced to recall in hopes of restoring order. "The courts [Parlements] have been recalled but haven't yet reconvened because there's so much disagreement. . . . No one knows what to believe."[3]

From early 1789 on, the sparse staccato style of Pélagie's letters to Provence conveys vivid insights into that year's historic events. She writes from hearsay rather than direct evidence, and her level of political consciousness is average for a woman of her privileged caste, but she initially displays greater liberalism and compassion than many of her milieu. "All is agreed for the Estates General; for the sake of the public good, God will it to remain that way,"[4] she wrote Gaufridy about the convocation of the assembly, which was opposed by many aristocrats. In April, in the urgent tone of a Parisian bringing world-shaking news to a sleepy provincial backwater, she wrote her friend a particularly colorful account of that month's most tumultuous event—the sacking of the home and factories of M. Réveillon, a wealthy wallpaper manufacturer who had recently infuriated the working class by advocating lower wages as a means of reducing the national debt.

> If your province is in a state of alarm, sir, this week Paris is not any less distressing. The Faubourg Saint-Antoine and that of Saint-Marceau, where I live, have been the stage of the revolt.

The pretext: one Réveillon, who is said to have spoken inconsiderately concerning the Third Estate [lower classes]. . . .

A lot of riffraff, shoeless, half naked, many of whom were later whipped and branded, forced the factories to dismiss their workers. Their meeting place was here, in the faubourg; they were armed with thick sticks, metal utensils, and even wooden boards. The first day, they charged into Faubourg Saint-Antoine, into the house of said Réveillon, who himself had fled. . . . They broke everything, drank the wine, the liqueurs, even house-painting chemicals, which poisoned some of them. . . . The following day, they pillaged and plundered many [other] houses, turning over coaches, forcing people to give them all their money.

In order not to be harassed by them, you had to say that you came from the Third Estate. . . . Their numbers grew to eight thousand. . . . Two regiments of cavalry had to be called.

They were shot at; many were killed; a few were hanged, others were jailed. Many more innocent persons perished than guilty ones: crowds of onlookers, people hanging out of their windows. As the evildoers demolished roofs, threw tiles and stones on troops, the infantry stood by a wall and fired. . . . They couldn't act otherwise. . . .

Right now I'm hearing street rumors that are as inconceivable for their absurdity as for their brazenness. Troops have been doubled in strength everywhere; they're standing by, ready to charge into any place where the riots might start again. The Estates General are still scheduled to convene on Monday; they will meet for a procession that will head for the church of Saint-Esprit, to hear a mass that is badly needed to cool heads. [5]

(The Réveillon riots, too, had a direct impact on Sade's schedule, for M. Réveillon was offered refuge at the Bastille to enjoy optimum protection from the mobs. For reasons of security, prison authorities again canceled prisoners' customary walks, a restriction that incited Sade to pen the following letter to his jailers: "Since the frequent visits received by M. Réveillon force me to spend my customary walking hour in the bathroom, until M. Réveillon returns to his *boutique* I beg the major to change my hour in the courtyard to one on the ramparts." [6])

Mme de Sade's next letter concerned a particularly stormy meeting of the Estates General, which had convened at Versailles in May.

M. de Mirabeau attempted to speak last time, but the king
dismissed the session; if he hadn't done so, he would have been
booed; everyone was ready for that. M. de Mirabeau had said
that M. Necker offers hope and faith, but that he [Mirabeau]
demands charity.

Oh, French people, how frivolous you are! You show us
the leash and you prove that you need to be led. . . .

The city is filled with troops. . . . Rumors abound; it's impossible to determine what's true. What is dreadful is the extreme misery of the poor.

Many people have starved to death because of a dearth of
payments or delays in small payments. One should never cease
to pay incomes in Paris; people should be given at least enough
with which to buy bread.[7]

In the third week of June, the clergy voted to ally itself with the
Third Estate, which comprised 98 percent of the population. It had
renamed itself National Assembly and had already won the support of
many powerful liberal aristocrats. Louis XVI, in angry response, ordered
the Estates General's meeting place closed. On June 20, finding the
doors of their assembly hall locked, the deputies moved on to the royal
tennis court nearby, the historic Jeu de Paume. There, under the presidency of France's greatest astronomer, Jean-Sylvain Bailly, the delegates
swore not to adjourn until they had produced a constitution for France.
Mme de Sade reflects on those events in an increasingly alarmed and
conservative tone (out of sheer weakness, she tells Gaufridy, she is writing from her bed).

The assemblies have reconvened. The Third Estate . . .
desires to pass judgment on the rights of the nobility and the
clergy. Those two estates do not wish it so; they pass edicts left
and right and constantly lose time quarreling.

The king wants to forbid this session until he has held a
general meeting, and that is right because the Third Estate . . .
has inflamed the mob with its harangues. . . .

Here, amid the people, it is said that there's a plan to hang
the "little hats"—that's the way priests are referred to; a few
of them have been insulted. . . .

There's a furious faction against M. Necker. Sensible people don't know what to think of him and are waiting to pass
judgment.[8]

It is a pity that we have no letters from Mme de Sade for the following four historic weeks. The day after her last missive, the king ordered his royal guard to disband the Estates General. The Third Estate objected. A group of progressive nobles, which included France's most popular military man, General Lafayette, placed their hands on their swords in support of the deputies. "We shall leave our places only under the threat of bayonets,"[9] Mirabeau announced. The king had to back down again. Facing growing insubordination from his own troops, Louis secretly called sixteen extra regiments to Paris, most of them Swiss and German mercenaries, to intimidate the assembly. On July 11, 1789, he ignited the Revolution by dismissing the more progressive members of his royal council, including the people's idol, Necker.

Since the general thrust of the following days' events is well known, it is time to backtrack a few weeks and catch up with the Marquis de Sade in his jail cell at the Bastille.

THE MARQUIS took a keen interest in the convening of the Estates General. Basing himself on his knowledge of demography, that spring he had jotted down in a journal the numbers of delegates he assumed each "estate" would send to the assembly: "Clergy—134; Nobility—180; Third—191."[10] Given his isolation, it is not surprising that his numbers were totally off target. Against the king's will, recent legislation had greatly increased the number of delegates from the Third Estate. The actual composition of the Estates General that convened in May of 1789 gave 291 seats to the clergy, 250 to the nobility, 577 to the Third Estate. Sade might have been piqued to learn that the greatest star of the National Assembly's progressive wing was his detested kinsman Comte de Mirabeau, who, although he was a noble, had been elected by the Third Estate of his Avignon district.

The turmoil of Paris streets may have interested the marquis more than any legislative details. Reacting angrily against the king's call for added troops, Parisians had demonstrated daily since the end of June on Faubourg Saint-Antoine, a traditional meeting place for political dissenters, which was situated directly below Sade's cell. By this time, the Bastille's cannons were loaded. On July 1, Sade—the sole inmate left in the "Liberté" tower—was so furious that his walks on the ramparts had again been canceled for security reasons that he decided to harangue the crowds milling below his cell window. The following day, Commander de Launay wrote to the minister of state, complaining about the marquis's political debut:

His walks on the tower having been suspended because of the circumstances, he stood at his window at noon and shouted at the top of his lungs that the prisoners were being assassinated, their throats cut, and that they must be rescued. These noisy shouts and accusations were made repeatedly. This is a moment when this man would be very dangerous to keep here. . . . I believe it is my duty, sir, to advise you that it is necessary to transfer this prisoner to Charenton or to some similar institution, where he would be less of a threat to public order.[11]

One of the prison guards, and Sade's own account, would add a picturesque detail to de Launay's report. In order to broadcast his call to rebellion more dramatically, Sade had used part of his urinal equipment—a long metal funnel, through which he disposed of his "waters" into the fortress's moat—as a loudspeaker. The government responded swiftly to de Launay's appeal. The night after he had issued his request, six armed guards burst into Sade's cell at one A.M. After sealing the doors of his cell to safeguard his belongings, they threw him into a coach, barely dressed, not allowing him to bring any possessions. "As naked as a worm"—or so he put it—he was taken to the Convent of the Brothers of Charity at Charenton, five miles from Paris, which served as a primitive jail in which the more turbulent political inmates mingled with violent criminals and the insane. His mood upon arriving at Charenton is best captured by the following letter, written on July 9 to Commissioner Chénon, the police official responsible for the Bastille district.

I, Louis Aldonze Donatien, Comte de Sade, Chief of Staff in the cavalry . . . taking as witness God, justice, and mankind, to observe the execrable vexations, menaces, injuries, ill treatment, and thievery committed toward me and my possessions on the night of 3 to 4 July 1789, by a band of insolent bandits brought to the cell I occupied at the Bastille, who without showing any orders announced that they were executing the ministerial despotism so horribly prevalent throughout France, and who under that deceptive, dangerous, and criminal pretext proceeded to transfer me into an asylum for the insane, with whom I have been ignobly mingled . . . even though my own sanity, thank heavens, has never been impaired.

I, the undersigned, declare . . .

That, obliged to surrender to force, I take advantage of the first occasion I have to protest against this tyrannical, un-

just, improper, barbaric measure, which is an obvious outrage
to the constitution of the French monarchy, and I swear that
the first use I will make of my liberty will be to denounce,
either to the nation, if it still exists, or to our courts of law, the
infamous violence through which I have been victimized. . . .
[These are] injustices so extreme that they are not equaled in
the most scandalous annals of Oriental despotism.

Drafted in an insane asylum, surrounded by the insane, at
Charenton this 9th of July, 1789.

The Comte de Sade.[12]

Attached to this protest was an affidavit giving Commissioner
Chénon the right to open the seals of his Bastille cell in the presence of
Mme de Sade, so that she might secure its contents. These are among
the few communications from Sade known to have survived his nine
months of detention at Charenton. Until the spring of the following
year, his circumstances can only be surmised from the flow of political
events.

NEWS OF NECKER'S DISMISSAL had spread through the capital by July
12, 1789, and was wreaking havoc. By noon, tens of thousands of citizens
were marching through the streets carrying busts of their two current
heroes, Necker and the king's radical first cousin, the Duc d'Orléans.
Mobs were assailing the Hôtel de Ville, grabbing ammunition. The
bourgeois militia formed that spring to protect the burgeoning rebellion
from government attack—it was being called the national guard and
would be led by Lafayette—was being reinforced by defecting army
troops.

By the morning of the fourteenth, a crowd was marching on that
symbol of royal despotism, the Bastille, where de Launay's pitiful rein-
forcements consisted of one hundred ten men, eighty of them retired
invalids. Shortly after noon, upon inviting a delegation of citizens into
the prison, de Launay promised not to attack the intruders unless his
soldiers were fired on first. But the delegation of rebels lingered in the
fortress; the crowd grew impatient, suspecting a trap. When a second
group of citizens entered one of the fortress's interior courtyards, seeking news of their comrades, de Launay thought he was being attacked
and ordered his men to shoot. Ninety-eight people were killed.

News of the carnage spread swiftly through the city, and from then
on there was no way of stopping a bloodbath. Several detachments of
the new national guard marched on the Bastille with cannons it had

seized from the government. In midafternoon, de Launay surrendered his fortress to the mob, which rushed into the bastion to liberate its seven remaining inmates—four forgers, a libertine nobleman, and two lunatics, one of whom was certain that he was Julius Caesar. De Launay had been promised safe conduct to the Hôtel de Ville but was killed on the way, at Place de Grève, where a scullery boy hacked off his head with a pocket knife and placed his trophy on top of a pike.

Nothing in the Bastille was spared the plunder that followed its capture. Demolition of the hated bastion, which had been scheduled for the end of the year, began within a few days. Sade's six-hundred-book library, his clothes, family portraits, and, most important to him, many of his manuscripts, were either stolen or destroyed. "I had been extremely busy in the Bastille; everything was torn up, burned, carried off, pillaged," he would write Gaufridy some months later. "For the loss of my manuscripts I have shed tears of blood! . . . Beds, tables, chests of drawers, can be replaced, but not ideas. . . . No, my friend, no, I will never be able to describe my despair at this loss." [13]

Earlier Sade biographers have deplored Mme de Sade's negligence in the loss of her husband's papers. But a recently discovered memoir written by former police chief Le Noir suggests that she lost no time in following the marquis's orders concerning the contents of his cell. She received Sade's communication from Commissioner Chénon on July 13 and made an appointment to go to the Bastille with him the very next morning. [14] According to Le Noir, on the morning of the fourteenth, while Chénon was drawing up the papers to bring to Mme de Sade, "the beginning of an insurrection" obliged him to postpone his appointment with her. "This incident saved the commissioner's life," Le Noir added laconically, "and perhaps Mme de Sade's."

By the evening of the fourteenth, seizure of the old regime's most formidable emblem had spread terror among France's privileged classes. Within three days, most princes of the blood and some of its most powerful nobility, such as Sade's childhood playmate Prince de Condé, had left Paris to seek refuge abroad. A far more modest member of the elite, Mme de Sade expressed her dread by transferring her power of attorney to Commissioner Chénon, asking him to retrieve her husband's possessions from the Bastille himself, in such a way that "they not be exposed to pillage and to public view." In an unusually shaky, scrawled hand—her letter is preserved at the National Archives—she added that she did not want to be "held responsible anymore for papers and effects of her husband, having personal reasons for desiring not to be responsible for them." [15] She announced that she was leaving for the country, presumably to her parents' country home in Normandy, and would remain away until "tranquillity" was restored.

The provinces, however, were no safer than the capital. In the countryside as in large towns, the sudden emigration of thousands of nobles led to a huge rise in unemployment. Much private property was plundered by bands of starving peasants and vagrants. Throughout the summer and fall, the phenomenon known as the "Great Fear" caused hundreds of thousands of citizens to arm against the dual threat of brigands and foreign invaders. The letters Pélagie wrote to Gaufridy in September, when she shuttled back and forth between the city and her parents' estate, give an inkling of the prevailing chaos.

> There's a constant lack of bread. The confusion is equal to that of the Tower of Babel. . . .
> It all reminds me of an overflowing torrent, or of a watch whose mainspring is broken. All the reasoning and calculations in the world won't set it right; it's the main spring that must be replaced. . . .
> Everyone carries arms, and a lot of people have fled to Great Britain. . . .
> It is a great strain . . . to distrust everybody one meets . . . to listen to threats of violence. It would be much better to be a galley slave; at least you'd know what you were expected to do.
> Poverty is greatly on the rise; commerce is at a low point; no taxes are being collected.[16]

"The support of the army and of the nobility has been lost," she wrote the same month, "and no good can come of that."[17]

On October 8, 1789, Mme de Sade wrote her friend in Provence about yet another demonstration. Angered by the king's continuing defiance of the National Assembly and above all incited by the high price of bread, Parisian working women organized a march on Versailles on October 5. Within a few hours, it had drawn tens of thousands of citizens. Although it was initially announced as a "march for bread," the demonstrators' goal soon became far more ambitious: in order to gain greater control over him, they would force Louis XVI to move the remnants of his court to Paris. At the cost of a few lives, this was accomplished the following day, when the procession led the king and his family back to their new quarters, the Louvre, "palace of [Louis's] ancestors"[18] as the popular press put it. Three days later, Pélagie, whose sympathies with "the people" were waning fast, described the episode to Gaufridy:

> I fled Paris with my daughter and a maid, following the general exodus in a rented coach, in order not to be caught up by the women of the people who forcibly dragged women out of their houses to kidnap the king at Versailles, and obliged them to walk on foot through the rain, the shit, etc. I arrived safely at my destination. The king is in Paris; he was led to the city, the heads of two of his bodyguards carried on top of pikes, all the way to the Louvre. Everyone in Paris is overjoyed, because they think the king's presence will bring them more bread.[19]

Pélagie's report, again, is based on hearsay; no women were witnessed being "forcibly dragged out of their houses," and she says nothing about the sheer immensity of the symbol-laden procession: the cortege of some sixty thousand persons that returned to Paris included the entire membership of the National Assembly; innumerable cartloads of flour and wheat; the king's own disarmed soldiery, who from that day on were forced, like the royal family itself, to wear the revolutionaries' tricolor cockade; the triumphant Paris women who had organized the march, some armed with pikes or sitting astride cannons; rebellious soldiers carrying the heads of two of the king's private guard, killed that morning while attempting to keep the mob from invading the royal apartments; and, among many other constituencies, large contingents of Lafayette's national guard, who had speared loaves of bread on the tips of their bayonets.

Later that month, Mme de Sade wrote to Provence about the anxiety that continued to prevail throughout rural France during the "Great Fear."

> I'm in the country, not because I fear the gallows but in order not to die of hunger, and because I'm penniless. . . . My older son arrived on leave. I'm holding him on a close rein for fear that he'll fall prey to vagabonds, etc. A local butcher has been massacred. Horrors are happening that make you tremble; a few culprits have been hanged. That does not restore the dead to life. If one could stop the marauders! There are so many of them that it makes you tremble. It is said that an infernal conspiracy has been unmasked.[20]

Her concerns remain unallayed the following month, November 1789.

We're menaced every day with carnage. As compliant as the clergy and some of the nobility are, they're still resented. . . . When you go to bed you're never sure what's going to happen the next day. Two days ago, at the Palais-Royal, shoe buckles and earrings were confiscated, people were forced to turn their pockets inside out on the pretext that they were contributing to the national coffer.[21]

The next important historic events Pélagie comments on are those of early February 1790, when Louis XVI appeared at the National Assembly, dressed in a simple black suit, and swore an oath to "defend and maintain constitutional liberty" and bring up his son as "a true constitutional monarch."[22] Pélagie offers some descriptions of the Revolution's fixation on oath swearing and of the euphoria that greeted Louis XVI's most recent capitulation.

One now prays for God in the streets and shouts "God save the king!" in churches. A Te Deum will be sung [at mass] on Sunday. The National Assembly will attend.

New oaths are being sworn in the middle of public places. The ramparts are all lit up. . . . In the enthusiasm of having sworn the oath . . . a man who raised his hand to give the oath said that if asked to, he would have raised his foot. Then he raised his hand on behalf of his employers, saying that they were not "istocrates."[23]

The following month, Pélagie wrote a more somber letter, about the paranoia spreading among privileged classes.

There was horrible carnage in Meaux [forty kilometers northeast of Paris]; it's said that the mayor was hanged and the bishop has fled. Misery is so extreme, it couldn't be otherwise. The password to evildoing is to say "He's an aristocrat; he wants to rescue the king," and you're hanged without a trial.[24]

These nine months of stormy reports constitute a barely documented period of the Sades' relations, for no missives that may have been exchanged between the spouses have been found. (One suspects that the marquis's communications were as imperious and wrathful as they'd ever been.) There is only one significant mention of Sade in official documents, a letter written in January 1790 by the prior of the convent of Charenton, who, like every other jail warden who had ever been in charge of Sade, pleaded to be disburdened of this rambunctious captive. "I beg the National Assembly to relieve me of this inmate, or else permit me to place him in solitary confinement in order to protect this house from the misfortunes with which he menaces it."[25]

As for Mme de Sade, she makes only two references to her husband during his detention. In a letter of August 1789, she simply informs Gaufridy that "M. de Sade is faring well." In March 1790, she intimates to Gaufridy that although she remains concerned about her husband, she wishes to be relieved of some of her responsibilities concerning his affairs. "I ask you to be vigilant concerning M. de Sade's interests and am persuaded of the gratitude he'll retain for you."[26]

Within a few weeks, Mme de Sade would finally express her true state of mind.

XXV

Liberation!!

*It's nature I wish to outrage. . . . I would like to vio-
late its plans, reverse its course, vanquish the stars
that float throughout it, ravage whatever serves it . . .
insult it, in sum, in all its manifestations.*

—*Justine*

☐

THE RELEASE of all prisoners jailed on *lettres de cachet* had been a priority
of the Revolution's pioneers, but the National Assembly, having greater
crises to resolve, took no direct action on the issue until March 13, 1790.
On that day, pressured by an obscure young deputy from northern
France, a small, scholarly man with delicate features named Maximilien
Robespierre, the assembly voted to free all such prisoners within six
weeks, with the exception of lunatics and those sentenced to death.

Five days later, on March 18, Sade's sons, now twenty and twenty-
two, went to the asylum of Charenton to inform their father of the
decree. The prisoner had not seen his children for some fourteen years.
He received permission from the prior of the convent to take a walk with
his boys for a few hours and to entertain them for dinner. This encounter
between father and sons may have been very emotional; but the only
recorded family reaction to Sade's release was a skeptical comment by
Mme de Montreuil. "I hope that he'll be happy, but I doubt if he knows
how to be,"[1] she quipped when her grandsons told her they were going
to visit their father. A few days later, she expressed her ambivalent emotions about Sade's release in a terse note to Gaufridy: "You've probably
seen . . . the National Assembly's decrees concerning the *lettres de cachet*.
Its phrasing could permit exceptions. The issue is whether . . . [these ex-
ceptions] should be invoked by families. I've come to think that [families]
must remain neutral and leave the government to decide as it deems fit."

In effect, she was cautiously accepting Sade's freedom but not necessarily her daughter's continued marriage. "You surely wouldn't advise
[Mme de Sade] to continue suffering all she's suffered."[2]

And so on April 1, 1790, the Marquis de Sade was released. He wore
a black ratteen coat and had with him no possessions beyond a mattress
and a gold coin in his pocket. He had been twenty-seven years old at the
time of his Easter Sunday caper with Rose Keller, thirty-two when he
frolicked with the Marseilles prostitutes, thirty-six when he began his
term at Vincennes. Now he was about to turn fifty, a balding, graying
man dressed in rags, who had grown so obese that by his own admission
he could "barely move about."

He made his way to the convent of Saint-Aure and asked to see his
wife of nearly twenty-seven years, still hoping to spend the rest of his
days with her. But in an about-face as absolute as the fervor of her
previous devotion, Pélagie refused to appear. She sent down a message
informing her husband that she never wished to see him again.

The next day, she wrote Gaufridy the following note: "M. de Sade
is free since yesterday, Good Friday. He wants to see me, but I answered
that I am still aiming for a separation; that's the only way."[3]

So many questions arise about this change of heart.

Was Pélagie quite simply exhausted, having struggled for a quarter
of a century against society's scorn, the blackmail of prostitutes, the
rigor of government and prison bureaucracies, her husband's rages and
gargantuan demands, her mother's fury, the peasants of La Coste, her
creditors everywhere? Her conscience and innate kindness having led her
to stand by Sade during his darker days, did his liberation now release
her from all obligations?

Or was God at issue, and the pressure of the very devout community
that her husband, ironically, had ordered her to join? Her innate piety
having greatly cooled during her years with the apostate marquis, had
her confessors finally convinced her that she must now repent for the
odious deeds she had committed for his sake, that her religious duties
held precedence over her marital ones? Once the love of her life ceased
to move her to pity, had she committed herself to the salvation of her
soul?

Moreover, how would the products of the marquis's erotic imagination strike a woman undergoing a spiritual conversion? In the months
before the fall of the Bastille, Pélagie, sitting alone in her little attic
room, is bound to have perused the writings he had passed on to her
(one of them was the early draft of his extremely salacious novel *Justine*)
and been appalled.

Or else should we see Mme de Montreuil as the dominant force at this moment of her daughter's life? For over a decade she had repeatedly urged Pélagie to leave her husband; Pélagie had continually refused. Was she able to capitulate to her mother's pressure only when her mystical need to aid a victim ceased?

For years this woman of limited learning but great shrewdness had been transformed by an exalted passion, had been impelled, as her mother once put it, to love "beyond all limits." Like innumerable wives of our own time who have suffered through years of psychic battering, she had been led to a breaking point by an accumulation of griefs—her husband's repeated threats and insults, the painful acknowledgment of her own blundering dedication. Her infatuation waning, her illusions about her husband dissolving, she had returned to her natural gravity, to being the conformist, prosaic creature she had been as a girl.

She may have stopped seeing her husband because she knew him well enough to dread that he might seduce her once again. Perhaps she was afraid not so much of him as of her own inclination to servility, terrified of the very force of her love, which had never waned in twenty-seven years.

More pragmatically, she must have feared that Sade's return threatened her children's future well-being, which was sure to be jeopardized. Pélagie's powerful maternal instinct, so repressed during all the years she placed her husband's well-being above all else, suddenly asserted itself and triumphed over all other duties.

And what about those upheavals so often experienced by women at midlife? Pélagie was in her late forties, infirm beyond her years, barely able to walk without help, feeling the plague of age in every inch of her spirit and her body.

All of that, all of it. And much more that has to do with 1789.

Mme de Sade might well have wandered through the streets of Paris on that fateful day of July 14 when she was scheduled to go to the Bastille and seen some of its harrowing events with her own eyes. Even if she had stayed home, for the past year she had glimpsed, and heard reports of, angry mobs demonstrating in most every area of the nation; patrician revolutionaries joining the unshod in seizing government buildings; royal guards and innocent bystanders slaughtered by wrathful hordes. And if her own husband had incited the crowds beneath his prison window to rebellion, what could this innately timid, decorous, conservative woman still hold sacred and secure? She finally made her choice: her family, her God, whatever measure of security and peace she could still salvage for her old age.

So one might say that the events of 1789 were the catalysts of Pélagie's transformation, consolidating the authority of her mother and her confessors. She had been seized by that "Great Fear" which gripped the nation and was living through a great inner fear of her own, a terror of her painful past and her uncertain future. Donatien, in her eyes, was now part of the mobs that were insulting and deriding her religion and her monarch, menacing all that her family most treasured—material property, the privileges of newly acquired caste. Those forces were threatening to dissolve the safe, stately maternal order of the Présidente de Montreuil's world, and ultimately that is where Pélagie belonged.

In Pélagie's own account, her conversion was not so sudden. The word to watch for in that note to Gaufridy written the day after her husband's release is "still": "I am *still* aiming for a separation." The marquis's own comments concerning his wife's defection also intimate that her change of heart was gradual. "For a very long time I'd been noticing a certain attitude on the part of Mme de Sade, when she came to see me at the Bastille, which caused me anxiety and grief," he would write Gaufridy a few months after he was set free. "The need I had of her led me to dissimulate, but every aspect of her conduct alarmed me. I clearly discerned the instigation of her confessor, and to tell you the truth, I foresaw that my freedom would bring about a separation."[4]

Pélagie further clarified her decision two months later, when she wrote her Provençal friend Gaufridy the following:

> I'm still holding to my decision to seek a separation. This follows long and carefully considered reflections. . . . M. de Sade, if he probes his conscience, is bound to see justice in my motives and acknowledge that it could not be otherwise. As for scandal, he's a master at it. I'll only say what he forces me to say, to justify myself. *But I'll say it if he forces me to.*[5]

The emphasis is Pélagie's, and the nasty threat of blackmail is consistent with the loathing that Mme de Sade now seemed to feel for her husband. Like many persons who have broken away from a religious cult, she had begun to proselytize fiercely against her former idol.

SO THE MARQUIS DE SADE is now destitute, homeless, suddenly wifeless, on the night of Good Friday, 1790. He had always been resourceful. Immediately after being turned away by his spouse, he knocked at the door of an old acquaintance, M. de Milly, his Paris business agent, who took him in for three days and loaned him enough money to survive on for a few more. Sade moved on to the Hôtel du Bouloir, near what is now Rue Saint-Honoré. His state of mind in the weeks that followed his release is displayed in his first letters to Gaufridy, who would henceforth take Pélagie's place as the principal recorder of Sade's consciousness.

> I left Charenton, to which I had been transferred from the Bastille, on Good Friday. Better the day, better the deed! Yes, my dear lawyer, that was the day when I regained my liberty. So I have made a vow to celebrate it for the rest of my life, and instead of indulging, when we should be weeping and wailing, in the usual festivities—hapless strolls, which current custom condones with scant respect to religion—instead, I say, of sharing in such worldly vanities, every time the forty-fifth day of Lent brings round a Good Friday, I shall fall on my knees, pray, and thank God . . . resolve to mend my ways and keep my word to it.[6]

The tone is playful, the religious resolves are ironic. What is more genuine, in Sade's first weeks of freedom, are those ascetic emotions familiar to many former prisoners but very unexpected for this particular inmate: disgust for all manifestations of the flesh, and a desire for a renewed form of confinement—the monastic life. He wrote his friend:

> All my sensations and appetites have been extinguished. I no longer have any taste or love for anything; the world which I was mad enough to regret strikes me as so boring, so sad! . . . There are times when I feel inclined to become a Trappist monk, and some fine day I may well disappear without anyone knowing what has become of me. Never have I been so misanthropic as I've been since I've again mingled with mankind.[7]

But a few weeks later, his gregariousness returned. He wrote Gaufridy that his misanthropy had "somewhat abated," that the despair of not being able to communicate his ideas for thirteen years had led to "a real need to talk," and a Trappist establishment "would no longer suit me too well."[8]

And however indigent, seedy, and obese the marquis had become, such was his magnetism that within weeks of reentering society he was again capturing the affection of charming women. His first conquest was a winsome divorcée called the Présidente de Fleurieu (her estranged husband was the president of the Lyons Treasury), who installed him in a little flat down the street from her own, on present-day Rue Bonaparte. A dramatist, she had had a play produced by the Comédie Française, which could not have failed to impress the stagestruck Sade. In her company he enjoyed "good air, a good view, good society," and became acquainted with some of France's most famous actors, such as Talma and Molé, who would help him to have his plays read at the best theaters. Describing his relationship with Mme de Fleurieu to Gaufridy, he made it clear that it was strictly platonic: she was forty years old, he commented, and "since there's ninety years between the two of us there could not be any danger. . . . No sentiment other than friendship enters our liaison," he continued, "no more impure pleasures . . . nothing improper; all that disgusts me now as much as it used to inflame me in the past."[9]

Within weeks of regaining freedom, Sade was also enjoying an elegant social life with Delphine de Clermont-Tonnerre. Her mother, a first cousin of the marquis's mother, had been a lady-in-waiting to Louis XVI's sister Mme Elizabeth; her husband, Comte Stanislas de Clermont-Tonnerre, was one of the aristocrats most engaged in revolutionary reform. These relatives lavished him with "thoughtfulness and kindness," and at their home he found "peace, tranquillity, and the most stoic philosophy."[10]

But those were not his most important social triumphs. The most glorious of his new conquests—he met her the summer of his release, and they moved in together a few months later—was a gentle, modest woman named Constance Quesnet, who would radically alter the course of his life. Whatever bad luck Donatien had had with the law he amply made up for with his good luck in love. With Constance Quesnet he would enjoy the sweetest and most steadfast familial bonds he had ever known. She would stay at his side for the rest of his quarter of a century on earth, and throughout that time she would remain as shrewdly protective, as passionately dedicated to him, as his wife had ever been.

IT IS A PITY that we do not know more about Constance Quesnet, whose baptismal name prefigures her fidelity of character. We have no portrait of her, and since she was a poor correspondent, we have only a handful of her letters as direct testimony of her thoughts. What we do know is that she was thirty-three when she met the marquis; that she had once been an actress; that she was separated from her husband, a merchant who had recently left for America; and that she had a son, Charles, six years old at the time of her meeting with Sade, whom the marquis would bring up with far more steadfast devotion than he ever displayed to his own children. We also know that Constance was very impressionable and prone to fainting fits; the name Sade would give her shortly after their meeting, "Sensible," translates not to the English "sensible" but to "sensitive" or even "hypersensitive."

For the rest of Constance's qualities we must trust the testimony of Sade, who had never been a fool about human nature. He would cele- brate her, in dedicating to her his novel *Justine,* as being "both the example and the honor of your gender, uniting the fairest and most enlightened mind to the most sensitive soul."[11] He would bring up her son to venerate his mother and would eulogize Sensible to him in the following words: "I've often told you that your mother is the kind of companion whom nature offers only once in a lifetime and whose loss is irreplaceable. . . . In sum, dear friend, such a companion is of supernatu- ral character."[12]

Early on in his liaison with Sensible, Sade made it clear to M. Reinaud, his friend in Provence, that this, too, was a platonic relation- ship, that his arrangement with Constance was a "liaison of conve- nience." Reinaud having suspected him of yet another fling with an actress, Sade wrote:

> Nothing as virtuous as my little ménage!! First of all, not a word of love; she's simply a good and honest bourgeoise, amiable, gentle, witty, who . . . agreed to take charge of my little household . . . not a word of flirtation. . . .
>
> Could I skim my pot-au-feu, oversee my butcher's bills, when I'm buried in my study in the midst of Molière, Marivaux . . . whom I look up to, admire, and shall never approximate? Don't I need a companion to whom I can read my work in the heat of creation? Well, my friend fulfills all of those functions. God keep her, notwithstanding the amazing cabal that con- stantly labors to deprive me of her. . . . My only fear is that, made impatient by so many base Montreuilian maneuvers, the poor creature will leave me in disgust.[13]

The reference to the Montreuils' "cabal" is a clear instance of Sade's paranoia. His former in-laws never attempted to sever him from Sensible and were probably thrilled to have him out of their way. What is genuine in those lines is the great joy brought him by the first domesticity he had known in some decades. His letters of 1791 are filled with descriptions of his cozy new household. Constance and he shared a narrow little three- floor house, to which they had separate entrances. "Pretty enough to be admired by Parisians, whose eyes are jaded to luxury," it was in an elegant district, on Rue Neuve-des-Mathurins, not far from what is now Faubourg Saint-Honoré and Place Vendôme.

Revolution does not seem to have diminished the marquis's gluttony and love for creature comforts. He sent to La Coste for Provençal
delicacies of jams and preserved fruit, for some of his furniture, curtains,
lamps, slipcovers. Sitting in slippers at his work desk, he had a view over
a small garden, and he generally felt like "a good fat priest in his rec-
tory." In addition, as an aspiring dramatist he now had free access to
theaters, and there were three or four houses he could "dine in" (we
can assume that these were noblemen's houses, like the Clermont-
Tonnerres', where he went without Sensible). An "honest and very car-
ing" companion and good wine in his cellar—these are the ingredients
for perfect happiness, he wrote Gaufridy.

So the libertine in Sade seems to have died, and debauches might
henceforth be relegated to his fictions. One could see this transformation
as Mme de Montreuil's ultimate triumph: thirteen years of prison had
turned the rake into a sedate, bourgeois eunuch.

NOTWITHSTANDING the contentment brought by Constance, there remained a somber side to the marquis's life as a free man: the bitterness
and wounded pride caused by Pélagie's defection, and his resulting penury; his rage at her alleged mishandling of his manuscripts; his wrath
toward the Montreuils, whom he blamed for the breakup of his marriage: "Those rascals . . . those monsters . . . forced my wife to leave me.
She had no wish to do so. . . . They left no stone unturned in forcing
her to take this step." [14]
Sade's letters to Gaufridy elaborate bitterly on his plight as an abandoned husband:
"Oh, Mme de Sade, what a revolution in your soul! What horrible
actions!" he wrote, a few weeks after being set free. ". . . My dear lawyer,
if you knew the indignities this woman is imposing on me!" [15] And he
lamented soon thereafter:

> The sensitive and touchy Mme de Sade has refused to see
> me. Another woman might have remarked: "He's unhappy,
> and I must comfort him"; her feelings are governed by no such
> logic. I haven't lost enough, she wants to ruin me, she's trying
> to divorce me. By this inconceivable process . . . she's set on
> bringing shame and misfortune upon myself and her children
> so that she may live or delightfully vegetate . . . in a convent,
> where some father confessor doubtless consoles her. . . . Were
> this woman to receive advice from my most mortal enemy it
> could not be worse or more dangerous. [16]

In the same weeks, he vents his wrath about his lost books:

> What is irreparable, *fifteen volumes of my works in manu-script* all ready to hand to the printer, all these effects . . . were put under seal by the officer of the Bastille, but Mme de Sade *dined, went to the toilet,* confessed, and fell asleep. Finally, on 14 July in the morning she imagined the time had come to have the seal broken and have my effects sent. . . . Unfortunately the day she chose to wake out of her lethargy was the same as that on which a mob of people advanced on the Bastille and assassinated the governor and all the officers, which meant that all entry was barred and all my effects were looted. I ask you, my dear lawyer, whether such behavior is not atrocious and whether Mme de Sade, who had ten days in which to act, can be forgiven for allowing me to be robbed of my possessions, including the manuscripts for which I mourn every day in tears of blood.[17]

Yet another hyperbole. Sade's claim that all the texts he wrote in prison were lost is greatly exaggerated. He started presenting the plays he had written in jail to the Comédie Française a few weeks after he was set free, and he published *Justine* and *Aline et Valcour* in the following five years. So Pélagie had obviously brought drafts of these works out of the Bastille weeks before the fortress was seized, and sent them on to him shortly after he was set free. But he never acknowledged Pélagie's rescue of those works. And although the Sades would occasionally exchange letters concerning the financial details of their separation, and may even have glimpsed each other from a distance while visiting their children, it appears that they never again met face-to-face.

The Sades' divorce settlement specified that Donatien pay Pélagie four thousand livres a year—interest on her hundred-thousand-livre dowry, which he had spent during their marriage. Alleging that Pélagie had kept the money he inherited from his mother (which, Pélagie claimed with good reason, had subsidized Sade's room and board in jail), he never paid her back a cent he owed her and kept complaining that her family had willfully ruined him. "My poor father used to say, 'I'm marrying my son to the daughter of tax collectors to make him rich,' and in fact they've ruined me."[18] After the spring of 1790, most of their correspondence consisted of acrimonious financial disputes. Pélagie would reply to his requests for money with lashing notes that displayed how fully she had returned to her parents' fold: "I've already had the honor of telling you that since you're not paying me a cent on what you owe me, it would be impossible for me to deposit anything into your account. As for my family, it has nothing to do anymore with your affairs; and if you attack them, they will always answer you with the truth, as they've done all along." [19]

Only one civil exchange between the former spouses has been recorded: in 1791, the marquis asked Gaufridy to send Mme de Sade several barrels of La Coste's excellent olive oil.

IN THE WEEKS after his release, Sade repeated his laments concerning his wrecked marriage and financial disasters to his two surviving aunts in Provence, whom he had turned to often during crises. The first relative he wrote to was the aging Abbess Gabrielle Éléonore of Cavaillon; his letters to her display genuine tenderness and a need for the maternal pity once offered him by his wife.

> Dear good aunt whom I've always adored, there's so much sorrow in my heart that it's impossible not to confide in a friend as beloved as you. . . . I who'd married to have company in my old age, here I am abandoned, isolated, and reduced to the same sad fate in which my poor father ended his last days, of all the fates of old age the one I feared the most. [20]

Sade's affection for his more glamorous relation, the wealthy, brilliant widow Mme de Villeneuve, was more ambiguous, being tinged with self-interest. He had long hoped she would remember him in her will. Honest enough to deride his own rapaciousness, he summed up his ambivalent emotions toward her with a quixotic sentence: "I wish her to live as long as possible, in order not to suffer from two sorrows: that of losing her and that of being *disinherited*." [21] Mme de Villeneuve's great attachment to her nephew was less equivocal. She had never shown much interest in her three daughters, two of whom were nuns and none of whom amused her, and she looked on Donatien as the son she had always wished for. She was the only member of the Sade clan to berate Mme de Montreuil publicly, writing her a letter in which she deplored her role in persuading Pélagie to separate. The Présidente sent a caustic, finely honed reply:

> It is cruel, madame, that the first time in my life that you've done me the honor of acknowledging me is upon an occasion when I cannot accommodate you. . . . You will ob-

serve that it is precisely for having followed the principles which you presently ask me to follow that my indulgent kindness . . . was abused . . . and incited the misfortunes that plagued my family. . . . There are wounds, madame, that never heal.[22]

Donatien's attachment to his aunts was one of many bonds that were drawing him back to Provence. He started planning a return trip a few weeks after getting out of jail, proudly writing to Gaufridy that he would come to La Coste as soon as possible to introduce his sons to the lawyer. But however eagerly he anticipated this trip, Donatien had to postpone it many times. Revolutionary politics were particularly agitated in Provence, and they grew even stormier in 1791 when France annexed the papal states. Sade did not wish to die "on the democratic gallows," as he put it in one letter. He would not be able to see his estates again for seven years.

It is not totally impossible that Mme de Sade and her daughter returned to southern France before Sade. Their whereabouts during the more dangerous revolutionary years can only be guessed. In 1792, when convents throughout France began to close, the two women moved on to the Montreuils' flat on Rue Madeleine, now Rue Boissy d'Anglas. Upon the onset of the Terror, in 1793, Pélagie and her daughter went into hiding in the countryside, where it was far easier to avoid persecution, and they may well have traveled south. Donatien's veiled comment to Gaufridy that "Our little nieces have been forced to leave the Clermont convent, which has been closed, and to seek refuge in Marseilles"[23] could have referred to them, or to other female relations. Whatever part of the French countryside they found shelter in, Pélagie and Madeleine-Laure, like the Montreuils, managed to survive the Revolution's most dangerous years, 1793 and 1794. They were fortunate to be spared, for by that time Pélagie's two sons and all her siblings had left France, and the Terror would savagely persecute many citizens whose relatives had emigrated.

For the time being, we must take leave of Pélagie as a central character of the Sadeian epic. Having survived greater measures of passion and devotion than most women experience in ten lifetimes, she returned to being the placid, conventional creature she had been before she met Donatien de Sade. Reclusion, religious devotion, the petty groveling of a provincial Catholic life, would now be the measure of her days. Her marriage had been her work of art: for good or for worse, it was solely through Pélagie's love and dedication that the Marquis de Sade's talents were able to flower and become part of the Western heritage. There lies the principal legacy of this potentially intrepid soul, whose saga leads us once more to marvel at (or to deplore) the phenomenon of female malleability.

Although she will make another cameo appearance, it is also time to bid adieu to the Présidente de Montreuil. One marvels equally at her amazing wits and at the fidelity of her rage, without which the Marquis de Sade would never have become a writer and would have remained ignored as just another tedious debauchee.

XXVI

The Active Citizen

O God, since it is engraved in your great book that
you gave me life to serve as fodder for bitches and as
pasture for pigs . . . at least allow your holy will to
turn me into an example to my peers and let the vile
criminals . . . realize that, having had little success
with me, they will see their own infamies revealed.
. . . Amen.

—"Evening Prayer to God," Vincennes, 1782

☐

THE PARIS that Sade returned to in 1790 had become a perpetual festival of liberation. In the summer of that year, brightly colored posters filled the city's public places, hawking the promises of various political factions. At street corners, salesmen of patriotic souvenirs peddled miniature Bastilles, which hung from lapels, bracelets, and watch fobs, or from the belts of the greatly simplified dresses that were the *dernier cri* of women's fashion. "Liberty trees" festooned with great bands of blue, white, and red ribbon abounded, tricolor emblems symbolizing the new national motto of "liberty, equality, fraternity" adorned hats, coats, men's sleeves. Even hairstyles had changed radically since 1789, and coiffures now went unpowdered, in a mode called *à la citoyenne*. Household objects were equally politicized: porcelain and china were decorated with patriotic sayings or symbols, as were teacups, snuffboxes, shaving mirrors, even chamber pots.

The atmosphere was one of boundless civic activism. A few weeks after Sade's release, the capital was divided into forty-eight geographical districts or sections—each of them with its own legislative assembly— which encouraged citizens' participation in local and national politics. It was by immediately joining such an association that Sade survived the political dangers of the next few years.

Some jailbirds come out of their confinement broken in spirit, their endurance depleted, and take years to revive their appetite for life. Sade was not one of them. The most striking attributes he displayed after his release were adaptability and shrewd opportunism. After a brief flirtation with the notion of a monastic life, Sade sprang back and dedicated himself wholeheartedly to a single goal—political survival. The first step he took toward that end was to sign up as an "active citizen" in his district of Paris, Section Vendôme. The members of its assembly met every ten days in an abandoned church that stood at what is currently 2 and 4 Rue de la Paix. To claim this membership, he gave up all signs of the noble origins he had once so vaunted and registered as "Louis Desade, man of letters." He would soon make himself even more plebeian, and go as just plain "Louis Sade." The character traits he evolved for his new identity were models of republican virtue. The old caprices gave way to rigorous discipline, arrogance to deference, flamboyance to self-effacing modesty. If this transformation seems like a triumph of self-will, one should note that the Revolution offered the outcast his only chance to reintegrate himself into society.

The strategy was effective. For a member of the high-ranking aristocracy, Sade's rise to power within his political district was extraordinary. He grew so skilled at revolutionary rhetoric, referring to his secretly beloved king as "a traitor, a rascal," and raving about "the great republican family we have just founded," that he soon became his section's official scribe. His political writings, which he referred to as "civic productions," were so popular among his colleagues that copies were often sent to the other districts of Paris and, on occasion, to the entire constituency of the French army.

But the patriotism of the former marquis—for that is what we must now call him—went far beyond rhetoric. He became the busybody of his district and often its oracle. He frequently took on the twenty-four-hour "guard duty" assigned to trusted male citizens. ("Citizen, comrade," such a directive would enjoin, "thou wilt go to headquarters, fully armed, on 15 Nivôse at 11 A.M. sharp to stand thy 24-hour watch."[1]) He would prove his revolutionary virtue by serving as his section's commissar for cavalry and for the reorganization of hospitals. In one characteristic assignment of winter 1792, when the young republic, in its euphoria of renewal, abolished Christian and pagan nomenclature at every level of national life, Sade was given the task of renaming all the streets of his district. He rebaptized Rue Saint-Honoré as Rue de la Convention, Rue des Capucines as Rue des Citoyennes Françaises, Rue Saint-Nicolas as

Rue des Hommes Libres, Rue Caumartin as Rue du Peuple Souverain, and he effected other martial christenings, such as Rue Spartacus, Rue Gracchus, Rue Caton.[2] The document in which Sade listed these new street names, which is preserved at France's National Archives, shows that this particular accomplishment was popular with the leaders of his district: *"Le Conseil Général applaudit ce travail,"* they commented on Sade's report. Sade was eventually named secretary of his section, and at the start of the Terror he even served briefly as its president.

It was on the basis of this patriotic veneer that the surrealists, when they resuscitated their "divine marquis" in the 1930s, asserted that "the revolution found him devoted body and soul," and praised him for "adapt[ing] his genius to that of a people delirious with strength and freedom."[3] To fashion this simplistic image of a man whose ideology remained essentially conservative, whose fictional heroes abused their victims (as he had attempted to do at La Coste) with the impunity of feudal lords, they skimmed the rhetorical froth off Sade's public writings; and in the process, they totally overlooked the complex, ambiguous statements he made in his correspondence.

In May 1790, for instance, Sade wrote to the Provençal lawyer Reinaud:

> Don't take me for a fanatic. . . . I protest that I'm merely impartial, angered by having lost a great deal, still more angry to see my sovereign in irons, baffled that you gentlemen in Provence don't realize that no good can come about . . . when the monarch's authority is constrained by thirty thousand simpletons armed with twenty cannon; but in point of fact I regret the ancien régime very little; assuredly it made me too miserable for me to lament it. Well, there's my profession of faith for you, and I make it without fear. . . .

Devoid of any illusions concerning the Revolution's interface of liberation and terror, Sade went on to deplore the blood being shed by republican forces in the south of France, where royalists were persecuted with particular violence.

> Valence, Montauban, Marseilles are theaters of horror in which cannibals daily enact melodramas that make your hair stand on end. For a long time I've been saying that this gentle and lovely nation . . . always poised between cruelty and fanaticism, would display its true character as soon as the occasion arose! Enough said; one must be prudent in one's correspon-

dence, for never did "despotism" unseal as many letters as "liberty" is unsealing.[4]

Hardly the words of a man "devoted body and soul" to the Revolution. In December of the following year, Sade wrote, even more ambiguously, to Gaufridy: "For me as a man of letters, the obligation to write daily, at times for one side, at times in favor of another, creates a mobility of opinion that informs my entire way of thinking."

The clearest summation of the former marquis's political beliefs, and of his icy disdain for both the former and the present regimes, appears in the same letter to his lawyer:

> I'm anti-Jacobin [the dominant radical faction, led by Robespierre]; I hate them to death; I adore the king, but I detest the ancient abuses; I like a great many articles of the Constitution, others revolt me. I wish the nobility to regain its luster, because it helps no one to have deprived us of it; I wish the king to be the head of the nation; I do not want a national assembly but want two chambers, as in England. . . . There's my profession of faith. What does that make me? Aristocrat or democrat? Tell me, if you please, lawyer, for I don't know.[5]

In point of fact, these convictions were consistent with the ideology Sade had held to all his life. Like much of the ancient provincial nobility, which had never lived at Versailles, Sade greatly distrusted absolutism. Given his conservative nostalgia for feudal times, and the years he had spent in royal jails, he resented the French Crown's power far more vehemently than most of his peers. Yet set in the political landscape of 1790, he was a garden-variety constitutional monarchist, still loyal to "his" monarch but requesting parliamentary curbs on royal authority. The year of his release, he joined an important political coalition founded on just those principles by his cousin Clermont-Tonnerre, the Society of Friends of a Constitutional Monarchy. He acted on the same credos the following year when he applied for service in the king's Constitutional Guard, a unit intended to ensure the legality of the king's actions as well as to protect him. (He never received the commission, perhaps because of his disgraceful past, and his request would cause him much trouble in later years.)

One should also note the elitist opinions, often carefully veiled in jest, that Sade expressed in his first year of freedom. On July 14, 1790, for example, he poked fun at the lavish festival held on the first anniversary of the fall of the Bastille: "I was in the best place but still was drenched with six hours of rain . . . which goes to prove that God had just declared himself an aristocrat."[6] He showed his distaste for the rabble a few months later on the occasion of the burial of his kinsman Mirabeau, known as "The Liberator," whose sudden death was initially suspected to have been caused by poisoning: "The populace flows toward public spectacles in order to interrupt them. . . . Good Parisians, content to see that the liberator died such a beautiful death, ceased to menace the aristocrats whom they earlier held responsible for this great misfortune."[7]

Another proof of Sade's conservatism was his reaction to the revolutionary government's decision, in 1792, to abolish aristocratic privileges and titles by destroying all the genealogical material stored in public archives. Sade immediately wrote his steward in Mazan, M. Ripert, to safeguard his own family's papers by storing them in "a dry place where no living being can find them."[8] So rather than adopt the surrealists' absurd model of a "marquis sans-culottes," one should see him as an aristocrat in sentiment, a cynic in his view of history, and the most prudent of bourgeois in his lifestyle. Secretly fearful of any threat to his property, shedding hidden tears over the beheading of fellow nobles, relentlessly opportunistic in his public stances, the *ci-devant* marquis (the adjective was used officially to designate former noblemen) was an unswerving moderate horrified by political excess.

ONE FEATURE of the Revolution particularly pleased Sade. He was finally able to declare himself a writer. Unlike the old regime, under which professions were deemed unsuitable to true "gentlemen," the new society required every citizen to make a living. Upon his being set free, one of Sade's earliest moves was to join the Society of Authors, founded two decades previously by Beaumarchais. The first literary genre he set his cap on was drama: beyond the fact that it was more remunerative than other forms, his highest ambition was, as always, to be a popular, respected dramatist. Within two months of his release, he had already submitted one of the dramas he had written in jail, *Oxtiern,* to the Comédie Française. Over the following three years he would propose a score of other plays to Paris theaters, all of them strikingly chaste works, devoid of rape, torture, or any other form of cruelty, in which vice is punished and social conventions are venerated.

But his career as a dramatist was overall a failure. Of the three works accepted at the Comédie Française, only *Oxtiern* and *Le Suborneur* were ever played, and both of them had a mixed reception. Although one critic declared that it had "interest and energy,"[9] *Oxtiern* was booed by spectators who found its rhetoric too close to that of the old regime, and the play was suspended after two performances. *Le Suborneur,* produced in 1792, met a similar fate, being repeatedly interrupted by rioting citizens. Its demise, in fact, incited Sade to make yet another derogatory comment about the masses who were taking over the Revolution. Speaking of the obligatory wearing of the Phrygian-style bonnets radical factions had recently imposed on citizens, he wrote to Gaufridy: "The Jacobins were responsible for the failure of a play of mine last month, for the simple reason that it was written by a *ci-devant.* They all wore red bonnets; it was the first time that was seen. . . . I was fated to be their first victim." [10]

It could be said that this society dramatist manqué looked on his pornographic works as a *travail alimentaire* (the French euphemism for "potboiler"), a means of financial support resorted to when he suffered setbacks in his career as a "respectable" author. Disappointed by his failure to have an immediate hit onstage, Sade began in late 1790 to revise one of the three full-length novels he had written in jail, *Les Infortunes de la Vertu,* which he retitled *Justine ou les Malheurs de la Vertu.* It would be the first of his works to be published. But as with much fiction of the genre, its author remained uncited and its frontispiece indicated an imaginary printing press in Holland, which was a haven, in Sade's time, for illicit literature (it was actually published by M. Girouard, Rue Bout-du-Monde, Paris). Sade had high hopes for *Justine.* Pornography continued to flourish in the first two years of the Revolution as a vehicle for antiroyalist propaganda. "A novel of mine is currently being published, but it is too immoral to be sent to a man as devout and decent as you are," he wrote in confidence to Reinaud. "I needed money, my editor asked me to make it *very spicy,* and I sauced it up enough to infect the devil." [11] (Yet another of Sade's subterfuges, this one intended to stress his penury and retain Reinaud's esteem. He had actually drafted many of those "spicy" scenes years earlier, at the Bastille, perhaps looking forward to making money out of them when he was freed.)

This ironic morality tale on the predicament of "the unfortunate individual biped," [12] as Sade refers to humanity, is a philosophical novel on the model of Voltaire's *Candide,* in which the protagonist endures a series of calamities that are designed to disprove a moral tenet. Just as Candide retains trust in Pangloss's optimism throughout many cruel twists of fate, so the unswervingly righteous Justine, orphaned at age fourteen, maintains her belief in God and in charity throughout the abuses she suffers at the hands of numerous bloodthirsty villains. But in Sade's hands, this popular motif of eighteenth-century European fiction —the futility of human virtue and the all too frequent triumph of vice—

is exemplified by scenes of barely tolerable cruelty. Among Justine's tribulations: falsely accused of theft by her first employer, she flees jail and is raped in a forest. She finds work as a ladies' maid in a noble family's castle but is forced to leave when her employer's woman-hating homosexual nephew threatens to kill her because she will not assist him in the murder of his aunt. Sheltered by a doctor who initially seems benign, she is persecuted by him when she tries to keep him from killing his own child. Escaping once more, she makes a pilgrimage to a monastery, where she becomes the victim of four depraved monks who practice monstrous sexual tortures on every woman they capture.

"Dear God," Justine exclaims in the middle of her tribulations, "is it possible that each time my heart is moved to virtuous action the most hideous punishments befall me?"[13] The victim of merciless, unwarranted accidents, a female forerunner of Kafka's Absurd Man, our heroine is viciously exploited each time she offers help or affection. Upon each new calamity, she is thrust back once more into one of those repressive gated compounds—heavily guarded fortresses, convents, jails—that are the staples of Sade's fictions and are projections of the author's own imprisoned state. Justine's successive calamities serve to undermine a fundamental Christian tenet: the belief that a natural leaning toward charity is fundamental to the individual and that there is a providence that looks after the good and the pious. She next falls into the hands of Comte de Gernande, a notorious vampire whose keenest erotic pleasure is to bleed women, including his own wife, to death. Fleeing yet again, she is promised shelter by a man whose life she has just saved, only to be enslaved by his band of counterfeiters. Finally rescued from her cycle of misfortunes by her wealthy long-lost sister, Juliette, who has prospered by leading a life of debauch diametrically opposed to Justine's, our heroine at last begins to enjoy a safe and happy family existence. But a few weeks into her liberation she is killed, at the age of twenty-seven, by a bolt of lightning. So merciless is Justine's fate, so relentless is her suffering at the hands of omnipotent tormentors that one could be tempted to see this as Sade's most autobiographical novel: seeing the innumerable times Sade begged his sexual partners to whip him, it can be argued that he is quite as much of a masochist as he is a sadist, and that his fantasies of torture are as geared to experiencing pain as they are to inflicting it. As his ardent admirer Gustave Flaubert would put it some decades later about his own heroine, Sade might well have said, *"Justine, c'est moi."*

Justine typifies the malicious subversion of Enlightenment ideas—most particularly Rousseau's—that prevails throughout Sade's work. He espouses the *philosophes'* belief in living in accordance with nature, but he sets their credo on its head and denies their doctrine of nature's inherent goodness. In his pessimistic reversal, nature is cruel and evil; we can save ourselves only by emulating its corruption and making egoism our principal moral guide. "[Nature's] movement is nothing but a perpetual sequence of crimes. . . . If crime serves it, if nature desires crimes, can they offend her?"[14] As in all Sade's fictions, the author is overly eager to convert us to this cynical message, to expose the vacuity of Enlightenment optimism. As he harangues us with lectures on the relativity of mores, on the practice of infanticide in China, or on theft and sodomy in Greece, his narrative all too often drowns in his villains' constant theorizing (in her brilliant book *The Sadeian Woman*, Angela Carter writes that Sade's protagonists have "the infernal loquacity of the damned"). Only *Justine*'s ending—Sade's concession to the growing puritanism of the Revolution—retains a dose of conventional morality: Justine's sister Juliette, overwhelmed by the sorrow of her sibling's death, sees the tragedy as "a warning from the Almighty to listen to the voice of remorse." She expiates her past sins by forsaking all worldly goods and joining the Carmelite order, soon becoming "as exemplary for her piety as she is for her wisdom and the purity of her morals."[15]

Fueled as it was by Sade's vengeful rage at the society that had deprived him of freedom, even in the context of eighteenth-century pornography *Justine* was strong stuff. "If it falls into your hands, burn it and don't read it; I'm disavowing it,"[16] Sade wrote to Reinaud about his first published novel, only half in jest. He was all too aware of *Justine*'s potential political dangers, and to his last day he denied that he had written it. The book had a distinct underground success and was extremely influential. Some literary historians believe it provided the inspiration for M. G. Lewis's *The Monk*, a pivotal work in the Novel of Terror genre. And it went through half a dozen editions in the following decade. But most reviewers savaged it, and its bad press would have serious political consequences for Sade in later years. Writing in the literary supplement *Affiches, annonces et avis divers, ou Journal général de France,* one critic admitted that "the imagination which produced this monstrous work . . . is rich and brilliant," and that the book might safely be read by those "wise and mature men whose experience and becalmed passions make them invulnerable to danger." But it qualified these cautious accolades with very negative caveats:

> All that is most unleashed, indecent, even disgusting, is heaped into this bizarre novel. . . . The reading of it is both exhausting and revolting. It is difficult to not often close the book out of disgust and indignation. . . . This is, at the least, a dangerous work. . . . Flee this venal book the way you would

flee an eye-pleasing dish that cloaks a subtle poison! Virtuous parents, hide it from the sight of your children! It is not even fitting for mature eyes.[17]

Not having fulfilled his initial hopes for a literary renown that would help to "rehabilitate" his social standing, Sade had to be content with more private familial joys. For a while he even tried to find them among his children.

AT THE TIME of his release from jail, Sade had attempted to be an affectionate *père de famille*. His daughter, his least favorite child, was living with her mother at the convent of Sainte-Aure, and he visited her there several times in those first months. He seemed to care about these reunions, for his correspondence shows that he struggled with the mother superior for the right to see Madeleine-Laure alone, without her supervision. These meetings, alas, confirmed Pélagie's negative reports about the girl. As she approached the age of twenty, Madeleine-Laure seemed fated to be an old maid. She was gauche and heavyset, with a stubby, flattened nose and a jowly, expressionless face; her mental faculties did not redeem her. "I assure you that my daughter, Mlle de Sade, is just as ugly as I'd told you. I've seen her three or four times recently," the marquis wrote Gaufridy in the summer of 1790. "I've looked her over carefully, and I assure you that in both mind and body she's simply a big fat farm girl. She lives with her mother, who truly does not endow her with any style or wit."[18]

Sade's relationship to his sons, who like most young nobles in 1790 France were serving in the king's army, was bound to be more emotional and more prone to disappointment. Delusions were the stuff of his life, and he seemed to have fantasized that he could instantly regain intimacy with two young men in their early twenties whom he had not seen since their childhood. In view of their father's egoism and the antipaternal propaganda to which they had been subjected by Mme de Montreuil, it is amazing that the young Sades evolved any kind of a bond with their parent. Their initial conduct seemed dutiful enough: Louis-Marie, for instance, went to Charenton a few days after his father was freed, to retrieve his personal effects. Yet a few weeks after his release, Donatien summed up his impressions of his children in terms that were already wary.

"You'll find my children extremely gentle and intelligent but cold," he wrote Gaufridy. "You won't see them entering a poor man's house as I do at La Coste, to ask about his career, his resources, and his family, and so they will never win affection. I note with sorrow that they have a touch of the Montreuil haughtiness, and I would have preferred to see them have a bit more of the Sade energy." [19]

Donatien's attitude to his sons grew even more guarded when, like the majority of high-ranking nobles, they protested the Revolution by emigrating. This was a choice that for a variety of reasons their father seems never to have considered. Unlike wealthier patricians, he derived his only revenue from his lands, and emigration would have deprived him of this income. There were subtler motivations for his decision to remain in France. He had loathed absolutism more fiercely than most of his peers, and although Sade the man detested violence, the savagery of his writings, and their unremittingly catastrophic view of history, intimate that many aspects of the Revolution might have fascinated Sade the writer.

The great exodus of French aristocrats incited by the upheavals of 1789, which would amount to some 150,000 persons, occurred in three major phases. In the summer and fall of 1789, the princes of the blood and France's most ardently monarchist families left the country. In the summer of 1790, after the National Assembly abolished hereditary titles, numerous aristocrats departed. In the summer of 1791, after the royal family's own botched escape attempt heightened the people's hatred for nobles, a large third wave, which included some three-quarters of the royal army, left France to seek exile abroad. After a period of toleration, the revolutionary regime began to look upon these "émigrés" as implacable enemies and enacted a series of increasingly repressive measures. As of April 1792, the property of any person who had left France after July 1789 and had not returned in one month's time was confiscated. By October of that year, exiles would be banished in perpetuity and sentenced to death.

The young Sades departed late. Louis-Marie left for Germany in 1791. Donatien-Claude-Armand followed him the following spring and went on to Malta to rejoin his religious order, the Knights Templar. By that time, a French citizen was compromised by the mere fact of having an émigré relative. And throughout the revolutionary years, Sade's attitude to his offspring fluctuated wildly, depending on his solipsistic appraisal of what impact they were having on his political survival.

In 1791, after reporting to Gaufridy that twenty-four-year-old Louis-Marie had resigned his army post and left for Germany, Donatien gave the following portrait of his two sons: "The oldest . . . is anxious, turbulent, harboring a secret sorrow. . . . He wishes to go to the ends of the earth; he detests his own country. . . . The chevalier is far calmer and better behaved." [20] It was clear that Sade was currently favoring the chevalier because he had not yet followed in his brother's footsteps abroad. A few months later, in his next mention of his sons, he made a radical turnabout. Suspecting Donatien-Claude-Armand of trying to inherit money from his aunt Mme de Villeneuve, Sade raged about a recent visit he had made to Provence: "M. le Chevalier just made a trip for which I won't ever forgive him. . . . I like neither crooks nor spies. . . . Never could his brother have been capable of such an infamy."[21] A while later, after Pélagie, with whom he occasionally exchanged news of their children, reassured him that Donatien-Claude-Armand's trip was not motivated by any self-interest, the chevalier reentered his father's good graces, and this time the blame was put on the Montreuil clan at large: "It's not the chevalier's goodwill I doubt, but that of many people who influence him. . . . Having been left young and impressionable in the Montreuils' care, he's capable of many little infamies."[22]

A few weeks later still, in March of 1792, the chevalier, who was serving as aide-de-camp to a prominent royalist general, made a surprise visit that pleased his father greatly. "He'd just written me from 160,000 leagues away, and suddenly here he is, bursting into my room and embracing me. . . . He was carrying an important letter. . . . We hardly had four or five hours together."[23]

But Sade's paternal emotions were mercurial at best: a few months later, his opinion was once more reversed. "The chevalier deserted, and in a vile way," he wrote when Donatien-Claude-Armand left France, defecting from his regiment without having taken official leave as his brother had. "The older one behaved a bit better. . . . Possessed with a wife and children, here I am alone in the world like a bachelor. That's just what I'd always feared."[24] By the following year, when the National Convention had passed a law that defined emigration as "a crime . . . in time of war" and confirmed the death penalty for any émigré who fell into the hands of the republic, government policy toward émigrés' parents hardened, and Sade's sons began directly to threaten his survival. He then felt compelled to disown them officially. This is just one of the many public denigrations he would make: "Armed, like my brethren, to defend my fatherland, and armed in my heart because I'd rather give my life a thousand times than see despotism . . . rise again in France, it is not fitting for my sons to arm themselves against me. If they're not here within fifteen days . . . I disinherit them."[25]

Sade's parental emotion had never been steadfast, and the Revolution did not foster filial and paternal bonds. Apart from his amazingly faithful feelings for Constance Quesnet, after his liberation from jail there was only one sentiment Sade could express with total sincerity: his lust for money.

□   □

THOSE WHO LOSE their libidinal drive, through trauma or through the natural process of aging, will often find it replaced by a new set of fixations. In Sade's case, sexual impulses seemed to have been supplanted by a growing obsession with money. His lawyer, Gaufridy, was bound to become his new whipping boy on this quest. Having already succeeded Pélagie as his confidant and alter ego, the lackadaisical provincial barrister now replaced her as the principal victim of Sade's extravagant material demands and of his rages.

For now that Sade was deprived of Pélagie's financial support, his source of income, beyond *Justine*'s slim earnings, was the revenue from his lands. His finances were worsened by his prodigality, for he lavished far more funds on his Paris nest than his income warranted. To oversee his finances directly, he tried desperately to make a trip to Provence in the company of the "gentle . . . pious, very reserved"[26] Constance, whom he yearned to introduce to the Gaufridys. In 1792, he carefully described the kind of travel conditions he wished his lawyer to arrange for them, showing that the Revolution had not diminished his obsession with food and other domestic comforts. "We'd like to find accommodations at the home of bourgeois over forty years old. . . . We need two bedrooms with a toilet, good beds, a study or salon attending those rooms. . . . For dinner we shall wish for a soup, a boiled meat, an entrée, a sweet course, good ordinary wine; nothing to speak of for lunch, and a dish of vegetables for supper."[27]

This cozy trip was scheduled for early 1793. But that year's increasingly turbulent political events made travel virtually impossible. Since Sade remained unable to control his finances directly—it had been agreed that Gaufridy would send him some three thousand livres every three months—his correspondence with the lawyer became a series of hysterical supplications, which turned readily to invectives when the sums did not arrive on time.

The egoism Sade displayed in his relationship with Gaufridy is made all the more blatant by the fact that in 1791, the lawyer became a hunted man. Like many devout Catholics of his generation in Provence, he was a passionate royalist, sufficiently committed to take part in a counterrevolutionary monarchist plot. Arrested several times, convicted by a revolutionary tribunal but always managing to escape, Gaufridy sought refuge in Marseilles, Lyons, and Toulon between 1792 and 1793, when those cities were held by royalist troops. Sometimes he and his sons, who shared their father's sympathies, had to hide in the caverns of the Lubéron countryside, seldom spending more than a night in one site. Throughout Gaufridy's struggle to survive, Sade continued to batter him relentlessly with demands and condemnations.

In early 1792, he wrote, "Go on, crinkle your forehead, crease your eyebrows, say 2 or 3 times, '*Ah, ché peste d'homme és isso!*' [Provençal for 'What a pest of a man he is!'] . . . Listen to me, lawyer, it was a heavy blow. . . . The dear marquise got away with 4,800 francs and left 4,000 francs, and an equal amount of debts, to her husband." [28]

In July 1792, when Gaufridy had gone into hiding: "In the name of heaven, money, money, money." [29]

In May 1793, when Gaufridy was still in flight from Republican troops:

> You're letting me die of starvation. . . . I can't forgive you these miserable delays; they turn me into a beggar. . . . I only survive by going out to dinner left and right. . . . What I ask of you is *money*, what I want is *money*, what I need is *money*. . . . Do what you wish with Saumane, Mazan, La Coste! Cut . . . sell . . . raise hell, carry on like the devil, but send me money. . . .
>
> You're wrong to say that you can't take on any responsibilities; the assignment I've given you, and my trust, give you the right to take on any responsibility, except that of making me wait. [30]

Sade's pleas had become all the more frenzied in the fall of 1792, after the sack of his castle at La Coste. This pillaging, which not only stripped the house of all of its furniture but also demolished doors, windows, floors, many of its partitions and walls, was not executed by Costains. The culprit was a baker from Apt with high political ambitions, who pretended to requisition La Coste's furnishings "for the nation" and used a horde of citizens from outside the village for the raid. Although sacking the mansions of nobles, triggered by the vicious attacks against aristocrats being staged in Paris, was a frequent pastime that summer throughout France, some Costains seem to have resented the devastation of Sade's property. The village mayor, Sambuc, whose family had tried hard to protect Sade before his 1777 arrest and who had been away the day the demolition began, publicly denounced the raid at a community meeting. Sambuc and other village officials sent Sade "fraternal" greetings and their assurance that they would thenceforth do all they could to safeguard his property. "Everyone in the area longs to see you," they added. "Your contemporaries and your childhood friends have never ceased to cherish your memory. And they long for the moment, as we do, when they'll have the pleasure of embracing you." [31]

This message was as warm a greeting as the average *seigneur* could have hoped for in 1792. But it does not appear to have represented the feelings of most of Sade's Provençal acquaintances. In the following months, Sade would learn that he had mistakenly been listed in the Bouches-du-Rhône department as having emigrated. Upon his vehement protests, his name was struck off that list. But in 1793, when part of the vast Bouches-du-Rhône region was split in two, creating the new Vaucluse department, the deletion was not transcribed onto the Vaucluse émigré rolls; they continued to list Sade as having left France. He was never successful in correcting the error, which was most probably traceable to the ill will of local officials. And since the major part of his estates lay in the new Vaucluse department (a minority of his holdings, such as the farm at Arles, still lay in the Bouches-du-Rhône), this bureaucratic foul-up would have disastrous repercussions for him.

The sack of La Coste plunged Sade into great sorrow. As with many of his misfortunes, he put the blame on Gaufridy, who was still fleeing for his life. "In leaving Provence, you left trouble and discord; everyone is going to profit by your absence to ruin me." [32] (Gaufridy would at this point have been put to death if he had returned to Provence.) Sade continued:

> No more La Coste for me! What a loss! It is beyond words. There was enough in that castle to furnish six more! . . . I'm in despair! If you hadn't been so long in your damned communications, I would have saved the whole thing! . . . At the moment when you only needed to have patience for six months, you do me a bloody turn. . . . Here you are gone, and my business abandoned, and I in the most dreadful constraints. . . . For God's sake return to Provence. [33]

Continuing to plead for Gaufridy's return, he tried a novel tactic —expressing concern for his friend's health. "Persons accustomed to Provence have very great difficulty surviving in the Lyons air. . . . It is obvious that you're in great need of a cathartic." [34]

No results. He offered Gaufridy room and board at his home in Paris, the most dangerous city for any royalist to venture to, and promised the dissident some lascivious distractions. "I beg you, come to convalesce in Paris, at 20 Rue des Mathurins. . . . If six doses of Palais-Royal [the city's most famous prostitution site] don't heal you, I'll be responsible."

Few men have better exemplified the egoism attributed to writers.

XXVII

A Letter to the King

*Yes, I admit I'm a libertine: I've conceived every-
thing one can conceive in that genre, but I've surely
not done all I've imagined and surely will never
do it. I'm a libertine, but I'm not a criminal or a
murderer.*

—Letter to Mme de Sade, 1781

□

ON THE EVENING of the longest day of the year 1791, June 20, the royal
family, having recently been forbidden to travel the twenty kilometers
from Paris to Saint-Cloud and realizing that they had become captives,
furtively set out to flee France. The expedition had long been favored by
Marie-Antoinette and her closest advisers. That spring, the king, shaken
by the hostile mobs who had stopped him from leaving the capital, and
growing anxious about his family's safety, had finally agreed to attempt
an escape.

The flight plan provided for the royal family to head for Montmédy
—a town some two days' travel northeast of Paris, on the frontier of the
Austrian Netherlands—where a large contingent of foreign and royalist
troops would provide security. The project demanded imaginative dis-
guises: the royal children's governess, Mme de Tourzel, traveled in a
separate carriage as "Baronne Korff," in whose name passports to Frankfurt had been supplied to the entire party. The king, wearing a plain
round hat, posed as the baroness's valet, "Durand," while the queen
masqueraded as the governess of the baroness's children. The family's
hope was that once they were out of France, a coalition of foreign powers
led by Marie-Antoinette's brother, the Emperor of Austria, would restore the king's authority through military force.

But the royal escape went awry from the start. Attempting to leave the palace soon after midnight, Marie-Antoinette, dressed in a modest black coat, lost her way in the vicinity of the Tuileries and was nearly an hour late for the departure of the royal coach. By late afternoon, only one-third of the way along the scheduled escape route, additional mishaps, such as broken carriage wheels, caused a delay of several hours in the family's rendezvous with their scheduled army escorts. The Flight to Varennes, as the ill-fated expedition came to be called, may have been doomed from the start by the vigilance of the populace. At eight P.M., when the royal family was barely halfway to the frontier, news of the escape had already spread to the region they were crossing, and a postmaster at the village of Saint-Ménehould recognized the king from his portrait on a coin. A few hours later, when the party arrived at Varennes, the cobbled streets were filled with angry crowds and national guardsmen. And soon after midnight, Louis XVI, quietly saying, "*Eh, bien,* I am indeed your king," to an elderly judge who had fallen to his knees in bewildered obeisance, surrendered again to the national will.

In Paris, mobs defaced or smashed public signs that bore the king's name. A placard placed at a gate of the Tuileries palace read *Maison à Louer,* "House for Rent." The citizen most responsible for the king's conduct, Lafayette, who in all probability had been totally ignorant of the monarch's escape plans, was excoriated by the more radical members of government. The royals' return to Paris, on June 25, could not have been grimmer. Escorted back to the capital by thousands of armed citizens and soldiers, met by contingents of national guardsmen who had crossed their rifles in midair as a sign of defiance, they reentered the city amid a silent crowd of three hundred thousand persons.

As Louis's coach crossed the Place de la Révolution (formerly Place Louis XV, presently Place de la Concorde), a citizen rushed up and tossed a letter into the carriage. Sade would later assert that he was that man. Even if this is another instance of his mythmaking and the missive never reached the royal coach, Sade did write a letter to Louis XVI upon the occasion of his humiliating return. In fact, it was Sade's first official political tract, issued by his publisher, Girouard, a few days after the Varennes fiasco. This eight-page pamphlet was entitled "Address of a French Citizen to the King of the French."

> Were you leaving France as an emigrant? Did you intend to go vegetate in some obscure part of Europe? Did you wish to return to France fully armed and return to Versailles atop mounds of dead men? . . . For have no doubt, sir, there isn't a single Frenchman . . . who wouldn't prefer death to the restoration of your abusive despotism. . . .

You protest your plight, you say that you're moaning in your chains. . . . Finding yourself unhappy in conditions that would offer felicity to many others, deign to meditate . . . on those sad individuals whom you, with a single signature, . . . tore from a tearful family and thrust for life into the cells of those dreadful bastilles which are spread throughout your kingdom. . . . When one has permitted such great evils, Sire, one must know how to suffer light ones.

The most violent of Sade's attacks was directed against Marie-Antoinette.

If it is true, as it seems to be, that it is your companion who advised you, don't expose her any more to the hatred of the French; learn to sever yourself from her. . . . Dispatch her back to her country, which sent her here only to distill more thoroughly the destructive and venomous hatred it's had for us throughout history. . . . Make this sacrifice; it is essential to your happiness, your tranquillity; it will return to you the love of the French people, which you never merited to lose when you conducted yourself according to your own conscience.

In 1791, it was still safe for Sade to end his communication in the conciliatory tone of a citizen who believed in a constitutional monarchy. He blamed Louis XVI's transgression on his corrupt entourage:

All are disposed to forgive you. . . . Listen to what is being said, Sire: It is not you who betrayed us . . . this flight was the work of your priests and courtesans . . . never would you have conceived this project without them. Seize this goodwill, Sire, to regain the hearts you have embittered. . . . The French empire can only be governed by a monarch. But that monarch, elected by a free nation, must subject himself faithfully to the law.[1]

The king's bungled escape opened a new page in the course of the Revolution. Shortly after his return to Paris, it was discovered that in recent months Louis had written a long letter to his cousin the King of Spain, disavowing the reformist decrees he had been compelled to sign since 1789. Along with the Varennes debacle, this document eroded whatever love and respect the French still had for their monarch, and deepened the split between the country's moderate and radical factions.

The sense of national emergency was heightened the following year by France's declaration of war against Austria, a conflict that the king had desired as a potential way of overthrowing the Revolution. But the early campaigns were botched. Prussia soon joined Austria's side in the conflict, and enemy armies imposed stinging defeats on French troops and invaded French soil.

Meanwhile tensions mounted between Louis XVI and the Legislative Assembly—now France's central lawmaking body—as he vetoed the majority of its decrees. In June 1792, a mob of red-bonneted Parisians, pikes in hand, assailed the royal family in the Tuileries, demanding that the king's veto be abolished. Louis agreed to don the revolutionaries' symbolic red bonnet and to drink a toast to the people, but he refused to give up his veto. In the following months, violent food riots spread throughout the country, triggered by a fifty percent decline in the value of the recently introduced paper currency, the *assignat*. It is the concurrence of these crises that brought about the bloody events of August 10, when tens of thousands of provincial militiamen and Parisian sans-culottes—a newly powerful social faction, which would alter the course of the Revolution—converged on the Tuileries, demanding the abolition of the monarchy.

The sans-culottes who masterminded the "Second Revolution" of August 10, whom Sade greatly disdained, were radically different from the bourgeois and intellectuals who had pioneered the uprisings of 1789. Their name denoted their contempt for a potent class symbol—the culottes, or knee breeches, traditionally worn above silk stockings by wealthy bourgeois and nobles. Primarily self-employed journeymen, artisans, and small shopkeepers, literate but highly suspicious of intellectuals, the sans-culottes tended to puritanism and inflammatory rhetoric. So far they had been denied most forms of political emancipation and had not even been allowed membership in the sections, which required a certain level of income and was initially restricted to the more educated middle class—jurists, doctors, men of letters. Thus sans-culottes differed as greatly from the Jacobins, who drew heavily from those professions and whose archetypal leader was the elitist and decorous Robespierre, as they did from bourgeois and nobles. It was the sans-culottes who replaced the traditional Monsieur or Madame form of address with *Citoyen* and imposed the familiar *tu* upon all classes of society. Their radical egalitarianism was summed up in a song that went as follows: "One must shorten the tall ones/And stretch out the small ones./Everyone at the same height—/There's the true delight." (*"Il faut raccourcir les géants/ Et rendre les petits plus grands./Tous à la même hauteur—/Voilà le vrai bonheur."*)[2]

After massacring the king's private guard and the commander of the national guard, the mob of sans-culottes that invaded the Tuileries on August 10 tore, burned, and destroyed most symbols of the Bourbons' two-hundred-year reign. They went on to invade the homes of many nobles, including that of the thirty-five-year-old Stanislas de Clermont-Tonnerre, Sade's cousin, whom they murdered in particularly savage fashion, throwing him from a window and dragging his mutilated body back to his wife. In the following days, the assembly voted to abolish the institution of kingship and ordered the royal family moved to the jail of the Temple. It named an executive council, which would rule until a new legislative body, the National Convention, was elected. Of the men who came to prominence that summer, the most powerful, Robespierre, was a member of Sade's own district, Section Vendôme, as was his acolyte Saint-Just.

Some three weeks after the August 10 massacre, hordes of sans-culottes forced their way into several Paris jails, indiscriminately murdering women and children along with aristocrats, common criminals, and "refractory" priests who had refused to take an oath to the new constitution. One of the mob's victims was Marie-Antoinette's closest friend, the Princesse de Lamballe, whose horribly disfigured head was paraded before the jail cells of the former king and queen—now referred to as the Capets—at the Temple.

SADE'S REACTIONS to this populist takeover and to the bloody "Second Revolution" of 1792 are chronicled in his letters to Gaufridy. He remained the consummate survival artist, growing increasingly duplicitous in his rhetoric. Continuing to play the role of committed patriot, he participated with growing fervor in his Section Vendôme, which that autumn was renamed Section des Piques and grew to be Paris's most radical district. Rarely did he hint at any apprehension concerning the Revolution's increasingly violent course. Only one explicit statement to that effect remains on record. A fortnight after the massacres of August 10, Sade deplored the murder of his kinsman and close friend, Clermont-Tonnerre. "The events of the tenth deprived me of everything," he wrote to Provence, "parents, friends, protection, solace; three hours deprived me of all that surrounds me; I'm alone!"[3] (In fact, he was never "alone" in those years, Constance being always at his side.) A few weeks later, Sade betrayed his true state of mind by greatly exaggerating the number of civilians killed on September 3 (they amounted to some 1,250) and expressing intense pity for the sans-culottes' victims:

Ten thousand prisoners perished in the day of September 3. Nothing equals the horrors of the massacres that were committed. The *ci-devant* Princesse de Lamballe was one of the victims; her head, atop a pike, was offered to the sight of the king and queen, and her unfortunate body . . . [was] sullied by infamies of the most ferocious debauch; all refractory priests were slaughtered, among them the Archbishop of Arles, the most virtuous and respectable of men.[4]

This particular letter is as curious as any of Sade's documents. Government authorities had recently begun to scrutinize citizens' mail, and right above the statement "nothing equals the horror of the massacres," Sade scribbled the words: "But they were just." This was a safety device now essential to saving his skin. So notwithstanding his private admission of loss to Gaufridy, the events of August 10 prompted Sade to indulge in increasingly fraudulent double talk. Just a week after the August events, for instance, he took care to write to the three parties to whom fate had linked him most closely—his wife, his children, his in-laws. In these letters, which were motivated by the increased persecution of those citizens whose relatives had emigrated, he took his strongest stand to date against his sons' defection.

He wrote to Mme de Sade on August 18:

I'd like to know what they're doing in Germany. Are they serving a treacherous and scoundrel king who, with the most vile cowardice, simultaneously betrayed the nation he'd sworn to uphold and the friends who were defending him? I'd instantly disclaim them as my sons if I thought them to be attached to such rascals. Let them return, madame, let them return, let them embrace their father's cause. I'm a citizen and a patriot, madame, and have always been so.[5]

Great political dexterity on the part of one who only five days earlier complained that the events of summer 1792 had deprived him of everything. Equal duplicity, and a heightened sans-culottish tone, is displayed in the letter Sade wrote directly to his sons:

You are serving a traitor, a wretch who, during the tenth of this month, a day forever etched in history, committed treason against both the people upon whom he opened fire and the friends who had stood by his side to defend him.

. . . Only imbeciles could any longer serve the cause of such a knave.[6]

Sade had these letters signed by witnesses. It is more than probable that they were never sent and were merely intended to protect him in case of trouble. Notwithstanding his long isolation from the public sphere, his political sense had remained astute. He clearly foresaw the results of the populist takeover. A great irony of Sade's life, in fact, is that the sans-culottes' rise to power was simultaneous with his own rise to eminence in the revolutionary ranks. The man who had ranted against the foulness of an underclass "freshly emerged from the mire" now excelled at hobnobbing with butchers, bakers, and pharmacists. He mounted the podium, the obligatory red bonnet on his head, to offer support to his cocitizens' petitions, displayed his fine singing voice as he joined them in patriotic songs, collaborated diligently in the drafting of increasingly radical petitions to the National Convention. Sade's certificate of residence, the closest thing an eighteenth-century Frenchman had to a passport, was signed by a saddlemaker, a carpenter, a cook, and a draper.

Might Sade's success with the "people" be rooted in his lifelong distrust for members of his own caste and his preference for mingling with the modest petits bourgeois of his Provençal villages? However we explain it, it is on record that Sade was elected to his first term as secretary of Section Vendôme/des Piques in the fall of 1792, after its membership had been radicalized by a massive incursion of sans-culottes. He was probably more repelled than any other member of his section by populist militancy, but he realized that the diligence which had enabled his survival so far did not suffice anymore, that thenceforth he must not only run with the wolves but also howl with them.

So in the fall of 1792, two months after the sans-culottes' takeover, Sade was made his section's commissar for cavalry and for hospital reform. (His colleagues in the group overseeing the latter issue included a lemonade maker and a male midwife.) His report on hospitals was so well considered that it was sent on to all forty-eight sections of Paris. The pride he took in his success is displayed in the following notes to Gaufridy:

> D'you know that I'm highly considered in my district now? Not a day goes by when I'm not called on. . . . I barely have an hour left to myself. . . . It is clear, gentlemen of the provinces, that you're not yet UP TO THE GREATNESS of the

Revolution. . . . I don't have one aristocratic pretension left, and I'm up to my neck, heart and soul, in revolution.[7]

Some months later, he would become one of the section's twenty judges, an appointment that he once more rejoiced about to his Provençal friend.

> I'm a judge, yes, a judge! . . . You see that I'm maturing and beginning to grow wise . . . but please felicitate me, and above all don't fail to send money to *Sir Judge,* or . . . *I'll condemn you to death!* Spread the news about in the countryside so that they can at last realize I'm a good patriot, for I swear that I'm truly so, body and soul.[8]

Sade left no commentary on the execution of Louis Capet. A majority of the National Convention, the legislative body that came to power in the fall of 1792, voted for the former king's death sentence. The yeas included that of Louis's first cousin the Duc d'Orléans, who had become a committed revolutionary under the name Philippe-Égalité. The night before his death, after exchanging final embraces with his family, the onetime monarch had a hearty last supper of chicken, vegetables, wine, and a sweet biscuit accompanied by a glass of Malaga. According to his valet, he fell into a deep sleep as soon as his head touched the pillow.[9]

The next morning, January 21, 1793, Louis Capet, accompanied by a silent contingent of eighty thousand soldiers, made the hour-and-a-half journey from the Temple to Place de la Révolution. As he mounted the steps to the guillotine, referred to by the sans-culottes as the "scythe of equality,"[10] he leaned on his confessor, the Irish priest Edgeworth de Firmont. Shortly before he laid his head on the block, the prisoner tried to address the crowd, but a crescendo of drums drowned out his voice. The blade fell at 10:22 A.M. A band of citizens danced briefly around the scaffold, shouting "Long live the republic! Long live liberty! Long live equality!"

The only sign of dissent against Louis's death was the assassination, the day before the execution, of a very popular deputy, Louis Michel Le Peletier, who had voted for the king's death sentence. The culprit, a former member of the king's guard, who shot his victim in a café at the Palais-Royal, belonged to the dwindling monarchist faction that still dared to remain in France. But the nation's general mood was one of apathy rather than indignation.

Equal indifference attended the execution of Marie-Antoinette, who nine months later, in October 1793, would show exemplary stoicism at the scaffold. Upon that occasion there was once more a great chasm between Sade's public and private voices. He seems to have spoken his true mind in a notebook entry, jotted a few days after her execution, in which he clearly identifies with the ill-fated monarch and displays the depth of his sorrow for her death. He entitled this entry, written in the former queen's assumed voice, "Words of Marie-Antoinette at the Conciergerie": "The ferocious beasts that surround me daily invent some humiliation which makes my fate all the more horrible. . . . They count my sighs with bliss, and quench their thirst with my tears."[11]

In an official report written some months later to the Committee of General Security, however, Sade would declare: "The punishment of L'Autrichienne was just."[12]

XXVIII

President for a Day

*There is a need to create more gentle laws, and above
all to abolish for all time the atrocity of the death
sentence, for any law that deprives a man of life is
worthless, unjust, intolerable.*

—*Philosophy in the Boudoir*

☐

IN APRIL 1793, an exquisite opportunity for revenge against Sade's most
hated oppressors, his former in-laws, came his way. The Montreuils, who
had lived in his district all along, came into sharp criticism from members
of Section des Piques. This explains the totally unexpected visit in April
from the Président de Montreuil, who came to call as Sade sat in his
section office on what is now Rue de la Paix. Though there is evidence
that Sade, as secretary of his district, had recently taken pleasure in
intercepting the Montreuils' mail, the two men had not seen each other
for fifteen years. We are not privy to their conversation. But it is certain that the Président had come to ask for a favor, if not beg for his
life. All the Montreuils' children with the exception of Pélagie had
emigrated, and the Revolutionary Tribunal, founded that spring to
eliminate "enemies of the people," had begun to arrest the parents
of émigrés. We know that the visit lasted for an hour and that it was
very civil. "It all occurred as prettily as possible," Citizen Sade wrote
Citizen Gaufridy. "I foresaw the day when he would invite me to
dinner." [1]

The Président visited again the following week, when Sade had been
named a judge of his section. In succeeding months he returned twice
to attend public sessions of Section des Piques. "I have Papa Montreuil
in my lair," [2] Sade commented to Gaufridy on one of those occasions.
That July, Sade was elected president of his section. The post, which

rotated on a weekly basis, briefly offered great power, and the Montreuils were all the more trapped in their former relative's "lair."

Sade's references to his in-laws throughout these episodes remain oblique. But he did record the fact that at the very first meeting he chaired, he opposed a motion that came up for vote, and gave up his presidency in protest. It is safe to assume that the disputed issue concerned the death penalties being imposed on certain residents of Sade's district and that he resigned because he refused to sign a warrant that would have put his in-laws to death. "The meeting was so stormy that I couldn't take it anymore! . . . I was obliged to relinquish my presidency," Sade wrote to Gaufridy the next day. "They wished me to put to the vote a horror, an inhumanity. I adamantly refused. Thank God, I've washed my hands of it." He continued, "During my presidency, I inscribed the Montreuils on a list of citizens to be spared. If I'd said a word, they would have been lost. I remained silent. That's the kind of revenge I chose!"[3]

This quixotic act of clemency was not motivated by any sudden surge of forgiveness. For the past year, Sade had been very conscious of his power over the Montreuils and liked to joke about the ironic reversal of their fates. "If I find any trace of aristocracy [in their lodgings] . . . I will not spare them," he had quipped to Gaufridy upon ordering a search of the Montreuils' residence, once more deriding their bourgeois origins. "Did you have a good laugh, lawyer?"[4] "They are wretches, acknowledged scoundrels, whom I could destroy with one word if I so wished," he had also written to his friend. "But I pity them; I return disdain and indifference for all the ills they've done me."[5] Notwithstanding his bent for describing cruelty in his fictions, throughout his life Sade had been a committed opponent of the death sentence. His indulgence toward his in-laws was far more ideological than any act of personal charity.

Yet one still marvels at the nature of this encounter between the once powerful old couple—M. de Montreuil was about to turn eighty, the Présidente was seventy-two—and their now powerful former victim. Did the aging spouses debate which of them was going to make the initial visit? Did Citizen Montreuil try to persuade his wife that she should try to recapture Sade's affection, and did she demur, mindful of their burden of mutual hatred? As the Président was graciously offered a chair, did the two men begin their talk with comments on the weather (any mention of the Sade sons and other émigré relatives was obviously taboo), or the dearth of good cheese and wine in the capital? Did either of the Montreuils feel gratitude for Sade's act of clemency? And were they capable of sensing the full irony of the situation? This is one of the few times that Sade evokes our admiration. Thanks to him, the Montreuils survived the Terror, only serving some three months in jail. (M. de Montreuil died six months after his release, in January 1795. The Présidente survived him by six years, dying in 1801.)

SADE DID NOT have to pay for his leniency quite yet. During most of the autumn of 1793, his status as a revolutionary remained intact. It was then that he received the greatest honor yet granted him: he was asked to give the funeral oration for the first two martyrs of the Revolution. One was the radical deputy Le Peletier, assassinated in January by a monarchist; the other was Jean-Paul Marat, publisher of the rabble-rousing *L'Ami du Peuple (Friend of the People)* and one of the Revolution's most bloodthirsty vampires, who had been stabbed in his bathtub that July by Citizeness Charlotte Corday. The ceremony that honored them was marked by as much pomp and circumstance as any held since 1789. The two-hour procession, which was attended by tens of thousands, included entire regiments of cannoneers, drummers, and infantrymen; representatives from all forty-eight sections of Paris; battalions of young women holding salvers of burning incense; numerous delegates from the National Convention; two catafalques surmounted by huge plaster busts of the victims and carried by citizens dressed in antique Roman dress; hundreds of children holding aloft crowns of laurel; and, bringing up the rear guard, the co-orators, Citizens Louis Sade and Pierre Moussard, a fellow member of Section des Piques.

Having arrived at Place Vendôme/des Piques, where he was scheduled to speak, Sade slowly mounted the speakers' podium, on which the dead heroes' incense-shrouded busts now rested. To fully appreciate the moral context of his oration, one should keep in mind a few of Marat's public statements. He had asserted that "to preserve himself, a human being has the right to attack the property, the freedom, even the life of his peers. . . . He has the right to oppress, to put in chains, to massacre."[6] In another passage, eerily akin to the most violent moments of Sade's fictions, Marat had claimed that "rather than die from hunger," it was our prerogative to "cut the throat and devour the palpitating flesh"[7] of other human beings. "Citizens," Sade's discourse began:

> For truly republican hearts, the most urgent duty is the gratitude that is due to great men. From the flowering of this sacred act are born all the virtues necessary to the upholding and the glory of the state. . . . Marat! Le Peletier! . . . Those who celebrate you now, and the voices of future centuries, will only

add to the homages offered you today. . . . Sublime martyrs of liberty, already enshrined in the temple of Memory, it is there that, always revered by humans, you will fly above them, like the benevolent stars that light their way. . . .

A final tribute to the two heroes:

> Those famous men whom we mourn are breathing again; our patriotism is resurrecting them; I glimpse them in our midst. . . . I hear them announce the dawn of those serene and tranquil days, more superb than ancient Rome ever was, when [Paris] will become . . . the bane of despots, the temple of the arts, the motherland of all free men.[8]

Sade's eulogy was so admired that it was sent out not only to the forty-seven other districts of Paris but also to the National Convention and to the entire republican army. One is led to wonder what might have been Sade's true state of mind as he spoke these apalling inanities. Was this tribute to a repugnant ogre another opportunistic charade inspired by Sade's impulse to save his skin? If so, is the author indulging in his gift for pastiche, and do we hear a glacial snicker behind his parody of sans-culottes clichés? We can be certain of only one thing: Sade enjoyed himself immensely on occasions such as the Marat carnival. Having never achieved the success he craved in the professional theater, he now had a far larger audience—tens of thousands—to admire his ringing voice and magnetic presence. And the frequency with which Section des Piques chose him as their official orator suggests that his rhetorical and dramatic skills greatly helped him to overcome, for a while, the hazards of a quasi-royal pedigree.

SADE'S POLITICAL APOGEE coincided with Robespierre's rise to absolute power and the beginning of the Terror. In the fall of 1793, Robespierre, head of the nation's ruling council, the Committee of Public Safety, established an emergency dictatorship. Sade's fate would be closely linked to this leader's political whims.

Robespierre was called "The Incorruptible," because of his monastic lifestyle and his much vaunted probity. ("He would pay someone to offer him gold in order to be able to say that he refused it,"[9] one of his contemporaries quipped.) Although Robespierre detested the sans-culottes' egalitarianism, he had managed to exploit their fervor to suit his ends and became such an idol of the Parisian masses that he got away with wearing the powdered wigs and decorous attire of the old regime. His dictatorship was made possible by the grave dangers facing France. By fall 1793, Lyons had fallen to the opposition, Toulon was under royalist and British control, the economic crisis was severe. The psychoses bred by military defeats and an abiding terror of monarchist plots led the sans-culottes to agitate ceaselessly for more repressive measures.

Under the reign of Terror and of "Virtue" promulgated by Robespierre, who was a far greater prig than Louis XVI, a new level of puritanism spread through the nation. Prostitutes were driven off the street, and all pornography was banned on the grounds that "immorality is the basis of despotism." The "virtuous man in the bosom of his family,"[10] who was duty-bound to inform on his neighbors, became the new national ideal. In the final three months of 1793, Paris's prison population tripled, from some 1,500 persons to over 4,500.[11]

Sade's own fall from grace may have had as much to do with his virulent atheism, and the process of "de-Christianization" current in France, as with his noble origins. Ironically, he might have accelerated his downfall by indulging in one of his very few expressions of public candor. The antireligion campaign under way since the autumn of 1793 —the beginning of "Year II" on the revolutionary calendar instituted to purify society of its past—had recently grown violent. In many areas of the country, atheist militants such as the Jacobin commissar Joseph Fouché rampaged through churches, smashed or burned altarpieces and stained-glass windows, organized processions in which citizens spat at crucifixes, and replaced statues of the saints with busts of Marat and Le Peletier. Posters with the motto "Death Is But an Eternal Sleep" were plastered on walls throughout the country. In November 1793, the church of Notre Dame, rebaptized the "Temple of Reason," was the site of a great Greco-Roman festival, at which busts of Voltaire, Franklin, and Rousseau were enthroned in the transept.

And so Citizen Sade, not sufficiently attuned to The Incorruptible's mercurial tactical shifts, felt safer than ever when he went to the National Convention on the morning of November 15, 1793 (25 Brumaire, in the new calendar), to launch one of his attacks against the Almighty. It was just a month after he had spoken his tribute to Marat and Le Peletier, and he was very proud that his section had once more chosen him as its official speaker to address this popular issue. Obligatory red bonnet on his head, spectacles perched on his nose, the obese nobleman slowly mounted the podium to deliver his talk, whose official title was "A Petition from Section des Piques to the Representatives of the French People." Having waited briefly for the Convention's clamor to subside, he started reading a ten-minute address, which, among many other insults to the faith of his fathers, referred to the Virgin Mary as the "Galilean courtesan."

> Man is finally enlightened. . . . Reason takes the place of Mary in our hearts, and the incense that used to burn to an adulterous woman will from now on be lit only at the feet of that Goddess [Reason] which severed our chains. . . .
>
> For a long while philosophy secretly derided the foolish trickeries of Catholicism; but it was allowed to raise its voice only in the cells of the Bastille, where ministerial despotism could quickly silence it. . . .
>
> Only a republican government, by destroying the royal scepter, could abolish a bloodthirsty religion. . . .
>
> Let symbols of morality be placed, in each church, upon the same altar where vain vows used to be pledged to a chimera. Let these emblems, while firing our hearts, make us pass from idolatry to wisdom; let filial piety, greatness of soul, courage, equality, good faith, love of the fatherland . . . let all these virtues, erected in each of our ancient temples, become the only objects of our veneration.[12]

Sade, for the first time in his political career, was talking straight, expressing sincere convictions. Twenty years back, in his *Voyage d'Italie*, he had mocked religion as childish "baubles" that catered to the credulity of the weak. Belief in a Supreme Being is "an inexhaustible source of murders and of crimes,"[13] he had written in his early draft of *Aline et Valcour*. "Religion is a phantom invented by men's infamy, which has no other goal but to deceive them or to arm them against each other," he had written in *Justine*.[14] In November 1793, such views still met with considerable success at the Convention. There was ringing applause from the deputies, who voted to send Sade's text to the Committee of Public Instruction.

What Sade failed to realize—this was his first major misjudgment, the first time, in fact, that he seemed out of touch with the Revolution's volatile course—is that the Jacobins were deeply split on the issue of "de-Christianization." The all-powerful Robespierre, supported by another national idol, Danton, had turned against it. To paraphrase the familiar phrase "more Catholic than the Pope," Sade blundered by being more atheistic than the commissars. The Incorruptible, who often agonized over the Revolution's increasingly violent course, was particularly shocked by the savagery of recent attacks against Christianity. Along with his more urbane acolytes, he realized that religious sentiment was still powerful in most of the population and that such excesses threatened to scandalize Europe and lose France the little foreign support it had left. To those of his colleagues who had coined the phrase "Death Is But an Eternal Sleep" Robespierre would soon retort that death, quite the contrary, was "the beginning of immortality."[15]

So less than a week after Sade publicly attacked the Almighty, Robespierre made a speech at the Jacobin Club calling a halt to the antireligion campaign. The thrust of revolutionary thought, he would elaborate over the next weeks, was freedom of conscience. Attacking "those who make a religion of atheism," the fastidiously bewigged jurist, speaking in his calm, clipped voice, quoted a phrase already made famous by Voltaire: "If God did not exist, we would have to invent him." The words of Robespierre that might have bewildered Sade more than any other, however, were the following: "Atheism is aristocratic. . . . The notion of a great Being who watches over oppressed conscience and who punishes crime is the one held by the People."[16] And that is how the cult of a Supreme Being became the French government's party line in December of 1793, how atheism became branded "counterrevolutionary," and how many of its militants came to be considered "enemies of the republic."

"If atheism wishes martyrs, let them say so, and my blood will be theirs," a protagonist of Sade's next novel would say. As if acting on that offer, at ten-thirty A.M. on 18 Frimaire, Year II (December 8, 1793), two armed members of Sade's section appeared at his home. In the presence of his faithful companion, Constance, he was served with an arrest warrant. He did not seem greatly surprised. "Citizens, I know nothing finer than obedience to the law," he told his colleagues. "Do your duty."[17] Throughout the fall months, Sade seems to have had many premonitions of danger. They were based in part on the growing excesses of the Terror, in part on the fact that he still had not managed to get his name deleted from the Vaucluse émigré list. In previous weeks, he had taken numerous precautions. He had tended assiduously to his civic duties. He had written to the minister of the interior to ask for a copy of the July 1789 letter from the commander of the Bastille, the ill-fated de Launay, accusing Sade of dangerously rebellious behavior. He had chided Gaufridy for not abiding by revolutionary protocol and forgetting to use the Citizen form of address in his letters. He had inveighed once more against his sons for having emigrated. "I called them . . . I pleaded with them to share my gratitude. Futile summons . . . dreadful despair! The monsters . . . fled me; they refused to acknowledge their father." He even pledged to father a second brood of offspring, in hope that "their education and sentiments might console me for all the misfortunes heaped on me by the first ones." [18]

But these precautions had come to naught. On that December day of 1793, after politely greeting his captors and making sure that three crucial manuscript pages of his novel *Aline et Valcour* would be sent to his publisher, Sade was taken to a Paris prison called Les Madelonnettes. The official registry documented Sade's arrival at the jail, a former convent, which had also served as a correctional institution for prostitutes:

> On Frimaire 18 second year of the republic one and indivisible
>
> François Desade, fifty-three years of age, native of Paris, man of letters residing at Rue de la Ferme des Mathurins No. 20
>
> Height five feet two inches, hair and eyebrows grayish blond, high balding forehead, light-blue eyes, nose average, small mouth, round chin, face oval and full
>
> Has been brought to this house as a suspect on grounds of an arrest warrant. . . . To be kept here until new orders. [19]

Citizen Sade remained at the crowded Madelonnettes for several weeks, confined to a filthy latrine, before being moved to another jail. Although their creature comforts did not begin to approach the Bastille's, all the prisons to which he would be shunted offered plenty of polished talk and learned discussion, for by this time a major part of the French intelligentsia was behind bars. Alongside Sade at Madelonnettes were several prominent actors of the Comédie Française, a handful of army generals, a former minister of war, and a member of the Académie Française, France's leading archaeologist, Abbé Barthélemy. Sade had little time—only eight days of January 1794—to acquaint himself with fellow inmates at his next jail, the Prison des Carmes, where Napoleon's future wife, Joséphine de Beauharnais, would sojourn later that year, at the time her husband, Vicomte de Beauharnais, went to the guillotine. Other distinguished guests awaited him at his next site of detention, Saint-Lazare, among them the painter Hubert Robert, who memorialized the penitentiary in one of his finest works, the remarkable *Corridor dans la prison Saint-Lazare,* which can be seen today at the Musée Carnavalet.

It was not until March 1794 that an official indictment was issued against Sade (one of the document's signatories was the Terror's official artist, David, a close friend of Robespierre's and a member of the Committee for General Security). It contained the following allegations:

Sade, a "ci-devant comte," had two years previously petitioned for service in Louis XVI's constitutional guard.

He had maintained "correspondences with enemies of the republic." (This was one of the more concrete accusations in the document, obviously based on the letters he exchanged with the militant monarchist Gaufridy.)

Sade was "in every way a very immoral and suspect man, not worthy of society." The sources cited for this accusation were shamelessly outdated—a 1768 scandal sheet report on the Arcueil incident, a 1778 issue of the gossip sheet "The British Spy."

There were several other allegations. Sade had once opposed a vote of censure against a prominent member of the centrist Girondist faction, former Minister Roland. He was cited as being "an enemy of republican groups, constantly making comparisons drawn from Greek and Roman history" (under the influence of the vehemently anti-intellectual sansculottes, such classical allusions, immensely popular at the beginning of the Revolution, were now being censured). And he was berated for having "feigned patriotism" at the meetings of his section; this accusation was accompanied by the wry comment that "none of them [the members of Section des Piques] were his dupes."[20]

How many of Sade's political faux pas are left unstated in this document! To cite only a few omissions: the abrupt manner in which he gave up the directorship of his section the previous summer, in protest against some "inhuman" measure; his probable intervention in favor of the Montreuils; his open opposition to one of Robespierre's proposed measures, a universal military draft; the publication of his novel *Justine*, which, though issued anonymously, many suspected him of having authored, and which was cited a few weeks after his arrest as a "dangerous and abominable" work.[21] And what about Sade's manifesto against the Supreme Being, delivered at the Convention a bare six days before Robespierre announced that "Atheism is aristocratic"? Given that very few high-ranking noblemen still living in France had survived the autumn of 1793 (the late king's cousin the Duc d'Orléans, a.k.a. Philippe-Égalité, had been beheaded a few weeks before Sade's arrest), it is remarkable that Sade remained free as long as he did. His rhetorical and literary gifts must indeed have been highly prized.

He tried, of course, to defend himself. As soon as he had read through the list of charges, he wrote numerous reports to the Committee for General Security, listing his credentials as a patriot. Chronicling the suffering imposed on him by the ancien régime, he appealed to his peers' own patriotism: "The sufferings of a true patriot are the delight of all enemies of the revolution. . . . My heart is pure, my blood is ready to flow for the happiness of the republic."[22] "The unfortunate Sade . . . has moaned . . . in jail merely for having displeased the infamous aristocracy."[23] He emphasized his loathing for Louis XVI, "the most cowardly, deceitful, and infamous tyrant," whose head he saw fall "like a true republican."[24]

Sade once more disavowed his aristocratic origins, claiming that he had "never once set foot at court"[25] (about the only truth in the entire cluster of documents) and that his ancestors "were for a long time engaged in the honorable farming trade." He also lied outlandishly about his children, stating that he had not seen them since 1772, "not since the crib, so to speak," that he was ignorant of their whereabouts, and that if they had emigrated, he condemned them "to public execra- tion."[26] And he asserted that he was only waiting for his divorce to become legalized to marry Citizeness Constance Quesnet, "the daugh- ter of a tailor, one of Paris's most excellent patriots."[27]

Seldom had Sade displayed his chicanery more abundantly than in these attempts at self-exoneration, sent every few weeks to various government agencies and preserved in France's National Archives. He even underscored his early display of patriotic fervor by claiming that he had "collaborated in the seizure of the Bastille."[28] (He had been whisked off to Charenton ten days before the fortress fell.)

"I previously loved the Revolution in theory, I now adore it through gratitude. . . ."[29] "Since the Revolution my life has been marked by repeated sacrifices. . . ."[30] "Sade moaned in the dreadful dun- geons of the Bastille; how could he not cherish the reign of liberty?"[31]

But in 1794, even the most sycophantic rhetoric could not reduce any citizen's prison time. And so Sade was moved on to yet another site of detention, in a suburb of Paris, close to the large open space, Place du Trône Renversé, that is now called Place de la Nation. He would later describe this new jail, Picpus, as an "earthly paradise" compared with his three previous lodgings. Located in a former mansion of the famous courtesan Ninon de Lenclos, Picpus was the Ritz of revolutionary jails, its room and board exorbitantly expensive (Constance found some way to foot the bill). Here he enjoyed good food, daily newspaper delivery, a ten-acre garden rich with flowers, vineyards, and fruit trees—in his own words, "beautiful house . . . elite society, amiable women." Among the inmates were the philosopher Volney, the son of France's greatest zoolo- gist, Comte Buffon, and the author of *Les Liaisons Dangereuses,* Chod- erlos de Laclos (this high-ranking army officer, a moralistic family man who disapproved of all libertines, did not seem to hit it off with Sade).

But the dearest company of all at Picpus was that of Constance, for this was the first of Sade's prisons which she was allowed to visit. Wearing the obligatory tricolor cockade on her hat or her lapel, his beloved "Sensible" came to his jail on foot, as Pélagie had for so many years, to bring him cheer and delicacies.

Picpus would soon receive far less desirable guests. In June 1794, the week Robespierre held his great Festival of the Supreme Being and set fire to a symbolic effigy of "the monster of atheism"—"that monster," in his words, "which the spirit of kings vomited upon France"[32] —the Terror reached its height. Even though the need for emergency rule was greatly diminished by the victories French troops were winning on all fronts, the guillotine's schedule intensified. During the "Great Terror," between June 9 and July 27, more than thirteen hundred seventy suspects would be put to death, triple the rate of previous months. When citizens complained of the dreadful stench caused by mass executions, the guillotine was moved from Place de la Révolution in mid-Paris to Barrière du Trône, just a few hundred yards from the Picpus jail. Since the city's cemeteries were filled to capacity, a huge ditch was dug in the unusually large garden of Sade's prison to accommodate a mass grave.

It was the hottest summer of the century. Over the following weeks, more than thirteen hundred corpses would be buried and thousands of containers filled with blood would be dumped in that ditch of the Picpus garden. It lay right under the inmates' cell windows. The great mid-nineteenth-century historian Michelet, who spoke to many survivors of the Terror, described these burial grounds:[33] "The sight of Picpus was intolerable. The clay pushed everything back, refused to hide anything. Everything stayed on the surface. The liquid putrefaction floated above all and boiled under the July sun. . . . Whitewash was thrown down, but so maladroitly that it made things still worse."[34]

The citizens who lived near Picpus complained about the smell, which spread for miles around. Their petition to the Committee of Public Safety protested "the pestilentially decomposing corpses of those aristocrats who, having been enemies of the people during their lifetime, now continue to kill it after their death."[35] But the city government merely had a wooden platform built on top of the mass grave and recommended that juniper, thyme, and sage be burned to allay the reek. Throughout those summer weeks, the inmates of Picpus, forced to live with these macabre vestiges of Robespierre's Great Terror, lost much of their former contact with the outside world. In the last half of June, newspapers were forbidden in the jail, visits were banned, the few letters that trickled in were heavily censored.

Little of Sade's correspondence has survived this period; he would chronicle Picpus only after his release: "All of a sudden, the guillotine was placed right close to our windows, and its cemetery in the very middle of our garden," he would report, considerably increasing the recorded number of victims. "We saw 1,800 interred in 35 days, a third of them from my unfortunate house." [36]

Sade himself escaped the guillotine by a hair's breadth. On July 26, 1794 (8 Thermidor, Year II), Robespierre's fearsome public prosecutor, Fouquier-Tinville, drew up a list of twenty-eight "enemies of the people," over a third of them former nobles, who were scheduled for "judgment" on the following morning. "Sade, former count, captain of Capet's guards in 1792, has corresponded with enemies of the republic," [37] a key clause of the document read.

Early on the following morning, July 27, a bailiff of the Revolutionary Tribunal proceeded to various Paris jails to take the twenty-eight accused to court. Sade was one of five prisoners on the prosecutor's roster who failed to respond to the roll call, were marked "absent" on the list, and did not have to board the dreaded tumbril that carried victims to the guillotine. He was in luck. By evening, most of the citizens rounded up by that bailiff had fallen to the "scythe of equality" that stood a few hundred yards from Citizen Sade's lodgings; he went to bed that night with no inkling that he had almost been laid in the mass grave below his window.

What facilitated Sade's miraculous escape? The most obvious explanation is bureaucratic mayhem: Sade may well have been marked "absent" because his name was called out at one of the prisons in which he had previously been held. But it is even more likely that he bought his way to safety through Constance's help. Bribes had become increasingly commonplace as the nation turned against the Terror. Constance was an extremely efficient and street-wise citizen, and subsequent events proved that she had highly placed acquaintances both on the Committee for General Security and in the Convention, particularly a deputy from Sade's home district of Bonnieux named Stanislas Rovère. It is likely that the tribunal bailiff had also been well compensated for not calling out Sade's name. For the rest of his life, Sade would attribute his survival to the "adorable woman" who saved him from the "revolutionary scythe." [38]

On the day of Sade's close brush with death—9 Thermidor, a legendary date in French history—a coalition of anti-Robespierre legislators, following an efficient plan of action, arrested the leader and several of his acolytes during a session of the National Convention. By the following evening, 10 Thermidor, Robespierre, Saint-Just, and scores of their supporters had also fallen to the scythe. They were executed, without a trial, before yet another bloodthirsty mob, to the sound of resounding applause. Rebutting two of the country's most militant atheist agitators, Robespierre, in his last recorded speech, had exclaimed, "No, Chaumette, no, Fouché, death is not an eternal sleep. . . ."

The coup had been brought about by a motley group of Convention delegates, who, impressed by the French army's current successes (the strategic Mediterranean port town of Toulon had recently been recaptured by a young officer named Napoleon Bonaparte), saw no further reason for emergency measures. Some of them were sickened by the bloodshed of the past year, others were diehard militants, resentful of the curbs Robespierre had imposed on their rampages. Whatever their political stripe, these politicians, among whom Paul de Barras would gain particular prominence, were terrified for their own lives and looked forward to fulfilling their venal ambitions.

One can imagine the elation with which Sade and his fellow inmates learned the following morning of Robespierre's end. Jubilation spread through the capital. "People were hugging each other in the streets," a survivor of the Terror wrote in his memoirs. "[They] were so surprised to find themselves still alive that their joy turned to frenzy." [39]

A few weeks after The Incorruptible's downfall, Section des Piques petitioned the new members of the Committee of General Security to liberate Sade, with warm assurances of his "adherence to the principles of a good patriot." [40] But in Paris alone several thousand prisoners were demanding to be freed, and the requests took many months to be processed. (Lafayette's wife was not released until the spring of 1795, and then only upon the intervention of the American ambassador to Paris, James Monroe.)

Sade was freed on October 15, 1794, under the short-lived "Thermidorian" regime that preceded the Directory and marked the swan song of the revolutionary era. The same wry contentment with which he had described his release from the Bastille informed his first letter to Gaufridy, who himself had narrowly escaped being one of the Terror's thirty thousand victims.

> The death of the scoundrels has dissipated every cloud, and the calm we're about to enjoy will heal all our wounds. . . . My name was on the list, and I would have passed under the guillotine . . . but the hand of justice seized the new Scyllas of France. . . . Thanks to the solicitude, as ardent as it was agile, of the amiable companion who has shared my heart and my life for the last five years, I was finally set free. [41]

Yet one senses a new touch of moral fatigue in Sade's communications, as well as a heightened sense of the human tragedy inevitable to most survivors of the French Terror. "My national detention," he also wrote to his friend, "*the guillotine under my eyes,* did me a hundred times more harm than all the imaginable bastilles ever did."[42]

XXIX

"Sade,
Who Is Not Without Talents"

*Frenchmen, Europe awaits you, to deliver you of both
the scepter and the censer.*

—*Philosophy in the Boudoir*

□

"The dancing craze was quite sudden, spontaneous, and frightening," a survivor of the Terror wrote about the summer and autumn months that followed it. "Hardly had the scaffolds been taken down, with the draining well still showing its gaping mouths to frightened passersby . . . and the ground still soaked with the human blood poured over it, when public dances began to be organized all over the capital."[1]

Robespierre's puritan rule was followed by some of the century's most hedonistic years. Concerts and lavish dinner parties took the place of guard duty and district meetings. In the 1794–95 season alone, six hundred forty-four public dance halls were opened in the capital. The extravagant attire of Paris's *Merveilleuses* and *Incroyables*—euphemisms for the fashion icons of each gender—were meticulously described in the nation's press. At the opulent Thermidorian salons, where the mode of antique dress was launched, Convention deputies mingled with patrician survivors and speculators grown rich on supplying France's busy armies. It was chic in 1795 to proclaim royalist sympathies and boast of one's arduous jail term under the Terror. Thousands of conservative, long-haired young dandies known as the "Gilded Youth," or *muscadins*, patrolled the streets, swinging their gilt-pommeled canes and spitting at citizens suspected of Jacobin sympathies. The red cap quickly went out of fashion. Marat's remains were taken out of the Pantheon and unceremoniously dumped. Usage of the familiar *tu* would be increasingly frowned on. Place des Piques soon became Place Vendôme, and as a token of national unity, Place de la Révolution was renamed Place de la Concorde. "Balls, spectacles, have replaced prisons and revolutionary committees," wrote the prominent statesman Talleyrand, who returned in 1796 from two years of exile in the United States. "Swarms of light-headed young men . . . dance while talking of politics and sigh after the monarchy as they savor ices or yawn before fireworks." [2]

The Directory regime instituted in October 1795, based on a fragile alliance of moderate republicans and constitutional monarchists, soon became dependent on the army for its support and was disrupted by frequent coups d'état. Dominated by a brand-new class of profiteers, the Directory was marked by as much venality and corruption as any period of French history, and its gaiety masked great despair. The harvests of 1794 and 1795 were disastrous. The winters that followed were the harshest in memory, and the Seine froze over for weeks at a time, blocking major supply routes for food and lumber.

Between January and April of 1795, the abolition of price controls caused the cost-of-living index to double. The *assignat* paper currency declined to one-tenth of its previous value, making the most basic staples unaffordable.

Beggars swarmed the streets; queues at bakeries formed at one A.M.; countless families died of cold; the suicide rate was unprecedented. Most citizens outside of the large-scale merchant aristocracy, especially persons living on private incomes, like Sade, were ruined. "There's no firewood; one dies of hunger on 25 livres a day," [3] he wrote from the home on Rue Neuve-des-Mathurins he had shared with Constance Quesnet since 1791 and returned to after his latest release from jail. Part of his land—his main source of revenue—had been confiscated during his detention. It was so cold in his flat, he noted in a letter to Gaufridy, that he was obliged to put his ink on top of a double boiler to keep it from freezing. In fact, Sade was so hard-pressed that a few months after leaving Picpus, he wrote a letter to a government official beseeching him for some form of employment, however modest. (In signing this letter, he again uses the archaic Provençal spelling of the baptismal name his parents had intended for him, Aldonze.)

> Citizen delegate,
>   Aldonze Sade, man of letters, having lost all his literary property during the siege of the Bastille, where ministerial despotism had detained him for many years . . . and having suffered innumerable losses during the Revolution, losses that he is far from regretting, since it is to that cause that he owes his

freedom . . . nevertheless admits to you that he has no means of livelihood.

Being well traveled in parts of Europe, possibly useful to the composition or editing of a literary work, to the direction or the maintenance of a library, a government office or a museum, Sade, in sum, who is not without talents, implores your justice and your goodwill, and begs you to find him work.[4]

In this speculators' paradise that left Sade and many of his compatriots dispossessed, much remained unchanged. Government harassment, though far less lethal than under the Terror, was still prevalent. In a nation veering from left to right like a drunken ship, one could be persecuted by promonarchist commissars one month and, after a leftist minicoup, be harassed just as harshly by Jacobins. The power of prerevolutionary France's magistrate class, its ability to lobby for most any favor, remained virtually intact and was beautifully exemplified by Sade's in-laws. Released, with amazing swiftness, right after Thermidor, Mme de Montreuil had remained as agile as ever at wielding her influence. She was able to secure most of her children and grandchildren's well-being by getting them struck off the émigré lists, thus absolving them from a stigma that would discredit thousands of citizens, including her former son-in-law, into the nineteenth century.

There were many reasons why it was in the interest of the Directory regime to harass émigrés. Their confiscated lands were prime sources of national revenue; their return might increase the growing tide of royalist sentiment; the prospect of the émigrés' return from exile was a nightmare to buyers of "national properties" who feared that their rights of ownership would be challenged. This chaotic government policy, which fluctuated widely according to the vagaries of internal politics and was all too frequently reversed in favor of persons with money or contacts, touched on the most bitter irony of Sade's post-Terror years. Although he was the only member of the Sade-Montreuil clan who had both stayed in France and "served the Revolution," Donatien was also the only one who could not manage to have his name deleted from the émigré list—Vaucluse officials could not be persuaded to correct their previous mistake. Beyond its political dangers, this accusation much aggravated his financial problems, since it gave the government reason to continue sequestering most of his estates. A year after his release, Sade and Constance had to give up their Paris house and move to Clichy, a suburban village where they found a modest flat for three hundred livres a month. And by 1795, Sade was once more plaguing Gaufridy with the familiar refrain: Money, money, money! Lease, sell any part of my lands you can! Sade was all the more desperate because he still could not get to Provence to attend to his finances directly. Travel to that region remained hazardous because the "White Terror"—reprisals against those suspected of having been Robespierre's acolytes—was waged there with particular ferocity. Moreover, Gaufridy now had a political excuse for his lethargy: he could plead that his record as a monarchist made it dangerous for him to pressure any of Sade's debtors.

And so although in the fall of 1795 Gaufridy managed to sell part of Sade's holdings in Saumane to one of his own relatives, Sade's complaints would henceforth grow increasingly piercing. Gaufridy's apathy was "cruel and unpardonable," his laziness was "barbaric," his sloth "execrable and criminal,"[5] he was exclusively responsible for Sade's poor state of health: "My doctor tells me that all my illnesses come from the horrible anxiety in which you maintain me."[6] Throughout these years, Sade's missives make it clear that his close brush with death during the Terror had not diminished his outlandish egoism. Upon hearing, in 1795, that Gaufridy had just lost one of his sons, he wrote him: "In weeping for the dead, don't let the living die of hunger, that's where your negligence is leading me!"[7]

And yet however monstrous this self-centeredness, for once there was a clear disparity between the lawyer's heartless indolence and the considerable efforts Sade made on Gaufridy's behalf. Upon his own release from jail, he had taken pains to safeguard the lawyer from any punishment his monarchist sympathies might have incurred. Working through Constance's acquaintances in government, he had even bribed a Provençal member of the Committee for General Security with a specie far more desirable than the wobbly *assignat:* he arranged for two pretty young women from the Apt region to join the official in Paris, ostensibly to serve as domestic helpers. And so Citizen Sade, as skilled as ever at the art of emotional blackmail, could now compare Gaufridy's sloth to the energetic efforts made in his behalf, asserting that the lawyer was causing Constance and Donatien to die of hunger. "How long will you allow . . . Sensible, poor Sensible . . . to dine on a glass of sweetened water, poor Sensible who on the way to [doing an errand for you] at the police station in horrible weather, just yesterday said, 'I'm going to get this done because M. Gaufridy worries so.' "[8]

There was a gleam of hope in Sade's finances at the end of 1796, when he was finally able to sell La Coste. However ardently he yearned for Provence, this sale did not seem to grieve him the way it might have in earlier years. Since the sacking of La Coste, certain emotions toward his family domains had changed. He now claimed that his affections focused on Saumane, the vast, eerie fortress in which he spent happy childhood years with his uncle Abbé de Sade. "It's Saumane I'm mad about," he wrote Gaufridy shortly after being freed from Picpus. "I'll go and end my days there. . . . I've four years more to work in Paris, at the end of which . . . I'll go to die at Saumane."[9]

The buyer of La Coste, Stanislas Rovère, was most probably the politician who had helped Sade escape the guillotine in 1794. He was now a prominent delegate to one of two citizens' conclaves that in the fall of 1795 replaced the National Convention and served as legislative bodies under the five-member Directory. Rovère, a prototype of the Directory era's corruption and cynicism, had saved his skin during the Terror by being one of Robespierre's most militant and bloodthirsty henchmen but had turned against him at Thermidor. By 1796, he had veered to the right again (his true proclivity) and become a royalist agitator in the Council of Ancients. Like countless other shady specula- tors of that decade, Rovère was making a considerable fortune by buying large tracts of émigrés' properties with flimsy *assignat* tender and exact- ing the revenue on them in metal currency. One of his delusions of grandeur was the creation of a landed dynasty in the area around his native Bonnieux. He paid Sade 79,000 livres for La Coste, and the sum would have served Sade well if it had not been for his former wife, who came out of hiding to zero in on the sale. There was a wealth of financial obligations, stipulated in their divorce settlement, which she had not been able to enforce during the chaos of the revolutionary years. She would see to it that Sade could not pocket much of the money he had earned from the sale of La Coste.

PÉLAGIE AND HER DAUGHTER had hidden in the countryside through- out the Terror. Seeing the reprisals still being taken against many aristo- crats under the Directory, Pélagie did not communicate with anyone outside her immediate family until 1796, when her son Louis-Marie, who was very protective of her and all too aware of her "kind, adorable, but weak"[10] character, alerted her about the sale of La Coste. She reemerged that year with a letter to Gaufridy that elaborated on her former hus- band's failure to pay his debts.

"My goal is to retain as much money as possible for my children, and therefore to not lose anything of what is owed me," she wrote the lawyer. "This is between us, and I'd be grateful . . . if you could answer me without compromising yourself; it's very essential for my children to retain a safe and honest man in their father's affairs."[11] (Throughout her correspondence with Gaufridy, Pélagie would continue to use revolu- tionary protocol: "My gratitude for your attachment," so she signed off one letter, "is always foremost among the sentiments of esteem and consideration with which I remain your cocitizen." [12])

Gaufridy was moved by Pélagie's plight. A devoted family man, he had long been appalled by Sade's failure to pay his debts to his former wife, so he started acting as double agent, carefully going against Sade's orders when they ran counter to the interests of Pélagie and her children. As a result of this vigilance, Donatien was forced to reinvest his La Coste earnings in land elsewhere in France, thus enabling Pélagie to transfer her lien to his new holdings. Most of his cash was used to purchase some four hundred hectares of nationalized farmland near Paris, in the Chartres and Malmaison areas. He was able to retain a small part of the La Coste money, however, to engage in an important subterfuge: he bought a house in a Paris suburb, Saint-Ouen, in the name of Constance Quesnet. The stratagem not being immediately evident to his former wife or to Gaufridy, they enjoyed a year of peace in bourgeois comfort.

An inventory of the couple's house drawn up in the late 1790s lists the following amenities: a living room graced with a marble fireplace, several sofas, and matching easy chairs; a dining room with a round walnut table that could seat twelve; two bathrooms, one of them equipped with two tubs; three upstairs bedrooms—monsieur's, madame's, and young Charles Quesnet's; madame's boudoir, its walls hung in blue moiré; monsieur's book-filled study, with boiserie walls on which hung tapestries later described in police reports as "representing the principal obscenities of the novel *Justine*"; [13] and a spacious garden, in which Sensible raised chickens, geese, and rabbits. In these cozy quarters, Donatien and Constance—he as obese and lordly as ever, she unfailingly attentive to him and still given to fainting fits—seem to have enjoyed a conventional and reclusive existence. Jeopardized by the Vaucluse's erroneous émigré list, Sade had abstained from any political activity since his release from Picpus and had tried to keep as low a profile as possible.

How we yearn to have an equally precise portrayal of Donatien's emotional life with Constance! But the nature of their relationship—to what degree it had remained the pragmatic "arrangement" Sade originally claimed it to be, how much mutual affection, or even passion, had developed—remains mysterious. Events of later years would prove that he was not totally liberated from the erotic whims of his youth. How were those impulses manifested in his ménage with Sensible? Had his bonds with her begun as platonic and grown physical? Or might she have continued to resist his advances and had he sublimated his lust through his writings? His dedication to her, in the foreword of *Justine*, makes a point of her primness, depicting her as a woman who, "detesting the sophistry of libertinage and impiety, constantly combat[s] them through her action and discourse."[14] So how did this supposedly prudish woman react to the more risqué objects of her household, such as the obscene tapestries that hung on the walls of her companion's study? And how did she respond to his writings, such as the 1791 *Justine,* the very salacious 1795 *Philosophy in the Boudoir*? Most mysterious, what was at the root of this winsome woman's attachment to a turbulent, ill-tempered, increasingly destitute older man?

All we have to go on is the unflagging devotion Constance displayed for her companion's causes, and her keen desire to ingratiate herself to his friends. (*"Mon fils . . . vous sanbrasse de tous son coeur il desire bien ardament de vous voir et moi jai le maime sentiment,"*[15] "My son . . . embraces you with all his heart, and as for me, I have the same feeling," she would write Gaufridy in her primitive spelling.) As for Sade, whose allusions to Constance remain worshipful, there are only a few oblique hints that they ever shared a more physical intimacy than he acknowledged to his friends in Provence. Sade biographers have pointed to an entry from his journals of the following decade: "Once, when she offered me something I didn't like, I reproached my friend for having forgotten my tastes. 'You're wrong,' she said, 'to reproach me for forgetting your tastes; what is certain is that I'll never forget the taste you have for me.' "[16] But these are slim pickings.

The delights of Sade's domestic life could not have escaped Gaufridy. And at some point he must have expressed his desire to protect the interests of Mme de Sade and her children, for his employer would soon criticize him for taking their side: "Don't always put my family, my children, ahead of me . . . for I have no family, even less any children, and all those relatives . . . continue to behave too wretchedly toward me for me to have the least sentiment toward them."[17] Sade's relations with his offspring were as turbulent as ever.

AT THE TIME of his release from Picpus, Sade had got along extremely well with his older boy, Louis-Marie, just as he had after his 1790 release from Louis XVI's jails. Although Mme de Montreuil most probably did the groundwork for deleting evidence of her grandson's emigration to Germany, the father further ensured his son's safety: he spread the story that Louis-Marie had spent the years 1792–94 "traveling throughout France, learning botany and engraving, disciplines through which he plans to earn a living."[18] Since mail was still intercepted by the government and his own reputation remained extremely suspect, Sade was careful to refer to his offspring, in his correspondence, under the code name "Vogel," German for "bird." His initial affection for Louis-Marie is evidenced by his anxiety concerning the young man's safety during the Vendémiaire (October) uprising of 1795. At that time, royalist factions rebelled against the recently declared "Constitution of Year III," which favored leftist republican candidates for the new legislative bodies. The dissidents were brutally put down by France's current political stars. One of the new strongmen was twenty-six-year-old Lieutenant General Napoleon Bonaparte, who later that month assumed command of the entire Army of the Interior; the other was former Vicomte de Barras, a key player in the downfall of Robespierre, who was about to be named a member of the Directory and for the next few years would be the country's virtual ruler. Louis-Marie, fighting, this time, on the republican side under Barras and Bonaparte, was in the thick of the fray. On the day of the insurrection, his father expressed his anxiety in a letter to Gaufridy: "One hears that the number of dead and wounded on both sides is considerable. . . . I perhaps suffered a dreadful loss; you know who was there, and I have no news from this young man." [19]

The following spring, Sade described his older son in glowing terms in a letter to Provence: "[He is] a very amiable boy who comes often to see me. I love him very much. . . . Very dynamic, idolizing the arts, uniquely preoccupied by painting and music, he doesn't hide the fact that as soon as the peace is signed he will want no other fatherland but the entire world. . . . He'd be off to New England now if I didn't hold him back." [20] In fact, at that time the two men got along so well that Louis-Marie scolded Gaufridy about the small sums he was forwarding to his father, taking him to task for "bad jokes that are not in fashion." [21]

Sade's attitude toward his two other children continued to be negative. He had once again made attempts to integrate Madeleine-Laure into his new family, asking her to lunch with his widowed relative Delphine de Clermont-Tonnerre, to meet Mme Quesnet. But he found her to be "as stupid and narrow-minded as a goose" [22] and eventually dismissed her as "a girl . . . for whom I wouldn't make the smallest sacrifice . . . the idol of her mother, who has created all kinds of troubles for me." [23] His younger son, Donatien-Claude-Armand, who had spent several of the revolutionary years in Malta, collecting rare seashells, and had then moved on to Russia to serve as an officer in Czar Alexander I's cavalry, did not get any higher ratings: "[He] could not be less concerned about me, gives me no sign of life, does not even write; I doubt if we'll ever see each other again." [24]

So in those years Sade's parental emotions focused on Louis-Marie and was analogous to the complex love-hate relationship he had once had with his own father. The very traits shared forty years earlier by Comte de Sade and the young marquis—profligacy, impetuousness, egoism, deviousness, quarrelsomeness, all accompanied by great charm—had been carried unto the third generation. Though he did not seem to inherit the older Sades' penchant for deviance, "Citizen Sade, artist," as Louis-Marie officially listed himself, was like them a restless and reckless fellow and very much a ladies' man. His paramour, for several years in the 1790s, was a lively Caribbean-born divorcée and fellow painter, known only as Mme Raynal de S., whom he addressed as "Mimi." Louis-Marie's artistic and bohemian bent, a trait particularly appreciated by his father, was apparent by the time he returned from exile. Within a year he was making a modest living as a painter and engraver, but he was also composing music and dabbling in literature. There was something both passionate and unfocused about Louis-Marie, and even his closest friend, a writer named Alexandre de Cabanis, took him to task: "It's time you begin to center on something," Cabanis would write young Sade in 1801. "All careers are open to you, and you're not following any of them with any success. . . . You've tried the arts . . . you've tried the sciences. . . . You don't have a second to lose if you want to achieve something in life." [25]

Like his grandfather, Louis-Marie seemed to love the beau monde of Paris. His considerable social ambitions, and his aspiration for a "good marriage," were hampered by his father's dreadful reputation, and this was bound to sour the men's relationship. In the late 1790s, Louis-Marie was turned down by Victorine de Chastenay, a prominent young woman of letters who had recently translated Mrs. Ann Radcliffe's *The Mysteries of Udolpho;* some decades later, in her memoirs, she would write about the problematic Sade men in the following manner:

"The son of a too famous madman—how else to describe him—whose depravity approaches the ferocious . . . is wise, honest, and even amiable . . . but I [reflected] on the terrifying risk of giving birth to the grandson of the man-phenomenon who shortly thereafter was incarcerated. . . . I refused Mr. Sade, who was not startled." [26]

Louis-Marie's relations with his father had already been damaged when he protected his mother's interests upon the sale of La Coste. The stigma cast on his marital prospects by his father were bound to worsen things. Within a few years of Sade's release, the two were again estranged. By 1798, Sade would refer to Louis-Marie as "that scoundrel who claims to be my son," a "monster," a "dragon," "the greatest egoist and meddler who ever lived." [27]

□   □

HE HAD ONCE MORE found a great solace, and also an attempted means of subsistence, in the writing of books. Now that he avoided all political activity, Sade had more time than ever for literature. One of his biographers estimates that between 1795 and 1801 he wrote an average of twenty to thirty pages a day, twice his rate of creativity during his years in royal jails.

Yet since his release from Picpus, Sade's literary career had been disappointing. The first book he had published since the 1791 *Justine,* which had had a definite *succès de scandale,* was the ultrachaste *Aline et Valcour,* originally drafted at the Bastille. It had been issued in the summer of 1795; and although the author had revised it extensively, striving to give it "that male and severe character which befits a free nation," it had made no mark. Its utopia of an egalitarian republican France was far better suited to the patriotic fervor of 1791 than to the cynical hedonism of the Directory. Sade may have made a bad mistake in not issuing it directly after his 1790 release; in 1795, it was barely noticed.

But Sade persevered. Later that year, in strict anonymity, he published a far more scabrous work, *La Philosophie dans le Boudoir,* which along with *The 120 Days of Sodom* and the forthcoming *Juliette* was one of his most innovative novels. It is blessedly short compared with the others, a mere 182 pages, in a current English-language edition, compared with *120 Days'* 483 and *Juliette'*s 1,190. Apart from the last scene, it is the merriest, least cruel of Sade's books. It is the one in which sexology, comedy, and politics are most harmoniously blended and in which he best displays his great gift for parody. *Boudoir'*s structure, a series of seven dialogues throughout which adult roués gleefully corrupt an enthusiastic teenager, is a pastiche of the conversational form long used in erotic literature, and also of eighteenth-century classroom didacticism. ("This little tongue below is called a clitoris." [28]) The central characters of this ABC of corruption are the profligate nobleman Dolmancé, described by his friends as "the most dissolute, the most dangerous man" of his time; [29] Mme de Saint-Ange, a depraved bisexual beauty in her mid-twenties who is determined to "fill [a] pretty little head with the principles of the most outrageous libertinism"; [30] and their prey, the delectable fifteen-year-old Eugénie, who in one afternoon session becomes as wickedly libertine as her elders. "Ah, you're tearing me. . . . I sense that pain is imperceptibly metamorphosing into pleasure. . . . I'm coming! I'm in the most delicious ecstasy!" [31] Eugénie exclaims, in a succinct summation of Sadeian pain/pleasure principles, as she is simultaneously penetrated by Dolmancé, Mme de Saint-Ange, and the latter's sexually prodigious gardener. *Boudoir*'s epigraph, "The mother will *pre-scribe* the reading [of this book] to her daughter," is a pun on the epigraph to a notorious pamphlet of 1791 entitled "Les Fureurs Utérines de Marie-Antoinette, femme de Louis XVI," which reads: "The mother will *proscribe* the reading to her daughter."

As the title indicates, philosophizing is as essential to Mme de Saint-Ange's boudoir as the roués' debauch. Dolmancé and Saint-Ange take respite from their sexual acrobatics by expounding on several pivotal Sadeian themes: the imperative of subverting parental authority ("In a century in which the rights of man have been so bountifully widespread, young women should not continue to see themselves as their families' slaves" [32]); the superiority of sodomy over traditional sexual intercourse; the abolition of all dominance in the institution of marriage ("It's as unjust to possess a woman exclusively as it is to possess slaves" [33]); and the general supremacy of sexual pleasure in human life ("Whatever situation a woman is in, my dear, she should have no goal, no occupation, no desire, other than being fucked from morning to night" [34]).

Like all of Sade's novels, *Boudoir* presents a utopia of permanent arousal replete with extravagant effects—Mme de Saint-Ange boasts of having had intercourse with twelve thousand men in the span of twelve years and of once being "fucked ninety times in twenty-four hours, as often from the front as from the back." [35] Such legendary feats suit the book's mythical time frame, which merges aspects of the ancien régime and the Directory. The novel's physical setting is clearly of the former era: guests arrive in liveried coaches and address each other in the formal *vous;* Mme de Saint-Ange's capable gardener, the only character addressed as *tu,* is sent out of the room when seditious ideas are discussed ("Leave us, Augustin, this is not for you . . . but don't go far; we'll ring when we want you back" [36]). Yet there is mention of the Constitution of 1795 and of the solidly bourgeois "respect for property" fundamental to the Directory era; and Paris's Palais-Royal complex, a center for both political and erotic activity throughout the decade, already bears its mid-1790s name of Palais-Égalité. This hybrid historical aura enabled Sade to indulge in the boldest and most modernist literary ploy of his career: the insertion, midbook, of a seventy-five-page polemical tract entitled "Français, encore un effort si vous voulez être républicains" ("Frenchmen, One More Effort if You Wish to Be Republicans"), which is read aloud, as an entr'acte, by Mme de Saint-Ange's younger brother. The title of the pamphlet, and its recall of the sans-culottes' patriotic clichés, suggest that the author meant it to be a pastiche of revolutionary principles. If it is read as satire, "One More Effort" is nothing less than a reductio ad absurdum of the doctrines expounded by Sade's bête noire, Robespierre. It might well be seen, in fact, as the writer's ultimate revenge against the puritanical dictator whose regime nearly cost him his head, and against the Enlightenment philosopher Rousseau, who had the greatest influence on the tyrant's ideology.

The roguish central argument of "One More Effort" is that the newborn French republic, having been founded on the dreadful crime of regicide, can survive only if it continues to be based on all other forms of crime—calumny, theft, rape, incest, and murder. "The republic is already criminal," Sade writes, "and if it wished to pass from the violent state to the gentler one, it would fall into inertia and ruin." [37] What is equally scandalous about this passage of *Boudoir* is that it takes a pivotal social fixation of the ancien régime's elite—the satisfaction of sensual appetites—and places it at the heart of postrevolutionary political discourse. Since the political liberation brought by the Revolution is meaningless without sexual freedom, a truly republican state, "One More Effort" preaches, must be founded on the satisfaction of sexual impulses; one of its imperatives is the institution of public bordellos in which both sexes can satisfy their erotic drive. Fucking well will make you into a better republican (in the 1790s' sense of that word) because it is "a means of purging the dose of despotism that nature had placed in [our] hearts" [38]—a despotism which, if left unfulfilled, would be redirected unto another person.

Philosophy in the Boudoir, notwithstanding its relatively comic tone, is not devoid of grimly aggressive impulses. In the book's denouement, the newly debauched ingenue finds the following revenge against her authoritarian mother: she rapes her with a dildo, has her raped again and sodomized by a syphilitic valet, and sews up both her orifices to ensure the onset of infection. This is one of the many moments in Sade's fiction that express the author's abhorrence of the maternal principle, of the entire process of procreation. It is tempting to surmise that this detested female is modeled on the Présidente de Montreuil, and that the book's violent ending was further fueled by his resentment of his own glacial mother.

Yet another perverse aspect of *Philosophy in the Boudoir* is Sade's continued subversion of Jean-Jacques Rousseau. His reversal of Rousseau's view of nature's goodness, already articulated in *Justine,* is here given a political spin. Whereas the state institutions provided by Rousseau's Social Contract allow us to recapture some of the goodness and innocence we enjoyed in our original "nature," Sade sees all governments as evil because they thwart and curb our innate cruelty. According to Enlightenment principles, the argument continues, it is precisely that cruelty which we must retain and cultivate in order to be true to "nature." "Cruelty . . . is the first sentiment imprinted in us by nature. The child breaks his toys, bites his nurse's nipple, strangles his bird, long before he's reached the age of reason. . . . Cruelty is far more natural among savages than it is in civilized man." [39] Sade's only practical alternative is the institution of "more gentle laws," which alone can create a gentler society. "New laws must be so mild, so few, that all men, of whatever character, can easily bend to them." [40] It is worth noting that Sade's views of human character are as pessimistic as Thomas Hobbes's—"*Homo Homini Lupus*"—but lead him to the opposite conclusions: absolute license as against absolute authority.

Like all Sade's works, *Philosophy in the Boudoir* raises the problem of the author's intent. Is he writing on a level of subversive irony or of deliberately obscure subterfuge? Does Sade take any of these wacky ideas seriously? To what degree are they incited by his often buffoonish exhibitionism, his desire to startle, jolt the reader into considering some extremist positions on libertarian individualism? The social and sexual anarchy touted in *Boudoir*, its disavowal of private property and its cordial support of theft, totally contradict the decorous British-style parliamentary system Sade held to in real life, the feudal possessiveness he expressed for his own family properties, the hysterical jealousy he displayed concerning his former wife.

The only passages of *Boudoir* unquestionably written in earnest are the articulations of Sade's atheism ("we relegate [such a God] forever into oblivion, whence the infamous Robespierre wished to take it" [41]). But then earnestness and consistency are the last features we should expect from this bastard child of the Enlightenment. One of the most maddening and modernist aspects of Sade's writing is that he has programmed himself to foil most methods of decoding and typification. Having robbed us of all the traditional pacts of trust between reader and writer, having also cracked, through his excesses, any traditional critical grid through which we might evaluate him, he forces us to play his own game, which works through principles of fluidity, indeterminacy, and sadomasochistic traumatization. "It does not matter whether or not our procedures will please or displease the object of our desires," the author states in *Philosophy in the Boudoir*, in what might serve as a summation of his aesthetic tenets. "The real issue is to shake up our nerves by as violent a shock as possible. . . . There's no doubt that pain affects us far more keenly than pleasure. . . . The shocks will be of far more vigorous vibration." [42]

THE DIRECTORY'S nouveaux riches had a taste for scabrous pornography, yet *Philosophy in the Boudoir* went relatively unnoticed. It may well

have been swamped by the profusion of literature, both chaste and pro-
fane, that flooded the market when the Terror's stringent censorship
rules were lifted. Between 1795 and the early months of 1797, the following works were published in Paris: Mme de Staël's first books of fiction;
two novels by Sade's colleague in pornography Restif de la Bretonne; translations of works by Goethe, Ann Radcliffe, and William
Godwin, which soon became cult books; and M. G. Lewis's notorious
novel of satanism, incest, and torture, *The Monk*. Several important
works by French authors who died during the Terror, Condorcet and
Chamfort among them, were issued posthumously in 1795. In 1796, two
seminal texts of Diderot's, *La Religieuse* and *Jacques le Fataliste,* would
be published. These are merely the books that retain some standing in
the Western canon; one can imagine the variety of now forgotten best-
sellers that competed in the mid-1790s with the anonymously published
Philosophy in the Boudoir. Moreover, *Boudoir,* which purported to have
been written by "the author of *Justine,*" was probably printed in expensive, very limited editions, which ended up in the libraries of a few
Thermidorian parvenus.

And so the following year, with his income still seriously limited,
Sade undertook what might well be the most extensive pornographic
enterprise of his century. This was a ten-volume series, lavishly illustrated
with one hundred obscene engravings, titled *La Nouvelle Justine ou les
Malheurs de la Vertu, suivie de L'Histoire de Juliette, sa soeur* (its last
volumes constitute what is known in English translations as *Juliette*). It
is probable that it was printed a few volumes at a time, by a number of
different editors, between 1797 and 1801. The chaos of the Directory era
makes precise dating of this particular work difficult; the chronology of
the series is further muddled by the strategy of predating frequently
used by publishers of erotica. The four-volume *Nouvelle Justine,* a vastly
enlarged and considerably more obscene version of its 1791 namesake,
was issued first. Its denouement is markedly different from the earlier
rendering: after being rescued by her wicked, wealthy sister, Juliette, the
heroine is brought back to her sibling's château, where she is forced to
mingle with a band of libertines who set out to destroy her because of
her intolerable virtue. As for the unsurpassably scandalous *Juliette,* it was
in all likelihood published between 1798 and 1801. Its publication would
seal Sade's fate.

SOME EIGHT MONTHS after the sale of La Coste, in the spring of 1797,
Sade was finally able to return to Provence. This long-projected visit—
his first in nineteen years, which he undertook with Constance and her

thirteen-year-old son—was the only hope he had of shaking up Gaufridy and establishing some order in his finances. The little family first headed for Apt, where they were received with great warmth by the Gaufridy clan. After a few days, Sade left his companions in his friends' care and began a tour of his remaining estates.

He went first to Saumane, where his foul temper incited a considerable scandal. The trouble arose over the paltry sum of twenty-nine livres, a fee owed him by a local resident that had been turned over to the National Treasury because of Sade's alleged émigré status. Without scrutinizing the facts, Sade accused the regional tax collector, one M. Perrin, of having pocketed the sum and threatened to "denounce [him] to the Directory as a swindler."[43] Perrin, in rebuttal, went directly to the regional tribunal of Avignon to accuse Sade of defamation and calumny. The court found Sade guilty on all charges and reminded him of the continuing dangers of offending government officials; he was fined a whopping fifteen hundred livres. Sade, too broke to afford that sum, ate crow and annulled most of his fine by making an official retraction, apologizing profusely to M. Perrin, and attesting to his "probity and honesty." Having maintained striking self-control during the more dangerous years of the Revolution, Sade had assumed since Thermidor that he could safely give free rein to his tantrums, and was proved wrong.

Sade next visited Mazan, where he had practiced his dramatic talents a quarter of a century earlier with his repertory troupe. It was his least favorite property, and it did not rise in his esteem when its citizens visited him, in the company of sheriffs, to confront him with a large and ancient list of family debts, including overlooked bills from the local physician, Dr. Terris, and even some forty-year-old arrears left unpaid by his prodigal uncle the abbé. Throughout his trip, Sade was forced to confront the hostility of the Provençals he had looked on, before 1789, as his vassals, and the difficulty of extracting any revenue from them. He realized that whether the collecting was done by him or by Gaufridy, the newly powerful local peasants were avenging humiliations imposed on them by many generations of Sades and would always find some subterfuge to get around their debts. Moreover, Sade, like many other revolutionary nobles, was caught in the mercurial politics of the Directory. While the more Jacobin citizens still resented him as an "aristo," the more conservative abhorred him as a Jacobin commissar.

Whatever thoughts Sade might have entertained about Provence for his retirement years were thoroughly dispelled by this journey. He never visited La Coste, the domain he had treasured above all others. Was he wary of returning to a site charged with such happy and wretched memories? Or was he simply in a hurry to return to the Gaufridys in Apt, missing Constance? His devotion to her was more evident than ever during his stay in Provence. Not having heard from her as often as he hoped during their brief separation, he stated his concern, in a note to Gaufridy, that she was "forgetting ancient pleasures when presented with new ones."[44] (This is construed by some as another suggestion that their relationship was more than platonic.)

Before returning to Paris, Sade would make one more fruitless expedition in an attempt to sell his estate in Arles, Mas de Cabannes. The Provençal town of Beaucaire, whose yearly fair had long been one of France's liveliest, was held in late July, and one of its most prominent attractions was its real estate auction. Since transactions held at country fairs were not always formally recorded, Sade had a chance of pocketing the money without Mme de Sade knowing about it. But the stratagem did not work, for he had underestimated his lawyer's probity and his devotion to Pélagie. The fertile, modestly priced land failed to elicit so much as one offer. It seems that Gaufridy's son, who at Sade's request had accompanied him on his trip to the Beaucaire fair, was under orders from his father to sabotage any auction bids on the estate. This earned Gaufridy the gratitude of Mme de Sade, who wrote to thank him for having avoided "a sale harmful to the interests of M. Sade and of his children."[45] Louis-Marie also expressed his appreciation, thanking the lawyer for "another great favor you've done the family."[46]

Donatien and Constance were away from Paris for three and a half months. Most of their journey home went without a hitch. "Good weather, good trip, charming mood of Sensible, not the least anxiety, not the least fainting fit,"[47] he noted in a letter on the way back to Paris, always anxious about his companion's health. But shortly before they reached the capital, during an overnight stop at an inn near Paris, they heard disturbing news concerning France's latest political upheaval. Reacting to the recent elections to the Council of Ancients and Council of Five Hundred, which had shown a resounding victory for the increasingly powerful monarchist movement, on 18 Fructidor (September 4, 1797) the left-leaning members of the Directory had staged a coup d'état. Effected, once more, by the predominantly republican army under the guidance of Barras—he was the only politician who would serve on the Directory throughout its four-year existence—the putsch annulled the elections. At the cost of eroding popular support, Barras deposed two of his co-directors and one-third of the recently elected deputies, and exiled scores of the dissidents to Guyana. One of the outcasts was deputy Rovère, the new owner of La Coste, who within eighteen months would die in exile, without ever having spent a night in his new domain.

Barras's coup equally threatened Sade. Under this new "Directorial

Terror," control of the press was greatly increased, informing against fellow citizens once more became the order of the day. Restrictions against émigrés were again greatly tightened. The new emergency regime decreed that those émigrés who had returned were to leave the country or be tried by a military tribunal (in the following eighteen months, one hundred sixty émigrés would be sentenced to death in Paris alone[48]). However reclusively they had lived since the end of the Great Terror, Donatien and Constance had retained considerable political savvy. ("God forbid that a *military government* . . . might replace under a prettier name all the horrors of *the revolutionary regime*,"[49] Sade had written presciently to Provence a few months after he left his last jail.) And this newest coup posed so many dangers that upon hearing of it, Constance, according to her companion, "came close to falling into a faint."[50]

There was now only one person in France who could possibly help Sade—Barras himself. The biographical affinities between the former Marquis de Sade and the former Vicomte de Barras must have been obvious to both men. Both were scions of the ancient Provençal nobility, both were notorious libertines; Barras had even boasted that he was a distant cousin of Donatien.

THE DIRECTORY has been as maligned as any period of French history for its debauchery, economic chaos, and corruption (there are some parallels with post-Communist Russia). One of its many paradoxes is that Barras, its most dissolute figure, was also its most gifted politician. A tall, flamboyant bon vivant with a mane of wavy black hair, this former Jacobin had built up a vast fortune through the *douceurs,* or bribes, offered him by prosperous army contractors. He was also famous for quickly wearying of his lovers and excelled at arranging good matches for his former mistresses. One former paramour, Joséphine de Beauharnais, he had passed on to young Napoleon Bonaparte, serving as witness at their 1796 wedding. After a stint with the wife of a prominent fellow Thermidorian, the beautiful Teresa Tallien, who was known as "Notre Dame de Thermidor" because of her incessant lobbying on the issue of amnesty for émigrés, he had settled her with one of France's wealthiest banking magnates.

In his leisure time, "King Barras" lived like an Oriental satrap in his country mansion an hour from Paris, where he entertained requests for amnesty on the part of other prominent émigrés. In 1796, he had granted Mme de Staël the right to return from Great Britain as long as she remained at the estate of her lover, Benjamin Constant. Pressured by

Staël to obtain a high government post for her former lover, Talleyrand, after his return from the United States, Barras eventually appointed him foreign minister. Barras had been very selective about what kind of citizens he wished to reintegrate into French society. Some 150,000 persons had left France since 1789; of the 17,000 who would request amnesty in 1797, only some 1,500 would receive it.[51]

It was this virtual dictator Sade would have needed to contact, after the Fructidor coup, to be expunged from the émigré list that was ruining his chances for a stable life. One word to Barras on the part of a popular Paris figure like Mme Tallien or Mlle de Chastenay, both of whom had persuaded the leader to grant amnesty to literally hundreds of true émigrés, would have done the trick. Now, having long ago chosen to disdain the power of family or peer networks, for the umpteenth time Sade found himself lacking significant political contacts. In this instance Louis-Marie could have intervened for him through Mlle de Chastenay. But although young Sade did write directly to Barras, pleading for help in rectifying the "cruel situation"[52] of his father's alleged émigré status, he was apparently reluctant to use his social contacts to plead for the "madman," as Mlle de Chastenay referred to Sade: it might have further weakened his chances for *un beau mariage*. In fact, Louis-Marie, like his brother, would soon attempt to minimize associations with his father by altering his name to Sade-Romanil.

Since their contacts in political circles were now next to nil—Rovère was dying in Guyana—the best Constance and Donatien could do was persuade a high-ranking police official to send Barras a memorandum concerning Sade's émigré plight. Since Sade had deliberately maintained a very low profile since Thermidor, this step, by making him conspicuous, carried its own hazards. In a letter to Gaufridy, he expressed his apprehension about coming to Barras's attention:

> It's yet another worry, another anxiety, to be brought to light this way. Barras, who is from Avignon, does he know of me? [Barras was actually from the Var region of Provence.] If he knows of me, how does he think of me? And what will he do, based on the information he might have of me? . . . My excellent revolutionary record plays in my behalf . . . but the old adventures, in the eyes of a fellow Provençal?[53]

Sade's fears were well founded. Men of Barras's ilk have seldom had any scruples about slandering fellow debauchees; his views of Sade were clearly stated in the memoirs he would write and publish some decades later:

If something could justify a state prison like the Bastille, legal and ethical principles would [suggest] that the Marquis de Sade might merit being imprisoned there. . . . This person is so aberrant that one could look on him as an anomaly of the human race. The system he dared to set forth, in writings not deprived of talent, had already been preceded in various countries by hideous practices that had provoked general horror but had not been submitted to punishment.

There follows an attack on Sade's work, whose basic thesis—that such books aim to corrupt the citizenry—remains unchanged to this day among many moralists.

According to his way of thinking, the pleasures of the senses do not consist of reciprocally agreeable sensations but are based on the imposition of the greatest possible pain. . . . To acquire disciples, to strengthen them in their criminal ways, he tried to demonstrate, in the novelistic genre . . . that the evils of the world are reserved for those whom we call virtuous and the crowns of felicity are bestowed on the vicious; that it has been thus since Adam and will always be thus.[54]

So Barras simply sent on Sade's request to his Ministry of Police, with a request for a "prompt report." Although Sade's petition emphasized that he was asking not for an amnesty but simply for a "rectification"; although he made it clear that he had not only remained in France since 1789 but had seldom even left the Paris region; and although his request was accompanied by over one hundred official documents testifying to his continuing residence in France—certificates of residence, tax receipts, affidavits of serving in citizens' assemblies, copies of patriotic writings—the Ministry of Police ruled against him. Its grounds were that Citizen Sade had failed to prove that the man still listed on the Vaucluse émigré list was the same man referred to in all those impressive papers, for the simple reason that the documents *bore too great a variety of first names.*

The police officials' reasoning was not unfounded. By both happenstance and design, for decades Sade's identity had been marked by an unusual variety of appellations. One remembers that his parents, who did not bother to attend his baptism, had intended him to be called Donatien Aldonse Louis and that out of ignorance or forgetfulness the domestics who carried him to church had him baptized, instead, Donatien Alphonse François. Over the years, the marquis had varied these names with striking capriciousness. He had used the initially intended Louis because of its associations to royalty (all the Bourbon kings had been called Louis), and the Provençal "Aldonse" (for which he preferred the more archaic spelling "Aldonze") out of feudal pride. In his earlier, scandalous years, he had successively utilized each of these names, or reshuffled their sequence, with the intent of covering up his traces from the authorities: Plain Donatien. Plain Aldonse or Aldonze. Plain François. Plain Louis, the name he gave himself during his stint as a revolutionary patriot. And also, used simultaneously or consecutively for the past forty years, Aldonse Louis; Aldonze-Louis; Donatien Alphonse Louis; François Aldonze Donatien Louis; Aldonze François, the name cited in his certificate of residence; Louis Aldonze Donatien François, the name he often used in Provence, which was listed on the disastrous Vaucluse roster of émigrés; and Donatien Alphonse François, his baptismal name, on which he would settle in 1800 and with which he would sign the few of his writings he acknowledged. The process of Sade's naming is further complicated by the fact that he occasionally added hyphens between these appellations ("Donatien-Aldonze-François"), even though they had not been specified in his certificate of baptism. Government authorities and some of his early biographers followed this erroneous usage.

Was this babel of names a pragmatic tactic that originated in the young Sade's need to evade authority? (He had fled to Italy in 1774 under the pseudonym "Comte de Mazan.") Could it be linked to his equally bizarre reluctance to abide by tradition on the issue of his title of nobility? (He had continued to call himself Marquis after his father's death, when family protocol decreed that he should have switched to Comte.) Or should we also see it as evidence of his elusive sense of identity, or even of a split personality? The government agencies ruling on the status of émigrés seemed to be wise to these psychological undercurrents. "It is inconceivable," their report concluded, "that this individual has ignored his own true surnames to the point of even calling himself, in a petition signed by his own hand, Louis-Aldonze-Donatien-François; such a disparity has not been clarified enough and gives grounds for doubts that there is a perfect identity." [55]

Beyond Barras's hostility and Sade's lack of high-placed connections, his failure to have his name removed from the Vaucluse émigré list can probably be explained by enmities on the rural, Provençal level: local bureaucrats still working out ancient vendettas against his arrogant family, local parliamentarians still prejudiced by his past reputation as the regional Bluebeard, new enemies like the tax collector M. Perrin, whom he'd wrongly accused of graft. The Directory era was notorious for its vicious settling of accounts, and any of these factions could easily have caused him to be retained on the list. Threatened with enforced exile or a criminal trial, Sade could only obtain medical certificates attesting to his poor health. Such a temporary measure could suspend all police action on grounds of illness and place a citizen under the scrutiny of a government functionary. For once in his life, Sade struck gold. The man assigned to him, a Commissar Cazade, instantly fell under Sade's spell and remained protective of him for the rest of his years as a free man.

Yet there remained the despair of poverty. In the winter of 1797–98, a few months after Constance and Donatien's return from Provence, the furniture in their Saint-Ouen house was seized by creditors. Constance had to sell her clothes to buy food. Sade played out his last card— appealing to the mercy of his estranged wife. In a pathetic letter, he suggested an arrangement whereby he would hand over all his Provençal properties in exchange for her paying him a modest yearly pension. "It's to your soul, your sensibility, that I appeal," he ended this forlorn plea. "Must I dread a refusal?"[56] A refusal he received, of course. He had gambled on the possibility of sentiment, and there wasn't an ounce of that left in the increasingly deaf, crippled Pélagie.

His diatribes against his family grew more vehement than ever. "Fatal children! Cruel and accursed spouse!" he wrote to Gaufridy, in another futile entreaty for cash. "I am far worse off, in my despair, than those unfortunates plunged into the torments of hell. Money, in God's name, money!"[57]

A few months later, in autumn 1798, penury forced Sade and Constance to leave their Saint-Ouen house and live apart. She moved in with charitable friends. Sade went to stay with one of his farmers in the Beauce area, receiving room and board in exchange for a little money the farmer owed him. But upon having discharged his debt, his host brusquely asked him to leave. After a few weeks of literally begging in the countryside, Sade moved to Versailles, for the simple reason that it had the cheapest cost of living in France. There he survived the winter months in the back of an attic, taking care of Constance's son, Charles. According to Sade's letters to Gaufridy, which often exaggerated his plight, the two lived on "a few carrots and beans," occasionally getting some firewood on credit. Their misery was such that Constance took food for them from her friends' table, hiding it in her pocket. To evade creditors, Sade was now calling himself Citizen Charles, a name cribbed, this time, from Constance's son. In order to better support the boy, he occasionally found work as a prompter at a Versailles theater, earning forty sous a day. For a while he was also fed by a restaurateur, M. Brunelle, "a poor innkeeper who, through charity, agrees to give me a bit of soup."[58] And yet he took this misery stoically, emphasizing all that Constance was doing for him. "It's mighty little to compensate for the worries and expenses undergone by the unfortunate mother, who braved the most horrid weather to run daily in search of appeasing creditors and seeing me struck off lists," he wrote to Provence. "In truth, this woman is an angel sent to me from heaven to keep me from being totally destroyed by the calamities visited on me by my enemies." [59]

The winter over, Sade again swallowed his pride and tried one more time to move his former wife to pity. He arranged for her to meet with Constance and a prominent Paris lawyer. But upon hearing of the rendezvous, Louis-Marie Sade sabotaged his father's plan, prevailing on the lawyer and on his mother to cancel the meeting. Sade's rage at Louis-Marie, "that traitor," "that scoundrel who calls himself my son," now knew no bounds. "There are few examples in the world of conduct as atrocious and barbaric as that of this villain," he wrote to Gaufridy. "He knows my situation; he came to contemplate my misery and not only refused to come to my aid but even ruined Mme Quesnet's ventures." [60] One thinks, inevitably, of King Lear. "They've ruined me," Sade wrote. "They'll ruin me yet." [61]

THE FOLLOWING YEAR, after yet another political upheaval, Sade was left to the mercy of a brand-new regime and of a new police minister. Esteemed by some historians as an administrative genius, by others as "one of the most sadistic and versatile political actors and opportunists in French history," [62] the former school principal Joseph Fouché had been one of Robespierre's earliest supporters. As delegate to the National Convention from his native Nantes, he rose to eminence during the Terror through the brutality with which he repressed royalists in Lyons. His execution of some two thousand citizens in the span of a few weeks and his frequent use of the phrase "Terror, salutary terror, is the order of the day," [63] earned him the epithet "Executioner of Lyons." Chameleonic enough to escape the persecutions suffered by many of Robespierre's acolytes after the leader's demise, he returned to power in the spring of 1799, when the political chaos that had prevailed in France since Thermidor reached its zenith. Barras, grown too dissolute and discredited to stage any more coups, had lost much of his former authority, and the Directory was again locked in a power struggle with the two councils. Many of France's most influential men were now paving the way for France's rising political star, Napoleon Bonaparte, by advocating a stronger executive. In July of 1799, the directors attempted to resolve the crisis with a total overhaul of government ministries; they appointed two eminent Bonapartists to key posts, assigning foreign affairs to Talleyrand and the police to Fouché, who instantly set out to reorganize and strengthen his department.

Several aspects of this fearsome politician's background would be pertinent to his dealings with Sade. Fouché, a member of Section des Piques throughout the revolutionary years, was already more than aware of the former marquis. He was a harsh censor, and following his appointment to the Ministry of Police ordered sixty of Paris's seventy-three periodicals closed down. He was a great believer in the value of long-term experience, and a sizable part of his police force would be composed of survivors from Sartine's and Le Noir's administrations, who were bound to have a keen memory of Sade. Finally, Fouché, like many Jacobins, was an austere puritan and gave the highest priority to reforming the Directory's corrupt morals.

It is significant that the spate of attacks that singled out *Justine* as the decade's most infamous book began the month after Fouché assumed power. One of the first invectives, published in the periodical *L'Ami des Lois* in August 1799, took the form of an obituary. Written by a former Benedictine friar turned gossip columnist, it announced that Sade, the author of *Justine,* had just died, and described him as having possessed "the most depraved heart, most degraded spirit, most bizarrely obscene imagination."[64] Sade quickly published a reply, which asserted that he was alive and well, and angrily denied authorship of "the infamous *Justine.*" But the former monk, undeterred, soon attacked him even more viciously in another tabloid, *Le Tribunal d'Apollon,* a periodical whose only redeeming grace was that it candidly described itself as "injuriously libelous, biased, and defamatory, written by a group of literary pygmies."[65] "One is told that Sade is dead, but his acolytes are not," the defrocked cleric ranted. "It is said that he organized a society of debauchees in Paris who put into practice the horrifying precepts propounded in his books. Useful and observing police spies, take heed!"[66] Some of Sade's retorts to these attacks carried his old seigneurial verve: "I'm not dead, and it's with a powerful stick that I should stamp the unequivocal proof of my existence on your royalist shoulders," he raged. "A reasonable being, barked at by curs of your sort, spits on them and walks by."[67]

It is likely that the attacks that began to lash out at Sade after Fouché assumed power drew on a particularly injurious essay recently published about him in the influential émigré press. Written by a specialist in Immanuel Kant who was exiled in Germany, Charles Villers, it had commented on the enormous influence of *Justine* and attested to the number of editions the novel had had throughout Europe: "It is asked for, sought out, it is spreading . . . the most cruel poison circulates with the most fatal abundance." Villers's article had gone on to elaborate (the surest way to rouse his fellow émigrés' hostility) on Sade's record as a revolutionary. "He is to literature what Robespierre was to the revolution," Villers wrote. "It is said that when this tyrant, and . . . his ministers . . . felt some remorse . . . and the pen fell from their hands as they were confronted with the numerous decrees they had to sign, they went to read a few pages of *Justine,* and returned to affix their signatures to the death warrants." [68]

In the late 1790s, Sade's revolutionary fervor, his pornographic bent, and his allegedly murderous impulses were being linked together with increasing frequency. Restif de la Bretonne's popular novel *Monsieur Nicolas* focused on a far sexier Jacobin hero than Robespierre, Danton, who, Restif gibed, "read *Justine* to masturbate." Restif, himself no paragon of rectitude, may have launched the most abusive invectives against Sade to date, making frequent allegations of his colleague's murderous impulses toward women. "O government, restrain this scoundrel, who if he were read by soldiers could cause the death of 20,000 women." [69]

Sade was aware of how dangerous such published attacks could be at a time when Fouché's police force was tightening its control of the press and of national mores. "We know that Moses' record is in perfect order and that he never emigrated," he had already written Gaufridy the previous spring, "but the Directory will not judge him on that; they'll judge him on his *morality.* Moses is an *immoral* man." [70]

Morality would become an even more pressing national issue in October 1799, three months after Fouché came to power, when Napoleon Bonaparte returned from his Egyptian campaign and staged his own sensational coup d'état. Revolted by the growing chaos and corruption of the Directory, French citizens had begun to look on the military hero as the only leader able to restore order and regenerate the nation. Overlooking the ruthlessness with which he had looted his way through Italy to amass a vast personal fortune, the dazzling publicity stunts with which he had cosmeticized his defeats in the Near East, they hailed Bonaparte as a reincarnation of republican virtues. When news of his landing in Fréjus reached Paris, theaters interrupted performances to announce his return. Tens of thousands of cheering citizens greeted him at every stop on his way to the capital. Within three weeks of the thirty-year-old general's return to Paris, he had engineered the dispersion of the Council of Ancients and the Council of Five Hundred; the members of the Directory had been forced, or bribed, to resign; and a three-member Consulate had been instituted, backed by a laconic constitution that concentrated most of the power in the hands of the First Consul, Napoleon Bonaparte.

If there is one aspect of the Napoleonic ethos that would most directly affect Sade's fate, it was Bonaparte's exaggerated Mediterranean patriarchalism, his belief in the supremacy of marriage and of family, and even of the Church. As puritanical in many ways as Louis XVI, and far more authoritarian, Bonaparte, despite his personal agnosticism, saw the Church as essential to the maintenance of law and order: "Deprive the people of their faith, and you'll be left with nothing but highway robbers."[71] In sum, the "Citizen Consul" 's moralistic views of society accorded perfectly with those of Minister Fouché and of his equally stern right-hand man, the brutally efficient police prefect of Paris, Dubois. One of Bonaparte's first executive measures was to increase these supercops' powers, encouraging them to enforce a widespread purification of national morals and to create the most efficient police system Europe had yet known. In the wake of Bonaparte's rigorous new censorship policies, several dozen additional newspapers were suppressed, and Paris's thirty theaters were reduced to eight; no dramatic work could thenceforth be produced in the country without the First Consul's approval. One can well imagine what repercussions such policies could have on the life of a pornographer.

IT WAS IN THIS CLIMATE of renewed puritanism that Sade would enter the nineteenth century. His continued efforts to rectify the Vaucluse émigré list, which continued to block most of his revenue, came at a moment when he was just about reduced to begging. "Sixty years old, infirm and destitute,"[72] he described himself in yet another letter to the Ministry of Justice that pleaded for a correction of his émigré record. And to Provence: "I'm literally dying of hunger, totally naked, obliged to commit sordidness to survive, yes, *sordidness!* I was driven to strip and sell the furnishings of my son's room because I lacked bread. . . . I stole from him."[73] We're not told which son's quarters he had looted, and we have no way of knowing whether he was once more giving in to his bent for outlandish exaggeration. What we do know is that at the dawn of the new century, in the "eighth year of liberty of the Republic One and Indivisible," January 1800, Sade was so down-and-out that he checked into the Versailles hospital in order not to "die at a street corner."[74] Young Charles Gaufridy, who was now sharing his aging father's task of administering Sade's affairs, had recently written him that he had some money for him but was deliberately taking his time sending it. "Public charity has assented to shelter me in a hospital. I'm dying of hunger," Sade raged in reply. "What stage of ferocity have all of you reached to leave me in such despair?"[75] Later that month, Sade wrote that he was living "in an unheated hospital, eating the bread of the poor."[76] "Dying of cold and hunger at the Versailles hospital,"[77] preceded his signature the following week. The next month, he cursed that Gaufridy *fils* deserved to be struck by lightning for being "treacherous and mean enough" to exploit Sade's "good faith and misery."[78]

In February, as Sade's situation grew still more dire, relations with the Gaufridys came to a breaking point. The same day that policemen took over his house in Saint-Ouen for failure to pay his debts, a bailiff served him with an arrest warrant issued by an innkeeper for yet other unpaid bills. For once, the couple's tribulations caused Constance to fall into a true faint; she remained unconscious for two hours and ran high fevers for the next several days. Writing to the elder Gaufridy's sister, Sade complained that he did not even have the means "to offer her the most basic medical necessities or a cup of broth. . . . A dreadful jail will be my asylum, a cold tomb that of my worthy and respectable companion!"[79] It is these miseries that incited him to accuse Gaufridy of outright theft and even to challenge him to a duel—the gentlemen were now, respectively, in their sixties and seventies. This time Gaufridy resigned for good, refusing to change his mind when he received more of Sade's and Constance's emotional pleas. "Embrace me, dear lawyer, as heartily as I embrace you, and I promise there will be no more ire in our hearts,"[80] his old friend wrote. "Forgive a man who is in despair and who in the past two years has exploited all resources to sustain himself,"[81] Constance had recently pleaded.

Rather than relent, the lawyer wrote a lengthy response elaborating on the harassments he had suffered for decades at Sade's hands and the "disgust" he had long experienced upon receiving his "injurious and menacing" missives. He admitted that he had often refused to read them, since they "only had the result of revoking all will to action, rather than invoking it."[82]

That summer, Constance and the friendly government official in charge of Sade's "surveillance," Commissar Cazade, took a short trip to Provence to see what they could do about Sade's finances. Chronicling Gaufridy's thirty years of negligence, Cazade reported that "a worse record of mismanagement would be hard to come by."[83] There would be no more communication between Sade and his onetime friend for many years.

□   □

IN THE PAST YEAR, Sade had known only one happy moment: in the last weeks of 1799, just before he checked into the Versailles hospital, *Oxtiern* had finally been staged, Sade himself in the role of the warmhearted innkeeper, Fabrice. The circumstances had been extremely modest—an amateur troupe in Versailles played it for a few nights as a benefit performance for indigent members of the community, and the proceeds may well have gone to the playwright. But it had brought Sade solace. Whatever remained of his vainglory led him to boast, in a letter to Provence, that his drama had enjoyed "an enormous success."[84]

The rest of his literary career, however, was not faring well. In October 1800, there was another powerful attack against Sade. This time it was aimed at his recently published *Les Crimes de l'Amour,* an innocuous collection of short stories preceded by a very impressive literary essay, "Reflections on the Novel," which is superior to many of the works it prefaces. Although it featured the staples of gothic fictions— incest, violent murders in isolated fortresses—*Les Crimes de l'Amour* was devoid of explicit erotic scenes. In fact, it was so relatively chaste that it was the first book for which Sade used his full name: whereas the superproper *Aline et Valcour* had only carried the byline "by citizen S***," *Les Crimes de l'Amour* was "by D. A. F. Sade, author of *Aline et Valcour.*" But the moral tone of Napoleon's and Fouché's new France made it fashionable for critics of all possible ideological stripes to attack Sade; and even this demure work was dissected in a prominent literary review as "a detestable book by a man suspected of having written a yet more horrible one." (The reference is to *Juliette,* which had probably been in the process of clandestine publication for some three years.) "What is the use of these depictions of triumphant crime?" the same critic, one M. Villeterque, protested, deploring the book's gothic excesses. "They create evil inclinations in the mean man, deprive the virtuous man of good ones . . . cause cries of discouragement in the weak. . . . They are useless and dangerous. . . . I could not read without indignation these four volumes of revolting atrocities."[85]

This time Sade responded in a pamphlet rather than in the periodical press; by now no respectable publication would risk publishing him. Grandly asserting that such attacks were no more affecting to a true man of letters than "the barking heard in a farmyard," he described M. Villeterque as "a penny-a-liner" who "defamed, calumniated, ranted, to make a living."[86]

But a few seasons of similar invectives had done their harm. For five years Sade had been protected by the chaos in the ranks of the Directory's corrupt and inept police force. Times had changed. Within a year of Bonaparte's takeover, the vice squads of "the first modern state," as

Napoleonic France came to be called, had become ruthlessly efficient. On the morning of March 6, 1801, the police raided the offices of Sade's publisher, Nicolas Massé, while Sade was there on business. They seized hundreds of Sade's manuscripts and arrested both men. Going on to Sade's house in Saint-Ouen, where he was able to make a tearful farewell to Constance, they seized yet more papers, and some paintings and tapestries "representing the most obscene subject matter." They then dragged him to the local prefecture, where he would be kept for six weeks before being transferred to a more spacious but equally humiliating institution. A report drawn up later by Paris police prefect Dubois, the second-highest-ranking man in Fouché's organization, detailed the circumstances of the raid:

In the early days of Ventôse Year IX [end of February 1801], I had been informed that Sade, ex-marquis, notorious for having authored the infamous novel *Justine,* was imminently planning to publish an even more horrendous work, called *Juliette.* I had him arrested the 15th of that very month [March 6] at the offices of his publisher, where I knew he was expected, manuscript in hand.[87]

In this memorandum, we are told that Fouché and Dubois had decided that a court trial was out of the question, since any legal process pertaining to Sade would "cause a scandal that would not be justified by a strong enough punishment." In their view, it was safer to "punish him administratively" (a favorite euphemism of Napoleon's police) and "forget him for a long while" at Sainte-Pélagie, one of the city's most crowded jails. This procedure of "forgetting" was common under the Consulate. Citizens in any way embarrassing to the government were quietly imprisoned, without trial or any form of public debate, and often detained for the rest of their days. The poet Théodore Désorgues was "deposed" at Sainte-Pélagie the same year as Sade for having written the couplet "The great Napoleon / Is a great chameleon"; he remained incarcerated until his death a decade later.

Sade's arrest and the subsequent seizure of thousands of copies of *Juliette* from numerous printing presses, bookbinders, and bookstores in the Paris region constituted one of the first major cleanup operations of the Napoleonic era, and it was clearly a carefully planned trap. Massé, his publisher, was released a few days later, upon informing the police of a warehouse where hundreds more copies of *Juliette* were kept. Sade would focus on this point in the first of his numerous petitions for freedom, which inevitably began with a vigorous denial of his ever having authored *Justine, Juliette,* or any other scabrous books, and went on to comment upon the increasing despotism of Napoleon's rule.

> [Whereas] Massé, the publisher of the work, who printed, sold, [and] is still selling it, has been released, I have been moaning in Paris's most horrible prison. . . . According to the law, one cannot be held captive more than ten days without due trial. . . . I ask for due process. . . . What is this arbitrariness . . . is it for this that we have just sacrificed, for twelve years, our lives and our fortunes?[88]

Sade was now sixty-one years old. He had enjoyed eleven years of freedom since the age of thirty-seven. Beyond Constance, who had nearly fainted at the sight of the police squad escorting her companion and had sworn never to abandon him, there seemed to be no one willing to come to his aid, least of all his children. Writing in the following weeks to his younger brother, Donatien-Claude-Armand, who was still exiled in Russia, to inform him of the death of their grandmother, Mme de Montreuil, Louis-Marie de Sade had this to say:

> All I can tell you is that our grandmother has been right in every way and we've been wrong to act in the least way against her. The last ten years will cost us profound and eternal sorrows. . . . [Our father] has many obligations to our mother. . . . I won't even speak to him about you, since he's very indiscreet and very dangerous.[89]

XXX

Society

> *If the manner in which I've painted crime afflicts*
> *you and makes you moan, your conversion is not far*
> *off, and I wrought the change I desired in you. But*
> *if its truth irritates you, if it leads you to curse the*
> *author ... Unfortunate one! You've recognized*
> *yourself, and you'll never change.*
>
> —*The Crimes of Love*

☐

WHO WAS JULIETTE, one might well ask, that she had so aroused the fury of Napoleon's henchmen? What kind of creature was this latest figment of Sade's imagination, to have caused such commotion? Rereading her saga, with its repeated scenes of infanticide and cannibalism, in 1998, any one of us might be as appalled as the emperor's censors were in 1801. We might keep in mind that at a time when the dread of female power was reaching its peak, *Juliette* was all the more menacing to Fouché's prudish commissars because it is dominated by violently depraved lesbian and bisexual women.

Juliette is the wicked older sister of the virtuous, ill-fated Justine, whose tribulations Sade first recounted in his 1791 *Justine, or The Misfortunes of Virtue*. Initially corrupted, in her early teens, by the mother superior of her convent, who expels her from the abbey when she is left penniless by her parents' death, Juliette follows the nun's advice to make her living as a prostitute. She soon becomes the mistress of two very powerful and corrupt men, Noirceuil and the minister of state Saint-Fond. The latter, described as "very false, very treacherous, very libertine, very ferocious,"[1] particularly enjoys roasting the bodies of young virgins on spits and serving them up for dinner. Sponsored by these two scoundrels and her equally bloodthirsty sapphic lover, Clairwil, Juliette is initiated into a secret group, the Society of the Friends of Crime, a dark, parodic version of the numerous secret societies that flourished in France in the revolutionary era. And she begins a career of theft, rape, pillage, and murder that will be crowned with every possible kind of triumph and fortune.

Juliette runs into her first great peril when she refuses to cooperate with one of her lover's pet schemes. Saint-Fond, who like many of Sade's male protagonists is obsessed with the dangers of overpopulation (some Sade scholars have called the author a precursor of Malthus), wants to starve to death two-thirds of the French populace by decimating the nation's food supplies. Even for Juliette, this "execrable plan" goes too far. "However corrupted I was, the idea made me shudder. . . . Here's a career to start over again. . . . Oh, fatal virtue! I managed once to be duped by you!" [2] Threatened by Saint-Fond's vengeance, she escapes to Italy and starts to amass another fortune in the company of a new lover, the shrewd brigand Sbrigani, and a band of lesbian acolytes.

A series of real-life historical personages Juliette encounters in Italy, each endowed with numerous fictional attributes, enter the narrative. There is Grand Duke Leopold of Tuscany, brother of "the first whore of France," [3] as Juliette refers to Marie-Antoinette, who conceives dozens of children each month with the members of his large harem, "solely for the delicious pleasure of destroying them." [4] There is Catherine II of Russia, who demands to be sodomized by her lover, the international gangster Brise-Testa, while she watches her son being tortured to death. There is the homicidal couple who run the Kingdom of Naples, Ferdinand IV and his wife, Marie-Caroline; the latter, a sister of Marie-Antoinette, arranges to be simultaneously penetrated by several men while watching the decapitation of a twelve-year-old girl she has just raped.

And there is the atheistic Pope Pius VI, accustomed to being sodomized at least twenty-five times a day, who inspires the most surreal apostatic vision to be found in Sade's oeuvre. Surrounded by hundreds of masturbating and copulating priests and monks, the Pope, who in real life was one of history's most virtuous pontiffs, holds a black mass, during which he performs the sexual act with Juliette on the main altar of Saint Peter's. Juliette's Vatican seduction provides her biggest loot to date. The Pope and his boon companions having fallen into a drunken stupor after raping and murdering seventy adolescent virgins of both sexes, Juliette absconds with the entire papal treasury and heads south, sensing that "it is prudent to leave Rome." [5]

It is in the Naples region, where Juliette is reunited with her lover Clairwil, that the heroine's malfeasances reach their orgiastic peak. Sated with the sexual favors of their paramour Olympe Borghese, Juliette and Clairwil casually throw her into the pit of Vesuvius and consummate their love on the rim of the volcano as they hear their companion's body cascade into its depths. After dozens of equally gruesome and gratuitous crimes, all narrated with that icy sobriety which characterizes much of Sade's prose style, Juliette, wealthier than ever since she absconded with the entire royal treasury of Naples, returns to France. She is reunited with Noirceuil, and the couple's omnipotence is now assured. The King of France rewards Noirceuil's career of pillage and bloodshed by making him prime minister and handing him "the reins of government." "I admit it, I passionately love crime," Juliette concludes. "Exempted as I am from all religious fears, knowing how to set myself above the law through my wits and my wealth, what power, divine or human, can ever stand in the way of my desires?"[6]

Throughout *Juliette*'s narrative, monotonously frenetic orgies alternate with long panegyrics on themes already elaborated in Sade's earlier works: the salubriousness of anarchy; the supremacy of hedonistic egoism as the only moral law; our tragic solitude, our utter lack of connectedness to other humans; and a stoic, if not cynical, acquiescence to the survival of the fittest. ("All beings are born isolated and without any need of each other. Leave men be in their natural state, don't civilize them, and each of them will find his food, his sustenance, without needing his peers."[7]) But *Juliette* also provides some of Sade's most succinct summations of the metaphysical underpinnings of his work, of their grim materialism and reductionism. In his atomistic views, which continue to be overwhelmingly influenced by Holbach's *Système de la Nature,* states of reality are merely transmutations of matter, rearrangements of "thousands and thousands of portions of different substances which reappear in all sorts of figurations."[8] His rigid determinism leads him to refute all notions of free will: we are solely what our physical constitution dictates that we be. "All our ideas originate in physical and material causes that are outside our control and depend on our physical makeup and on the exterior objects that sway it. . . . All our character resides in the action of the nervous fluid, and the difference between a rascal and an honest man consists exclusively of the physical essences that compose this fluid."[9]

Juliette further offers the most phantasmagoric, surreal passages of Sade's oeuvre. We witness a scene in which Juliette and Clairwil celebrate Good Friday by holding a mass orgy at a Carmelite convent, where they are serviced by relay races of seventy monks and novices wielding their own prodigious organs and innumerable dildos. We encounter Minsky, an omnivorous Muscovite giant who owns a private guillotine, whose ejaculations shoot twenty feet upward, and whose mobile dining-room furniture—tables, armchairs, candelabra—is composed of hundreds of "artistically arranged"[10] naked girls. Equally extravagant is the portrait of the sorceress Durand, Juliette's most beloved mistress, whose finger-length clitoris can penetrate women as efficaciously as any male organ and who boasts that she can destroy the entire planet in six minutes through her magical skill with poisonous plants. But above all the novel is dominated by the mythic monstrosity of its female protagonists, insatiable maenads drenched with blood and sperm, who lose all human density and seem to merge into the volcanic forces that fill their surreal landscape.

However fantastical its aura, *Juliette* may well be as autobiographical as *Justine*. Its Italian passages are heavily drawn from the travel notes Sade compiled in the 1770s. Juliette's obsession with money expresses a fixation perhaps more central to Sade's last decades than sexuality ("How divine to roll in gold and be able to say, while counting your riches . . . 'With this, all my illusions can be realized, all my fantasies satisfied, no woman will resist me, no desire will remain unfulfilled' "[11]). And in no book did Sade more maliciously censure the corruption often existing in governing elites—those same ministerial elites who had repeatedly deprived him of his freedom—than in his portraits of Noirceuil and Saint-Fond, the latter of whom "doled out *lettres de cachet* upon his most mercurial whims" and was "unsurpassably skilled at the art of stealing from the national treasury."[12]

Juliette was the culmination of a large body of work, written in the brief span of some fifteen years, in which Sade expressed several ideas that were quite novel to Western thought. Beyond advancing the most extreme doctrine of individual liberty ever set forth, he proposed a revolutionary view of the human psyche. Breaking with his contemporaries, who had limited their scrutiny to the surface of observed behavior, he explored those more hidden inclinations that we now call the subconscious. Perpetually deriding Enlightenment pieties concerning natural "goodness," he emphasized the grim ambivalence of erotic and destructive impulses, of love and hate, that color most human attachments. A century before Freud, this hardheaded pessimist discerned that the manner in which these conflicting drives were repressed or fulfilled might provide the master plan of every individual personality. He saw that the dual forces of Eros and Thanatos, as Freud would later call them, coexist in self-love as well as in the love of others and that our impulse to self-destruction can be as powerful as our instinct of self-preservation. And in the terrifying orgies of his fictions he gave free rein to those darker inclinations, to the impulses that can compel us to regress, if only in our fantasies, to an archaic, animal-like stage, liberated from even the most fundamental taboos—incest, cannibalism—imposed by civilization.

Sade's most lucid twentieth-century commentator, the British philosopher Stuart Hampshire, sees him as "a serious figure in the history of thought" because he was the first to understand "the non-logical, or contradictory, nature of men's original attachments" and because he dared to discard all "civilized restraints"[13] in expressing his insights. I would add that notwithstanding his heinous, deplorable, seldom surpassed misogyny, Sade was also prophetic in his androgynous views of erotic conduct. Few thinkers since Plato have more eloquently argued that heterosexual relations are not any more "normal" than homosexual ones. Somewhat like advocates of contemporary "Queer Theory," Sade championed a highly polymorphous view of human eroticism, in which heterosexuality was only one possible expression of libidinal impulses, one fragment of the sexual spectrum available to human needs.

These are bold ideas. I leave the reader to imagine the effect that the books in which they are stated, particularly *Juliette,* might have had on the prim Jacobins, many of them former Robespierrean terrorists, like Fouché, who filled the higher ranks of France's police ministry in 1801.

THE PRISON OF SAINTE-PÉLAGIE, where Sade was transferred in April 1801 after six weeks in the police lockup, was yet another former convent that had served as a political jail under the Terror. In the 1790s, it had lodged two prominent revolutionaries, Mme Roland and the poet André Chénier, and it now housed numerous citizens whose writings or attitudes Bonaparte deemed unfitting. One of its most distinguished guests, in the early 1800s, was the young belletrist Charles Nodier, who two decades later became France's foremost apostle of Romanticism. He was sent to Sainte-Pélagie and a few other institutions for having published a satiric ode on Bonaparte called *La Napoléone*[14] and asserts having encountered Sade there. Although Nodier's description might be based on others' eyewitness accounts—his dates of detention do not quite correspond to Sade's—his haunting portrait is one of those inventions that, in the hands of a good writer, can be truer than fact.

At first I only noticed his enormous obesity, which hampered his movements without preventing him from displaying traces of grace and elegance in his demeanor and language. His tired eyes still retained vestiges of brilliance and refinement, which were occasionally reanimated like the dying sparks of extinguished coals. . . . This prisoner merely passed by me. I only remember that he was polite to the point of obsequiousness, that his affability verged on the unctuous, and that he spoke respectfully of all that is respectable.[15]

None of Sade's letters from his two years at Sainte-Pélagie have survived. We know merely that its regime was relaxed enough to allow Constance's visits a few times a week and to tolerate the activities of a lively literary group, which called itself Dîners de Sainte-Pélagie and met every five days over the evening meal. Limited to nine members, in honor of the nine Muses, the group's participants read to each other from their works, and Sade soon became its president.

But this companionship was short-lived. There was no more Revolution to keep Sade on the straight and narrow, and two years into his stay at Sainte-Pélagie he seems to have strayed. In the spring of 1803, a group of young rowdies arrested for disorderly conduct were locked up in Sade's corridor, and he was accused, in police lingo, of attempting to "sate his brutal passion" upon them and of "using all means suggested by his depraved imagination to seduce and corrupt them."[16] Given the state of paranoia prevailing in any jail, and the French police's fixation on Sade, such accusations could have been based on a vast spectrum of actions, from verbal innuendos to outright attempts at sexual contact. But the police strengthened their case by reporting that they had seized, in Sade's cell, "an enormous wax instrument . . . which showed traces of its ignoble introduction."[17] (An indication that Sade's libido was not totally extinguished, this was clearly a primitive version of the *prestiges* he had resorted to at the Bastille.) Sade was moved to a jail far worse than any he'd ever been in, the notorious Bicêtre, known as "the riffraffs' Bastille."

Bicêtre was the nadir of Sade's last decades, a sordid and filthy compound, part hospital and part jail, in which paralytics, epileptics, the mentally retarded, and the totally demented mingled with assassins, thieves, and prostitutes. This time round, Sade's family, led by his older son, vehemently protested the government's choice of lodgings. Louis-Marie may well have been in favor of having his father put away for the rest of his life, but it had to be in a "correct" place, and Bicêtre brought what the Sades feared most—dishonor. As police prefect Dubois would later put it, "his wife and sons desired him to leave an establishment whose name spelled opprobrium."[18] Having decided that it was a tad more honorable to have Sade incarcerated on grounds of insanity than for writing obscene books, they asked to have him committed to the most famous asylum of the time, Charenton, five kilometers out of Paris.

The Fouché-Dubois team, who had considered far more awesome alternatives—the sinister fortress of Ham, in Picardy, and Brittany's equally grim Mont-Saint-Michel—acceded to the family's wishes. To preserve some modicum of respectability for their decision, Fouché and Dubois even invented a mental disease for their ward, "libertine dementia."[19] They institutionalized Sade at Charenton under yet another imaginative classification: "patient of the police."

Charenton is the establishment where the marquis had been sent in July 1789 when he was shunted out of the Bastille. Closed, like all convents, for several years of the revolutionary era, the Charenton facility was reopened toward the end of the Directory years as a center for "the healing of the insane"[20] and placed directly under the supervision of the Ministry of the Interior. By the time Sade reached it, it was already looked on as a model institution of its kind. Its population had grown from a few dozen persons to several hundred; its accommodations had tripled in size; the more agitated and obstreperous patients had been isolated into separate facilities, and the remaining inmates had been segregated according to their type of ailments—melancholia, persecution mania, retardation. By 1803, Charenton had become a favorite of many patrician families who, like the Sades, needed to institutionalize their kin. Its transformation was attributable to its director, a man who, ironically, was about to offer Sade some of the most tolerable years of his life.

FRANÇOIS SIMONET DE COULMIER, a former priest two years Sade's junior, was born into the high bourgeoisie of Burgundy. He rose to political eminence as a deputy from the Third Estate in 1789, when he made fiery speeches to the Estates General about the misery of the poor, and was later defrocked by the Church for siding, albeit as a moderate, with the Revolution. He remained in hiding during the height of the Terror, committed himself early on to Bonaparte, and was named head of Charenton soon after it reopened. Often working at his own expense, he made it his life's mission to reform the institution, and under his rule Charenton became the first asylum in France devoted to the treatment of mental problems. Although it retained some brutal and archaic treatments for the more violent cases of dementia, such as straitjackets and immersion in icy baths, it was also the first to emphasize "psychological cures" over millennia-old physical remedies such as diets, bleedings, or purges. Charenton was equally distinguished from other asylums by its good food and humane nursing care, and it came to be looked on as the vanguard of what would soon be called psychiatry. Although professional

doctors often criticized Coulmier's eccentric curative methods and anarchic administrative style, by the time Sade came into his charge he was
considered a pioneer in the area of mental health and had received that
honorific bauble of Napoleon's creation, the Legion of Honor.

There was another singular feature about Coulmier that was bound
to color his relationship with the world and with the patrician inmate
whom he would favor extravagantly over all other patients: Coulmier
suffered from severe physical disadvantages. He was less than four feet
tall and rather hunchbacked, with twisted legs, bulging eyes, and a dis-
proportionately large head. Yet he was graced with refined manners and
a superior cultivation. A considerable dandy and a great snob, he had a
voyeuristic interest in sexuality and an insatiable passion for the theater.
Those last few traits alone could have encouraged his fascination for his
notorious patient the Marquis de Sade. (One might now resurrect the
title, for in the early 1800s, First Consul Bonaparte, as he conspired to
become Emperor, had begun to re-create an aristocratic caste.)

At Charenton, Sade's family would pay one of the most expensive
room rates in the asylum—three thousand livres a year—but this bought
many amenities. The marquis enjoyed a two-room suite with a view over
the community's spacious, well-tended park and the river Marne. He
had once more been allowed to bring his own artworks and furnishings,
which included a four-poster bed and a chaise longue upholstered
in yellow velvet. The pictures he hung on his walls were very telling:
Nattier's portrait of his father, Comte de Sade, in full army regalia, and
miniatures of his mother, of his older son, Louis-Marie, and of his late
sister-in-law Anne-Prospère de Launay. His library of over two hundred
fifty books would eventually include an eighty-nine-volume set of Voltaire, the collected writings of Seneca, Suetonius, Tacitus, Cervantes,
and Rousseau, Chateaubriand's *The Genius of Christianity,* and the few
of his novels whose authorship he acknowledged, such as *Aline et Valcour* and, in later years, *La Marquise de Ganges.*

The marquis was allowed to walk about the garden whenever he
wished and to fraternize with fellow inmates—he employed them as
copyists for his writings and in later years, when his eyesight was failing,
readily found patients willing to read the newspaper to him. He was
permitted to receive business associates such as his lawyers, tenants, and
farmers (he was frequently visited by the foreman of Mazan, Ripert, and
by a M. Lenormand, who overlooked his holdings in Versailles and to
whom he would refer in his will). And he could host lunch and dinner
parties in his rooms, where he seems to have entertained several times a
week.

Within a year of the marquis's admission, Coulmier would grant

Sade a far more outlandish privilege: Constance Quesnet was allowed to move into Charenton to keep him company and was given rooms adjoining his. She was listed in the asylum's rosters as his illegitimate daughter, and Sade often carried the paternal role playing into his journals, referring to her as "my daughter," when he did not denote her as "Md." or "Madame." Relations between the two companions, for the next few years, seemed to remain idyllic. Constance's son, Charles, had settled near the asylum. There was a semblance of family life. Sade's monumental egoism broke down whenever Sensible fell ill. When she ailed, he nursed her with dedication, kept a fastidious day-by-day chronicle of her fevers, coughs, and bowel movements, and was devastated whenever she raised the possibility that he would survive her: "In the first week of her illness my dear friend told me some powerful and devastating things which led me to tears as soon as I found myself alone. . . . 'Do you absolutely desire me to live?' she asked me one day, as if to thank me for my care. Another time she said, 'You won't keep me for long. . . .' Yet another time she told me, looking at me meaningfully: 'I knew that you'd bury me.' "

"Oh, no," goes the last line of that journal entry, in the marquis's own voice, "for I shall follow you." [21]

Sade's comments about Constance in his last will and testament, which he made out at Charenton in 1806 and which bestowed to her whatever worldly goods he had left, were equally ardent: "I wish to witness to this lady my extreme gratitude for the devotion and the sincere friendship she lavished on me from August 25, 1790, until the day of my death," the document states, "a devotion offered not only with delicacy and disinterestedness but also with the most courageous energy, since, under the Terror, it is she who rescued me from the revolutionary scythe all too ominously hovering over my head." [22]

ONCE AT CHARENTON, Constance lobbied more energetically than ever for Sade's release. A request she wrote to the Ministry of Justice in 1804 is one of the few of her letters that have survived. The marquis might have hoped that her primitive spelling and syntax would move the authorities' pity: *"Le nomé Sade vous suplie de luis a corder sa liberté a netan privé depuis trois ans sur de simple soupson,"* [23] it states: "Said Sade begs you to grant him freedom having been deprived of it for three years on grounds of simple suspicion." The missive having remained unanswered, "Sade, man of letters," wrote the next petition for mercy himself, addressing it directly to police minister Fouché. According to the increasingly monarchic protocol of Napoleon's entourage, the former

revolutionary, whose terrorist reprisals even Robespierre deemed excessive, was now addressed as "Monseigneur" and "Your Excellency."
Would "Monseigneur" Fouché consider the suffering of "a sexagenarian
interned for four years without any due process?"[24] Sade implored.
Hardly a plight to move the stony-hearted Fouché. He passed the letter
on to his subalterns and ten days later, Paris police prefect Dubois issued
a report stating that Sade should remain indefinitely at Charenton,
"where his family desires him to remain," because his character was
"inimical to all submission."[25]

Sade tried another venue. Addressing his next plea to the "Senato-
rial Commission for Individual Liberty," he resorted once more to his
record as a patriot, blaming his incarceration on "a horrendous coalition
of relatives" who had opposed the Revolution and emigrated. "These
dishonest people . . . adroitly profited by the little credit they enjoyed
upon their return to France to destroy the one who had refused to follow
them. Thus began the story of my misfortunes, of their lies . . . and of
my chains."[26] Still no response. Faced with the government's continuing
intransigence, Sade found his principal solace in his complex friendship
with Coulmier.

Relations between the authoritarian administrator and the fractious
marquis, whose impatience and paranoia were always aggravated by internment, were bound to be complex. As a former priest and an amateur
psychiatrist, Coulmier was both exasperated and intrigued by his inmate's provocations; as a snob, he was proud of having him in his charge.
And if he judged Sade to be genuinely deranged, he seemed determined
to heal him. Yet he clearly remained torn between his fascination for
the nobleman, whose entrancing conversation was certainly unique at
Charenton, and the need to protect his establishment by retaining the
goodwill of the Interior Ministry.

The beginning of their relationship was stormy. Sade was clearly
aware of the spell he'd cast on Coulmier and seemed to enjoy testing his
limits. In his first two years at Charenton, his temper and insolence were
so intolerable that the director had begged the Interior Ministry, and
also the marquis's younger son, to be relieved of him. "It is impossible
to deal with someone so choleric. . . . He called me a clown, a calumnia-
tor, a thief, and a thousand other invectives far more atrocious."[27]
Whenever his guest's temper flared, the director would discipline him
by withdrawing crucial privileges—visits, newspapers—and would even
confine him to his room. Sade, realizing that he was jeopardizing essential comforts, gradually drew back his claws. For their last eight years
together, the two men enjoyed increasingly cordial, even affectionate,

relations as they collaborated on one of the more bizarre dramatic experiments of recent times, the theater of Charenton.

Coulmier had long been engrossed by the therapeutic potential of theatrical performance. Moreover, this interest was shared by Charenton's chief physician, Dr. Gastaldy, a man of Provençal origin who had considerable sympathy for Sade. "We looked for means to dispel [the patients'] ailments by innocent games, concerts, dances, comedies, in which they could act," Coulmier would write. "These occupations kept them active and dispelled melancholy, the all too frequent source of delirium."[28]

Whether Coulmier or Sade first thought of the idea of staging plays at the asylum, Coulmier assigned Sade to design and oversee the building of the theater, giving him a free hand in the project. The facilities that opened at Charenton in 1805 included a full-size stage and orchestra pit, and could house an audience of over three hundred. In the middle of the spectators' section was a row of loges, which were reserved for Sade, Coulmier, and a few other favored members of the Charenton community. (Constance had seven places in her loge.) On either side of the orchestra pit were tiers of steps reserved for the asylum patients, who were segregated by gender and were carefully selected from the less agitated members of the community.

The Charenton theater was a much more grandiose enterprise than Sade's amateur troupe in Provence. The marquis chose and directed the plays, assigned the roles, took on many of the parts himself, designed sets and costumes, coached the actors in the art of declamation, and served as the troupe's artistic director and public relations manager. His repertory had nothing to do with the experimental psychodramas described in Peter Weiss's play *Marat/Sade*. They were, to the contrary, chaste, conventional, Marivaux-type society dramas. The schedule, however, was demanding: performances were held once a month throughout the year and usually featured a double bill, combining a drama with a comedy or an opera. One marvels at the energy Sade still managed to summon for this venture. No task was too lowly for him. When shorthanded, he served as prompter, usher, and general handyman, sewing up costumes, repairing sets and curtain pulleys. On the evenings of the premieres, he played host in his most seigneurial manner, standing at the door of the asylum to greet the spectators, making small talk, chatting about the forthcoming performance, and generally spreading enthusiasm for his venture.

Although Sade's troupe included Parisian professionals such as Mme Saint-Aubin, a popular star of the Opéra Comique, the bulk of it was recruited among Charenton's patients. (Retired actress Constance Quesnet was also given important roles.) And it is this use of the insane as thespians that undoubtedly turned the Charenton troupe into a *succès de scandale* of the Paris region. The house was usually sold out. At one typical performance, for which one hundred eighty-six seats had been reserved, the spectators included the mayor of Charenton, the town's chief notary, the local surgeon, the priest of the local parish, and a fairly impressive array of Paris intelligentsia and society figures, which included Mme Cochelet, lady-in-waiting to Napoleon's stepdaughter, Hortense de Beauharnais, Queen of Holland. Each of these persons had reserved between two and seven seats, for it had become the fashion, especially among trendy literati, to travel to Charenton and see asylum inmates mount the stage. *"Le tout Paris* ran there for years, some out of curiosity, others to judge the effects of this admirable method of healing insanity,"[29] wrote Professor Esquirol of France's most prominent hospital, the Salpetrière, a pioneer in scientific psychiatry. (His use of "admirable" was ironic; like many doctors, Esquirol was highly dubious of the Charenton spectacles' curative properties, even though he had never attended them and was merely informed by hearsay.)

Although we have no information on how many cures these spectacles may have effected, we know that they were accompanied by considerable social activities. To the great delight of Coulmier, dinner parties would often attend the spectacles, some held in Charenton's public rooms, others in Coulmier's or Sade's lodgings.

One eyewitness to the festivities was the journalist and vaudevillian Armand de Rochefort, who was one of some sixty guests invited to a pretheater supper in 1812. Directly to his left, he recorded, sat "an old man with an inclined head and a fiery gaze," whose "white crowning hair gave him a venerable air that imposed respect."

> He spoke to me several times, with such spirited verve and such a richness of wit that I found him very sympathetic. When I rose from the table, I asked my other dinner partner who was that amiable man. . . . At that name, I fled from him with as much terror as if I'd been bitten by the most venomous serpent. I knew that this unfortunate old man was the author of a wretched novel in which all the deliriums of crime were presented under the guise of love.[30]

After the dinner attended by Rochefort, Marivaux's *Fausses Confidences* was performed, a play featured that same season in Paris with the famous Mlle Mars in the leading role. Rochefort was pleasantly surprised by the distinction of the Charenton performance, particularly by the dramatic gifts of "the madwoman" who played the starring role, "with an ease, a flawlessness of memory, that amazed all observers." "All ended without error in the midst of applause, surprise, and startlement," Rochefort summed up his evening at Charenton. ". . . After seeing such wonders there, I needed to flee this establishment to safeguard my own sanity." [31]

The theatrical ventures of Sade's last decade yielded far more precise verbal portrayals of his physique and personality than were ever drawn in his youth. One Labouisse-Rochefort (no relation to Armand de Rochefort) attended a performance in which Sade himself acted a lead role. "This actor is very fat, very obese, very cold, very heavy," the spectator commented. "This is a large lump of a man, a short, ugly fellow whose face is a shameful ruin." At the play's end, Labouisse learned the identity of the actor. He expressed his horror:

> Oh, heavens! Do I dare say it? It was . . . it was, yes, Comte de Sade! . . . That infamous scoundrel!!! . . . Amusements, pleasures, honors [were being offered to] one whose presence must revolt all sentient beings . . . and without shame, some habitués even applauded him! Even a few women!! . . . What a distressing example! What catastrophic tolerance! What criminal delirium! [32]

The most haunting portrait of all is drawn from the memory of a then aspiring young actress, Mlle Flore. She had gone to the asylum not only because of its troupe's growing renown but because of her desire to meet "the diamond of the Opéra Comique," the famous Mme Saint-Aubin, who not only acted in Charenton productions but also helped Sade rehearse his actors. After commenting on M. de Coulmier's physique ("a four-feet-tall dwarf whose short deformed legs supported an enormous torso") and the performance of Mme Quesnet ("a woman of a certain age who nevertheless affected youth and coquetry . . . [and] had relations with one of the house's pensioners"), Mlle Flore gives this portrait of the marquis in 1811 or so.

> This man, whom I regarded as a kind of curiosity, like one of those monstrous creatures one sees in cages, was the all too famous Marquis de Sade, author of several books whose names one cannot even speak and whose only claim is to have insulted good taste and morality. . . . He had a rather handsome head, a bit too long, an aquiline nose . . . a narrow mouth, a promi-

nent lower lip. The corners of his mouth displayed a disdainful smile. His small but brilliant eyes were partly shielded by a powerful brow surmounted by thick eyebrows. His creased eyelids hung over the corners of his eyes like those of a cat. He was coiffed in the Louis XV fashion, his hair lightly curled and perfectly powdered, and this hair was still all his, even though he was then 74 [Mlle Flore mistakes Sade's age by a few years]. . . . His bearing was that of a man of the highest society. . . . He had retained majestic manners and much wit.[33]

Sade drew all the more attention to himself by masterminding Charenton's social activities. Dr. Ramon, a young physician very sympathetic to the marquis, who was assigned to Charenton in later years, reported that "gatherings, balls, concerts," were frequently held at the asylum and that these "festivities, soirees, spectacles, were all organized by Sade."[34] In this late flowering of his dramatic career, the marquis and his equally stagestruck friend Coulmier especially enjoyed entertaining pretty Parisian actresses for dinner in their lodgings. One particular trace of their gallantries is a billet-doux Sade wrote to Mme Saint-Aubin and folded into her dinner napkin at one of his soirees. (His fancy for her seems to have been returned—she often brought him delicacies such as freshly killed turkeys.)

> *Saint-Aubin, Thalia's charming favorite,*
> *Your subtle game is played with heart and spirit!*
> *Who can be surprised by such dual art,*
> *When all of one's spirit comes from the heart?*[35]

Flattery seemed to be the order of the day at Charenton. Of the several plays staged there that were written by Sade himself, the only one that has survived is an occasional piece produced in 1810 for Coulmier's birthday, *Fête de l'Amitié*. The hero's name, Meilcour, is an anagram of the asylum director's. Sade and Constance Quesnet played the roles, tellingly, of a happily married couple, M. and Mme de Blinval. There is only one reference to madness in the play—Momus, the Roman deity of insanity, and a few of his demented prisoners are restored to health by the healing powers of the wise, humane Meilcour, whom Sade celebrates in many saccharine stanzas, one of which follows.

> *We yearn to offer our homages*
> *To our charming protector.*
> *Our gifts would be paltry tokens*

Of what inspires our ardor;
But there is nothing finer
Than our hearts' gentle offers;
One better pleases this amiable man
Through wishes than through flowers.[36]

Sade would write many such sycophantic verses during his stay at Charenton. Perhaps the most startling are those he wrote for Cardinal Maury, the archbishop of Paris, when he visited the asylum in 1812.

Like our Lord's Holy Son,
Blessed by uncommon good,
In the guise of a mortal
You have overcome misfortune,
With the fullness of your grace,
Always firm and always fair,
Under the pontiff's purple robe
Do not scorn the sorrows of Job.[37]

The ultimate irony of Sade's life is that only repressive regimes could force him to be this compliant, this amenable, to protocol and social graces. It took the Terror, and later his detainment at Charenton, to reconcile him to the courtly compromises a "social life" requires—courtesy, dissimulation, flattery, tact. He was finally socialized, toward the end of his life, through a community of persons rejected by society as insane.

But this relative serenity remained fragile. A few years into his stay at Charenton, Sade, having obtained Coulmier's permission, attended Easter mass at the parish church of Charenton and passed the holy bread and the donation dish among the congregation. Even this devout little frolic was too much for Napoleon's officials. "Under no pretext can you allow him to leave the asylum without a formal authorization on my part," police prefect Dubois fulminated two days later in a letter to Coulmier. "Haven't you realized that the sheer presence of such a man only inspires horror and incites public disarray?"[38] The reprimand deprived the Paris area of one of its more surreal visions: the obese old atheist, thrilled to have been permitted a modest excursion, gravely passing the ritual plates among his fellow parishioners, feigning devotion as he genuflected at the altar. Under the growing autocracy and prudishness of Napoleon's rule, government authorities were increasingly appalled that a Jacobin-leaning defrocked priest with bizarrely experimental attitudes to mental health was cohosting parties and spectacles—

in a government institution!—with the most infamous nobleman of his generation. And the nobleman's family was not about to take his side.

SADE'S RELATIONS with his offspring had remained mostly strained since his incarceration at Charenton. Madeleine-Laure, living placidly at her mother's side in their family estate at Echauffour, had long ago given up thoughts of marriage. Her father couldn't have been far off the mark when he described her as "pickled in stupidity and piety,"[39] although he had not seen her for some years.

Sade's younger son, Donatien-Claude-Armand, returned from Russia in 1803 and applied for service in Napoleon's army, but he was turned down because he had emigrated. In 1805, he petitioned for amnesty on that issue, taking care to request that he not be "confused with D. A. F. de Sade, detained on grounds of his writings." (He had recently deleted the "Donatien" from his name, to further minimize any association with his father, and now called himself simply Armand de Sade.) He was allowed to live "under surveillance" at Echauffour with his sister and his mother, who had always favored him over her older son. ("I kiss you with pleasure and not with chagrin, as I do your brother,"[40] Pélagie had written Armand in 1802.) Though it is hard to know whether it was genuine, Armand was now manifesting great piety. When he was still in his thirties—he would live on for another forty years, into the mid-nineteenth century—he set aside a goodly sum of money to have a mass said every year after his death at the Echauffour parish church and offered a lamp that was to be lit on all major holidays in honor of the Virgin Mary. Over the years, he revealed himself to be a child of the Montreuils: cold, conformist, penny-pinching, lacking in imagination, he was constantly in conflict with the only true Sade of his generation, his impetuous, brilliant brother.

Louis-Marie's correspondence shows that he had poor relations with both his sister and his mother. He described Madeleine-Laure as a feebleminded woman who did everything "by fits and starts, without rhyme or reason."[41] The distaste was mutual. His sister refused even to come down to meals when he visited Echauffour. As for Pélagie, he criticized her enduring tendency to be "victimized by all who surround her," particularly deploring the way she was being "reduced to servitude" by her own servant, who ruled her household and whom he judged to be "a bitch of the first order, hypocritical, underhanded, pretending to pamper my mother but constantly betraying her."[42] Pélagie, on her part, fretted about what she described as Louis-Marie's "deranged state" and lamented that "to my misfortune, I'll never find filial emotions in him."[43]

In those years, Louis-Marie was beginning a promising literary career. In the spring of 1805, he published the first sections of his *Histoire du peuple français* in which he intended eventually to record the entire span of his nation's past. His first three volumes, which ranged from pre-Roman times to the tenth century, were praised for their elegant style and scrupulous erudition. The elder Sade seemed intensely proud of this achievement. There were long periods in which Louis-Marie experienced great intellectual camaraderie with his father. He visited him at the asylum fairly often, took him out for walks in the park, borrowed books from his library, and even attended some of the Charenton spectacles. Yet their relations remained ambivalent. Because of his father's bad name, a "fine" marriage continued to remain beyond Louis-Marie's reach. In 1805, when he turned thirty-eight, his peers pressured him increasingly on this issue. "Hurry up, you're getting old," one friend warned. "Take a gentle and even a stupid wife; it's the only way of retaining independence in a marriage."[44]

In addition to the general aura of scandal that had led Mlle de Chastenay to keep her distance, after Sade entered Charenton Louis-Marie bore the stigma of his father's alleged "insanity" (such ailments were still regarded as hereditary). Without the financial security that only a good marriage could bring him, in 1805 Louis-Marie rejoined the army, and he fought in many of the Napoleonic battles whose names now grace the avenues of Paris, notably Jena and Friedland, suffering substantial wounds at the latter engagement.

The latent conflicts between the Sade brothers grew to a climax in 1808, when Armand upstaged Louis-Marie by finding a very profitable bride. A distant cousin, she was a daughter of Comte de Sade d'Eyguières, a far wealthier and more respectable branch of the family than the marquis's. The bride was so plain and, for that time, so advanced in age —thirty-six—that her parents had ceased to be particular and were as eager for the match as the groom. Obese and cross-eyed, Louise-Gabrielle-Laure de Sade d'Eyguières, who was called Laure, was as ungainly as her future sister-in-law, Madeleine-Laure, with whom she quickly became friends. ("Our Laures are getting on terrifically,"[45] Armand's prospective mother-in-law wrote.) Mme Bimard de Sade d'Eyguieres was so eager to get her ugly duckling married that she readily found a way to justify her choice of son-in-law—the merit of the Montreuil clan: "We've been happy to see that he bore, from his father, only the name and that he carries all of his mother's virtues. This is what attached us to him."[46]

The match perfectly suited the ambitions of the venal Armand. Beyond their wealth, the Sade d'Eyguières family had always had the contacts to overcome their own shady political past. Even though Comte d'Eyguières, in the 1790s, had been a leader of the counterrevolution in Provence and had subsequently immigrated to Italy with his family, he was now in perfect standing with the authorities. Having received a full certificate of amnesty in 1802, he had gone on to live at one of his several ancestral castles, at Condé-en-Brie, in the Champagne area, east of Paris, a real estate asset that his prospective son-in-law was bound to find seductive.

So in accordance with the protocol of the times, on a spring day of 1808 the younger Sade went to Charenton to ask his father's consent for his marriage. Sade's incarcerations had not diminished his shrewdness. He immediately saw a way to bargain with his son, replying that he would give his consent only if the family made a formal promise to lobby vigorously for his release. Armand seemed to agree to the trade-off and went home to arrange for his father's signing of the proper papers. But the very morning after his brother's visit, Louis-Marie burst into Sade's Charenton lodgings and announced that the marriage was a trap: Armand and his future in-laws, he warned his father, were intending to have him moved to the bleak fortress of Ham, or the equally forbidding Mont-Saint-Michel. Terrified, the marquis reversed his earlier decision and tried to add extravagant clauses to his papers of consent, which Armand found unacceptable. A deadlock occurred, caused, predictably, by grossly materialistic concerns: besides suffering loss of face in society because his younger brother had married ahead of him, Louis-Marie was terrified that his mother would give away his share of the family funds to Armand as a wedding gift.

Enter Mme Bimard de Sade d'Eyguières, as resourceful and cunning a mother-in-law as Mme de Montreuil ever was. She quickly found a way to bypass Sade's refusal. Since the marquis had never been taken off the Vaucluse émigré list, he was still deprived of all civil rights. Who needed his consent? A few letters to the Ministry of Justice did the trick. No matter that the entire Sade d'Eyguières family had not only emigrated but actively fought against the republic, while the marquis remained in France with an exemplary patriotic record: the ministry ruled against him. Anyone not officially struck off the émigré lists or amnestied, the ruling stated, "is denied the rights which the Napoleonic Code offers to all French citizens. . . . Children, if they wish to marry, must proceed just as they would if their father did not exist."[47]

But Sade had lost none of his fighting spirit. He decided to sue, and his younger son was served notice to appear in court. However flimsy the prisoner's chances of winning such a trial, the Sade d'Eyguières family dreaded the publicity any legal action could arouse and convinced Armand to seek reconciliation with his father. An agreement was finally reached. On a sunny July day, a police official—or someone who posed as such—came to pick up Sade at the Charenton asylum and take him to the town notary's office, where Sade formalized his assent to his son's marriage. It is possible that he made this accommodation for the sheer pleasure of seeing a bit of landscape, a bit of street life, beyond the precincts of his asylum, as he had not been outside its walls since that Easter Sunday four years earlier when he had attended mass at the Charenton parish church.

But even this family outing aroused the wrath of Napoleon's police ministry, a sign of the vigilance with which Sade was being observed. An admonition was once more issued by Dubois, who apparently had never authorized any policeman to accompany Sade to the notary's office. "I'm startled, monsieur," he wrote Coulmier, "that you deferred with such nonchalance to a commissar . . . from whom you should have requested a written order, before putting him in charge of *a man who is under your care and who under no pretext is allowed to leave the asylum.*" The letter was signed "Counselor of State, Prefect, Count of the Empire DUBOIS."[48] Dubois and his superior, Fouché, had been among the first to benefit from Napoleon's new practice of doling out titles of nobility; the once enraged revolutionary Joseph Fouché had been offered a huge parcel of land in northern Italy and was now called Duke of Otranto.

Meanwhile the émigré farce continued. Of the 150,000 citizens who had originally been listed as having left France, by the end of 1810 only 3,000 had not been pardoned, Sade among them. He would finally receive "amnesty" and be struck off the lists in 1811, three years before Napoleon's final defeat and the restoration of the Bourbon monarchy. This long-delayed rectification would be motivated not by any governmental clemency or familial decency but by Armand's cupidity. As Sade grew older and feebler, his son perceived the material advantage of having the émigré stigma lifted: he, rather than the state, might inherit whatever could be rescued from his father's estate upon his death.

As for Armand's marriage, all was well that ended well. Notwithstanding the bride's relatively advanced age, this generation of Sades was to beget four children; the first, a girl, was not surprisingly named Laure-Émilie.

AND THEN TRAGEDY STRUCK the family. In 1809, Louis-Marie, traveling through northern Italy en route to rejoining his regiment in Corfu, was ambushed by a group of Neapolitan nationalists and shot through the head. Forty-two years old, he had only begun to fulfill his considerable talents. All of the documents found on him were enclosed by his father into a large gray envelope and marked, in a large, trembling hand, "Papers found on my son after his death." They included a letter in which the marquis gave Louis-Marie permission to marry any woman he might choose, on the condition that "he never lose sight of the birth and station he inherited from his ancestors."[49] The loss must have been dreadful. Theirs had been a tumultuous relationship but never an indifferent one. Louis-Marie had been the only member of the immediate family with whom his father could truly exchange ideas, the only one with whom he had shared moments of genuine affection. In recent years, the two of them—the bold, adventurous Sades—had often banded together against the cautious, philistine Montreuils. And during their periods of accord, Sade referred to his oldest child with intense pride and admiration, without a trace of the disdain that marked his attitude to Armand. In the last request for clemency he made before learning of his son's death—it was addressed to Napoleon himself, "His Majesty Emperor and King"—he had boasted of Louis-Marie's recent army record.

> Sir de Sade, head of a family in which, to his consolation, he sees his son distinguishing himself in our armies, has spent almost nine years in three consecutive prisons, living the most unfortunate existence. He is seventy years old, nearly blind, afflicted with gout, suffering rheumatism in his chest and stomach, which causes him horrible pain. Certificates from the Charenton house . . . attest to the truth of this and justify his finally claiming his liberty, with the promises that there will never be any regret for granting it to him. He dares to proclaim that he remains, with the most profound respect, Your Majesty's very humble, obedient servant and subject.[50]

We have no record of Sade's reaction to the news of Louis-Marie's death. There is only one trace of Sade's grief—an angry note to his younger son, scolding him for the brusque manner in which he informed his mother of Louis-Marie's death. "Do you wish it said of you that you killed both your parents, one by bringing him misery, the other by [afflicting her] with grief? Just wait . . . just wait, your own son will seek a revenge. Remember that such atrocities never go unpunished."[51]

The year after Louis-Marie's death, in 1810, Pélagie succumbed, at age sixty-nine, to an obstruction of the gallbladder. She had been an invalid for much of the past decade. Two years earlier, grown totally blind, she had already been too ill to attend Armand's marriage. Her daughter, Madeleine-Laure, would survive her by over thirty years and end her days in her narrow, pious life at Echauffour. The two women's remains are buried together in the new cemetery of that village, where they were transported in our own century. Their gravestone bears the following epitaph:

> Here lie the remains of Mlle Laure Madeleine de Sade, deceased at the Château of Echauffour on January 18 1844 at the age of 73, buried at the side of her mother, Mme Renée Pélagie de Montreuil, Marquise de Sade, both of them as virtuous as they were charitable. Pray to God for the repose of their souls.

Sade's reaction to the death of the woman who had "loved him beyond one's wildest expectations," as Pélagie's mother once put it; who had encouraged his bizarre literary gifts and sacrificed much of her life to fight for his freedom; and in whom he had confided his deepest griefs and most outrageous deviances, is not chronicled either. Throughout his years at Charenton, the most intimate records of Sade's inner life are found in three documents: a journal entry, a letter to his oldest friend, Gaufridy, and an epitaph he wrote for himself while at the hospice.

In a telling passage of his journals from January 1808, Sade expressed his longing for his father, with whom he'd had a relationship strikingly similar to the one he had with his own son: "Anniversary of my father's death; I think about him all day long and go to bed offering him my tears. Ah! if he had lived on, would he have tolerated all the stupidities inflicted on me??"[52]

Sade's letter to Gaufridy was written in 1806, after a silence of nearly six years. Its apparent aim was to assure that the clauses of his will, drafted that year, be closely followed and that Constance remain his only heir. But at the end, in a uniquely unguarded moment, this very private man suddenly unleashed his emotions and expressed deep nostalgia for his youth, his Provence, his once beloved La Coste, for the park and orchards he had so meticulously tended, for his closest childhood friend.

> How is all your family faring? Have you had pleasant occasions in your family, good advancements for your boys, marriages for your daughters?
> How is the kind and honest Mme Gaufridy? And how are

you, my dear lawyer, you, my contemporary, my childhood companion, how are you?

. . . A few details on La Coste, on those I have loved, on . . . Paulet, etc. Is it true that Mme Rovère is not living at the château? And what state is it in, that poor château? And my poor park, does it still bear a recognizable trace of me? My relatives in Apt, how are they?

Perhaps you would presently like a word about me? Well then! *I am not happy,* but I am well. That's all I can answer to a friend who, I hope, still inquires about me.[53]

Yours for life,
SADE

In order not to reveal his incarceration, Sade gave Gaufridy a somewhat distorted address: "Care of M. de Coulmier, president of the canton and member of the Legion of Honor, at Charenton-Saint-Maurice, department of the Seine."

Finally, there is the marquis's epitaph, also written in the Charenton years, and phrased with an aloof irony far more habitual to his style:

> Wayfarer,
> *Kneel down and pray*
> *For the most unhappy of men.*
> *Born in the century that passed away,*
> *Died in the one we're now in.*
>
> *Despotism with its hideous face,*
> *Fought against him every day:*
> *Under monarchy it was so base*
> *As to make his life its prey.*
>
> *Under the Terror it came again,*
> *Setting him on the edge of a pit;*
> *Under the Consulate it returned, and*
> *Sade once more was fatally hit.*[54]

XXXI

Last Curtain Calls

*I have only one enemy to fear . . . the inconstant and
vagabond European, . . . seeing elsewhere riches more
precious than his own, . . . turbulent, ferocious, anxious, . . . catechizing the Asiatic, enchaining the African, exterminating the citizen of the new world,
and still searching in the midst of oceans unfortunate
islanders to subjugate.*

—*Aline et Valcour*

☐

"WHAT DISTINGUISHES Napoleon's reign, among all nations and all
histories, is its abuse of arbitrariness and illegality," Charles Nodier, the
man of letters who claimed to have encountered Sade at Sainte-Pélagie,
wrote in his memoirs. "By the end of the Consulate [1804], judicial
process, at first violently infringed on, came to be so disdained that one
could not call for it without inciting derision. . . . Places of detention
became insular colonies, cast beyond the bounds of society, in which all
rights had been lost."[1] It is this feature of the Napoleonic regime that
Sade never seemed to acknowledge fully as he continued to pen his
complaints, to write out his chimerical requests for amnesty.

These requests had become all the more futile in 1806, when one of
Sade's two Charenton protectors, the liberal Dr. Gastaldy, died after
attending a sumptuous supper at the home of the archbishop of Paris. A
renowned gastronome, Gastaldy had helped himself four times to a dish
of braised salmon he particularly fancied, and he suffered fatal consequences.

He was replaced by a man of radically opposite temperament. Antoine Royer-Collard, a dour, methodical, highly conservative man,
whose brother was a prominent royalist militant, immediately started

contesting most of Coulmier's methods. Royer-Collard was as austere in his ways as Coulmier was hedonistic; and few aspects of the director's rule shocked him more than his theater, his incessant entertaining, and, above all, the extravagant privileges he gave his favorite inmate, the Marquis de Sade, who in no time became Royer-Collard's whipping boy.

Is it any wonder? How would a stern, repressive moralist look on this renowned libertine who had been granted outlandish privileges by the fawning Coulmier? Who seemed to dictate the entire social tone of the asylum, holding literary discussion groups with its inmates, directing its theater, exchanging gallantries over fine suppers with Paris's prettiest actresses? Who had long "corrupted public mores"[2] and, moreover, was enjoying a seemingly incestuous liaison with a woman who claimed to be his own daughter? What "moral" impact on Charenton's inmates and on society at large, Royer-Collard might well have asked, did Sade's presence have at a hospice directly accountable to Napoleon's Ministry of the Interior?

It is most probably due to Royer-Collard's hostile reports that Fouché's police, a year after the doctor's arrival in Charenton, staged a raid on Sade's quarters. The reason officially given for the foray was to check whether, in Minister Fouché's words, Sade was composing "a licentious work . . . which might even depict events concerned with foreign policy."[3] Though none of Sade's manuscripts posed that kind of threat, after a thorough search of his rooms and of Constance's quarters the police did confiscate armloads of his writings, along with yet another wax "instrument," similar to the one they had seized at Sainte-Pélagie. Among the documents were manuscripts of the book he had been working on throughout his stay at Charenton, a novel described by the authorities as "more dreadful even than *Juliette* . . . a series of unspeakable obscenities, blasphemies, and villainies." The work referred to was the particularly ill-fated *Les Journées de Florbelle*, the rewritten version of a novel originally entitled *Les Conversations au Château de Charmelle*, which had been confiscated upon Sade's arrest in 1801 and which the world would never read: for it would be destroyed by the police, in Armand de Sade's presence and upon his request, after his father's death. Armand is also believed to have destroyed hundreds of Sade's letters, and many other works of fiction seized in 1807.

Coulmier did his best to console Sade for this loss, visiting him daily for hours at a time in the following weeks, but the June 1807 raid seems to have affected him deeply and aggravated his tendency to paranoia. "My poor daughter," he noted in his journal, referring to Constance, "was very affected by this seizure, and this afflicted me all the more because I have no closer friend in the world."[4] Sade's "signals"—the numerical delusions that had marked his stays at Vincennes and the Bastille, and returned with a vengeance after he'd entered Charenton— reappeared more frequently than ever in his journals. "Many 'ones' were signaled," he recorded shortly after the police foray, when Louis-Marie visited him for dinner. "[My son] brought me back the first volume of *Les Crimes de l'Amour,* borrowed the first volume of *Histoire de France,* I was given one extra dish for dinner, Md. [Constance] took her first music lesson, my son spoke about his first volume."[5]

Another effect of the raid was a radical change in the tone of Sade's writings. His remaining three books are terribly proper little historical novels. *La Marquise de Ganges,* which was issued in 1813, and was the only one of these late works published in the author's lifetime, concerns a great Provençal beauty of Louis XIV's reign who was victimized and ultimately assassinated by her evil brothers-in-law. The other two, which would not be published until the 1960s, are set in the Middle Ages, feudal times for which Sade had always felt an affinity. *Histoire Secrète d'Isabelle de Bavière* concerns the dissolute and bloodthirsty wife of France's mad king Charles VI. *Adélaïde de Brunswick* chronicles an eleventh-century Saxon princess who was falsely accused of infidelity by her husband and ended up dying in a convent, a denouement that Sade graced with the following piety: "We believe her to rest in the bosom of a God who forgives all repentant sinners."[6]

And the police raid of 1807 was a prelude to far more serious threats. In 1809, Dr. Royer-Collard protested to "Monseigneur" Fouché, Duke of Otranto, that Sade's very presence at Charenton was a scandal. He elaborated on the disgraces brought to a government institution by a man made "too famous" by his "audacious morality." "His delirium is that of vice," he stated, "and it is not in an establishment reserved for the medical treatment of alienation that this kind of delirium can be cured." Royer-Collard judged it all the more outrageous that the "infamous author" directed a theater at the asylum, and he asked that Sade be transferred to a place where inmates would not be constantly confronted by his "profound corruption."[7]

For the next few months, a tug-of-war would be waged. On one side was Fouché's second in command, Dubois, who, incited by Royer-Collard, repeatedly issued orders for Sade's transfer to the grim fortress of Ham. "The memory of his former libertinage," so a memo of Royer-Collard's to Dubois had protested, "and the kind of superiority he exercises over the direction of the theater," warranted him to be assigned to "another site of reclusion."[8] In the opposite camp stood Sade's family, who, once more motivated by a striving for respectability, lobbied furiously to retain him at the elite Charenton asylum. An important intervention, directly to Fouché, was made by Armand's mother-in-law, Mme Bimard de Sade d'Eyguières, who on the whole was kind to Sade and tried to reform him by sending him edifying books such as a Chateaubriand volume on Christianity.

The most decisive mediator was the inmate's cousin Delphine, the widow of Stanislas de Clermont-Tonnerre, who was now married to one of France's most powerful nobles, the Marquis de Talaru. She had been visiting Sade at Charenton since his first years there. An eccentric, dynamic woman who had intervened successfully for many citizens with problematic records, she seemed to have been the only one of Donatien's relatives, beyond Louis-Marie, who genuinely cared for him. She was a personal friend of Fouché, and in April of 1809 paid a visit to the minister that dealt the final blow to Royer-Collard's schemes. Countermanding Dubois's earlier orders, Fouché signed a decree ordering that the inmate should be retained "indefinitely" at Charenton.

To WHAT DEGREE was the Emperor of the French involved in these decisions concerning Sade? By 1809, Napoleon was confronted with far more weighty matters than the repression of aging libertines. The "legitimist" movement led by the pro-Bourbon nobility was gathering strength, Spain was rebelling violently against his rule, his own nation was increasingly resentful of his incessant wars, and the coalition of enemy powers was growing day by day. But we know that Napoleon was aware of the marquis. On two occasions, in 1811 and 1812, he would sign with his own hand the ministerial decrees that ordered Sade to remain in detention (the indefatigable Delphine had continued to lobby for his release). And in the memoir that documents the exile of his last years, Las Cases's *Mémorial de Sainte-Hélène,* the emperor, probably referring to *Justine,* stated that he had "leafed through the most abominable book that a depraved imagination ever conceived: a novel that even at the time of the Convention had so revolted public morals that [the author] had been jailed."[9]

Delphine de Talaru would continue to do as much as she could to ease her cousin's last years, even sending him fine old wine from her own cellar when he claimed the asylum's wine was adulterated. She was a godsend to him, for Royer-Collard's influence could only grow with the ascendance of the pro-Bourbon movement and the resulting shake-up in Napoleon's ministries. In 1810, Fouché, who had grown resigned to Sade's remaining peacefully at Charenton, was fired for having engaged in secret peace negotiations with the British and was replaced by an officer of Napoleon's personal guard; and the Ministry of the Interior was given to the very conservative Comte de Montalivet. A few weeks after taking his post, Montalivet ordered Sade lodged in separate quarters, kept incommunicado (even from Mme Quesnet), and forbidden the use of pencil, pen, ink, or any other writing implements, on grounds that "he suffered from the most dangerous kind of folly; that his communication with other inmates posed incalculable dangers; that his writings are not less demented than his conduct and his speech."[10] Continuing to defend Sade, Coulmier protested that he was not a jailer and that his inmate was "twice unfortunate," having been made destitute by his family, who had profited by his detention to rob him. Coulmier's objection was overridden, and Delphine had to come to the rescue again, with a personal visit to Montalivet; she convinced him to have the quarantine partially lifted. Sade was allowed to walk about during the hours when inmates were confined indoors, and was again permitted to see Mme Quesnet, as long as no other inmate saw them together.

And so Sade continued the increasingly prosaic life of the old pensioner—dull, dispiriting days marked by financial worries, trivial quarrels with asylum wardens over lack of coffee or firewood, the petty intrigues inevitable to this kind of small, stifling community. They are recorded in the little that remains of his Charenton journals, which document only some fourteen months of the years 1807–8 and the last four months of his life, July to November 1814. (Sade seems to have kept diaries throughout his years at the asylum, but police confiscations and his son's autos-da-fé took care of the missing volumes.)

Throughout his last six years at Charenton a chief source of consolation, beyond his dramatic productions, was his visits with the asylum chaplain, an enlightened cleric who is several times cited in Sade's surviving diaries as "calming [him] down" or "consoling"[11] him. If this seems like curious company for a hard-line atheist, one should remember Sade's lifelong fascination for theology and his close friendships with the parish priests of La Coste and of the neighboring village of Oppède, both of whom had protected him during his tribulations in Provence.

But in light of the increasing conservatism of Napoleon's troubled regime, how long could such tense compromises last? How long could Sade go on ruling the roost at Charenton, the worshipful Coulmier at his side, and continue to fulfill his life's ambition by running a fashionable dramatic group? The ax would fall in May 1813, when the Charenton theater was closed by ministerial decree. Coulmier's own days were numbered. Although his tolerance and empathy had made him very popular among inmates and staff in the first decade of his tenure, there had been increasing complaints by patients, most probably encouraged by Royer-Collard, concerning the director's relaxed mores and his favoritism toward Sade. "What would you say about a hospital in which balls and concerts, and occasionally splendid dinners, are given two or three times a week," read the most militant of the anti-Coulmier petitions sent to the Ministry of Justice, "while unfortunate patients are treated like criminals, most of them bedded on straw like dogs, with a tiny bit of worn blanket for cover?" [12]

An equally harmful report—and a far more influential one—was issued by one Hippolyte de Colins, a retired cavalry officer and licensed veterinarian, who in 1812 painted a grim portrait of the institution for the Minister of the Interior. He singled out Sade, Director de Coulmier's closest friend, as "a monster doomed to public execration . . . a creature whom I could not dignify as a man." What incited Colins's greatest indignation was that one of Sade's dramatic productions featured the author's couplets in praise of the imperial family and of the King of Rome: "Should such a rascal be allowed to praise all that France holds most sacred!" [13]

BY 1814, there was far more at issue than these hostile reports. The career of any aging Bonapartist such as Coulmier—he had just turned seventy-three—would be threatened by that year's events. On April 11, six months after his Grande Armée was torn to shreds at the disastrous battle of Leipzig, a few days after enemy armies entered Paris, Napoleon was forced to abdicate. Since Leipzig, pro-Bourbon loyalties had increased at an amazing pace. "Many people were converting . . . overnight . . . [to] the idea of returning to the ancien régime and to the Bourbons," wrote the memoirist Victorine de Chastenay. "Ladies wore rings freshly engraved with 'Domine, Salvum fac regem,' 'Lord protect the king.' " [14] And a few weeks after the emperor's surrender, Louis XVIII—the younger brother of Louis XVI—entered Paris in a horse-drawn coach with a few members of his family and his immediate entourage, including Sade's distant cousin, that childhood playmate responsible for his very first exile, Prince de Condé, who since 1789 had been an indefatigable leader of the royalist opposition and its most dynamic military hero.

Such an upheaval was bound to revolutionize the workings of all government institutions. Two days after Louis XVIII's return to Paris, the Ministry of the Interior was offered to the prominent monarchist Abbé de Montesquiou. A few weeks later, upon Dr. Royer-Collard's recommendation, Coulmier was replaced as director of the Charenton asylum by the lawyer Roulhac de Maupas, the doctor's own son-in-law, who thenceforth followed all his dictates. In a September 1814 memo to the Ministry of Justice, for instance, Maupas stated his outrage concerning Sade's freedom to communicate freely with the inmates; the fact that some of them came to his room to read the newspaper particularly incensed him. He also noted that the notoriously stingy Armand de Sade was refusing to pay a debt of some eight thousand francs to the hospice.

There was little left to cheer Sade. After his favorite son's death, his relations with Armand had grown stormier. Yet another dispute arose when Sade sold the last of his Provençal mansions, Mazan, to his former overseer, Ripert. Because of the lien their late mother had over his lands and income, Sade's son and daughter now claimed the revenue, which the marquis was of course loath to give them. Sade also complained that by failing to pay his father's full pension, Armand caused him to be deprived of sufficient firewood and candles, of proper domestic help, even of the barber's services. "Through unpardonable cruelty, you close your eyes to all my sufferings," he wrote his son. "Would you love the child your wife is carrying if he treated you this way? Well, I promise that's the way it will be [for you]." [15] (One should take these accusations with a grain of salt: although the detestably bigoted, avaricious Armand may well have cut down on his father's luxuries, it is probable that he never let him in dearth of true necessities, if only because of his obsessive concern with appearances.)

Sade's liaison with Constance, meanwhile, had lost its former serenity. As early as 1808, she had been going to Paris every few weeks, staying two or three days at a time. But in 1812, the couple's financial constraints forced her to take on some kind of wage-earning job: she left Charenton far more frequently and for longer periods. Constance worked as hard for her friend as ever, and many of her trips may have been undertaken at his behest. The marquis was still trying to get his plays performed; and she lobbied, unsuccessfully, with several Paris theaters—the Odéon, the Comédie Française, the Feydeau—to produce his works. We know that in 1814 she called on Béchet, the Paris editor who had published Sade's superproper *Marquise de Ganges,* to bring him the manuscript of a new novel, probably *Isabelle de Bavière* or *Adélaide de Brunswick*.

Yet the couple seems not to have preserved their former harmony. Sade's journals often refer to Constance's increasingly long absences and mention her "surprise visits" to him, her "singular and ridiculous" [16] statements, their temperamental scenes. He forthrightly noted "a few disputes with Md. (Madame)" and, in one unusual instance of remorse, admitted that "I'm the one who was wrong." [17]

But during his last year at Charenton, there was an even more striking reason for the marquis's unease with his companion of many years: at the age of seventy-four, for the first time in some decades, he had fallen in love.

HIS INAMORATA was a seventeen-year-old laundress, Magdeleine Leclerc, whose comeliness he had been noticing for a few years. The girl's mother, an employee of Charenton, had clearly played the role of procuress, encouraging her daughter to flirt with the old codger. We know little about Magdeleine beyond the fact that she was greedy about food, loved chocolate, and was of delicate health; that she received a maximum of three francs for each of her rendezvous with the inmate; and that she was temperamental, sometimes ardent toward him, sometimes cool.

The relationship was not altogether happy. Sade was often tormented by the sense that he was Magdeleine's dupe and that her mother's interests prevailed over any affection the girl had for him. At times Magdeleine reminded him of "one of those spies, placed near condemned men, who attempt to glean their secrets." [18] As if he were having a liaison with a great lady, he complained of "her coldness, her insouciance in pleasure and in conversations," and noted that "there was more forthrightness and honesty in her when she was a child." [19] Yet Magdeleine did seem to have a certain fondness for her protector, the kind a tolerant teenager might have for a doddering uncle given to pinching behinds.

Sade was intensely jealous. Magdeleine had to promise to attend no balls, take no baths, share no visits with men or with friends of her older sister, and she had to renew these promises at each visit. His journal also indicates that he gave Magdeleine lessons in reading, writing, and singing and loaned her books from his library, sometimes improper ones such as the eighteenth-century pornographic classic *Portier des Chartreux*. Their carnal encounters—whatever they consisted of, he referred to them as "little games"—were recorded in his notebooks with a special sign, "Ø," which seems to have signified the act of sodomization. "The Ø was started but not followed up," [20] he jotted down in July 1814, an understandable fiasco, given his age.

Constance does not seem to have been happy about this pitiful interlude and gave it, at best, a mixed reception. In August of 1814, she "spoke angelically about MGL, doesn't seem to want to be much of a bother." [21] Some weeks later, the older woman's jealousy seems to have deepened, and she burst into his room, "making a scene because she thought [Magdeleine] was there." [22] This sheds light on the domestic tensions of Sade's last years. But it certainly does not explain why Constance was absent from Charenton during the last week of her companion's life.

Magdeleine Leclerc made her final visit to Sade on November 27, 1814. She stayed two hours. "She said she had been at no balls and promised not to go to any, told me she would be 18 the following month," he jotted in his journal. "She lent herself as usual to our little games, she promised to return next Sunday or Monday, thanked me for all I was doing for her, and made it evident that she was faithful to me and had no thought of being inconstant."[23] On that November Sunday, Sade had begun to have great pains in his chest and lower abdomen, and he recorded that his young friend seemed "very sensitive" to his discomfort.

The following days, in increasing pain, Sade kept to his room. On Thursday, December 1, he started to run a fever and couldn't walk. He was carried to smaller quarters and put in the care of an orderly. Throughout the week his decline was carefully monitored by a remarkable nineteen-year-old medical student, L.-J. Ramon, who had arrived earlier that month to serve an internship at the asylum and would eventually become its chief physician. He described the aging inmate as he knew him just before his last illness:

> I often met him, walking by himself with a heavy and dragging step, very negligently dressed, in the corridor adjoining his apartment. I never saw him talking to anyone. When I passed him I saluted him, and he responded with an icy politeness that dismissed any notion of entering into conversation. . . . Nothing would have led me to suspect that he was the author of *Juliette* and *Justine*. My only impression of him was that of a haughty, morose nobleman.

This passage of Ramon's memoir of Sade, published half a century later, when the doctor himself was in his seventies, ended with the following remarks:

> I must emphasize that I never heard anything said about M. Sade, who enjoyed great freedom of communication with the world outside, which could in any way justify the reputation created by his writings or by the misdeeds of which he was accused.[24]

Ramon knew Sade well enough to be fully apprised of his relationship with Constance Quesnet and had had a chance to observe them together. Thus there is an inexplicable lacuna in his record of Sade's last days: why was Constance not at his side?

In one of his last journal entries, the marquis mentioned a talk he had with her on Saturday, November 26, the day before Magdeleine's last recorded visit. She may well have gone back to Paris after that weekend for her usual round of errands. But since the capital was merely an hour away, why did someone not alert her to Sade's state when he grew worse? Was she unreachable because she had suddenly undertaken a more distant trip—to Provence, for instance—to take care of some business for the marquis? Or might their quarrels have grown more bitter in previous weeks as she sulked about his fling with the teenager? Or else is it possible that Armand, knowing that his father had left his scant worldly goods to Constance and hoping still to wheedle a few pennies for himself, gave orders that she not be informed of his illness? In these last days, the woman who throughout a quarter of a century had stood constantly by Sade remains more mysterious than ever.

At the end of the week, Sade's condition deteriorated swiftly. In addition to his stomach ailments, he suffered from acute asthma, severe edema of the lungs, and hypertension. On Friday, December 2, Armand came to his father's bedside. Their relations seemed to have improved in the last month—a fortnight earlier, Armand had written his father that he had much enjoyed reading *La Marquise de Ganges*. Before leaving on Friday, Armand asked Dr. Ramon to watch his father round the clock. Though such care was beyond the call of his duties, the young doctor agreed. As he went into Sade's room at dusk, he met the asylum chaplain, who had been visiting the patient daily since the onset of his illness. The priest seemed "satisfied, if not edified" by his last visit with Sade and mentioned that they had made an appointment for the following day.

Sade seems to have faced his end serenely. Could it be that his austerely materialistic (and classically Stoic) view of "nature" helped him to meet his end more peacefully? As he saw it, nothing is ever born or truly dies, since death is merely a change of form. He had written about the nature of death in one of *Juliette*'s several chaste footnotes:

> One should call regeneration, or rather transformation, that particular change we see in matter. It is neither lost, nor spoiled, nor corrupted, by the different shapes it takes; and perhaps one of the principal causes of its force and vigor lies in these seeming destructions, which render it more subtle and offer it the liberty to form new miracles. In sum, matter does not destroy itself to take on new forms, any more than . . . a

square of wax when it is reshaped into a circle. Nothing is more natural than these perpetual resurrections, and it is not more unusual to be born twice than to be born once. All in the world is resurrection: caterpillars are reborn as butterflies; a seed is resuscitated as a tree; all animals buried in the earth are resuscitated in grass, in plants, in worms, and feed other animals, with whose substance they eventually merge.[25]

That last Saturday of the marquis's life, Ramon settled by his patient's bedside, giving him small sips of herbal tea and syrup to relieve the acute congestion of his lungs. Sade's breathing became more labored as the evening wore on. At ten P.M., Dr. Ramon, having walked about the room after giving his patient a drink, noticed that the sounds of rasping breath had suddenly stopped. "Hearing no noise and surprised by the silence,"[26] he realized that Sade had breathed his last.

The following day, the director of Charenton advised His Excellency the Minister of Police of Sade's death. He stated that he did not deem it necessary to seal off the rooms of the deceased, since "young M. de Sade's probity is so evident that we can trust him to destroy any dangerous papers that might be found there." The same day, two employees of Charenton went to the local *mairie* (the equivalent of our town hall) to draw up the death certificate: "December 3, noon. . . . We attest . . . the death, in this commune, of Donatien Alphonse francois, Comte Desade [*sic*], man of letters. . . ."[27]

In his will of 1806, Sade had made precise geographic stipulations concerning his place of burial. Though he subsequently sold the land he had specified for his grave site, he never bothered to change that clause of his will. So one should read the following passage for the general thrust of his intentions and for its lucid consistency with the views of death he had expressed in his writings, rather than for its geographic particulars.

> I absolutely forbid that my body be opened, on any pretext whatever. I most earnestly entreat that it be guarded for forty-eight hours in the room in which I shall die, reposing in a wooden bier which will only be nailed shut at the end of the prescribed 48 hours. . . . During that interval, I wish that a message be sent to M. Le Normand, wood merchant, 1 boulevard de l'Égalité, Versailles, to ask him to come himself, with a cart, to transfer my body under his escort, in said cart, to the woods in my lands at Malmaison, commune of Émancé, near

Épernon, where I wish it to be placed, without any ceremony whatever, at the entrance of said woods, in the first thicketed copse on the right. . . . He could be accompanied in this ceremony, if he wishes, by those of my relatives or friends who, without any formality whatever, might offer me this last sign of attachment. After the grave is covered, acorns will be sown there in such a way that once the site of said grave is again overgrown, and the vegetation over it is once more as thick as it was before, all traces of my tomb will disappear from the face of the earth, just as I hope all trace of my memory will be erased from the memory of men, with the exception of those few who kindly continued to love me until the last moments, fond memories of whom accompany me into the grave.

D. A. F. de Sade[28]

The location of Sade's intended grave is now too urbanized to be recognizable, but it was still rural in the 1920s, when his pioneer biographer, Maurice Heine, was able to recognize and describe the site. "The place is severe and melancholy, and is made surprising by its air of great solitude. . . . In a few instants, we feel that we have forgotten all, and have been forgotten."[29]

Armand de Sade's one gesture of respect for his father's wishes was to forbid the dissection of his body. Otherwise, he countermanded all his father's orders. Sade received a cheap but complete Christian funeral, complete with mass, incense, candles, sexton, etc., and was buried in the cemetery of the Charenton asylum, with a stone cross over his grave. Armand's behavior toward his father's memory did not improve with the years. For decades he refused to pay off the debts for his father's room and board; in 1831, he would be taken to court by the hospice, prompting Charenton's director to describe him as "the disgraceful heir who refuses to fulfill the sacred obligation of providing his father's food."[30]

Several years after Sade's death, the cemetery of the Charenton asylum was dug up. At that time, Ramon, by now a fully qualified doctor at the institution, took Sade's skull home, with the intention of making phrenological studies of it. Shortly thereafter he was visited by an eminent German phrenologist, Dr. Spurzheim, who persuaded him to loan him the skull and promised to send him a cast of it. But not long afterward the phrenologist died, and Ramon never saw the skull again. It had been in Ramon's possession long enough, however, for him to draw up a short report, a copy of which has survived:

"Beautiful development of the arch of the cranium (theosophy, goodwill); no exaggerated protuberance in the temples (no ferocity); no protuberances behind and over the ears (no aggressive drives); cerebellum of moderate dimensions, no exaggerated distance from one mastoid to the other (no excess in erotic impulses).

"In sum," the good doctor ended his report, "his skull was in every way similar to that of a father of the Church." [31]

Epilogue

An unrestricted satisfaction of every need presents itself as the most enticing method of conducting one's life, but this . . . soon brings its own punishment.

—Sigmund Freud,
Civilization and Its Discontents

The history and the tragedy of our era really begin with [Sade]. . . . Our times have . . . blended, in a curious manner, his dream of a universal republic and his technique of degradation.

—Albert Camus, *The Rebel*

☐

SADE'S WISH for the anonymity of his tomb was fulfilled. His desire to be "erased from the memory of men" was not.

1825: "Justine . . . could have been prestigious only at a time when morality, laws, religion, were all undermined to their foundations. . . . After dishonoring himself through so many obscenities, [Sade] could not help but support a revolution which in some way consecrated them."[1]

1834: "Let's take a close look at this strange phenomenon, an intelligent man who drags himself on his knees through fantasies that could not even have been invented by a savage drunk on spirits and human blood. . . . Everywhere you see this man, you smell an odor of sulfur, as if he had swum across the lakes of Sodom."[2]

1839: "One of the glories of France, a martyr . . . who reached his calvary only after being incarcerated in half a dozen jails . . . the very high and powerful seigneur de Sade."[3]

1839: "The author of unnameable books, which caused more rav-

ages than the plague. . . . A Martyr! A martyr!! The Marquis de Sade a
martyr!!'"[4]

A MISFIT EVERYWHERE within his lifetime, a pariah even within his
own caste, Sade would for decades after his death be simultaneously
stigmatized by the excesses of the monarchy and of the Terror. The
coalition of bourgeois capitalists and repatriated émigrés who took
power under the Bourbon Restoration saw him as an emblem of the
bloodshed unleashed in 1789, as "one of the most odious fruits of the
revolutionary crisis."[5] Good republicans such as Michelet, the theorist
of revolutionary fraternity and idolizer of "The People," demonized
him as a symbol of ancien régime corruption: "That such a man still
lived—there was no better proof of the need to destroy the hideous
arbitrariness of the old monarchy," Michelet wrote in 1848. "He was a
professor emeritus of crime. Societies end with such monstrous events:
the Middle Ages with Gilles de Retz [Rais], the famous killer of children;
the ancien régime with Sade, apostle of assassins."[6]

Communal phobias are inevitably fed by myths. In an apocryphal
pseudomemoir published in the 1830s, a prominent member of Paris
society, the Marquise de Créqui, alleged that upon Sade's flight to Italy
in the 1770s, "the corpses of a young man and young woman, totally
pierced with holes . . . attached to each other with knots of pink silk
ribbons,"[7] were found in a pond near La Coste. In the memoirs of his
middle age, one of Sade's former persecutors, Paul Barras, asserted that
"numerous skeletons"[8] had been found in Sade's house at Saint-Ouen
when the police arrested him in 1801. For many years, similar details of
Sade's fiction were transposed into his life without any mention that he
was a writer. Ironically, only when the word *sadisme* officially entered the
French lexicon as a designation for his writings (this occurred in the
1834 edition of the *Dictionnaire universel,* which defined the term as "a
monstrous and antisocial system revolting to nature"[9]) did the stigma
begin to fade. Now that he was officially categorized as a novelist, it
might be possible to see him as someone who imagined, rather than
acted out, his "turpitudes."

Sade's books, however, were extremely difficult to find in the repressive aura of the Restoration, which lasted until 1830, when King Charles
X, Louis XVI's ultrareactionary youngest brother, was overthrown and
was replaced by his benign cousin Louis-Philippe. Under the far more
permissive reign of that monarch, *Justine* seems to have gone through
several more clandestine editions, which were highly prized by French
and foreign literati, particularly the British. Moreover, those years

marked the peak of French Romanticism. Its attendant symptoms—
adulation of the Byronic outlaw, fascination with the more morbid impulses, general exaltation of excess—were bound to enlarge Sade's read-
ership. By the late 1830s, even Sade's most embattled detractors were
admitting his influence. "The Marquis de Sade is everywhere," the influential critic-essayist Jules Janin wrote in his epochal attack of Sade,
Monographie d'un scorpion, which unwittingly created an unprecedented
surge of interest in the marquis's writings. "He is in all bookstores, on
certain mysterious and hidden shelves, which are readily discovered.
It's one of those books usually found behind a volume of Saint John
Chrysostom or Pascal's *Pensées.*" [10] "I would affirm . . . that Byron and
Sade (forgive me the parallel) may have been our contemporaries' greatest sources of inspiration—one visible and prominent, the other clandestine," Sainte-Beuve wrote in 1843. "When reading some of our
fashionable novelists, if you want the secret stairs, the master key, don't
ever lose that last one." [11]

The marquis's reputation among the avant-garde was growing so
fast that in 1839, Gustave Flaubert, then only eighteen years old, was
desperately trying to purchase books by "that honest writer." "I much
like to see men . . . such as Nero, such as the Marquis de Sade," he
wrote a friend that year. "Those monsters explain history for me, they
are its complement, its apogee, its morality. . . . Believe me, they're great
men, immortals." [12] The marquis would exert his spell on Flaubert
throughout his life. "In Flaubert there is truly an obsession with de
Sade; he racks his brains to find sense in that madman," the Goncourts
wrote in an 1861 journal entry. "In one of his finest paradoxes, he even
says [Sade] is the latest word in Catholicism." [13] (Even the Goncourts,
however, looked on *Juliette* as "an illness to be studied.")

Baudelaire would be equally smitten. "To understand evil, one must
always return to de Sade, that is, to *natural man,*" [14] he jotted in his
journal; and "Evil aware of itself less horrible and closer to healing than
evil ignoring itself . . . G. Sand inferior to Sade." [15] No one expressed
greater adulation of Sade than the dandyish eccentric Petrus Borel, a
mascot of French Romanticism, who epitomized the morbid extravagances of that movement (he eventually committed suicide by letting
himself die of sunstroke). The hero of his historical fantasy *Madame
Putiphar,* a brother of Byron's prisoner of Chillon, meets Sade when
he's released from the Bastille and hails him as "the illustrious author of
a book which you all loudly defame, and which you all carry in your
pockets." [16]

From the first generation of Romantics on, Sade was lionized by
many who were rebelling against authority and bourgeois conformism,

or who feigned doing so. An excerpt of "Frenchmen, one more effort if you want to be republicans," from *Philosophy in the Boudoir,* was handed out at the Paris barricades during the Revolution of 1848. The British poet Algernon Charles Swinburne, an atheist and a political radical who found considerable pleasure in passive flagellation, was introduced to the marquis's writings a decade later by the belletrist Monckton Milnes (Lord Haughton), whose outstanding collection of erotica included every available edition of Sade. Swinburne's initial eulogies of the marquis, the "adorer of the phallus," as he called him, were as impassioned as those of his French colleagues. Comparing the "mystic pages of the martyred Marquis de Sade" to those of William Blake, he referred to him as "an illustrious and ill-requited benefactor of humanity." [17] It was inevitable that the marquis would be flaunted, on both sides of the Channel, by many other practitioners of fin de siècle Decadence, which dealt with world-weariness, with perversions, and all forms of neuroses.

The next important steps in Sade's rehabilitation were taken by psychiatrists rather than literati, in Germany rather than Britain or France. The first prominent medical treatise to refer to Sade was Krafft-Ebing's *Psychopathia Sexualis,* published in 1895, which, while condemning the marquis's "sensuality and cruelty," [18] saw his aberrations as an illness whose study would be of great scientific value. And it was in Germany that Sade's most systematically outrageous work had been preserved for posterity.

ON AN UNDOUBTEDLY tumultuous day in July 1789, shortly after Sade had been whisked from his cell at the Bastille, the forty-foot-long original manuscript of *The 120 Days of Sodom* was snatched up by a citizen named Arnoux de Saint-Maximin, about whom nothing is known beyond the fact that he had the wisdom not to destroy the curious document. He passed it on to the family of one Marquis de Villeneuve-Trans, with which it stayed for three generations, whence it migrated, through the clandestine intermediaries of a Paris bookseller and a Berlin psychiatrist named Iwan Bloch, into the hands of a German bibliophile. It was in Germany that Dr. Bloch, in 1904, published the first limited edition (180 copies) of *The 120 Days.* [19] In his introduction, signed with the pseudonym Eugene Düehren, Bloch lavished praise on the author, describing him as "one of the most remarkable men of the eighteenth century, or even of modern times . . . a true wellspring of scientific insights and novel notions for doctors, economists, and moralists. . . . His works show how closely linked our life is to the sexual instinct, which, as he had recognized . . . influences the near totality of human relationships." [20]

And so *The 120 Days* lay dormant in Berlin for the first decades of our century, its gruesome fantasies accessed by just a few bibliophiles. Few members of the French avant-garde were more eager to have the manuscript returned to Sade's homeland than the poet Guillaume Apollinaire, whose trust in the subconscious, in artistic coincidence, and in chance arrangements of words heralded many tenets of the "surrealist" movement (although the term was not used for another several years, he is said to have coined it). Apollinaire had been supporting himself by writing introductions to editions of erotica and had eagerly read the marquis in the *enfer,* or "forbidden section," of the Bibliothèque Nationale. His 1909 edition of Sade—selected pages from *Philosophy in the Boudoir, The Crimes of Love, Justine,* and *Juliette*—further enhanced the marquis's reputation among the French intelligentsia, particularly those who a decade later were to found the surrealist movement. "The time has come for those ideas which germinated in the infamous aura of libraries' forbidden shelves to blossom," Apollinaire wrote in his introduction to Sade, "and this man who seemed to count for nothing in the nineteenth century could well dominate the twentieth." [21] But Apollinaire went off to World War I before his work on Sade could come to fruition. He suffered a serious head wound and died, greatly weakened, of influenza two days before the armistice, at the age of thirty-eight.

Shortly before his death, Apollinaire had befriended a scholar and aesthete named Maurice Heine, with whom he shared many friends among the future surrealists. The two men had agreed to collaborate, as soon as the war was over, in researching and publishing Sade's dispersed works. Sade studies have had their share of eccentrics, and Heine, a member of the Communist Party, was no exception. He once fired a gun into the air at a party congress, presumably in protest against some edict issued by the Soviet Union, and accidentally wounded his wife, who subsequently left him. He went on to serve as editor of the Communist newspaper *L'Humanité* but was soon expelled from the Party, and its paper, for protesting yet other Soviet policies. He thenceforth dedicated himself exclusively to Sade's resurrection, supporting himself, in part, by working for the art dealer Ambroise Vollard.

By that time the surrealists, initially introduced to Sade by Apollinaire, had enshrined the "Divine Marquis"—so they called him—as the central figure of their pantheon. They were drawn to his conjunction of sexual freedom and political liberty, his search for the absolute in all forms of pleasure, his anarchic opposition to the traditional bonds imposed by family, church, and state.

It was through the surrealist movement that Heine met Vicomte Charles de Noailles, who happened to be married to the eccentric amateur painter and art collector Marie-Laure de Noailles—a direct descendant, through three generations of women, of the Marquis de Sade. Her grandmother Comtesse de Chévigné, Armand de Sade's oldest daughter, had been the primary model for Proust's Duchesse de Guermantes. Her mother made a marriage of convenience to her father, the millionaire Maurice Bischoffsheim. Marie-Laure herself, who seemed to have inherited her ancestor's voracious erotic appetites and his bent for scandal, and was the first of his descendants to take pride in him, had also made an arranged marriage, to the charming homosexual art patron de Noailles.

This immensely cultivated couple, who were to assemble one of Europe's great private art collections and, as a recent biographer of Marie-Laure puts it, were "affably prepared to subsidize the denunciation of their way of life,"[22] were among the surrealists' earliest supporters. They underwrote the movement's most radical publications and ventures, such as Luis Buñuel and Salvador Dalí's film *L'Age d'or,* which is based on Sade's *The 120 Days.* It was due to this fortuitous alliance of *vieille France* lineage and radical aesthetics that Charles and Marie-Laure de Noailles, in 1929, sent Heine to Germany in search of the original manuscript of *The 120 Days.*

The mission was successful. Upon his return, Heine published the first accurate edition of the book, in a tiny edition of 396 copies. Heine spent the 1930s traveling throughout France in search of the marquis's papers, prowling in hundreds of provincial libraries, searching numerous family attics for his hero's correspondence. Toward the end of his life (this man of eminent compassion and gentleness would die of starvation in the first year of World War II, having lavished his meager earnings on food for his numerous cats), he often visited with a young Paris editor, Gilbert Lely. Lely became as obsessively dedicated to the marquis as Heine. Lely's excessive adulation has with good reason been derided— he referred to Sade as "the most atrociously calumniated genius in the history of mankind," "a moralist whose depth is not surpassed even by the genius of Friedrich Nietzsche."[23] But in the postwar years Lely produced a voluminous body of Sade research, which became a foundation for all subsequent studies. Lely, in fact, was so obsessed with his idol that during the war years, when his Jewish origins forced him to go into hiding in the countryside, he sought refuge in the vicinity of La Coste and Bonnieux, the Provençal villages most intimately connected with the "Divine Marquis."

However, Lely would not have been able to fulfill his mission without the cooperation of yet another dedicated Sade researcher, this one a male descendant of the marquis.

□　　□

THE MARQUIS DE SADE's great-great-grandson Comte Xavier de Sade, a genial, courtly man who is now in his late seventies, spent most of his youth in the Champagne area of France, east of Paris, at the château of Condé-en-Brie, where his great-grandfather Armand spent his last forty years. At our first meeting, Comte de Sade emphasized that in order to avoid scandalous associations, the title Marquis had not been used in the Sade family since the infamous author's death. For his first twenty-six years, as a matter of fact, Xavier de Sade, who is descended from the writer through three generations of men, had never even heard that he had an ancestor named the Marquis de Sade, or that any of his forebears had written books. "Any mention of the marquis had been strictly forbidden in my family for over a century," he recalls. Moreover, Comte de Sade's father, Bernard George Marie de Sade, died when Xavier was twelve, and his mother, "who cared about little else than hunting and shooting," had heartily disliked her husband's relatives.

There was one small hint during young Xavier's childhood, however, that some family secret was being hidden from him: every few months, his mother would pull out a miniature portrait that she kept locked in a chest of drawers of the living room and show it furtively to a few of her guests. "What is that, Maman?" her son asked several times as he was growing up. "None of your business," she would reply, or "You're too young." As a teenager in the 1930s, young Sade was also aware that two gentlemen, Vicomte Charles de Noailles and M. Maurice Heine, had tried to visit his family at Condé-en-Brie and had been rudely turned away. "Apparently my mother literally barred the door to them," Comte de Sade says today. "She couldn't stand the Noailles family."

Then came the Second World War. In 1941, Xavier de Sade, then twenty years old, was interned in a German work camp. Soon after his return, he married. The young couple, who had set up residence at the family home at Condé-en-Brie, decided to spend their honeymoon in Provence, where the bridegroom vaguely knew his ancestors came from. "Why are you going to that horrible place?" his mother wanted to know. The honeymooners, however, were very taken with the beauty of the villages they visited—Saumane, La Coste—and decided to return often.

A year or so after Comte de Sade's marriage, a group of journalists assigned to do a story on the French aristocracy for *France-Dimanche* arrived at Condé-en-Brie, asking to interview him. "And that is the first time I ever heard of my ancestor the writer," he recalls today. "I was very embarrassed by my ignorance." His mother's family, he recounts, immediately tried to suppress the information imparted by the journalists. "My mother's brother—a bachelor, a dreadful man—told me, 'If you ever, ever speak about your great-great-grandfather, you will be damned!' But after the reportage was published in *France-Dimanche,* Gilbert Lely descended upon me, and I began to learn all about my forebear the marquis."

Comte de Sade knew that during the war years part of the château's library had been walled up by his mother, and later ransacked by German troops. Upon being apprised of his notorious ancestor, he searched through that area of the house, which had remained in a dire state of disarray, and found a jumble of suitcases and boxes filled with family papers. Among them were thousands of the marquis's documents and letters, and in 1947 he began to work on them with Lely. They would find many more boxes. Comte de Sade eventually signed a contract with one of France's most distinguished publishers, Arthème Fayard, to issue them. And that was the beginning of Sade biography as we know it. His mother's family remained as hostile as ever to Comte de Sade's scandalous ancestor. "When I wanted to call my oldest son Donatien," he recalls today, "my uncle threatened to disinherit me."

Decades later, Comte Xavier de Sade, who now lives in a manor house a few miles from Tours and vacations in his *mas* in Provence, forty minutes from La Coste, has not yet finished sorting out his ancestor's papers. He never got to meet his third cousin Marie-Laure de Noailles, who died in 1970, and it is doubtful that he would have approved of her style of life. He did not follow the debates that raged in the postwar years concerning the allegations that Sade's writings presented a "hallucinatory prefiguration of Nazism" and heralded "the world of concentration camps." [24] He has been mostly indifferent to the distinguished scholarly writings—by Maurice Blanchot, Philippe Sollers, Roland Barthes, Jacques Lacan, among many others—that countered those charges and subverted any political analysis of Sade's writings by appraising them as "pure text." Helped in recent years by one of France's most distinguished literary scholars, Maurice Lever, Comte de Sade just dug in and stayed at work in his attic, finding yet more letters from Pélagie, from Mme de Montreuil, from the Sade children, from scores in their entourage, through which we can now begin to re-create Sade's world.

"One has to do this kind of work drop by drop," he says. "I've spent decades in that attic; I've lived with a beeper belt around my waist." Decades ago, Comte de Sade, who is a devout Catholic, tried to read his ancestor's fiction, but it "left him cold." "The correspondence is by far the best part of his writings," he asserts.

Comte de Sade's dedication to the Marquis de Sade remains unlimited, his pride in him intense. Like many French bibliophiles, he is chagrined that the manuscript of *The 120 Days of Sodom,* was stolen from the Noailles family's collection. It has again left France and is currently in the hands of a Swiss collector. And he is happy that unlike the Noailles' offspring, his own five children take a keen interest in the marquis. "My youngest son, Thibault, wrote his doctoral dissertation on Sade. My son Hughes baptized one of his sons Donatien. My oldest granddaughter, at the age of eighteen, asked to have her name changed to Sade. My grandson Dmitri, who is twelve, can tell you all about the marquis." And like his ancestor, Comte de Sade, a high-ranking member of the Association of the French Nobility, a group dedicated to studying the origins and history of the French aristocracy, is extremely proud of his family's ancient lineage. "How could you not want to know about the Marquis de Sade!" he exclaimed during one of our talks. "He's descended from King Saint Louis!"

Comte de Sade is the first member of his family since the death of the writer to take on the title Marquis. He uses it casually, occasionally, as a tribute to his ancestor. "When people ask me whether I prefer to be called Comte de Sade or Marquis de Sade," he says, "I give them a visiting card. Some of the cards say 'Comte,' the others say 'Marquis'— in Provence they prefer 'Marquis.' I don't care which title people use. What really matters to me is that I'm descended from very ancient aristocracy, that I'm descended from King Saint Louis."

YOU CAN STAND AT LA COSTE, today, at that southern rim of the castle wall where the Marquis and Marquise de Sade had their apartments, and enjoy the view they had from their bedroom windows. Looking straight down and east in the particularly glorious month of April, you will see, for miles on end, groves of pink and white cherry trees, budding vineyards interspersed with crimson poppies and violet Judas trees. Southward and two miles beyond, the village of Bonnieux tumbles down its hillock toward the Lubéron range, whose slopes yield some of the Vaucluse's loveliest wines. Left and northward, majestic forests of spruce and oak, more hilltop hamlets, and orchards redolent with rosemary, thyme, and lavender stretch into the distance toward the snow-capped peaks of the Ventoux range.

The rest of La Coste, a steep-pathed pinnacle of pale-golden stone surmounted by the savage ruins of Sade's castle, is equally unaltered from his time. Even the village's population, about 360 souls, remains about the same as in 1780. Its citizens are inbred and fiercely individualistic, and they delight in showing you those features of their village which have not changed. They take you to a field on the marquis's former property to see a tiny brook called the Riaille, which only two centuries ago Costains jumped, packages of playing cards in their pockets, to cross into neighboring papal territories—Bonnieux, Ménerbes—for a night of gambling. They preen on their left-wing politics: the same Communist mayor ran the town for fifty years of our century. They are proud, as the marquis would have been, of their anticlericalism—in this predominantly Protestant and highly secularized community, there are not enough observing Catholics to warrant a working church. In the deep verdant valley that lies south of Sade's castle, Costains will show you the site where thousands of Waldensians were murdered in the sixteenth century by the neighboring feudal lord Baron d'Oppède. Mme Appy, a retired judge and the scion of one of the two oldest Protestant families in town, lives on land owned by her family for five centuries; with delighted malice in her eyes, she will tell you that the Baron d'Oppède came to his own end "in a state of exquisite suffering" and guides you through her cellar, in which many prominent Protestant leaders hid during the sixteenth-century wars of religion.

Thanks to La Coste's abiding loveliness, after the last legal restrictions on the publication of Sade's works were lifted in the 1960s, his reputation went the way of most flesh in the second half of our century: he became a tourist attraction, with the happy result that his village grew steadily in prosperity.

As his works were being published in scores of foreign languages—they would eventually be included in France's prestigious Pléiade edition—the marquis's name began to draw thousands of tourists to La Coste. Several of its struggling farms were converted into charming bed-and-breakfasts. Whether they had ever read a word of his or not, many visitors found La Coste such an amiable place that they eventually settled there, and nearly half of its official residents are now foreigners. In 1975, a popular American art school was founded a few hundred feet below Sade's castle—the School of the Arts in France, now administered by Bard College, whose sixty participants occupy almost a third of the village. Restaurants in neighboring villages started serving dishes with names such as *Mousse glacée aux fruits confits d'Apt et son coulis d'orange à la Sade*. A local vintner began to manufacture a regional wine called Cuvée du Divin Marquis. On top of the rocky plateau surrounding the castle, where the marquis cultivated his beloved fruit trees and boxwood labyrinths, a scattering of tourist cars and buses are nearly always parked, and in season, camera-laden Japanese abound. The village, which for decades had no commercial establishments whatever, now boasts a bakery, a news-and-tobacco store, and a few bistros, of which the most popular is called Café de Sade.

Unlike their more prudish forebears, contemporary Costains express opinions ranging from bemused tolerance to fierce pride when queried about the marquis. To Liliane Ségura, who owns and manages the Café de Sade, the sexual *frisson* evoked by this native son brings the community plenty of added business: "Thousands are drawn here by the romance of his name—the romance of the illicit." "We're proud of his status as a man of letters, we're proud that he turned us into the *village des intellos* [the intellectuals' village]," says Elise Severat, who runs the news-and-tobacco store. Bernard Lamy, a native of Strasbourg who moved to La Coste thirty years ago and runs Bonne Terre, one of the village's most attractive bed-and-breakfasts, agrees: "His odor of sulfur draws the crowds, particularly the Germans." As for the mayor of La Coste, Gilbert Grégoire, he finds Sade the writer "boring and repetitious" but comes to Citizen Sade's defense: "He never committed the crimes he describes in his books. . . . Anyone has the right to jazz it up in his own home."

But here is what might give the marquis the greatest pleasure of all: at midcentury, the château of La Coste and its surrounding terrain were purchased by a progressive-minded local schoolteacher, Henri Bouër. His widow, who still owns it, has recently offered to bequeath it to the Institut de France, and there is speculation that a "Musée Sade" might eventually be installed in a reconstructed room of the castle. With admirable dedication, the Bouërs spent decades partially restoring Sade's domain and built a large theater in the stone quarries just below the château. With a seating capacity of sixteen hundred, the Théâtre de La Coste now has the largest public auditorium in the whole of the Vaucluse, equaled only by the outdoor theater in Avignon's Palais des Papes. Jazz festivals, ballet performances, and contemporary plays have been produced there most every summer. The marquis's ambition to make La Coste a thespian mecca was finally realized, and one recent dramatic venture might have particularly enthralled him: a "fantastical melodrama" about a love affair between the Marquis de Sade and Saint Teresa de Avila, at whose denouement the saint follows the accursed writer into hell. The production, which originated at La Coste, received enthusiastic reviews and went on to tour in Berlin, Rouen, and Bucharest.

Strolling through the ruins of Sade's château, I've often imagined the bemusement the marquis would have expressed upon hearing of this posthumous success.

As I SEARCHED in Provence for the places most familiar to Sade's childhood, I stood often on the banks of the Fontaine de Vaucluse, a few minutes' ride from his family estates at La Coste and Saumane. It is here, in a little house by the water's edge, whose site is said to have remained intact, that Petrarch, according to local legend, nursed his unrequited passion for Laure de Sade. It is here that little Donatien accompanied Abbé de Sade as the scholar documented the poet's sorrowing love for their ancestor.

Set in a narrow gorge surmounted by steep cliffs that are strikingly akin to the sinister landscapes of Sade's fiction, the Fontaine de Vaucluse, one of the world's most powerful resurgent springs, first comes to sight as a round, calm pool of eerie greenness—a lustrous peacock-feather green, the most radiant green I've seen in any liquid element. And then, from the edge of that deceptively tranquil basin, its waters bound down the mountain with thunderous speed, becoming a torrent, generating huge mounds of white spume, surging over rocks and wooded banks with an imperiousness that always strikes me as Dionysian and utterly male.

After its first vertiginous half mile, this foaming green fury flattens out and flows into the plain, becoming a powerful river, the Sorgue. The stream is so forceful that until early medieval times, its numerous tributaries created extensive swamplands, pernicious to the local population. But eventually these waters were coerced into irrigating thousands of acres of vineyards and cherry and melon groves, and some of Provence's richest valleys were created. The area prospered as large bladed wheels set upon the river empowered the industries that spun or dyed cotton and hemp, the mills that processed grain, paper, and olive oil, the engines that tanned leather and furs. And as I stood at the Fontaine de Vaucluse one day, watching the green cascade romping savagely toward the tame, thriving valley below, I was struck by its affinities with the cycle of Sade's life: sexuality and water power are only two of the countless manifestations of energy that humankind must curb and rechannel in order to survive. This, I realized, was one of the lessons of the marquis's fate.

For until his thirty-sixth year, Sade had inundated all that surrounded him with the rage of his desires, mastered the women he coveted as readily as the torrent sculpts its rocky beds, overpowered all obstacles in his catastrophic path . . . until the day when his society, at the behest of one powerful woman, imprisoned him, and he soon began filling tens of thousands of pages with the most audacious texts ever to flow out of any author's pen.

The fury of water unleashed at this site continues to be a central emblem. Sade's energies had to be dammed up and channeled, because he never grasped the fundamentals of civilized life: which have to do with accepting, with a measure of serenity, the ultimate necessity of compromise.

Few men would have been more reluctant than Sade to admit that the central program of civilization is to repress instinct and replace the power of the individual with the power of community. Few would have been less ready to accept the "ordinary human unhappiness"—Freud's phrase—that results from such restraints.

Instead this virtuoso of lust and nihilistic despair demanded round-the-clock ecstasy, fortunes to spend, palaces besides, continual felicity. With Pélagie acquiescing like some cosmic wet nurse to his every longing, he howled like an infant to be readmitted to the paradise of instant gratification, constantly schemed for yet stronger orgasms, yet more baroque choreographies of desire.

And so he remained torn, throughout his life, by the conflict between his actual impotence and his dreams of omnipotence. He became a borderline psychotic because he refused the Great Neurotic Compromise most of us docilely accept.

It is precisely in these pitiful shortcomings that Sade's visionary gifts lay. It is his crude insistence on expressing humankind's most bestial urges, on speaking out what most of us barely dare to admit, on mirroring the primal impulse we've all had, at some point, to claw at the taboos of our own caged lives, that makes him an occasionally fascinating and very modern writer.

Yet as I stood at the torrent of Fontaine de Vaucluse on my last visit there, the line from his writings that rose most urgently to mind was not a blazing depiction of sexual orgy but a flat, brief sentence that he scrawled, in his last years, to Gaufridy. *"I am not happy,"* he wrote, underlining those four words, "but I am well."

"I am not happy, but I am well." In this phrase Donatien might have finally made some grim little adjustment to reality. I stood by the side of the torrent he'd so often visited as a child, wanting to know: how many of us have been truly happy, how many have been merely well? Might not all of life be a constant compromise between those two poles —enjoying the primal satisfactions of being happy, accepting the repressions essential to being well?

What a conservative fable, I reflected, with which to conclude the saga of one of the first great rebels of modern times.

Notes

FOREWORD

1. Guillaume Apollinaire, *Les diables amoureux,* vol. 2 of *Oeuvres complètes* (Paris: Ballant et Lecat, 1966), 231. (Henceforth referred to as **Apollinaire.**)

2. Jules Michelet, *Histoire de la révolution française,* 2 vols. (Paris: Gallimard, Pléiade edition, 1952), vol. 2: 847. (Henceforth referred to as **Michelet, vol. 1, Michelet, vol. 2.**)

3. Gilbert Lely, *Morceaux choisis de DAF de Sade* (Paris: Pierre Seghers, n.d.), xxxiv.

4. Frederic Soulié, *Les mémoires du diable* (Paris: Michel Lévy frères, 1858), vol. 1: 88–90.

5. Aldous Huxley, *Ends and Means* (New York: Greenwood Press, 1937), 314.

6. Sade to his wife, Nov. 24, 1783. Sade, *Oeuvres complètes,* ed. Gilbert Lely, 16 vols. (Paris: Cercle du livre précieux, 1966–67), vol. 12: 415–17. (Henceforth referred to as *OC.*)

I: YOUTH

1. All epigraph citations used throughout the text, except those that head the prologue and the epilogue, are from Sade's works.

2. Archives de la Commune de Saumane, Registre BB 6, copy in collection of Maurice Lever, Paris. Cited in Maurice Lever, *Donatien Alphonse François, Marquis de Sade* (Paris: Librairie Arthème Fayard, 1991), 61. (Henceforth referred to as **Lever.**)

3. Sade, *Aline et Valcour,* in Sade, *Oeuvres,* ed. Michel Delon, 2 vols. (Paris: Gallimard, Pléiade edition, 1990, 1995), vol. 1: 403. (Henceforth referred to as **Pléiade.**)

4. *Mazan: Histoire et vie quotidienne d'un village comtadin* (Editions "Le Nombre d'Or," 1979), 131.

5. For the debate concerning the relationship between Petrarch and Laure de Sade, see Lever, 18.

6. Sade, *Aline et Valcour,* Pléiade, vol. 1: 403.

7. It is impossible to know at what precise moment Donatien left his grandmother's house in Avignon to live with his uncle. Estimates vary between four and seven years of age.

8. Sade, *Les cent vingt journées de Sodome,* Pléiade, vol. 1: 58.

9. Voltaire, *Correspondance,* ed. Théodore Besterman, 12 vols. (Paris: Gallimard, Pléiade edition, 1977), vol. 1: 443.

10. Mme du Châtelet to Francesco Algarotti, Aug. 27, 1738. *Lettres de la Marquise du Châtelet,* ed. Théodore Besterman, in vol. 1 (Geneva, Institut et Musée
Voltaire), 250. Cited in Lever, 64.

11. Voltaire, *Correspondance,* vol 1: 443.

> *Ah tout prêtre que vous serez,*
> *seigneur, seigneur, vous aimerez;*
> *fussiez vous Évêque ou Saint-Père,*
> *vous aimerez et vous plairez:*
> *voilà votre vrai ministère.*
> *Vous aimerez et vous plairez*
> *et toujours vous réussirez*
> *et dans l'Église et dans Cythère.*

12. *Encyclopaedia Britannica,* 1976 ed., "Micropedia" entry on Avignon.

13. Cited in Gilbert Lely, *Vie du marquis de Sade* (Paris: Éditions Jean-Jacques
Pauvert and Éditions Gallimard, 1965), 16. (Henceforth referred to as **Lely, *Vie*.**)

14. Sade to Abbess Gabrielle-Éléonore de Cavaillon, July 1765. *OC,* vol. 12: 24.

15. Sade, *Aline et Valcour,* Pléiade, vol 1: 403.

16. Books and illustrations discussed in *The Invention of Pornography,* ed. Lynn
Hunt (New York: Zone Books, 1993), 15, 17, 21, 31, 37. See also Robert Darnton's
remarkable work, *The Forbidden Best Sellers of Pre-Revolutionary France* (London
and New York: W. W. Norton, 1995).

II: THE FATHER

1. Bibliothèque de l'Arsenal, Paris (manuscript of the Bastille Archives, 10265).
Cited in Lever, 35.

2. *Bibliothèque Sade (I) Papiers de Famille, 1721–1760,* ed. Maurice Lever (Paris:
Fayard, 1993), 22. (Henceforth referred to as ***Bibliothèque Sade I.***)

3. Charles Kunstler, *La vie quotidienne sous la Régence* (Paris: Hachette, 1960),
87.

4. Ibid.

5. *Mémoires du Maréchal-Duc de Richelieu,* vol. 1 (Paris: Firmin-Didot, 1889),
278. Cited in Lever, 47.

6. Sade, *La philosophie dans le boudoir,* ed. Gilbert Lely (Paris: Christian Bourgois, 1972), 264.

7. Kunstler, *La vie quotidienne,* 90.

8. Comte de Sade (addressee unknown), Oct. 1754. *Bibliothèque Sade I,* 650.

9. Comte de Sade (addressee unknown), Feb. 24, 1754. Ibid., 635.

10. Comte de Sade to Mme de Raimond, Dec. 31, 1758. Ibid., 816.

11. Sade Family Archives. Cited in Lever, 39–42.

12. Ibid.

13. Comte de Sade (addressee unknown), Feb. 10, 1745. *Bibliothèque Sade I,*
305.

14. Marquis d'Argenson, *Journal et mémoires,* 9 vols. (Paris: E.-J.-B. Rathery,
1859–67), vol. 3: 260. Cited in Lever, 49.

15. Pauvert, Jean-Jacques, *Sade vivant,* 3 vols. (Paris: Éditions Robert Laffont,
1986), vol. 1, *Une innocence sauvage, 1740–1777,* 21. (Henceforth referred to as **Pauvert, vol. 1, 2, 3.**)

16. Sade Family Archives. Cited in Lever, 36.

> *J'ai tous les goûts quand je vous rend hommage,*
> *J'y trouve en même temps la femme et le garçon,*
> *J'adore en vous une femme volage,*
> *Un ami sage, un aimable giton.*
>
> *Comme un habitant de Sodome*
> *Je fais la femme avec un homme,*
> *C'est ce qui vous met en fureur.*
> *Mais pourquoi vous fâcher, Mesdames?*
> *Vous seules faites mon bonheur:*
> *Je suis très homme avec les femmes.*

17. Ibid., 23.

III: WILD OATS

1. Cited in Lever, 71.
2. Pauvert, vol 1: 47, note 1.
3. *Petits et grands théâtres du Marquis de Sade,* ed. Annie Le Brun (Paris: Paris Art Center, 1989), 016. (Henceforth referred to as *Petits et Grands Théâtres.*)
4. Ibid., 017.
5. Sade, *Reflections on the Novel,* in *The 120 Days of Sodom and Other Writings,* comp. and trans. Richard Seaver and Austryn Wainhouse (New York: Grove Weidenfeld, 1966), 106.
6. Mme de Raimond to Comte de Sade, Sept. 8, 1753. *Bibliothèque Sade I,* 613.
7. Mme de Raimond to Comte de Sade, Sept. 8, 1753, and Sept. 22, 1753. Ibid., 612–14.
8. Mme de Saint-Germain to Comte de Sade, n.d., Sade Family Archives, Lever 79.
9. Sade to his wife, Feb. 3, 1784, in Sade, *Lettres et mélanges littéraires écrits à Vincennes et à la Bastille, avec des lettres de Madame de Sade, de Marie-Dorothée de Rousset et de diverses personnes,* 3 vols., ed. Gilbert Lely and Georges Daumas (Paris: Éditions Borderie, 1980), vol. 3: 71. (Henceforth referred to as *LML,* vol. 1, 2, 3.)
10. Jan. 22, 1781. Ibid.
11. *Extraordinaire de la Gazette,* June 27–28, 1756. Cited in Lever, 83.
12. Comte de Sade to Mme de Raimond, April 1757. *Bibliothèque Sade I,* 738.
13. Mme de Raimond to Comte de Sade, April 1757. Sade Family Archives. Cited in Lever, 85.
14. Comte de Sade to Mme de Raimond, April 27, 1758. *Bibliothèque Sade I,* 757.
15. Sade to Mlle de Rousset, May 12, 1779. *LML,* vol 1: 69.
16. M. de Castéja to Comte de Sade, 1759, Bibliothèque Nationale, Paris: Manuscrits Nouvelles acquisitions françaises 24384, fo. 305. (Henceforth referred to as **BNnaf.**) Cited in *OC,* vol. 12: 8–9 (where this individual is referred to as "Castéra").
17. Sade to Abbé Amblet, April 1759. *OC,* vol. 12: 7.
18. Sade to his father. Ibid., 9–13.
19. Sade, *Journal inédit, deux cahiers retrouvés du journal inédit du Marquis de Sade (1807, 1808, 1814) suivis en appendice d'une notice sur l'hospice de Charenton par Hippolyte de Colins* (Paris: Gallimard, 1970), 43 (Aug. 21, 1807). (Henceforth referred to as *Journal inédit.*)

20. Pauvert, vol 1: 66.

21. March 16, 1763, *Archives de l'Armée*. Cited in Pauvert, vol 1: 53.

22. Comte de Sade to Abbé de Sade, Feb. 2, 1763. *Bibliothèque Sade (II) Papiers de Famille, 1761–1815* (Paris: Fayard, 1995), 39. (Henceforth referred to as *Bibliothèque Sade II*.) Original source BNnaf 24384, fos. 287–88.

23. Comte de Sade to Abbé de Sade, [April?] 6, 1763, BNnaf 24384, fos. 310–11. Also in *Bibliothèque Sade II*, 47.

24. Comte de Sade to Gabrielle-Laure de Sade, May 15, 1763. BNnaf 24384, fos. 262–63. Also in *Bibliothèque Sade II*, 56.

IV: SETTLING DOWN

1. Comte de Sade to Gabrielle-Laure de Sade, late 1762. BNnaf 24384, fos. 279–80. Also in *Bibliothèque Sade II*, 36.

2. The precise French term of Comte de Sade's appointment was "lieutenant general."

3. Pauvert, vol. 1, 75.

4. Comte de Sade to Abbé de Sade, March–April 1763. BNnaf 24384, fo. 286. Also in *Bibliothèque Sade II*, 44.

5. Comte de Sade to Abbé de Sade, spring 1763. Ibid., fos. 310–11. Also in *Bibliothèque Sade II*, 47.

6. Comte de Sade to Abbé de Sade, May 15, 1763. Ibid., fos. 302–3. Also in *Bibliothèque Sade II*, 55.

7. Comte de Sade to Gabrielle-Laure de Sade, May 15, 1763. Ibid., fos. 262–63. Also in *Bibliothèque Sade II*, 56.

8. Lely, *Vie*, 51. Lely identifies him as *"syndic des nobles du Comtat Venaissin."*

9. Cited in a letter from Comte de Sade to Gabrielle-Laure de Sade, late 1762, *Bibliothèque Sade II*, 36. (To my knowledge, the original of this letter from the young marquis has not been identified—it is merely cited by his father in a missive sent to his brother in late 1762.)

10. Sade to Mlle de Lauris, April 6, 1763. *OC*, vol. 12: 13.

11. Comte de Sade to Gabrielle-Laure de Sade, May 2, 1763. BNnaf 24384, fo. 267. Also in *Bibliothèque Sade II*, 53.

12. Comte de Sade to Abbess de Saint-Laurent, May 15, 1763. Ibid., fos. 262–63. Also in *Bibliothèque Sade II*, 56.

13. Comte de Sade to Abbé de Sade, May 15, 1763. Ibid., fos. 302–3. Also in *Bibliothèque Sade II*, 55.

14. Comte de Sade to Abbé de Sade, April 19–20, 1763. Ibid., fos. 306–7. Also in *Bibliothèque Sade II*, 52.

15. Comte de Sade to Gabrielle-Laure de Sade, April 19, 1763. BNnaf 24384, fos. 277–87. Also in *Bibliothèque Sade II*, 51.

16. Comte de Sade to Abbé de Sade, May 15, 1763. Ibid., fos. 302–3. Also in *Bibliothèque Sade II*, 55.

17. Comte de Sade to Gabrielle-Laure de Sade, May 1763. Ibid., fos. 262–63. Also in *Bibliothèque Sade II*, 56.

18. Comte de Sade to Abbé de Sade, March 17, 1763. Ibid., fo. 281. Also in *Bibliothèque Sade II*, 43.

19. Comte de Sade to Gabrielle-Laure de Sade, April 19, 1763. Ibid., fos. 277–78. Also in *Bibliothèque Sade II*, 51.

20. Mme de Montreuil to Abbé de Sade, May 26, 1763. Ibid., fos. 448–49. Also in *Bibliothèque Sade II*, 60.

21. Ibid.

22. Mme de Sade to her husband, Oct. 3, 1778. *LML,* vol. 2: 149.

23. Mlle de Rousset to Gaufridy, Nov. 27, 1778, in *Correspondance inédite du Marquis de Sade, de ses proches et de ses familiers,* ed. Paul Bourdin (Paris: Librairie de France, 1929), 129. (Henceforth referred to as **Bourdin**.)

24. Bourdin, xxx.

25. Mme de Montreuil to Abbé de Sade, May 16, 1763. BNnaf 24384, fos. 406–7. Also in *Bibliothèque Sade II,* 57.

26. Mme de Montreuil to Abbé de Sade, May 26, 1763. Ibid., fos. 408–9. Also in *Bibliothèque Sade II,* 60.

27. The basic unit of French eighteenth-century currency was the livre, or pound, which can be multiplied by four to arrive at a very approximate equal sum (in terms of purchasing power) to the contemporary dollar.

28. Mme de Montreuil to Abbé de Sade, Oct. 20, 1763. BNnaf 24384, fos. 410–12. Also in *Bibliothèque Sade II,* 75.

29. Comte de Sade to Abbé de Sade, June 2, 1763. Ibid., fos. 308–9. Also in *Bibliothèque Sade II,* 61.

30. Mme de Montreuil to Abbé de Sade, Sept. 14, 1763. Ibid., fos. 414–15. Also in *Bibliothèque Sade II,* 70–1.

31. Ibid.

32. Mme de Montreuil to Comte de Sade, Sept. 24, 1763. *Bibliothèque Sade II,* 73.

33. Comte de Sade to Abbé de Sade, Sept. 21, 1763. BNnaf 24384, fo. 318. Also in *Bibliothèque Sade II,* 72.

34. Comte de Sade to Gabrielle-Laure de Sade, June–July 1763. Cited in Pauvert, vol. 1: 90.

35. Comte de Sade to Gabrielle-Laure de Sade, Oct. 8, 1763. BNnaf 24384, fo. 269. Also in *Bibliothèque Sade II,* 74.

36. Mme de Montreuil to Abbé de Sade, Oct. 20, 1763. Ibid., fos. 410–12. Also in *Bibliothèque Sade II,* 76.

37. Kunstler, *La vie quotidienne,* 146.

38. Feb. 16, 1778. *LML,* vol. 2: 127.

39. July 24, 1781. Ibid., 292.

40. July 30, 1785. Ibid., 368.

41. Mme de Sade to her husband, Jan. 4, 1778. Ibid., 123.

42. Mme de Sade to Gaufridy, May 9, 1777. *Bibliothèque Sade II,* 189.

43. Mme de Montreuil to Abbé de Sade, Sept. 14, 1763. BNnaf 24384, fos. 414–15. Also in *Bibliothèque Sade II,* 71.

44. Mme de Montreuil to Abbé de Sade, Oct. 20, 1763. Ibid., fos. 410–12. Also in *Bibliothèque Sade II,* 77.

45. Comte de Sade to Abbé de Sade, June 2, 1763. Ibid., fos. 308–9. Also in *Bibliothèque Sade II,* 61.

V: *THE FIRST OUTRAGE*

1. Comte de Sade to Abbé de Sade, Nov. 15, 1763. BNnaf 24384, fo. 312. Also in *Bibliothèque Sade II,* 78.

2. The most complete account of this episode is given in Lely, *Vie,* 79.

3. Ibid.

4. Ibid.

5. Ibid.

6. Lever, 130.

7. Jacques Michel, *Du Paris de Louis XV à la marine de Louis XVI: L'oeuvre de Monsieur de Sartine* (Paris: Les Éditions de l'Érudit, 1983), 63.

8. Lever, 127.

9. Sade, *La philosophie dans le boudoir*, 119.

10. Sade to M. de Sartine, Oct. 29, 1763. Lely, *Vie*, 83–40.

11. Sade to M. de Sartine, Nov. 2, 1763. *OC*, vol. 12: 17.

12. Mme de Montreuil to Abbé de Sade, Jan. 21, 1764. BNnaf 24383, fos. 416–17. Also in *Bibliothèque Sade II*, 83.

VI: A PEACEFUL INTERLUDE

1. *OC*, vol. 14: 23–5.

2. Lely, *Vie*, 87.

3. The name is alternately spelled Colet, Collet, Colette. I use the "Colet" version employed by Lely and Lever.

4. Sade to Mlle Colet, July 16, 1764. *OC*, vol. 12: 19.

5. Ibid., 20.

6. The sum denoted is 25 louis a month. Throughout this text I use the equivalents offered by the *Petit Larousse* dictionary, which estimates the louis to be worth 24 livres (a French pound, as noted earlier, can be multiplied by four to get its approximate equivalent in contemporary dollars).

7. Lely, *Vie*, 92.

8. Sade to his wife, May 21, 1781. *OC*, vol. 12: 324.

9. Lely, *Vie*, 93.

10. The sum cited here is one thousand écus, yet another monetary species, which *Larousse* estimates to be worth three livres.

11. Mme de Montreuil to Abbé de Sade, Aug. 26, 1765. BNnaf 24383, fos. 459–60. Also in *Bibliothèque Sade II*, 109.

12. Sade to Mlle Colet, early January 1765. *OC*, vol. 12: 22.

13. Sade to Mme de Montreuil, Feb. 1777. Ibid., 111.

14. Ibid.

VII: LA COSTE

1. According to a historian of the region, Henri Fauville, author of *La Coste: Sade en Provence* (Aix-en-Provence: Édisud, 1984), La Coste's population was 80 percent Protestant. (This volume henceforth referred to as **Fauville**.)

2. Comte de Sade to Gabrielle-Laure de Sade, July 24, 1763. BNnaf 24383, fo. 273. Also in *Bibliothèque Sade II*, 66.

3. Fauville, 51.

4. Lely, *Vie*, 97.

5. Ibid., 99.

6. Sade to Abbess Gabrielle-Éléonore de Cavaillon, July 1765. *OC*, vol. 12: 24.

7. Mme de Montreuil to Abbé de Sade, May 20, 1765. BNnaf 24384, fos. 442–43. Also in *Bibliothèque Sade II*, 100.

8. Mme de Montreuil to Abbé de Sade, July 17, 1765. Ibid., fos. 452–53. Also in *Bibliothèque Sade II*, 104.

9. Mme de Montreuil to Abbé de Sade, Aug. 8, 1765. Ibid., fos. 454–56. Also in *Bibliothèque Sade II*, 110.

10. Mme de Montreuil to Abbé de Sade, Aug. 26, 1765. Ibid., fos. 459–60. Also in *Bibliothèque Sade II*, 109.

11. Mme de Montreuil to Abbé de Sade, Sept. 16, 1765. Ibid., fos. 463–64. Also in *Bibliothèque Sade II*, 110.

12. Ibid.

13. Mme de Montreuil to Abbé de Sade, Nov. 7, 1765. BNnaf 24384, fos. 457–58. Also in *Bibliothèque Sade II*, 113.

14. Ibid.

15. Lely, *Vie*, 104.

16. Ibid.

17. Sade to Mlle de Beauvoisin, January 1766. *OC*, vol. 12: 25.

18. Sade to his wife, April 21, 1777. Ibid., 129.

19. The contents of Sade's library at La Coste are listed in Fauville, 68.

20. Abbé de Sade to Mme de Montreuil, June 1, 1776. Lely, *Vie*, 106.

21. Sade Family Archives. Cited in Lever, 155.

22. Ibid.

23. Mme de Montreuil to Abbé de Sade, Jan. 30, 1767. BNnaf 24384, fos. 418–19. Also in *Bibliothèque Sade II*, 122.

24. Mme de Montreuil to Abbé de Sade. Lely, *Vie*, 109.

25. "Consul" was the prerevolutionary term used for a community's assistant mayor.

26. Fauville, 72.

27. Lely, *Vie*, 109.

VIII: *EASTER SUNDAY*

1. This account of the Keller episode is based on the 1768 criminal court proceedings published in Maurice Heine, *Le Marquis de Sade* (Paris: Gallimard, 1950), 153–202 (henceforth referred to as **Heine**); and also on Gilbert Lely's rendering of the court transcript, Lely, *Vie*, 122–26.

2. Sade to Abbé de Sade, April 12, 1768. *OC*, vol. 12: 28.

3. Mme de Saint-Germain refers to the fact that the Arcueil incident occurred on Easter Sunday.

4. Mme de Saint-Germain to Abbé de Sade, April 18, 1768. Lely, *Vie*, 131.

5. Lely, *Vie*, 138.

6. Ibid., 139.

7. Inspector Marais to Comte de Saint-Florentin, minister of the king's household, April 30, 1768. Municipal Library of Reims, collection Tarbié. Cited in Lever, 173.

8. Mme de Montreuil to Abbé de Sade, April 26, 1768. Cited in Lely, *Vie*, 139, and more fully in Pauvert, vol 1: 197.

9. Lever, 172.

10. Mme de Montreuil to Abbé de Sade, June 13, 1768. BNnaf 24384, fos. 420–21. Also in *Bibliothèque Sade II*, 128.

11. *Gazette d'Utrecht*, May 3, 1768. Cited in Pauvert, vol 1: 181, note 1.

12. Benedetta Craveri, *Madame du Deffand and Her World* (Boston: David Godine, 1994), 335.

13. Simeon Prosper Hardy, *Mes loisirs, ou Journal d'évènements tels qu'ils parviennent à ma connaissance*. BNnaf 6680. Cited in Lever, 179.

14. Comtesse de Sade to M. de Sartine, May 24, 1768. Lever, 177.

15. M. de Saint-Florentin to Comtesse de Sade, Nov. 16, 1768. Pauvert, vol 1: 199.

16. Mme de Montreuil to Abbé de Sade, Nov. 19, 1768. BNnaf 24384, fos. 402–403. Also in *Bibliothèque Sade II*, 129.

17. Mme de Montreuil to Abbé de Sade, March 2, 1769. Ibid., fos. 424–27. Also in *Bibliothèque Sade II*, 134.

18. Mme de Montreuil to Abbé de Sade, March 4, 1769. Ibid., fos. 440–41. Also in *Bibliothèque Sade II*, 134–35.

19. Mme de Montreuil to Abbé de Sade, April 17, 1769. Ibid., fos. 446–48. Also in *Bibliothèque Sade II*, 136.

20. Mme de Montreuil to Abbé de Sade, June 29, 1769. Ibid., fos. 422–23. Also in *Bibliothèque Sade II*, 137.

21. Ibid.

22. Sade, *Voyage de Hollande en forme de lettres*. *OC*, vol. 16: 87–108.

23. M. de Saint-Florentin to Mme de Montreuil, March 24, 1770. Lely, *Vie*, 149.

24. Mme de Montreuil to Abbé de Sade, April 27, 1771. *Bibliothèque Sade II*, 136.

25. Sade to Maître Fage, notary at Apt, early 1771. Jean Desbordes, *Le vrai visage du Marquis de Sade* (Paris: Éditions de la Nouvelle Revue Critique, 1939), 90. (Henceforth referred to as **Desbordes**.)

26. Sade to Maître Fage, May 1771. BNnaf 24384. Cited in Pauvert, vol. 1: 236.

IX: A WINTER IN PROVENCE

1. Olivier Bernier, *Louis the Beloved: The Life of Louis XV* (New York: Doubleday, 1984), 245.

2. Sade Family Archives. Lever, 193.

3. Lely, *Vie*, 169–70.

4. Ibid., 167.

5. Mlle de Launay to Abbé de Sade, Nov. 7, 1771. BNnaf 24384, fos. 473–74. Also in *Bibliothèque Sade II*, 138–39.

6. A phrase from an unidentified letter of Mlle de Launay, cited in a letter from Abbé de Sade, note 7.

7. Abbé de Sade to Mlle de Launay, winter 1771–72. BNnaf 24384, fos. 324–25. Also cited in Lever, 194.

8. Collection of Maurice Lever. Lever, 193.

9. See *Petits et grands théâtres*, 047. The names of the actors Sade tried to recruit are listed—three of them were the greatest stars of the Comédie Française.

10. Sade to M. Girard of Lourmarin, 1771–72. Cited in Guillaume Apollinaire, *L'oeuvre du Marquis de Sade* (Paris: Collection des Classiques Gallants, 1909), 33.

11. Pauvert, vol 1: 245.

12. Ibid., 246.

13. "Inventaire du linge de M. de Sade," Dec. 1, 1771. BNnaf 24384, fos. 475–76.

14. Bourdin, xxii.

15. Fauville, 89.

16. Mme de Montreuil to Gaufridy, May 29, 1772. BNnaf 24384, fos. 428–29. Also in *Bibliothèque Sade II,* 140.

X: THE ORGY

1. This account of the Marseilles episode is based on Maurice Heine's publication of the court testimony of June 1772, Heine, 127–50, and on Gilbert Lely's rendering of the events described in the transcript, Lely, 181–85.
2. Lely, *Vie,* 185.
3. Mme de Montreuil to Gaufridy, March 12, 1776. Sade Family Archives. Lever, 209.
4. Sade, *Le président mystifié,* in *Historiettes, contes et fabliaux* (Paris, 1927 ed.), 166–67. Also in Lely, *Vie,* 189.
5. Notarized petition, 1774, dictated to Gaufridy, outlining Mme de Sade's griefs against Mme de Montreuil. BNnaf 24384, fo. 595. Partially published in Bourdin, 9.
6. Ibid.
7. Louis de Bachaumont, *Mémoires secrets pour servir à l'histoire,* 36 vols. (London, 1771–87), vol. 6, July 25, 1772. This popular memoirist was the founder of the "Journal de Bachaumont," which was compiled by large teams of correspondents scattered throughout France and published in samizdat form. Bachaumont died in 1771 and could not have collated this note on Sade himself, as attributed in some sources. Cited in Lever, 212–13.
8. M. de Saint-Florentin to M. de Montyon, July 15, 1772. Pauvert, vol 1: 263. (This author seldom bothers to cite his bibliographical sources.)
9. Lever, 197.
10. Diary of M. de Montreuil, private collection. Cited in Lever, 198.
11. Pauvert, vol 1: 261.
12. Maurice Lever, *Les bûchers de Sodome* (Paris: Fayard, 1985), 335–81.
13. Sade, *Les cent vingt journées de Sodome,* Pléiade, vol. 1: 254.

XI: THE PRISONER

1. Mme de Sade, notarized petition of 1774, cited above. Bourdin, 9.
2. Lever, 220.
3. Lely, *Vie,* 205.
4. Commander de Launay to Governor de La Tour, Jan. 1, 1773. Lely, *Vie,* 206.
5. Mme de Montreuil to Comte Ferrero de La Marmora. Ibid., 208.
6. M. de Launay to Comte de La Tour, Feb. 5, 1773. Ibid., 211–12.
7. Sade to Comte de La Tour, Feb. 14, 1773. Ibid., 213.
8. Samia I. Spencer, ed., *French Women and the Age of Enlightenment* (Bloomington: Indiana University Press, 1984), 1.
9. Ibid., 363.
10. Mme de Montreuil to Comte de La Marmora, Jan. 10, 1773. Lely, *Vie,* 207.
11. Mme de Sade to Comte de La Tour, March 5, 1773. Pauvert, vol. 1: 307.
12. Mme de Sade to King Victor Amadeus III of Sardinia, March 18, 1773. Ibid., 308, note 1. (King Charles Emmanuel III had died on Feb. 20, 1773, and been succeeded by Victor Amadeus III.)
13. Comte de La Marmora to Comte de La Tour, March 8, 1773. Lely, *Vie,* 219.

14. Comte de La Marmora to Comte de La Tour, March 26, 1773. Ibid., 223.

15. M. de Launay to Comte de La Tour, March 26, 1773. Ibid., 224.

16. Sade to de Launay, April 15, 1733. Ibid., 225.

17. Sade to Comte de La Tour, March 19, 1773. Ibid., 222.

18. Comte de La Tour to Chevalier de Mouroux (de La Tour is citing Commander de Launay's communication concerning Sade), April 17, 1773. Ibid., 226.

XII: ON THE LAM

1. Inventory of personal effects left by Sade at the fortress of Miolans. *OC,* vol. 15: 57–9.

2. Comte de la Marmora to Comte de La Tour (citing a letter sent him by Mme de Montreuil), May 14, 1733. Lely, *Vie,* 230.

3. Father Testanière to Mme de Montreuil, June 30, 1775. *Bibliothèque Sade II,* 176.

4. Deposition by Mme de Sade, 1774. Bourdin, 9–12.

5. Bourdin, xxx.

6. Aeschylus, *The Oresteia,* trans. Robert Fagles (New York: Penguin, 1984), 226. I am aware that the translator's phrase "blood-dimmed tide" (above) occurs in Yeats's "The Second Coming."

7. Mme de Montreuil to Mme Necker, Feb.–March, 1774. *Bibliothèque Sade II,* 165.

8. Maître Fage to Mme de Montreuil, Jan. 3, 1774. *Bibliothèque Sade II,* 159–62.

9. Maître Fage to Mme de Montreuil, Jan. 7–8, 1774. Ibid., 162–63.

10. Mme de Montreuil to Maître Fage, Jan. 12, 1774. Ibid., 163–64.

11. Lever, 252.

12. Bernier, *Louis the Beloved,* 249.

13. Mme de Sade to Gaufridy, July 29, 1774. Bourdin, 14.

14. Ibid.

15. Lely, *Vie,* 238.

16. Sade to Gaufridy, n.d. (probably summer 1774). Bourdin, 13.

17. Ibid.

18. Mme de Sade to Gaufridy, Sept. 3, 1774. Ibid., 15.

19. I'm deeply indebted to the splendid contributions of Dr. Sheldon Bach, particularly to his essay "A Dream of the Marquis de Sade," coauthored with Lester Schwartz, M.D. In Sheldon Bach, *Narcissistic States and the Therapeutic Process* (Northvale, N.J.: Jason Aronson, 1985), 129–50.

20. For these insights into Sade I'm also indebted to Janine Chasseguet-Smirgel's "The Narcissistic Function of Masochism (and Sadism)," *International Journal of Psychoanalysis, London Congress Papers* 56, part 1 (1975), published by Baillière-Tindall for the Institute of Psychoanalysis, London.

21. Sade to his wife, May 10, 1782. *LML,* vol. 3, "148 Lettres Inédites du Marquis de Sade," 112.

22. Sade, *Les cent vingt journées de Sodome,* Pléiade, vol. 1: 28.

23. Sade to his wife, late 1784. *OC,* vol. 12: 449–51.

24. Sade to Gaufridy, Dec. 1774. *OC,* vol. 12: 67.

XIII: The Last Fling of Liberty

1. Bourdin, introduction to entries of 1775, 19.
2. Sade, *La philosophie dans le boudoir,* 24.
3. Fauville, 105.
4. Ibid., 104.
5. Mme de Sade to Abbé de Sade, Feb. 1775. Lely, *Vie,* 244.
6. Ibid.
7. Abbé de Sade to Gaufridy, March 28, 1775. Bourdin, 29.
8. Fauville, 108.
9. Lely, *Vie,* 251.
10. Mme de Montreuil to Gaufridy, April 8, 1775. Bourdin, 30–2.
11. Mme de Montreuil to Abbé de Sade, Nov. 22, 1774. Pauvert, vol. 1: 355–57.
12. Abbé de Sade to Gaufridy. Bourdin, 32.
13. Abbé de Sade (addressee unknown), Dec. 13, 1775. Bourdin, 47.
14. Sade to Gaufridy, n.d. (probably spring 1775). Ibid., 33.
15. Mme de Montreuil to Gaufridy, July 26, 1775. Ibid., 39.
16. Sade, *Voyage d'Italie, ou Dissertations critiques, historiques et philosophiques sur les villes de Florence, Rome et Naples, 1775–1776,* ed. Maurice Lever (Paris: Librairie Arthème Fayard, 1995).
17. Ibid., 64.
18. Ibid., 72.
19. All of Chiara Moldetti's letters to Sade are published in Lever, appendix 8, 837–47.
20. Sade, *Voyage d'Italie,* 177.
21. Ibid., 186.
22. Ibid.
23. Sade to Gaufridy, n.d. (probably fall 1775). Bourdin, 44.

XIV: The Trap

1. Fauville, 116.
2. Mme de Montreuil to Gaufridy, April 29, 1775. Bourdin, 33.
3. Abbé de Sade to M. Ripert, Nov. 10, 1775. Ibid., 46.
4. Sade to Gaufridy, Sept. 29, 1775. Ibid., 43.
5. Mme de Sade to Gaufridy, Nov. 27, 1776. Ibid., 59–60.
6. Fauville, 122. Only this faithful chronicler of La Coste history mentions the detail of Trillet's drinking, which is attested to in the legal depositions of several witnesses.
7. Sade to Gaufridy, n.d. (probably late fall 1776). Bourdin, 66–8.
8. Ibid.
9. Mme de Montreuil to Gaufridy, Jan. 21, 1777. Ibid., 77.
10. Reinaud to Gaufridy, Jan. 8, 1777. Ibid., 79–80.
11. Mme de Sade to Gaufridy, Jan. 10, 1777. Ibid., 80.
12. Sade to an abbé, between Feb. 8 and 13, 1777. *OC,* vol. 12: 107.
13. Mme de Montreuil to Gaufridy, March 4, 1777. Bourdin, 82.
14. Abbé de Sade to Gaufridy, Feb. 23, 1777. Ibid., 80.

XV: The Child of the Government

1. Mme de Sade to her husband, Feb. 15, 1777. *LML,* vol. 2: 101.
2. Mme de Sade to Gaufridy, Feb. 25, 1777. Bourdin, 81.
3. Mme de Sade to Gaufridy, March 19, 1777. Ibid., 82.
4. Mme de Sade to her husband, early March 1777. *LML,* vol. 2: 103.
5. Mme de Sade to her husband, June 14, 1777. Ibid., 105.
6. Sade to his wife, April 17, 1781. *LML,* vol. 3: 84.
7. Mme de Sade to her husband, June 26, 1777. *LML,* vol. 2: 105.
8. Mme de Sade to Gaufridy, June 4, 1777. Bourdin, 86.
9. Mme de Sade to her husband, July 28, 1777. *LML,* vol. 2: 107.
10. Mme de Sade to her husband, July 26, 1777. Ibid., 106.
11. Mme de Sade to her husband, June 14, 1778. Ibid., 132.
12. Mme de Sade to her husband, Dec. 3, 1777. Ibid., 118.
13. Mme de Sade to her husband, also Dec. 3, 1777. Ibid., 116.
14. Sade to his wife, April 18, 1777. *OC,* vol. 12: 124.
15. Mirabeau, *Des lettres de cachet et des prisons d'état* (Hamburg [Paris], 1782), 43–6. Cited in Lely, *Vie,* 296–97.
16. Sade to his wife, March 6, 1777. *OC,* vol. 12: 113–16.
17. Ibid.
18. Sade to his wife, late Feb. 1777. Lely, *Vie,* 269.
19. Sade to his wife, April 18, 1777. *OC,* vol. 12: 122.
20. Sade to Le Noir, n.d. (probably March–April 1777). Desbordes, 176–77.
21. Sade to his wife, 1777. Pauvert, vol. 2: 43.
22. Ibid., 60.
23. Sade to his wife, n.d. Sade Family Archives. Lever, 302.
24. Sade to his wife, March 14, 1779. Pauvert, vol. 2: 41.
25. Sade to his wife, Dec. 17, 1777.
26. Sade to his wife, n.d. Desbordes, 170.
27. Sade to his wife, June 16, 1777. Pauvert, vol. 2: 63.
28. Sade to his wife, June 15, 1777. *LML,* 59.
29. Sade to his wife, October 1777. Ibid., 62.
30. Mme de Sade to her husband, n.d. Desbordes, 174.
31. Sade's scribbling on margin of letter from his wife cited in Pauvert, vol. 2: 44.
32. Sade to his wife, n.d. Pauvert, 53.
33. Sade to Mme de Montreuil, late Feb. 1777. *OC,* vol. 12: 113.
34. Sade to Mme de Montreuil, March 13, 1777. Ibid., 117.
35. Sade to Mme de Montreuil. Sade Family Archives. Lever, 302.
36. Sade to Mme de Montreuil, May 25, 1778. Pauvert, vol. 12: 62.
37. Mme de Sade to Gaufridy, May 9, 1777. Bourdin, 85.
38. Mme de Montreuil to Gaufridy, June 3, 1777. Ibid., 86–7.
39. Mme de Sade to her husband, Dec. 30, 1777. *LML,* vol. 2: 121.
40. Mme de Sade to her husband, Feb. 16, 1778. Ibid., 127.
41. Mme de Sade to her husband, April 9, 1778. Ibid., 129.
42. Mme de Sade to her husband, May 17, 1778. Ibid., 131.

XVI: Freedom, Almost

1. Lely, *Vie,* 278.
2. Sade to Gaufridy, July 18, 1778. *OC,* vol. 12: 139.

3. Lever, 313.
4. Gothon (Anne Marguerite Duffé) to Sade. Bourdin, 107.
5. Lever, 316.
6. The account that follows is based on Lely's rendering of Marais's testimony, in Lely, *Vie,* 283–85.
7. Sade to Gaufridy, July 18, 1778. Bourdin, 109–12.
8. Sade to Gaufridy, July 18, 1778. *OC,* vol. 12: 133.
9. Sade to Gaufridy, after July 18, 1778. Ibid., 138.
10. Reinaud to Sade, July 1777. Sade Family Archives. Lever, 318–19.
11. Mme de Villeneuve to Sade, July 26, 1777. Ibid., 319.
12. Gabrielle-Éléonore de Sade to Sade, summer 1777. Ibid., 320.
13. Marguerite-Félicité de Sade to Sade, summer 1777. Ibid., 321.
14. Gabrielle-Laure de Sade to Sade, summer 1777. Ibid., 320.
15. Mme de Sade to Gaufridy, July 27, 1778. Bourdin, 114.
16. Mme de Sade to her husband, n.d., probably early August 1777. Ibid., 112.
17. Lever, 325.
18. Mme de Montreuil to Gaufridy, Aug. 1, 1778. Bourdin, 116.
19. Mme de Montreuil to Mme de Sade, Aug. 13, 1778. Ibid., 121.
20. Sade to Gaufridy, early August 1778. *OC,* vol. 12: 140–41.

XVII: AN UTTERLY CHASTE ROMANCE

1. Sade to Rousset, April 1779. *LML,* vol. 1: 63.
2. Rousset to Sade, Dec. 29, 1778. Ibid., 322.
3. Rousset to Sade, Dec. 30, 1778. Ibid., 324.
4. Rousset to Sade, April 30, 1779. Ibid., 346.
5. Sade to his wife, Oct. 21, 1778. *OC,* vol. 12: 173.
6. Sade to Rousset, March 22, 1779. Ibid., 190.
7. Ibid., 187.
8. Sade to his wife, March 22, 1779. Ibid., 197.
9. Sade to Gaufridy, Sept. 1778. Bourdin, 124.
10. Sade to Gaufridy, mid-Aug. 1778. *OC,* vol. 12: 141.
11. Sade to Gaufridy, early Aug. 1778. Ibid., 140.
12. Sade to his wife, Sept. 1778. Ibid., 158.
13. Pauvert, vol. 2: 102, note 1.
14. This entire episode is recounted by Sade to his wife in a long letter written between Sept. 7 and 28, 1778. *OC,* vol. 12: 151–61.
15. Ibid.
16. Mme de Montreuil to Gaufridy, Sept. 15, 1778. Bourdin, 126.
17. Sade to his wife, Sept. 7 to 28, 1778. *OC,* vol. 12: 152.
18. Mme de Sade to Rousset, Sept. 7, 1778. Bourdin, 125.

XVIII: "MONSIEUR LE 6," 1778–84

1. Attributed to the Marquis de Carioccoli, ambassador from the court of Naples to the court of France. Cited in Pauvert, vol. 2: 15.
2. Simon Schama, *Citizens: A Chronicle of the French Revolution* (New York: Vintage Books, 1990), 212.
3. Cited in Pauvert, vol. 2: 16. (For all translations of rhymed material in this

book—Sade's verse as well as the doggerel variety such as this one—deep gratitude
to Cleve Gray.)

4. Ibid.

5. Ibid.

6. François Furet and Mona Ozouf, eds., *A Critical Dictionary of the French
Revolution*, trans. Arthur Goldhammer (Cambridge, Mass.: Harvard University
Press, 1989), 240.

7. Albert Camus, *The Rebel*, trans. Anthony Bower (New York: Vintage International, 1991), 36.

8. Rousset to Gaufridy, Nov. 15, 1780. Bourdin, 160.

9. Rousset to Gaufridy, Oct. 21, 1780. Ibid., 159.

10. Rousset to Sade, Dec. 26, 1778. *LML*, vol. 1: 320.

11. Rousset to Sade, Dec. 29, 1778. Ibid., 324–25.

12. Sade's poem was sent on by Mlle de Rousset to Gaufridy in a letter of Jan.
1, 1779. Bourdin, 137.

> *Ce sera par les soins touchants*
> *D'une amitié sincère et pure*
> *Présent divin, que la nature*
> *Nous fit pour nous dédommager*
> *Ou plutôt pour nous alléger*
> *Les maux, les chagrins qu'elle donne.*
> *Dieu charmant dont en vous, ma bonne,*
> *Le temple saint elle érigea*
> *Souffrez qu'un culte délicat*
> *Aille la seul lui rendre hommage,*
> *Et qu'il en reçoive pour gage,*
> *Au lieu des myrtes de l'amour*
> *Que le plaisir fane en un jour,*
> *Cette couronne qu'elle érige*
> *À des feux purs et sans prestige. . . .*

13. Rousset to Sade, Jan. 18, 1779. *LML*, vol. 1: 330.

14. Rousset to Sade, April 24, 1779. Ibid., 338.

15. Many of the underlinings in Sade's letters to Rousset indicate that he is
quoting from her letters to him. This particular phrase indicates that Rousset and
Sade had candidly discussed the marquis's practice of masturbation.

16. Sade to Rousset, April 1779. *LML*, vol. 1: 65.

17. Sade to Rousset, March 22, 1779. *OC*, vol. 12: 183.

18. Sade to Rousset, quoted at length in a letter from Rousset to Sade dated
Nov. 30, 1778. *LML*, vol. 1: 317.

19. Rousset to Sade, April 24, 1779. Ibid., 339.

20. Sade to Rousset, May 1779. *OC*, vol. 12: 217.

21. Rousset to Gaufridy, Jan. 26, 1779. Bourdin, 138–92.

22. Rousset to Sade, May 11, 1779. *LML*, vol. 1: 351.

23. Rousset to Gaufridy, Nov. 9, 1779. Bourdin, 149.

24. Mirabeau, *Des lettres de cachet et des prisons d'État* (Hamburg [Paris],
1782), 43–6. (Like many works critical of the government in that decade, the edition
was published clandestinely in Paris, with a foreign imprint.) An eloquent passage
of the book is cited in Lely, *Vie*, 304.

25. Sade to his wife, July 27, 1780. *OC*, vol. 12: 251.

26. Sade to his wife, Oct. 8, 1778. Ibid., 167.

27. Mirabeau, *Des lettres*. Cited in Lely, *Vie*, 306.

28. Sade to his wife, May 21, 1781. *OC*, vol. 12: 322.

29. Ibid., 325.

30. *LML*, vol. 3: 41.

> *Ci-gît le geôlier de Vincennes,*
> *Petit, vilain, cocu, hargneux.*
> *Qui fit ses délices des peines*
> *Et des larmes des malheureux.*
>
> *La terre en connait la réclame.*
> *Passant, tu vois tout ici-bas:*
> *Ne t'informe pas de ton âme,*
> *Car ce jean-foutre n'en eut pas.*

31. Sade to his wife, June 25, 1780. *OC*, vol. 12: 245.

32. The Sade-Mirabeau altercation is eloquently described by Lely in *LML*, vol. 2: 47–8.

33. Sade, *Juliette*, vol. 1: 481.

34. Sade to his wife, Dec. 14, 1780. *OC*, vol. 12: 258.

35. Sade to his wife, March 22, 1779. Ibid., 196.

36. Sade to his wife, Oct. 21, 1778. Ibid., 172.

37. Sade to his wife, Jan. 7, 1779. *LML*, vol. 3: 15.

38. Sade to his wife, March or April 1779. *OC*, vol. 12: 198.

39. The Sades followed a widespread custom of the French upper classes, who often kept their offspring until the age of six or seven under the supervision of the same woman who had been their wet nurse; the great majority of such caregivers lived in the country, where the air was considered far more salubrious for young children.

40. Sade to his wife, Oct. 21, 1778. *OC*, vol. 12: 172.

41. Mme de Sade to her husband, April 30, 1779. *LML*, vol. 2: 193.

42. Mme de Sade to her husband, Dec. 10, 1778. Ibid., 164.

43. Sade to Rousset, Jan. 1779. *OC*, vol. 12: 190.

44. Mme de Sade to her husband, April 14, 1779. *LML*, vol. 2: 189.

45. Ibid., 190.

46. Mme de Sade to her husband, Feb. 16, 1778. Ibid., 127.

47. All of the Sade children's letters to their father are cited from *LML*, vol. 1: 408–12.

48. La Jeunesse to Sade, Sept. 14, 1779. Bibliothèque de l'Arsenal, 12455, fos. 558–63. Cited in Lever, 346.

49. Lely, *Vie*, 317.

50. La Jeunesse to Sade, Sept. 1779. Ibid., 316.

51. Ibid., 317.

52. Sade to La Jeunesse, Oct. 4, 1779. *OC*, vol. 12: 218.

53. Sade to La Jeunesse (Martin Quiros), Jan. 1780. Ibid., 229.

> *Qui, de Bacchus ou de l'amour*
> *Remporte aujourd'hui la victoire?*
> *Quoi! de les fêter tour à tour*
> *Voulez vous obtenir la gloire?*

54. Mme de Sade to Gaufridy, May 24, 1785. Bourdin, 212.

55. Mme de Sade to Gaufridy, June 16, 1785. Ibid.

56. Sade to his wife, Feb. 17, 1779. *OC*, vol. 12: 181.

57. I'm indebted to René de Ceccatty's excellent recent work, *Laure et Justine* (Paris: Éditions JC Lattès, 1996), 12–29, for these insights into Sade's "Laura"

dream. And I want to emphasize again how crucial Dr. Sheldon Bach's reading of this dream (in his *Narcissistic States and the Therapeutic Process*) has been to my understanding of Sade.

58. Sade to his wife, July 3, 1780. *LML*, vol. 3: 47.

59. Sade to his wife, Sept. 1780. Ibid., 60.

60. Sade to his wife, early April 1781. Ibid., 80.

61. Sade to his wife, Feb. 1783. *OC*, vol. 12: 375.

62. Sade to his wife, Feb. 20, 1781. Ibid., 266.

63. Sade to his wife, Feb. 8, 1779. Ibid., 174.

64. Sade to his wife, May 1779. Ibid., 207.

65. Sade to his wife, Dec. 30, 1780. Ibid., 261.

66. Sade to his wife, Oct. 1781. Ibid., 334.

67. Rousset to Gaufridy, Jan. 26, 1779. Bourdin, 139.

68. Ibid.

69. For this missive and all the letters between the marquise and her mother that follow: Sade Family Archives. Lever, 352–55. The letters were exchanged between Dec. 1778 and Feb. 1779.

70. Sade to his wife, May 16, 1779. *OC*, vol. 12: 207.

71. Sade to his wife, Dec. 14, 1780. *OC*, vol. 12: 258.

72. Sade to his wife, May 9, 1779. *LML*, vol. 1: 67.

73. Sade to his wife, Oct. 1778. *LML*, vol. 3: 154.

74. Sade to his wife, March 18, 1783. *OC*, vol. 12: 378.

75. *LML*, vol. 1: 151–53.

76. Sade to his wife, June 15, 1783. *LML*, vol. 3: 147.

77. Sade, *Juliette*, vol I: 284.

78. Sade, *La nouvelle Justine*. Pléiade vol. II: 862.

79. Sade to his wife, Dec. 14, 1780. *OC*, vol. 12: 256.

80. Ibid., 260.

81. Sade to his wife, 1782 or 1784. Cited in Pauvert, vol. 2: 363.

82. Sade to his wife, Nov. 23–24, 1783. *OC*, vol. 12: 412–17.

83. Sade to his wife, Oct. 4, 1778. Ibid., 164–65.

84. Mme de Sade to her husband, May 21, 1779. *LML*, vol. 2: 193.

85. Sade to his wife, 1781–82. Pauvert, vol. 2: 317–18.

86. See Sade's *L'almanach illusoire*, in *LML*, vol. 1: 283, left col.

87. Sade to his wife, May 1779. *OC*, vol. 12: 209.

88. Sade to his wife, late 1784. Ibid., 449–51.

89. Beauvoir, *Must We Burn de Sade?*, 31.

90. Sade to his wife, July 1783. Cited in Pauvert, 400. (This is another of the innumerable instances in which this biographer does not cite his source.)

91. Sade to his wife, late June 1781. *LML*, vol. 3: 92.

92. Ibid.

93. Mme de Sade to her husband, Sept. 30, 1783. *LML*, vol. 2: 336.

94. Ibid.

95. Mme de Sade to her husband, Dec. 13, 1783. Ibid., 346.

96. The annotation is made on a letter from Mme de Sade written to her husband on June 29, 1781. *LML*, vol. 2: 283.

97. Comment made on Mme de Sade's letter to her husband of Sept. 9, 1779, *LML*, vol. 2: 215. (His annotation is documented on 231, note 121, of the same volume.)

XIX: The Jealous Husband

1. Sade to his wife, July–Sept. 1781. *OC*, vol. 12: 327.
2. Sade to his wife, 1781. Lely, *Vie*, 341.
3. Mme de Sade to her husband, Aug. 1781. Ibid., 348.
4. Mme de Sade to her husband, July 24, 1781. *LML*, vol. 2: 293.
5. Mme de Sade to her husband, Aug. 8, 1781. Ibid., 297.
6. Mme de Sade to Rousset, Aug. 18, 1781. Bourdin, 173.
7. Lely, *Vie*, 347.
8. Sade to his wife, June 1782. *OC*, vol. 12: 360.
9. Mme de Sade to her husband, July 21, 1782. *LML*, vol. 2: 289.
10. Sade to his wife, Jan. 22, 1781. *LML*, vol. 3: 71.
11. Sade to his wife, 1782. *OC*, vol. 12: 372.
12. Sade to Rousset, April 17, 1782. Ibid., 351.
13. Ibid.
14. Mme de Sade to Rousset. Bourdin, 172.
15. Sade to his wife, June 1782. *OC*, vol. 12: 361.
16. Mme de Sade to Gaufridy, Sept. 12, 1784. Bourdin, 206.
17. Ibid.
18. Sade to his wife, Aug. 8, 1787. *LML*, vol. 1: 114.
19. Sade to his wife, Feb. 20, 1784. *LML*, vol. 3: 182.
20. Sade to his wife, late Nov. 1783. *OC*, vol. 12: 419.
21. Rousset to Gaufridy, Sept. 6, 1782. Bourdin, 188.
22. Rousset to Gaufridy, Jan. 2, 1782. Bourdin, 189.
23. Sade to Rousset, Jan. 26, 1782. Ibid., 181.
24. Rousset to Sade, March 22, 1782. *LML*, vol. 1: 359–60.
25. Rousset to Gaufridy, Oct. 21, 1780. Bourdin, 159.
26. Rousset to Gaufridy, Oct. 23, 1780. Ibid., 161.
27. Rousset to Gaufridy, Oct. 21, 1780. Ibid., 159.
28. Rousset to Sade, June 1782. *LML*, vol. 1: 367.
29. Sade to Rousset, May 1783. *OC*, vol. 12: 387. (My gratitude again to Cleve Gray for his translation of this particularly difficult poem.)
30. The elision indicates the verb *branler*, "to masturbate."
31. Mme de Sade to Rousset, n.d., probably late 1782. Bourdin, 185.
32. Mme de Sade to Rousset, Feb. 7, 1783. Ibid., 196.
33. Rousset to Gaufridy, 1783. Ibid., 194.
34. Mme de Sade to Gaufridy, July 14, 1784. Ibid., 198.
35. Sade to his wife, March 8, 1784. *OC*, vol. 12: 433.
36. Ibid.

XX: The Tower of Liberty: 1784–89

1. François Furet and Denis Richet, *La révolution française* (Paris: Hachette 1973), 33. For reasons that escape me, the authors' original phrase, *"masochisme collectif,"* is translated in the American edition (*The French Revolution* [New York: Macmillan, 1977], 26) as "refined masochism." (American edition henceforth referred to as **Furet and Richet**.)
2. Pauvert, vol. 2: 405.
3. Sade to his wife, early Nov. 1783. *OC*, vol. 12: 410.
4. Sade to his wife, Sept. 15, 1783. *LML*, vol. 3: 156.
5. Sade to his wife, July 1783. *OC*, vol. 12: 397.

6. Cited in Pauvert, vol. 2: 413.

7. Sade to his wife, July 1783. *OC,* vol. 12: 395.

8. Sade to his wife, April 20, 1783. Ibid., 384.

9. Sade to his wife, 1781. Ibid., 345.

10. Sade to his wife, March 26, 1783. Ibid., 382.

11. Sade to his wife, May 21, 1781. Ibid., 325.

12. Sade to Rousset, April 26, 1783. Ibid., 385.

13. Sade to his wife. Lely, *Vie,* 382, note 1.

14. Pauvert, vol. 2: 477.

> *Vous qui semblable à l'astre adoré des humains,*
> *Y répandez la bienfaisance*
> *Et par vos agréments y changez les chagrins*
> *En des instants de jouissance.*

15. Sade to his wife, Aug. 24, 1783. *LML,* vol. 3: 155.

16. Sade to his wife, n.d. *LML,* vol. 1: 137.

17. Sade to his wife, Oct. 24, 1787. Ibid., 123.

18. Sade to his wife, March 1787. Ibid., 110.

19. Mme de Sade to her husband, April 18, 1787. *LML,* vol. 2: 371.

20. Mme de Sade to her husband, Aug. 20, 1787. Ibid., 372.

21. Sade to his wife, Aug. 14, 1787. *LML,* vol. 1: 114.

22. Sade to his wife, May 16, 1781. *LML,* vol. 3: 90–1.

23. Mme de Sade to her husband, May 14, 1783. *LML,* vol. 2: 335.

24. Mme de Sade to her husband, Aug. 1782. Lely, *Vie,* 361.

25. Mme de Sade to her husband, April 3, 1781. *LML,* vol. 2: 273.

26. Sade to his wife, Nov. 1783. *LML,* vol. 3: 169.

27. Sade to his wife, Aug. 24, 1787. *OC,* vol. 12: 457.

28. Sade to his wife, June 8, 1784. Ibid., 443.

XXI: *Reading and Writing: The Budding Novelist*

1. Sade to his wife, June 15, 1783. *LML,* vol. 3: 147.

2. Sade to his wife, c. March 28, 1781. *OC,* vol. 12: 283.

3. Sade to his wife, July 1783. Ibid., 396.

4. Sade to his wife, Nov. 1783. Ibid., 418.

5. Sade to Abbé Amblet, spring 1784. Ibid., 442.

6. Mme de Sade to her husband, May 18, 1781. *LML,* vol. 2: 278.

7. Mme de Sade to her husband, March 25, 1781. Ibid., 271.

8. Sade to Abbé Amblet, Jan. 1782. *OC,* vol. 12: 347.

9. Deleuze, Gilles, *Coldness and Cruelty,* and von Sacher-Masoch, Leopold, *Venus in Furs* (New York: Zone Books, 1991), 60.

10. Sade, *Les cent vingt journées de Sodome,* Pléiade, vol. 1, 39.

11. Ibid.

12. Ibid., 69.

13. Georges Bataille, *Literature and Evil,* trans. Alastair Hamilton (New York: Marion Boyars, 1985), 116.

14. Sade, *Aline et Valcour,* Pléiade, vol. 1: 387.

15. Ibid., 701.

16. Ibid.

17. Madame de Sade to her husband, "Observations sur le roman d'*Aline et Valcour,*" May–June 1789. *LML,* vol. 2: 387–402.

18. Pauvert, vol. 2: 478–79, note 2.
19. Sade to his wife, Dec. 2, 1786. *LML,* vol. 1: 103.

XXII: The Children, the Future

1. Mme de Sade to Rousset, Jan. 13, 1782. Bourdin, 182.
2. Mme de Sade to Gaufridy, June 16, 1785. Ibid., 212.
3. Sade to his wife, early Jan. 1784. *OC,* vol. 12: 420.
4. Sade to Louis-Marie de Sade, early Jan. 1784. Ibid., 422.
5. Sade to his wife, April 1784. *LML,* vol. 3: 189.
6. Sade to his wife, after Jan. 10, 1784. *OC,* vol. 12: 423.
7. Ibid.
8. Sade to his wife, week of July 3, 1783. *OC,* vol. 12: 390.
9. Sade to his wife, Oct. 24, 1787. *LML,* vol. 1: 122.
10. Donatien-Claude-Armand de Sade to his mother, Feb. 13, 1789. *Bibliothèque Sade II,* 287.
11. Mme de Sade to her mother. Ibid., 257.

XXIII: A Royal Scandal and Its Aftermaths

1. This accounting of the Diamond Necklace Affair is principally drawn from Furet and Richet; from Simon Schama, *Citizens* (New York: Vintage, 1990) 203–10; and from Stefan Zweig, *Marie-Antoinette,* trans. Eden Paul and Cedar Paul (London: Cassell, 1952).
2. Mme de Sade to Gaufridy, Dec. 2, 1785. Bourdin, 214.
3. Sade to M. de Crosne, lieutenant general of police, Sept. 1785. *LML,* vol. 1: 88. (De Crosne had replaced Le Noir in the post earlier that year.)
4. Sade to his wife, Jan. 20, 1787. *LML,* vol. 1: 109.
5. Mme de Sade to M. Cauchy, first secretary of police, Nov. 1788. *LML,* vol. 2: 374.
6. Sade to his wife, Oct. 24, 1787. *LML,* vol. 1: 122.
7. Mme de Sade to Gaufridy, Oct. 22, 1788. Bourdin, 238.
8. Sade to his wife, Oct. 1788. *OC,* vol. 12: 460.
9. Mme de Sade to Gaufridy, Nov. 21, 1788. Bourdin, 239.
10. Mme de Sade to Gaufridy, May 11, 1789. Ibid., 247.
11. Sade to his wife, 1787. *OC,* vol. 12: 459.
12. Mme de Sade to her husband, Dec. 29, 1788. *LML,* vol. 2: 374.
13. Commander de Launay to Lieutenant General of Police de Crosne, July 7, 1788. Lely, *Vie,* 389–90.
14. Mme de Sade to her husband, Dec. 29, 1788. *LML,* vol. 2: 374.
15. Mme de Sade to Bastille commander de Launay, Dec. 31, 1788. Ibid., 377.
16. Mme de Sade to her husband, June 1789. Lever, 393 (no attribution given).

XXIV: The Revolution According to Madame de Sade

1. John Hardman, *Louis XVI* (New Haven: Yale University Press, 1993), 126.
2. Mme de Sade to Gaufridy, June 15, 1788. Bourdin, 235.
3. Mme de Sade to Gaufridy, Sept. 12, 1788. Ibid., 236.
4. Mme de Sade to Gaufridy, Feb. 25, 1789. Ibid., 244.

5. Mme de Sade to Gaufridy, May 1789. Ibid., 245.

6. Sade to Major de Losme, May 29, 1789. *LML,* vol. 1: 134.

7. Mme de Sade to Gaufridy, May 11, 1789. Bourdin, 247.

8. Mme de Sade to Gaufridy, June 22, 1789. Ibid., 248.

9. Furet and Richet, 73.

10. Sade's notation in a journal, spring 1789. *LML,* vol. 1: 133.

11. Commander de Launay to M. de Villedeuil, July 2, 1789. Lely, *Vie,* 398.

12. Sade to Commissioner Chénon, July 9, 1789. Sade, *Lettres inédites et documents,* ed. Jean-Louis Debauve (Paris: Éditions Ramsay/Jean-Jacques Pauvert, 1990), 207.

13. Sade to Gaufridy, spring 1790. Bourdin, 264–65.

14. This order of events is confirmed in a letter of former Lieutenant General of Police Le Noir, found by Robert Darnton in the municipal library of Orléans and described in his article "Les Papiers de Sade et la Prise de la Bastille," *Annales Historiques de la Révolution Française* 202 (Oct.–Dec. 1970), 666.

15. Mme de Sade to Commissioner Chénon, July 19, 1789, Arch. Nat., O^1, 596.

16. Mme de Sade to Gaufridy, Sept. 17, 1789. Bourdin, 250.

17. Mme de Sade to Gaufridy, Sept. 29, 1789. Ibid., 251.

18. Cited in Schama, *Citizens,* 468.

19. Mme de Sade to Gaufridy, soon after Oct. 5, 1789. Bourdin, 252.

20. Mme de Sade to Gaufridy, Oct. 24, 1789. Ibid.

21. Mme de Sade to Gaufridy, Nov. 26, 1789. Ibid., 253.

22. Schama, *Citizens,* 502.

23. Mme de Sade to Gaufridy, Feb. 13, 1790. Bourdin, 260.

24. Mme de Sade to Gaufridy, March 11, 1790. Ibid., 261.

25. Pauvert, vol. 2: 524.

26. Mme de Sade to Gaufridy, March 17, 1790. Pauvert, vol. 2: 527. (No source cited.)

XXV: *LIBERATION!!*

1. Lely, *Vie,* 454.

2. Mme de Montreuil to Gaufridy, March 23, 1790. Private collection, unpublished letter. Cited in Lever, 736, note 13.

3. Mme de Sade to Gaufridy, April 2, 1790. Bourdin, 260.

4. Sade to Gaufridy, n.d. (probably late May 1790). Ibid., 269.

5. Mme de Sade to Gaufridy, June 13, 1790. Ibid., 272.

6. Sade to Gaufridy, April 12, 1790. Ibid., 263.

7. Sade to Gaufridy, May 1790. Ibid., 264.

8. Sade to Gaufridy, n.d. (probably spring 1790). Ibid., 269.

9. Sade to Gaufridy, n.d. (probably late spring 1790). Ibid., 271.

10. Ibid.

11. Sade, *Justine ou les malheurs de la vertu* (Paris: Gallimard, 1981), 51.

12. Sade to Charles Quesnet, 1803. *OC,* vol. 12: 598.

13. Sade to Reinaud, June 12, 1791. Bourdin, 289.

14. Sade to Reinaud, May 19, 1790. Ibid., 266.

15. Sade to Gaufridy, n.d. (probably early June 1790). Desbordes, 257.

16. Sade to Gaufridy, spring 1790. Bourdin, 265.

17. Sade to Gaufridy, n.d. (probably May 1790). Ibid., 269.

18. Sade to Gaufridy, Feb. 15, 1792. Ibid., 310.

19. Mme de Sade to her husband, March 13, 1793. Sade Family Archives. Cited in Lever, 503.

20. Sade to Gabrielle-Éléonore de Sade, April 1790. BNnaf 24384, fos. 438–39. Cited in Lever, 437.

21. Sade to Gaufridy, n.d. (probably 1791). Bourdin, 311.

22. Mme de Montreuil to Mme de Villeneuve, May 22, 1790. Sade Family Archives. Cited in Lever, 440.

23. Sade to Gaufridy, summer 1793. Pauvert, vol. 3: 49.

XXVI: THE ACTIVE CITIZEN

1. National guard unit of Section des Piques to Citizen Sade, Jan. 1, 1795. Lely, *Vie*, 543.

2. Arch. Nat., F^7: 4775^9.

3. Paul Éluard, in *La révolution surréaliste* 8 (Dec. 1, 1926), 8–9. Cited in Lever, 454.

4. Sade to Reinaud, May 19, 1790. Bourdin, 267.

5. Sade to Gaufridy, Dec. 5, 1791. Ibid., 301.

6. Sade to Gaufridy, July 14, 1790. Ibid., 272.

7. Sade to Gaufridy, April 5, 1791. Ibid., 286.

8. Sade to Ripert, June 18–19, 1791. BNnaf 24384, fo. 16.

9. *Le Moniteur,* Nov. 6, 1791. Cited in Pauvert, vol. 3: 583.

10. Sade to Gaufridy, April 7, 1792. *OC,* vol. 12: 509.

11. Sade to Reinaud, June 12, 1791. Ibid., 488.

12. Sade, *Justine,* 53.

13. Ibid., 314.

14. Ibid., 134.

15. Ibid., 413.

16. Sade to Reinaud, June 12, 1791. *OC,* vol. 12: 488.

17. *Affiches, annonces et avis divers, ou Journal général de France,* Sept. 27, 1792. Cited in Pauvert, vol. 2: 592.

18. Sade to Gaufridy, Aug. 18, 1790. Lely, *Vie,* 464.

19. Sade to Gaufridy, late May 1790. *OC,* vol. 12: 479.

20. Sade to Gaufridy, Oct. 4, 1791. Ibid., 492.

21. Sade to Gaufridy, Feb. 6, 1792. Bourdin, 309.

22. Sade to Gaufridy, n.d. (probably late winter 1792). Ibid., 310.

23. Sade to Gaufridy, April 7, 1792. Ibid., 313.

24. Sade to Gaufridy, n.d. (probably May or June 1792). Ibid., 316.

25. Sade to Gaufridy, Aug. 18, 1792. Ibid., 319.

26. Sade to Gaufridy, June 12, 1791. Ibid., 289.

27. Sade to Gaufridy, n.d. (probably early 1792). Ibid., 316–17.

28. Sade to Gaufridy, early Jan. 1792. *OC,* vol. 12: 506.

29. Sade to Gaufridy, July 10, 1792. Ibid., 318.

30. Sade to Gaufridy, May 5, 1793. Bourdin, 340.

31. May 3, 1792. Arch. Nat., F^7: 4954^3, fo. 122.

32. Sade to Gaufridy, Oct. 14, 1792. Bourdin, 330.

33. Sade to Gaufridy, n.d. (probably Oct. 1792). Ibid., 332.

34. Sade to Gaufridy, Nov. 7, 1792. Ibid., 335.

XXVII: A LETTER TO THE KING

1. Sade, "Adresse d'un citoyen de Paris au roi des Français," *Opuscules Politiques. OC,* vol. 9: 69–74.
2. Cited in Pauvert, vol. 2: 631.
3. Sade to Gaufridy, Aug. 25, 1792. Bourdin, 322.
4. Sade to Gaufridy, Sept. 6, 1792. Ibid., 323.
5. Sade to his wife, Aug. 18, 1792. Ibid., 320.
6. Sade to his sons, Aug. 18, 1792. Ibid., 321.
7. Sade to Gaufridy, Oct. 30, 1792. Ibid., 334.
8. Sade to Gaufridy, April 13, 1793. Ibid., 340.
9. The description of the king's execution is drawn from Furet and Richet, 166.
10. Ibid., 190.
11. Sade, *Notes Littéraires. OC,* vol. 15: 15.
12. Sade to the Committee of General Security, June 24, 1794. Arch. Nat., F[7]: 4775[9].

XXVIII: PRESIDENT FOR A DAY

1. Sade to Gaufridy, April 6, 1793. Bourdin, 339.
2. Sade to Gaufridy, July 23, 1793. Lely, *Vie,* 506.
3. Sade to Gaufridy, Aug. 3, 1793. Bourdin, 342.
4. Sade to Gaufridy, Oct. 30, 1792. Ibid., 333.
5. Sade to Gaufridy, July 10, 1792. Ibid., 318.
6. Marat, *Projet de déclaration des droits de l'homme et des citoyens,* Aug. 1793. Cited in Pauvert, vol. 3: 69.
7. Cited in Hugues Jallon, *Sade: Le corps constituant* (Paris: Éditions Michalon, 1997), 66.
8. Sade, *Opuscules Politiques. OC,* vol. 11: 119–22.
9. Furet and Ozouf, *A Critical Dictionary,* 300.
10. Section des Piques, "Discours servant de rapport à l'épuration de ladite société," Jan. 31, 1794. Cited in Pauvert, vol. 3: 110.
11. *Encyclopaedia Britannica,* 1976 ed., entry on "France, History of," 642.
12. Sade, *Opuscules Politiques. OC,* vol. 11: 129.
13. Sade, *Aline et Valcour.* In Pléiade, vol. 1: 624.
14. Sade, *Justine,* 378.
15. Cited in Schama, *Citizens,* 778.
16. Robespierre's speech of Nov. 22, 1793, to the Jacobin Club, cited in Lever, 524. (Precursor of his *Rapport des idées religieuses et morales avec les principes republicains,* 18 Floréal 1794.)
17. Report of the Section des Piques. In *OC,* vol. 2: 391–92.
18. Sade to the members of the Convention, cited in a letter from Sade to Gaufridy, n.d. Bourdin, 348–49.
19. Lely, *Vie,* 519.
20. March 8, 1794, table of request for information on Sade sent by the Committee for General Security to the Committee of Surveillance, Section des Piques, and filled out by the latter group (Arch. Nat., F[7]: 4775[9]).
21. Meister, *Correspondance littéraire,* in Michel Delon, "Meister lecteur de Sade," in *Du Baroque aux Lumières* (Paris: Rougerie, 1986). Cited in Pauvert, vol. 3: 121.

22. Dec. 29, 1793. All the following letters from Sade are cited in the same "carton" of the Archives Nationales as those designated by note 20 above: Arch. Nat., F⁷: 4775⁹. The numbering of the documents in this file is very sporadic, and I can do no more than give the date of each letter.

23. Aug. 10, 1794. Ibid.

24. Rough draft of letter sent June 24, 1794. Ibid.

25. June 24, 1794. Ibid.

26. March 18, 1794. Ibid.

27. Ibid.

28. June 24, 1794. Ibid.

29. March 18, 1794. Ibid.

30. Sept. 30, 1794. Ibid.

31. Aug. 17, 1794. Ibid.

32. June 8, 1794. Cited in Pauvert, vol. 3: 150. (No source cited.)

33. The site of the Picpus garden, and even of the mass grave, is now a privately run shrine. It can be visited by ringing at the front door of the convent at 35 Rue de Picpus.

34. Michelet, *Histoire de la révolution française*, vol. 2: 928.

35. *Cited in Lely, Vie,* 539, note 1. (Lely gives a book entitled *Le Jardin de Picpus* as his source for this quote, but offers no details on the publication.)

36. Sade to Gaufridy, Nov. 1794. Bourdin, 361.

37. Hector Fleischmann, *Réquisitoires de Fouquier-Tinville* (Paris, 1911), 144–157.

38. Sade, last will and testament. *OC,* vol. 10: 221.

39. Furet, 217–18.

40. Section des Piques to the Committee of General Security, Sept. 30, 1794. Arch. Nat., F⁷: 4775⁹, doc. 13.

41. Sade to Gaufridy, Nov. 19, 1794. Bourdin, 360.

42. Sade to Gaufridy, Jan. 20, 1795. Ibid., 365.

XXIX: "SADE, WHO IS NOT WITHOUT TALENTS"

1. Furet and Richet, 232.

2. Talleyrand, letter of July 5, 1797. Cited in Ibid., 340.

3. Sade to Gaufridy, Jan. 6, 1795. Bourdin, 363.

4. Sade to Jacques-Antoine Rabaut-Pommier, Feb. 26, 1795. *OC,* vol. 12: 550. Original text in BNnaf 24390, fo. 459.

5. Sade to Gaufridy, March 5, 1799. Bourdin, 431.

6. Sade to Gaufridy, June 24, 1796. *OC,* vol. 12: 562.

7. Sade to Gaufridy, Jan. 31, 1795. Bourdin, 365.

8. Sade to Gaufridy, Dec. 7, 1798. Ibid., 417.

9. Sade to Gaufridy, July 6, 1794. Ibid., 376.

10. Louis-Marie to Armand de Sade, April 20, 1801. *Bibliothèque Sade II,* 418.

11. Mme de Sade to Gaufridy, March 5, 1796. Bourdin, 402.

12. Mme de Sade to Gaufridy, Jan. 10, 1797. Ibid., 418.

13. Sept. 7, 1803, report by Police Prefect Dubois. Arch. Nat., F⁴: 3119.

14. Sade, *Justine ou les malheurs de la vertu* (Paris: Gallimard, 1981), 51.

15. Constance Quesnet to Gaufridy, Jan. 21, 1798. Bourdin, 421.

16. Sade, *Notes littéraires,* Oct. 31, 1801. *OC,* vol. 2: 31.

17. Sade to Gaufridy, Oct. 27, 1799. *OC,* vol. 12: 587.

18. Sade to Gaufridy, May–June 1795. Bourdin, 373.

19. Sade to Gaufridy, Oct. 5, 1795. Ibid., 383.

20. Sade to Gaufridy, April 19, 1796. Ibid., 388.

21. Louis-Marie de Sade to Gaufridy, Oct. 27, 1795. Ibid., 387.

22. Sade to Gaufridy, Jan. 16, 1798. Ibid., 419.

23. Sade to Gaufridy, April 19, 1796. Ibid., 388.

24. Ibid.

25. Alexandre de Cabanis to Louis-Marie de Sade, Oct. 18, 1801. *Bibliothèque Sade II*, 431.

26. *Madame de Chastenay, Mémoires*, ed. Guy Chaussinand-Nogaret (Paris: Librairie Académique Perrin, 1987). Cited in Pauvert, vol. 3: 231.

27. Sade to Gaufridy, Jan. 24, 1798 (Year VII). Bourdin, 429.

28. Sade, *La philosophie dans le boudoir*, 43. (Throughout my discussion of this book, I use what I feel should be the proper English translation of its title, *Philosophy in the Boudoir*, departing from the title used in Richard Seaver's and Austryn Wainhouse's standard Grove edition of the text, *Philosophy in the Bedroom*. There is a vast difference, to my mind, between the nuances evoked by the words "boudoir" and "bedroom.")

29. Ibid., 19.

30. Ibid., 25.

31. Ibid., 105–6.

32. Ibid., 66.

33. Ibid.

34. Ibid., 73.

35. Ibid., 92.

36. Ibid., 190.

37. Ibid., 257.

38. Ibid., 228.

39. Ibid., 123.

40. Ibid., 216.

41. Ibid., 200.

42. Ibid., 119.

43. Lely, *Vie*, 555.

44. Pauvert, vol. 3: 217; original source not given.

45. Mme de Sade to Gaufridy, Jan. 10, 1798. Bourdin, 418.

46. Louis-Marie de Sade to Gaufridy, Dec. 15, 1797. Ibid., 417.

47. Sade to Gaufridy, Oct. 27, 1797. Sade Family Archives. Cited in Lever, 561.

48. Furet and Richet, 369.

49. Sade to Gaufridy, Aug. 5, 1795. Bourdin, 375.

50. Sade to Gaufridy, Oct. 27, 1797. Sade Family Archives. Cited in Lever, 563.

51. Furet and Richet, 329.

52. Louis-Marie de Sade to Barras, June 26, 1799. Debauve, 605.

53. Sade to Gaufridy, Jan. 17, 1798. Bourdin, 418.

54. Paul de Barras, *Mémoires*, ed. George Duruy (Paris: Hachette, 1895), 56.

55. Bureau de Révision, March 1, 1799. Cited in Lely, *Vie*, 567.

56. Sade to his estranged wife, early Jan. 1798. Sade Family Archives. Cited in Lever, 567.

57. Sade to Gaufridy, spring 1798. Bourdin, 421.

58. Sade to François Gaufridy, Feb. 13, 1799. BNnaf 18312, fos. 28–9.

59. Ibid. (This portion of the letter is excerpted in Bourdin, 430.)

60. Sade to Gaufridy, Jan. 24, 1799. Bourdin, 428.

61. Sade to Gaufridy, July 2, 1798. Ibid., 423.

62. Alan Schom, *Napoleon Bonaparte* (New York: HarperCollins, 1997), 251.

63. Ibid., 253.

64. *L'ami des Lois,* Aug. 29, 1799. Cited in Françoise Laugaa-Traut, *Lectures de Sade* (Paris: Arman Colin, 1973), 51.

65. The full title and self-description of the publication is *Le Tribunal d'Apollon ou Jugement en dernier ressort de tous les auteurs vivants; libelle injurieux, partial et diffamatoire; Par une Société de Pygmées littéraires* (Paris: Marchand, Libraire, Palais-Égalité, Galerie Neuve). Cited in Lely, *Vie,* 569, and Laugaa-Traut, 55.

66. *Le Tribunal d'Apollon* 2, no. 10 (1799), 193–97. Cited in Lely, *Vie,* 569, and Laugaa-Traut, 55.

67. Sade in *L'ami des Lois,* Sept. 24, 1799. Cited in Laugaa-Traut, 52.

68. Charles Villers, *Spectateur du Nord,* Dec. 1797, vol. 4: 407.

69. Restif de la Bretonne, *Monsieur Nicolas* (Paris: Éditions de la Pléiade, 1989), vol. 4: 269–71.

70. Sade to Gaufridy, March 30, 1799. Bourdin, 430.

71. Furet and Ozouf, *A Critical Dictionary of the French Revolution,* 282.

72. Sade to the Ministry of Justice, April 15, 1800. Lely, *Vie,* 574.

73. Sade to Gaufridy, Oct. 27, 1799. *OC,* vol. 12: 588.

74. Sade to Gaufridy, Jan. 3, 1800. Ibid., 589.

75. Ibid.

76. Sade to Gaufridy, Jan. 17, 1800. Ibid., 590–91.

77. Sade to Gaufridy, Jan. 26, 1800. Ibid., 591.

78. Sade to Charles Gaufridy, Feb. 1, 1800. Ibid., 592.

79. Sade to "citoyenne Mademoiselle Archias," Feb. 22, 1800. Ibid., 593.

80. Sade to Gaufridy, May 28, 1800. Bourdin, 444.

81. Constance Quesnet to Gaufridy, Aug. 3, 1799. Ibid., 433.

82. Gaufridy to Sade, May 17, 1800. Sade Family Archives. Lever, 581.

83. Lely, *Vie,* 574.

84. Ibid., 572.

85. *Journal des arts, des sciences et de littérature,* 90 (Oct. 22, 1800), 281–84. Cited in Laugaa-Traut, 60.

86. Sade, *L'Auteur des "Crimes de l'amour" à Villeterque, folliculaire* (Paris: Massé, 1800–1).

87. Arch. Nat., F⁷: 3119 (Fichiers de Police, "Travail du 20 Fructidor An XII" [Sept. 7, 1803]).

88. Sade to "Citizen Fouché," May 20, 1802. *OC,* vol. 12: 597.

89. Louis-Marie de Sade to Claude-Armand de Sade, April 18, 1802. *Bibliothèque Sade II,* 418.

XXX: SOCIETY

1. Sade, *Juliette,* vol. 1: 241.

2. Ibid., 566.

3. Ibid., vol. 2: 24.

4. Ibid.

5. Ibid., 205.

6. Ibid., 578.

7. Ibid., vol. 1: 211.

8. Ibid., vol. 2: 173.

9. Ibid., 78.

10. Ibid., 600.

11. Ibid., vol. 1: 350.

12. Ibid., 241.

13. Stuart Hampshire, *Modern Writers and Other Essays* (New York: Alfred A. Knopf, 1970), 56–62.

14. Lever, 594.

15. Charles Nodier, *Souvenirs, episodes et portraits de la restauration et de l'empire*, vol. 2 (Paris: 1831), 52.

16. This is the same Dubois memorandum that was noted at the end of the last chapter, Arch. Nat., F^7: 3119.

17. Ibid.

18. Arch. Nat., F^7: 3129. Sept. 2, 1808.

19. Arch. Nat., F^7: 3119.

20. Lely, *Vie*, 633.

21. Sade, *Journal inédit*, 66.

22. BNnaf 24384, fos. 599–602. Cited in Lely, *Vie*, 689.

23. Arch. Nat., F^7: 6294, pièce 27.

24. Sade to Fouché, June 10, 1806. Ibid., pièce 20.

25. Arch. Nat., F^4: 3119.

26. Sade to Commission sénatoriale de la liberté individuelle, June 19, 1805. Arch. Nat., O^2 (Maison de l'Empereur-Sénatoreries) 1430.

27. *Bibliothèque Sade II*, 488.

28. François Simonet de Coulmier, *Précis sur la maison de santé de Charenton*, Archives Départementales du Val de Marne, AJ2100. Cited in Lever, 607.

29. Jean-Etienne Esquirol, *Mémoire historique et statistique sur la maison royale de Charenton*, Paris 1835. Cited in Lever, 645–46.

30. Armand de Rochefort, *Mémoires d'un vaudevilliste* (Paris: Charlieu et Huillery, 1863). Cited in *Petits et grands théâtres*, 088.

31. Ibid.

32. Auguste Labouisse-Rochefort, *Voyage à Saint-Léger, campagne de M. le chevalier de Boufflers, suivi du voyage à Charenton et des notes contenant des particularités sur toute la famille Boufflers* (Paris: C-J Trouvé, 1827), 154. Cited in Sade, *Oeuvres* (Pléiade), xxix–xxxii, and in Lever, 613.

33. *Mémoires de Mlle Flore, artiste du théâtre des Variétés*, 3 vols. (Paris: Comptoir des Imprimeurs Unis, 1845), vol. 2: 172–84. Cited in *Petits et grands théâtres*, 089. The exact year of Mlle Flore's visit to Charenton is not known.

34. L.-J. Ramon, *Notes sur M. de Sade*, Dec. 1867. *OC*, vol. 2: 47.

35. Lely, *Vie*, 647.

> *"Saint-Aubin, de Thalie aimable favorite,*
> *Dans ton jeu délicat que d'âme et de chaleur!*
> *Pourquoi donc s'étonner de ce double mérite,*
> *Quand tout l'esprit est dans le coeur?"*

36. Sade, *Théâtre*, ed. Jean-Jacques Brochier, 35 vols. (Paris: J. J. Pauvert, 1970), vol. 4: 432–42.

> *Nous brûlons d'offrir nos hommages*
> *À notre charmant protecteur.*
> *Nos dons seront de faibles gages*
> *De ce qu'inspire notre ardeur;*

Mais il n'est rien de préférable
À la plus douce offrande des coeurs;
On plaît mieux à cet homme aimable
Par des voeux que par des fleurs.

37. Lely, *Vie*, 651.

Semblable au fils de l'éternel
Par une bonté peu commune
Sous l'apparence d'un mortel,
Venant combler l'infortune,
Votre âme pleine de grandeur,
Toujours ferme, toujours égale,
Sous la pourpre pontificale,
Ne dédaigne point le malheur.

38. Dubois to Coulmier, *Archives de la maison nationale de Charenton.* Cited in Lever, 602.

39. Sade to François Ripert, Sept. 10, 1810. Cited in Debauve, 530.

40. Mme de Sade to Armand de Sade, Aug. 25, 1802. *Bibliothèque Sade II,* 469.

41. Louis-Marie de Sade to Armand de Sade, April 1803. Ibid., 482.

42. Louis-Marie de Sade to Armand de Sade, April 20, 1801. Ibid., 418.

43. Mme de Sade to Claude-Armand de Sade, Aug. 25, 1802. Ibid., 468.

44. M. de Miscault to Louis-Marie de Sade, Jan. 4, 1805. Ibid., 494.

45. Mme Bimard de Sade to Armand de Sade, Feb. 15, 1808. Ibid., 550. Comtesse de Sade d'Eyguières is referred to perplexingly in some family correspondence as "Mme Bimard," her maiden name. I've fused her maiden name and her married name to avoid confusion.

46. Mme Bimard de Sade to M. de Vallery (Armand's maternal uncle), July 14, 1808. Ibid., 564.

47. Sade Family Archives. Cited in Lever, 626.

48. Municipal Library of Avignon, Collection "Requien." Cited in Lever, 628.

49. Document of the French Military of Justice, Sade Family Archives. Cited in Lever, 633.

50. From Sade to "Napoleon Bonaparte, His Majesty Emperor and King, Protector of the Confederate of the Rhine," June 17, 1809. *OC,* vol. 12: 605.

51. Sade to Claude-Armand, Dec. 5, 1809. Sade Family Archives. Cited in Lever, 633.

52. Sade, *Journal inédit,* 50.

53. Sade to Gaufridy, 1806, *OC,* vol. 12: 606.

54. Sade, *Epitaphe de D.-A.-F. Sade, détenu sous tous les régimes.* In *Notes littéraires. OC,* vol. 2: 20.

Agenouille-toi pour prier
Près du plus malheureux des hommes.
Il naquit le siècle dernier
Et mourut au siècle où nous sommes.

Le despotisme au front hideux
En tous les temps lui fit la guerre:
Sous les rois ce monstre odieux
S'empara de sa vie entière;
Sous la Terreur il reparaît

Et met Sade au bord de l'abîme;
Sous le Consulat il renaît;
Sade en est encore la victime.

XXXI: LAST CURTAIN CALLS

1. Charles Nodier, *Souvenirs de la révolution et de l'empire* (Paris: Nouvelles Éditions, 1850), vol. 2: 10–12.
2. Arch. Nat., F⁷: 3129.
3. BN dossier, cited in Pauvert, vol. 3: 376. (This author never gives any denotations more precise than a "BN" or "AN" in his meager and spotty footnotes, and I failed to find this reference.)
4. Sade, *Journal inédit,* 38.
5. Ibid., 46.
6. Sade, *Adélaide de Brunswick. OC,* vol. 12: 79.
7. Dr. Royer-Collard to Police Minister Fouché, 1808. Arch. Nat., F⁷: 6294, pièce 18.
8. Ibid.
9. Emmanuel de Las Cases, *Mémorial de Sainte-Hélène* (Paris: Flammarion), vol. 2: 598.
10. Interior Minister de Montalivet to M. de Coulmier, Oct. 18, 1810. Municipal Library of Avignon, Collection "Requien." Cited in Lever, 635.
11. Sade, *Journal inédit,* 41, 47, 69.
12. Arch. Nat., F¹⁵: 2608.
13. H. de Colins, *Notice sur l'établissement consacré au traitement de l'aliénation mentale, établi à Charenton, près PARIS,* published in *Journals inédits,* 116–17.
14. Schom, *Napoleon Bonaparte,* 683.
15. Sade to Armand de Sade, May 18, 1810. Sade Family Archives. Cited in Lever, 641.
16. Sade, *Journal inédit,* 90.
17. Ibid., 94.
18. Ibid., 82.
19. Ibid.
20. Ibid., 40.
21. Ibid., 83.
22. Ibid., 94.
23. Ibid., 95.
24. L.-J. Ramon, *Notes sur M. de Sade. OC,* vol. 2: 47.
25. Sade, *Juliette,* vol. 2: 177.
26. Ramon, *Notes. OC,* vol. 2: 42.
27. Lely, *Vie,* 687.
28. BNnaf 24384, fos. 599–602. Most complete version in Lely, *Vie,* 688–90.
29. Heine, *Sade,* 353–54.
30. Lely, *Vie,* 692.
31. Ramon, *Notes. OC,* vol. 2: 43.

EPILOGUE

1. Louis-Gabriel Michaud, *Biographie universelle ancienne et moderne,* vol. 39 (1825): 472–80.

2. Jules Janin, "Le Marquis de Sade," *Revue de Paris,* 1834: 321–22. Cited in Laugaa-Traut, 125.

3. Petrus Borel, *Madame Putiphar,* 1877–1878 ed., vol. 2. Cited in Laugaa-Traut, 140.

4. Laugaa-Traut, 125.

5. Charles de Villers, in *Spectateur du Nord,* vol. 4 (Dec. 1797): 407. Cited in Sade, Pléiade, Vol. I, xxiii.

6. Michelet, *La révolution française,* vol. 2: 486.

7. *Souvenirs de la marquise de Créqui de 1710 à 1800,* vol. 3 (Paris 1849), 111–12. Cited in Fauville, 93.

8. Barras, *Mémoires de Barras,* vol. 1: 56. Cited in Sade, Pléiade, vol. 1, xl.

9. Boiste, *Dictionnaire universel,* 8th ed., 1834. Cited in Laugaa-Traut, 107.

10. Jules Janin, *Monographie d'un scorpion, Revue de Paris,* 1834: 331–47. Cited in Laugaa-Traut, 129.

11. Sainte-Beuve, "A few truths about the Situation in Literature." In Laugaa-Traut, 132.

12. Gustave Flaubert to Ernest Chevalier, July 15, 1839. Flaubert, *Correspondance* (Paris: Gallimard, Pléiade edition, 1973), vol. 1: 47.

13. Edmond and Jules de Goncourt, *Journal* (Paris: Laffont, 1989), entry of April 9, 1861, 683.

14. Baudelaire, *Oeuvres complètes* (Paris: Gallimard, Pléiade edition, 1961), 521.

15. Ibid., 148.

16. Borel, *Madame Putiphar.* In Laugaa-Traut, 140.

17. James Pope-Hennessy, *James Monckton Milnes* (London: Constable, 1951), 147.

18. R. Krafft-Ebing, *Psychopathia Sexualis* (Paris: Georges Carré, 1895), 79. Cited in Laugaa-Traut, 169.

19. Eugene Düehren (Dr. Iwan Bloch), *Le Marquis de Sade et son temps,* trans. from the German by Dr. A. Weber-Riga (Berlin: Barsdorf; Paris: Michalon, 1901).

20. Cited in Apollinaire, 230.

21. Ibid., 231.

22. James Lord, *Six Exceptional Women* (New York: Farrar, Straus & Giroux, 1993), 90.

23. Heine, Introduction by Gilbert Lely, 9, 11.

24. "Doit on brûler le Divin Marquis?" in *Le Nouvel Observateur,* March 2, 1966.

Bibliography

I. Original Archives

Archives Nationales, Paris (**Arch. Nat.**)
    Series F^7 (Police générale—Cartons): 3119, 3129, 4775^9, 4953^4, 4954^3, 6294
    Series O^1 (Maison du roi): 305, 393, 404
    Series O^2 (Maison de l'Empereur-Sénatoreries): 1430
Bibliothèque de l'Arsenal, Paris: Manuscript of Bastille Archives 10255: Dossier
    "Comte de Sade"; and 10265: Dossier "Abbé de Sade"
Bibliothèque Nationale, Paris: Manuscrits Nouvelles acquisitions françaises 24384–
    24393 (**BNnaf**)
Sade Family Archives (as cited in Maurice Lever, *Sade*).

II. Works by Sade (editions used)

Bibliothèque Sade (I) Papiers de Famille, le règne du père (1721–1760). Edited by
    Maurice Lever. Paris: Librairie Arthème Fayard, 1993. (***Bibliothèque Sade I***)
Bibliothèque Sade (II) Papiers de Famille, le marquis et les siens (1761–1815). Edited
    by Maurice Lever. Paris: Librairie Arthème Fayard, 1995. (***Bibliothèque Sade
    II***)
Correspondance inédite du Marquis de Sade, de ses proches et de ses familiers. Edited
    by Paul Bourdin. Paris: Librairie de France, 1929. (**Bourdin**)
Histoire de Juliette ou les prospérités du vice. 2 vols. Paris: Éditions Pauvert, 1987.
    (**Juliette**)
Histoire secrète d'Isabelle de Bavière, reine de France. Paris: Gallimard, 1953.
*Journal inédit, deux cahiers retrouvés du journal inédit du Marquis de Sade (1807,
    1808, 1814), suivis en appendice d'une notice sur l'hospice de Charenton par Hippo-
    lyte de Colins*. Paris: Gallimard, 1970. (***Journal inédit***)
Justine ou les malheurs de la vertu. Paris: Gallimard, 1981. (**Justine**)
Lettres inédites et documents. Edited by Jean-Louis Debauve. Paris: Éditions Ram-
    say/Jean-Jacques Pauvert, 1990.
*Lettres et mélanges littéraires écrits à Vincennes et à la Bastille, avec des lettres de
    Mme de Sade, de Marie-Dorothée de Rousset et de diverses personnes*. Edited by
    Gilbert Lely and Georges Daumas. 3 vols. Paris: Éditions Borderie, 1980. (***LML
    1, LML 2, LML 3***)
La Marquise de Ganges. Paris: Éditions Autrement Littératures, 1994.
La nouvelle Justine ou les malheurs de la vertu. 2 vols. Paris: Union Générale d'Édi-
    tions, 1978.

Oeuvres. Edited by Michel Delon. 2 vols. Paris: Gallimard, Bibliothèque de la Pléiade, 1990, 1995. **(Pléiade, vol. 1, Pléiade, vol. 2)**

Oeuvres complètes du Marquis de Sade. Edited by Gilbert Lely. 16 vols. Paris: Cercle du livre précieux, 1966–67. (**OC, vol. 1, vol. 2, vol. 3, etc.**)

La philosophie dans le boudoir. Edited by Gilbert Lely. Paris: Christian Bourgois, 1972.

Théâtre. Edited by Jean-Jacques Brochier. 4 vols. Paris: J. J. Pauvert, 1970.

Voyage d'Italie, ou Dissertations critiques, historiques et philosophiques . . . Edited by Maurice Lever. Paris: Librairie Arthème Fayard, 1995.

In English

Juliette, compiled and translated by Richard Seaver and Austryn Wainhouse. New York: Grove Weidenfeld, 1968.

Justine, Philosophy in the Bedroom, and Other Writings. Compiled and translated by Richard Seaver and Austryn Wainhouse. New York: Grove Weidenfeld, 1965.

The Marquis de Sade: Selected Letters. Edited by Margaret Crosland. Translated by W. J. Strachan. New York: October House, 1966.

The 120 Days of Sodom and Other Writings. Compiled and translated by Richard Seaver and Austryn Wainhouse. New York: Grove Weidenfeld, 1966.

The Passionate Philosopher: A Marquis de Sade Reader. Edited and translated by Margaret Crosland. London: Peter Owen Publishers, 1991.

III. GENERAL BIBLIOGRAPHY

Aeschylus. *The Oresteia.* Translated by Robert Fagles. New York: Penguin Books, 1984.

Allison, David B., and Mark S. Roberts, with Allen S. Weiss. *Sade and the Narrative of Transgression.* Cambridge, Eng.: Cambridge University Press, 1995.

d'Alméras, Henri. *Le Marquis de Sade: L'homme et l'écrivain.* Paris: Albin Michel, 1906.

Anonymous. *Le portier des Chartreux.* Paris: Babel, Actes Sud, 1993.

Apollinaire, Guillaume. Oeuvres Complètes, 2 vols. Paris: Ballantet Lecat, 1966.

Bach, Sheldon. *Narcissistic States and the Therapeutic Process.* New Jersey: Jason Aronson, 1985.

Barthes, Roland. *Sade, Fourier, Loyola.* Translated by Richard Miller. New York: Hill and Wang, 1976.

Bataille, Georges. *Literature and Evil.* Translated by Alastair Hamilton. New York: Marion Boyars, 1985.

Beauvoir, Simone de. *Must We Burn de Sade?* Translated by Annette Michelson. London: Peter Nevill, 1953.

Berlin, Isaiah, ed. *The Age of Enlightenment.* New York: New American Library, 1956.

Bernier, Olivier. *Louis the Beloved: The Life of Louis XV.* New York: Doubleday, 1984.

Biver, Paul, and Marie-Louise Biver. *Abbayes, monastères, couvents de femmes à Paris, des origines à la fin du XVIIIème siècle.* Paris: Presses Universitaires de France, 1975.

Blanchot, Maurice. *Sade et Restif de la Bretonne.* Le Regard Littéraire, Paris: Éditions Complexe, n.d.

Brochier, Jean-Jacques. *Théâtre de Sade.* Paris: J. J. Pauvert, 1970.

Bruni, René. *Villages du Lubéron.* Tome II, *Lacoste, Ménerbes, Oppède.* Marguerittes: Éditions de l'Equinoxe, 1993.

Camus, Albert. *The Rebel.* Translated by Anthony Bower. New York: Vintage International Books, 1991.

Camus, Michel, ed. *Colloques Sade: Château de Cerisy.* Paris: Belfond, 1983.

Carter, Angela. *The Sadeian Woman and the Ideology of Pornography.* New York: Pantheon Books, 1978.

Casanova, Antoine, and Claude Mazauric. *Vive la révolution.* Paris: Messidor/Éditions sociales, 1989.

Ceccatty, René de. *Laure et Justine.* Paris: Éditions JC Lattès, 1996.

Centre Aixois d'études et de recherches sur le dix-huitième siècle. *Le Marquis de Sade.* Paris: Librairie Armand Colin, 1968.

Chanover, E. Pierre. *The Marquis de Sade: A Bibliography.* Metuchen, N.J.: The Scarecrow Press, 1973.

Châtelet. *Lettres de la Marquise du Châtelet.* Edited by Théodore Besterman. Geneva: Institut et musée Voltaire, n.d.

Clap, Sylvestre. *Fontaine de Vaucluse.* Marguerittes: Éditions de l'Equinoxe, 1992.

———. *L'isle sur la Sorgue.* Marguerittes: Éditions de l'Equinoxe, 1993.

Clébert, Jean-Paul. *Guide de la Provence mystérieuse.* Bourges: Les Guides Noirs, Éditions Sand, 1992.

Craveri, Benedetta. *Madame du Deffand and Her World.* Translated by Teresa Waugh. Boston: David R. Godine, 1994.

Crosland, Margaret. *Sade's Wife: The Woman Behind the Marquis.* London: Peter Owen Publishers, 1995.

Cryle, Peter. *Geometry in the Boudoir: Configurations of French Erotic Narrative.* Ithaca and London: Cornell University Press, 1994.

Darnton, Robert. *The Forbidden Best-Sellers of Pre-Revolutionary France.* London and New York: W. W. Norton, 1995.

———. *The Great Cat Massacre and Other Episodes in French Cultural History.* New York: Basic Books, 1984.

Deleuze, Gilles. *Coldness and Cruelty.* With Sacher-Masoch, Leopold von. *Venus in Furs.* New York: Zone Books, 1991.

Delpech, Jeanine. *La passion de la Marquise de Sade.* Paris: Éditions Planète, 1970.

Desbordes, Jean. *Le vrai visage du Marquis de Sade.* Paris: Éditions de la Nouvelle Revue Critique, 1939. **(Desbordes)**

Duby, Georges, ed. *Histoire de la France: Des origines à nos jours.* Paris: Larousse, 1995.

Fauville, Henri. *La Corte: Sade en Provence.* Aix-en-Provence: Édisud, 1984.

Fauville, Henri. *La Coste: Sade en Provence.* Aix-en-Provence: Édisud, 1984.

Foucault, Michel. *The History of Sexuality.* Vol. I: *An Introduction.* Translated by Robert Hurley. New York: Vintage Books, 1990.

Frappier-Mazur, Lucienne. *Writing the Orgy: Power and Parody in Sade.* Translated by Gillian C. Gill. Philadelphia: University of Pennsylvania Press, 1996.

Freud, Sigmund. *Civilization and Its Discontents.* Translated by James Strachey. New York: W. W. Norton, 1961.

Furet, François, and Mona Ozouf, eds. *A Critical Dictionary of the French Revolution.* Translated by Arthur Goldhammer. Cambridge, Mass.: Harvard University Press, 1989.

Furet, François, and Denis Richet. *La révolution française.* Paris: Hachette, 1973. American ed.: *The French Revolution.* New York: Macmillan, 1977. **(Furet and Richet)**

Ginisty, Paul. *La Marquise de Sade.* Paris: Bibliothèque-Charpentier, 1901.

Godechot, Jacques. *La vie quotidienne en France sous le directoire.* Paris: Librairie Hachette, 1977.

Gorer, Geoffrey. *The Life and Ideas of the Marquis de Sade.* New York: W. W. Norton, 1963.

Goulemot, Jean M. *Ces livres qu'on ne lit que d'une main.* Paris: Minerve, 1994.

Hampshire, Stuart N. *Modern Writers and Other Essays.* New York: Alfred A. Knopf, 1970.

Hanly, Margaret Ann Fitzpatrick. *Essential Papers on Masochism.* New York and London: New York University Press, 1995.

Hardman, John. *Louis XVI.* New Haven: Yale University Press, 1993.

Hayman, Ronald. *De Sade: A Critical Biography.* New York: Thomas Y. Crowell, 1978.

Heine, Maurice. *Le Marquis de Sade.* Paris: Librairie Gallimard, 1950.

Huët, Marie-Hélène. *Mourning Glory: The Will of the French Revolution.* Philadelphia: University of Pennsylvania Press, 1997.

Hunt, Lynn. *The Family Romance of the French Revolution.* Berkeley and Los Angeles: University of California Press, 1992.

——, ed. *The Invention of Pornography: Obscenity and the Origins of Modernity, 1500–1800.* New York: Zone Books, 1993.

——, ed. *Eroticism and the Body Politic.* Baltimore and London: Johns Hopkins University Press, 1991.

Jallon, Hugues. *Sade: Le corps constituant.* Paris: Éditions Michalon, 1997.

Klossowski, Pierre. *Sade mon prochain.* Précédé de *Le philosophe scélérat.* Paris: Éditions du Seuil, 1967.

Kunstler, Charles. *La vie quotidienne sous la Régence.* Paris: Hachette, 1960.

Laborde, A. M. *Le Marquis et la Marquise de Sade.* American University Studies. New York: Peter Lang, 1990.

Lacan, Jacques. *Écrits II.* Paris: Éditions du Seuil, 1971.

Laugaa-Traut, Françoise. *Lectures de Sade.* Paris: Arman Colin, 1973.

Le Brun, Annie. *Les châteaux de la subversion.* Paris: Pauvert aux Éditions Garnier Frères, 1982.

——. *Soudain, un bloc d'abîme: Sade.* Paris: Pauvert, 1986. American ed.: *Sade: A Sudden Abyss.* San Francisco: City Lights Books, 1990.

——, ed. *Petits et grands théâtres du Marquis de Sade.* Paris: Paris Art Center, 1989.

Lely, Gilbert. *Morceaux choisis de Donatien-Alphonse-François Marquis de Sade.* Paris: Pierre Seghers, n.d.

——. *Vie du Marquis de Sade.* Paris: Jean-Jacques Pauvert and Gallimard, 1965.

Lennig, Walter. *Portrait of de Sade: An Illustrated Biography.* Translated by Sarah Twohig. New York: Herder and Herder, 1971.

Lever, Maurice. *Les bûchers de Sodome.* Paris: Fayard, 1985.

Lever, Maurice. *Donatien Alphonse François, Marquis de Sade.* Paris: Librairie Arthème Fayard, 1991. American ed.: *Sade: A Biography.* Translated by Arthur Goldhammer. New York: Farrar, Straus & Giroux, 1993. **(Lever)**

Michel, Jacques. *Du Paris de Louis XV à la marine de Louis XVI. L'Oeuvre de Monsieur de Sartine.* Vol. I: *La vie de la capitale.* Paris: Les Éditions de l'Érudit, 1983.

Michelet, Jules. *Histoire de la révolution française.* 2 vols. Paris: Gallimard, Bibliothèque de la Pléiade, 1952.

Mirabeau. *Ma conversion.* Paris: Union générale d'Éditions, 1995.

———. *Le rideau levé.* Paris: Babel, Actes Sud, 1994.

Mishima, Yukio. *Madame de Sade.* Translated from the Japanese by Donald Keene. New York: Grove Press, 1967.

Obliques. Special Issue No. 12–13. Edited by Michel Camus. Paris: Borderie, 1977.

Ozouf, Mona. *Les mots de femmes.* Paris: Librairie Arthème Fayard, 1995.

Paglia, Camille. *Sexual Personae.* New York: Vintage Books, 1991.

Pauvert, Jean-Jacques. *Sade vivant: Une innocence sauvage.* 3 vols. Paris: Éditions Robert Laffont, 1986. **(Pauvert)**

Paz, Octavio. *Un au-delà érotique: Le Marquis de Sade.* Translated by Jean-Claude Masson. Paris: Arcades, 1994.

Abbé du Prat. *Vénus dans le cloître.* Paris: Babel, Actes Sud, 1994.

Praz, Mario. *The Romantic Agony.* Translated by Angus Davidson. 2d ed. London: Oxford University Press, 1970.

Ribeiro, Aileen. *Fashion in the French Revolution.* New York: Holmes & Meier Publishers, 1988.

Roger, Philippe. *Sade, La philosophie dans le pressoir.* Paris: Grasset, 1976.

Sacher-Masoch, Leopold von. *Venus in Furs and Selected Letters.* Translated by Uwe Moeller and Laura Lindgren. New York: Blast Books, 1989.

Sawhney, Deepak Narang, ed. *The Divine Sade.* Warwick, Eng.: PLI-Warwick Journal of Philosophy, University of Warwick, 1994.

Schama, Simon. *Citizens: A Chronicle of the French Revolution.* New York: Vintage Books, 1990.

Schom, Alan. *Napoleon Bonaparte.* New York: HarperCollins, 1997.

Sgard, Jean, ed. *L'Écrivain devant la Révolution, 1780–1800.* Grenoble: Université Stendhal de Grenoble, 1990.

Shattuck, Roger. *Forbidden Knowledge: From Prometheus to Pornography.* New York: St. Martin's Press, 1996.

Singer, Irving. *The Nature of Love, Courtly and Romantic.* Chicago: University of Chicago Press, 1984.

Sollers, Philippe. *Sade contre l'être suprême,* précédé de *Sade dans le temps.* Paris: Gallimard, 1996.

Spencer, Samia I., ed. *French Women and the Age of Enlightenment.* Bloomington: Indiana University Press, 1984.

Thomas, Chantal. *Sade, l'oeil de la lettre.* Paris: Payot, 1978.

Voltaire, François-Marie Arouet. *Correspondance.* Edited by Théodore Besterman. 12 vols. to date. Paris: Gallimard, Bibliothèque de la Pléiade, 1977.

Weiss, Peter. *The Persecution and Assassination of Jean-Paul Marat as Performed by the Inmates of the Asylum of Charenton Under the Direction of the Marquis de Sade.* English version by Geoffrey Skelton. Verse adaptation by Adrian Mitchell. Chicago: Dramatic Publishing Company, 1965.

Yalom, Marilyn. *Blood Sisters: The French Revolution in Women's Memory.* New York: Basic Books, 1993.

Zweig, Stefan. *Marie Antoinette.* Translated by Eden Paul and Cedar Paul. London: Cassell, 1952.

IV. PERIODICALS

Archives Nationales. *Paris: Les Lieux de la Révolution.* 12 dossiers: 20 copies of written and illustrated documents from the Revolution. Printed for the bicentennial. Paris, 1989.

Chasseguet-Smirgel, Janine. "Reflexions on the Connexions Between Perversion and Sadism." *International Journal of Psycho-analysis and Bulletin of the International Psycho-Analytical Association* 59 (1978): 27–35.

Cohen, Sydney. "The Origin and Function of Sadistic Behavior." *Journal of Contemporary Psychotherapy* 2, no. 1 (Summer 1969): 3–7.

Ferguson, Frances. "Sade and the Pornographic Legacy." *Representations* 36 (Fall 1991).

Frappier-Mazur, Lucienne. "A Turning Point in the Sadean Novel: The Terror." *PLI Warwick Journal of Philosophy,* Coventry, 1994.

Klossowski, Pierre. "Élements d'une étude psychanalytique sur le Marquis de Sade." *Revue Française de Psychanalyse* 6, no. 3–4 (1933): 458–74.

Lee, Vera. "The Sade Machine." *Studies on Voltaire and the Eighteenth Century* 158 (1972).

Lesse, Stanley, ed. "Sadism Revisited." *American Journal of Psychotherapy* 30 (1976): 631–40.

Michaels, Colette V. "The Source of Excess and the Excesses of Sadian Rhetoric: From the Cosmic to the Comic." *Studies on Voltaire and the Eighteenth Century* 265 (1989).

Le Nouvel Observateur. Doit on brûler le Divin Marquis? March 2, 1966.

O'Reilly, Robert F. "Language and the Transcendent Subject in Three Works of the Marquis de Sade: *Les 120 journées de Sodome, La philosophie dans le boudoir,* and *Justine.*" *Studies on Voltaire and the Eighteenth Century* 249 (1987).

Roger, Philippe. "Rousseau selon Sade ou Jean-Jacques travesti." *Dix-Huitième Siècle* 23 (1991): 381–403.

Stolorow, Robert D. "The Narcissistic Function of Masochism (and Sadism)." *International Journal of Psycho-analysis and Bulletin of the International Psycho-Analytical Association* 56, part I (1975): 441–47.

Tel Quel 28, Winter 1967. "La pensée de Sade."

Williams, David. "Another Look at the Sadean Heroine: The Prospects of Femininity." *Essays in French Literature* 13 (November 1976).

Yale French Studies 35, 1965.

Acknowledgments

My first and foremost debt is to Maurice and Evelyne Lever, brilliant scholars and wonderful friends, who have been a prime source of inspiration and guidance. No studies of Sade can anymore proceed without taking into account Professor Lever's remarkable studies, which include the most extensive archival research since the generation of Maurice Heine and Gilbert Lely. It is his work, and his detailed documentation of the Sade family, that made the execution of this work possible. Evelyne Lever, the gifted biographer of Marie-Antoinette and Philippe-Égalité, has also been a great source of help. Her expertise in the social history of eighteenth-century France, particularly as it relates to the lives of women, has been invaluable. I thank both Evelyne and Maurice for the initial encouragement they gave to this project, and to the wise advice they gave throughout.

My next debt of gratitude is once more to my dearest mentor and friend, Ethel Woodward de Croisset, my perennial hostess in Paris, who for over two decades has sheltered, fed, and nurtured me during my research trips to France. Ethel, whose late husband, Philippe de Croisset, was a direct descendant of the Marquis de Sade, displayed an ardent curiosity in this particular project, even accompanying me on my forays into Provence. Her deep knowledge of French society, past and present, was always a source of inspiration.

I'm not sure I could have brought this book to fruition, or generally survived the last four years, without the help of my gifted friend and researcher, Sari Goodfriend, whose patient cheerfulness and efficiency are coupled with a talent for composing perfect footnotes and accomplishing the most painstaking archival work in lightning time. Deep gratitude also to Amy Larocca, who assisted me during my last bouts of research in Paris. The shrewdness and street-wisdom she displayed in helping me to master the Byzantine complexities of the Archives Nationales' computer system and of the Bibliothèque Nationale's card files were downright uncanny, and the dedication she brought to every moment of our work together was memorable.

Equal gratitude to my friend George Lechner, whose help in completing my inquiries was invaluable; to Jonathan Fasman, whose perfect pitch for prose helped me greatly in the very last days of shaping my draft; and to Oliver Bernier for his wonderful thoughtfulness.

I give thanks to the residents of Provence who assisted me in my research into the history of La Coste and its relationship to Sade: Gilbert Grégoire, its mayor; Jacques Pialat, Crystal Woodward and Georges Adrien, and Caryn Merveille, who offered valuable historical and sociological background on the region; Nora Bouër, the owner of the Château de La Coste, who shared with me many documents concerning the history of the marquis's property; Elise Severat, whose interpretations of the community were very helpful; Liliane Ségura, who fed me many a scrumptious *coq au vin* at her establishment, the Café de Sade; Ruth Middleton Murry, my hostess in Vénasque, whose hospitality and wisdom much sustained me; and Antoine de Gebbelin, the unfailingly thoughtful owner of "Le Relais du Procureur," which was my second home during my extended stays at La Coste.

Of the persons in France who helped to document this book, I am particularly indebted to Comte de Sade, the marquis's direct descendant, for the graciousness with which he received me at his home and generously shared the history of the Sade family archives.

I also extend profound gratitude to those scholars and friends who were generous enough to read my book in manuscript form: my angelic reader-in-residence, Claire Bloom; my severe and scrupulous critic-in-residence, Luke Gray; Sarah Plimpton and Robert O. Paxton, dear walking companions and my mentors in many issues of French history; Lynn Hunt of the University of Pennsylvania, Lucienne Frappier-Mazur, also of Penn, and Marie-Hélène Huët of the University of Michigan at Ann Arbor, who each gave my manuscript the kind of rigorous reading every independent scholar dreams of; Dr. Sheldon Bach of New York City, whose insights into the marquis's more than bizarre psyche were very precious; Hendon Chubb, whose knowledge of French eighteenth-century history and dedication to the art of accuracy are a perpetual source of wonder; and my friend and neighbor Michael Pollan, whose formidable editorial eye helped me to detect, and, hopefully, to correct, several thematic shortcomings.

When dealing with a figure as problematic as Sade, the biographer owes special gratitude to those writers and scholars, past or present, whose pioneering research laid the groundwork for all ensuing studies. Guillaume Apollinaire, Gilbert Lely, Maurice Heine, and now Maurice

Lever, are in that category. Beyond their writings, the texts that have given me the most precious insights into Sade's psychology and oeuvre are Octavio Paz's *Un au-delà érotique: Sade;* Maurice Blanchot's *Sade et Restif de la Bretonne;* Roland Barthes's *Sade, Fourier, Loyola;* Philippe Roger's *La Philosophie dans le pressoir;* Philippe Sollers's, Chantal Thomas's and Michel Delon's writings on the marquis; and Hugues Jallon's recent study *Sade: Le corps constituant.* In the Anglo-American tradition, I'd like to acknowledge my debt to Angela Carter's *The Sadeian Woman,* which argues, fearlessly if not always convincingly, that Sade is useful to women because he exposes the deep-seated misogyny of our society; to Stuart Hampshire's remarkable reflections on the marquis; to Camille Paglia's chapter on Sade in *Sexual Personae;* and also to Roger Shattuck's *Forbidden Knowledge,* whose stubborn and individualistic views are to be appreciated.

A few reflections on my process of documentation: Apart from the material cited in Arthur Goldhammer's recent translation of Maurice Lever's *Sade,* and two meager selections of letters published in Great Britain in the 1960s, to my knowledge very little of the marquis's correspondence, and almost none of his family's, has been published in English. More often than not, I worked in virgin territory; and the reader can assume that all prose translations of documents and letters are my own (my husband, Cleve Gray, valiantly took on the translation of Sade's often wretched verse, which I include in my footnotes in the original French). The passages from Sade's essays and fictional works cited in this book are also my own translations, with one exception: for practical reasons, I used the English-language rendition of Sade's *Idées sur les romans (Reflections on the Novel)* published thirty-five years ago by Richard Seaver and Austryn Wainhouse in their handsome Grove Press edition.

A word about the French editions of Sade I worked with: I turned to the recent Pléiade volumes of Sade's novels for quoting from *Aline et Valcour, Les 120 Journées de Sodome,* and *La Nouvelle Justine.* If only for reasons of continuity and general convenience (volume two of the Pléiade did not come out until 1995, two years after I started my research) I used various contemporary paperback editions for other pivotal novels —*La Philosophie dans le boudoir, Justine, Juliette.* And I referred to the sixteen-volume Cercle du Livre Précieux edition (1966) for Sade's polemical pamphlets and numerous other minor writings.

I look on footnotes as a communal service of sorts. For the comfort of future Sade chroniclers and of my own conscience I have attempted to indicate, as often as possible, the primary as well as the secondary sources of my citations. Being a great believer in the talismanic power of the scripted word, I also looked at many original manuscripts of those Sade letters and documents that are in the collections of the Bibliothèque Nationale and the Archives Nationales. A direct viewing of the words "horreur, horreur" impulsively scribbled by Mme de Sade on the margin of a La Coste laundry list, a glimpse of the spidery, neurotically fastidious script in which her enigmatic sister wrote her flirtatious notes to the Abbé de Sade, throw a far richer light on the Sades' family drama than any critical text ever could. The folio numbers of these manuscripts are not always clearly indicated; I've documented them to the best of my abilities.

As always, deep gratitude to my editor of the past twenty-four years, Alice Mayhew, whose enthusiasm and encouragement made this book possible; and to Elizabeth Stein, who brought her formidable precision and dedication to the process of producing it. Also at Simon & Schuster, my gratitude to Lydia Buechler and Marge Horvitz, whose kind patience and awesome copy-editing skills surmounted many onerous problems posed by the formatting of eighteenth-century French idioms; and to Natalie Goldstein and Kate Lewin for their magnificent work in assembling the photographic material. Finally, I thank my dear friends and agents, Anne and Georges Borchardt, for the encouragement and support they've shown me throughout the years; and my husband, Cleve Gray, for constantly re-offering me, over the past decades, the gift of life.

And of course to Alex, beloved mentor of my youth, who is the godfather of this book, having allowed me to read Sade at an unconscionably early age, when many of us read him for all the wrong reasons.

—August 1998
Warren, Connecticut

Index

Photo Credits

FOR THE BEST IN PAPERBACKS, LOOK FOR THE

In every corner of the world, on every subject under the sun, Penguin represents quality and variety—the very best in publishing today.

For complete information about books available from Penguin—including Puffins, Penguin Classics, and Arkana—and how to order them, write to us at the appropriate address below. Please note that for copyright reasons the selection of books varies from country to country.

In the United Kingdom: Please write to *Dept. EP, Penguin Books Ltd, Bath Road, Harmondsworth, West Drayton, Middlesex UB7 0DA.*

In the United States: Please write to *Penguin Putnam Inc., P.O. Box 12289 Dept. B, Newark, New Jersey 07101-5289* or call 1-800-788-6262.

In Canada: Please write to *Penguin Books Canada Ltd, 10 Alcorn Avenue, Suite 300, Toronto, Ontario M4V 3B2.*

In Australia: Please write to *Penguin Books Australia Ltd, P.O. Box 257, Ringwood, Victoria 3134.*

In New Zealand: Please write to *Penguin Books (NZ) Ltd, Private Bag 102902, North Shore Mail Centre, Auckland 10.*

In India: Please write to *Penguin Books India Pvt Ltd, 11 Panchsheel Shopping Centre, Panchsheel Park, New Delhi 110 017.*

In the Netherlands: Please write to *Penguin Books Netherlands bv, Postbus 3507, NL-1001 AH Amsterdam.*

In Germany: Please write to *Penguin Books Deutschland GmbH, Metzlerstrasse 26, 60594 Frankfurt am Main.*

In Spain: Please write to *Penguin Books S. A., Bravo Murillo 19, 1° B, 28015 Madrid.*

In Italy: Please write to *Penguin Italia s.r.l., Via Benedetto Croce 2, 20094 Corsico, Milano.*

In France: Please write to *Penguin France, Le Carré Wilson, 62 rue Benjamin Baillaud, 31500 Toulouse.*

In Japan: Please write to *Penguin Books Japan Ltd, Kaneko Building, 2-3-25 Koraku, Bunkyo-Ku, Tokyo 112.*

In South Africa: Please write to *Penguin Books South Africa (Pty) Ltd, Private Bag X14, Parkview, 2122 Johannesburg.*